Quantitative Aptitude

An ideal book for preparation of:
- Management entrance test like CMAT, CAT, MAT, IGNOU, etc.
- SSC Combined Preliminary Exam
- Examination conducted by UPSC including CDS / NDA
- Bank PO Exam (especially conducted by IBPS)
- Railway Recruitment Board Exam
- L.I.C. / G.I.C. Recruitment Exam
- Campus Recruitment Test

Quantitative Aptitude

Shripad Deo

ALLIED PUBLISHERS PVT. LTD.
New Delhi • Mumbai • Kolkata • Lucknow • Chennai
Nagpur • Bangalore • Hyderabad • Ahmedabad

ALLIED PUBLISHERS PRIVATE LIMITED

1/13-14 Asaf Ali Road, **New Delhi**–110002
Ph.: 011-23239001 • E-mail: delhi.books@alliedpublishers.com

47/9 Prag Narain Road, Near Kalyan Bhawan, **Lucknow**–226001
Ph.: 0522-2209942 • E-mail: lko.books@alliedpublishers.com

17 Chittaranjan Avenue, **Kolkata**–700072
Ph.: 033-22129618 • E-mail: cal.books@alliedpublishers.com

15 J.N. Heredia Marg, Ballard Estate, **Mumbai**–400001
Ph.: 022-42126969 • E-mail: mumbai.books@alliedpublishers.com

60 Shiv Sunder Apartments (Ground Floor), Central Bazar Road,
Bajaj Nagar, **Nagpur**–440010
Ph.: 0712-2234210 • E-mail: ngp.books@alliedpublishers.com

F-1 Sun House (First Floor), C.G. Road, Navrangpura,
Ellisbridge P.O., **Ahmedabad**–380006
Ph.: 079-26465916 • E-mail: ahmbd.books@alliedpublishers.com

751 Anna Salai, **Chennai**–600002
Ph.: 044-28523938 • E-mail: chennai.books@alliedpublishers.com

5th Main Road, Gandhinagar, **Bangalore**–560009
Ph.: 080-22262081 • E-mail: bngl.books@alliedpublishers.com

3-2-844/6 & 7 Kachiguda Station Road, **Hyderabad**–500027
Ph.: 040-24619079 • E-mail: hyd.books@alliedpublishers.com

Website: www.alliedpublishers.com

© 2014, Allied Publishers Pvt. Ltd.

No part of the material protected by this copyright notice may be reproduced or utilized in any form or by any means, electronic or mechanical including photocopying, recording or by any information storage and retrieval system, without prior written permission from the copyright owners. The views expressed in this volume are of the individual contributors, editor or author and do not represent the view point of the Centre.

ISBN: 978-81-8424-878-4

Published by Sunil Sachdev and printed by Ravi Sachdev at Allied Publishers Pvt. Ltd. (Printing Division), A-104 Mayapuri Phase II, New Delhi-110064

Preface

'Quantitative Aptitude' is the cornerstone of most of the competitive examinations, as well as for all MBA entrance examinations. Undoubtedly, aptitude tests the skill and ability to do faster calculations in a stipulated duration.

This book on 'Quantitative Aptitude' is formulated with an objective to benefit all the aspirants who plan to appear for competitive exams. The language in the book is kept very simple purposefully, so that every student can easily understand the techniques of aptitude problem solving in just one reading. More than 1200 problems on different topics of quantitative aptitude are fully solved with detail explanation. The chapters in this book start with introductory theory and important formulae to remember, followed by solved examples and finally exercise and its solution.

In most of the existing books which are in circulation in market the sequence of problems in the exercise is haphazard, but in this book exercise problems are starting with easy level and slowly approaching towards the difficult level as we proceed. This approach of easy to difficult and clubbing the same variety of problems together will make it any student to learn the topics thoroughly. Also, very sincere efforts are done to include questions in the exercises which are parallel to the questions asked in Bank PO exam, RRB exam and Management entrance exam as well as tests conducted by private companies in campus recruitment for engineering students.

Further, in any competitive examination, solving time is the major constraint. Moreover, how to solve aptitude questions is not significant in such examinations. The most important aspect is to solve a question in a fraction of minute, using shortcut methods. Every possible effort has been made to include exceptional methods and tricks of problem solving which are taught in coaching centers, so that students will learn best possible techniques of quickly finding the answer. It is hoped that the subject matter in this book will increase the confidence among the candidates and the book will help them like an ideal teacher.

I convey my gratitude to the entire management of Allied Publishers Pvt. Ltd. for taking all pains in the publication of this book.

Any constructive suggestion for further improvement of the book will be gratefully acknowledged and highly appreciated.

Shripad Deo

Contents

Preface .... *v*

1. Numbers 1
2. L.C.M. and H.C.F. 46
3. Simplification 68
4. Surds and Indices 95
5. Simple Equations 110
6. Ratio-Proportion-Variation 145
7. Percentage 175
8. Profit and Loss 205
9. Partnership 237
10. Average 251
11. Alligation or Mixture 271
12. Time and Work 295
13. Pipes and Cistern 327
14. Chain Rule 347
15. Time and Distance 363
16. Problem on Trains 392
17. Boats and Streams 417
18. Permutation and Combination 432
19. Probability 452
20. Clocks 472
21. Calendars 487
22. Simple and Compound Interest 504
23. Stocks and Shares 530
24. Height and Distance 544
25. Perimeter and Area 555
26. Volume and Surface Area 588
27. Number Series 619
28. Data Interpretation 632

1
Numbers

CLASSIFICATION OF REAL NUMBERS

- **_Natural Numbers:_** Natural numbers are the numbers from where we normally start counting.
  Natural numbers $\Rightarrow$ 1, 2, 3, 4, 5, 6, ...

- **_Whole Numbers:_** Whole number also contains all natural numbers with zero included in to.
  Whole numbers $\Rightarrow$ 0, 1, 2, 3, 4, 5, 6, ...

- **_Integers:_** Integers consists of zero, as well as positive and negative natural numbers. In the problem of numbers, we often use the word 'number' to mean an 'integer'.
  Integers $\Rightarrow$ ..., –5, –4, –3, –2, –1, 0, 1, 2, 3, 4, 5, ...

- **_Rational Numbers:_** The rational or fractional numbers are the numbers which are technically regarded as ratios (divisions) of integers. In other words a number which can be expressed in the form of a/b where 'a' and 'b' are integers and $b \neq 0$ is called a rational number. All integers as well as fractions are rational numbers.
  Rational numbers $\Rightarrow$ ... –3, $-\frac{2}{5}$, $-\frac{1}{3}$, 0, $\frac{4}{3}$, 2, 5, ...

- **_Irrational Numbers:_** The numbers which are not rational but which can be represented by a point on the number line are called irrational numbers.
  Irrational numbers $\Rightarrow$ $\sqrt{2}$, $\sqrt{5}$, $\sqrt[3]{7}$, $\sqrt[4]{12}$

EVEN AND ODD NUMBERS

- **_Even Numbers:_** Numbers which are divisible by 2 or which when divided by 2 gives zero as a remainder are called even numbers.
  Even numbers $\Rightarrow$ 2, 4, 6, 8, 10, 12, 14, ... etc.
  Please note that every even number ends with 0, 2, 4, 6, or 8. Also the sum or difference of any two even numbers is always even.

- **_Odd Numbers:_** Numbers which are not divisible by 2 are called as odd numbers.
  Odd numbers $\Rightarrow$ 1, 3, 5, 7, 9, 11, 13, ... etc.
  Please note that every odd number ends with 1, 3, 5, or 7. Also the sum or difference of any two odd numbers is always even, while the sum or difference of an odd and even number is always odd.

PRIME, COMPOSITE AND CO-PRIME NUMBERS

- *Prime Numbers:* Integers can be a prime number or a composite number. A number other than 1 which dose not have any factor apart from one and itself is called a prime number. For example 2, 3, 5, 7, 11, 13, etc. are prime numbers. Every prime number greater than 3 can be written in the form of '$6k + 1$' or '$6k - 1$', where k is an integer.

- *Composite Numbers:* Any number other than 1, which is not a prime number, is called a composite number. In other words, a composite number is a number which has factors other than one and itself. For example 4, 6, 8, 9, 10, 12, etc. are composite numbers. Please note that the number '1' is neither prime nor composite and the only even prime number is '2'.

- *Co-prime Numbers:* Two numbers are said to be co-prime or relative primes if they do not have any common factor other than 1. In other words co-prime numbers are those numbers whose highest common factor is 1. For example {3, 4}, {12, 25}, {16, 55} are the sets of co-prime numbers.

FACE VALUE AND LOCAL VALUE OF A DIGIT IN A NUMBER

- *Face Value:* The face value of a digit in a number is its own value, at whatever place it may be. For example in the number 945, the face value of 9 is 9, face value of 4 is 4 and face value of 5 is 5.

- *Local Value:* The local value (or place value) of a digit in a number is the value that is attained by that digit due to its position in the number. For example in the number 945, local value of 9 is 900, local value of 4 is 40 and local value of 5 is 5.

DIVISIBILITY TEST

- *Divisibility by 2:* A number is divisible by 2 if its unit place (or last digit) is 0, 2, 4, 6, or 8.
  For example 3564, 8976, 4520 are all divisible by 2.

- *Divisibility by 4:* A number is divisible by 4 if its last two digits are divisible by 4.
  For example 45<u>28</u>, 79<u>512</u>, 77<u>00</u> are all divisible by 4 as their last two digits are divisible by 4.

- *Divisibility by 8:* A number is divisible by 8 if its last three digits are divisible by 8.
  For example 75<u>128</u>, 79<u>512</u>, 19<u>000</u> are all divisible by 8 as their last three digits are divisible by 8.

- *Divisibility by 3:* A number is divisible by 3 if sum of its digits is a multiple of 3.
  For example 9213 is divisible by 3 as sum of digits (*i.e.,* $9 + 2 + 1 + 3 = 15$) is a multiple of 3. Similarly 7452 and 11430 are also divisible by 3 as their sum of digits is a multiple of 3.

- *Divisibility by 9:* A number is divisible by 9 if sum of its digits is a multiple of 9.
  For example 5472 is divisible by 9 as sum of digits (*i.e.,* $5 + 4 + 7 + 2 = 18$) is a multiple of 9. Also every number which is divisible by 9 is necessarily divisible by 3, but a number which is divisible by 3 may or may not be divisible by 9.

- ***Divisibility by 5:*** A number is divisible by 5 if its last digit is either zero or 5.

  For example 425, 650, 885 are all divisible by 5 as their unit place is either 0 or 5.

- ***Divisibility by 6:*** A number is divisible by 6 if it is divisible by both 2 and 3. Here 2 and 3 are the co-prime or relative prime factors of 6.

  For example 180, 204, 3324 are all multiples of 6 as these numbers are divisible by 2 and 3.

- ***Divisibility by 7:*** If the unit place digit of a number is doubled and is subtracted from remaining number, and if this difference is divisible by 7, then the number is said to be divisible by 7.

  For example 595 is divisible by 7 as follows:

  $59 - 2(5) = 49$, which is a multiple of 7.

- ***Divisibility by 10:*** A number will be divisible by 10 if its unit place is zero.

  For example 1450, 8990, 1200 are divisible by 10 as their unit place is 0.

- ***Divisibility by 11:*** A number is divisible by 11 if sum of alternate digits is same or they differ by multiples of 11.

  For example the number 2453 is divisible by 11 as follows:

  2 4 5 3   As $2 + 5 = 7$ and $4 + 3 = 7$. Here sum of alternate digits is same.

  The number 3572646 is also divisible by 11 as follows:

  3 5 7 2 6 4 6   As $3 + 7 + 6 + 6 = 22$ and $5 + 2 + 4 = 11$. Here the sum differs by 11.

NUMBERS IN SERIES

- Finding the sum of first 'n' natural numbers

  $$1 + 2 + 3 + \ldots + n = \frac{n(n+1)}{2}$$

- Finding the sum of squares of first 'n' natural numbers

  $$1^2 + 2^2 + 3^2 + \ldots + n^2 = \frac{n(n+1)(2n+1)}{6}$$

- Finding the sum of cubes of first 'n' natural numbers

  $$1^3 + 2^3 + 3^3 + \ldots + n^3 = \left(\frac{n(n+1)}{2}\right)^2$$

- *Numbers in Arithmetic Progression (A.P.):* Numbers are said to be in arithmetic progression if they increase or decrease by a common difference.

  For example: 1, 5, 9, 13, 17, 21, 25, …

  15, 10, 5, 0, –5, –10, –15, …

  The first term of an arithmetic progression is denoted by 'a' and the common difference is denoted by 'd'. Common difference can be found as the difference between any term and its previous term. Therefore the arithmetic progression will appear as follows:

  $a, a + d, a + 2d, a + 3d, a + 4d, a + 5d, \ldots$

Finding n^{th} term of arithmetic progression:

$T_n = a + (n-1)d$

Finding sum of n terms of arithmetic progression:

$S_n = \dfrac{n}{2}$ [First term + Last term]

Substituting first term as 'a' and last term (or n^{th} term) as '$a + (n-1)d$'

$S_n = \dfrac{n}{2}[2a + (n-1)d]$

Finding arithmetic mean of n terms:

A.M. $= \dfrac{S_n}{n}$ or $\dfrac{\text{(First term + Last term)}}{2}$

- *Numbers in Geometric Progression (G.P.):* Numbers are said to be in geometric progression if they increase or decrease by a common ratio.

    For example: 2, 4, 8, 16, 32, 64, 128, ...

    $\dfrac{1}{3}, \dfrac{1}{9}, \dfrac{1}{27}, \dfrac{1}{81}, \dfrac{1}{243}, \dfrac{1}{729}, ...$

The first term of a geometric progression is denoted by 'a' and the common ratio is denoted by 'r'. Common ratio can be found by dividing any term with its previous term. Therefore geometric progression will appear as follows:

$a, ar, ar^2, ar^3, ar^4, ar^5, ...$

Finding n^{th} term of geometric progression:

$T_n = ar^{n-1}$

Finding sum of n terms of geometric progression:

$S_n = \dfrac{a(r^n - 1)}{(r-1)}$ \quad if $r > 1$

$S_n = \dfrac{a(1 - r^n)}{(1-r)}$ \quad if $r < 1$

Finding the sum of terms of geometric progression up to infinity:

$S_\infty = \dfrac{a}{1-r}$ \quad Only if $r < 1$

Finding geometric mean of n terms:

G.M. $= \sqrt[n]{T_1 \times T_1 \times T_1 \times ...... \times T_n}$

NUMBER OF FACTORS OF A NUMBER

If N is a composite number then we need to factorize N such that:

$N = a^p \times b^q \times c^r$

Where a, b and c are the prime factors and p, q, r are positive integers, then number of factors of N is given by the expression:

Number of factors = $(p + 1)(q + 1)(r + 1)$

For example: $360 = 2^3 \times 3^2 \times 5^1$

Hence 360 has $(3 + 1)(2 + 1)(1 + 1)$ i.e., 24 factors including 1 and the number 360 itself.

POWER CYCLE

The last digit (or unit place) of the power of any number follow a cyclic pattern i.e., they repeat after certain number of steps. Lets take an example by writing down powers of 2 as follows:

$2^1 = 2$
$2^2 = 4$
$2^3 = 8$
$2^4 = 16$
$2^5 = 32$
$2^6 = 64$
$2^7 = 128$
$2^8 = 256$
$2^9 = 512$

Hence the last digit in the powers of 2 follows a specific cyclic pattern i.e., 2, 4, 8, 6 and the same digits are repeated after every fourth power. Suppose if we want to find out the last digit of 2^{24} we can easily find out as follows:

$2^{24} = 2^{4K} \Rightarrow$ Last digit will be 6. $\qquad (\because$ cycle repeats after every 4th power)

$2^{25} = 2^{4k+1} \Rightarrow$ Last digit will be 2.

$2^{26} = 2^{4k+2} \Rightarrow$ Last digit will be 4.

$2^{27} = 2^{4k+3} \Rightarrow$ Last digit will be 8 and so on.

In similar way powers of 3 also follows a cyclic pattern as shown below:

$3^1 = 3$
$3^2 = 9$
$3^3 = 27$
$3^4 = 81$
$3^5 = 243$
$3^6 = 729$
$3^7 = 2187$
$3^8 = 6561$

Hence the last digit in the powers of 3 follows a specific cyclic pattern i.e., 3, 9, 7, 1 and the same digits are repeated after every fourth power.

Let us list down the power cycle for every digit as follows:

Number		Last digit of nth power of number			
n		n^1	n^2	n^3	n^4
2	$\Rightarrow$	2	4	8	6
3	$\Rightarrow$	3	9	7	1
4	$\Rightarrow$	4	6	4	6
5	$\Rightarrow$	5	5	5	5
6	$\Rightarrow$	6	6	6	6
7	$\Rightarrow$	7	9	3	1
8	$\Rightarrow$	8	4	2	6
9	$\Rightarrow$	9	1	9	1

SUCCESSIVE DIVISION OF NUMBER

If a number is divided by a divisor we get a quotient and we may or may not get a remainder. If the quotient of the first division is used as a dividend in the next division, such a division is called successive division. A successive division process may continue up to any number of steps until the quotient in a division becomes zero for the first time. For example if a number 198 is successively divided by the divisors 7, 5 and 4 the remainders are 2, 3 and 1 respectively as shown below:

$$7\overline{)198}\begin{array}{c}28\\ \underline{14}\\ 58\\ \underline{56}\\ 2\end{array}\quad\Rightarrow\quad 5\overline{)28}\begin{array}{c}5\\ \underline{25}\\ 3\end{array}\quad\Rightarrow\quad 4\overline{)5}\begin{array}{c}1\\ \underline{4}\\ 1\end{array}$$

Hence in case of successive division a question may be asked to find out a smallest number which when divided successively by 7, 5 and 4 the remainders are 2, 3 and 1 respectively. Let us carry out the same process in a reverse way to find out the number.

Divisors	Remainder
7	2
5	3
4	1

Assuming the quotient of final division as x, it is seen that when the final dividend is divided by 4 the remainder is 1.

∴ The 3rd dividend = $4x + 1$ (∵ Dividend = Divisor × Quotient + Remainder)

Now this $(4x + 1)$ will be the quotient if 2nd dividend is divided by 5 and the remainder is 3.

∴ The 2nd dividend = $5(4x + 1) + 3$

Now this [5(4x + 1) + 3] will be the quotient if 1st dividend (or original number) is divided by 7 and the remainder is 2.

∴ The 1st dividend = 7[5(4x + 1) + 3] + 2

Substituting the value of x as 1 to get smallest number.

∴ The 1st dividend (original number) = 7[5(4x + 1) + 3] + 2
= 7[5(4(1) + 1) + 3] + 2
= 198.

LARGEST POWER OF A NUMBER IN N!

Factorial of a number N is defined as the product of numbers from 1 to N. Factorial N is written as 'N!'. If the task is to find out the largest power of 2 or 3 in 100! or how many 2's and 3's exist in 100! can be found by dividing the number 100 successively as follows:

2	100
2	50
2	25
2	12
2	6
2	3
2	1
	0

3	100
3	33
3	11
3	3
3	1
	0

Therefore the largest power of 2 in 100! can be obtained by adding all the quotients *i.e.*, 50 + 25 + 12 + 6 + 3 + 1 = 97

Hence 2^{97} exist in 100!

In a similar way the largest power of 3 in 100! can be obtained by adding all the quotients *i.e.*, 33 + 11 + 3 + 1 = 48

Hence 3^{48} exist in 100!

Please note that this method is applicable only if the number whose largest power is to be found out is a prime number. If the number is not prime, then we have to write the number as the product of prime numbers, find the largest power of each factor separately. Then the smallest among the largest power of these factors of the given number will give the largest power required.

For example if we need to find out the largest power of 6 in 100! or how many 6's are there in 100! can be found as follows:

$\quad$ 6 = 2 × 3

Number of 2's in 100! = 97
Number of 3's in 100! = 48

Hence the largest power of 6 in 100! is minimum of 48 and 97 *i.e.*, 48 or 6^{48} exist in 100!

RULES PERTAINING TO $(x^n + a^n)$ OR $(x^n - a^n)$

1. When n is odd $(x^n + a^n)$ is always divisible by $x + a$
2. When n is odd or even $(x^n - a^n)$ is always divisible by $x - a$
3. When n is even $(x^n - a^n)$ is always divisible by $x + a$
4. $(x^n + 1)$ will be divisible by $(x + 1)$ only when n is odd.

SOLVED EXAMPLES

Example 1

How many of the following numbers are divisible by 66?
    (a) 1056   (b) 1256   (c) 1584
    (d) 1846   (e) 4708   (f) 5412

Solution

$66 = 11 \times 3 \times 2$

For a number to be divisible by 66 it must be also divisible by 11, 3 and 2 which are the co-prime factors of 66.

(a) 1056

Test for $11 \Rightarrow (1 + 5) - (0 + 6) = 0$.
As sum of alternate digits is equal the number 1056 is divisible by 11.
Test for $2 \Rightarrow$ As last digit is even hence divisible by 2.
Test for $3 \Rightarrow$ Sum of digits $1 + 0 + 5 + 6 = 12$.
As sum of digits is a multiple of 3, hence the number is divisible by 3.
$\therefore$ 1056 is divisible by 66.

(b) 1256

Test for $11 \Rightarrow (2 + 6) - (1 + 5) = 2$.
As sum of alternate digits differ by 2, the number 1256 is not divisible by 11.
$\therefore$ 1256 is not divisible by 66.

(c) 1584

Test for $11 \Rightarrow (1 + 8) - (5 + 4) = 0$.
As sum of alternate digits is equal the number 1584 is divisible by 11.
Test for $2 \Rightarrow$ As last digit is even hence divisible by 2.
Test for $3 \Rightarrow$ Sum of digits $1 + 5 + 8 + 4 = 18$.
As sum of digits is a multiple of 3, hence the number is divisible by 3.
$\therefore$ 1584 is divisible by 66.

(d) 1846

   Test for $11 \Rightarrow (8 + 6) - (1 + 4) = 9$.

   As sum of alternate digits differ by 9 the number 1846 is not divisible by 11.

   ∴ 1846 is not divisible by 66.

(e) 4708

   Test for $11 \Rightarrow (7 + 8) - (4 + 0) = 11$.

   As sum of alternate digits differ by 11 the number 4708 is divisible by 11.

   Test for $2 \Rightarrow$ As last digit is even hence divisible by 2.

   Test for $3 \Rightarrow$ Sum of digits $4 + 7 + 0 + 8 = 19$.

   As sum of digits is not a multiple of 3, hence the number is not divisible by 3.

   ∴ 4708 is not divisible by 66.

(f) 5412

   Test for $11 \Rightarrow (5 + 1) - (4 + 2) = 0$.

   As sum of alternate digits is equal the number 5412 is divisible by 11.

   Test for $2 \Rightarrow$ As last digit is even hence divisible by 2.

   Test for $3 \Rightarrow$ Sum of digits $5 + 4 + 1 + 2 = 12$.

   As sum of digits is a multiple of 3, hence the number is divisible by 3.

   ∴ 5412 is divisible by 66.

Example 2

If a six digit number $47a51b$ is divisible by 72, then find the minimum value of a.

Solution

$72 = 8 \times 9$

For a number to be divisible by 72 it must be also divisible by both 8 and 9 which are the co-prime factors of 72.

Test for $8 \Rightarrow$ Last 3 digits i.e., $51b$ should be a multiple of 8, hence $b = 2$.

Test for $9 \Rightarrow$ Sum of digits $(19 + a)$ should be a multiple of 9, hence $a = 8$.

∴ Minimum value of $a = 8$.

Example 3

Find the total number of prime factors in the product $4^9 \times 5^5 \times 7^7$.

Solution

$4^9 \times 5^5 \times 7^7 = (2^2)^9 \times 5^5 \times 7^7$
$= 2^{18} \times 5^5 \times 7^7$

∴ Number of prime factors $= 18 + 5 + 7 = 30$

Example 4

Find the smallest number with which 360 should be multiplied
(a) To make it a perfect square?
(b) To make it a perfect cube?

Solution

(a) To make it a perfect square
Factorizing the number 360 as:
$360 = 2^3 \times 3^2 \times 5^1$

From the factorization it seems that to make a number as a perfect square there is a shortage of one 2 and one 5.
$(2^3 \times 3^2 \times 5^1) \times 2 \times 5 \Rightarrow 2^4 \times 3^2 \times 5^2$

Hence the smallest number with which 360 should be multiplied to make it a perfect square is 10.

(b) To make it perfect cube
Factorizing the number 360 as:
$360 = 2^3 \times 3^2 \times 5^1$

From the factorization it seems that to make a number as a perfect cube there is a shortage of one 3 and two 5's.
$(2^3 \times 3^2 \times 5^1) \times 3 \times 5^2 \Rightarrow 2^3 \times 3^3 \times 5^3$

Hence the smallest number with which 360 should be multiplied to make it a perfect cube is 75.

Example 5

What is the unit digit in the following products?
(a) $354 \times 864 \times 169 \times 273$
(b) $(666)^{55} \times (444)^{22}$

Solution

(a) $354 \times 864 \times 169 \times 273$
Unit digit in the given product = Unit digit in the product $(4 \times 4 \times 9 \times 3) = 2$.

(b) $(666)^{55} \times (444)^{22}$
Unit digit of $(666)^{55}$ = Unit digit of 6^{55}
$= 6$ ∵ Any power of 6 will give 6 in unit place
Unit digit of $(444)^{22}$ = Unit digit of 4^{22}
$= 6$ ∵ Even power of 4 will give 6 in unit place
Unit digit in the given product = Unit digit in the product $(6^{55} \times 4^{22})$
$= 6 \times 6 = 6.$

Example 6

If a, b, c, d, e, f, g are 7 single digit distinct numbers and they satisfy following condition:

$$\begin{array}{cccc} & a & b & 3 \\ + & d & e & \\ \hline & b & f & g \end{array} \qquad \begin{array}{cccc} & a & b & 3 \\ - & d & e & \\ \hline & & f & g \end{array}$$

Find: (a) Value of a.
(b) Value of g.

Solution

(a) Finding value of a

If a two digit number is subtracted from a three digit number, and the resulting number is of two digits, implies that $a = 1$.

(b) Finding value of g

The variable e can be either less than 3 or greater than 3.
If $e < 3$
Assuming $e = 1$. Then addition will give $g = 4$ and subtraction will give $g = 2$.
Assuming $e = 2$. Then addition will give $g = 5$ and subtraction will give $g = 1$.
As we are not getting unique value of g, hence $e < 3$ is not possible.
If $e > 3$
In addition $3 + e = g$ ... (1)
In subtraction $13 - e = g$ ... (2)
Equating the LHS of equation (1) and (2)
$3 + e = 13 - e$
$\therefore \quad e = 5$
Hence, $g = 8$.

Example 7

A number when divided successively by 5 and 8 gives respective remainders of 2 and 3. What will be the remainder when original number is divided by 27?

Solution

Divisors	Remainder
5	2
8	3

Assuming the quotient of second division as x, it is seen that when the final dividend is divided by 8 the remainder is 3.

$\therefore$ The 2nd dividend $= 8x + 3$ ($\because$ Dividend = Divisor × Quotient + Remainder)

Now this $(8x + 3)$ will be the quotient if 1st dividend is divided by 5 and the remainder is 2.

∴ The 1ˢᵗ dividend (or original number) $= 5(8x + 3) + 2 = 40x + 17$

Substituting the value of x as 1 to get smallest number.

The required number $= 40(1) + 17 = 57$

If 57 is divided by 27, the remainder is 3.

Example 8

How many times the number 7 is present in 300!?

Solution

The number of 7's existing in 300! can be found by dividing the number 300 successively by 7 as follows:

```
7 | 300
7 |  42
7 |   6
  |   0
```

Therefore the largest power of 7 in 300! can be obtained by adding all the quotients i.e., $42 + 6 = 48$.

Hence 7^{48} exist in 300!

Example 9

The difference between two numbers is 677. On dividing the larger number with smaller, we get 8 as quotient and 5 as remainder. Find the smaller number.

Solution

Let the smaller number be n. Then larger number will be $(n + 677)$

∴ $n + 677 = 8n + 5$ (∵ Dividend = Divisor × Quotient + Remainder)

   $7n = 672$ $n = 96$

Example 10

Find the sum of all odd numbers lying between 100 and 200.

Solution

The numbers are 101, 103, 105, …, 199

This is an arithmetic progression with first term i.e., $a = 101$ and the common difference i.e., $d = 2$.

Let us find out the number of terms in this series as follows:

$$T_n = a + (n-1)d$$
$$199 = 101 + (n-1)2$$
$$n - 1 = \frac{199 - 101}{2}$$
$$\therefore \quad n = 50$$

The sum of these 50 terms is:

$$S_{50} = \frac{50}{2} [T_1 + T_{50}] = 25 \times [101 + 199] = 7500.$$

EXERCISE

1. Which one of the following is not a prime number?
   (a) 41 (b) 61
   (c) 71 (d) 91

2. Which one of the following is a prime number?
   (a) 49 (b) 69
   (c) 79 (d) 99

3. Which one of the following is a prime number?
   (a) 307 (b) 429
   (c) 489 (d) 651

4. Find the smallest number that must be added to 593846 to make it divisible 9.
   (a) 1 (b) 4
   (c) 6 (d) 9

5. The smallest 4 digit number exactly divisible by 44 is:
   (a) 1008 (b) 1012
   (c) 1032 (d) 1044

6. The difference between the local value and the face value of 5 in the number 3785694 is:
   (a) 5000 (b) 5694
   (c) 5689 (d) 4995

7. The difference between the local value and the face value of 2 in the number 7585294 is:
   (a) 292 (b) 294
   (c) 198 (d) 200

8. The difference between the local value and the face value of 4 in the number 9545278 is:
   (a) 40000 (b) 45278
   (c) 39996 (d) 45274

9. What is the remainder when a number 56897328937 is divided by 25?
   (a) 2	(b) 7
   (c) 12	(d) 17

10. What is the remainder when 7596328 is divided by 9?
    (a) 1	(b) 2
    (c) 4	(d) 6

11. What is the last digit in the product of first 25 odd natural numbers?
    (a) 1	(b) 3
    (c) 5	(d) 7

12. If $a + b = 30$ and $a \times b = 176$, find $a^3 + b^3$.
    (a) 10060	(b) 11060
    (c) 11160	(d) 11600

13. The sum of first 50 natural number is:
    (a) 1100	(b) 1275
    (c) 1850	(d) 2550

14. The sum of first 30 even natural numbers is:
    (a) 465	(b) 680
    (c) 930	(d) 985

15. The sum of the squares of first 20 even natural numbers is:
    (a) 2870	(b) 5740
    (c) 8610	(d) 11480

16. The smallest number that should be subtracted from 4456 to make it divisible by 6 is:
    (a) 2	(b) 4
    (c) 6	(d) 8

17. If a three digit number $5x2$ is divisible by 6, then x should be:
    (a) 1	(b) 2
    (c) 3	(d) 4

18. Which natural number nearest to 4855 is divisible by 75?
    (a) 4850	(b) 4825
    (c) 4875	(d) 4900

19. Find the smallest number that must be added to 6873 to make it divisible by 12.
    (a) 1	(b) 3
    (c) 5	(d) 7

20. Which of the following number is divisible by 24?
    (a) 75318	(b) 45156
    (c) 15804	(d) 34512

21. The sum of two numbers is 14 and their product is 48. How much is the sum of reciprocal of these numbers?
    (a) 24/7
    (b) 7/24
    (c) 1/14
    (d) 1/24

22. In a division sum, the remainder is 0. As student by mistake taken the divisor by 23 instead of 32 and obtained 96 as quotient. What is the correct quotient?
    (a) 36
    (b) 45
    (c) 64
    (d) 69

23. In a division sum, the divisor is 6 times the quotient and 2 times the remainder. If the remainder is 15, what is the dividend?
    (a) 115
    (b) 164
    (c) 165
    (d) 176

24. In a division sum, the divisor is 8 times the quotient and 4 times the remainder. If the remainder is 24, what is the dividend?
    (a) 1152
    (b) 1164
    (c) 1170
    (d) 1176

25. The 6 digit number $123a7b$ is divisible by 36. Find the minimum value of a.
    (a) 8
    (b) 5
    (c) 3
    (d) 1

26. Find the number of three digit numbers which are divisible neither by 2 nor by 3?
    (a) 300
    (b) 320
    (c) 350
    (d) 400

27. Which of the following numbers can be expressed as a power of 5?
    (a) 3926145
    (b) 1953125
    (c) 7863915
    (d) 5698725

28. If $N + 2$ is a three digit odd number, then which among the following must be always a three digit even number?
    (a) $N + 1$
    (b) $N - 1$
    (c) $N + 3$
    (d) All of these

29. The sum of all prime numbers from 1 to 50 is:
    (a) odd number
    (b) even number
    (c) prime number
    (d) both (a)&(c)

30. The difference between a two digit number and the sum of its digits is always a multiple of:
    (a) 6
    (b) 10
    (c) 9
    (d) 11

31. How many factors dose the number 5184 have?
    (a) 35
    (b) 36
    (c) 37
    (d) 38

32. How many numbers are there between 1 to 5880 which can divide 5880 leaving a remainder as zero?
    (a) 46
    (b) 47
    (c) 48
    (d) 50

33. The square root of 15876 is:
    (a) 124
    (b) 126
    (c) 136
    (d) 144

34. The cube root of 85184 is:
    (a) 34
    (b) 44
    (c) 42
    (d) 38

35. The cube root of 74088 is:
    (a) 38
    (b) 42
    (c) 48
    (d) 52

36. The difference between a three digit number and a number formed by reversing its digits is always divisible by:
    (a) 6
    (b) 11
    (c) 9
    (d) Both (b)&(c)

37. The sum of two numbers is 176. 4 times one number is equal to 7 times the other. The bigger of the two numbers is:
    (a) 104
    (b) 112
    (c) 132
    (d) 126

38. A number is doubled and 9 is added. If the resultant is tripled, it becomes 165. What is that number?
    (a) 15
    (b) 18
    (c) 23
    (d) 27

39. Find a number such that when 15 is subtracted from 7 times the number, the result is 10 more than twice the number.
    (a) 5
    (b) 7
    (c) 8
    (d) 11

40. If a four digit number $2x48$ is exactly divisible by 44, then find the value of x.
    (a) 2
    (b) 0
    (c) 6
    (d) 9

41. If the number $85x3675$ is completely divisible by 55, then the smallest whole number in place of x will be:
    (a) 2
    (b) 5
    (c) 7
    (d) 9

42. If the 5 digit number $976ab$ is divisible by 90, then $(a + b) = ?$
    (a) 4
    (b) 5
    (c) 7
    (d) 9

43. How many prime numbers are there in first 50 natural numbers?
    (a) 12
    (b) 13
    (c) 15
    (d) 16

44. The difference between two numbers is 1000. On dividing the larger number with smaller, we get 16 as quotient and 25 as remainder. Find the larger number.
    (a) 1045
    (b) 1050
    (c) 1065
    (d) 1085

45. On dividing a number by 65, we get 42 as a remainder. On dividing the same number by 13, what will be the remainder?
    (a) 3
    (b) 4
    (c) 7
    (d) 11

46. On dividing a number by 336, we get 90 as a remainder. On dividing the same number by 28, what will be the remainder?
    (a) 3
    (b) 4
    (c) 6
    (d) 11

47. On dividing a number by 270, we get 100 as a remainder. On dividing the same number by 18, what will be the remainder?
    (a) 3
    (b) 4
    (c) 7
    (d) 10

48. A 3-digit number $45P$ is added to another 3-digit number 968 to give a 4-digit number $141Q$, which is divisible by 11. Then $P + Q$ is:
    (a) 7
    (b) 9
    (c) 9
    (d) 10

49. Find the smallest number with which 157500 should be multiplied to make it a perfect square?
    (a) 7
    (b) 14
    (c) 35
    (d) 70

50. What is the largest power of 24 that can divide 80!?
    (a) 26
    (b) 36
    (c) 54
    (d) 78

51. What is the largest power of 32 that can divide 100!?
    (a) 16
    (b) 19
    (c) 21
    (d) 24

52. What is the largest power of 81 that can divide 810!?
    (a) 10
    (b) 50
    (c) 100
    (d) 101

53. $19^{75} + 21^{75}$ is a multiple of:
    (a) 19
    (b) 20
    (c) 21
    (d) 40

54. Which of the following number divides $17^{2n} - 11^{2n}$ for all positive integer values of n is:
    (a) 6   (b) 28
    (c) 121   (d) 168

55. Which one of the following is the common factor of $(61^{37} + 37^{37})$ and $(61^{61} + 37^{61})$?
    (a) $(61 + 37)$ (b) $(36 - 37)$
    (c) $(61^{37} + 37^{37})$ (d) Only 1

56. What will be in the unit place of 9853^{42}?
    (a) 1   (b) 3
    (c) 7   (d) 9

57. What will be in the unit place of 77^{77}?
    (a) 1   (b) 3
    (c) 7   (d) 9

58. What is the unit digit of $(39^{11} - 32^{11})$?
    (a) 1   (b) 5
    (c) 7   (d) 8

59. What will be in the unit place of $45^{8} + 19^{11} - 62^{18}$?
    (a) 0   (b) 3
    (c) 7   (d) 9

60. What will be in the unit place of $44^{11} \times 55^{11}$?
    (a) 0   (b) 5
    (c) 6   (d) 8

61. What will be in the unit place of $57^{142} \times 82^{161} \times 93^{172}$?
    (a) 1   (b) 3
    (c) 8   (d) 9

62. The number 50! will end with how many zeros?
    (a) 1   (b) 5
    (c) 10   (d) 12

63. On dividing a number by 7, we get 4 as a remainder. What will be the remainder when the square of this number is divided by 7?
    (a) 1   (b) 2
    (c) 3   (d) 4

64. If N is a natural number which when divided by 9 gives 5 as a remainder. What will be the remainder when $2N$ is divided by 9?
    (a) 1   (b) 3
    (c) 5   (d) 7

65. If N is a natural number which when divided by 12 gives 3 as a remainder. What will be the remainder when $5N$ is divided by 12?
    (a) 1   (b) 3
    (c) 5   (d) 7

66. A Number N when divided by 7 leaves 2 as a remainder. When N^2 is divided by 7, the remainder is:
   (a) 2
   (b) 4
   (c) 5
   (d) 6

67. A Number N when divided by 11 leaves 7 as a remainder. When N^2 is divided by 11, the remainder is:
   (a) 2
   (b) 4
   (c) 5
   (d) 6

68. Which of the following numbers will completely divide $(64^9 - 1)$?
   (a) 8
   (b) 9
   (c) 64
   (d) 65

69. What will be remainder when $(51^{51} + 51)$ is divided by 52?
   (a) 1
   (b) 51
   (c) 50
   (d) 49

70. A number when successively divided by 7 and 9 gives respective remainders as 3 and 4. What will be the remainder when the same number is divided by 5?
   (a) 1
   (b) 2
   (c) 3
   (d) 4

71. A number when divided successively by 4 and 5 leaves remainders 1 and 4 respectively. When it is successively divided by 5 and 4, then the respective remainders will be:
   (a) 1, 2
   (b) 2, 3
   (c) 3, 2
   (d) 4, 3

72. A number was successively divided by 5, 6 and 7. The remainders obtained were 4, 3 and 1 respectively. Find the number.
   (a) 144
   (b) 199
   (c) 259
   (d) 274

73. A number when divided by 5, 7 and 8 leaves respective remainders of 2, 4 and 6. Find smallest such three digit number.
   (a) 272
   (b) 327
   (c) 502
   (d) 512

74. Which term of the arithmetic progression 3, 7, 11, ..., is 63?
   (a) 10
   (b) 16
   (c) 7
   (d) 9

75. Which term of the geometric progression 3, $3\sqrt{3}$, 9, ... is 81?
   (a) 5th
   (b) 8th
   (c) 6th
   (d) 7th

76. The sum of all two digit numbers divisible by 5 is:
   (a) 865
   (b) 920
   (c) 945
   (d) 975

77. Find the sum of the integers between 1 and 200 that are multiples of 7.
    (a) 2742
    (b) 2546
    (c) 2842
    (d) 2646

78. What will be the maximum sum of 44, 42, 40, 38, ...?
    (a) 504
    (b) 506
    (c) 502
    (d) 512

79. The sum of the three numbers in an AP is 39 and the sum of the squares of the three numbers is 515. Find the smallest of the three numbers.
    (a) 9
    (b) 12
    (c) 11
    (d) 10

80. How many terms of the series $\sqrt{3} + 3 + 3\sqrt{3} + ...$ add up to $39 + 13\sqrt{3}$?
    (a) 5
    (b) 9
    (c) 6
    (d) 7

81. After striking the floor, a rubber ball rebounds to half of the height from which is has fallen. Find the total distance that it travels before coming to rest, if it has been gently dropped from a height of 128 meters.
    (a) 128 m
    (b) 384 m
    (c) 256 m
    (d) 420 m

82. The geometric mean of 1, 2, 4, 8, and 16 is:
    (a) 32
    (b) 16
    (c) 8
    (d) 4

83. Find the number of common terms in following series of numbers:
    Series 1 $\Rightarrow$ 3, 6, 9, 12, 15, 18, ..., 120
    Series 2 $\Rightarrow$ 5, 10, 15, 20, 25, ..., 120
    (a) 8
    (b) 10
    (c) 15
    (d) 24

84. If all 4's are replaced by 5, then algebraic sum of numbers from 1 to 100 (both inclusive) is:
    (a) 5050
    (b) 5060
    (c) 5160
    (d) 5150

85. If all 4's are replaced by 6, then algebraic sum of numbers from 1 to 60 (both inclusive) is:
    (a) 1830
    (b) 2030
    (c) 2040
    (d) 2042

86. Find the values of $-1^2 + 2^2 - 3^2 + 4^2 - 5^2 + 6^2 - ... - 19^2 + 20^2$.
    (a) 420
    (b) 630
    (c) 210
    (d) 190

87. The number of digits in $(2XY)^4$ where $2XY$ is a three digit number is:
    (a) 9
    (b) 10
    (c) 11
    (d) can't say

KEYS

1. (d)	2. (c)	3. (a)	4. (a)	5. (b)	6. (d)	7. (c)	8. (c)
9. (c)	10. (c)	11. (c)	12. (c)	13. (b)	14. (c)	15. (d)	16. (b)
17. (b)	18. (c)	19. (b)	20. (d)	21. (b)	22. (d)	23. (c)	24. (d)
25. (c)	26. (a)	27. (b)	28. (a)	29. (b)	30. (c)	31. (a)	32. (a)
33. (b)	34. (b)	35. (b)	36. (d)	37. (b)	38. (c)	39. (a)	40. (d)
41. (c)	42. (b)	43. (c)	44. (c)	45. (a)	46. (c)	47. (d)	48. (d)
49. (a)	50. (a)	51. (b)	52. (d)	53. (d)	54. (d)	55. (a)	56. (d)
57. (c)	58. (a)	59. (a)	60. (a)	61. (c)	62. (d)	63. (b)	64. (a)
65. (b)	66. (b)	67. (c)	68. (b)	69. (c)	70. (d)	71. (b)	72. (c)
73. (d)	74. (b)	75. (d)	76. (c)	77. (c)	78. (b)	79. (c)	80. (c)
81. (b)	82. (d)	83. (a)	84. (c)	85. (d)	86. (c)	87. (b)	

SOLUTIONS

Solution 1

91 is not a prime number as it is a product of 13 and 7.

Choice (d)

Solution 2

79 is a prime number.

Choice (c)

Solution 3

307 is a prime number.

Choice (a)

Solution 4

The divisibility test for 9 says that the sum of digits must be a multiple of 9.

$5 + 9 + 3 + 8 + 4 + 6 = 35$

Hence if we add 1 to the number, the sum will become 36 which is a multiple of 9.

Choice (a)

Solution 5

The smallest 4 digit number is 1000. Let us divide 1000 with 44.

$$\begin{array}{r} 22\\ 44{\overline{\smash{)}\,1000}}\\ \underline{88}\\ 120\\ \underline{88}\\ 32 \end{array}$$

As the remainder is 32, so to make the number divisible by 44 either we need to subtract 32 from 1000 or add 12 to it ($\because$ 32 + 12 = 44).

$\therefore$ Smallest 4 digit number divisible by 44 = 1000 + 12 = 1012.

Choice (b)

Solution 6

(Local value of 5) – (Face value of 5) = 5000 – 5 = 4995.

Choice (d)

Solution 7

(Local value of 2) – (Face value of 2) = 200 – 2
= 198.

Choice (c)

Solution 8

(Local value of 4) – (Face value of 4) = 40000 – 4
= 39996.

Choice (c)

Solution 9

The remainder of any number divided by 25 is the remainder of the number formed by its last two digits divided by 25. The number formed by last two digits is 37. So, the remainder will be 12.

Choice (c)

Solution 10

The remainder of any number divided by 9 is the remainder of the sum of its digits divided by 9. The sum of the digits of the number 7596328 is 40. So, the remainder will be 4.

Choice (c)

Solution 11

The 3rd odd natural number is 5. The number 5 multiplied with any other odd number will give a number whose last digit is always 5.

Choice (c)

Solution 12

$a^3 + b^3 = (a + b)(a^2 - ab + b^2)$
$= 30 \times (a^2 + b^2 - ab)$
$= 30 \times [(a + b)^2 - 2ab - ab]$
$= 30 \times [(a + b)^2 - 3ab]$
$= 30 \times [30^2 - 3 \times 176]$
$= 11160.$

Choice (c)

Solution 13

The sum of first n natural number is $\dfrac{n(n+1)}{2}$

$\therefore$ Sum of first 50 natural numbers $= \dfrac{50 \times 51}{2} = 1275.$

Choice (b)

Solution 14

Sum $= 2 + 4 + 6 + \ldots + 60$
$= 2(1 + 2 + 3 + \ldots + 30)$
$= 2 \times \dfrac{30 \times 31}{2}$
$= 930.$

Choice (c)

Solution 15

Sum $= 2^2 + 4^2 + 6^2 + \ldots + 40^2$
$= 2^2 (1^2 + 2^2 + 3^2 + \ldots + 20^2)$
$= 2^2 \times \dfrac{20(20+1)(40+1)}{6}$ $\because \sum n^2 = \dfrac{n(n+1)(2n+1)}{6}$
$= 4 \times \dfrac{20 \times 21 \times 41}{6}$
$= 11480.$

Choice (d)

Solution 16

$6 = 2 \times 3$

For a number to be divisible by 6, it must be also divisible by both 2 and 3 which are the co-prime factors of 6.

Divisibility test for 2 $\Rightarrow$ As the last digit is even the number divisible by 2.
Divisibility test for 3 $\Rightarrow 4 + 4 + 5 + 6 = 19$, hence the number is not divisible by 3.

Here we need to subtract 2, 4, 6 or 8 from the number to make the sum of digits a multiple of 3.

Subtracting 2 from the number, resulting number 4454 is not divisible by 3.

Subtracting 4 from the number, resulting number 4452 is divisible by 3.

Choice (b)

Solution 17

$6 = 2 \times 3$

For a number to be divisible by 6, it must be also divisible by both 2 and 3 which are the co-prime factors of 6.

Divisibility test for 2 $\Rightarrow$ As the last digit is even the number divisible by 2.
Divisibility test for 3 $\Rightarrow (5 + x + 2)$ must be a multiple of 3. Hence x must be 2.

Choice (b)

Solution 18

$75 = 25 \times 3$

For a number to be divisible by 75, it must be also divisible by both 25 and 3 which are the co-prime factors of 75. For a number to be divisible by 25 the last 2 digits must be '00', '25', '50' or '75'.

The number 4850 is divisible by 25 but not divisible by 3.

The number 4825 is divisible by 25 but not divisible by 3.

The number 4875 is divisible by both 25 and 3, hence divisible by 75.

Choice (c)

Solution 19

$12 = 3 \times 4$

If the number is divisible by both 3 and 4 it will be divisible by 12 also because 3 and 4 are the co-prime factors of 12.

Divisibility test for 3 $\Rightarrow$ Sum of 6, 8, 7 and 3 is 24 which is a multiple of 3.

Divisibility test for 4 ⇒ Last 2 digits *i.e.,* 73 is not divisible by 4 or gives a remainder 1 when divided by 4. Hence if we add 3 to the number the last 2 digits will be 76 which is a multiple of 4.

Choice (b)

Solution 20

$24 = 3 \times 8$

For a number to be divisible by 24, it must be also divisible by both 3 and 8 which are the co-prime factors of 24.

Checking option (a)
Divisibility test for 3   ⇒ $7 + 5 + 3 + 1 + 8 = 24$, hence the number is divisible by 3.
Divisibility test for 8   ⇒ 318 is not divisible by 8, hence the number is not divisible by 8.

Checking option (b)
Divisibility test for 3   ⇒ $4 + 5 + 1 + 5 + 6 = 21$, hence the number is divisible by 3.
Divisibility test for 8   ⇒ 156 is not divisible by 8, hence the number is not divisible by 8.

Checking option (c)
Divisibility test for 3   ⇒ $1 + 5 + 8 + 0 + 4 = 18$, hence the number is divisible by 3.
Divisibility test for 8   ⇒ 804 is not divisible by 8, hence the number is not divisible by 8.

Checking option (d)
Divisibility test for 3   ⇒ $3 + 4 + 5 + 1 + 2 = 15$, hence the number is divisible by 3.
Divisibility test for 8   ⇒ 512 is divisible by 8, hence the number is also divisible by 8.

∴ The number 34512 is divisible by 24 as it is divisible by both of its co-primes.

Choice (d)

Solution 21

Let the numbers be *a* and *b*. Then, $a + b = 14$ and $a \times b = 48$

$$\therefore \frac{a+b}{ab} = \frac{14}{48}$$

$$\frac{1}{b} + \frac{1}{a} = \frac{7}{24}.$$

Choice (b)

Solution 22

Number (or Dividend) $= 23 \times 96 = 2208$

Correct quotient $= \frac{2208}{32} = 69.$

Choice (d)

Solution 23

Divisor = 2 × Remainder = 2 × 15 = 30
Divisor = 6 × Quotient

∴ Quotient = Divisor/6 = 30/6 = 5

Dividend = (Divisor × Quotient) + Remainder
= (30 × 5) + 15
= 165.

Choice (c)

Solution 24

Divisor = 4 × Remainder = 4 × 24 = 96
Divisor = 8 × Quotient

∴ Quotient = Divisor/8 = 96/8 = 12

Dividend = (Divisor × Quotient) + Remainder = (96 × 12) + 24 = 1176.

Choice (d)

Solution 25

36 = 4 × 9

For a number to be divisible by 36, it must be also divisible by both 4 and 9 which are the co-prime factors of 36.

Divisibility test for 4 ⇒ The last 2 digits must be either 72 or 76, hence $b = 2$ or 6

Consider the number 123a72

Divisibility test for 9 ⇒ Sum of digits *i.e.*, $(15 + a)$ must be divisible by 9 for which $a = 3$.

Consider the number 123a76

Divisibility test for 9 ⇒ sum of digits *i.e.*, $(19 + a)$ must be divisible by 9 for which $a = 8$.

∴ Minimum value of $a = 3$.

Choice (c)

Solution 26

From 100 to 999, there are 900 three digits numbers.

Numbers divisible by 2 = $\frac{1}{2} \times 900 = 450$

Numbers divisible by 3 = $\frac{1}{3} \times 900 = 300$

Numbers divisible by both 2 and 3 = $\frac{1}{6} \times 900 = 150$

Numbers divisible by either 2 or 3 = (450 + 300) − 150 = 600
∴ Numbers which are divisible neither by 2 nor by 3 = 900 − 600 = 300.

Choice (a)

Solution 27

$5^3 = 125$
$5^4 = 625$
$5^5 = 3125$
$5^6 = 15625$

The higher powers of 5 will end with 125 or 625. Also any power of 5 in never divisible by 3 or 9. Option (a), (c) and (d) are divisible by 3.

Choice (b)

Solution 28

| $N + 2$ | $\Rightarrow$ | 101 | to | 999 | |
| ∴ N | $\Rightarrow$ | 99 | to | 997 | |

Option (a)

| $N + 1$ | $\Rightarrow$ | 100 | to | 998 | we get only 3-digit even numbers. |

Option (b)

| $N − 1$ | $\Rightarrow$ | 98 | to | 996 | we may get 2-digit even number. |

Option (c)

| $N + 3$ | $\Rightarrow$ | 102 | to | 1000 | we may get 4-digit even number. |

Choice (a)

Solution 29

There are 15 prime numbers from 1 to 50 as follows:

2, 3, 5, 7, 11, 13, 17, 19, 23, 29, 31, 37, 41, 43 and 47.

Sum = 2 + (14 odd prime numbers)
    = 2 + even number
    = even number.

Choice (b)

Solution 30

Let two digit number = $10x + y$

∴ $10x + y − (x + y) = 9x − 9y = 9(x − y)$

Hence it will be always a multiple of 9.

Choice (c)

Solution 31

If a number N is factorized as:

$$N = a^p \times b^q \times c^r \text{ where } a, b, \text{ and } c \text{ are prime factors, then}$$

Number of factors $= (p + 1)(q + 1)(r + 1)$

$$5184 = 2^6 \times 3^4$$

$\therefore$ Number of factors $= (6 + 1)(4 + 1)$
$= 35.$

Choice (a)

Solution 32

The numbers which can divide a number leaving a remainder as zero are the factors of that number. If a number N is factorized as:

$$N = a^p \times b^q \times c^r \text{ where } a, b, \text{ and } c \text{ are prime factors, then}$$

Number of factors $= (p + 1)(q + 1)(r + 1)$

$$5880 = 2^3 \times 3^1 \times 5^1 \times 7^2$$

$\therefore$ Number of factors $= (3 + 1)(1 + 1)(1 + 1)(2 + 1)$
$= 48$

If 1 and 5880 are excluded, the factors are 46.

Choice (a)

Solution 33

Factorizing the number 15876 as:

$$15876 = 2^2 \times 3^4 \times 7^2$$

Hence square root of $15876 = 2 \times 3^2 \times 7 = 126$

Choice (b)

Solution 34

Factorizing the number 85184 as:

$$85184 = 2^6 \times 11^3$$

Hence cube root of $85184 = 2^2 \times 11 = 44.$

Choice (b)

Solution 35

Factorizing the number 74088 as:

$$74088 = 2^3 \times 3^3 \times 7^3$$

Hence cube root of $74088 = 2 \times 3 \times 7 = 42$.

Choice (b)

Solution 36

Let the three digit number $= 100x + 10y + z$
So the reversed number $= 100z + 10y + x$

Difference $= (100x + 10y + z) - (100z + 10y + x)$
$= 99x - 99z = 99(x - z)$

Hence the difference will be divisible by both 9 and 11.

Choice (d)

Solution 37

Let the two numbers be A and B.

$$4A = 7B \text{ or } \frac{A}{B} = \frac{7x}{4x}$$

$$A + B = 176$$
$$7x + 4x = 176$$

$\therefore \quad x = \frac{176}{11} = 16$

So the bigger number, $A = 7 \times 16 = 112$.

Choice (b)

Solution 38

Let the number be N

If the number is doubled and 9 is added to it the it will be $2N + 9$

$3 \times (2N + 9) = 165$

$\therefore \quad N = 23.$

Choice (c)

Solution 39

Let the number be N

If the number is multiplied by 7 and 15 is subtracted from it, then it will be $7N - 15$

$7N - 15 = 2N + 10$

$\therefore \quad 5N = 25 \; N = 5.$

Choice (a)

Solution 40

44 = 4 × 11

If the number 2x48 is exactly divisible by 44, then it must be also divisible by 4 and 11 which are the co-prime factors of 44. As the last 2 digits are already divisible by 4, hence we need to only check the divisibility for 11.

2x48

Sum of alternate digits $\Rightarrow 2 + 4$
$\Rightarrow x + 8$

To make the number divisible by 11, the sum of alternate digits must be same or differ in the multiple of 11. If we consider sum of alternate digits as equal i.e., $x + 8 = 2 + 4$ then x will be negative which is not possible.

∴ $(x + 8) - (2 + 4) = 11$

∴ $x = 9$.

Choice (d)

Solution 41

55 = 5 × 11

If the number 85x3675 is exactly divisible by 55, then it must be also divisible by 5 and 11 which are the co-prime factors of 55. As the last digit is already 5, hence we need to only check the divisibility for 11.

Sum of alternate digits $\Rightarrow 8 + x + 6 + 5$
$\Rightarrow 5 + 3 + 7$

As the sum of alternate digits should be equal or differ by a multiple of 11

$(8 + x + 6 + 5) - (5 + 3 + 7) = 11$

$19 + x - 15 = 11$

∴ $x = 7$

Choice (c)

Solution 42

90 = 9 × 10

For a number to be divisible by 90, it must be also divisible by both 9 and 10 which are the co-prime factors of 90. For a number to be divisible by 10 the last digit 'b' must be zero.

Divisibility test for 9 $\Rightarrow 9 + 7 + 6 + a + 0 = 22 + a$ must be a multiple of 9.

∴ $a = 5$

The required sum $a + b = 5 + 0 = 5$

Choice (b)

Solution 43

The 15 prime numbers in first 50 natural numbers as follows:

2, 3, 5, 7, 11, 13, 17, 19, 23, 29, 31, 37, 41, 43 and 47.

Choice (c)

Solution 44

Let the smaller number be n. Then larger number will be $(n + 1000)$

$\therefore \quad n + 1000 = 16n + 25 \quad\quad (\because \text{Dividend} = \text{Divisor} \times \text{Quotient} + \text{Remainder})$
$\quad\quad 15n = 975$
$\quad\quad n = 65$

Hence larger number = 1065.

Choice (c)

Solution 45

Let the number be n and k be the quotient when it is divided by 65.

$n = 65k + 42$
$\quad = (13 \times 5k) + (13 \times 3) + 3$
$\quad = 13(5k + 3) + 3$

Hence if the number is divided by 13 the remainder obtained is 3.

Choice (a)

Solution 46

Let the number be n and k be the quotient when it is divided by 336.

$n = 336k + 90$
$\quad = (28 \times 12k) + (28 \times 3) + 6$
$\quad = 28(12k + 3) + 6$

Hence if the number is divided by 28 the remainder obtained is 6.

Choice (c)

Solution 47

Let the number be n and k be the quotient when it is divided by 270.

$n = 270k + 100$
$\quad = (18 \times 15k) + (18 \times 5) + 10$
$\quad = 18(15k + 5) + 10$

Hence if the number is divided by 18 the remainder obtained is 10.

Choice (d)

Solution 48

$$\begin{array}{r} 4\ 5\ P \\ +\ 9\ 6\ 8 \\ \hline 1\ 4\ 1\ Q \end{array} \Rightarrow P + 8 = Q \quad \Rightarrow P - Q = 8$$

Also, $141Q$ is divisible by 11, therefore taking the difference of addition of alternate digits as follows:

$(4 + Q) - (1 + 1) = 11$

∴ $Q = 9$

Hence $P = 1$

So, $P + Q = 10$.

Choice (d)

Solution 49

Factorizing the number 157500 as:

$157500 = 2^2 \times 3^2 \times 5^4 \times 7^1$

From the factorization it seems that to make a number as a perfect square there is a shortage of one 7.

$(2^2 \times 3^2 \times 5^4 \times 7^1) \times 7 \Rightarrow 2^2 \times 3^2 \times 5^4 \times 7^2$

Hence the smallest number with which 157500 should be multiplied to make it a perfect square is 7.

Choice (a)

Solution 50

$24 = 2^3 \times 3$

The largest power of 2 or number of 2's existing in 80! can be found by dividing the number 80 successively by 2 as follows:

2	80
2	40
2	20
2	10
2	5
2	2
2	1
	0

Therefore the largest power of 2 in 80! can be obtained by adding all the quotients i.e., 40 + 20 + 10 + 5 + 2 + 1 = 78. So number of 2^3 will be one-third of 78 i.e., 26.

The largest power of 3 or number of 3's existing in 80! can be found by dividing the number 80 successively by 3 as follows:

```
3 | 80
3 | 26
3 |  8
3 |  2
  |  0
```

Therefore the largest power of 3 in 80! can be obtained by adding all the quotients i.e., 26 + 8 + 2 = 36.

Number of $2^3 \Rightarrow 26$
Number of $3 \Rightarrow 36$

Hence largest power of 24 that can divide 80! is 26.

Choice (a)

Solution 51

$32 = 2^5$

The largest power of 2 or number of 2's existing in 100! can be found by dividing the number 100 successively by 2 as follows:

```
2 | 100
2 |  50
2 |  25
2 |  12
2 |   6
2 |   3
2 |   1
  |   0
```

Therefore the largest power of 2 in 100! can be obtained by adding all the quotients i.e., 50 + 25 + 12 + 6 + 3 + 1 = 97. Hence 2^{97} exist in 100!

$$2^{97} = 2^{95} \times 2^2$$
$$= (2^5)^{19} \times 2^2$$
$$= (32)^{19} \times 2^2.$$

Choice (b)

Solution 52

$81 = 3^4$

The largest power of 3 or number of 3's existing in 810! can be found by dividing the number 810 successively by 3 as follows:

3	810
3	270
3	90
3	30
3	10
3	3
3	1
	0

Therefore the largest power of 3 in 810! can be obtained by adding all the quotients *i.e.*, $270 + 90 + 30 + 10 + 3 + 1 = 404$. Hence 3^{404} exist in 810!

$$3^{404} = (3^4)^{101} = (81)^{101}.$$

Choice (d)

Solution 53

When n is odd, $(x^n + a^n)$ is always divisible by $(x + a)$.

∴ $(19^{75} + 21^{75})$ must be a multiple of $(19 + 21)$.

Choice (d)

Solution 54

$17^{2n} - 11^{2n} = 289^n - 121^n$

$(x^n - a^n)$ is always divisible by $(x - a)$ for all positive values of n.

Hence $289^n - 121^n$ is divisible by 168.

Choice (d)

Solution 55

When n is odd, $(x^n + a^n)$ is always divisible by $(x + a)$.

∴ Each one of $(61^{37} + 37^{37})$ and $(61^{61} + 37^{61})$ is divisible by $(61 + 37)$.

Choice (a)

Solution 56

Unit place of 9853^{42} = Unit place of 3^{42}

The powers of 3 will give unit place as 3, 9, 7, 1 repeatedly.

Unit place of $3^{42} = 3^{4K+2}$ $\because$ Unit digit repeats after every 4th power of 3.
$\phantom{Unit place of 3^{42}} = 9.$

Choice (d)

Solution 57

Unit place of 77^{77} = Unit place of 7^{77}

The powers of 7 will give unit place as 7, 9, 3, 1 repeatedly.

Unit place of $7^{77} = 7^{4K+1}$ $\because$ Unit digit repeats after every 4th power of 7.
$\phantom{Unit place of 7^{77}} = 7.$

Choice (c)

Solution 58

Unit digit of $(39^{11} - 32^{11})$ = Unit digit of 9^{11} – Unit digit of 2^{11}

Unit digit of $9^{11} = 9$ $\because$ Any odd power of 9 is 9 in unit place.

Unit digit of $2^{11} = 2^{4k+3} = 8$ $\because$ Power cycle of 2 follows a pattern 2, 4, 8, 6.

$\therefore$ Unit place of $(39^{11} - 32^{11}) = 9 - 8$
$\phantom{\therefore Unit place of (39^{11} - 32^{11})} = 1.$

Choice (a)

Solution 59

Unit place of $45^8 + 19^{11} - 62^{18}$ = (Unit place of 5^8) + (Unit place of 9^{11}) – (Unit place of 2^{18})

Unit place of $5^8 = 5$ $\because$ Unit place of any power of 5 is always 5.
Unit place of $9^{11} = 9$ $\because$ Unit place of any odd power of 9 is 9.
Unit place of $2^{18} = 2^{4k+2}$
$\phantom{Unit place of 2^{18}} = 4$ $\because$ Unit digit repeats after every 4th power of 2.

$\therefore$ Unit place of $45^8 + 19^{11} - 62^{18} = 5 + 9 - 4 = 0$.

Choice (a)

Solution 60

Unit digit of $(44)^{11}$ = Unit digit of 4^{11}
$\phantom{Unit digit of (44)^{11}} = 4$ $\because$ Any odd power of 4 will give unit digit as 4

Unit digit of $(55)^{11}$ = Unit digit of 5^{11}
= 5   ∵ Any power of 5 will give unit digit as 5

Unit digit in the given product = Unit digit in the product $(4^{11} \times 5^{11})$
= 4 × 5 = 0.

Choice (a)

Solution 61

Unit digit of $(57)^{142}$ = Unit digit of 7^{4k+2}
= 9   ∵ Unit digit repeats after every 4th power of 7.

Unit digit of $(82)^{161}$ = Unit digit of 2^{4k+1}
= 2   ∵ Unit digit repeats after every 4th power of 2.

Unit digit of $(93)^{172}$ = Unit digit of 3^{4k}
= 1   ∵ Unit digit repeats after every 4th power of 3.

Unit digit in the given product = Unit digit in the product $(7^{142} \times 2^{161} \times 3^{172})$
= 9 × 2 × 1 = 8.

Choice (c)

Solution 62

The number of zeros coming at the end of 50! depends on the largest power of 5, because as every 5 gets multiplied with an even number we get zero at the end.

The largest power of 5 or number of 5's existing in 50! can be found by dividing the number 50 successively by 5 as follows:

5	50
5	10
5	2
	0

Therefore the largest power of 5 in 50! can be obtained by adding all the quotients *i.e.,* 10 + 2 = 12. Hence 50! ends with 12 zeros.

Choice (d)

Solution 63

Let the number be x and on dividing x by 7, we get k as quotient and 4 as remainder.

∴ $x = 7k + 4$
      $x^2 = (7k + 4)^2 = (49k^2 + 56k + 16) = 7(7k^2 + 8k + 2) + 2$

∴ On dividing x^2 by 7, we get 2 as remainder.

Choice (b)

Solution 64

Let k be the quotient when N is divided by 9.

$\therefore \qquad N = 9k + 5$

Then, $\qquad 2N = 18k + 10$
$\qquad\qquad\quad = 9(2k + 1) + 1$

Thus when $2N$ is divided by 9, the remainder is 1.

Choice (a)

Solution 65

Let k be the quotient when N is divided by 12.

$\therefore \qquad N = 12k + 3$

Then, $\qquad 5N = 60k + 15$
$\qquad\qquad\quad = 12(5k + 1) + 3$

Thus when $5N$ is divided by 12, the remainder is 3.

Choice (b)

Solution 66

Let k be the quotient when N is divided by 7.

$\therefore \qquad N = 7k + 2$

Then, $\qquad N^2 = (7k + 2)^2$
$\qquad\qquad\quad = 49k^2 + 28k + 4$
$\qquad\qquad\quad = 7(7k^2 + 4k) + 4$

Thus, if N^2 is divided by 7, the remainder is 4.

Choice (b)

Solution 67

Let k be the quotient when N is divided by 11.

$\therefore \qquad N = 11k + 7$

Then, $\qquad N^2 = (11k + 7)^2$
$\qquad\qquad\quad = 121k^2 + 154k + 49$
$\qquad\qquad\quad = 11(11k^2 + 14k + 4) + 5$

Thus, if N^2 is divided by 11, the remainder is 5.

Choice (c)

Solution 68

$(x^n - 1)$ will be divisibly by $(x + 1)$ only when n is even.

$(64^9 - 1) = [(8^2)^9 - 1] = (8^{18} - 1)$, which is divisible by $(8 + 1)$, i.e., 9.

Choice (b)

Solution 69

$(x^n + 1)$ will be divisible by $(x + 1)$ only when n is odd.

$\therefore (51^{51} + 1)$ will be divisible by $(51 + 1)$

$\therefore (51^{51} + 1) + 50$, when divided by 52 will give 50 as remainder.

Choice (c)

Solution 70

Divisors	Remainder
7	3
9	4

Assuming the quotient of second division as x, it is seen that when the final dividend is divided by 9 the remainder is 4.

$\therefore$ The 2nd dividend $= 9x + 4$ ($\because$ Dividend = Divisor × Quotient + Remainder)

Now this $(9x + 4)$ will be the quotient if 1st dividend is divided by 7 and the remainder is 3.

$\therefore$ The 1st dividend (or original number) $= 7(9x + 4) + 3$
$= 63x + 31$

Substituting the value of x as 1 to get smallest number.

The required number $= 63(1) + 31 = 94$

If 94 is divided by 5, the remainder is 4.

Choice (d)

Solution 71

Divisors	Remainder
4	1
5	4

Assuming the quotient of second division as x, it is seen that when the final dividend is divided by 5 the remainder is 4.

$\therefore$ The 2nd dividend $= 5x + 4$ ($\because$ Dividend = Divisor × Quotient + Remainder)

Now this $(5x + 4)$ will be the quotient if 1st dividend is divided by 4 and the remainder is 1.

∴ The 1st dividend (or original number) = 4(5x + 4) + 1 = 20x + 17

Substituting the value of x as 1 to get smallest number.

The required number = 20(1) + 17 = 37

If the number 37 is divided by 5 and 4 successively:

$$5 \overline{)37} \atop \underline{35} \atop 2 7 \Rightarrow 4 \overline{)7} \atop \underline{4} \atop 3 1$$

The remainders are 2 and 3 respectively.

Choice (b)

Solution 72

Divisors	Remainder
5	4
6	3
7	1

Assuming the quotient of third division as x, it is seen that when the final dividend is divided by 7 the remainder is 1.

∴ The 3rd dividend = 7x + 1   (∵ Dividend = Divisor × Quotient + Remainder)

Now this (7x + 1) will be the quotient if 2nd dividend is divided by 6 and the remainder is 3.

∴ The 2nd dividend = 6(7x + 1) + 3

Now this [6(7x + 1) + 3] will be the quotient if 1st dividend (or original number) is divided by 5 and the remainder is 4.

∴ The 1st dividend = 5[6(7x + 1) + 3] + 4

Substituting the value of x as 1 to get smallest number.

∴ The 1st dividend (original number) = 5[6(7x + 1) + 3] + 4
= 5[42x + 9] + 4
= 210x + 49
= 210(1) + 49
= 259.

Choice (c)

Solution 73

Divisors	Remainder
5	2
7	4
8	6

Assuming the quotient of third division as x, it is seen that when the final dividend is divided by 8 the remainder is 6.

$\therefore$ The 3rd dividend = $8x + 6$ ($\because$ Dividend = Divisor $\times$ Quotient + Remainder)

Now this ($8x + 6$) will be the quotient if 2nd dividend is divided by 7 and the remainder is 4.

$\therefore$ The 2nd dividend = $7(8x + 6) + 4$

Now this $[7(8x + 6) + 4]$ will be the quotient if 1st dividend (or original number) is divided by 5 and the remainder is 2.

$\therefore$ The 1st dividend (original number) = $5[7(8x + 6) + 4] + 2$
$\qquad\qquad\qquad\qquad\qquad\qquad\qquad = 5[56x + 46] + 2$
$\qquad\qquad\qquad\qquad\qquad\qquad\qquad = 280x + 232$

Substituting the value of x as 1 to get smallest number.

Required number = $280(1) + 232 = 512$.

Choice (d)

Solution 74

3, 7, 11, ...

First term of the A.P. $\Rightarrow a = 3$

Common difference $\quad \Rightarrow d = 4$

$\qquad\qquad T_n = a + (n - 1)\, d$
$\qquad\qquad 63 = 3 + (n - 1)\, 4$
$\qquad\qquad n - 1 = \dfrac{63 - 3}{4}$

$\therefore \qquad\qquad n = 16.$

Choice (b)

Solution 75

3, $3\sqrt{3}$, 9, ...

First term of the G.P. $\Rightarrow a = 3$

Common ratio $\qquad \Rightarrow r = \dfrac{3\sqrt{3}}{3} = \sqrt{3}$

$\qquad\qquad T_n = a\, r^{n-1}$
$\qquad\qquad 81 = 3(\sqrt{3})^{n-1}$
$\qquad\qquad 27 = 3^{(n-1)/2}$

$$3^3 = 3^{(n-1)/2}$$

$$\therefore \quad \frac{n-1}{2} = 3$$

$$n = 7$$

So, 81 is the 7th term of given geometric progression.

Choice (d)

Solution 76

The two digit numbers divisible by 5 are: 10, 15, 20, ..., 95.

This is an arithmetic progression with first term *i.e.*, $a = 10$ and the common difference *i.e.*, $d = 5$.

Let us find out the number of terms in this series as follows:

$$T_n = a + (n-1)d$$
$$95 = 10 + (n-1)5$$
$$n - 1 = \frac{95 - 10}{5}$$

$$\therefore \quad n = 18$$

The sum of these 18 terms is:

$$S_{18} = \frac{18}{2}[T_1 + T_{18}]$$
$$= 9 \times [10 + 95] = 945.$$

Choice (c)

Solution 77

The multiples of 7 are: 7, 14, 21, ..., 196

This is an arithmetic progression with first term *i.e.*, $a = 7$ and the common difference *i.e.*, $d = 7$.

Let us find out the number of terms in this series as follows:

$$T_n = a + (n-1)d$$
$$196 = 7 + (n-1)7$$
$$n - 1 = \frac{196 - 7}{7}$$

$$\therefore \quad n = 28$$

The sum of these 28 terms is:

$$S_{28} = \frac{28}{2}[T_1 + T_{28}]$$
$$= 14 \times [7 + 196] = 2842.$$

Choice (c)

Solution 78

44, 42, 40, 38, ...

This is decreasing arithmetic progression in which the sum will be maximum if we consider the terms up to zero, because after that the value of terms will be negative.

Let us find out the number of terms in this series as follows:

$$T_n = a + (n-1)d$$
$$0 = 44 + (n-1) \times -2$$
$$n - 1 = \frac{-44}{-2}$$
$$\therefore \quad n = 23$$

The maximum sum of these 23 terms is:

$$S_{23} = \frac{23}{2}[T_1 + T_{23}]$$
$$= \frac{23}{2} \times [44 + 0] = 506.$$

Choice (b)

Solution 79

Let the three numbers be $a - d, a, a + d$.

Sum of three numbers:
$$a - d + a + a + d = 39$$
$$3a = 39$$
$$\therefore \quad a = 13$$

Sum of squares of three numbers:
$$(a-d)^2 + a^2 + (a+d)^2 = 515$$
$$a^2 - 2ad + d^2 + a^2 + a^2 + 2ad + d^2 = 515$$
$$3a^2 + 2d^2 = 515$$
$$3(13)^2 + 2d^2 = 515$$
$$d^2 = 4$$
$$d = \pm 2.$$

So smallest of the three numbers will be 11.

Choice (c)

Solution 80

The given series is a geometric progression.

First term *i.e.,* $\quad a = \sqrt{3}$

Common ratio i.e., $r = \dfrac{3}{\sqrt{3}} = \sqrt{3}$

$$S_n = \dfrac{a(r^n - 1)}{(r - 1)}$$

$$39 + 13\sqrt{3} = \dfrac{\sqrt{3}(3^{\frac{n}{2}} - 1)}{(\sqrt{3} - 1)}$$

$$(39 + 13\sqrt{3})(\sqrt{3} - 1) = \sqrt{3}(3^{\frac{n}{2}} - 1)$$

$$-39 + 26\sqrt{3} + 39 = \sqrt{3}(3^{\frac{n}{2}} - 1)$$

$$26 = 3^{\frac{n}{2}} - 1$$

$$3^{\frac{n}{2}} = 27$$

$$3^{\frac{n}{2}} = 3^3$$

$\therefore \quad \dfrac{n}{2} = 3$

$$n = 6$$

Hence 6 terms in the progression will add up to $39 + 13\sqrt{3}$.

Choice (c)

Solution 81

Distance traveled by the rubber ball $= 128 + 2(64) + 2(32) + 2(16) + \ldots \infty$

$\qquad = 128 + 2\,[64 + 32 + 16 + \ldots \infty]$

$\qquad = 128 + 2\left[\dfrac{64}{1 - 1/2}\right] \qquad \because S_\infty = \dfrac{a}{1-r}$

$\qquad = 128 + 2\,[128] = 384$ m.

Choice (b)

Solution 82

As there are 5 terms, geometric mean can be found as:

$\text{G.M.} = \sqrt[5]{1 \times 2 \times 4 \times 8 \times 16}$

$\qquad = \sqrt[5]{1 \times 2^1 \times 2^2 \times 2^3 \times 2^4}$

$\qquad = \sqrt[5]{2^{10}} = 2^{10 \times \frac{1}{5}} = 4.$

Choice (d)

Solution 83

Series 1 ⇒ 3, 6, 9, 12, 15, 18, ..., 120
Series 2 ⇒ 5, 10, 15, 20, 25, ..., 120

In series-1 numbers are incrementing with a difference of 3, while in series-2 numbers are incrementing with a difference of 5. Therefore the common terms will be incrementing with a difference which is LCM (least common multiple) of 3 and 5 *i.e.,* 15.

Series of common terms will be: 15, 30, 45, 60, 75, 90, 105, and 120

Hence 8 terms will be common.

Choice (a)

Solution 84

Sum of first 100 natural numbers = $\frac{100 \times 101}{2}$ = 5050

The number 4 will appear in unit place 10 times as follows:

04, 14, 24, ..., 94 ⇒ 05, 15, 25, ..., 95

Increment in total as 4 is replaced by 5 at unit place = 1 × 10 = 10

The number 4 will appear in tens place 10 times as follows:

40, 41, 42, 43, ..., 49 ⇒ 50, 51, 52, 53, ..., 59

Increment in total as 4 is replaced by 5 at tens place = 10 × 10 = 100

Total sum = 5050 + 10 + 100 = 5160.

Choice (c)

Solution 85

Sum of first 60 natural numbers = $\frac{60 \times 61}{2}$ = 1830

The number 4 will appear in unit place 6 times as follows:

04, 14, 24, ..., 54 ⇒ 06, 16, 26, ..., 56

Increment in total as 4 is replaced by 6 at unit place = 2 × 6 = 12

The number 4 will appear in tens place 10 times as follows:

40, 41, 42, 43, ..., 49 ⇒ 60, 61, 62, 63, ..., 69

Increment in total as 4 is replaced by 6 at tens place = 20 × 10 = 200

Total sum = 1830 + 12 + 200 = 2042.

Choice (d)

Solution 86

$$\begin{aligned}
\text{Sum} &= -1^2 + 2^2 - 3^2 + 4^2 - 5^2 + 6^2 - \ldots - 19^2 + 20^2 \\
&= (-1^2 + 2^2) + (-3^2 + 4^2) + (-5^2 + 6^2) + \ldots + (-19^2 + 20^2) \\
&= 3 + 7 + 11 + 15 + \ldots + 39 \\
&= 3 + (7 + 11 + 15 + \ldots + 39) \\
&= 3 + \frac{9}{2} \times [7 + 39] \qquad \because S_n \text{ in A.P} = \frac{n}{2} \times [\text{First term} + \text{Last term}] \\
&= 210.
\end{aligned}$$

Choice (c)

Solution 87

$(2XY)^4$ must be at least $(200)^4$ and less than $(300)^4$.

$(200)^4$ as well as $(300)^4$ both have 10 digits.

$\therefore (2XY)^4$ has 10 digits.

Choice (b)

2

L.C.M. and H.C.F.

FACTORS AND MULTIPLES

If a number M divides another number N giving zero as the reminder, then we say that M is a hat factor of N. Also we can say that N is a multiple of M.

LEAST COMMON MULTIPLE (L.C.M.)

Least Common Multiple (LCM) of two or more numbers is the least number which is divisible by each of these numbers. Let us consider two numbers as 6 and 8, and we need to find their LCM.

Multiples of 6 are 6, 12, 18, 24, 30, 36, 42, 48, and so on.

Multiples of 8 are 8, 16, 24, 32, 40, 48, 56, 64, and so on.

We can see that the common multiples are 24, 48, then it will be 72 and so on, but the least among those is 24. Hence we say LCM of 6 and 8 being 24.

There are two methods of finding LCM of a given set of numbers:

1. *Factorization Method*—Resolve each one of the given numbers into a product of prime factors. Then, LCM is the product of highest powers of all the factors.
2. *Division Method*—Arrange the given numbers in a row in any order. Divide by a number which divides exactly at least two of the given numbers and carry forward the numbers which are not divisible. Repeat the above process till no two of the numbers are divisible by the same number except one. The product of the divisors and the undivided numbers is the required LCM of the given numbers.

HIGHEST COMMON FACTOR (H.C.F.)

Highest Common Factor (HCF) is the largest factor of two or more given numbers. HCF is also called Greatest Common Divisor (GCD). Let us consider two numbers as 18 and 30, and we need to find their HCF.

Factors of 18 are 1, 2, 3, 6, 9, and 18.

Factors of 30 are 1, 2, 3, 5, 6, 10, 15, and 30.

Although factors 1, 2, 3, and 6 are common, but highest among these will be called as HCF (or GCD) *i.e.,* 6.

There are two methods of finding HCF of a given set of numbers:
1. *Factorization Method*—Express the each one of the given numbers as the product of prime factors. Then HCF will be product of least powers of common prime factors.
2. *Division Method*—Suppose we have to find the H.C.F. of two given numbers, divide the larger by the smaller one. Now, divide the divisor by the remainder. Repeat the process of dividing the preceding number by the remainder last obtained till zero is obtained as remainder. The last divisor is the required HCF.

L.C.M AND H.C.F. PRODUCT RULE

Product of two numbers = Product of LCM and HCF

Let's take any two numbers, suppose 9 and 12.

$\quad$ LCM = 36 and HCF = 3

So, as per the rule:

$\quad 9 \times 12 = 36 \times 3$

Also LCM is a multiple of HCF or HCF is a factor of LCM.

CO-PRIME OR RELATIVE PRIME

Two numbers are said to be co-primes or relative primes if they do not have any common factor other than 1 or their HCF is 1. For example, the numbers 14 and 15 do not have any common factors other than 1 and hence they are co-primes. Please note that none of the two numbers may individually be prime but still they can be said to be co-prime if their HCF is 1.

L.C.M AND H.C.F. OF FRACTIONS

The LCM of a fraction can be found as:

$\quad$ LCM = LCM of Numerator/HCF of Denominator

The HCF of a fraction can be found as:

$\quad$ HCF = HCF of Numerator/LCM of Denominator.

LCM AND HCF FORMS

LCM Form 1

Any number N which when divided by A, B, or C leaving the same remainder R in each case will be of the form:

$\quad N = $ (LCM of A, B and C) + Remainder

Lets take a number N which when divided by 4 or 5 leaves a remainder 2 in each case, then N can be found as:

$\quad N = $ (LCM of 4 and 5) + 2

Smallest such number N will be 22. Other possible values of N are 42, 62, 82, 102, and so on which can be found as follows:

$$N = (\text{LCM of 4 and 5}).k + 2$$

Where $k = 1, 2, 3, 4$, and so on.

LCM Form 2

Any number N which when divided by A, B, or C leaving the respective remainders as P, Q and R where $(A-P) = (B-Q) = (C-R) = D$ (say), will be of the form:

$$N = (\text{LCM of } A, B, \text{ and } C) - D$$

In this form of problems we observe that the remainders are not same as like Form 1, but there is a common difference D between divisor and remainder. Lets take a number N which when divided by 4 leaves a remainder 1 or when divided by 5 leaves a remainder 2, then N can be found as:

$$N = (\text{LCM of 4 and 5}) - D$$
$$N = 20 - 3 = 17$$

Smallest such number N will be 17. Other possible values of N are 37, 57, 77, 97, 117 and so on which can be found as follows:

$$N = (\text{LCM of } A, B, \text{ and } C).k - D$$

Where $k = 1, 2, 3, 4$, and so on.

LCM Form 3

In this form of problems the remainders will not be same and even the differences between each of the given divisors and corresponding remainders also will not remain the same. Let us take an example and see how to solve this type of problems:

A number N when divided by 4 leaves a remainder 2, but when divided by 5 leaves a remainder 4. The number N can be written as:

$$N = 5k + 4 \text{ (as 4 is remainder when divided by 5)}$$

As this number leaves a remainder 2 when it is divided by 4, so if we subtract 2, then the left over number will be divisible by 4. So, $N = 5k + 2$ is divisible by 4.

- If $k = 0$ then $N = 2$
- If $k = 1$ then $N = 7$
- If $k = 2$ then $N = 12$, which is divisible by 4.

Hence 2 is the smallest possible value of k which satisfy the condition, and so the number:

$$N = 5k + 4 = 5(2) + 4 = 14.$$

HCF Form 1

The largest number N which divides A, B and C giving remainders as P, Q and R respectively can be found as:

$$N = \text{HCF of } (A - P), (B - Q), \text{ and } (C - R)$$

Let us take the numbers as 17, 23, and 34 when divided by a number N leaves remainders as 2, 3 and 4 respectively can be found as:

N = HCF of $(17 - 2)$, $(23 - 3)$, and $(34 - 4)$
N = HCF of 15, 20, 30
$N = 5$.

HCF Form 2

The largest number N which divides A, B and C giving same remainder can be found as:

N = HCF of $(B - A)$ and $(C - B)$

Let us take the numbers as 14, 26, and 62 when divided by a number N leaves same remainders in each case can be found as:

N = HCF of $(26 - 14)$ and $(62 - 26)$
N = HCF of 12 and 36
$N = 4$.

SOLVED EXAMPLES

Example 1

Find the LCM of 24, 36, and 45 by:
1. Factorization Method
2. Division Method.

Solution

1. Factorization Method
   $24 = 8 \times 3 = 2^3 \times 3$
   $36 = 4 \times 9 = 2^2 \times 3^2$
   $45 = 9 \times 5 = 3^2 \times 5$

   LCM = Product of highest powers of 2, 3 and 5
   $= 2^3 \times 3^2 \times 5 = 360$.

2. Division Method

3	24	36	45
3	8	12	15
2	8	4	5
2	4	2	5
	2	1	5

   LCM = Product of divisors × Undivided numbers left
   $= 3 \times 3 \times 2 \times 2 \times 2 \times 5 = 360$.

Example 2

Find the HCF of 48, 72, and 144 by:
1. Factorization Method
2. Division Method.

Solution

1. Factorization Method

$$48 = 2^4 \times 3$$
$$72 = 2^3 \times 3^2$$
$$144 = 2^4 \times 3^2$$

HCF = Product of least powers of common factors *i.e.,* 2 and 3
$$= 2^3 \times 3$$
$$= 24$$

2. Division Method

$$48\overline{)72}\genfrac{}{}{0pt}{}{1}{} \Rightarrow 24\overline{)48}\genfrac{}{}{0pt}{}{2}{}$$
$$\underline{48} \underline{48}$$
$$24 0$$

So, HCF of 48 and 72 is 24.

$$72\overline{)144}\genfrac{}{}{0pt}{}{2}{}$$
$$\underline{144}$$
$$0$$

So, HCF of 72 and 144 is 72.

Hence HCF of 48, 72 and 144 will be HCF of 24 and 72 *i.e.,* 24.

Example 3

Find the LCM and HCF of $\dfrac{4}{9}, \dfrac{6}{27}$

Solution

$$\text{LCM} = \dfrac{\text{LCM}(4, 6)}{\text{HCF}(9, 27)} = \dfrac{12}{9}$$

$$\text{HCF} = \dfrac{\text{HCF}(4, 6)}{\text{LCM}(9, 27)} = \dfrac{2}{27}$$

Example 4

The HCF of two numbers is 6 and their LCM is 72. If one of the numbers is 18, find the other.

Solution

Product of two numbers = Product of LCM and HCF

$18 \times N = 72 \times 6$

$N = \dfrac{72 \times 6}{18} = 24$

Example 5

Find the smallest two digit number which when increased by 2 becomes divisible by both 5 and 8.

Solution

In this case we need to first find out the smallest two digit number which is divisible by both 5 as well as 8 (*i.e.,* their LCM). From this number we need to subtract 2, so that whenever we increase it by 2 it becomes divisible by both 5 and 8.

Required number = (LCM of 5 and 8) − 2 = 40 − 2 = 38.

Example 6

Find the largest four digit number which is exactly divisible by 5, 6 and 8.

Solution

The largest four digit number is 9999.

Required number must be divisible by LCM of 5, 6 and 8 *i.e.,* by 120.

On dividing 9999 by 120, we get remainder as 39.

So, required number = 9999 − 39 = 9960.

Example 7

Find the smallest five digit number which is exactly divisible by 12, 15 and 18.

Solution

The smallest five digit number is 10000.

Required number must be divisible by LCM of 12, 15 and 18.

$12 = 2^2 \times 3$
$15 = 3 \times 5$
$18 = 2 \times 3^2$
LCM = $2^2 \times 3^2 \times 5 = 180$

On dividing 10000 by 180, we get remainder as 100.

So, required number = 10000 − 100 + 180 = 10080.

Example 8

Find the smallest three digit number which when divided by 9 or 15 leaves a remainder 5 in each case.

Solution

As the remainder is same if N is divided by 9 or 15, the problem can be solved as:

$N =$ (LCM of 9 and 15).$k +$ Remainder

$N = 45.k + 5$

If we take $k = 1$ or 2, we get a two digit number. Taking $k = 3$,

$N = 140$.

Example 9

Find the largest four digit number which when divided by divided by 4, 5, and 6 leaves remainder as 1, 2 and 3 respectively.

Solution

Here remainders are not same, but there is a common difference between divisor and remainder i.e., $(4 - 1) = (5 - 2) = (6 - 3) = 3$

$N =$ (LCM of 4, 5, 6).k $-$ Common difference between divisor and remainder

$N = 60.k - 3$

To find out smallest four digit number k should be 17.

$N = 60(17) - 3 = 1020 - 3$
$= 1017$.

Example 10

Find the largest number which divides 74, 112 and 162 leaving remainders as 2, 4 and 6 respectively.

Solution

Let the number be N. All the three numbers 74, 112 and 162 are not divisible by N as they leave remainders. If we subtract these remainders from that respective numbers i.e. $(74 - 2)$, $(112 - 4)$ and $(162 - 6)$, the resulting numbers will be divisible by N.

Therefore, $N =$ HCF of 72, 108, 156

$72 = 2^3 \times 3^2$

$108 = 2^2 \times 3^3$

$156 = 2^2 \times 3 \times 13$

So, HCF $= 2^2 \times 3 = 12$.

Example 11

Find the largest number which can divide 30, 51, and 79 leaving the same remainder 2 in each case.

Solution

Method 1: The Required number = HCF of (51 – 30), (79 – 51)
= HCF of 21, 28
= 7

This method is useful if the remainder is not given.

Method 2: The Required number = HCF of (30 – 2), (51 – 2), (79 – 2)
= HCF of 28, 49, 77
= 7.

Example 12

The HCF of two numbers is 10 and their LCM is 120. Find the numbers.

Solution

If the HCF of two numbers is 10, the numbers can be $10x$ and $10y$, where x and y are co-primes.

Product of two numbers = Product of LCM and HCF

$$10x \times 10y = 120 \times 10$$
$$x \times y = 12$$

As x and y are co prime, the only possibility of x and y can be 3 and 4. Hence the numbers are 30 and 40.

Example 13

From a domestic airport flight for Delhi depart at frequency of every 3 hrs, while the flight for Mumbai depart at a frequency of every 5 hrs. Both the flights departed together on Sunday 7:00 a.m. Find the day and time when both the flights will again depart together after Sunday 7:00 a.m.

Solution

The frequency when both Delhi and Mumbai flights will depart together will be the LCM of 3 and 5 *i.e.,* after every 15 hrs.

So, 15 hrs after Sunday 7:00 a.m. *i.e.,* Sunday 10:00 p.m.

Example 14

Find the least number of apples which can be exactly distributed between 12, 15, 20, or 25 students.

Solution

The required number of apples should be a number which must be exactly divisible by 12, 15, 20 and 25 and that too it must be least, so it must be LCM.

3	12	15	20	25
4	4	5	20	25
5	1	5	5	25
	1	1	1	5

LCM = 3 × 4 × 5 × 5 = 300 apples.

Example 15

There are some chocolates with the teacher. If these chocolates are distributed equally between 6, 7, 8, 9 or 12 students every time 1 chocolate is left. Find the number of chocolates.

Solution

The number of chocolates should be a figure which is divisible by 6, 7, 8, 9, and 12 leaving remainder as 1, or in other words it should be (LCM of 6, 7, 8, 9 and 12) + 1

2	6	7	8	9	12
2	3	7	4	9	6
3	3	7	2	9	3
	1	7	2	3	1

LCM = 2 × 2 × 3 × 7 × 2 × 3 = 504

Therefore number of chocolates = 504 + 1 = 505.

EXERCISE

1. The fraction $\frac{144}{504}$ when expressed in lowest terms will be:
   (a) $\frac{6}{7}$
   (b) $\frac{4}{7}$
   (c) $\frac{2}{7}$
   (d) $\frac{3}{7}$

2. The HCF of $2^4 \times 3^2 \times 5$, $2^3 \times 5^2$, and $2^2 \times 3 \times 5$ will be:
   (a) $2^2 \times 3^2 \times 5^2$
   (b) $2^2 \times 5$
   (c) $2^4 \times 3^2 \times 5^2$
   (d) $2 \times 3 \times 5$

3. The LCM of $2^3 \times 3^2 \times 5 \times 7$, $2^3 \times 5^2 \times 7$, and $2^2 \times 3^2 \times 5$ will be:
   (a) $2^3 \times 3^2 \times 5 \times 7$
   (b) $2^3 \times 3^2 \times 5^2 \times 7$
   (c) $2^2 \times 3^2 \times 5$
   (d) $2 \times 3 \times 5 \times 7$

4. The HCF of 154, 196 and 308 is:
   (a) 14
   (b) 22
   (c) 28
   (d) 44

5. The HCF of 324, 576 and 784 is:
   (a) 4
   (b) 6
   (c) 8
   (d) 12

6. The LCM of 12, 18 and 27 is:
   (a) 216
   (b) 108
   (c) 81
   (d) 162

7. The LCM of $\frac{18}{35}$ and $\frac{2}{40}$ is:
   (a) 2/5
   (b) 18/40
   (c) 9/5
   (d) 18/5

8. The HCF of $\frac{9}{10}$, $\frac{12}{25}$ and $\frac{18}{35}$ is:
   (a) 3/5
   (b) 3/35
   (c) 3/350
   (d) 3/8750

9. The LCM is how many times the HCF of $\frac{8}{15}$ and $\frac{12}{25}$?
   (a) 45
   (b) 60
   (c) 75
   (d) 90

10. Which of the following fraction is the largest?
    (a) $\frac{5}{12}$
    (b) $\frac{7}{15}$
    (c) $\frac{11}{20}$
    (d) $\frac{17}{30}$

11. Which of the following fraction is the least?
    (a) $\frac{3}{5}$
    (b) $\frac{7}{10}$
    (c) $\frac{8}{15}$
    (d) $\frac{11}{20}$

12. Which of the following is a pair of co-primes numbers?
    (a) 8, 18
    (b) 9, 16
    (c) 27, 30
    (d) All of the above

13. Which of the following pairs are not co-primes numbers?
    (a) 9, 20
    (b) 12, 27
    (c) 12, 39
    (d) All of the above

14. Two numbers are in the ratio of 7:10 and their HCF is 3, then the numbers are:
    (a) 70, 100 (b) 14, 20
    (c) 21, 30 (d) 7, 10

15. The product of two numbers is 605. If the H.C.F. of these numbers is 11, then the greater number is:
    (a) 11 (b) 22
    (c) 55 (d) 121

16. The product of two numbers is 6300. If the HCF. of these numbers is 15, then the largest number is:
    (a) 60 (b) 75
    (c) 90 (d) 105

17. The HCF of two numbers is 11 and their L.C.M. is 7700. If one of the numbers is 308, then the other is:
    (a) 275 (b) 341
    (c) 242 (d) 374

18. Three number are in the ratio of 3 : 5 : 8 and their LCM is 7200. Their HCF is:
    (a) 60 (b) 120
    (c) 240 (d) 400

19. The least number that should be added to 397, so that the number becomes exactly divisible by 4, 5 and 6:
    (a) 23 (b) 27
    (c) 33 (d) 37

20. The least number that should be subtracted from 2055, so that the number becomes exactly divisible by 15, 20 and 24:
    (a) 5 (b) 15
    (c) 25 (d) 35

21. Find the largest four digit number which is exactly divisible by 12, 15, 27, and 40.
    (a) 9820 (b) 9940
    (c) 9750 (d) 9720

22. Find the smallest five digit number which is exactly divisible by 20, 35, and 49.
    (a) 10200 (b) 10380
    (c) 10780 (d) 10980

23. The LCM of three different numbers is 585. Which of the following cannot be the HCF?
    (a) 15 (b) 39
    (c) 95 (d) 117

24. The HCF and LCM of two numbers are 26 and 234. If the first number is divided by 13, the quotient is 3 and remainder is zero. The second number is:
    (a) 13 (b) 39
    (c) 78 (d) 156

25. Find the largest three digit number which when diminished by 7 becomes divisible by 8, 14 and 20.
    (a) 847
    (b) 867
    (c) 927
    (d) 987

26. Find the smallest three digit number which when divided by 15 or 25 leaves a remainder as 5 in each case.
    (a) 110
    (b) 130
    (c) 155
    (d) 165

27. There are some fruits on a tree. If a farmer plucks 21 fruits every day, then 4 fruits are left on tree at the end. If he plucks 24 fruits every day, then 7 fruits are left on the tree at the end. Find the total number of fruits on the tree.
    (a) 147
    (b) 151
    (c) 168
    (d) 171

28. A number if divided by 4, 5, 6, and 7 leaves remainders as 3, 4, 5, and 6 respectively. Find the number.
    (a) 101
    (b) 321
    (c) 409
    (d) 419

29. Find the smallest number which when divided by 7 leaves a remainder 3 and when divided by 5 leaves a remainder of 2.
    (a) 17
    (b) 24
    (c) 27
    (d) 32

30. Find the largest number which divides 49, 74 and 115 leaving remainders as 1, 2 and 3 respectively.
    (a) 4
    (b) 8
    (c) 12
    (d) 16

31. Find the largest number which divides 925 and 965 leaving remainders as 15 and 20 respectively.
    (a) 15
    (b) 25
    (c) 35
    (d) 45

32. Find the greatest number that will divide 43, 95 and 187 so as to leave the same remainder in each case.
    (a) 4
    (b) 7
    (c) 12
    (d) 23

33. Find the largest number, with which, when 472, 832 and 1372 are divided the remainders are same.
    (a) 56
    (b) 90
    (c) 140
    (d) 180

34. The product of two numbers is 1024. If their HCF is 16, then find the ratio of their LCM and HCF.
    (a) 4:1
    (b) 3:1
    (c) 2:1
    (d) None of these

35. There are some chocolates with the teacher. If he distributes them equally among 10, 16 or 20 children he is left with 1 chocolate in each case. If he distributes the chocolates equally among 23 children, he would not have any chocolates left. How many chocolates the teacher has?
    (a) 96
    (b) 113
    (c) 156
    (d) 161

36. How many minimum numbers of identical square tiles are required to cover a rectangular floor of dimensions 180 feet by 204 feet?
    (a) 144
    (b) 255
    (c) 275
    (d) 345

37. Four bells commence tolling together and toll at intervals of 6, 12, 18, and 24 seconds respectively. In 60 minutes, how many times do they toll together?
    (a) 41
    (b) 50
    (c) 51
    (d) 60

38. Three persons A, B and C start from the same point to run around a circular track around a stadium in same direction. The running speed of A, B and C is 10, 15, and 20 m/sec, and the length of track is 300 m. After how much time they will meet at the start point again?
    (a) 22.5 sec
    (b) 45 sec
    (c) 60 sec
    (d) Never meet at start point.

39. From a certain city, buses start for four different places every 15, 20, 25 and 30 minutes starting from 8:00 a.m. At what time, for the first time after 8:00 a.m., would all the buses start together again?
    (a) 10:00 a.m.
    (b) 11:00 a.m.
    (c) 12:00 noon
    (d) 1:00 p.m.

40. If a light beeps every 10th second starting from 11 a.m., find the number of times it will glow from 11 a.m. to 1 p.m. (inclusive of both the ends).
    (a) 720
    (b) 721
    (c) 719
    (d) 722

KEYS

1. (c)	2. (b)	3. (b)	4. (a)	5. (a)	6. (b)	7. (d)	8. (c)
9. (d)	10. (d)	11. (c)	12. (b)	13. (c)	14. (c)	15. (c)	16. (d)
17. (a)	18. (a)	19. (a)	20. (b)	21. (d)	22. (c)	23. (c)	24. (d)
25. (a)	26. (c)	27. (b)	28. (d)	29. (a)	30. (b)	31. (c)	32. (a)
33. (d)	34. (a)	35. (d)	36. (b)	37. (c)	38. (c)	39. (d)	40. (b)

SOLUTIONS

Solution 1

At first we need to find the HCF of 144 and 504

$$144 = 2^4 \times 3^2$$
$$504 = 2^3 \times 3^2 \times 7$$
$$HCF = 2^3 \times 3^2 = 72$$

Therefore $\dfrac{144}{504} = \dfrac{72 \times 2}{72 \times 7} = \dfrac{2}{7}$.

Choice (c)

Solution 2

HCF = Product of least powers of common factors *i.e.*, 2 and 5 = $2^2 \times 5$.

Choice (b)

Solution 3

LCM = Product of highest powers of all factors = $2^3 \times 3^2 \times 5^2 \times 7$.

Choice (b)

Solution 4

$$154 = 2 \times 7 \times 11 \quad 196 = 2^2 \times 7^2 \quad 308 = 2^2 \times 7 \times 11$$

HCF = Product of least powers of common factors = $2 \times 7 = 14$.

Choice (a)

Solution 5

$$324 = 2^2 \times 3^4 \quad 576 = 2^6 \times 3^2 \quad 784 = 2^4 \times 7^2$$

HCF = Product of least powers of common factors = $2^2 = 4$.

Choice (a)

Solution 6

By method of division:

3	12	18	27
3	4	6	9
2	4	2	3
	2	1	3

LCM = $3 \times 3 \times 2 \times 2 \times 1 \times 3 = 108$.

Choice (b)

Solution 7

LCM = LCM of Numerator/HCF of Denominator

LCM = LCM of 18 and 2/HCF of 35 and 40 = 18/5.

Choice (d)

Solution 8

HCF = HCF of Numerator/LCM of Denominator

HCF = HCF of 9, 12 and 18/LCM of 10, 25 and 35 = 3/350.

Choice (c)

Solution 9

LCM = LCM of Numerator/HCF of Denominator
LCM = LCM of 8 and 12/HCF of 15 and 25 = 24/5
HCF = HCF of Numerator/LCM of Denominator
HCF = HCF of 8 and 12/LCM of 15 and 25 = 4/75.

Answer = $\dfrac{LCM}{HCF} = \dfrac{24/5}{4/75} = 90.$

Choice (d)

Solution 10

Let us first find out the LCM of denominators *i.e.,* 12, 15, 20 and 30 is 60.

Multiplying each fraction with the LCM of denominator.

$\dfrac{5}{12} \times 60 = 25$

$\dfrac{7}{15} \times 60 = 28$

$\dfrac{11}{20} \times 60 = 33$

$\dfrac{17}{30} \times 60 = 34.$

Choice (d)

Solution 11

The LCM of denominators *i.e.,* 5, 10, 15 and 20 = 60

Multiplying each fraction with the LCM of denominator.

$\dfrac{3}{5} \times 60 = 36$

$\frac{7}{10} \times 60 = 42$

$\frac{8}{15} \times 60 = 32$

$\frac{11}{20} \times 60 = 33.$

Choice (c)

Solution 12

For 8 and 18, HCF = 2, so they are not co-primes
For 9 and 16, HCF = 1, so they are co-primes
For 27 and 30, HCF = 3, so they are not co-primes.

Choice (b)

Solution 13

For 9 and 20, HCF = 1, so they are co-primes
For 12 and 27, HCF = 1, so they are co-primes
For 12 and 39, HCF = 3, so they are not co-primes.

Choice (c)

Solution 14

Let the two numbers be $7x$ and $10x$, where x is the highest common factor, so the numbers will be 21 and 30.

Choice (c)

Solution 15

If the HCF of two numbers is 11, the numbers can be $11x$ and $11y$, where x and y are co-primes.

Product of two numbers = Product of LCM and HCF

$\quad 11x \times 11y = 605$
$\quad\quad x \times y = 5$

As x and y are co prime, the only possibility of x and y can be 1 and 5. Hence the numbers are 11 and 55.

Choice (c)

Solution 16

If the HCF of two numbers is 15, the numbers can be $15x$ and $15y$, where x and y are co-primes.

Product of two numbers = Product of LCM and HCF

$15x \times 15y = 6300$

$x \times y = 6300/225 = 28$

As x and y are co prime, the only possibility of x and y can be 4 and 7. Hence the numbers are 60 and 105.

Choice (d)

Solution 17

Product of two numbers = Product of LCM and HCF

$308 \times x = 7700 \times 11$

So, $x = 275$.

Choice (a)

Solution 18

Let the three numbers be $3x$, $5x$, and $8x$. LCM of these numbers will be $120x$

$120x = 7200$

So, $x = 60$ which is the highest common factor.

Choice (a)

Solution 19

The LCM of 4, 5, and 6 is 60. So any number which is in multiple of 60 will be divisible by 4, 5 and 6. The number 397 if divided by 60 leaves a remainder 37. So to make the number divisible by 60, further 23 should be added to it.

Choice (a)

Solution 20

The LCM of 15, 20, and 24 is:

$15 = 3 \times 5$
$20 = 2^2 \times 5$
$24 = 2^3 \times 3$
LCM $= 2^3 \times 3 \times 5$
$= 120$

So any number which is in multiple of 120 will be divisible by 15, 20 and 24. The number 2055 if divided by 120 leaves a remainder 15. So to make the number divisible by 120, 15 should be subtracted.

Choice (b)

Solution 21

The LCM of 12, 15, 27 and 40 is:

2	12	15	27	40
2	6	15	27	20
3	3	15	27	10
5	1	5	9	10
	1	1	9	2

LCM = $2 \times 2 \times 3 \times 5 \times 9 \times 2 = 1080$

The largest four digit number is 9999. If this number is divided by 1080, the remainder is 279.

Hence, required number = 9999 − 279 = 9720.

Choice (d)

Solution 22

The LCM of 20, 35, 49 is:

5	20	35	49
7	4	7	49
	4	1	7

LCM = $5 \times 7 \times 4 \times 7 = 980$

The smallest five digit number is 10000. If this number is divided by 980, the remainder is 200. Hence we need to add further 780 to 10000 to get the smallest five digit number.

Hence, required number = 10000 + 780 = 10780.

Choice (c)

Solution 23

LCM is always a multiple of HCF. The number 585 is divisible by 15, 39 and 117 but not by 95.

Choice (c)

Solution 24

The first number = Divisor × Quotient + Remainder = 39

Product of two numbers = Product of LCM and HCF
$39 \times N_2 = 26 \times 234$
$N_2 = 156$.

Choice (d)

Solution 25

Required number = (LCM of 8, 14 and 20).$k + 7$

2	8	14	20
2	4	7	10
	2	7	5

LCM = $2 \times 2 \times 2 \times 7 \times 5 = 280$

So, required number = $280.k + 7$

If we take $k = 3$ we get largest three digit number.

Required number = 847.

Choice (a)

Solution 26

Required number = (LCM of 15 and 25).$k + 5 = 75.k + 5$

Taking $k = 2$, the number will be 155.

Choice (c)

Solution 27

Let the number of fruits be N, if this number is divided by 21 we get the remainder as 4, and if it is divided by 24 remainder is 7. Here remainders are different, but still there is a common difference between divisor and remainder *i.e.,* $(21 - 4) = (24 - 7) = 17$.

N = (LCM of 21 and 24) – Common difference between divisor and remainder
$N = 168 - 17 = 151$.

Choice (b)

Solution 28

As we can observe in this question that even if the remainders are different, but there is a common difference between divisor and remainder *i.e.* $(4 - 3) = (5 - 4) = (6 - 5) = (7 - 6) = 1$.

N = (LCM of 4, 5, 6 and 7) – Common difference between divisor and remainder
$N = 420 - 1 = 419$.

Choice (d)

Solution 29

As the remainders are different, and the difference between divisor and remainder is not same, so the problem can be solved as follows:

N = Divisor × Quotient + Remainder

$N = 7 \times k + 3$

If this number is divided by 5 we get the remainder as 2. If we subtract 2 from the number, it will be obviously divisible by 5.

So, $N_1 = 7 \times k + 1$ is divisible by 5.

Now to make this number N_1 divisible by 5, k should be 2. So, substituting value of $k = 2$ and finding N

$$N = (7 \times 2) + 3$$
$$= 17.$$

Choice (a)

Solution 30

Let the number be N. All the three numbers 49, 74 and 115 are not divisible by N as they leave remainders. If we subtract these remainders from that respective numbers *i.e.,* $(49 - 1)$, $(74 - 2)$ and $(115 - 3)$ the resulting numbers will be divisible by N.

Therefore, $N =$ HCF of 48, 72 and 112
$$48 = 2^4 \times 3$$
$$72 = 2^3 \times 3^2$$
$$112 = 2^4 \times 7$$
So, HCF = 8.

Choice (b)

Solution 31

Let the number be N. Both the numbers 925 and 965 are not divisible by N as they leave remainders. If we subtract these remainders from that respective numbers *i.e.,* $(925 - 15)$ and $(965 - 20)$ the resulting numbers will be divisible by N.

Therefore, $N =$ HCF of 910 and 945
$$910 = 2 \times 5 \times 7 \times 13$$
$$945 = 3^3 \times 5 \times 7$$
So,   HCF $= 5 \times 7$
$$= 35.$$

Choice (c)

Solution 32

Taking the difference between any two numbers out of the three numbers:
$$95 - 43 = 52$$
$$187 - 95 = 92$$

The required number is the HCF of these two differences *i.e.,* HCF of 52 and 92 which is 4.

Choice (a)

Solution 33

Taking the difference between any two numbers out of the three numbers:

$832 - 472 = 360$
$1372 - 832 = 540$

The required number is the HCF of these two differences *i.e.,* HCF of 360 and 540 which is 180.

Choice (d)

Solution 34

Product of two numbers = Product of LCM and HCF
$1024 = 16 \times$ LCM

So, LCM = 64
LCM : HCF = 64 : 16
= 4 : 1.

Choice (a)

Solution 35

If the chocolates as distributed equally among 10, 16 or 20 children, 1 chocolate is left.

So number of chocolates = (LCM of 10, 16, and 20).$k + 1 = 80.k + 1$

If we take $k = 1$, number of chocolates will be 81, which will satisfy the above condition, but this number is not divisible by 23.

Hence taking $k = 2$, number of chocolates will be 161, which will satisfy the above condition as well as this number also divisible by 23.

Choice (d)

Solution 36

The size (or length) of square tile will be a HCF of 180 and 204.

$180 = 2^2 \times 3^2 \times 5$
$204 = 2^2 \times 3 \times 17$
HCF $= 2^2 \times 3 = 12$

So, each square tile will be of size 12 feet × 12 feet.

Number of tiles required $= \dfrac{180 \times 204}{12 \times 12} = 255$.

Choice (b)

Solution 37

The frequency when all the bells commence tolling together will be LCM of 6, 12, 18 and 24 = 72 seconds.

Number of times they commence tolling together in 60 min $= \left(\dfrac{60 \times 60}{72}\right) + 1$

$= 50 + 1 = 51$ times.

Choice (c)

Solution 38

Time after which they will meet at the start point will be LCM of time taken by individually to complete one lap.

Time taken by A to reach the start point (or complete a lap) = 300/10 = 30 sec.

Time taken by B to reach the start point (or complete a lap) = 300/15 = 20 sec.

Time taken by C to reach the start point (or complete a lap) = 300/20 = 15 sec.

Time after which they will be together at start point = LCM of 30, 20 and 15 = 60 sec.

Choice (c)

Solution 39

Time after which buses start together = LCM of 15, 20, 25 and 30

Time required = 300 min or 5 hrs *i.e.,* at 1:00 p.m.

Choice (d)

Solution 40

Time from 11 a.m. to 1 p.m. = 120 min or 7200 sec.

Number of times light beeps (inclusive of both ends) $= \left(\dfrac{7200}{10}\right) + 1 = 721$.

Choice (b)

3
Simplification

SEQUENCE OF SIMPLIFICATION

To simplify arithmetic expressions, which involve various operations like brackets, multiplication, division, addition, etc. a particular sequence has to be followed. For example: What is the result of $5 + 4 \times 2$?

Is it 18 or 13? Well, the result is 13, because in these arithmetic operations multiplication has to be done before addition. The hierarchy of arithmetic operations is given by a rule called BODMAS rule in which operations have to be carried out in the order in which they appear in the word as follows:

- B → Brackets
- O → Of
- D → Division
- M → Multiplication
- A → Addition
- S → Subtraction

SIMPLIFICATION OF DECIMAL FRACTIONS

Fractions in which denominators are in the powers of 10 are known as decimal fractions. For example: 0.1, 0.05, 2.25 etc. are the decimal fractions.

Conversion of Decimal to Vulgar Fraction

The numerator of fraction is the number formed by removing the decimal point, and denominator is the power of 10 which depends upon the number of digits after decimal point. The resulting fraction is then reduced to its lowest terms.

Thus, $0.1 = \frac{1}{10}$; $0.05 = \frac{5}{100} = \frac{1}{20}$; $2.25 = \frac{225}{100} = \frac{9}{4}$.

Addition and Subtraction of Decimal Fraction

The given numbers are so placed under each other that the decimal point lie in one column. The numbers so arranged can be added or subtracted in the usual way.

For example: 368.475 – 18.25 →

```
   3 6 8 . 4 7 5
 -   1 8 . 2 5
   ─────────────
   3 5 0 . 2 2 5
```

Multiplication of Decimal Fraction by Powers of 10

After multiplication, the decimal point is shifted to the right by as many places as is the power of 10.

For example: $3.68475 \times 1000 = 3684.75$.

Multiplication of Decimal Fractions

The product is taken by converting the decimal fractions to vulgar fraction, by keeping their denominators in the power of 10. Then the resulting product in vulgar fraction can be converted to decimal fraction by shifting the decimal point towards left by as many digits as the power of 10 in the denominator.

For example: $0.05 \times 40.3 = \dfrac{5}{100} \times \dfrac{403}{10} = \dfrac{2015}{1000} = 2.015$.

Division of Decimal Fractions

The division is taken by multiplying both the dividend and the divisor by suitable power of 10. Then the resulting number in vulgar fraction can be converted to decimal fraction by shifting the decimal point towards left by as many digits as the power of 10 in the denominator.

For example: $0.935 \div 1.7 = \dfrac{0.935 \times 10^3}{1.7 \times 10^3} = \dfrac{935}{17 \times 10^2} = \dfrac{55}{10^2} = 0.55$.

Recurring Decimals

A decimal in which a digit or a set of digits is repeated continuously is called a recurring decimal. A recurring decimal is represented by putting a bar over the repeating digits.

For example: $\dfrac{1}{3} = 0.3333333\ldots = 0.\overline{3}$

$\dfrac{7}{11} = 0.63636363\ldots = 0.\overline{63}$

All recurring decimals are rational numbers and can be expressed in the form of *p/q*, where *p* and *q* are integers.

SOME BASIC FORMULAE

- $(a + b)^2 = a^2 + 2ab + b^2$
- $(a - b)^2 = a^2 - 2ab + b^2$
- $(a^2 - b^2) = (a + b)(a - b)$
- $(a + b)^3 = a^3 + b^3 + 3ab(a + b) = a^3 + b^3 + 3a^2b + 3ab^2$
- $(a - b)^3 = a^3 - b^3 - 3ab(a - b) = a^3 - b^3 - 3a^2b + 3ab^2$
- $a^3 + b^3 = (a + b)(a^2 - ab + b^2)$
- $a^3 - b^3 = (a - b)(a^2 + ab + b^2)$
- $(a^3 + b^3 + c^3 - 3abc) = (a + b + c)(a^2 + b^2 + c^2 - ab - bc - ac)$.

SOLVED EXAMPLES

Example 1

Find the value of $\frac{2}{3} of 45 \div 5 \times \left[\left(3^4 - 1\right) \div 2^4\right]$

Solution

Applying BODMAS rule we have,

$$\frac{2}{3} \text{ of } 45 \div 5 \times \left[\left(3^4 - 1\right) \div 2^4\right] = 30 \div 5 \times \left[(81 - 1) \div 2^4\right]$$

$$= 6 \times \left[80 \div 2^4\right]$$

$$= 6 \times \left[\frac{80}{16}\right] = 30.$$

Example 2

Find the value of $5 + 6 \times \frac{1}{3}$ of $9 - \left(4 - \frac{5}{8} + 2\frac{7}{8} + \frac{3}{4}\right)$

Solution

Applying BODMAS rule we have,

$$5 + 6 \times \frac{1}{3} \text{ of } 9 - \left(4 - \frac{5}{8} + 2\frac{7}{8} + \frac{3}{4}\right) = 5 + 18 - \left(4 - \frac{5}{8} + \frac{23}{8} + \frac{3}{4}\right)$$

$$= 23 - \left(\frac{32 - 5 + 23 + 6}{8}\right)$$

$$= 23 - \left(\frac{56}{8}\right) = 23 - 7 = 16.$$

Example 3

If $2\frac{2}{5} + 1\frac{3}{5} - 1\frac{2}{x} = 2\frac{1}{3}$, then find the value of x.

Solution

$$2\frac{2}{5} + 1\frac{3}{5} - 1\frac{2}{x} = 2\frac{1}{3}$$

$$\Rightarrow \frac{12}{5} + \frac{8}{5} - 1\frac{2}{x} = \frac{7}{3}$$

$$\Rightarrow 4 - 1\frac{2}{x} = \frac{7}{3}$$

$\Rightarrow$ $\qquad 1\dfrac{2}{x} = 4 - \dfrac{7}{3}$

$\Rightarrow$ $\qquad 1\dfrac{2}{x} = \dfrac{12-7}{3}$

$\Rightarrow$ $\qquad 1\dfrac{2}{x} = \dfrac{5}{3}$

$\Rightarrow$ $\qquad 1\dfrac{2}{x} = 1\dfrac{2}{3}$

$\therefore$ $\qquad x = 3.$

Example 4

Find the value of $1 + \dfrac{1}{1 + \dfrac{1}{1 + \dfrac{1}{1 - \dfrac{1}{2}}}}$

Solution

$$1 + \dfrac{1}{1 + \dfrac{1}{1 + \dfrac{1}{1 - \dfrac{1}{2}}}} = 1 + \dfrac{1}{1 + \dfrac{1}{1 + \dfrac{1}{\frac{1}{2}}}} = 1 + \dfrac{1}{1 + \dfrac{1}{1 + 2}}$$

$$= 1 + \dfrac{1}{\frac{4}{3}} = 1 + \dfrac{3}{4} = \dfrac{7}{4}.$$

Example 5

Convert the following recurring decimals to fraction:
1. $0.\overline{7}$
2. $0.9\overline{63}$
3. $2.\overline{6}$

Solution

1. $0.\overline{7}$

   Let $\qquad x = 0.\overline{7}$

   $\therefore \qquad 10x = 7.\overline{7}$

   $\Rightarrow \qquad 10x - x = 7.\overline{7} - 0.\overline{7}$

   $\Rightarrow \qquad 9x = 7$

   $\Rightarrow \qquad x = \dfrac{7}{9}.$

2. $0.9\overline{63}$

   Let $x = 0.9\overline{63}$

   $\therefore \quad 10x = 9.\overline{63}$

   $\therefore \quad 1000x = 963.\overline{63}$

   $\Rightarrow \quad 1000x - 10x = 963.\overline{63} - 9.\overline{63}$

   $\Rightarrow \quad 990x = 954$

   $\Rightarrow \quad x = \dfrac{954}{990} = \dfrac{53}{55}.$

3. $2.\overline{6}$

   $2.\overline{6} = 2 + 0.\overline{6}$

   Let $x = 0.\overline{6}$

   $\therefore \quad 10x = 6.\overline{6}$

   $\Rightarrow \quad 10x - x = 6.\overline{6} - 0.\overline{6}$

   $\Rightarrow \quad 9x = 6$

   $\Rightarrow \quad x = \dfrac{2}{3}$

   So, $2.\overline{6} = 2 + \dfrac{2}{3} = \dfrac{8}{3}.$

Example 6

Simplify the expression: $\dfrac{(48+35)^2 - (48-35)^2}{48 \times 35}$

Solution

The given expression is in the form of $\dfrac{(a+b)^2 - (a-b)^2}{ab}$ where $a = 48$ and $b = 35$

$$\dfrac{(a+b)^2 - (a-b)^2}{ab} = \dfrac{a^2 + b^2 + 2ab - a^2 - b^2 + 2ab}{ab}$$

$$= \dfrac{4ab}{ab} = 4$$

$\therefore \quad \dfrac{(48+35)^2 - (48-35)^2}{48 \times 35} = 4.$

Example 7

Evaluate: $\dfrac{80 \times 8 \times 0.8 \times 0.08 \times 0.008}{0.04 \times 0.002}$

Simplification

Solution

$$\frac{80 \times 8 \times 0.8 \times 0.08 \times 0.008}{0.04 \times 0.002} = \frac{80 \times 8 \times \frac{8}{10} \times \frac{8}{100} \times \frac{8}{1000}}{\frac{4}{100} \times \frac{2}{1000}}$$

$$= \frac{\frac{8 \times 8 \times 8 \times 8 \times 8}{10^5}}{\frac{8}{10^5}}$$

$$= \frac{8 \times 8 \times 8 \times 8 \times 8}{10^5} \times \frac{10^5}{8}$$

$$= 4096.$$

Example 8

Find the value of $\sqrt{\dfrac{0.064 \times 0.0004 \times 6.25}{0.0081 \times 0.036}}$

Solution

$$\sqrt{\frac{0.064 \times 0.0004 \times 6.25}{0.0081 \times 0.036}} = \sqrt{\frac{\frac{64}{1000} \times \frac{4}{10000} \times \frac{625}{100}}{\frac{81}{10000} \times \frac{36}{1000}}}$$

$$= \sqrt{\frac{64}{1000} \times \frac{4}{10000} \times \frac{625}{100} \times \frac{10000}{81} \times \frac{1000}{36}}$$

$$= \frac{8 \times 2 \times 25}{10 \times 9 \times 6} = \frac{20}{27}.$$

EXERCISE

1. The value of $50 \times 5 - 150 + 500 \div 25$ is:
   (a) 24   (b) 120
   (c) 350   (d) 950

2. The value of $729 \div 27 \times 20 + 60$ is:
   (a) 61.35   (b) 270
   (c) 600   (d) 2160

3. The value of $5 - \left[5 - \{5 - 5(5 + 5)\}\right]$ is:
   (a) 15   (b) –25
   (c) –50   (d) –45

4. Which mathematical operator should come in place of '?' in the equation 3? 6 − 15 ÷ 3 = 13.
   (a) +
   (b) −
   (c) ×
   (d) ÷

5. The value of $50 - 10[4 + 6\{4 - 4(10 - 6) + 10\} - 20] \div 2$ is:
   (a) 125
   (b) 190
   (c) 180
   (d) 192

6. The value of $\dfrac{120 \times 12 - 110 \times 11}{80 \times 6 - 70 \times 7}$ is:
   (a) −12
   (b) −23
   (c) −31
   (d) −36

7. The value of $\dfrac{46 - 12(9 \div 3) + 2}{4 - 5 \times 2 + 8}$ is:
   (a) 6
   (b) 8
   (c) 9.5
   (d) 11.5

8. The value of $8\dfrac{1}{3} + 5\dfrac{4}{5} - 7\dfrac{2}{15}$ is:
   (a) 7
   (b) $6\dfrac{1}{15}$
   (c) $5\dfrac{7}{15}$
   (d) $4\dfrac{3}{5}$

9. If $4\dfrac{2}{5} + 3\dfrac{4}{5} - x = 1$, then the value of x is:
   (a) $4\dfrac{3}{5}$
   (b) $6\dfrac{3}{5}$
   (c) $7\dfrac{1}{5}$
   (d) $7\dfrac{4}{5}$

10. If $5\dfrac{2}{3} - 3\dfrac{1}{6} - x = 1$, then the value of x is:
    (a) $1\dfrac{1}{2}$
    (b) $1\dfrac{1}{3}$
    (c) $1\dfrac{1}{6}$
    (d) $1\dfrac{1}{12}$

11. The difference of $6\dfrac{2}{3}$ and its reciprocal is equal to:
    (a) $\dfrac{29}{60}$
    (b) $\dfrac{391}{60}$
    (c) $\dfrac{37}{60}$
    (d) $\dfrac{41}{60}$

12. If $5\frac{1}{4} \times 5\frac{1}{x} = 28$, the value of x is:
    (a) 3
    (b) 4
    (c) 5
    (d) 6

13. Find: $8\frac{1}{10}$ of $2\frac{7}{9}$ of $8\frac{2}{3}$
    (a) 135
    (b) 162
    (c) 174
    (d) 195

14. Find the value of $2 + \cfrac{1}{2 + \cfrac{1}{2 + \cfrac{1}{2 - \frac{1}{2}}}}$

    (a) $\frac{19}{46}$
    (b) $\frac{8}{19}$
    (c) $\frac{19}{8}$
    (d) $\frac{46}{19}$

15. If $x + \cfrac{1}{4 - \cfrac{1}{3 - \cfrac{1}{1 - \frac{1}{2}}}} = 1$, then the value of x is:

    (a) $\frac{1}{3}$
    (b) $\frac{2}{3}$
    (c) $\frac{1}{2}$
    (d) $\frac{1}{4}$

16. If $\cfrac{2 \div 2\frac{2}{3}}{4 \div 2\frac{2}{3}} + x = 2 \times \left(5\frac{2}{3} \div 2\frac{5}{6}\right)$, then the value of x is:

    (a) $2\frac{1}{2}$
    (b) $3\frac{1}{4}$
    (c) $3\frac{1}{2}$
    (d) $4\frac{1}{2}$

17. If $0.\overline{6}$ is converted to fraction, the result is:
    (a) $\frac{1}{3}$
    (b) $\frac{2}{3}$
    (c) $\frac{1}{6}$
    (d) $\frac{2}{9}$

18. If $0.\overline{25}$ is converted in to fraction, the result is:
    (a) $\dfrac{1}{4}$
    (b) $\dfrac{5}{18}$
    (c) $\dfrac{5}{99}$
    (d) $\dfrac{25}{99}$

19. If $0.\overline{065}$ is converted into fraction, the result is:
    (a) $\dfrac{65}{99}$
    (b) $\dfrac{65}{990}$
    (c) $\dfrac{65}{1000}$
    (d) $\dfrac{65}{999}$

20. If $0.1\overline{5}$ is converted to fraction, the result is:
    (a) $\dfrac{5}{33}$
    (b) $\dfrac{3}{20}$
    (c) $\dfrac{1}{6}$
    (d) $\dfrac{7}{45}$

21. If $0.1\overline{575}$ is converted to fraction, the result is:
    (a) $\dfrac{18}{145}$
    (b) $\dfrac{27}{115}$
    (c) $\dfrac{26}{165}$
    (d) $\dfrac{25}{126}$

22. If $2.3\overline{7}$ is converted to fraction, the result is:
    (a) $\dfrac{107}{45}$
    (b) $\dfrac{100}{37}$
    (c) $\dfrac{105}{37}$
    (d) $\dfrac{117}{50}$

23. If $22.\overline{22}$ is converted to fraction, the result is:
    (a) $\dfrac{200}{11}$
    (b) $\dfrac{200}{9}$
    (c) $\dfrac{200}{13}$
    (d) $\dfrac{200}{17}$

24. The value of $(0.\overline{2} + 0.\overline{3} + 0.\overline{4} + 0.\overline{5})$ is:
    (a) $1.\overline{4}$
    (b) $1.\overline{5}$
    (c) $1.\overline{75}$
    (d) $1.\overline{45}$

25. The value of $(4.\overline{37} - 3.\overline{29})$ is:
    (a) $1.\overline{08}$
    (b) $1.\overline{17}$
    (c) $1.\overline{18}$
    (d) $0.\overline{66}$

26. The value of $(3.\overline{3} \times 0.0\overline{9})$ is:
    (a) $0.\overline{27}$
    (b) $0.\overline{3}$
    (c) $0.\overline{6}$
    (d) $0.\overline{297}$

27. The value of $(2.\overline{7} \div 0.\overline{15})$ is:
    (a) $\dfrac{45}{7}$
    (b) $\dfrac{55}{6}$
    (c) $\dfrac{55}{3}$
    (d) $\dfrac{65}{4}$

28. If $x + \dfrac{1}{x} = 2$, then $x^2 + \dfrac{1}{x^2}$ is:
    (a) 1
    (b) 2
    (c) 4
    (d) 1/2

29. Simplify: $\dfrac{(63+56)^2 - (63-56)^2}{63 \times 56}$
    (a) 4
    (b) 7
    (c) 14
    (d) 63×56

30. Simplify: $\dfrac{(35+25)^2 + (35-25)^2}{35 \times 35 + 25 \times 25}$
    (a) 2
    (b) 4
    (c) 875
    (d) 1750

31. Simplify: $\dfrac{45 \times 45 \times 45 + 50 \times 50 \times 50}{45 \times 45 + 50 \times 50 - 45 \times 50}$
    (a) 5
    (b) 95
    (c) 2250
    (d) 4500

32. The value of $\dfrac{1.8 \times 22.5 \times 0.0216}{0.36 \times 0.15}$ is:
    (a) 16.2
    (b) 1.62
    (c) 0.162
    (d) 0.0162

33. The value of $\dfrac{1.44 \times 0.0256}{0.04 \times 0.016 \times 1.2}$ is:
    (a) 4.8
    (b) 24
    (c) 48
    (d) 96

34. The value of $\dfrac{5 \times 1.2 - 4 \times 0.15}{1.35}$ is:
    (a) 2.25
    (b) 3
    (c) 3.5
    (d) 4

35. Simplify: $\dfrac{0.02 \times 0.3 + 0.03 \times 0.2}{0.06}$

   (a) 0.2 (b) 1
   (c) 1.2 (d) 2

36. Evaluate: $\dfrac{(5.75)^2 - (3.25)^2}{7.75 - 5.25}$

   (a) 7.5 (b) 9
   (c) 10.5 (d) 8

37. Evaluate: $\dfrac{(3.44)^2 - (2.56)^2}{4.7 - 3.2}$

   (a) 1.62 (b) 3.52
   (c) 4.44 (d) 6.26

38. If $\dfrac{225}{0.225} = \dfrac{22.5}{x}$, then value of x is:

   (a) 0.0225 (b) 0.00225
   (c) 2.25 (d) 0.225

39. Evaluate: $\dfrac{50 \times 5 \times 0.5 \times 0.05 \times 0.005}{0.0025 \times 0.025}$

   (a) 25 (b) 250
   (c) 500 (d) 625

40. The value of $\dfrac{(0.03)^2 + (0.45)^2 + (0.075)^2}{(0.003)^2 + (0.045)^2 + (0.0075)^2}$ is:

   (a) 0.1 (b) 10
   (c) 100 (d) 1000

41. Find the value of $\dfrac{8.84^3 - 5.34^3}{8.84^2 + 5.34^2 + 8.34 \times 5.34}$

   (a) 2 (b) 3.5
   (c) 4.24 (d) 6.14

42. Simplify: $\dfrac{(3.21)^3 + 5.37(3.21)^2 + 9.63(1.79)^2 + (1.79)^3}{(3.21)^2 + 2 \times 3.21 \times 1.79 + (1.79)^2}$

   (a) 1.25 (b) 2.5
   (c) 5 (d) 25

43. Simplify: $\dfrac{2.7^2 - 2 \times 1.2 \times 1.5}{1.2^2 + 1.5^2}$

   (a) 1 (b) 1.2
   (c) 2 (d) 2.7

44. Simplify: $\dfrac{(0.5)^4 - (0.3)^4}{(0.5)^2 + (0.3)^2}$

   (a) 0.16 (b) 0.3
   (c) 0.8 (d) 1

45. The square root of $0.\overline{4}$ is:

   (a) 0.02 (b) $0.\overline{2}$
   (c) $0.\overline{6}$ (d) $0.\overline{8}$

46. The cube root of 0.000125 is:

   (a) 0.5 (b) 0.05
   (c) 0.005 (d) 0.0005

47. Simplify: $\sqrt{93 + \sqrt{41 + \sqrt{69 - \sqrt{25}}}}$

   (a) 10 (b) 11
   (c) 12 (d) 13

48. If $\sqrt{\dfrac{671-95}{75-39}} \div \sqrt{\dfrac{289-145}{389-164}} + \sqrt{x} = 10$, then x is:

   (a) 9 (b) 16
   (c) 25 (d) 36

49. If $\sqrt{\dfrac{25}{81} - x} = \dfrac{4}{9}$, then x is:

   (a) $\dfrac{1}{9}$ (b) $\dfrac{5}{9}$
   (c) $\dfrac{5}{27}$ (d) $\dfrac{5}{81}$

50. If $\dfrac{\sqrt{162}}{x} = \sqrt{\dfrac{72}{25}}$, then x is:

   (a) 5 (b) $5\sqrt{2}$
   (c) $\dfrac{5}{2}$ (d) $\dfrac{15}{2}$

51. The value of $\dfrac{\sqrt{112} - \sqrt{80}}{\sqrt{63} - \sqrt{45}}$ is:

   (a) $1\dfrac{1}{3}$ (b) $1\dfrac{2}{3}$
   (c) $2\dfrac{1}{3}$ (d) $2\dfrac{2}{3}$

52. The value of $\dfrac{2\sqrt{27} - \sqrt{75} + \sqrt{12}}{\sqrt{108} - \sqrt{48}}$ is:

   (a) $1\dfrac{1}{2}$
   (b) $2\dfrac{1}{2}$
   (c) $\sqrt{3}$
   (d) $2\sqrt{3}$

53. $\left(\sqrt{5} - \dfrac{1}{\sqrt{5}}\right)^2$ simplifies to:

   (a) $2\dfrac{1}{5}$
   (b) $2\dfrac{3}{5}$
   (c) $3\dfrac{1}{5}$
   (d) $4\dfrac{2}{5}$

54. $\dfrac{\sqrt{5} + \sqrt{3}}{\sqrt{5} - \sqrt{3}}$ simplifies to:

   (a) 2
   (b) $2 + \sqrt{15}$
   (c) $4 + \sqrt{15}$
   (d) $2\sqrt{15}$

55. The value of $\sqrt{\dfrac{0.081 \times 0.0001 \times 6.25}{0.0025 \times 0.064}}$ is:

   (a) $\dfrac{3}{2}$
   (b) $\dfrac{3}{4}$
   (c) $\dfrac{5}{16}$
   (d) $\dfrac{9}{16}$

56. The value of $\sqrt{\dfrac{(0.055)^2 + (0.077)^2}{(0.0055)^2 + (0.0077)^2}}$ is:

   (a) 0.01
   (b) 0.1
   (c) 10
   (d) 100

KEYS

1. (b)	2. (c)	3. (d)	4. (c)	5. (b)	6. (b)	7. (a)	8. (a)
9. (c)	10. (a)	11. (b)	12. (a)	13. (d)	14. (d)	15. (b)	16. (c)
17. (b)	18. (d)	19. (d)	20. (d)	21. (c)	22. (a)	23. (b)	24. (b)
25. (a)	26. (b)	27. (c)	28. (b)	29. (a)	30. (a)	31. (b)	32. (a)
33. (c)	34. (d)	35. (a)	36. (b)	37. (b)	38. (a)	39. (c)	40. (c)
41. (b)	42. (c)	43. (a)	44. (a)	45. (c)	46. (b)	47. (a)	48. (c)
49. (a)	50. (d)	51. (a)	52. (a)	53. (c)	54. (c)	55. (d)	56. (c)

SOLUTIONS

Solution 1

$$50 \times 5 - 150 + 500 \div 25 = 250 - 150 + 20$$
$$= 120.$$

Choice (b)

Solution 2

$$729 \div 27 \times 20 + 60 = 27 \times 20 + 60$$
$$= 540 + 60 = 600.$$

Choice (c)

Solution 3

$$5 - \left[5 - \{5 - 5(5+5)\}\right] = 5 - \left[5 - \{5 - 5(10)\}\right]$$
$$= 5 - \left[5 - \{5 - 50\}\right]$$
$$= 5 - \left[5 - \{-45\}\right]$$
$$= 5 - [50] = -45.$$

Choice (d)

Solution 4

$$3 \;?\; 6 - 15 \div 3 = 13$$
$$\Rightarrow \quad 3 \;?\; 6 - 5 = 13$$
$$\Rightarrow \quad 3 \;?\; 6 = 13 + 5$$
$$\Rightarrow \quad 3 \;?\; 6 = 18$$
$$\therefore \quad ? = \times$$

Choice (c)

Solution 5

$$50 - 10\left[4 + 6\{4 - 4(10-6) + 10\} - 20\right] \div 2 = 50 - 10\left[4 + 6\{4 - 4 \times 4 + 10\} - 20\right] \div 2$$
$$= 50 - 10\left[4 + 6\{4 - 16 + 10\} - 20\right] \div 2$$
$$= 50 - 10\left[4 + 6\{-2\} - 20\right] \div 2$$
$$= 50 - 10\left[4 - 12 - 20\right] \div 2$$
$$= 50 + 280 \div 2 = 190.$$

Choice (b)

Solution 6

$$\frac{120 \times 12 - 110 \times 11}{80 \times 6 - 70 \times 7} = \frac{1440 - 1210}{480 - 490}$$
$$= -23.$$

Choice (b)

Solution 7

$$\frac{46 - 12(9 \div 3) + 2}{4 - 5 \times 2 + 8} = \frac{46 - 12 \times 3 + 2}{4 - 10 + 8}$$
$$= \frac{46 - 36 + 2}{4 - 10 + 8}$$
$$= \frac{12}{2} = 6.$$

Choice (a)

Solution 8

$$\frac{25}{3} + \frac{29}{5} - \frac{107}{15} = \frac{25}{3} + \frac{29}{5} - \frac{107}{15}$$
$$= \frac{125 + 87 - 107}{15}$$
$$= \frac{105}{15} = 7.$$

Choice (a)

Solution 9

$$4\frac{2}{5} + 3\frac{4}{5} - x = 1$$
$$\Rightarrow \quad \frac{22}{5} + \frac{19}{5} - x = 1$$
$$\Rightarrow \quad \frac{41}{5} - x = 1$$
$$\Rightarrow \quad x = \frac{41}{5} - 1$$
$$\Rightarrow \quad x = \frac{36}{5}$$
$$\Rightarrow \quad x = 7\frac{1}{5}.$$

Choice (c)

Solution 10

$$5\frac{2}{3} - 3\frac{1}{6} - x = 1$$
$$\Rightarrow \frac{17}{3} - \frac{19}{6} - x = 1$$
$$\Rightarrow \frac{34-19}{6} - x = 1$$
$$\Rightarrow x = \frac{15}{6} - 1$$
$$\Rightarrow x = \frac{9}{6} = 1\frac{1}{2}.$$

Choice (a)

Solution 11

Value of $6\frac{2}{3} = \frac{20}{3}$

Reciprocal of $6\frac{2}{3} = \frac{3}{20}$

Difference $= \frac{20}{3} - \frac{3}{20} = \frac{391}{60}.$

Choice (b)

Solution 12

$$5\frac{1}{4} \times 5\frac{1}{x} = 28$$
$$\Rightarrow \frac{21}{4} \times \frac{5x+1}{x} = 28$$
$$\Rightarrow \frac{5x+1}{x} = \frac{16}{3}$$
$$\Rightarrow 3(5x+1) = 16x$$
$$\Rightarrow 15x + 3 = 16x$$
$$\Rightarrow x = 3.$$

Choice (a)

Solution 13

$8\frac{1}{10}$ of $2\frac{7}{9}$ of $8\frac{2}{3} = \frac{81}{10} \times \frac{25}{9} \times \frac{26}{3} = 195.$

Choice (d)

Solution 14

$$2 + \cfrac{1}{2+\cfrac{1}{2+\cfrac{1}{2-\cfrac{1}{2}}}} = 2 + \cfrac{1}{2+\cfrac{1}{2+\cfrac{2}{3}}} = 2 + \cfrac{1}{2+\cfrac{3}{8}} = 2 + \frac{8}{19} = \frac{46}{19}.$$

Choice (d)

Solution 15

$$x + \cfrac{1}{4-\cfrac{1}{3-\cfrac{1}{1-\cfrac{1}{2}}}} = 1 \Rightarrow x + \cfrac{1}{4-\cfrac{1}{3-2}} = 1 \Rightarrow x + \frac{1}{4-1} = 1$$

$$\Rightarrow x + \frac{1}{3} = 1 \quad \Rightarrow x = 1 - \frac{1}{3} \quad \Rightarrow x = \frac{2}{3}.$$

Choice (b)

Solution 16

$$\frac{2 \div 2\frac{2}{3}}{4 \div 2\frac{2}{3}} + x = 2 \times \left(5\frac{2}{3} \div 2\frac{5}{6}\right) \quad \Rightarrow \frac{2 \div \frac{8}{3}}{4 \div \frac{8}{3}} + x = 2 \times \left(\frac{17}{3} \div \frac{17}{6}\right)$$

$$\Rightarrow \frac{2 \times \frac{3}{8}}{4 \times \frac{3}{8}} + x = 2 \times \left(\frac{17}{3} \times \frac{6}{17}\right) \quad \Rightarrow \frac{\frac{3}{4}}{\frac{3}{2}} + x = 2 \times 2$$

$$\Rightarrow \frac{1}{2} + x = 4 \quad\quad\quad\quad \Rightarrow x = \frac{7}{2} = 3\frac{1}{2}.$$

Choice (c)

Solution 17

Let $\quad\quad\quad\quad x = 0.\overline{6}$
∴ $\quad\quad\quad\quad 10x = 6.\overline{6}$
$\Rightarrow \quad\quad 10x - x = 6.\overline{6} - 0.\overline{6}$
$\Rightarrow \quad\quad\quad\quad 9x = 6$
$\Rightarrow \quad\quad\quad\quad x = \frac{2}{3}.$

Choice (b)

Solution 18

Let $x = 0.\overline{25}$

$\therefore \quad 100x = 25.\overline{25}$

$\Rightarrow \quad 100x - x = 25.\overline{25} - 0.\overline{25}$

$\Rightarrow \quad 99x = 25$

$\Rightarrow \quad x = \dfrac{25}{99}.$

Choice (d)

Solution 19

Let $x = 0.\overline{065}$

$\therefore \quad 1000x = 65.\overline{065}$

$\Rightarrow \quad 1000x - x = 65.\overline{065} - 0.\overline{065}$

$\Rightarrow \quad 999x = 65$

$\Rightarrow \quad x = \dfrac{65}{999}.$

Choice (d)

Solution 20

Let $x = 0.1\overline{5}$

$\therefore \quad 10x = 1.\overline{5}$ and $100x = 15.\overline{5}$

$\Rightarrow \quad 100x - 10x = 15.\overline{5} - 1.\overline{5}$

$\Rightarrow \quad 90x = 14$

$\Rightarrow \quad x = \dfrac{7}{45}.$

Choice (d)

Solution 21

Let $x = 0.15\overline{75}$

$\therefore \quad 100x = 15.\overline{75}$ and $10000x = 1575.\overline{75}$

$\Rightarrow \quad 10000x - 100x = 1575.\overline{75} - 15.\overline{75}$

$\Rightarrow \quad 9900x = 1560$

$\Rightarrow \quad x = \dfrac{1560}{9900} = \dfrac{26}{165}.$

Choice (c)

Solution 22

$$2.\overline{37} = 2 + 0.\overline{37}$$

Let $\quad x = 0.\overline{37}$

$\therefore \quad 10x = 3.\overline{7}$ and $100x = 37.\overline{7}$

$\Rightarrow \quad 100x - 10x = 37.\overline{7} - 3.\overline{7}$

$\Rightarrow \quad 90x = 34$

$\Rightarrow \quad x = \dfrac{17}{45}$

$\therefore \quad 2.\overline{37} = 2 + \dfrac{17}{45} = \dfrac{90 + 17}{45} = \dfrac{107}{45}.$

Choice (a)

Solution 23

$$22.\overline{22} = 22 + 0.\overline{22}$$

Let $\quad x = 0.\overline{22}$

$\therefore \quad 100x = 22.\overline{22}$

$\Rightarrow \quad 100x - x = 22.\overline{22} - 0.\overline{22}$

$\Rightarrow \quad 99x = 22$

$\Rightarrow \quad x = \dfrac{2}{9}$

$\therefore \quad 22.\overline{22} = 22 + \dfrac{2}{9} = \dfrac{198 + 2}{9} = \dfrac{200}{9}.$

Choice (b)

Solution 24

Let $\quad a = 0.\overline{2} \qquad \therefore 10a = 2.\overline{2}$

$\Rightarrow \quad 9a = 2 \qquad \Rightarrow a = \dfrac{2}{9}$

Let $\quad b = 0.\overline{3} \qquad \therefore 10b = 3.\overline{3}$

$\Rightarrow \quad 9b = 3 \qquad \Rightarrow a = \dfrac{3}{9}$

Let $\quad c = 0.\overline{4} \qquad \therefore 10c = 4.\overline{4}$

$\Rightarrow \quad 9a = 4 \qquad \Rightarrow a = \dfrac{4}{9}$

Let $\quad d = 0.\overline{5} \qquad \therefore 10d = 5.\overline{5}$

$\Rightarrow \quad 9a = 5 \qquad \Rightarrow a = \dfrac{5}{9}$

$$\therefore 0.\overline{2}+0.\overline{3}+0.\overline{4}+0.\overline{5} = \frac{2}{9}+\frac{3}{9}+\frac{4}{9}+\frac{5}{9}$$
$$= \frac{14}{9} = 1.\overline{5}.$$

Choice (b)

Solution 25

$$4.\overline{37}-3.\overline{29} = (4+0.\overline{37})-(3+0.\overline{29})$$
$$= (4-3)+(0.\overline{37}-0.\overline{29})$$
$$= 1+\left(\frac{37}{99}-\frac{29}{99}\right)$$
$$= 1+\frac{8}{99}$$
$$= 1+0.\overline{08}$$
$$= 1.\overline{08}.$$

Choice (a)

Solution 26

$$3.\overline{3}\times 0.0\overline{9} = \left(3+\frac{3}{9}\right)\times\frac{9}{90}$$
$$= \frac{10}{3}\times\frac{1}{10}$$
$$= \frac{1}{3}$$
$$= 0.\overline{3}.$$

Choice (b)

Solution 27

$$2.\overline{7} \div 0.\overline{15} = \left(2+\frac{7}{9}\right)\div\frac{15}{99}$$
$$= \frac{25}{9} \div \frac{15}{99}$$
$$= \frac{25}{9} \times \frac{99}{15}$$
$$= \frac{55}{3}.$$

Choice (c)

Solution 28

$$\left(x+\frac{1}{x}\right)^2 = x^2 + \frac{1}{x^2} + 2$$

$\Rightarrow \quad (2)^2 = x^2 + \frac{1}{x^2} + 2$

$\Rightarrow \quad x^2 + \frac{1}{x^2} = 2.$

Choice (b)

Solution 29

The given expression is in the form of $\dfrac{(a+b)^2 - (a-b)^2}{ab}$ where $a = 63$ and $b = 56$

$$\frac{(a+b)^2 - (a-b)^2}{ab} = \frac{a^2 + b^2 + 2ab - a^2 - b^2 + 2ab}{ab}$$

$$= \frac{4ab}{ab} = 4.$$

Choice (a)

Solution 30

The given expression is in the form of $\dfrac{(a+b)^2 + (a-b)^2}{a^2 + b^2}$ where $a = 35$ and $b = 25$

$$\frac{(a+b)^2 + (a-b)^2}{a^2 + b^2} = \frac{a^2 + b^2 + 2ab + a^2 + b^2 - 2ab}{a^2 + b^2}$$

$$= \frac{2(a^2 + b^2)}{a^2 + b^2} = 2.$$

Choice (a)

Solution 31

The given expression is in the form of $\dfrac{a^3 + b^3}{a^2 + b^2 - ab}$, where $a = 45$ and $b = 50$

$$\frac{a^3 + b^3}{a^2 + b^2 - ab} = \frac{(a+b)(a^2 + b^2 - ab)}{a^2 + b^2 - ab} = a + b = 95.$$

Choice (b)

Solution 32

$$\frac{1.8 \times 22.5 \times 0.0216}{0.36 \times 0.15} = \frac{18 \times 225 \times 216}{36 \times 15 \times 100} = 16.2.$$

Choice (a)

Solution 33

$$\frac{1.44 \times 0.0256}{0.04 \times 0.016 \times 1.2} = \frac{144 \times 256}{4 \times 16 \times 12} = 48.$$

Choice (c)

Solution 34

$$\frac{5 \times 1.2 - 4 \times 0.15}{1.35} = \frac{5 \times \frac{12}{10} - 4 \times \frac{15}{100}}{\frac{135}{100}}$$

$$= \frac{6 - 0.6}{\frac{27}{20}} = 5.4 \times \frac{20}{27} = \frac{54}{10} \times \frac{20}{27} = 4.$$

Choice (d)

Solution 35

$$\frac{0.02 \times 0.3 + 0.03 \times 0.2}{0.06} = \frac{\frac{2}{100} \times \frac{3}{10} + \frac{3}{100} \times \frac{2}{10}}{\frac{6}{100}}$$

$$= \frac{\frac{6}{1000} + \frac{6}{1000}}{\frac{6}{100}}$$

$$= \frac{12}{1000} \times \frac{100}{6} = 0.2.$$

Choice (a)

Solution 36

$$\frac{(5.75)^2 - (3.25)^2}{7.75 - 5.25} = \frac{(5.75 - 3.25)(5.75 + 3.25)}{7.75 - 5.25} \quad \because a^2 - b^2 = (a+b)(a-b)$$

$$= \frac{2.5 \times 9}{2.5} = 9.$$

Choice (b)

Solution 37

$$\frac{(3.44)^2 - (2.56)^2}{4.7 - 3.2} = \frac{(3.44 - 2.56)(3.44 + 2.56)}{1.5} \quad \because a^2 - b^2 = (a+b)(a-b)$$

$$= \frac{0.88 \times 6}{1.5} = 0.88 \times 4 = 3.52.$$

Choice (b)

Solution 38

$$\frac{225}{0.225} = \frac{22.5}{x}$$

$$\Rightarrow \quad x = \frac{22.5 \times 0.225}{225}$$

$$\Rightarrow \quad x = \frac{\frac{225}{10} \times \frac{225}{1000}}{225}$$

$$\Rightarrow \quad x = \frac{225}{10} \times \frac{225}{1000} \times \frac{1}{225}$$

$$\Rightarrow \quad x = 0.0225.$$

Choice (a)

Solution 39

$$\frac{50 \times 5 \times 0.5 \times 0.05 \times 0.005}{0.0025 \times 0.025} = \frac{50 \times 5 \times \frac{5}{10} \times \frac{5}{100} \times \frac{5}{1000}}{\frac{25}{10000} \times \frac{25}{1000}}$$

$$= \frac{\frac{3125}{10^5}}{\frac{625}{10^7}} = \frac{3125}{10^5} \times \frac{10^7}{625} = 500.$$

Choice (c)

Solution 40

$$\frac{(0.03)^2 + (0.45)^2 + (0.075)^2}{(0.003)^2 + (0.045)^2 + (0.0075)^2} = \frac{(0.03)^2 + (0.45)^2 + (0.075)^2}{\left(\frac{0.03}{10}\right)^2 + \left(\frac{0.45}{10}\right)^2 + \left(\frac{0.075}{10}\right)^2}$$

$$= \frac{(0.03)^2 + (0.45)^2 + (0.075)^2}{\frac{1}{100} \times (0.03)^2 + (0.45)^2 + (0.075)^2} = 100.$$

Choice (c)

Solution 41

$$\frac{8.84^3 - 5.34^3}{8.84^2 + 5.34^2 + 8.34 \times 5.34} = \frac{(8.84 - 5.34)(8.84^2 + 5.34^2 + 8.34 \times 5.34)}{(8.84^2 + 5.34^2 + 8.34 \times 5.34)}$$

$$= 8.84 - 5.34 = 3.5.$$

Choice (b)

Solution 42

$$\frac{(3.21)^3 + 5.37(3.21)^2 + 9.63(1.79)^2 + (1.79)^3}{(3.21)^2 + 2 \times 3.21 \times 1.79 + (1.79)^2}$$

$$= \frac{(3.21)^3 + (1.79)^3 + 5.37(3.21)^2 + 9.63(1.79)^2}{(3.21)^2 + 2 \times 3.21 \times 1.79 + (1.79)^2}$$

$$= \frac{(3.21)^3 + (1.79)^3 + \left[3 \times 1.79 \times (3.21)^2\right] + \left[3 \times 3.21 \times (1.79)^2\right]}{(3.21)^2 + 2 \times 3.21 \times 1.79 + (1.79)^2}$$

$$= \frac{(3.21 + 1.79)^3}{(3.21 + 1.79)^2} \quad \because (a + b)^3 = a^3 + b^3 + 3ab^2 + 3ba^2$$

$$= \frac{5^3}{5^2} = 5.$$

Choice (c)

Solution 43

$$\frac{2.7^2 - 2 \times 1.2 \times 1.5}{1.2^2 + 1.5^2} = \frac{(1.2 + 1.5)^2 - 2 \times 1.2 \times 1.5}{1.2^2 + 1.5^2}$$

$$= \frac{1.2^2 + 1.5^2}{1.2^2 + 1.5^2} \quad \because (a + b)^2 - 2ab = a^2 + b^2$$

$$= 1.$$

Choice (a)

Solution 44

The given expression is in the form of $\dfrac{a^4 - b^4}{a^2 + b^2}$, where $a = 0.5$ and $b = 0.3$

$$\frac{a^4-b^4}{a^2+b^2} = \frac{(a^2-b^2)(a^2+b^2)}{a^2+b^2}$$
$$= a^2 - b^2 = (a+b)(a-b) = (0.8) \times (0.2) = 0.16.$$

Choice (a)

Solution 45

Let $\quad x = 0.\overline{4}$

$\therefore \quad 10x = 4.\overline{4}$

$\quad 9x = 4$

$\quad x = \dfrac{4}{9}$

So, square root of $\quad x = \dfrac{2}{3} = 0.\overline{6}$.

Choice (c)

Solution 46

$$\sqrt[3]{0.000125} = \sqrt[3]{\frac{125}{10^6}} = \frac{5}{10^2} = 0.05.$$

Choice (b)

Solution 47

$$\sqrt{93+\sqrt{41+\sqrt{69-\sqrt{25}}}} = \sqrt{93+\sqrt{41+\sqrt{69-5}}}$$
$$= \sqrt{93+\sqrt{41+\sqrt{64}}} = \sqrt{93+\sqrt{41+8}}$$
$$= \sqrt{93+\sqrt{49}} = \sqrt{93+7} = \sqrt{100} = 10.$$

Choice (a)

Solution 48

$$\sqrt{\frac{671-95}{75-39}} \div \sqrt{\frac{289-145}{389-164}} + \sqrt{x} = 10$$

$\Rightarrow \quad \sqrt{\dfrac{576}{36}} \div \sqrt{\dfrac{144}{225}} + \sqrt{x} = 10$

$\Rightarrow \quad \dfrac{24}{6} \div \dfrac{12}{15} + \sqrt{x} = 10$

$\Rightarrow \quad \dfrac{24}{6} \times \dfrac{15}{12} + \sqrt{x} = 10$

Simplification

$$\Rightarrow \quad 5 + \sqrt{x} = 10$$
$$\Rightarrow \quad \sqrt{x} = 5$$
$$\Rightarrow \quad x = 25.$$

Choice (c)

Solution 49

$$\sqrt{\frac{25}{81} - x} = \frac{4}{9}$$

$$\frac{25}{81} - x = \frac{16}{81}$$

$$x = \frac{25}{81} - \frac{16}{81}$$

$$x = \frac{1}{9}.$$

Choice (a)

Solution 50

$$\frac{\sqrt{162}}{x} = \sqrt{\frac{72}{25}}$$

$$\frac{\sqrt{81 \times 2}}{x} = \sqrt{\frac{36 \times 2}{25}}$$

$$\frac{9\sqrt{2}}{x} = \frac{6\sqrt{2}}{5}$$

$$x = \frac{5 \times 9\sqrt{2}}{6\sqrt{2}} = \frac{15}{2}.$$

Choice (d)

Solution 51

$$\frac{\sqrt{112} - \sqrt{80}}{\sqrt{63} - \sqrt{45}} = \frac{\sqrt{16 \times 7} - \sqrt{16 \times 5}}{\sqrt{9 \times 7} - \sqrt{9 \times 5}} = \frac{4\sqrt{7} - 4\sqrt{5}}{3\sqrt{7} - 3\sqrt{5}} = \frac{4(\sqrt{7} - \sqrt{5})}{3(\sqrt{7} - \sqrt{5})} = 1\frac{1}{3}.$$

Choice (a)

Solution 52

$$\frac{2\sqrt{27} - \sqrt{75} + \sqrt{12}}{\sqrt{108} - \sqrt{48}} = \frac{2\sqrt{9 \times 3} - \sqrt{25 \times 3} + \sqrt{4 \times 3}}{\sqrt{36 \times 3} - \sqrt{16 \times 3}} = \frac{6\sqrt{3} - 5\sqrt{3} + 2\sqrt{3}}{6\sqrt{3} - 4\sqrt{3}} = \frac{3\sqrt{3}}{2\sqrt{3}} = 1\frac{1}{2}.$$

Choice (a)

Solution 53

The expression is in the form of $(a + b)^2$, where $a = \sqrt{5}$ and $b = \dfrac{1}{\sqrt{5}}$

$$\left(\sqrt{5} - \dfrac{1}{\sqrt{5}}\right)^2 = 5 + \dfrac{1}{5} - 2 \times \sqrt{5} \times \dfrac{1}{\sqrt{5}}$$

$$= 5 + \dfrac{1}{5} - 2$$

$$= \dfrac{25 + 1 - 10}{5} = \dfrac{16}{5} = 3\dfrac{1}{5}.$$

Choice (c)

Solution 54

$$\dfrac{\sqrt{5} + \sqrt{3}}{\sqrt{5} - \sqrt{3}} \times \dfrac{\sqrt{5} + \sqrt{3}}{\sqrt{5} + \sqrt{3}} = \dfrac{\left(\sqrt{5} + \sqrt{3}\right)^2}{(5 - 3)}$$

$$= \dfrac{5 + 3 + 2\sqrt{15}}{2} = 4 + \sqrt{15}.$$

Choice (c)

Solution 55

$$\sqrt{\dfrac{0.081 \times 0.0001 \times 6.25}{0.0025 \times 0.064}} = \sqrt{\dfrac{\dfrac{81 \times 1 \times 625}{10^9}}{\dfrac{25 \times 64}{10^7}}} = \sqrt{\dfrac{81 \times 625}{10^9} \times \dfrac{10^7}{25 \times 64}}$$

$$= \sqrt{\dfrac{81 \times 25}{10^2 \times 64}} = \dfrac{9 \times 5}{10 \times 8} = \dfrac{9}{16}.$$

Choice (d)

Solution 56

$$\sqrt{\dfrac{(0.055)^2 + (0.077)^2}{(0.0055)^2 + (0.0077)^2}} = \sqrt{\dfrac{(0.055)^2 + (0.077)^2}{\left(\dfrac{0.055}{10}\right)^2 + \left(\dfrac{0.077}{10}\right)^2}}$$

$$= \sqrt{\dfrac{100\left[(0.055)^2 + (0.077)^2\right]}{(0.055)^2 + (0.077)^2}} = \sqrt{100} = 10.$$

Choice (c)

4
Surds and Indices

LAWS OF INDICES

(i) $a^n \times a^m = a^{(n+m)}$ (ii) $\dfrac{a^n}{a^m} = a^{(n-m)}$

(iii) $(a^n)^m = a^{nm}$ (iv) $(ab)^n = a^n \times b^n$

(v) $\left(\dfrac{a}{b}\right)^n = \dfrac{a^n}{b^n}$ (vi) $\dfrac{1}{a^n} = a^{-n}$

(vii) $a^0 = 1$

LAWS OF SURDS

(i) $\sqrt[n]{a} = a^{\frac{1}{n}}$ (ii) $\sqrt[n]{ab} = \sqrt[n]{a} \times \sqrt[n]{b}$

(iii) $\sqrt[n]{\dfrac{a}{b}} = \dfrac{\sqrt[n]{a}}{\sqrt[n]{b}}$ (iv) $\left(\sqrt[n]{a}\right)^n = a$

(v) $\left(\sqrt[n]{a}\right)^m = \sqrt[n]{a^m}$ (vi) $\sqrt[m]{\sqrt[n]{a}} = \sqrt[mn]{a}$

SOLVED EXAMPLES

Example 1

Solve: (i) $(81)^{-\frac{3}{4}}$ (ii) $(3125)^{\frac{2}{5}}$ (iii) $\left(\dfrac{8}{27}\right)^{-\frac{2}{3}}$

Solution

(i) $(81)^{-\frac{3}{4}} = (3^4)^{-\frac{3}{4}}$

$= 3^{\left(4 \times -\frac{3}{4}\right)} = 3^{-3}$

$= \dfrac{1}{3^3} = \dfrac{1}{27}$

(ii) $(3125)^{\frac{2}{5}} = \left(5^5\right)^{\frac{2}{5}} = 5^{\left(5\times\frac{2}{5}\right)} = 5^2 = 25$

(iii) $\left(\dfrac{8}{27}\right)^{-\frac{2}{3}} = \left(\dfrac{2^3}{3^3}\right)^{-\frac{2}{3}}$

$= \left(\dfrac{2}{3}\right)^{3\times-\frac{2}{3}} = \left(\dfrac{2}{3}\right)^{-2} = \dfrac{9}{4}.$

Example 2

If $5^n = (0.0016)^{-0.25}$, then find the value of n.

Solution

$$5^n = \left(\dfrac{16}{10000}\right)^{-\frac{1}{4}}$$

$\Rightarrow \quad 5^n = \left(\dfrac{2^4}{10^4}\right)^{-\frac{1}{4}}$

$\Rightarrow \quad 5^n = \left(\dfrac{2}{10}\right)^{4\times-\frac{1}{4}}$

$\Rightarrow \quad 5^n = \left(\dfrac{1}{5}\right)^{-1}$

$\Rightarrow \quad 5^n = 5^1$

$\Rightarrow \quad n = 1.$

Example 3

Find the value of $\left[7\times\left(64^{\frac{1}{6}} + 625^{\frac{1}{4}}\right)\right]^{-\frac{1}{2}}$

Solution

$\left[7\times\left(64^{\frac{1}{6}} + 625^{\frac{1}{4}}\right)\right]^{-\frac{1}{2}} = \left[7\times\left(2^{6\times\frac{1}{6}} + 5^{4\times\frac{1}{4}}\right)\right]^{-\frac{1}{2}}$

$= \left[7\times(2+5)\right]^{-\frac{1}{2}} = \left[7^2\right]^{-\frac{1}{2}} = 7^{-1} = \dfrac{1}{7}.$

Example 4

If $3^{n+1} = \dfrac{1}{27^{3-n}}$, then find the value of n?

Solution

$$3^{n+1} = \dfrac{1}{27^{3-n}}$$

$\Rightarrow \quad 3^{n+1} = \dfrac{1}{3^{3(3-n)}}$

$\Rightarrow \quad 3^{n+1} = \dfrac{1}{3^{9-3n}}$

$\Rightarrow \quad 3^{n+1} = 3^{3n-9}$
$\Rightarrow \quad n + 1 = 3n - 9$
$\Rightarrow \quad 2n = 10$
$\therefore \quad n = 5.$

Example 5

Find the value of $\dfrac{1}{1+x^{p-q}} + \dfrac{1}{1+x^{q-p}}$.

Solution

$$\dfrac{1}{1+x^{p-q}} + \dfrac{1}{1+x^{q-p}} = \dfrac{1}{1+\dfrac{x^p}{x^q}} + \dfrac{1}{1+\dfrac{x^q}{x^p}}$$

$$= \dfrac{1}{\dfrac{x^q+x^p}{x^q}} + \dfrac{1}{\dfrac{x^p+x^q}{x^p}}$$

$$= \dfrac{x^q}{x^q+x^p} + \dfrac{x^p}{x^p+x^q}$$

$$= \dfrac{x^q+x^p}{x^q+x^p} = 1.$$

Example 6

If $3^{n-1} + 3^{n+1} = 270$, then find the value of n^n.

Solution

$$3^{n-1} + 3^{n+1} = 270$$

$\Rightarrow \quad 3^{n-1}(1 + 3^2) = 270$

$\Rightarrow \qquad 3^{n-1}(10) = 270$
$\Rightarrow \qquad 3^{n-1} = 27$
$\Rightarrow \qquad 3^{n-1} = 3^3$
$\therefore \qquad n - 1 = 3$
$\Rightarrow \qquad n = 4$

So, the value of $n^n = 4^4 = 256$.

Example 7

If $x = 5 + 2\sqrt{6}$, then find the value of $\sqrt{x} - \dfrac{1}{\sqrt{x}}$.

Solution

$$\left(\sqrt{x} - \frac{1}{\sqrt{x}}\right)^2 = x + \frac{1}{x} - 2$$

$$= 5 + 2\sqrt{6} + \frac{1}{5 + 2\sqrt{6}} - 2$$

$$= 5 + 2\sqrt{6} + \frac{1}{5 + 2\sqrt{6}} \times \frac{5 - 2\sqrt{6}}{5 - 2\sqrt{6}} - 2$$

$$= 5 + 2\sqrt{6} + 5 - 2\sqrt{6} - 2 = 8$$

$\therefore \qquad \sqrt{x} - \dfrac{1}{\sqrt{x}} = \sqrt{8}$

$$= 2\sqrt{2}.$$

Example 8

Find the value of $\dfrac{\sqrt{5} + \sqrt{3}}{\sqrt{5} - \sqrt{3}} + \dfrac{\sqrt{5} - \sqrt{3}}{\sqrt{5} + \sqrt{3}}$.

Solution

$$\frac{\sqrt{5}+\sqrt{3}}{\sqrt{5}-\sqrt{3}} + \frac{\sqrt{5}-\sqrt{3}}{\sqrt{5}+\sqrt{3}} = \left(\frac{\sqrt{5}+\sqrt{3}}{\sqrt{5}-\sqrt{3}} \times \frac{\sqrt{5}+\sqrt{3}}{\sqrt{5}+\sqrt{3}}\right) + \left(\frac{\sqrt{5}-\sqrt{3}}{\sqrt{5}+\sqrt{3}} \times \frac{\sqrt{5}-\sqrt{3}}{\sqrt{5}-\sqrt{3}}\right)$$

$$= \frac{(\sqrt{5}+\sqrt{3})^2}{5-3} + \frac{(\sqrt{5}-\sqrt{3})^2}{5-3}$$

$$= \frac{5 + 3 + 2\sqrt{3}\sqrt{5}}{2} + \frac{5 + 3 - 2\sqrt{3}\sqrt{5}}{2}$$

$$= \frac{16}{2}$$

$$= 8.$$

EXERCISE

1. If $5^x = 3125$, then 3^{x-2} is:
   (a) 27
   (b) 81
   (c) 243
   (d) 729

2. The value of $(729)^{\frac{2}{3}}$ is:
   (a) 27
   (b) 81
   (c) 243
   (d) 729

3. If $\left(\sqrt{2}\right)^n = 128$, then value of n is:
   (a) 10
   (b) 12
   (c) 14
   (d) 16

4. The value of $\left(\sqrt{125}\right)^{\frac{2}{3}}$ is:
   (a) $\sqrt{5}$
   (b) 5
   (c) 25
   (d) 125

5. The value of $(0.04)^{-1.5}$ is:
   (a) 5
   (b) 25
   (c) 125
   (d) 625

6. The value of $\left(\dfrac{1}{343}\right)^{-\frac{2}{3}}$ is:
   (a) $\sqrt{7}$
   (b) 7
   (c) 49
   (d) 1/49

7. The value of $\dfrac{1}{(243)^{-\frac{2}{5}}} + \dfrac{1}{(196)^{-\frac{1}{2}}} + \dfrac{1}{(125)^{-\frac{2}{3}}}$ is:
   (a) 36
   (b) 48
   (c) 52
   (d) 64

8. The value of $3^{0.5} \times (27)^{0.5}$ is:
   (a) 3
   (b) 9
   (c) $3^{0.25}$
   (d) $6^{0.25}$

9. The value of $(125)^7 \div (25)^{10}$ is:
   (a) 5
   (b) 25
   (c) 125
   (d) 625

10. If $\left(\sqrt{\dfrac{3}{5}}\right)^{n+2} = \dfrac{125}{27}$, the value of n is:
    (a) 3
    (b) 4
    (c) –6
    (d) –8

11. If $2^{3x+3} = 2^{3x+1} + 48$, then find the value of x.
    (a) 0
    (b) ½
    (c) 1
    (d) 2

12. What is the value of x in the equation $3^{8x-1} - 27^{2x} = 0$?
    (a) 0
    (b) ½
    (c) 1
    (d) –1

13. Which is the largest among the following?
    (a) $2^{2^{2^2}}$
    (b) $2^{2^{22}}$
    (c) 2^{22^2}
    (d) 22^2

14. The value of x in the equation $2^{x^{(\sqrt{3})^2}} = 256$ is:
    (a) ½
    (b) 2
    (c) ³⁄₂
    (d) 4

15. The value of x in the equation $(9)^{4.5} \times (27)^2 \div (81)^{1.5} = 3^x$ is:
    (a) 6.5
    (b) 8
    (c) 9
    (d) 10.5

16. If $\left(\dfrac{7}{3}\right)^{2x+9} = \left(\dfrac{3}{7}\right)^{3-4x}$, then value of x is:
    (a) ³⁄₂
    (b) 3
    (c) 6
    (d) ⁹⁄₂

17. If $5^{n+2} = \dfrac{1}{625^{3-2n}}$, then the value of n is:
    (a) ½
    (b) 2
    (c) 3
    (d) 4

18. If $(\sqrt{5})^7 \times 5^4 = 25^n \times 25\sqrt{5}$, then the value of n is:
    (a) 2
    (b) ⁵⁄₂
    (c) 4
    (d) 5

19. If $7^{n-1} + 7^{n+1} - 2450 = 0$, then n is equal to:
    (a) 2
    (b) 3
    (c) –3
    (d) 4

20. If $5^{n-1} - 5^n + 500 = 0$, then the value of n^n is:
    (a) 64
    (b) 125
    (c) 256
    (d) 625

21. $\dfrac{(32)^{\frac{n}{5}} \times 2^{2n+1}}{4^n \times 2^{n-1}} = ?$
   (a) 2
   (b) 2^n
   (c) 4
   (d) 8

22. The value of $81^{0.2} \times 81^{0.4} \times 81^{0.6} \times 81^{0.8}$ is:
   (a) 3^2
   (b) 3^4
   (c) 3^6
   (d) 3^8

23. If $x = 3 + 2\sqrt{2}$, then $\sqrt{x} + \dfrac{1}{\sqrt{x}}$ is:
   (a) $2\sqrt{2}$
   (b) $3\sqrt{2}$
   (c) $2\sqrt{3}$
   (d) $3\sqrt{5}$

24. The value of $\dfrac{\sqrt{6}+\sqrt{2}}{\sqrt{6}-\sqrt{2}} + \dfrac{\sqrt{6}-\sqrt{2}}{\sqrt{6}+\sqrt{2}}$ is:
   (a) $\sqrt{2}\sqrt{6}$
   (b) $2\sqrt{2}\sqrt{6}$
   (c) 4
   (d) 8

25. The number of prime factors of $(81)^{\frac{3}{4}} \times (125)^{\frac{2}{3}} \times (216)^{\frac{4}{3}}$ is:
   (a) 7
   (b) 9
   (c) 11
   (d) 13

26. If $3^x = a$, $3^y = b$, $3^z = c$, then $3^{x-y+z-2}$ is:
   (a) $\dfrac{ac}{3b}$
   (b) $\dfrac{3ac}{b}$
   (c) $\dfrac{ac}{9b}$
   (d) $\dfrac{abc}{9}$

27. If $2^{x-y} = 32$ and $2^{x+y} = 128$, then the value of x is equal to:
   (a) 4
   (b) 5
   (c) 6
   (d) 7

28. If $3^x \times \sqrt[3]{9} = \sqrt[6]{81}$, then x is equal to:
   (a) 0
   (b) ½
   (c) –½
   (d) 1

29. The value of $\left(5^{p-q}\right)^{p+q} \cdot \left(5^{q-r}\right)^{q+r} \cdot \left(5^{r-p}\right)^{r+p}$ is:
   (a) 0
   (b) 1
   (c) 5
   (d) 5^2

30. The value of $\dfrac{3^{a+b} \cdot 3^{b+c} \cdot 3^{c+a}}{\left(3^a \cdot 3^b \cdot 3^c\right)^2}$ is:

(a) 0
(b) 1
(c) 3
(d) 3^{a+b+c}

KEYS

1. (a)	2. (b)	3. (c)	4. (b)	5. (c)	6. (c)	7. (b)	8. (b)
9. (a)	10. (d)	11. (c)	12. (b)	13. (b)	14. (b)	15. (c)	16. (c)
17. (b)	18. (b)	19. (b)	20. (c)	21. (c)	22. (d)	23. (a)	24. (c)
25. (d)	26. (c)	27. (c)	28. (a)	29. (b)	30. (b)		

SOLUTIONS

Solution 1

$$5^x = 3125 \Rightarrow 5^x = 5^5$$
$\therefore\ x = 5$
So, $3^{x-2} = 3^3 = 27.$
Choice (a)

Solution 2

$$(729)^{\tfrac{2}{3}} = (9^3)^{\tfrac{2}{3}} = 9^{\left(3 \times \tfrac{2}{3}\right)} = 81.$$

Choice (b)

Solution 3

$$\left(\sqrt{2}\right)^n = 128$$

$\Rightarrow \quad \left(2^{\tfrac{1}{2}}\right)^n = 2^7$

$\Rightarrow \quad 2^{\tfrac{n}{2}} = 2^7$

$\therefore \quad \dfrac{n}{2} = 7$

$n = 14.$

Choice (c)

Solution 4

$$\left(\sqrt{125}\right)^{\frac{2}{3}} = \left(125^{\frac{1}{2}}\right)^{\frac{2}{3}} = 125^{\left(\frac{1}{2}\times\frac{2}{3}\right)}$$

$$= 125^{\frac{1}{3}} = \sqrt[3]{125} = 5.$$

Choice (b)

Solution 5

$$(0.04)^{-1.5} = \left(\frac{1}{25}\right)^{-\frac{3}{2}}$$

$$= (25)^{\frac{3}{2}}$$

$$= \left(5^2\right)^{\frac{3}{2}}$$

$$= 5^3 = 125.$$

Choice (c)

Solution 6

$$\left(\frac{1}{343}\right)^{-\frac{2}{3}} = \left(\frac{1}{7}\right)^{3\times -\frac{2}{3}}$$

$$= \left(\frac{1}{7}\right)^{-2}$$

$$= 7^2 = 49.$$

Choice (c)

Solution 7

$$\frac{1}{(243)^{-\frac{2}{5}}} + \frac{1}{(196)^{-\frac{1}{2}}} + \frac{1}{(125)^{-\frac{2}{3}}} = \frac{1}{\left(3^5\right)^{-\frac{2}{5}}} + \frac{1}{\left(14^2\right)^{-\frac{1}{2}}} + \frac{1}{\left(5^3\right)^{-\frac{2}{3}}}$$

$$= \frac{1}{3^{-2}} + \frac{1}{14^{-1}} + \frac{1}{5^{-2}}$$

$$= 3^2 + 14 + 5^2$$

$$= 48.$$

Choice (b)

Solution 8

$$3^{0.5} \times (27)^{0.5} = 3^{\frac{1}{2}} \times \left(3^3\right)^{\frac{1}{2}} = 3^{\frac{1}{2}} \times 3^{\frac{3}{2}}$$

$$= 3^{\left(\frac{1}{2}+\frac{3}{2}\right)} = 3^2 = 9.$$

Choice (b)

Solution 9

$$(125)^7 \div (25)^{10} = (5^3)^7 \div (5^2)^{10}$$
$$= 5^{21} \div 5^{20} = 5.$$

Choice (a)

Solution 10

$$\left(\sqrt{\frac{3}{5}}\right)^{n+2} = \frac{125}{27}$$

$$\Rightarrow \left(\frac{3}{5}\right)^{\frac{n+2}{2}} = \left(\frac{5}{3}\right)^3$$

$$\Rightarrow \left(\frac{3}{5}\right)^{\frac{n+2}{2}} = \left(\frac{3}{5}\right)^{-3}$$

$$\therefore \frac{n+2}{2} = -3$$

$$\Rightarrow n+2 = -6$$
$$\Rightarrow n = -8.$$

Choice (d)

Solution 11

$$2^{3x+3} = 2^{3x+1} + 48$$
$$\Rightarrow 2^{3x+3} - 2^{3x+1} = 48$$
$$\Rightarrow 2^{3x+1}(2^2 - 1) = 48$$
$$\Rightarrow 2^{3x+1}(3) = 48$$
$$\Rightarrow 2^{3x+1} = 16$$
$$\Rightarrow 2^{3x+1} = 2^4$$
$$\therefore 3x + 1 = 4$$
$$\Rightarrow x = \frac{4-1}{3} = 1.$$

Choice (c)

Solution 12

$$3^{8x-1} - 27^{2x} = 0$$
$$\Rightarrow 3^{8x-1} = 27^{2x}$$
$$\Rightarrow 3^{8x-1} = (3^3)^{2x}$$
$$\Rightarrow 3^{8x-1} = 3^{6x}$$
$$\therefore 8x - 1 = 6x$$
$$\Rightarrow 2x = 1$$
$$\Rightarrow x = \tfrac{1}{2}.$$

Choice (b)

Solution 13

Evaluating option (a)

$$2^{2^{2^2}} = 2^{2^4} = 2^{16}$$

Evaluating option (b)

$$2^{2^{22}} = 2^{4194304}$$

Evaluating option (c)

$$2^{22^2} = 2^{484}$$

Evaluating option (d)

$$22^2 = 484$$

Hence $2^{2^{22}}$ seems to be the largest vale.

Choice (b)

Solution 14

$$2^{x^{(\sqrt{3})^2}} = 256$$
$$\Rightarrow 2^{x^3} = 2^8$$
$$\Rightarrow x^3 = 8$$
$$\Rightarrow x^3 = 2^3$$
$$\therefore x = 2.$$

Choice (b)

Solution 15

$$(9)^{4.5} \times (27)^2 \div (81)^{1.5} = 3^x$$
$$\Rightarrow (3^2)^{4.5} \times (3^3)^2 \div (3^4)^{1.5} = 3^x$$
$$\Rightarrow 3^9 \times 3^6 \div 3^6 = 3^x$$
$$\Rightarrow \frac{3^9 \times 3^6}{3^6} = 3^x$$
$$\Rightarrow 3^9 = 3^x$$
$$\therefore x = 9.$$

Choice (c)

Solution 16

$$\left(\frac{7}{3}\right)^{2x+9} = \left(\frac{3}{7}\right)^{3-4x}$$
$$\Rightarrow \left(\frac{7}{3}\right)^{2x+9} = \left(\frac{7}{3}\right)^{4x-3}$$
$$\therefore 2x + 9 = 4x - 3$$
$$\Rightarrow 2x = 12$$
$$\Rightarrow x = 6.$$

Choice (c)

Solution 17

$$5^{n+2} = \frac{1}{625^{3-2n}}$$
$$\Rightarrow 5^{n+2} = \frac{1}{(5^4)^{3-2n}}$$
$$\Rightarrow 5^{n+2} = \frac{1}{5^{12-8n}}$$
$$\Rightarrow 5^{n+2} = 5^{8n-12}$$
$$\therefore n + 2 = 8n - 12$$
$$\Rightarrow 7n = 14$$
$$\Rightarrow n = 2.$$

Choice (b)

Solution 18

$$(\sqrt{5})^7 \times 5^4 = 25^n \times 25\sqrt{5}$$
$$\Rightarrow \left(5^{1/2}\right)^7 \times 5^4 = (5^2)^n \times 5^2 \times 5^{1/2}$$

Surds and Indices

$\Rightarrow \quad 5^{\frac{7}{2}} \times 5^4 = 5^{2n} \times 5^{2+\frac{1}{2}}$

$\Rightarrow \quad 5^{\frac{7}{2}} \times 5^4 = 5^{2n} \times 5^{\frac{5}{2}}$

$\therefore \quad \frac{7}{2} + 4 = 2n + \frac{5}{2}$

$\Rightarrow \quad \frac{15}{2} = 2n + \frac{5}{2}$

$\Rightarrow \quad 2n = \frac{10}{2}$

$\Rightarrow \quad n = 5/2$.

Choice (b)

Solution 19

$7^{n-1} + 7^{n+1} = 2450$

$\Rightarrow \quad 7^{n-1}(1 + 7^2) = 2450$

$\Rightarrow \quad 7^{n-1}(50) = 2450$

$\Rightarrow \quad 7^{n-1} = 49$

$\Rightarrow \quad 7^{n-1} = 7^2$

$\therefore \quad n - 1 = 2$

$\Rightarrow \quad n = 3$.

Choice (b)

Solution 20

$5^{n-1} - 5^n = -500$

$\Rightarrow \quad 5^{n-1}(1 - 5) = -500$

$\Rightarrow \quad 5^{n-1} = 125$

$\Rightarrow \quad 5^{n-1} = 5^3$

$\therefore \quad n - 1 = 3$

$\Rightarrow \quad n = 4$

So, $4^4 = 256$.

Choice (c)

Solution 21

$$\frac{(32)^{\frac{n}{5}} \times 2^{2n+1}}{4^n \times 2^{n-1}} = \frac{(2^5)^{\frac{n}{5}} \times 2^{2n+1}}{2^{2n} \times 2^{n-1}} = \frac{2^n \times 2^{2n+1}}{2^{2n} \times 2^{n-1}}$$

$$= \frac{2^{3n+1}}{2^{3n-1}} = 2^{(3n+1)-(3n-1)} = 2^2 = 4.$$

Choice (c)

Solution 22

$$81^{0.2} \times 81^{0.4} \times 81^{0.6} \times 81^{0.8} = \left(3^4\right)^{\frac{1}{5}} \times \left(3^4\right)^{\frac{2}{5}} \times \left(3^4\right)^{\frac{3}{5}} \times \left(3^4\right)^{\frac{4}{5}}$$

$$= 3^{\frac{4}{5}} \times 3^{\frac{8}{5}} \times 3^{\frac{12}{5}} \times 3^{\frac{16}{5}} = 3^{\left(\frac{4}{5}+\frac{8}{5}+\frac{12}{5}+\frac{16}{5}\right)} = 3^8.$$

Choice (d)

Solution 23

$$\left(\sqrt{x} + \frac{1}{\sqrt{x}}\right)^2 = x + \frac{1}{x} + 2 = 3 + 2\sqrt{2} + \frac{1}{3+2\sqrt{2}} + 2$$

$$= 3 + 2\sqrt{2} + \frac{1}{3+2\sqrt{2}} \times \frac{3-2\sqrt{2}}{3-2\sqrt{2}} + 2$$

$$= 3 + 2\sqrt{2} + 3 - 2\sqrt{2} + 2 = 8$$

$\therefore \quad \sqrt{x} + \dfrac{1}{\sqrt{x}} = \sqrt{8} = 2\sqrt{2}.$

Choice (a)

Solution 24

$$\frac{\sqrt{6}+\sqrt{2}}{\sqrt{6}-\sqrt{2}} + \frac{\sqrt{6}-\sqrt{2}}{\sqrt{6}+\sqrt{2}} = \left(\frac{\sqrt{6}+\sqrt{2}}{\sqrt{6}-\sqrt{2}} \times \frac{\sqrt{6}+\sqrt{2}}{\sqrt{6}+\sqrt{2}}\right) + \left(\frac{\sqrt{6}-\sqrt{2}}{\sqrt{6}+\sqrt{2}} \times \frac{\sqrt{6}-\sqrt{2}}{\sqrt{6}-\sqrt{2}}\right)$$

$$= \frac{\left(\sqrt{6}+\sqrt{2}\right)^2}{6-2} + \frac{\left(\sqrt{6}-\sqrt{2}\right)^2}{6-2}$$

$$= \frac{6+2+2\sqrt{2}\sqrt{6}}{4} + \frac{6+2-2\sqrt{2}\sqrt{6}}{4} = \frac{16}{4} = 4.$$

Choice (c)

Solution 25

$$(81)^{\frac{3}{4}} \times (125)^{\frac{2}{3}} \times (216)^{\frac{4}{3}} = (3^4)^{\frac{3}{4}} \times (5^3)^{\frac{2}{3}} \times (6^3)^{\frac{4}{3}} = 3^3 \times 5^2 \times 6^4 = 3^7 \times 5^2 \times 2^4$$

Hence number of prime factors = 7 + 2 + 4 = 13.

Choice (d)

Solution 26

$$3^{x-y+z-2} = 3^x \cdot 3^{-y} \cdot 3^z \cdot 3^{-2} = \frac{3^x 3^z}{3^y 3^2} = \frac{ac}{9b}.$$

Choice (c)

Solution 27

$$2^{x-y} = 32 \Rightarrow 2^{x-y} = 2^5$$

∴ $x - y = 5$ ... (1)

$$2^{x+y} = 128 \Rightarrow 2^{x+y} = 2^7$$

∴ $x + y = 7$ ... (2)

Adding equation (1) and (2)

$$(x - y) + (x + y) = 5 + 7$$
$$2x = 12$$

∴ $x = 6.$

Choice (c)

Solution 28

$$3^x \times \sqrt[3]{9} = \sqrt[6]{81}$$

$\Rightarrow \quad 3^x \times \left(3^2\right)^{\frac{1}{3}} = \left(3^4\right)^{\frac{1}{6}}$

$\Rightarrow \quad 3^x \times 3^{\frac{2}{3}} = 3^{\frac{2}{3}}$

$\Rightarrow \quad 3^x = \dfrac{3^{\frac{2}{3}}}{3^{\frac{2}{3}}}$

$\Rightarrow \quad 3^x = 3^{\frac{2}{3} - \frac{2}{3}}$

$\Rightarrow \quad 3^x = 3^0$

∴ $x = 0.$

Choice (a)

Solution 29

$$\left(5^{p-q}\right)^{p+q} \cdot \left(5^{q-r}\right)^{q+r} \cdot \left(5^{r-p}\right)^{r+p} = 5^{p^2-q^2} \cdot 5^{q^2-r^2} \cdot 5^{r^2-p^2}$$

$$= 5^{\left(p^2-q^2\right)+\left(q^2-r^2\right)+\left(r^2-p^2\right)} = 5^0 = 1.$$

Choice (b)

Solution 30

$$\dfrac{3^{a+b} \cdot 3^{b+c} \cdot 3^{c+a}}{\left(3^a \cdot 3^b \cdot 3^c\right)^2} = \dfrac{3^{(a+b)+(b+c)+(c+a)}}{3^{2a} \cdot 3^{2b} \cdot 3^{2c}} = \dfrac{3^{2a+2b+2c}}{3^{2a+2b+2c}} = 3^0 = 1.$$

Choice (b)

5
Simple Equations

ABOUT EQUATIONS

A combination of variables and constants connected with arithmetic operators is an equation. A simple (or linear) equation is one where each variable occurs only in its first power and not in any higher powers. In general, we need as many equations as the variables we need to solve for. So, to find out the value of two unknown variables, we need two distinct equations (or two different conditions in the problem). To find out the value of three variables, we need three distinct equations, and so on.

There are wide variety of problem on equations but the general approach in solving these problems is most of the time same. The first step of solving is to assume a variable for what ever is asked. The second step is to frame an equation. This is the most important step, because a correctly framed equation will only give you the correct answer. The third step is solving the equation, and getting the answer.

Assuming a variable i.e., x, y, z …..
⇓
Framing an equation
⇓
Solving the equation and getting answer

SOLVED EXAMPLES

Example 1

If 20 is added from 2/5th of a number, the result is equal to sum of 44 and one-fourth of that number. What is the number?

Solution

Let the number be x. As per the condition mentioned in the problem, the equation will be as follows:

$$\frac{2}{5}x + 20 = 44 + \frac{1}{4}x$$

$$\Rightarrow \quad \frac{2}{5}x - \frac{1}{4}x = 44 - 20$$

$\Rightarrow$ $\qquad \dfrac{3}{20}x = 24$

$\therefore$ $\qquad x = \dfrac{24 \times 20}{3} = 160.$

Example 2

There are two numbers such that the sum of twice the first and thrice the second is 34, while the sum of thrice the first and twice the second is 31. Find the larger of the two numbers.

Solution

Let the first number be x and second number be y.

$\qquad 2x + 3y = 34$ ... (1)
$\qquad 3x + 2y = 31$ ... (2)

Multiplying equation (1) with 3 and equation (2) with 2.

$\qquad 6x + 9y = 102$ ... (3)
$\qquad 6x + 4y = 62$ ... (4)

Subtracting equation (4) from equation (3)

$\qquad (6x + 9y) - (6x + 4y) = 102 - 62$

$\Rightarrow \qquad 5y = 40$
$\therefore \qquad y = 8$

and $\qquad x = 5$

So, the larger of the two numbers is 8.

Example 3

In a two digit number, the unit digit exceeds the tens digit by 2. Also the number exceeds the sum of its digits by 18. Find the number.

Solution

Let the two digit number be $10x + y$; where x is the tens place and y is the unit place.

As per the 1st condition:

$\qquad y = x + 2$ ... (1)

As per the 2nd condition:

$\qquad 10x + y = (x + y) + 18$ ... (2)

Substituting y as $(x + 2)$ in equation (2)

$\qquad 10x + (x + 2) = x + (x + 2) + 18$
$\Rightarrow \qquad 11x + 2 = 2x + 20$

$$\Rightarrow \quad 9x = 18$$
$$\therefore \quad x = 2$$
and $\quad y = 4$

So, the required number is 24.

Example 4

The sum of numerator and denominator of a fraction is 11. If 1 is subtracted from the numerator and 4 is added to the denominator, it becomes 2/5. Find the fraction.

Solution

Let the fraction be $\frac{n}{d}$.

As per the 1st condition:
$$n + d = 11 \quad \ldots (1)$$
$$\Rightarrow \quad d = 11 - n$$

As per the 2nd condition:
$$\frac{n-1}{d+4} = \frac{2}{5} \quad \ldots (2)$$

$$\Rightarrow \quad 5(n-1) = 2(d+4)$$
$$\Rightarrow \quad 5n - 5 = 2d + 8$$
$$\Rightarrow \quad 5n - 2d = 13$$

Substituting $d = 11 - n$ in the above equation.
$$\Rightarrow \quad 5n - 2(11 - n) = 13$$
$$\Rightarrow \quad 5n - 22 + 2n = 13$$
$$\Rightarrow \quad 7n = 35$$
$$\therefore \quad n = 5$$
and $\quad d = 6$

So, the required fraction is $\frac{5}{6}$.

Example 5

Of the three numbers, the sum of first two is 30; the sum of second and third is 42 and the sum of third and twice the first number is 48. Find the first number.

Solution

Let the first, second and third number be F, S and T respectively. As per the given conditions in the problem, the equations will be as follows:

$$F + S = 30 \quad \ldots (1)$$
$$S + T = 42 \quad \ldots (2)$$
$$2F + T = 48 \quad \ldots (3)$$

Subtracting equation (2) from equation (1)
$$(F + S) - (S + T) = 30 - 42$$
$$F - T = -12 \quad \ldots (4)$$

Adding equation (3) and (4)
$$(2F + T) + (F - T) = 48 - 12$$
$$\Rightarrow \quad 3F = 36$$
$$\therefore \quad F = 12$$

So, the first number is 12.

Example 6

Four year ago age of Rajesh was three years more than thrice the age of his only son Rishi. Fifteen years hence Rajesh's age will be five years less than twice his son's age. Find the present age of Rishi.

Solution

Let the present age of Rajesh be x, and present age of his son Rishi be y.

As per the 1st condition:
$$x - 4 = 3(y - 4) + 3 \quad \ldots (1)$$
$$\Rightarrow \quad x - 4 = 3y - 12 + 3$$
$$\Rightarrow \quad x = 3y - 5$$

As per the 2nd condition:
$$x + 15 = 2(y + 15) - 5 \quad \ldots (2)$$

Substituting x as $(3y - 5)$ in equation (2)
$$(3y - 5) + 15 = 2(y + 15) - 5$$
$$\Rightarrow \quad 3y + 10 = 2y + 30 - 5$$
$$\therefore \quad y = 15$$

So, the age of Rishi is 15 years.

Example 7

A mother said to her daughter, "I was as old as you are at present the time of your birth". If the present age of mother is 42 years, then what was the age of daughter 6 years ago?

Solution

Let the present age of daughter be D. At the time of birth of daughter, the mother's age was equal to daughter's present age.

$\therefore \qquad 42 - D = D$

$\therefore \qquad 2D = 42$

$\Rightarrow \qquad D = 21$ years

So, age of daughter 6 years ago was 15 years.

Example 8

A bag has a total of 100 notes in denomination of ₹ 10, ₹ 20 and ₹ 50. The total value of the notes in the bag is ₹ 1600. If the number of ₹ 20 notes are doubled, then the total value of notes in the bag is would be ₹ 2000. Find the number of ₹ 50 notes in the bag.

Solution

Let the number of notes of ₹ 10, ₹ 20 and ₹ 50 be A, B and C respectively. As per the conditions given in the problem, the equations will be as follows:

$$A + B + C = 100 \qquad \ldots (1)$$
$$10A + 20B + 50C = 1600 \qquad \ldots (2)$$
$$10A + 40B + 50C = 2000 \qquad \ldots (3)$$

Subtracting equation (2) from equation (3),

$(10A + 40B + 50C) - (10A + 20B + 50C) = 2000 - 1600$

$$20B = 400$$

$\therefore \qquad B = 20$

Substituting the value of B in equation (1) and (2)

$$A + C = 80 \qquad \ldots (4)$$
$$A + 5C = 120 \qquad \ldots (5)$$

Subtracting equation (4) from equation (5)

$(A + 5C) - (A + C) = 120 - 80$

$$4C = 40$$

$\therefore \qquad C = 10$

So, there are 10 notes of ₹ 50 in the bag.

Example 9

Abhay and Bharat have some amount of money with them. If Abhay gives ₹ 20 to Bharat, then Abhay will have exactly half the amount as that of Bharat. If Bharat gives ₹ 30 to Abhay then they will have equal amounts. Find the amounts each had individually.

Solution

Let the amount of money with Abhay and Bharat be A and B respectively.

As per 1st condition:
$$A - 20 = \frac{1}{2}(B + 20) \qquad \ldots (1)$$
$$\Rightarrow \qquad 2A - 60 = B$$

As per 2nd condition:
$$A + 30 = B - 30$$
$$\Rightarrow \qquad A + 60 = B \qquad \ldots (2)$$

Equating the left hand sides of equations (1) and (2)
$$2A - 60 = A + 60$$
$$\therefore \qquad A = 120 \text{ and } B = 180.$$

Example 10

The expenses of a hostel are partly fixed and partly varying with the number of occupants. If there are 20 occupants, then each of the occupants has to bear ₹ 700 per month and if there are 5 more occupants, then the share of each occupant comes down by ₹ 30 per month. How many occupants would be there if share of each occupant is ₹ 600 per month?

Solution

Let the fixed cost be F and varying cost is V for N number of occupants.

$$F + \frac{V}{N} = \text{Per head expenses}$$

$$F + \frac{V}{20} = ₹\ 700 \qquad \ldots (1)$$

$$F + \frac{V}{25} = ₹\ 670 \qquad \ldots (2)$$

Subtracting equation (2) from equation (1)

$$\left(F + \frac{V}{20}\right) - \left(F + \frac{V}{25}\right) = 700 - 670$$

$$\Rightarrow \qquad \frac{V}{20} - \frac{V}{25} = 700 - 670$$

$$\Rightarrow \qquad \frac{5V - 4V}{100} = 30$$

$$\therefore \qquad V = 3000$$

and $\qquad F = 550$

The number of occupants needed to share per head ₹ 600 can be found as:

$$F + \frac{V}{N} = ₹\,600$$

$$550 + \frac{3000}{N} = 600$$

∴ $N = 60.$

EXERCISE

1. If three-fourth of a number is taken and 9 is added to it, the resulting number is 33. Find the number.
   (a) 24   (b) 32
   (c) 36   (d) 40

2. Four-fifth of a number is 6 more than its two-third. The number is:
   (a) 30   (b) 36
   (c) 45   (d) 48

3. One-third of one-fourth of a number is 3. Then five-sixth of the number is:
   (a) 24   (b) 30
   (c) 36   (d) 42

4. Find the number which when multiplied by 8 is increased by 175.
   (a) 20   (d) 24
   (c) 25   (d) 30

5. If the sum of one-third and one-fourth of a number exceeds three-eighth of that number by 10, the number is:
   (a) 24   (b) 36
   (c) 48   (d) 60

6. If 4 is subtracted from two-third of a number, the result is equal to sum of 6 and one-third of that number. Find the number,
   (a) 24   (b) 30
   (c) 33   (d) 36

7. Raju selected a positive number at random, and taken its square. He added the number with its square and the result obtained was 132. What number he must have selected?
   (a) 9   (b) 11
   (c) 12   (d) 13

8. A two digit number is such that it is 10 times the sum of digits. If the difference between the digits is 5, find the number.
   (a) 50   (b) 61
   (c) 72   (d) 35

9. Sum of the digits of a two digit number is 9. If 3 more than units digit would be half of tens digit, find the number.
   (a) 18
   (b) 63
   (c) 72
   (d) 81

10. The sum of the digits of two digit number is 9. If 27 is subtracted from the number the digits interchange there places. Find the number?
    (a) 36
    (b) 63
    (c) 45
    (d) 54

11. The sum of the digits of a two digit number is 9. The fraction formed by taking 3 less than the number as numerator and 3 more than the number as denominator is 7/8. Find the number?
    (a) 54
    (b) 27
    (c) 45
    (d) 63

12. Six times the denominator of a fraction is 2 less than 8 times the numerator and 10 times the numerator equals to 20 less than 10 times the denominator. Find the fraction.
    (a) 9/7
    (b) 7/9
    (c) 8/11
    (d) 9/11

13. The middle digit of a 3 digit number is 0 and the sum of the digits is 9. If 99 is added to the number, the digits interchange their places. Find the number?
    (a) 306
    (b) 504
    (c) 207
    (d) 405

14. Six times the sum of the digits of a two digit number is one less than the number and eight more than the number obtained by reversing the digits of the two digit number. What is the product of the digits?
    (a) 31
    (b) 12
    (c) 19
    (d) 61

15. A two digit number is obtained by either subtracting 12 from 4 times the sum of digits or by adding 6 to twice the difference of its digits. Find the number.
    (a) 14
    (b) 16
    (c) 18
    (d) 24

16. In a two digit number, if the sum of digits is 14 and the sum of reciprocals of the digits is 7/24, then find the product of digits.
    (a) 24
    (b) 45
    (c) 48
    (d) 36

17. There are four consecutive even numbers. The product of first and fourth is 216. What is the product of second and third? (All are positive)
    (a) 216
    (b) 220
    (c) 224
    (d) Data inadequate

18. The sum of two numbers is 20 and their product is 96. What will be the sum of their reciprocals?
    (a) 5/24
    (b) 7/20
    (c) 7/24
    (d) 11/36

19. If the difference of two numbers is 3 and the difference of their squares is 57, then the larger number is:
    (a) 8
    (b) 9
    (c) 11
    (d) 12

20. The sum of three consecutive numbers is 108. The greatest among these three numbers is:
    (a) 34
    (b) 37
    (c) 41
    (d) 43

21. What is the sum of two consecutive even numbers, the difference of whose squares is 44?
    (a) 18
    (b) 20
    (c) 22
    (d) 24

22. The sum of the two positive integers multiplied by the bigger number is 204 and their difference multiplied by the smaller number is 35. The numbers are:
    (a) 12, 5
    (b) 24, 10
    (c) 13, 4
    (d) 14, 3

23. There are two numbers such that sum of twice the first and thrice the second is 54, while the sum of thrice the first and twice the second is 61. The smaller of the two numbers is:
    (a) 6
    (b) 7
    (c) 8
    (d) 9

24. Of the three numbers, the sum of first two is 35; the sum of second and third is 50 and the sum of third and twice the first number is 60. The first number is:
    (a) 12
    (b) 15
    (c) 18
    (d) 20

25. Father was 20 years old when his son was born. If the present age of father is 5 times the age of son, how old the son is?
    (a) 3 years
    (b) 5 years
    (c) 8 years
    (d) 10 years

26. A father is twice as old as his son; 20 years back he was 12 times as old as his son, what are their present ages (in years)?
    (a) 24, 12
    (b) 44, 22
    (c) 48, 24
    (d) None of these

27. A is 2 years younger than B. If 7 years back, 5/6 times A's age exceeds 3/10 times B's age by 9 years, what is B's present age in years?
    (a) 25
    (b) 27
    (c) 28
    (d) None of these

28. Five years hence Raj's age will be thrice the age of Sam four years ago. Four years ago Raj's age was twice Sam's present age. Find the age of Sam and Raj in years.
    (a) 24, 8 (b) 8, 24
    (c) 46, 21 (d) 21, 46

29. 25 years hence Rohit will become 11 times as old as he was 25 years ago. Find the present age of Rohit?
    (a) 20 years (b) 50 years
    (c) 40 years (d) 30 years

30. Father's age is 2 more than twice the son's age. After 3 years the father's age would be 20 years less than thrice the son's age. Find the Father's present age?
    (a) 30 years (b) 34 years
    (c) 36 years (d) 32 years

31. Mother's age is equal to the sum of ages of her daughter and a 22 year old son. 22 years ago their average age was 24 years. Find the present age of mother.
    (a) 47 years (b) 51 years
    (c) 57 years (d) 69 years

32. 27 years ago a man's age was half his wife's present age. If sum of their present ages is 90 years, how much is the present age of man?
    (a) 42 years (b) 45 years
    (c) 48 years (d) 52 years

33. Sum of the ages of Ram and Shyam 18 years ago was half of the sum of their ages today. Presently, Ram is twice as old as Shyam. What is the present age of Ram?
    (a) 24 years (b) 36 years
    (c) 48 years (d) 54 years

34. 30 years ago Sailesh was $1/5^{th}$ of that he would be after 30 years. Find his present age.
    (a) 40 years (b) 45 years
    (c) 50 years (d) 60 years

35. At a certain place, there are some rabbits and some hens. The total number of heads are 78 and total number of legs are 240. Find the number of hens and rabbits respectively.
    (a) 36, 42 (b) 42, 36
    (c) 32, 46 (d) 46, 32

36. Abhay covers 10 Km/hr more than Prakash while driving. If Prakash doubles his speed, then he covers 15 Km/hr more than Abhay who is driving at his normal speed. What is Abhay's Speed?
    (a) 40 Km/hr (b) 45 km/hr
    (c) 25 Km/hr (d) 35 km/hr

37. In 1 hr, P walks twice the distance that Q walks. In 5 hrs, P walks 6 km more than Q walks in 8 hrs. How many kilometers dose Q walks per hour?
    (a) 2 km (b) 3 km
    (c) 4 km (d) 5 km

38. A is greater than B by one-third the sum of A and B. If B is increased by 40 it becomes greater than twice A by 10. Find A, B.
    (a) 30, 20
    (b) 20, 40
    (c) 60, 30
    (d) 20, 10

39. A shopkeeper has a few 100 gm weight and a few 500 gm weights. He can weigh a maximum of 8 kg in one weighing. If he has 20 pieces of weights, what is the maximum weight that he can weigh with only 100 gm weights?
    (a) 800 gm
    (b) 600 gm
    (c) 400 gm
    (d) 500 gm

40. Sharad has 15 coins consisting of 10 paise and 20 paise. If the total amount with him is ₹ 2, then how many 10 paise and 20 paise coins respectively dose he have?
    (a) 5, 10
    (b) 10, 5
    (c) 7, 8
    (d) 12, 3

41. A box contains certain number of coins of ₹ 1, ₹ 2 and ₹ 5. The total number of coins are twice the ₹ 5 coins and thrice the ₹ 2 coins. If the number of coins of ₹ 1 are 12, then how much is the total amount in the box?
    (a) ₹ 200
    (b) ₹ 240
    (c) ₹ 280
    (d) ₹ 320

42. Four friends A, B, C and D have 150 mangos among them. A has mangos equal to B and D together. C has half the mangos of what A has. How much do A and C have?
    (a) $A = 60, C = 30$
    (b) $A = 30, C = 60$
    (c) $A = 40, C = 20$
    (d) $A = 80, C = 40$

43. In 5 hours Anil walks 4 miles more than Bharat dose in 8 hours. In 7 hours, Bharat walks 2 miles more than Anil walks in 3 hours. How many miles dose Anil walks per hour?
    (a) 4
    (b) 6
    (c) 7
    (d) 8

44. A housewife, with a given amount, can buy either 10 mangos or 15 apples or 2 watermelons. Find the maximum number of apples which she can buy with 6 times the initial amount such that she gets each of the three varieties of fruits.
    (a) 75
    (b) 81
    (c) 60
    (d) cannot be determined

45. One third of the boys and one-half of the girls of a college are going out for a picnic. If the number of students going for picnic are 300, and out of these 100 are boys, then find the total number of students in the school.
    (a) 500
    (b) 800
    (c) 600
    (d) 700

46. In an examination consisting of 150 questions, 1 mark is given for every correct answer and one-fourth mark is deducted for every wrong answer. A student attempts all 150 questions and scores a total of 100 marks. Find the number of questions he marked wrong.
    (a) 45
    (b) 40
    (c) 50
    (d) 30

Simple Equations

47. Sam and Umesh have some amount of money with them. If Sam gives ₹ 10 to Umesh they will have equal amounts, if Umesh gives ₹ 20 to Sam, Sam will have an amount 4 times that of Umesh. Find the amounts each had individually.
    (a) ₹ 60, ₹ 40
    (b) ₹ 80, ₹ 60
    (c) ₹ 50, ₹ 30
    (d) ₹ 45, ₹ 75

48. The cost of 2 pineapple, 3 apples and 4 mangos together is ₹ 35. The cost of 4 pineapples, 6 apples and 7 mangos together is ₹ 66. Find the cost of a mango.
    (a) ₹ 2
    (b) ₹ 3
    (c) ₹ 4
    (d) ₹ 5

49. There are some apples in a basket. Amit took one-third of them. Vijay took one-third of the remaining and finally Karan took one-third of the remaining. If at the end there were 8 apples. Find the number of apples initially in the basket.
    (a) 27
    (b) 36
    (c) 24
    (d) 32

50. A man can feed his dog for a certain number of days with ₹ 1200. If the cost of feed of dog per day increases by ₹ 20, he can feed his dog 30 days less. Find the number of days he use to feed his dog earlier?
    (a) 60
    (b) 80
    (c) 50
    (d) 75

51. If the cost of each book is reduced by ₹ 10, a person can buy 30 more books for ₹ 1800. Find the original price of book?
    (a) ₹ 50
    (b) ₹ 60
    (c) ₹ 30
    (d) ₹ 40

52. Arjun is standing in a queue at a reservation counter. $1/6^{th}$ of the number of persons standing in front of him is equal to $4/7^{th}$ if the persons standing behind him. Find the minimum possible number of persons standing in that queue.
    (a) 28
    (b) 30
    (c) 32
    (d) 34

53. A man has sufficient money to buy 50 apples or 30 mangoes. If he decides to spend 90% of the money, and buys 9 mangoes, then how many apples he can buy?
    (a) 20
    (b) 24
    (c) 26
    (d) 30

54. A daily wages worker joins on 1st of a month and earns ₹ 60 every day, but spends ₹ 40 every alternate day starting from the second day. In how many days his saving will reach to ₹ 480?
    (a) 8 days
    (b) 10 days
    (c) 12 days
    (d) 13 days

55. The total cost of 4 chairs and 2 tables is ₹ 4600. If the cost of table is ₹ 50 more than chair, how much is the cost of each table?
    (a) ₹ 650
    (b) ₹ 700
    (c) ₹ 800
    (d) ₹ 900

56. Cost of an apple is ₹ 8, while cost of an orange is ₹ 6. Karan spend ₹ 46 on these fruits and purchased more number of apples than oranges. How many apples he buy?
    (a) 2 (b) 3
    (c) 4 (d) 5

57. The charges for hiring a car on rent are partly fixed and partly varying as per number of kilometers traveled. If the bill for traveling 45 km is ₹ 380 and for traveling 60 km is ₹ 440, then how much will be the bill for traveling 80 km?
    (a) ₹ 500 (b) ₹ 520
    (c) ₹ 580 (d) ₹ 600

58. The expenses of a mess are partly fixed and partly varying with the number of members. If there are 40 members in the mess, then it cost ₹ 450 per head. If there are 50 members in the mess, then it cost ₹ 430 per head. How many members should be there in mess, so that per head cost will be ₹ 400?
    (a) 60 (b) 70
    (c) 75 (d) 80

59. A certain number of notebooks were purchased for ₹ 450. If the shopkeeper offers a discount of ₹ 15 on each notebook, then 5 more notebooks can be purchased in the same amount. How many notebooks were purchased?
    (a) 10 (b) 15
    (c) 20 (d) 25

60. One-fourth of the boys and one-sixth of girls in a school appeared for scholarship exam. If the number of students appearing for scholarship exam are 150, and out of these one-third are girls, then how much is the strength of school?
    (a) 540 (b) 600
    (c) 700 (d) 860

KEYS

1. (b)	2. (c)	3. (b)	4. (c)	5. (c)	6. (b)	7. (b)	8. (a)
9. (a)	10. (b)	11. (c)	12. (b)	13. (d)	14. (b)	15. (b)	16. (c)
17. (c)	18. (a)	19. (c)	20. (b)	21. (c)	22. (a)	23. (c)	24. (b)
25. (b)	26. (b)	27. (b)	28. (d)	29. (d)	30. (b)	31. (c)	32. (c)
33. (c)	34. (b)	35. (a)	36. (d)	37. (b)	38. (d)	39. (d)	40. (b)
41. (b)	42. (a)	43. (a)	44. (b)	45. (d)	46. (b)	47. (a)	48. (c)
49. (a)	50. (a)	51. (c)	52. (c)	53. (d)	54. (c)	55. (c)	56. (d)
57. (b)	58. (d)	59. (a)	60. (c)				

SOLUTIONS

Solution 1

Let the number be x.

$$\frac{3}{4}x + 9 = 33$$

$$\Rightarrow \quad \frac{3}{4}x = 33 - 9$$

$$\therefore \quad x = 24 \times \frac{4}{3} = 32.$$

Choice (b)

Solution 2

Let the number be x.

$$\frac{4}{5}x - \frac{2}{3}x = 6$$

$$\Rightarrow \quad \frac{12x - 10x}{15} = 6$$

$$\therefore \quad x = \frac{6 \times 15}{2} = 45.$$

Choice (c)

Solution 3

Let the number be x.

$$\frac{1}{3} \times \frac{1}{4} \times x = 3$$

$$\therefore \quad x = 3 \times 3 \times 4 = 36$$

Five-sixth of number $= \frac{5}{6} \times 36 = 30.$

Choice (b)

Solution 4

Let the number be x.

$$8 \times x = x + 175$$

$$\Rightarrow \quad 7x = 175$$

$$\therefore \quad x = \frac{175}{7} = 25.$$

Choice (c)

Solution 5

Let the number be x.

$$\left(\frac{x}{3}+\frac{x}{4}\right)-\frac{3x}{8} = 10$$

$\Rightarrow \quad \frac{8x+6x-9x}{24} = 10$

$\Rightarrow \quad \frac{5x}{24} = 10$

$\therefore \quad x = \frac{10 \times 24}{5} = 48.$

Choice (c)

Solution 6

Let the number be x.

$$\frac{2x}{3} - 4 = \frac{x}{3} + 6$$

$\Rightarrow \quad \frac{2x}{3} - \frac{x}{3} = 10$

$\Rightarrow \quad \frac{x}{3} = 10$

$\therefore \quad x = 30.$

Choice (b)

Solution 7

Let the number be x.
Square of the number will be x^2.

$$x^2 + x = 132$$
$$x^2 + x - 132 = 0$$
$$x^2 + 12x - 11x - 132 = 0$$
$$(x+12)(x-11) = 0$$

$\therefore \quad x = 11 \text{ or } -12.$

Choice (b)

Solution 8

Let the two digit number be $10x + y$.

$$10x + y = 10(x + y)$$
$\Rightarrow \quad 10x + y = 10x + 10y$
$\Rightarrow \quad y = 0$

Also difference of digits is 5.

∴ $x - y = 5$
⇒ $x = 5$

So, the required number is 50.

Choice (a)

Solution 9

Let the two digit number be $10x + y$.

Sum of digits is 9.

$$x + y = 9$$
⇒ $$x = 9 - y$$

Also 3 more than units digit would be half of tens digit.

$$x + 3 = \frac{y}{2}$$
⇒ $$9 - y + 3 = \frac{y}{2}$$
⇒ $$12 = y + \frac{y}{2}$$

∴ $y = 8$ and $x = 1$

So, the required number is 18.

Choice (a)

Solution 10

Let the two digit number be $10x + y$.

Sum of digits is 9.

$$x + y = 9 \quad \ldots (1)$$

Also if 27 is subtracted to the number, the digits are interchanged (or number is reversed).

$$10x + y - 27 = 10y + x$$
⇒ $$9x - 9y = 27$$
⇒ $$x - y = 3 \quad \ldots (2)$$

Adding equation (1) and (2)

$$2x = 12$$
∴ $$x = 6$$
and $$y = 3$$

So, the required number is 63.

Choice (b)

Solution 11

Let the two digit number be $10x + y$.

Sum of digits is 9.

$$x + y = 9$$

$$\frac{10x + y - 3}{10x + y + 3} = \frac{7}{8}$$

$\Rightarrow \qquad 80x + 8y - 24 = 70x + 7y + 21$

$\therefore \qquad 10x + y = 45$

As the sum of digits of 45 is 9, hence 45 is the required number.

Choice (c)

Solution 12

Let the fraction be $\frac{n}{d}$.

As per 1st condition

$\Rightarrow \qquad 8n - 6d = 2$ ... (1)

As per 2nd condition

$\Rightarrow \qquad 10d - 10n = 20$

$\Rightarrow \qquad d - n = 2$ ... (2)

Equating equation (1) and (2)

$$8n - 6d = d - n$$

$$9n = 7d$$

$\therefore \qquad \frac{n}{d} = \frac{7}{9}.$

Choice (b)

Solution 13

Let the three digit number be $100x + 10y + z$.

As the middle digit is zero, so $y = 0$. The number will be $100x + z$.

As sum of digits is 9, so

$$x + z = 9 \qquad \qquad ...(1)$$

If 99 is added to the number, the digits are interchanged.

$$100x + z + 99 = 100z + x$$

$$99z - 99x = 99$$

$$z - x = 1 \qquad \qquad ...(2)$$

Solving equation (1) and (2)
$$z = 5 \text{ and } x = 4$$
So, the required number is 405.

Choice (d)

Solution 14

Let the two digit number be $10x + y$.

As per 1st condition

$\Rightarrow \quad\quad\quad 6(x + y) = 10x + y - 1$
$\Rightarrow \quad\quad\quad 6x + 6y = 10x + y - 1$
$\Rightarrow \quad\quad\quad 4x - 5y = 1$ ... (1)

As per 2nd condition

$\Rightarrow \quad\quad\quad 6(x + y) = 10y + x + 8$
$\Rightarrow \quad\quad\quad 6x + 6y = 10y + x + 8$
$\Rightarrow \quad\quad\quad 5x - 4y = 8$ ... (2)

Solving equation (1) and (2)
$$x = 4 \text{ and } y = 3.$$
So, product of digits = $4 \times 3 = 12$.

Choice (b)

Solution 15

Let the two digit number be $10x + y$.

As per 1st condition

$\Rightarrow \quad\quad\quad 10x + y = 4(x + y) - 12$
$\Rightarrow \quad\quad\quad 10x + y = 4x + 4y - 12$
$\Rightarrow \quad\quad\quad 6x = 3y - 12$
$\Rightarrow \quad\quad\quad 12x = 6y - 24$ ... (1)

As per 2nd condition

$\Rightarrow \quad\quad\quad 10x + y = 2(y - x) + 6$
$\Rightarrow \quad\quad\quad 10x + y = 2y - 2x + 6$
$\Rightarrow \quad\quad\quad 12x = y + 6$ ... (2)

Equating equation (1) and (2)
$$6y - 24 = y + 6$$
$$5y = 30$$
$\therefore \quad\quad\quad y = 6 \text{ and } x = 1$

So, the required number is 16.

Choice (b)

Solution 16

Let the two digit number be $10x + y$.

As sum of digits is 14,

$$\therefore \quad x + y = 14$$

Sum of reciprocals of digits is 24,

$$\frac{1}{x} + \frac{1}{y} = \frac{7}{24}$$

$$\Rightarrow \quad \frac{x+y}{xy} = \frac{7}{24}$$

$$\Rightarrow \quad \frac{14}{xy} = \frac{7}{24}$$

$$\therefore \quad xy = 48$$

So, product of digits is 48.

Choice (c)

Solution 17

Let the four consecutive even numbers be $2x, 2x + 2, 2x + 4$ and $2x + 6$.
The product of first and fourth:

$$2x(2x + 6) = 216$$
$$4x^2 + 12x - 216 = 0$$
$$x^2 + 3x - 54 = 0$$
$$x^2 + 9x - 6x - 54 = 0$$
$$(x + 9)(x - 6) = 0$$
$$\therefore \quad x = -9 \text{ or } 6$$

As the numbers are positive, taking $x = 6$.
So the numbers are 12, 14, 16, and 18.
Product of second and third number $= 14 \times 16 = 224$.

Choice (c)

Solution 18

If the sum of two numbers is 20 and product is 96, then the two numbers must be 12 and 8.

$$\text{Sum of their reciprocals} = \frac{1}{12} + \frac{1}{8}$$

$$= \frac{2+3}{24}$$

$$= \frac{5}{24}.$$

Choice (a)

Solution 19

Let the two numbers be x and y.

$$x - y = 3 \qquad \ldots (1)$$

As the difference of their squares is 57,

$$x^2 - y^2 = 57$$
$$(x - y)(x + y) = 57$$
$$3(x + y) = 57$$
$$\therefore \quad x + y = 19 \qquad \ldots (2)$$

Adding equation (1) and (2)

$$2x = 22$$
$$\therefore \quad x = 11$$

and $\quad y = 8$

So, the larger number is 11.

Choice (c)

Solution 20

Let the three consecutive numbers be $(x - 1), x, (x + 1)$

$$(x - 1) + x + (x + 1) = 108$$
$$3x = 108$$
$$\therefore \quad x = 36$$

So, the greatest number is 37.

Choice (b)

Solution 21

Let the two consecutive even numbers be $2x$ and $2x + 2$.

$$(2x + 2)^2 - (2x)^2 = 44$$
$$4x^2 + 8x + 4 - 4x^2 = 44$$
$$8x = 40$$
$$\therefore \quad x = 5$$

So, the numbers are 10 and 12, and their sum is 22.

Choice (c)

Solution 22

Let the two numbers be x and y.

As per 1st condition

$$\Rightarrow \quad x(x + y) = 204$$

$\Rightarrow$ $\qquad x^2 + xy = 204$
$\Rightarrow$ $\qquad xy = 204 - x^2$ ... (1)

As per 2nd condition
$\Rightarrow$ $\qquad y(x - y) = 35$
$\Rightarrow$ $\qquad xy - y^2 = 35$
$\Rightarrow$ $\qquad xy = 35 + y^2$ ... (2)

Equating equation (1) and (2)
$$204 - x^2 = 35 + y^2$$
$$x^2 + y^2 = 169$$

So, x and y must be 12 and 5. ($\because 12^2 + 5^2 = 13^2$).

Choice (a)

Solution 23

Let the two numbers be x and y.
$\qquad 2x + 3y = 54$ ... (1)
$\qquad 3x + 2y = 61$ ... (2)

Multiplying equation (1) with 2 and equation (2) with 3.
$\qquad 4x + 6y = 108$ ... (3)
$\qquad 9x + 6y = 183$ ... (4)

Subtracting equation (3) from (4)
$\qquad 5x = 75$
$\therefore \qquad x = 15$

Substituting value of x in equation (1)
$\qquad 2(15) + 3y = 54$
$\qquad 3y = 54 - 30$
$\therefore \qquad y = 8$

The smaller of the two numbers is 8.

Choice (c)

Solution 24

Let the first, second and third number be F, S and T respectively.
$\qquad F + S = 35$ ... (1)
$\qquad S + T = 50$ ... (2)
$\qquad 2F + T = 60$ ... (3)

Subtracting equation (1) from equation (2)
$\qquad (S + T) - (F + S) = 50 - 35$
$\qquad T - F = 15$ ... (4)

Subtracting equation (4) from (3)

$$(2F + T) - (T - F) = 60 - 15$$
$$3F = 45$$
$$\therefore F = 15.$$

Choice (b)

Solution 25

Let the present age of father be F and present age of son be S.

Father was 20 years old when his son was born, means father's age is 20 years more than son's age.

$$F = S + 20 \quad \ldots (1)$$

Also present age of father is 5 times the age of son.

$$F = 5S \quad \ldots (2)$$

Substituting $F = 5S$ in equation (1)

$$5S = S + 20$$
$$4S = 20$$
$$\therefore S = 5 \text{ years}.$$

Choice (b)

Solution 26

Let the present age of father be F and present age of son be S. As per the condition in the problem, the equations will be as follows:

$$F = 2S \quad \ldots (1)$$
$$(F - 20) = 12 (S - 20) \quad \ldots (2)$$

Substituting $F = 2S$ in equation (2)

$$(2S - 20) = 12 (S - 20)$$
$$2S - 20 = 12S - 240$$
$$10S = 220$$
$$\therefore S = 22 \text{ and } F = 44.$$

Choice (b)

Solution 27

As per the condition in the problem, the equations will be as follows:

$$A = B - 2 \quad \ldots (1)$$
$$\frac{5}{6}(A - 7) - \frac{3}{10}(B - 7) = 9 \quad \ldots (2)$$

$$\Rightarrow \quad \frac{25(A - 7) - 9(B - 7)}{30} = 9$$

$$\Rightarrow \quad 25A - 9B = 382$$
$$\Rightarrow \quad 25(B - 2) - 9B = 382 \text{ (Substituting } A = B - 2)$$
$$\Rightarrow \quad 16B = 432$$
$$\therefore \quad B = 27.$$

Choice (b)

Solution 28

Let the present age of Raj be R and present age of Sam be S. As per the condition in the problem, the equations will be as follows:

$$R + 5 = 3(S - 4) \qquad \ldots (1)$$
$$R - 4 = 2S \qquad \ldots (2)$$

Substituting $R = 2S + 4$ in equation (1)

$$(2S + 4) + 5 = 3(S - 4)$$
$$2S + 9 = 3S - 12$$
$$\therefore \quad S = 21$$
and $\quad R = 46.$

Choice (d)

Solution 29

Let the present age of Rohit be R.

$$R + 25 = 11(R - 25)$$
$$R + 25 = 11R - 275$$
$$10R = 300$$
$$\therefore \quad R = 30.$$

Choice (d)

Solution 30

Let the present age of father be F and present age of son be S. As per the condition in the problem, the equations will be as follows:

$$F = 2S + 2 \qquad \ldots (1)$$
$$(F + 3) = 3(S + 3) - 20 \qquad \ldots (2)$$
$$\Rightarrow \quad (2S + 2 + 3) = 3(S + 3) - 20$$
$$\Rightarrow \quad 2S + 5 = 3S + 9 - 20$$
$$\Rightarrow \quad S = 16$$
$$\therefore \quad F = 2(16) + 2$$
$$= 34 \text{ years.}$$

Choice (b)

Solution 31

Let the present age of mother be M and present age of daughter be D. As per the condition in the problem, the equations will be as follows:

$$M = D + 22 \qquad \ldots (1)$$

$$\frac{(M-22)+(D-22)}{2} = 24 \qquad \ldots (2)$$

Substituting M as $D + 22$ in equation (1)

$$\frac{(D+22-22)+(D-22)}{2} = 24$$

$$2D - 22 = 48$$
$$2D = 70$$
∴ $$D = 35$$

So, present age of mother = 35 + 22 = 57 years.

Choice (c)

Solution 32

Let the present age of man be M and present age of wife be W. As per the condition in the problem, the equations will be as follows:

$$M - 27 = \frac{W}{2} \qquad \ldots (1)$$

$$M + W = 90 \qquad \ldots (2)$$

Substituting W as $2(M - 27)$ in equation (2)

$$M + 2(M - 27) = 90$$
$$3M = 144$$
∴ $$M = 48 \text{ years.}$$

Choice (c)

Solution 33

Let the present age of Ram be R and present age of Shyam be S. As per the condition in the problem, the equations will be as follows:

$$R = 2S \qquad \ldots (1)$$

$$(R - 18) + (S - 18) = \frac{R+S}{2} \qquad \ldots (2)$$

Substituting R as $2S$ in equation (2)

$$(2S - 18) + (S - 18) = \frac{3S}{2}$$

$$\Rightarrow 3S - 36 = \frac{3S}{2}$$

$\Rightarrow$ $\qquad 6S - 72 = 3S$
$\Rightarrow$ $\qquad 3S = 72$
$\therefore$ $\qquad S = 24$
and $\qquad R = 48.$

Choice (c)

Solution 34

Let the present age of Sailesh be S.
$$S - 30 = \frac{1}{5}(S + 30)$$
$\Rightarrow \qquad 5S - 150 = S + 30$
$\Rightarrow \qquad 4S = 180$
$\therefore \qquad S = 45.$

Choice (b)

Solution 35

Let the number of rabbits be R and number of hens be H. As the number of heads are 78,
$$R + H = 78 \qquad \ldots (1)$$
Also the number of legs are 240,
$$4R + 2H = 240 \qquad \ldots (2)$$
Multiplying equation (1) with 2 and subtracting it from equation (2)
$\qquad (4R + 2H) - (2R + 2H) = 240 - 156$
$\Rightarrow \qquad 2R = 84$
$\therefore \qquad R = 42 \text{ and } H = 36$

So, the number of hens and rabbits are 36 and 42 respectively.

Choice (a)

Solution 36

Let the speed of Abhay be A km/hr and speed of Prakash be P km/hr. As per the condition in the problem, the equations will be as follows:
$$A = P + 10 \qquad \ldots (1)$$
$$2P = A + 15 \qquad \ldots (2)$$
Substituting A as $P + 10$ in equation (2)
$\qquad 2P = (P + 10) + 15$
$\therefore \qquad P = 25$
and $\qquad A = 35.$

Choice (d)

Solution 37

Let the speed of P is P km/hr and speed of Q is Q km/hr. As P walks twice the distance that Q walks in 1 hr,

$$P = 2Q \qquad \ldots (1)$$

Also in 5 hrs, P walks 6 km more than Q walks in 8 hrs,

$$5P = 8Q + 6 \qquad \ldots (2)$$

Substituting P as $2Q$ in equation (2)

$$5(2Q) = 8Q + 6$$
$$10Q = 8Q + 6$$
$$\therefore \quad Q = 3 \text{ km/hr.}$$

Choice (b)

Solution 38

As per 1st condition:

$$A - B = \frac{1}{3}(A + B) \qquad \ldots (1)$$

$$\Rightarrow \quad 3A - 3B = A + B$$
$$\Rightarrow \quad 2A = 4B$$
$$\Rightarrow \quad A = 2B$$

As per 2nd condition:

$$B + 40 = 2A + 10 \qquad \ldots (2)$$
$$\Rightarrow \quad B + 40 = 2(2B) + 10$$
$$\Rightarrow \quad B + 40 = 4B + 10$$
$$\Rightarrow \quad 3B = 30$$
$$\therefore \quad B = 10 \text{ and } A = 20.$$

Choice (d)

Solution 39

Let the number of weights of 100 gm are x and number of weights of 500 gm are y. As he has 20 pieces of weights,

$$x + y = 20 \qquad \ldots (1)$$

Also he can weigh a maximum of 8 kg using all the weights,

$$100x + 500y = 8000 \qquad \ldots (2)$$

Multiplying equation (1) with 100 and subtracting it from equation (2)

$$(100x + 500y) - (100x + 100y) = 8000 - 2000$$
$$\Rightarrow \quad 400y = 6000$$
$$\therefore \quad y = 15 \text{ and } x = 5$$

So, the maximum weight he can weigh using only 100 gm weights = 100 × 5 = 500 gm.

Choice (d)

Solution 40

Let the number of coins of 10 paise be x and the number of coins of 20 paise be y. As the total number of coins are 15,

$$x + y = 15 \qquad \ldots (1)$$

Also the total value of coins is ₹ 2 (200 paise)

$$10x + 20y = 200 \qquad \ldots (2)$$

Multiplying equation (1) with 10 and subtracting it from equation (2)

$$(10x + 20y) - (10x + 10y) = 200 - 150$$
$$\Rightarrow \qquad 10y = 50$$
$$\therefore \qquad y = 5 \text{ and } x = 10$$

So, the number of coins of 10 paise and 20 paise are 10 and 5 respectively.

Choice (b)

Solution 41

Let the total number of coins in the box are C.

Number of ₹ 1 coins = 12 (given)

Number of ₹ 2 coins = $\dfrac{C}{3}$ (∵ Total coins are thrice ₹ 2 coins)

Number of ₹ 5 coins = $\dfrac{C}{2}$ (∵ Total coins are twice ₹ 5 coins)

$$12 + \frac{C}{3} + \frac{C}{2} = C$$

$$\frac{72 + 2C + 3C}{6} = C$$

$$\therefore \qquad C = 72$$

So, the number of ₹ 2 coins are 24, while number of ₹ 5 coins are 36.

Total amount in the box = 12(1) + 24(2) + 36(5) = ₹ 240.

Choice (b)

Solution 42

As per the conditions mentioned in the problem, the equations will be as follows:

$$A + B + C + D = 150 \qquad \ldots (1)$$
$$A = B + D \qquad \ldots (2)$$
$$C = A/2 \qquad \ldots (3)$$

Substituting $B + D = A$ and $C = A/2$ in equation (1)

$$A + A + \frac{A}{2} = 150$$

$$\frac{5A}{2} = 150$$

∴ $$A = \frac{150 \times 2}{5} = 60$$

and $$C = \frac{60}{2} = 30.$$

Choice (a)

Solution 43

Let the speed of Anil be A miles/hr and Bharat be B miles/hr. As per the conditions mentioned in the problem, the equations will be as follows:

$$5A = 8B + 4 \quad \ldots (1)$$
$$\Rightarrow \quad 5A - 8B = 4$$
$$\Rightarrow \quad 15A - 24B = 12$$
$$7B = 3A + 2 \quad \ldots (2)$$
$$\Rightarrow \quad 7B - 3A = 2$$
$$\Rightarrow \quad 35B - 15A = 10$$

Adding equation (1) and (2)

$$(15A - 24B) + (35B - 15A) = 12 + 10$$
$$11B = 22$$
∴ $$B = 2$$
and $$A = 4.$$

Choice (a)

Solution 44

$$10 M = 15 A = 2 W$$

Let us assume the cost of 10 mangos, 15 apples or 2 watermelons as a value which is LCM of 10, 15 and 2 *i.e.,* ₹ 30

∴ $\quad 10 M = 15 A = 2 W = ₹ 30$
∴ $\quad M = ₹ 3, A = ₹ 2$ and $W = ₹ 15$

If she has 6 times of this amount ₹ 180 and she buys at least 1 mango and 1 watermelon, then:
Amount left = $180 - (3 + 15) = ₹ 162$

Maximum number of apples that can be purchased = $\frac{162}{2} = 81.$

Choice (b)

Solution 45

Let the total number of boys in the school be B and total number of girls be G.

Number of boys going for picnic = $\dfrac{B}{3}$

Number of girls going for picnic = $\dfrac{G}{2}$

Out of 300 students going or picnic, 100 are boys.

$\therefore \qquad \dfrac{B}{3} = 100$

$\Rightarrow \qquad B = 300$

$\therefore \qquad \dfrac{G}{2} = 200$

$\Rightarrow \qquad G = 400$

Number of students in the school = $B + G = 300 + 400 = 700$.

Choice (d)

Solution 46

Let the number of questions marked correct be C and number of questions marked wrong be W. As total questions attempted are 150,

$$C + W = 150 \qquad \ldots (1)$$

Also 1 mark is scored for every correct and one-fourth mark is lost for every wrong,

$$C - \dfrac{W}{4} = 100 \qquad \ldots (2)$$

Subtracting equation (2) from equation (1)

$$(C + W) - (C - \dfrac{W}{4}) = 150 - 100$$

$\Rightarrow \qquad W + \dfrac{W}{4} = 50$

$\Rightarrow \qquad \dfrac{5W}{4} = 50$

$\therefore \qquad W = \dfrac{50 \times 4}{5} = 40.$

Choice (b)

Solution 47

Let the amount with Sam be ₹ S and the amount with Umesh be ₹ U. If Sam gives ₹ 10 to Umesh they will have equal amounts;

$$S - 10 = U + 10 \qquad \ldots (1)$$

$\Rightarrow \qquad S = U + 20$

If Umesh gives ₹ 20 to Sam, Sam will have an amount 4 times that of Umesh;
$$S + 20 = 4(U - 20) \quad \ldots (2)$$
Substituting $S = U + 20$ in equation (2)
$$(U + 20) + 20 = 4(U - 20)$$
$\Rightarrow \quad U + 40 = 4U - 80$
$\Rightarrow \quad 3U = 120$
$\therefore \quad U = 40$
and $\quad S = 60$

So, Sam and Umesh has ₹ 60 and ₹ 40 with them respectively.

Choice (a)

Solution 48

$$2P + 3A + 4M = 35 \quad \ldots (1)$$
$$4P + 6A + 7M = 66 \quad \ldots (2)$$

Multiplying equation (1) with 2 and subtracting equation (2) from it.

$(4P + 6A + 8M) - (4P + 6A + 7M) = 70 - 66$

$\therefore \quad M = 4.$

Choice (c)

Solution 49

Let the number of apples in the basket initially be x.

After Amit took one-third of the apples:

Number of apples left = $\frac{2}{3}x$

After Vijay took one-third of the remaining apples:

Number of apples left = $\frac{2}{3} \times \frac{2}{3}x = \frac{4}{9}x$

Finally after Karan took one-third of the remaining apples:

Number of apples left = $\frac{2}{3} \times \frac{4}{9}x = \frac{8}{27}x$

As there are 8 apples left at the end:

$\therefore \quad \frac{8}{27}x = 8$

$\therefore \quad x = 27.$

Choice (a)

Solution 50

Let the cost of feed per day be C and the number of days in which he can feed the dog be D.

$$C \times D = 1200$$

$\Rightarrow \qquad C = \dfrac{1200}{D}$

As the cost of feed of dog per day increases by ₹ 20, he can feed his dog 30 days less.

$$(C + 20)(D - 30) = C \times D$$

$\Rightarrow \qquad CD + 20D - 30C - 600 = CD$

$\Rightarrow \qquad 20D - 30C = 600$

$\Rightarrow \qquad 20D - 30 \times \dfrac{1200}{D} = 600$

$\Rightarrow \qquad D^2 - 30D - 1800 = 0$

$\Rightarrow \qquad D^2 - 60D + 30D - 1800 = 0$

$\Rightarrow \qquad (D - 60)(D + 30) = 0$

$\therefore \qquad D = 60 \text{ or } -30.$

Choice (a)

Solution 51

Let the cost of book be C and the number book that can be purchased be B.

$$C \times B = 1800$$

$\Rightarrow \qquad C = \dfrac{1800}{B}$

If the cost of each book is reduced by ₹ 10, a person can buy 30 more books.

$$(C - 10)(B + 30) = C \times B$$

$\Rightarrow \qquad CB + 30C - 10B - 300 = CB$

$\Rightarrow \qquad 3C - B - 30 = 0$

$\Rightarrow \qquad 3C - \dfrac{1800}{C} - 30 = 0$

$\Rightarrow \qquad 3C^2 - 1800 - 30C = 0$

$\Rightarrow \qquad C^2 - 10C - 600 = 0$

$\Rightarrow \qquad C^2 - 30C + 20C - 600 = 0$

$\Rightarrow \qquad (C - 30)(C + 20) = 0$

$\therefore \qquad C = 30 \text{ or } -20.$

Choice (c)

Solution 52

B ←———— A ————→ F

Let the number of persons standing in front of him are F and number of persons standing behind him are B.

$$\frac{1}{6}F = \frac{4}{7}B$$

$$\frac{F}{B} = \frac{24}{7}$$

Minimum number of persons in the queue $= B + A + F$
$= 7 + 1 + 24 = 32$.

Choice (c)

Solution 53

Let the cost of each apple be A and cost of each mango be M.

$$50\,A = 30\,M$$

Let us assume the cost of 50 apples or 30 mangos as a value which is LCM of 50 and 30 *i.e.,* ₹ 150

$$50\,A = 30\,M = ₹\,150$$

∴ $\quad A = ₹\,3$ and $M = ₹\,5$

Amount the person want to spend $= \dfrac{90}{100} \times 150 = ₹\,135$

Money spent in buying 9 mangos $= 9 \times 5 = ₹\,45$

Number of apples he can buy in remaining money $= \dfrac{135 - 45}{3} = 30$.

Choice (d)

Solution 54

Earning on day 1 = ₹ 60

Earning on day 2 = ₹ 60 − ₹ 40 = ₹ 20

So, in every 2 days he is saving ₹ 80.

Number of day require to save ₹ 480 $= \dfrac{480}{80} \times 2 = 12$ days.

Choice (c)

Solution 55

Let the cost of each chair be C and cost of each table be T. As per the condition in the problem, the equations will be as follows:

$$T = C + 50 \qquad \qquad \ldots (1)$$

$$\Rightarrow \quad C = T - 50$$
$$4C + 2T = 4600 \quad \ldots (2)$$

Substituting C as $(T - 50)$ in equation (1)
$$4(T - 50) + 2T = 4600$$
$$\Rightarrow \quad 6T = 4600 + 200$$
$$\therefore \quad T = 800.$$

Choice (c)

Solution 56

Let the number of apples purchased are A and number of oranges purchased are R.
$$8A + 6R = 46$$
$$\Rightarrow \quad A = \frac{46 - 6R}{8}$$
If $\quad R = 1, A = 5$
If $\quad R = 5, A = 2$

But as number of apples purchased are more than oranges, so number of apples must be 5.

Choice (d)

Solution 57

Let the fixed cost be F and varying cost is V for traveling N km.
$$\therefore \quad F + NV = \text{Bill amount}$$
$$F + 45V = ₹ 380 \quad \ldots (1)$$
$$F + 60V = ₹ 440 \quad \ldots (2)$$

Subtracting equation (1) from equation (2)
$$(F + 60V) - (F + 45V) = 440 - 380$$
$$15V = 60$$
$$\therefore \quad V = ₹ 4 \text{ per km.}$$
and $\quad F = ₹ 200$

Bill for traveling 80 km $= F + NV = 200 + 80(4) = ₹ 520.$

Choice (b)

Solution 58

Let the fixed cost be F and varying cost is V for N number of members.
$$F + \frac{V}{N} = \text{Per head expenses}$$
$$F + \frac{V}{40} = ₹ 450 \quad \ldots (1)$$
$$F + \frac{V}{50} = ₹ 430 \quad \ldots (2)$$

Subtracting equation (2) from equation (1).

$$\left(F+\frac{V}{40}\right)-\left(F+\frac{V}{50}\right) = 450-430$$

$$\Rightarrow \quad \frac{V}{40}-\frac{V}{50} = 450-430$$

$$\Rightarrow \quad \frac{5V-4V}{200} = 20$$

$$\therefore \quad V = 4000$$
and $\quad F = 350.$

The number of members needed to share per head ₹ 400 can be found as:

$$F + \frac{V}{N} = ₹\,400$$

$$350 + \frac{4000}{N} = 400$$

$$\therefore \quad N = 80.$$

Choice (d)

Solution 59

Let the cost of each notebook be C and the number of notebooks purchased are N.

$$C \times N = 450$$

If the cost of each notebook is reduced by ₹ 15, then 5 more notebooks can be purchased.

$$(C-15)(N+5) = 450$$
$$\Rightarrow \quad CN - 15N + 5C - 75 = 450$$
$$\Rightarrow \quad 15N - 5C + 75 = 0$$
$$\Rightarrow \quad 15N - 5 \times \frac{450}{N} + 75 = 0$$
$$\Rightarrow \quad N^2 + 5N - 150 = 0$$
$$\Rightarrow \quad N^2 + 15N - 10N - 150 = 0$$
$$\Rightarrow \quad (N+15)(N-10) = 0$$
$$\therefore \quad N = -15 \text{ or } 10$$

So, the number of notebooks purchased are 10.

Choice (a)

Solution 60

Let the total number of boys in the school be B and total number of girls be G.

Number of boys appearing for scholarship = $\frac{B}{4}$

Number of girls appearing for scholarship = $\frac{G}{6}$

Out of 150 students appearing for scholarship, one-third *i.e.*, 50 are girls.

∴ $\qquad \dfrac{G}{6} = 50$

⇒ $\qquad G = 300$

∴ $\qquad \dfrac{B}{4} = 100$

⇒ $\qquad B = 400$

Number of students in the school = $B + G$ = 400 + 300 = 700.

Choice (c)

6

Ratio-Proportion-Variation

RATIO

Ratio is the relation which one quantity bears to another of same kind. The ratio of two quantities 'a' and 'b' is represented as $a : b$ and read as "a is to b". In this ratio the first term 'a' is called antecedent, and the second term 'b' is called consequent.

Ratio of any number of quantities is expressed after removing any common factors that all the terms of ratio have. For example if there is a ratio 6 : 15 : 21; so after taking the common factor 3 between them out the ratio becomes 2 : 5 : 7. Similarly, if the ratio between two or more quantities is given, then their actual values can be found by multiplying them with the required common factor. For example if the age of two persons is in the ratio of 3 : 4, we can take it as $3x$ and $4x$. In this case x is the common factor which can be found by simplifying the given condition in the problem.

Points to Note

- Duplicate ratio of $(a : b)$ is $(a^2 : b^2)$
- Sub-duplicate ratio of $(a : b)$ is $(\sqrt{a} : \sqrt{b})$
- Triplicate ratio of $(a : b)$ is $(a^3 : b^3)$
- Sub-triplicate ratio of $(a : b)$ is $(\sqrt[3]{a} : \sqrt[3]{b})$.

PROPORTION

When two ratios are equal, the four quantities involved in two ratios are said to be proportional. If $a : b = c : d$, we write $a : b :: c : d$ and we say that a, b, c, d are in proportion. Here a and d are called *extremes*, while b and c are called *means*. The relation is:

Product of means = Product of extremes

Points to Note

- If $a : b = c : d$, then d is called fourth proportional to a, b, c.
- If $a : b = b : c$, then c is called third proportional to a and b.
- Mean proportional between a and b is $\sqrt{ab}$
- If $\frac{a}{b} = \frac{c}{d} = \frac{e}{f}...$, then each of these ratio is equal to $\frac{a+c+e+....}{b+d+f+....}$

- If $\frac{a}{b} = \frac{c}{d}$, then:
  - The relation $\frac{a+b}{b} = \frac{c+d}{d}$ is called componendo
  - The relation $\frac{a-b}{b} = \frac{c-d}{d}$ is called dividendo
  - The relation $\frac{a+b}{a-b} = \frac{c+d}{c-d}$ is called componendo-dividendo.

VARIATION

Variation is the relation between the variables, stating that by changing value of one, how the value of other affects. The variation is categorized as follows:

- *Direct Variation*—One variable X is said to vary directly with another variable Y if with the increase of X, the variable Y also increases or with the decreases of X, the variable Y also decreases. It is expressed as:

  $X \alpha Y$

  $X = KY$

  Where, K is the constant of proportionality.

- *Inverse Variation*—One variable X is said to vary inversely with another variable Y if with the increase of X, the variable Y decreases or with the decreases of X, the variable Y increases. It is expressed as:

  $X \alpha \frac{1}{Y}$

  $X = \frac{K}{Y}$

  Where, K is the constant of proportionality.

- *Joint Variation*—If there are three variables X, Y and Z such that X varies with Y when Z is constant, and X also varies with Z when Y is constant, then X is said to vary jointly with Y and Z.

  $X \alpha Y$ (when Z is constant)

  $X \alpha Z$ (when Y is constant)

  As X is jointly varying with Y and Z, therefore:

  $X \alpha YZ$

  $X = K \times YZ$

  Where, K is the constant of proportionality.

SOLVED EXAMPLES

Example 1
If $A:B = 3:5$ and $B:C = 2:7$, find $A:B:C$.

Solution

As $A:B = 3:5$ and $B:C$ is $2:7$, so finding the common ratio as follows:

$$\begin{array}{ccc} A & B & C \\ 3 & 5 & \\ & 2 & 7 \\ \hline 6 & 10 & 35 \end{array}$$

By multiplying the ratio of $A:B$ by 2 and the ratio of $B:C$ by 5, the ratio of $A:B:C$ is obtained as 6:10:35.

Example 2
Divide 836 in the ratio of 4:7:11

Solution

Sum of ratio terms = $4 + 7 + 11 = 22$

First part = $\frac{4}{22} \times 836 = 152$

Second part = $\frac{7}{22} \times 836 = 266$

Third part = $\frac{11}{22} \times 836 = 418$.

Example 3
If $a:b = 3:5$, find $(4a + 5b) : (3b - 2a)$

Solution

$\frac{a}{b} = \frac{3x}{5x}$

$\frac{4a+3b}{3b-2a} = \frac{4(3x)+3(5x)}{3(5x)-2(3x)} = \frac{12x+15x}{15x-6x} = \frac{27x}{9x} = 3.$

Example 4
If A is 125% of B, B is 40% of C and C is 150% of D, then find $A:D$

Solution

A is 125% of B means $A = \frac{5}{4} B$ or $\frac{A}{B} = \frac{5}{4}$

B is 40% of C means $B = \frac{2}{5} C$ or $\frac{B}{C} = \frac{2}{5}$

C is 150% of D means $C = \frac{3}{2} D$ or $\frac{C}{D} = \frac{3}{2}$

$\therefore \frac{A}{D} = \frac{A}{B} \times \frac{B}{C} \times \frac{C}{D} = \frac{5}{4} \times \frac{2}{5} \times \frac{3}{2} = \frac{3}{4}.$

Example 5

Find:
1. The fourth proportional of 5, 7, 20
2. The third proportional of 8 and 12
3. The mean proportional between 0.12 and 0.48.

Solution

1. Fourth proportional

    Let the fourth proportional to 5, 7, 20 be x

    $5 : 7 :: 20 : x$

    $\frac{5}{7} = \frac{20}{x}$

    $\therefore x = \frac{20 \times 7}{5} = 28$

2. Third proportional

    Let the third proportional of 8 and 12 be x

    $8 : 12 :: 12 : x$

    $\frac{8}{12} = \frac{12}{x}$

    $\therefore x = \frac{12 \times 12}{8} = 18$

3. Mean proportional

    The mean proportional between 0.12 and 0.48 = $\sqrt{0.12 \times 0.48} = 0.24$.

Example 6

A sum of ₹ 4650 is distributed between three partners Ajay, Biju and Chiju in such a way that 2 times the share of Ajay, 3 times the share of Biju and 5 times the share of Chiju is equal. Find the share of A.

Solution

Let the share of three partners Ajay, Biju and Chiju be A, B and C respectively.

As per the given condition in the problem: $2A = 3B = 5C = K$

Let us select (or assume) the value of K which is divisible by 2, 3 and 5 say 30.

$\therefore 2A = 3B = 5C = 30$

So, $A = 15$, $B = 10$ and $C = 6$.

$A:B:C = 15:10:6$

A's share = $\frac{15}{31} \times 4650 = ₹\ 2250$.

Example 7

The ratio of boys and girls in a class is 8:5. If 10 boys leave the class and 15 new girls joins the class, the ratio of boys and girls will be 3:4. Find the number of boys and girls in the class initially.

Solution

Let the number of boys and girls initially in the class be $8x$ and $5x$ respectively.

$$\frac{8x-10}{5x+15} = \frac{3}{4}$$

$\Rightarrow \qquad 4(8x - 10) = 3(5x + 15)$
$\Rightarrow \qquad 32x - 40 = 15x + 45$
$\Rightarrow \qquad 17x = 85$
$\Rightarrow \qquad x = 5$

$\therefore$ Number of boys initially = $8x = 8 \times 5 = 40$

$\therefore$ Number of girls initially = $5x = 5 \times 5 = 25$.

Example 8

The income of A and B is in the ratio of 3:4, and the ratio of their expenses is 5:6. If B saves 25% of his income, find the ratio of their saving.

Solution

Let the incomes of A and B be $3x$ and $4x$ respectively.

Let the expenses of A and B be $5y$ and $6y$ respectively.

$\therefore$ Saving of $A = 3x - 5y$ ... (1)

$\therefore$ Saving of $B = 4x - 6y$ ... (2)

As B saves 25% of his income, therefore:
$$(4x - 6y) = 25\% \text{ of } 4x$$
$\Rightarrow \qquad (4x - 6y) = \frac{1}{4} \times 4x$

$\Rightarrow \qquad 4x - 6y = x$
$\Rightarrow \qquad 3x = 6y$
$\Rightarrow \qquad x = 2y$

Substituting $x = 2y$ in equation (1) and equation (2)
Saving of $A = 3(2y) - 5y = y$
Saving of $B = 4(2y) - 6y = 2y$
Ratio of saving of A and $B = y : 2y = 1 : 2$.

Example 9

Force of attraction between two bodies is inversely proportional to the square of distance between them. For a distance of 2 m, the force of attraction is 25 N. Find the force of attraction for a distance of 5 m.

Solution

As the force of attraction is inversely proportional to the square of distance:
$$F \propto \frac{1}{D^2}$$
$$F = \frac{K}{D^2}$$

When $\qquad D = 2\ m, F = 25\ N$
$$25 = \frac{K}{2^2}$$

$\Rightarrow \therefore \qquad K = 100$

When $\qquad D = 5\ m$
$$F = \frac{K}{D^2}$$
$$= \frac{100}{5^2} = 4\ N$$

So, when the distance between two bodies is 5 m, the force of attraction will be 4 N.

Example 10

The height of the cone varies directly as its volume when radius is constant and inversely as the square of its radius when volume is constant. Find the ratio of heights of two cones, if the second cone having twice the volume and thrice the radius of the first cone.

Solution

$H \alpha V$ ($\because R$ is constant)

$H \alpha \dfrac{1}{R^2}$ ($\because V$ is constant)

Applying joint variation:

$$H \alpha \dfrac{V}{R^2}$$

$$H = k\dfrac{V}{R^2}$$

Height of first cone $\Rightarrow H_1 = k\dfrac{V}{R^2}$

Height of second cone $\Rightarrow H_2 = k\dfrac{2V}{(3R)^2}$

Ratio of heights $\Rightarrow \dfrac{H_1}{H_2} = \dfrac{k\dfrac{V}{R^2}}{k\dfrac{2V}{(3R)^2}} = \dfrac{V}{R^2} \times \dfrac{9R^2}{2V} = \dfrac{9}{2}$.

EXERCISE

1. If $P:Q = 2:3$ and $Q:R = 5:7$, then $P:Q:R$ is:
   (a) 8:12:21 (b) 10:15:21
   (c) 4:6:14   (d) 6:9:21

2. If $2A = 3B = 5C$, then $A:B:C$ is:
   (a) 2:3:5   (b) 5:3:2
   (c) 15:10:6 (d) 15:10:8

3. If $2A = 3B$ and $2B = 3C$, then $A:C$ is:
   (a) 2:3   (b) 3:2
   (c) 4:9   (d) 9:4

4. If $A:B = 1:2$, $B:C = 2:3$, $D:C = 3:4$, find $A:D$
   (a) 4:9   (b) 1:4
   (c) 1:3   (d) 1:12

5. If A is 75% of B, B is 150% of C and D is 25% of C, then find $A:D$.
   (a) 5:2   (b) 5:3
   (c) 7:2   (d) 9:2

6. If $M:N = 3:2$, then $(M^2 - N^2) : (M^2 + N^2)$ is:
   (a) 5:7   (b) 7:11
   (c) 7:13   (d) 5:13

7. If 27:64 is the triplicate ratio of *a:b*, then *a:b* is:
   (a) 2:3
   (b) 3:2
   (c) 3:4
   (d) 4:3

8. If 2:3 is the sub-duplicate ratio of *a:b*, then the duplicate ratio of *a:b* is:
   (a) 4:9
   (b) 9:4
   (c) 16:81
   (d) 81:16

9. If $(a + 4) : (3a + 15)$ is the triplicate ratio of 2:3. Find a.
   (a) 1
   (b) 2
   (c) 3
   (d) 4

10. If $\frac{x}{2} = \frac{y}{3} = \frac{z}{5}$, then $\frac{x+y+z}{2x+2y}$ is equal to:
    (a) 1
    (b) 1.5
    (c) 2
    (d) 2.5

11. Find $a : b$ from the equation $8a^2 - 18ab + 9b^2 = 0$, if a/b is a proper fraction.
    (a) 1:3
    (b) 2:3
    (c) 3:4
    (d) 2:5

12. Three numbers are in the ratio 3:4:7 and their average is 28. The largest number is:
    (a) 35
    (b) 42
    (c) 49
    (d) 56

13. Three numbers are in the ratio 1:3:5 and their product is 3240. The sum of three numbers is:
    (a) 54
    (b) 63
    (c) 72
    (d) 81

14. What number should be added to the numbers in the ratio 5:6, so that the ratio becomes 8:9, and the sum of terms become 51?
    (a) 7
    (b) 8
    (c) 9
    (d) 31

15. A number 60 is divided into two parts such that 4 times the first part and 5 times the second part are in the ratio of 6:5. Find the first part.
    (a) 30
    (b) 32
    (c) 36
    (d) 40

16. Five times the first number is equal to three times the second number. Find the ratio of five times the sum of the numbers and twice their difference.
    (a) 5:2
    (b) 7:1
    (c) 8:3
    (d) 10:1

17. One-fourth of first number is equal to 40% of second number. Find the ratio of first and second number.
    (a) 6:5
    (b) 8:5
    (c) 5:12
    (d) 9:15

18. Three partner's P, Q and R share profits such that three times the share of P is equal to two times the share of Q which is equal to four times the share of R. Find the ratio of their shares.
    (a) 3:2:4
    (b) 3:6:4
    (c) 4:2:3
    (d) 4:6:3

19. A person divides ₹ 575 among his three kids in the ratio of $\frac{1}{2} : \frac{2}{3} : \frac{3}{4}$. Find the biggest share among the three portions.
    (a) 225
    (b) 200
    (c) 175
    (d) 150

20. The sides of a triangular ground are in the ratio of $\frac{3}{5} : \frac{2}{3} : \frac{4}{5}$. If the perimeter of triangular ground is 248 m, find the length of shortest side.
    (a) 72 m
    (b) 80 m
    (c) 90 m
    (d) 96 m

21. A person divides ₹ 2250 among his three sons A, B and C in such a way that $1/6^{th}$ of A's share, $1/4^{th}$ of B's share and $2/5^{th}$ of C's share are equal. Find A's share.
    (a) ₹ 960
    (b) ₹ 1080
    (c) ₹ 1150
    (d) ₹ 1280

22. The ratio of number of boys to girls in a class is 2:3. If 5 boys leaves the class and 5 girls join the class, the ratio becomes 1:2. Find the number of boys in the class initially.
    (a) 20
    (b) 30
    (c) 18
    (d) 24

23. In a bag, there are notes of ₹ 10, ₹ 20 and ₹ 50 in the ratio of 4:2:1. If the total amount in the bag is ₹ 260, how many ₹ 10 notes are there?
    (a) 4
    (b) 8
    (c) 12
    (d) 16

24. The ratio of three positive numbers is 2:3:5 and sum of their squares is 608. The sum of the numbers is:
    (a) 40
    (b) 50
    (c) 60
    (d) 70

25. The present age of Ram and Shyam is in the ratio of 3:5. After 10 years, the ratio of their ages will be 4:5. How much is the present age of Ram?
    (a) 6 years
    (b) 9 years
    (c) 12 years
    (d) 15 years

26. In a class of 40 students, the ratio of boys and girls 4:1. How many girls should join the class, so that the ratio of boys to girls is 2:3?
    (a) 25
    (b) 30
    (c) 36
    (d) 40

27. A certain amount of money was distributed among A, B and C in the ratio of 1:3:5. If C's share is ₹ 1025, then the total amount is:
    (a) ₹ 1765
    (b) ₹ 1845
    (c) ₹ 1920
    (d) ₹ 2250

28. A certain sum of money is distributed between four partners P, Q, R and S in the ratio of 3:5:6:9. If R received ₹ 1200 more than P, then how much money S have received?
    (a) ₹ 3600
    (b) ₹ 4500
    (c) ₹ 5400
    (d) ₹ 6300

29. A sum of ₹ 111 is distributed between P, Q and R in such a way that P got ₹ 3 more than Q and Q got ₹ 9 more than R. The ratio of their shares is:
    (a) 14 : 13 : 10
    (b) 15 : 12 : 10
    (c) 16 : 11 : 10
    (d) 14 : 12 : 11

30. A sum of ₹ 640 is distributed between A and B in such a way that $3/7^{th}$ of A's share is equal to $1/3^{rd}$ of B's share. How much amount dose B get?
    (a) ₹ 240
    (b) ₹ 300
    (c) ₹ 330
    (d) ₹ 360

31. Two numbers are respectively 25% and 50% more than the third number. The ratio of two numbers is:
    (a) 1:2
    (b) 2:1
    (c) 2:5
    (d) 5:6

32. The ratio of boys and girls in a class is 5:4. If the percentage increase in the number of boys and girls is 20% and 50% respectively, what will be the new ratio?
    (a) 1:1
    (b) 3:4
    (c) 1:2
    (d) 2:3

33. The fourth proportional to 3, 5, 15 is:
    (a) 18
    (b) 20
    (c) 25
    (d) 30

34. The third proportional to 0.4 and 0.6 is:
    (a) 0.2
    (b) 0.5
    (c) 0.8
    (d) 0.9

35. The mean proportional between 27 and 108 is:
    (a) 48
    (b) 54
    (c) 63
    (d) 68

36. The ratio of third proportional to 8 and 20, and the mean proportional between 64 and 9 is:
    (a) 15:8
    (b) 20:9
    (c) 24:15
    (d) 25:12

37. The mean proportional of two numbers P^2 and 9 is Q. The ratio of $\dfrac{P^2+Q^2}{P^2-Q^2}$ is:
    (a) 1:1
    (b) 3:2
    (c) 3:4
    (d) 5:4

38. The income of A and B are in the ratio of 3:2 and their expenditure is in the ratio 5:3. If each saves ₹ 1000 then A's income is:
    (a) 3000
    (b) 4000
    (c) 9000
    (d) 6000

39. The income of A and B are in the ratio of 4:3 and their expenditure is in the ratio of 5:4. Find the ratio of their saving if A spends three-fourth of his income.
    (a) 1:1
    (b) 4:3
    (c) 5:3
    (d) 3:1

40. The speed of three cars is in the ratio 2:3:4. The ratio between the time taken by these cars to travel the same distance is:
    (a) 2:3:4
    (b) 4:3:2
    (c) 6:4:3
    (d) 4:3:6

41. A cat takes 5 leaps for every 4 leaps of a dog, but 3 leaps of dog are equal to 4 leaps of cat. What is the ratio of the speed of cat to that of the speed of dog?
    (a) 11:15
    (b) 15:11
    (c) 15:16
    (d) 16:15

42. The mean proportional between two numbers is 24. The third proportional of the same numbers is 81. Find the greater of the two numbers.
    (a) 30
    (b) 36
    (c) 42
    (d) 48

43. ₹ 3,000 is distributed among P, Q and R such that P gets two-third of what Q and R together get, and R get one-half of what P and Q together get. Find R's share.
    (a) ₹ 750
    (b) ₹ 1000
    (c) ₹ 1200
    (d) ₹ 800

44. A mixture contains milk and water in the ratio 5:1. On adding 5 litres of water the ratio of milk to water becomes 5:2. The quantity of milk in the mixture is:
    (a) 16 litre
    (b) 25 litre
    (c) 22.75 litre
    (d) 32.5 litres

45. A cask contains a mixture of 49 litres of wine and water in the proportion 5:2. How much water must be added to it so that the ratio of wine to water may become 7:4?
    (a) 4
    (b) 5
    (c) 6
    (d) 7

46. A journey of 48 km performed by car, bus and scooter, the distance covered by the three vehicle in that order are in the ratio of 8:1:3 and charges per km in that order are in the ratio of 4:1:2. If the car charges being ₹ 8 per km, the total cost of journey is:
    (a) ₹ 924
    (b) ₹ 1000
    (c) ₹ 1200
    (d) None of these

47. The students in three sections of a class are in the ratio of 2:3:5. If 20 students are increased in each section, the ratio changes to 4:5:7. Find the total number of the students in three sections before the increase.

(a) 80 (b) 100
(c) 120 (d) 150

48. Value of x varies inversely as square of y. When y = 3 at that time x = 2. Find x when y is 6.
   (a) 1 (b) 1/2
   (c) 2/3 (d) 1/4

49. If x varies inversely as square root of y. When y is equal to 9 when x = 4, find x when y = 36.
   (a) 1 (b) 2
   (c) ½ (d) 1½

50. The weight of a cylinder varies directly the square of radius when the height is constant and with the height when the radius is constant. What is the ratio of radius of two cylinders of same weights whose heights are in the ration 9:25?
   (a) 5:3 (b) 25:9
   (c) 3:5 (d) 6:25

51. The cost of laying an underground cable L km long has two parts. One of the parts varies directly as L and other as L^2. If the cost of laying a cable 10 km is ₹ 2450 and 15 km long is ₹ 4725, then how much will be the cost of laying cable 20 km long?
   (a) ₹ 6650 (b) ₹ 6800
   (c) ₹ 7250 (d) ₹ 7700

52. The volume of a gas is inversely proportional to the pressure when temperature is constant and directly proportional to temperature when pressure is constant. When the temperature is 20 units and pressure is 30 units, volume is 260 units. Find the volume when temperature is 45 units and pressure is 65 units.
   (a) 270 units (b) 290 units
   (c) 300 units (d) 325 units

53. Volume of the sphere varies directly as cube of radius. If three metal spheres of radius 3 cm, 4 cm and 5 cm are melted and recast to one bigger sphere, the how much will be the radius of bigger sphere?
   (a) 5.5 cm (b) 6 cm
   (c) 6.5 cm (d) 7 cm

54. A is inversely proportional to 5 more that square root of B. When B = 25, A = 2. How much will be A when B = 100?
   (a) $\frac{1}{4}$ (b) $\frac{3}{2}$
   (c) $\frac{4}{3}$ (d) $\frac{2}{3}$

55. A precious stone worth ₹ 15000 is broken into two pieces whose weights are in the ratio 2:3. If the value of the stone is proportional to the square of its weight. Find the loss incurred because of the breakage.
   (a) ₹ 1800 (b) ₹ 2400
   (c) ₹ 7200 (d) ₹ 7800

KEYS

1. (b)	2. (c)	3. (d)	4. (a)	5. (d)	6. (d)	7. (c)	8. (c)
9. (d)	10. (a)	11. (c)	12. (b)	13. (a)	14. (c)	15. (c)	16. (d)
17. (b)	18. (d)	19. (a)	20. (a)	21. (b)	22. (b)	23. (b)	24. (a)
25. (a)	26. (d)	27. (b)	28. (a)	29. (a)	30. (d)	31. (d)	32. (a)
33. (c)	34. (d)	35. (b)	36. (d)	37. (d)	38. (d)	39. (c)	40. (c)
41. (c)	42. (b)	43. (b)	44. (b)	45. (c)	46. (d)	47. (b)	48. (a)
49. (b)	50. (a)	51. (d)	52. (a)	53. (b)	54. (c)	55. (c)	

SOLUTIONS

Solution 1

As $P:Q = 2:3$ and $Q:R$ is $5:7$, so finding the common ratio as follows:

$$\begin{array}{ccc} P & Q & R \\ 2 & 3 & \\ & 5 & 7 \\ \hline 10 & 15 & 21 \end{array}$$

By multiplying the ratio of $P:Q$ by 5 and the ratio of $Q:R$ by 3, the ratio of $P:Q:R$ is obtained as $10:15:21$.

Choice (b)

Solution 2

$$2A = 3B = 5C = K$$

Let us select (or assume) the value of K as a number which is divisible by 2, 3 and 5; say 30.

$$2A = 3B = 5C = 30$$

∴ $A = 15, B = 10$ and $C = 6$.

So, $A:B:C = 15:10:6$.

Choice (c)

Solution 3

If $2A = 3B$, then the ratio of A and B is:

$$\frac{A}{B} = \frac{3}{2}$$

If $2B = 3C$, then the ratio of B and C is:

$$\frac{B}{C} = \frac{3}{2}$$

$$\therefore \quad \frac{A}{C} = \frac{A}{B} \times \frac{B}{C} = \frac{3}{2} \times \frac{3}{2} = \frac{9}{4}.$$

Choice (d)

Solution 4

$$\frac{A}{B} = \frac{1}{2}, \frac{B}{C} = \frac{2}{3}, \frac{D}{C} = \frac{3}{4}$$

$$\therefore \frac{A}{D} = \frac{A}{B} \times \frac{B}{C} \times \frac{C}{D} = \frac{1}{2} \times \frac{2}{3} \times \frac{4}{3} = \frac{4}{9}.$$

Choice (a)

Solution 5

A is 75% of B means $A = \frac{3}{4} B$ or $\frac{A}{B} = \frac{3}{4}$

B is 150% of C means $B = \frac{3}{2} C$ or $\frac{B}{C} = \frac{3}{2}$

D is 25% of C means $D = \frac{1}{4} C$ or $\frac{C}{D} = \frac{4}{1}$

$$\therefore \quad \frac{A}{D} = \frac{A}{B} \times \frac{B}{C} \times \frac{C}{D}$$

$$= \frac{3}{4} \times \frac{3}{2} \times \frac{4}{1} = \frac{9}{2}.$$

Choice (d)

Solution 6

$$\frac{M}{N} = \frac{3x}{2x}$$

$$\frac{M^2 - N^2}{M^2 + N^2} = \frac{(3x)^2 - (2x)^2}{(3x)^2 + (2x)^2} = \frac{9x^2 - 4x^2}{9x^2 + 4x^2} = \frac{5x^2}{13x^2} = \frac{5}{13}.$$

Choice (d)

Solution 7

As 27:64 is the triplicate ratio of $a:b$

$$\therefore \quad \frac{a^3}{b^3} = \frac{27}{64}$$

$$\Rightarrow \quad \frac{a}{b} = \frac{3}{4}.$$

Choice (c)

Ratio-Proportion-Variation

Solution 8

As 2:3 is the sub-duplicate ratio of $a:b$

$$\therefore \quad \frac{\sqrt{a}}{\sqrt{b}} = \frac{2}{3}$$

$$\Rightarrow \quad \frac{a}{b} = \frac{4}{9}$$

Duplicate ratio of $a:b = \frac{4^2}{9^2} = \frac{16}{81}$.

Choice (c)

Solution 9

As $(a + 4) : (3a + 15)$ is the triplicate ratio of 2:3

$$\frac{a+4}{3a+15} = \frac{2^3}{3^3}$$

$$\Rightarrow \quad \frac{a+4}{3a+15} = \frac{8}{27}$$

$$\Rightarrow \quad 27(a + 4) = 8(3a + 15)$$
$$\Rightarrow \quad 27a + 108 = 24a + 120$$
$$\Rightarrow \quad 3a = 12$$
$$\therefore \quad a = 4.$$

Choice (d)

Solution 10

$$\frac{x}{2} = \frac{y}{3} = \frac{z}{5} = k$$

$$\therefore \quad x = 2k, y = 3k, \text{ and } z = 5k$$

$$\frac{x+y+z}{2x+2y} = \frac{2k+3k+5k}{2(2k)+2(3k)}$$

$$= \frac{10k}{4k+6k}$$

$$= 1.$$

Choice (a)

Solution 11

$$8a^2 - 18ab + 9b^2 = 0$$
$$\Rightarrow \quad 8a^2 - 12ab - 6ab + 9b^2 = 0$$
$$\Rightarrow \quad 4a(2a - 3b) - 3b(2a - 3b) = 0$$
$$\Rightarrow \quad (4a - 3b)(2a - 3b) = 0$$

$$4a - 3b = 0$$
$$\Rightarrow \quad 4a = 3b$$
$$\therefore \quad \frac{a}{b} = \frac{3}{4}$$
$$2a - 3b = 0$$
$$\Rightarrow \quad 2a = 3b$$
$$\therefore \quad \frac{a}{b} = \frac{3}{2}$$

As $a:b$ is a proper fraction, so it will be 3:4.

Choice (c)

Solution 12

Let the three numbers be $3x$, $4x$ and $7x$.
$$\frac{3x + 4x + 7x}{3} = 28$$
$$\Rightarrow \quad \frac{14x}{3} = 28$$
$$\therefore \quad x = \frac{28 \times 3}{14} = 6$$

So, the largest number i.e., $7x = 7 \times 6 = 42$.

Choice (b)

Solution 13

Let the three numbers be x, $3x$ and $5x$.
$$x \times 3x \times 5x = 3240$$
$$\Rightarrow \quad 15x^3 = 3240$$
$$\Rightarrow \quad x^3 = \frac{3240}{15}$$
$$\Rightarrow \quad x^3 = 216$$
$$\therefore \quad x = 6$$

So, the sum of three numbers $= x + 3x + 5x = 9x = 9 \times 6 = 54$.

Choice (a)

Solution 14

Let the numbers after addition be $8x$ and $9x$ respectively.
$$8x + 9x = 51$$
$$\Rightarrow \quad 17x = 51$$
$$\Rightarrow \quad x = 3$$

So, the resulting numbers after addition are 24 and 27.

If a number k is added to the numbers in the ratio 5:6, the resulting numbers are in the ratio of 8:9. In a similar way if the same number k is subtracted from the numbers in the ratio 8:9, we get the resulting numbers in the ratio 5:6.

$$\frac{24-k}{27-k} = \frac{5}{6}$$

$\Rightarrow \qquad 6(24-k) = 5(27-k)$
$\Rightarrow \qquad 144 - 6k = 135 - 5k$
$\Rightarrow \qquad k = 9.$

Choice (c)

Solution 15

Let the first part be F and second part be S.

$$F + S = 60 \qquad \ldots (1)$$

$$\frac{4F}{5S} = \frac{6}{5}$$

$\therefore \qquad \dfrac{F}{S} = \dfrac{6}{5} \times \dfrac{5}{4} = \dfrac{3}{2}$

Substituting F and S as $3x$ and $2x$ respectively in equation (1)

$$3x + 2x = 60$$
$$5x = 60$$
$\therefore \qquad x = 12$

So, the first part = $3x = 3 \times 12 = 36$.

Choice (c)

Solution 16

Let the first part be F and second part be S.

$$5F = 3S$$

$\therefore \qquad \dfrac{F}{S} = \dfrac{3x}{5x}$

Required ratio = $\dfrac{5(5x+3x)}{2(5x-3x)} = \dfrac{40x}{4x} = \dfrac{10}{1}$.

Choice (d)

Solution 17

Let the first part be F and second part be S.

As one-fourth of first number is equal to 40% of second number:

$$\frac{1}{4}F = \frac{40}{100}S$$

$$\frac{F}{S} = \frac{40}{100} \times 4$$

$$= \frac{8}{5}.$$

Choice (b)

Solution 18

$$3P = 2Q = 4R = K$$

Let us select (or assume) the value of K as a number which is divisible by 2, 3 and 4; say 12.

$$3P = 2Q = 4R = 12$$

∴ $$P = 4, Q = 6 \text{ and } R = 3$$

So, $P:Q:R = 4:6:3$.

Choice (d)

Solution 19

The ratio in which money is divided $= \frac{1}{2} : \frac{2}{3} : \frac{3}{4}$

Multiplying each term of ratio with LCM of 2, 3 and 4 *i.e.*, 12

The ratio in which money is divided $= \frac{1}{2} \times 12 : \frac{2}{3} \times 12 : \frac{3}{4} \times 12$

$$= 6 : 8 : 9$$

Biggest share $= \frac{9}{23} \times 575$

$$= ₹ 225.$$

Choice (a)

Solution 20

The ratio of sides $= \frac{3}{5} : \frac{2}{3} : \frac{4}{5}$

Multiplying each term of ratio with LCM of 3 and 5 *i.e.*, 15

The ratio of sides $= \frac{3}{5} \times 15 : \frac{2}{3} \times 15 : \frac{4}{5} \times 15$

$$= 9 : 10 : 12$$

Shortest side $= \frac{9}{31} \times 248$

$$= 72 \text{ m}.$$

Choice (a)

Solution 21

$$\frac{1}{6}A = \frac{1}{4}B = \frac{2}{5}C = K$$

∴ $A = 6K, B = 4K, C = 2.5K$

A's share $= \frac{6K}{12.5K} \times 2250 = ₹\, 1080.$

Choice (b)

Solution 22

Let the initial number of boys and girls in the class be $2x$ and $3x$ respectively.

$$\frac{2x-5}{3x+5} = \frac{1}{2}$$

⇒ $2(2x - 5) = 3x + 5$
⇒ $4x - 10 = 3x + 5$
∴ $x = 15$

So, the number of boys initially $= 2x = 2 \times 15 = 30$.

Choice (b)

Solution 23

Let the number of notes of ₹ 10, ₹ 20 and ₹ 50 be $4x$, $2x$ and x respectively. As total amount in the bag is ₹ 260, therefore:

$10(4x) + 20(2x) + 50(x) = 260$
⇒ $40x + 40x + 50x = 260$
⇒ $130x = 260$
∴ $x = 2$

So, number of notes of ₹ 10 $= 4x = 4 \times 2 = 8$.

Choice (b)

Solution 24

Let the three numbers be $2x$, $3x$ and $5x$.

$(2x)^2 + (3x)^2 + (5x)^2 = 608$
⇒ $4x^2 + 9x^2 + 25x^2 = 608$
⇒ $38x^2 = 608$
⇒ $x^2 = 16$
∴ $x = 4$

So, sum of the numbers $= 2x + 3x + 5x = 10x = 10 \times 4 = 40$.

Choice (a)

Solution 25

Let the present age of Ram and Shyam be $3x$ and $5x$ respectively. After 10 years, the ratio of their ages will be 4:5.

$$\therefore \quad \frac{3x+10}{5x+10} = \frac{4}{5}$$

$$\Rightarrow \quad 5(3x+10) = 4(5x+10)$$
$$\Rightarrow \quad 15x + 50 = 20x + 40$$
$$\Rightarrow \quad 5x = 10$$
$$\Rightarrow \quad x = 2$$

So, present age of Ram $= 3x$
$= 3 \times 2$
$= 6$ years.

Choice (a)

Solution 26

Let the number of boys and girls be $4x$ and x respectively. As the strength of class is 40, therefore:

$$4x + x = 40$$
$$\Rightarrow \quad 5x = 40$$
$$\Rightarrow \quad x = 8$$

Number of boys = 32

Number of girls = 8

Let the number of girls should join the class be n to make the ratio of boys to girls as 2:3.

$$\frac{32}{8+n} = \frac{2}{3}$$
$$\Rightarrow \quad 96 = 16 + 2n$$
$$\therefore \quad n = 40.$$

Choice (d)

Solution 27

Let the amount of money among A, B and C be x, $3x$ and $5x$ respectively.

As C's share $= ₹ 1025$
$\therefore \quad 5x = 1025$
$x = 205$

So, total amount $= x + 3x + 5x$
$= 9x = 9 \times 205$
$= ₹ 1845.$

Choice (b)

Solution 28

Let the amount of money distributed between P, Q, R and S be $3x$, $5x$, $6x$, and $9x$ respectively.

As R received ₹ 1200 more than P, therefore:
$$6x - 3x = 1200$$
$$\Rightarrow 3x = 1200$$
$$\Rightarrow x = 400$$

Amount of money received by $S = 9x$
$$= 9 \times 400$$
$$= ₹ 3600.$$

Choice (a)

Solution 29

Let the amount of money received by $R = x$
∴ Amount of money received by $Q = x + 9$
∴ Amount of money received by $P = (x + 9) + 3$
$$= x + 12$$

$$x + (x + 9) + (x + 12) = 111$$
$$\Rightarrow 3x + 21 = 111$$
$$\Rightarrow 3x = 90$$
$$\Rightarrow x = 30$$

P's share $= x + 12 = ₹ 42$
Q's share $= x + 9 = ₹ 39$
R's share $= x = ₹ 30$

So, $P:Q:R = 42:39:30 = 14:13:10$.

Choice (a)

Solution 30

$$\frac{3}{7}A = \frac{1}{3}B$$
$$\Rightarrow \therefore \quad \frac{A}{B} = \frac{7}{9}$$
$$A + B = 640$$
$$\Rightarrow 7x + 9x = 640$$
$$\Rightarrow 16x = 640$$
$$\Rightarrow x = 40$$

B's share $= 9x = 9 \times 40 = ₹ 360$.

Choice (d)

Solution 31

Let the first, second and third number be F, S and T respectively and assuming $T = 1$.

∴ $\quad F = 1.25$ and $S = 1.5$

So, the ratio of first and second number $= \dfrac{1.25}{1.5} = \dfrac{5}{6}$.

Choice (d)

Solution 32

Let the number of boys and girls in the class initially be $5x$ and $4x$ respectively.

Number of boys after 20% increase $= \dfrac{120}{100} \times 5x = 6x$

Number of girls after 50% increase $= \dfrac{150}{100} \times 4x = 6x$

New ratio of boys and girls $= 6x : 6x = 1:1$.

Choice (a)

Solution 33

The fourth proportional of 3, 5 and 15 can be found as:

$$\dfrac{3}{5} = \dfrac{15}{x}$$

∴ $\quad x = \dfrac{15 \times 5}{3} = 25.$

Choice (c)

Solution 34

The third proportional of 0.4 and 0.6 can be found as:

$$\dfrac{0.4}{0.6} = \dfrac{0.6}{x}$$

∴ $\quad x = \dfrac{0.6 \times 0.6}{0.4} = 0.9.$

Choice (d)

Solution 35

Mean proportional $= \sqrt{27 \times 108}$
$= \sqrt{3^6 \times 2^2}$
$= 54.$

Choice (b)

Solution 36

The third proportional to 8 and 20 can be found as:

$$\frac{8}{20} = \frac{20}{x}$$

$\therefore \quad x = \frac{20 \times 20}{8} = 50$

Mean proportional between 64 and 9 = $\sqrt{64 \times 9} = 24$

$\therefore$ Required ratio = $\frac{50}{24} = \frac{25}{12}$.

Choice (d)

Solution 37

As the mean proportional of P^2 and 9 is Q, therefore:

$$\sqrt{P^2 \times 9} = Q$$
$$P^2 \times 9 = Q^2$$
$$\frac{P^2}{Q^2} = \frac{9}{1}$$
$$\frac{P}{Q} = \frac{3}{1} \text{ or } P = 3x \text{ and } Q = x$$

$$\frac{P^2 + Q^2}{P^2 - Q^2} = \frac{(3x)^2 + x^2}{(3x)^2 - x^2} = \frac{9x^2 + x^2}{9x^2 - x^2} = \frac{10x^2}{8x^2} = \frac{5}{4}.$$

Choice (d)

Solution 38

Let the incomes of A and B be $3x$ and $2x$ respectively.
Let the expenses of A and B be $5y$ and $3y$ respectively.

$\therefore$ Saving of $A \Rightarrow 3x - 5y = 1000$ ... (1)

$\therefore$ Saving of $B \Rightarrow 2x - 3y = 1000$ ... (2)

As their savings are same, therefore:

$$3x - 5y = 2x - 3y$$
$$\Rightarrow \quad x = 2y$$

Substituting x as $2y$ in equation (1)

$$3(2y) - 5y = 1000$$
$\therefore \quad y = 1000 \text{ and } x = 2000$

So, A's income = $3x = 3 \times 2000 = ₹\,6000$.

Choice (d)

Solution 39

Let the incomes of A and B be $4x$ and $3x$ respectively.

Let the expenses of A and B be $5y$ and $4y$ respectively.

As A spends $3/4^{th}$ of his income,

$$5y = \frac{3}{4}(4x)$$

$\therefore \quad \frac{x}{y} = \frac{5}{3}$ or $x = 5k$ and $y = 3k$

∴ Saving of A = $4x - 5y = 4(5k) - 5(3k) = 5k$

∴ Saving of B = $3x - 4y = 3(5k) - 4(3k) = 3k$

Ratio of savings of A and B = $\frac{5k}{3k} = \frac{5}{3}$.

Choice (c)

Solution 40

Speed of three cars is in the ratio 2:3:4

As time and speed are inversely proportional, so the ratio of time taken by these three cars to travel same distance can be found as:

Required ratio = $\frac{1}{2} : \frac{1}{3} : \frac{1}{4}$

$= \left(\frac{1}{2} : \frac{1}{3} : \frac{1}{4}\right) \times 12$

$= 6 : 4 : 3$.

Choice (c)

Solution 41

As 3 leaps of dog are equal to 4 leaps of cat:

$$3D = 4C$$
$$\frac{C}{D} = \frac{3}{4}$$

So, the length of each leap taken by a cat and dog is in the ratio of 3:4.

Also cat takes 5 leaps for every 4 leaps of a dog:

∴ Speed of cat = $5 \times 3 = 15$

∴ Speed of dog = $4 \times 4 = 16$

Required ratio = $\frac{15}{16}$.

Choice (c)

Solution 42

Let the two numbers be x and y.

As the mean proportional of two numbers is 24:

$$\sqrt{xy} = 24$$

$\Rightarrow \qquad xy = 576$

As the third proportional of two numbers is 81:

$$\frac{x}{y} = \frac{y}{81}$$

$\Rightarrow \qquad \frac{y^2}{x} = 81$

$\Rightarrow \qquad \frac{y^2}{\frac{576}{y}} = 81$

$\Rightarrow \qquad y^3 = 46656$
$\Rightarrow \qquad y = 36$ and $x = 16$

So greater of the two numbers will be 36.

Choice (b)

Solution 43

As per the given conditions in the problem, the equations will be as follows:

$$P = \frac{2}{3}(Q+R)$$

$\Rightarrow \qquad 3P = 2Q + 2R \qquad \ldots (1)$

$$R = \frac{1}{2}(P+Q)$$

$\Rightarrow \qquad 2R = P + Q \qquad \ldots (2)$

Substituting $2R = P + Q$ in equation (1)

$3P = 2Q + 2R$
$\Rightarrow \qquad 3P = 2Q + P + Q$
$\Rightarrow \qquad 2P = 3Q$
$\Rightarrow \qquad \frac{P}{Q} = \frac{3}{2}$ or $\frac{P}{Q} = \frac{3x}{2x}$

Substituting P and Q as $3x$ and $2x$ respectively in equation (2)

$2R = P + Q$
$\Rightarrow \qquad 2R = 3x + 2x$
$\Rightarrow \qquad R = 2.5x$

P's share + Q's share + R's share = ₹ 3000
$$\Rightarrow 3x + 2x + 2.5x = 3000$$
$$\Rightarrow 7.5x = 3000$$
$$\Rightarrow x = 400$$
$$\therefore R\text{'s share} = \frac{2.5}{7.5} \times 3000 = ₹ 1000.$$

Choice (b)

Solution 44

Let the quantity of milk and water in the mixture initially be $5x$ and x litres respectively.
$$\frac{5x}{x+5} = \frac{5}{2}$$
$$\Rightarrow 10x = 5x + 25$$
$$\Rightarrow 5x = 25$$
$$\Rightarrow x = 5$$

So, the quantity of milk in the mixture = $5x = 5 \times 5 = 25$ litres.

Choice (b)

Solution 45

Let the quantity of wine and water in the cask initially be $5x$ and $2x$ litres respectively.
$$5x + 2x = 49$$
$$\Rightarrow 7x = 49$$
$$\Rightarrow x = 7$$
$\therefore$ Quantity of wine = $5x$ = 35 litres
$\therefore$ Quantity of water = $2x$ = 14 litres

Let W litres of water is added to make the ratio of wine to water as 7:4.
$$\frac{35}{14+W} = \frac{7}{4}$$
$$\Rightarrow 98 + 7W = 140$$
$$\Rightarrow 7W = 42$$
$$\Rightarrow W = 6 \text{ litres.}$$

Choice (c)

Solution 46

Let the distance traveled by car, bus and scooter be $8x$, x and $3x$ respectively.
$$8x + x + 3x = 48 \text{ km}$$
$$\Rightarrow 12x = 48$$
$$\Rightarrow x = 4$$

Distance traveled by car = $8x = 32$ km
Distance traveled by bus = $x = 4$ km
Distance traveled by scooter = $3x = 12$ km

Let the per km charges of car, bus and scooter be $4y$, y and $2y$ respectively.

As the car charges ₹ 8 per km,

$\therefore \quad\quad\quad\quad\quad\quad\quad 4y = 8$
$\Rightarrow \quad\quad\quad\quad\quad\quad\quad y = 2$

Charges of bus = y = ₹ 2 per km
Charges of scooter = $2y$ = ₹ 4 per km

Total cost of journey $\quad\quad = 32(8) + 4(2) + 12(4)$
$\quad\quad\quad\quad\quad\quad\quad\quad\quad = 256 + 8 + 48 =$ ₹ 312.

Choice (d)

Solution 47

Let the students in the three sections initially be $2x$, $3x$ and $5x$ respectively. After 20 students are added to each section the number of students in three sections will be $4x$, $5x$ and $7x$ respectively.

$\quad\quad (2x + 20) + (3x + 20) + (5x + 20) = 4x + 5x + 7x$
$\Rightarrow \quad\quad\quad\quad\quad\quad 10x + 60 = 16x$
$\Rightarrow \quad\quad\quad\quad\quad\quad 6x = 60$
$\therefore \quad\quad\quad\quad\quad\quad\quad x = 10$

Total number of students in three sections before increase
$\quad\quad\quad\quad\quad\quad = 2x + 3x + 5x = 10x = 100.$

Choice (b)

Solution 48

$$x \propto \frac{1}{y^2}$$

$$x = \frac{k}{y^2}$$

When $\quad\quad\quad\quad y = 3, x = 2$ (given)

$$2 = \frac{k}{3^2}$$

$\Rightarrow \therefore \quad\quad\quad\quad k = 36$
When $\quad\quad\quad\quad y = 6$

$$x = \frac{36}{6^2} = 1.$$

Choice (a)

Solution 49

$$x \propto \frac{1}{\sqrt{y}}$$

$$x = \frac{k}{\sqrt{y}}$$

When $\quad y = 9, x = 4$ (given)

$$4 = \frac{k}{\sqrt{9}}$$

$\Rightarrow \therefore \quad k = 12$

When $\quad y = 36$

$$x = \frac{12}{\sqrt{36}} = 2.$$

Choice (b)

Solution 50

$W \propto r^2$ (When h is constant)
$W \propto h$ (When r is constant)

Applying joint variation:

$$W \propto hr^2$$
$$W = k\, hr^2$$

As the heights of two cylinders are in the ratio of 9:25 and their weights are same:

$$W_1 = k \times 9 \times r_1^2$$
$$W_2 = k \times 25 \times r_2^2$$
$$W_1 = W_2$$
$$k \times 9 \times r_1^2 = k \times 25 \times r_2^2$$
$$\frac{r_1^2}{r_2^2} = \frac{25}{9}$$
$$\frac{r_1}{r_2} = \frac{5}{3}.$$

Choice (a)

Solution 51

Cost = Part-1 + Part-2
Part-1 $\propto L$ $\quad\Rightarrow$ Part-1 $= k_1 L$
Part-2 $\propto L^2$ $\quad\Rightarrow$ Part-2 $= k_2 L^2$

$\therefore \quad C = k_1 L + k_2 L^2$

As the cost of laying a cable 10 km is ₹ 2450 and 15 km long is ₹ 4725:
$$k_1 L + k_2 L^2 = 2450$$
$$10k_1 + 100k_2 = 2450$$
$$k_1 + 10k_2 = 245 \quad \ldots (1)$$
$$k_1 L + k_2 L^2 = 4725$$
$$15k_1 + 225k_2 = 4725$$
$$k_1 + 15k_2 = 315 \quad \ldots (2)$$

Subtracting equation (1) from equation (2)
$$(k_1 + 15k_2) - (k_1 + 10k_2) = 315 - 245$$
$$5k_2 = 70$$
∴ $\quad k_2 = 14$
and $\quad k_1 = 105$

Cost of laying the cable 20 km long
$$= 20k_1 + 400k_2 = 20(105) + 400(14)$$
$$= 2100 + 5600 = ₹ 7700.$$

Choice (d)

Solution 52

$$V \alpha\ T$$
$$V \alpha\ \frac{1}{P}$$

Applying joint variation:
$$V \alpha\ \frac{T}{P}$$
$$V = k\ \frac{T}{P}$$

When $V = 260$, $T = 20$ and $P = 30$ units
$$260 = k\ \frac{20}{30}$$
$$\Rightarrow \quad k = \frac{260 \times 30}{20} = 390$$

When $T = 45$ and $P = 65$ units
$$V = k\ \frac{T}{P} = 390 \times \frac{45}{65} = 270 \text{ units.}$$

Choice (a)

Solution 53

$$V \alpha\ r^3$$
$$V = kr^3$$
$$V_1 = k\ (3)^3 = 27k$$
$$V_2 = k\ (4)^3 = 64k$$
$$V_3 = k\ (5)^3 = 125k$$

Volume of the bigger sphere formed by melting small three spheres will be:
$$V = V_1 + V_2 + V_3$$
$$\Rightarrow V = 27k + 64k + 125k$$
$$\Rightarrow V = 216k$$
$$\Rightarrow kR^3 = 216k$$
$$\Rightarrow R^3 = 216$$
$$\Rightarrow R = 6 \text{ cm.}$$

Choice (b)

Solution 54

$$A \alpha \frac{1}{\sqrt{B}+5}$$
$$A = \frac{K}{\sqrt{B}+5}$$

When $B = 25, A = 2$
$$2 = \frac{K}{\sqrt{25}+5}$$
$\Rightarrow \therefore \quad k = 20$

When $B = 100$
$$A = \frac{20}{\sqrt{100}+5} = \frac{20}{15} = \frac{4}{3}.$$

Choice (c)

Solution 55

Let the weight of two broken pieces be $2x$ and $3x$. So the weight of original unbroken stone must be $5x$.
$$V \alpha W^2$$
$$V = kW^2$$

Value of original stone:
$$V = k(5x)^2$$
$$15000 = 25kx^2$$
$$\therefore \quad kx^2 = 600$$

Value of first piece of stone:
$$V_1 = k(2x)^2 = 4kx^2 = 4 \times 600 = ₹ 2400$$

Value of second piece of stone:
$$V_2 = k(3x)^2 = 9kx^2 = 9 \times 600 = ₹ 5400$$

Loss incurred due to breakage = Value of original stone − Sum of value of broken pieces
$$= 15000 - (2400 + 5400) = ₹ 7200.$$

Choice (c)

7
Percentage

INTRODUCTION

The word 'percent' implies 'out of 100'. Thus 'p' percent means p out of 100 and is written as $p\%$. This concept is developed to make comparison of fractions easier by equalizing the denominators of all fractions to hundred.

For example if two students A and B appeared for two different exams. Student A scored 30 marks out of 40 in his exam, while student B scored 38 marks out of 50 in other exam. Now we need to decide, who scored better?

Score of $A \Rightarrow \dfrac{30}{40} = \dfrac{30 \times 100}{40 \times 100} = \dfrac{(30 \times 100)/40}{100} = \dfrac{75}{100}$

Score of $B \Rightarrow \dfrac{38}{50} = \dfrac{38 \times 100}{50 \times 100} = \dfrac{(38 \times 100)/50}{100} = \dfrac{76}{100}$

Looking at the above calculations it is clear that B is better than A because A scored 75 out of 100 or 75%, while B scored 76 out of 100 or 76%. So with the aid of this concept of percentage we are able to bring them on a common platform (*i.e.,* out of 100) and decide who is better.

PERCENTAGE INCREASE OR DECREASE

Percentage increase can be found as:

$$\text{Percentage increase} = \dfrac{\text{Actual Increase}}{\text{Initial Value}} \times 100$$

$$= \dfrac{\text{Final Value} - \text{Initial Value}}{\text{Initial Value}} \times 100$$

Percentage decrease can be found as:

$$\text{Percentage decrease} = \dfrac{\text{Actual decrease}}{\text{Initial Value}} \times 100$$

$$= \dfrac{\text{Initial Value} - \text{Final Value}}{\text{Initial Value}} \times 100$$

The generalized formula for percentage change can be found as:

$$\text{Percentage change} = \dfrac{\text{Difference between Final and Initial Value}}{\text{Initial Value}} \times 100$$

STANDARD EXPRESSIONS ON PERCENTAGE

Price of a Item and its Consumption

If the price of an item increases by $R\%$, then the reduction in consumption to maintain a constant expenditure is given as:

$$\text{Reduction in consumption} = \left(\frac{R}{100+R} \times 100\right)\%$$

If the price of an item decreases by $R\%$, then increase in consumption to maintain a constant expenditure is given as:

$$\text{Increase in consumption} = \left(\frac{R}{100-R} \times 100\right)\%$$

Rise or Fall of Population over Years

If the present population of a town is P, and if it increases at the rate of $R\%$ per year, then:

$$\text{Population after } n \text{ years} = P\left(1+\frac{R}{100}\right)^n$$

$$\text{Population } n \text{ years ago} = \frac{P}{\left(1+\frac{R}{100}\right)^n}$$

Depreciation over a Period of Time

If the present cost of the machine (or vehicle) is P, and if it depreciates (reduces) at the rate of $R\%$ per year, then:

$$\text{Value after } n \text{ years} = P\left(1-\frac{R}{100}\right)^n$$

$$\text{Value } n \text{ years ago} = \frac{P}{\left(1-\frac{R}{100}\right)^n}$$

Comparison between Two

If A is $R\%$ more than B then:

$$B \text{ is less than } A \text{ by } \left(\frac{R}{100+R} \times 100\right)\%$$

If A is $R\%$ less than B then:

$$B \text{ is more than } A \text{ by } \left(\frac{R}{100-R} \times 100\right)\%$$

IMPORTANT SHORTCUTS ON PERCENTAGE

$\dfrac{1}{1} = 100\%$ $\dfrac{1}{2} = 50\%$ $\dfrac{1}{3} = 33.33\%$

$\dfrac{1}{4} = 25\%$ $\dfrac{1}{5} = 20\%$ $\dfrac{1}{6} = 16.66\%$

$\dfrac{1}{7} = 14.28\%$ $\dfrac{1}{8} = 12.5\%$ $\dfrac{1}{9} = 11.11\%$

$\dfrac{1}{10} = 10\%$ $\dfrac{1}{11} = 9.09\%$ $\dfrac{1}{12} = 8.33\%$

SOLVED EXAMPLES

Example 1

If $X = 20$ and $Y = 25$, then:

1. What percent of Y is X?
2. What percent of X is Y?
3. By what percent X is less than Y?
4. By what percent Y is greater than X?

Solution

1. In this case comparison is done with Y (word used in question is "of Y"). Hence value of Y will stay in the denominator.

   Required percentage = $\dfrac{20}{25} \times 100 = 80\%$

2. In this case comparison is done with X (word used in question is "of X"). Hence value of X will stay in the denominator.

   Required percentage = $\dfrac{25}{20} \times 100 = 125\%$

3. In this case comparison is done with Y; therefore value of Y will be in the denominator. As X is less than Y by an amount of 5, so it will be the numerator.

   Required percentage = $\dfrac{5}{25} \times 100 = 20\%$

4. In this case comparison is done with X; therefore value of X will be in the denominator. As Y is greater than X by an amount of 5, so it will be the numerator.

   Required percentage = $\dfrac{5}{20} \times 100 = 25\%$.

Example 2

Find:

1. 42 is what percentage of 168?
2. 36 is what percent of 80?
3. What percent of 175 is 91?
4. What percent of 40 is 60?

Solution

1. Required percentage = $\dfrac{42}{168} \times 100 = 25\%$

2. Required percentage = $\dfrac{36}{80} \times 100 = 45\%$

3. Required percentage = $\dfrac{91}{175} \times 100 = 52\%$

4. Required percentage = $\dfrac{60}{40} \times 100 = 150\%$.

Example 3

Find:

1. 140 m is what percent of 7 km?
2. 2 quintals is what percent of 5 metric tones?
3. 300 ml is what percent of 5 litres?

Solution

1. 1 km = 1000 m
   Required percentage = $\dfrac{140}{7000} \times 100 = 2\%$

2. 1 metric ton = 10 quintals
   Required percentage = $\dfrac{2}{50} \times 100 = 4\%$

3. 1 litre = 1000 ml
   Required percentage = $\dfrac{300}{5000} \times 100 = 6\%$.

Example 4

Evaluate:

1. 25% of 96 + 75% of 48
2. 28% of 450 + 45% of 280.

Solution

1. Sum $= \left(\dfrac{25}{100} \times 96 + \dfrac{75}{100} \times 48\right) = \left(\dfrac{1}{4} \times 96 + \dfrac{3}{4} \times 48\right) = 60$

2. Sum $= \left(\dfrac{28}{100} \times 450 + \dfrac{45}{100} \times 480\right) = \left(\dfrac{7}{25} \times 450 + \dfrac{9}{20} \times 480\right) = 342.$

Example 5

If the price of an article is increased by 20% and then reduced by 30%. If the final price of article is ₹ 420, then:

1. Find the initial price of article
2. Percentage change in price.

Solution

Let us begin the problem with the base of 100. Assuming the initial price of article as ₹ 100.

Initial price = ₹ 100

Increased by 20% = $100 \times \dfrac{6}{5}$ = ₹ 120

Reduced by 30% = $120 \times \dfrac{7}{10}$ = ₹ 84.

1. Initial price of article

    If initial price is ₹ 100, then final price is ₹ 84.

    If final price is ₹ 420, the initial price = $\dfrac{420 \times 100}{84}$

    = ₹ 500

2. Percentage change in price

    Initial price = ₹ 500

    Final price = ₹ 420

    Percentage change = $\dfrac{500 - 420}{420} \times 100$

    $= 19\dfrac{1}{21}\%.$

Example 6

To maintain constant expenditure on fuel, by what percent the consumption of petrol should be increased/reduced if:

1. Price of petrol increases by 10%
2. Price is petrol reduces by 10%

Solution

1. If price increases by 10%

   Reduction in consumption $= \dfrac{R}{100+R} \times 100 = \dfrac{10}{100+10} \times 100$

   $= \dfrac{1}{11} \times 100 = 9\dfrac{1}{11}\%$

2. If price reduces by 10%

   Increase in consumption $= \dfrac{R}{100-R} \times 100 = \dfrac{10}{100-10} \times 100$

   $= \dfrac{1}{9} \times 100 = 11\dfrac{1}{9}\%$.

Example 7

In an election between two candidates, 80% of the voters cast their votes, out of which 10% of the votes were invalid. The winning candidate got 65% of the valid votes and wins by a margin of 1512 votes. Find:

1. Total number of voters enrolled in that election
2. Number of valid votes
3. Number of invalid votes.

Solution

Let us begin the problem with the base of 1000. Assuming the total number of voters enrolled in the election as 1000.

Total votes polled $= 1000 \times \dfrac{80}{100} = 800$

Total valid votes $= 800 \times \dfrac{90}{100} = 720$

Votes in favor of winning candidate $= 720 \times \dfrac{65}{100} = 468$

Votes in favor of loosing candidate $= 720 \times \dfrac{35}{100} = 252$

Margin by which the candidate wins $= 468 - 252 = 216$

1. Total votes enrolled

   If 1000 voters are enrolled the winning candidate wins by a margin of 216 votes. In actual if the winning candidate wins by a margin of 1512, then:

   Total voters enrolled $= \dfrac{1512 \times 1000}{216} = 7000$

2. Number of valid votes

   Valid votes $= 7000 \times \dfrac{80}{100} \times \dfrac{90}{100} = 5040$

3. Number of invalid votes

   Invalid votes = $7000 \times \dfrac{80}{100} \times \dfrac{10}{100} = 560$.

Example 8

A machine was purchased 2 years ago whose value deprecates at the rate of 20% per annum. If the present value of machine is ₹ 94000, then:

1. What must be its value 2 years ago
2. What will be its value after 3 years.

Solution

1. Value 2 years ago $= \dfrac{P}{\left(1-\dfrac{R}{100}\right)^n} = \dfrac{94000}{\left(1-\dfrac{20}{100}\right)^2}$

   = ₹ 146875

2. Value after 3 years $= P\left(1-\dfrac{R}{100}\right)^n = 94000\left(1-\dfrac{20}{100}\right)^3$

   = ₹ 48128.

Example 9

Population of town increases at the rate of 10% every year. If the present population of the town is 24200, then:

1. What must be the population before 2 years?
2. What must be the population after 2 years?

Solution

Population before 2 years $= \dfrac{P}{\left(1+\dfrac{R}{100}\right)^n} = \dfrac{24200}{\left(1+\dfrac{10}{100}\right)^2}$

= 20000

Population after 2 years $= P\left(1+\dfrac{R}{100}\right)^n$

$= 24200\left(1+\dfrac{10}{100}\right)^2 = 29282.$

Example 10

In a tournament a hockey team is playing a total of 25 matches, keeping the winning target as 80% of total matches in the tournament. Out of first 10 matches the team enjoyed the success of winning 70% matches. What percentage of winning is required in the remaining matches to achieve the pre decided target?

Solution

Winning target of team = $25 \times \dfrac{80}{100}$ = 20 matches

	Matches	Won
Initial Matches played	10	7
Total matches	25	20 (target)

So, in the remaining 15 matches, the team must win 13 matches to achieve a final target of 20 matches.

Percentage of winning required in remaining matches = $\dfrac{13}{15} \times 100 = 86\dfrac{2}{3}\%$.

EXERCISE

1. The fraction $\dfrac{1}{5}$ is what percent of $\dfrac{1}{3}$?
   (a) 40% (b) 60%
   (c) 33.33% (d) 166.67%

2. 70% of $4\dfrac{2}{7}$ is:
   (a) $2\dfrac{1}{7}$ (b) $2\dfrac{3}{7}$
   (c) 3 (d) $3\dfrac{2}{7}$

3. 60% of 540 + 75% of ? = 864
   (a) 600 (b) 660
   (c) 720 (d) 780

4. 12.5% of 648 = ? × 27
   (a) 3 (b) 3½
   (c) 4 (d) 4½

5. 150% of 64 + 15% of 80 − ? = 90
   (a) 15 (b) 18
   (c) 22 (d) 27

6. 0.025 is what percent of 0.5?
   (a) 0.005% (b) 0.05%
   (c) 0.5% (d) 5%

7. What percent of a day is 4 hrs?
   (a) 25% (b) $33\dfrac{1}{3}\%$
   (c) $12\dfrac{1}{2}\%$ (d) $16\dfrac{2}{3}\%$

8. What is 50% of 20% of 2500?
   (a) 250
   (b) 450
   (c) 750
   (d) 800

9. 65% of 9560 = 50% of?
   (a) 12408
   (b) 12428
   (c) 12636
   (d) 12840

10. If 20% of R% of 15625 = 1250, then R is:
    (a) 30
    (b) 40
    (c) 45
    (d) 50

11. If R% of R is 49, then R is equal to:
    (a) 7
    (b) 49
    (c) 51
    (d) 70

12. If A scores 20% more than B, then by what percent B scores less than A?
    (a) $16\frac{2}{3}$ %
    (b) 20%
    (c) 22%
    (d) 25%

13. If A's salary is 6 times of B's salary. The percent by which B's salary is less than A's salary is:
    (a) 500%
    (b) $66\frac{2}{3}$ %
    (c) $83\frac{1}{3}$ %
    (d) $90\frac{2}{3}$ %

14. If 30% of a number is 63, then 300% of that number will be:
    (a) 189
    (b) 210
    (c) 420
    (d) 630

15. If 40% of a number is 300, then what percent of 300 is that number?
    (a) 150%
    (b) 250%
    (c) 300%
    (d) 600%

16. 60% of a number is added to 60, then the result is the number itself. The number is:
    (a) 60
    (b) 90
    (c) 150
    (d) 180

17. 60% of a number is 150. What is 84% of the number?
    (a) 180
    (b) 210
    (c) 224
    (d) 232

18. 35% of a number is 105. What is 15% of three times of the same number?
    (a) 105
    (b) 115
    (c) 120
    (d) 135

19. 39% of a number exceeds 19% of the same by 29. What is the number?
    (a) 145
    (b) 151
    (c) 165
    (d) 169

20. A number when increased by 12.5% becomes 63. Find the number.
    (a) 48
    (b) 56
    (c) 54
    (d) 60

21. A number when decreased by $16\frac{2}{3}$% becomes 205. Find the number.
    (a) 216
    (b) 240
    (c) 246
    (d) 252

22. A number if increased by $16\frac{2}{3}$% and then reduced by $12\frac{1}{2}$% becomes 98. The original number is:
    (a) 96
    (b) 98
    (c) 108
    (d) 112

23. Subtracting 5% of x from x is equivalent to multiplying x by how much?
    (a) 1/20
    (b) 11/20
    (c) 19/20
    (d) 21/20

24. In a fraction, the numerator is decreased by 25% and the denominator is increased by 20%, then the value of the fraction becomes 15/16. Find the original fraction.
    (a) 3/4
    (b) 3/5
    (c) 3/2
    (d) 3/9

25. The price of a book is increased from ₹ 80 to ₹ 96. By what percent dose the price increases?
    (a) 20%
    (b) 30%
    (c) 40%
    (d) 60%

26. If the price of a mobile handset is increased by 20%, and then a discount of 20% was offered. Find the percentage change in the price of hand set.
    (a) 2% increase
    (b) 2% decrease
    (c) 4% decrease
    (d) No change

27. The value of a land appreciates by 20% in the first year and by 30% in the second year. By what percent did the value of land appreciates in these two years?
    (a) 50%
    (b) 56%
    (c) 60%
    (d) 150%

28. A company produced 600 cars in the month of March and 750 cars in the month of April. Find the percentage increase in production, from March to April.
    (a) 15%
    (b) 20%
    (c) 25%
    (d) 30%

29. A mill produced 2100 m of cloth on a certain day. On the next day the manager decided to increase the production by $33\frac{1}{3}$%. Find how much meters of cloth is to be produced on the next day.
    (a) 700
    (b) 3100
    (c) 2500
    (d) 2800

30. Population of Mumbai is 4.5 times the population of Pune. What percent of India's population is the population of USA?
    (a) 11.11% (b) 9.09%
    (c) 22.22% (d) 450%

31. If the length of the rectangle is increased by 10% whereas breadth decreases by 10%. What is the percentage change in the area of rectangle?
    (a) 1% increase (b) 1% decrease
    (c) 10% decrease (d) No change

32. If the second and third number is 25% and 50% more than the first number, then what percentage of second number is the third number?
    (a) 150 (b) 100
    (c) 75 (d) 120

33. If the cost of cement bag is increased by 20% but its weight is reduced by 20%, then by what percent the price of cement is changed?
    (a) 0% (b) 20%
    (c) 40% (d) 50%

34. In an exam Arun scored 90 marks while Vishal scored 80 marks. By what percent Arun scored more than Vishal?
    (a) 10% (b) 12.5%
    (c) 9.09% (d) 11.11%

35. In the above problem by what percent Vishal scored less than Arun?
    (a) 10% (b) 12.5%
    (c) 9.09% (d) 11.11%

36. The population of a city increases by 30% every year. If the present population is 338000. What was the population two years ago?
    (a) 200000 (b) 220000
    (c) 250000 (d) 240000

37. If the price of 1 kg apples is ₹ 35 more than the price 1 kg mangoes. If 4 kg of apples and 4 kg of mangoes together cost ₹ 460, then by what percent the price per kg of apple is more than mangoes?
    (a) 46.67% (b) 35%
    (c) 65% (d) 87.5%

38. If price of sugar is increased by 25%, then find the percentage reduction in its consumption a housewife should do in order to maintain a constant expenditure.
    (a) 20% (b) 25%
    (c) 33.33% (d) 50%

39. To pass an exam a student need to score 65% of the total marks. A student scored 126 marks and failed by 30 marks. The maximum marks are:
    (a) 240 (b) 250
    (c) 260 (d) 280

40. In a test Ajay scored 25% and failed by 15 marks. In the same test, Vijay scored 35%, which is 15 marks more than the pass marks. Find the maximum marks of the test.
    (a) 250
    (b) 300
    (c) 320
    (d) 350

41. In a school 10% of the students did not appear for scholarship exam. Out of the appeared students 10% students are able to qualify the exam. If the disqualified students in the scholarship exam are 243, then how much is the strength of school?
    (a) 260
    (b) 300
    (c) 380
    (d) 420

42. A student multiplied a number by 2/3 instead of 3/2. What is the percentage error in the calculation?
    (a) 125%
    (b) 95%
    (c) $55\frac{5}{9}\%$
    (d) $45\frac{5}{9}\%$

43. 325 boys and 160 girls appeared for an exam. 24% of boys and 20% of girls passed the exam. The total number of student who failed are:
    (a) 245
    (b) 310
    (c) 360
    (d) 375

44. The ratio of salary of an employee in 2010 and 2011 is $1\frac{1}{3} : 2$. By what percent his salary of 2011 greater than salary of 2010?
    (a) $66\frac{2}{3}\%$
    (b) 60%
    (c) 50%
    (d) $33\frac{1}{3}\%$

45. The total strength of a class is 60. If 20% and 30% more boys and girls join the class then the strength increases to 76. Find the number of boys in the class initially.
    (a) 20
    (b) 36
    (c) 40
    (d) 46

46. The value of a machine decreases every year at the rate of 4% over that of previous year. If the value at the end of three years will be ₹ 13824, then find the present value.
    (a) ₹ 13120
    (b) ₹ 14575
    (c) ₹ 15625
    (d) ₹ 15824

47. The population of a town increases by 25% at the end of every year. During which of the following years will the population get doubled?
    (a) 2nd year
    (b) 3rd year
    (c) 4th year
    (d) 5th year

48. The population of a town increases at the rate of $33\frac{1}{3}\%$. If the present population is 16000, then how much was the population 2 years ago?
    (a) 9000
    (b) 10000
    (c) 12400
    (d) 28444

49. The price of a share in a stock market increases by 10%. After some time it decreases by 30% of its previous price and then again increases by 20% of its previous price at the time of closing. If the final price of share at the time of market closing is ₹ 1386, then how much was the initial price?
    (a) ₹ 1250
    (b) ₹ 1360
    (c) ₹ 1500
    (d) ₹ 1850

50. In a hostel 40% of the students are boys. 35% of the boys are non-vegetarians and 15% of the girls are vegetarians. What percent of total strength of hostel are non-vegetarian girls?
    (a) 35%
    (b) 51%
    (c) 65%
    (d) 85%

51. Raju saves 20% of his income. If he plans to increase his present saving by 25%, then by how much percentage should he reduce his present expenditure, if his income remains same?
    (a) 6.25%
    (b) 8%
    (c) 10%
    (d) 12.5%

52. Three persons A, B and C appeared for an exam. B scored 10% less than A, while C scored 20% less than A. By what percent B scored more than C?
    (a) 10%
    (b) 12.5%
    (c) 15%
    (d) 16.67%

53. Sam spends 60% of his annual salary and saves the remaining amount. In the next year if his salary is increased by 25% and he increased his spending by 20%. By what percentage did his saving increase?
    (a) 20%
    (b) 25%
    (c) 32.5%
    (d) 36.25%

54. The price of gold increased by the same percentage over the last four years. If at the beginning it was ₹ 512 per gram and at the end of four years it became ₹ 1250 per gram, then find the percentage increase ever year.
    (a) 10%
    (b) 15%
    (c) 20%
    (d) 25%

55. In an election, there were only two contestants A and B. A won the election. He secured 54% of the votes and won by a margin of 112 votes. If all the votes polled were valid, then how many votes were polled?
    (a) 1256
    (b) 1400
    (c) 1480
    (d) 1620

56. In an election between two candidates 10% of the votes polled were invalid. If the winning candidate got 52% of the total valid votes and wins by a majority of 160 votes, then how many valid votes other candidate got?
    (a) 1800
    (b) 1600
    (c) 1920
    (d) 2220

57. In an election involving two candidates, 36 votes were declared invalid. The winning candidate secures 60% and wins by a margin of 1680 votes. The total number of votes polled is:
(a) 8400
(b) 8436
(c) 8364
(d) 8636

58. The salaries of Prakash and Ramesh together amount to ₹ 24000. Prakash spends 85% of his salary and Ramesh spends 55% of his salary. If their savings are same, then how much is the salary of Prakash?
(a) ₹ 6000
(b) ₹ 16000
(c) ₹ 18000
(d) ₹ 20000

59. The present value of car is ₹ 600000. If the value of car depreciates at the rate of 20% every year, then what will be the value of car 3 years from now?
(a) ₹ 420400
(b) ₹ 307200
(c) ₹ 290800
(d) ₹ 280320

60. The value of the machine deprecates at the rate of 25% every year. It was purchased 3 years ago. If its present value is ₹ 6750, its purchase price was:
(a) ₹ 16000
(b) ₹ 16400
(c) ₹ 17200
(d) ₹ 18000

KEYS

1. (b)	2. (c)	3. (c)	4. (a)	5. (b)	6. (d)	7. (d)	8. (a)
9. (b)	10. (b)	11. (d)	12. (a)	13. (c)	14. (d)	15. (b)	16. (c)
17. (b)	18. (d)	19. (a)	20. (b)	21. (c)	22. (a)	23. (c)	24. (c)
25. (a)	26. (c)	27. (b)	28. (c)	29. (d)	30. (c)	31. (b)	32. (d)
33. (d)	34. (b)	35. (d)	36. (a)	37. (d)	38. (a)	39. (a)	40. (b)
41. (b)	42. (c)	43. (d)	44. (c)	45. (a)	46. (c)	47. (c)	48. (a)
49. (c)	50. (b)	51. (a)	52. (b)	53. (c)	54. (d)	55. (b)	56. (c)
57. (b)	58. (c)	59. (b)	60. (a)				

SOLUTIONS

Solution 1

Required percentage = $\dfrac{1/5}{1/3} \times 100 = \dfrac{1}{5} \times 3 \times 100 = 60\%$.

Choice (b)

Solution 2

Required percentage = $\dfrac{70}{100} \times 4\dfrac{2}{7} = \dfrac{70}{100} \times \dfrac{30}{7} = 3$.

Choice (c)

Solution 3

60% of $540 + 75\%$ of $x = 864$

$\dfrac{60}{100} \times 540 + \dfrac{75}{100} \times x = 864$

$324 + \dfrac{3}{4} x = 864$

$\therefore \quad x = \dfrac{864 - 324}{3/4} = 720$.

Choice (c)

Solution 4

12.5% of $648 = x \times 27$

$\dfrac{1}{8} \times 648 = x \times 27$

$\therefore \quad x = 3$.

Choice (a)

Solution 5

150% of $64 + 15\%$ of $80 - x = 90$

$\dfrac{150}{100} \times 64 + \dfrac{15}{100} \times 80 - x = 90$

$96 + 12 - x = 90$

$\therefore \quad x = 18$.

Choice (b)

Solution 6

Required percentage = $\dfrac{0.025}{0.5} \times 100 = 5\%$.

Choice (d)

Solution 7

Required percentage = $\dfrac{4}{24} \times 100 = 16\dfrac{2}{3}\%$.

Choice (d)

Solution 8

Required percentage = $\dfrac{50}{100} \times \dfrac{20}{100} \times 2500 = 250$.

Choice (a)

Solution 9

65% of $9560 = 50\%$ of x

$\dfrac{65}{100} \times 9560 = \dfrac{50}{100} \times x$

$\therefore \quad x = \dfrac{65 \times 9560}{50}$

$\quad\quad\quad = 12428$.

Choice (b)

Solution 10

20% of $R\%$ of $15625 = 1250$

$\dfrac{20}{100} \times \dfrac{R}{100} \times 15625 = 1250$

$\therefore \quad\quad\quad\quad R = 40$.

Choice (b)

Solution 11

$\dfrac{R}{100} \times R = 49$

$\quad\quad R^2 = 4900$

$\therefore \quad\quad R = 70$.

Choice (d)

Solution 12

Assuming score of $B = 100$

$\therefore$ Score of $A = 120$

Percentage by which B scores less than $A = \dfrac{20}{120} \times 100 = 16\frac{2}{3}\%$.

Choice (a)

Solution 13

Assuming B's salary as ₹ 100

$\therefore$ A's Salary = ₹ 600

Percent by which B's salary is less than A's salary = $\dfrac{500}{600} \times 100 = 83\frac{1}{3}\%$.

Choice (c)

Solution 14

Let the number be x

30% of $x = 63$

$\dfrac{30}{100} \times x = 63$

$\therefore \qquad x = 210$

300% of $x = 210 \times \dfrac{300}{100} = 630$.

Choice (d)

Solution 15

Let the number be x

40% of $x = 300$

$\dfrac{40}{100} \times x = 300$

$\therefore \qquad x = 750$

Required percentage = $\dfrac{750}{300} \times 100 = 250\%$.

Choice (b)

Solution 16

Let the number be x

60% of $x + 60 = x$

$\left(\dfrac{60}{100} \times x\right) + 60 = x$

Quantitative Aptitude

$$\frac{3x}{5} + 60 = x$$

$$\frac{2x}{5} = 60$$

∴ $x = 150$.

Choice (c)

Solution 17

Let the number be x

$$60\% \text{ of } x = 150$$

$$\frac{60}{100} \times x = 150$$

∴ $x = 250$

$$84\% \text{ of } x = \frac{84}{100} \times 250$$

$$= 210.$$

Choice (b)

Solution 18

Let the number be x

$$35\% \text{ of } x = 105$$

$$\frac{35}{100} \times x = 105$$

∴ $x = 300$

15% of $\quad 3x = \frac{15}{100} \times 900$

$$= 135.$$

Choice (d)

Solution 19

Let the number be x

$$(39\% \text{ of } x) - (19\% \text{ of } x) = 29$$

$$\frac{39x}{100} - \frac{19x}{100} = 29$$

∴ $x = \frac{29 \times 100}{20} = 145.$

Choice (a)

Solution 20

Let the number be x

$$x + 12.5\% \text{ of } x = 63$$
$$x + \frac{1}{8}x = 63$$
$$\frac{9}{8}x = 63$$
$$\therefore \qquad x = 56.$$

Choice (b)

Solution 21

Let the number be x

$$x - 16\tfrac{2}{3}\% \text{ of } x = 205$$
$$x - \frac{1}{6}x = 205$$
$$\frac{5}{6}x = 205$$
$$\therefore \qquad x = 246.$$

Choice (c)

Solution 22

$$16\tfrac{2}{3}\% = \frac{1}{6}$$
$$12\tfrac{1}{2}\% = \frac{1}{8}$$

Let us assume a number which is multiple of 6 and 8, say 48.

48 is increased by $16\tfrac{2}{3}\% \Rightarrow 48 \times \frac{7}{6} = 56$

56 is reduced by $12\tfrac{1}{2}\% \Rightarrow 56 \times \frac{7}{8} = 49$

$$48 \rightarrow 49$$
$$x \rightarrow 98$$

$$\therefore \qquad x = \frac{98 \times 48}{49} = 96.$$

Choice (a)

Solution 23

Let the number to be multiplied with x is n.

$$x - (5\% \text{ of } x) = n \times x$$

$$x - \frac{5}{100}x = n \times x$$

$$\frac{19}{20}x = n \times x$$

∴ $\quad n = \frac{19}{20}.$

Choice (c)

Solution 24

Let the original fraction be $\frac{n}{d}$

n is decreased by 25% $\Rightarrow \frac{3n}{4}$

d is increased by 20% $\Rightarrow \frac{6d}{5}$

Resulting fraction $= \dfrac{\frac{3n}{4}}{\frac{6d}{5}} = \dfrac{5n}{8d}$

$$\frac{5n}{8d} = \frac{15}{16}$$

∴ $\quad \dfrac{n}{d} = \dfrac{3}{2}.$

Choice (c)

Solution 25

Percentage increase in price $= \dfrac{96-80}{80} \times 100 = 20\%.$

Choice (a)

Solution 26

Let initial price of handset = ₹ 100

Price increased by 20% $= \dfrac{120}{100} \times 100 = ₹ 120$

Discount of 20% on increased price $= \dfrac{80}{100} \times 120 = ₹ 96$

Initial price = ₹ 100
Final price = ₹ 96

Percentage change $= \dfrac{100-96}{100} \times 100 = 4\%$ decrease.

Choice (c)

Solution 27

Let the initial price of land = ₹ 100

If price increases by 20% = $\frac{120}{100} \times 100$ = ₹ 120

If price further increases by 30% = $\frac{130}{100} \times 120$ = ₹ 156

If the cost of land reached to ₹ 156 from ₹ 100, then percentage increase in 2 years is 56%.

Choice (b)

Solution 28

Percentage increase in production = $\frac{750 - 600}{600} \times 100$ = 25%.

Choice (c)

Solution 29

Cloth produced on next day = 2100 + (33 $\frac{1}{3}$ % of 2100)

$\qquad$ = 2100 + $\frac{1}{3} \times 2100$

$\qquad$ = 2800 m.

Choice (d)

Solution 30

Let population of Pune $\quad$ = 100
And population of Mumbai = 4.5 × 100 = 450

Required percentage $\quad$ = $\frac{100}{450} \times 100$

$\qquad\qquad$ = $\frac{2}{9} \times 100$

$\qquad\qquad$ = 22.22%.

Choice (c)

Solution 31

Assuming the length and breadth both as 10 cm

∴ Original Area = 10 × 10 = 100 cm^2

As length is increased by 10%

∴ New length = 11 cm

As breadth is decreased by 10%

∴ New breadth = 9 cm
∴ New area = 11 × 9 = 99 cm²

Percentage change = $\frac{100-99}{100} \times 100$ = 1% decrease.

Choice (b)

Solution 32

Assuming First number = 100
∴ Second number = 125
and Third number = 150

Required percentage = $\frac{150}{125} \times 100$ = 120%.

Choice (d)

Solution 33

Let the initial cost of cement bag = ₹ 1000
Let the initial weight of bag = 10 kg

∴ Original price of cement = $\frac{1000}{10}$ = ₹ 100 per kg

New price of cement bag = ₹ 1200 (∵ 20% increase in price)
New weight of cement bag = 8 kg (∵ 20% decrease in weight)

∴ New price of cement = $\frac{1200}{8}$ = ₹ 150 per kg

Percentage change in price = $\frac{150-100}{100} \times 100$ = 50%.

Choice (d)

Solution 34

Score of Arun = 90
Score of Vishal = 80

Required percentage = $\frac{10}{80} \times 100$ = 12.5%.

Choice (b)

Solution 35

Required percentage = $\frac{10}{90} \times 100$ = 11.11%.

Choice (d)

Solution 36

If P is the present population and R is the percentage rise every year.

Population n years ago $= \dfrac{P}{\left(1+\dfrac{R}{100}\right)^n}$

$= \dfrac{338000}{\left(1+\dfrac{30}{100}\right)^2}$

$= 200000.$

Choice (a)

Solution 37

Let the cost of 1 kg of Apple $= A$
And the cost of 1 kg of Mangoes $= M$

$\qquad A - M = 35 \qquad \ldots (1)$
$\qquad 4A + 4M = 460 \qquad \ldots (2)$

Solving equation (1) and (2)

$A = 75$ and $M = 40$

Required percentage $= \dfrac{35}{40} \times 100 = 87.5\%.$

Choice (d)

Solution 38

If the price of a commodity increases by $R\%$, then

Percentage reduction in consumption $= \left(\dfrac{R}{100+R} \times 100\right)\% = \dfrac{25}{100+25} \times 100 = 20\%.$

Hence consumption should be reduced by 20% to maintain constant expenditure.

Choice (a)

Solution 39

Passing marks $= 126 + 30 = 156$
65% of Total marks $= 156$

$\dfrac{65}{100} \times$ Total marks $= 156$

$\therefore$ Total marks $= \dfrac{156 \times 100}{65} = 240.$

Choice (a)

Solution 40

Let passing marks = P
And total marks = T

Ajay $\Rightarrow \dfrac{25T}{100} = P - 15$ ... (1)

Vijay $\Rightarrow \dfrac{35T}{100} = P + 15$ ... (2)

Subtracting equation (1) from (2)

$$\dfrac{35T}{100} - \dfrac{25T}{100} = (P + 15) - (P - 15)$$

$$\dfrac{10T}{100} = 30$$

$\therefore \qquad T = 300.$

Choice (b)

Solution 41

Assuming the strength of school = 100

Number of students appeared for scholarship = $\dfrac{90}{100} \times 100 = 90$

Number of students qualified scholarship = $\dfrac{10}{100} \times 90 = 9$

If strength of school is 100, the disqualified students in scholarship exam are 81. In actual if the disqualified students are 243, then:

Strength of school = $\dfrac{243 \times 100}{81}$
$= 300.$

Choice (b)

Solution 42

As the student multiplied a number by 2/3 instead of 3/2, so let us assume a number which is divisible by both 2 as well as 3, say 6.

Calculated value = $6 \times \dfrac{2}{3} = 4$

Actual value expected = $6 \times \dfrac{3}{2} = 9$

Percentage error = $\dfrac{9-4}{9} \times 100$

$= 55 \dfrac{5}{9} \%.$

Choice (c)

Solution 43

Percentage of passing boys = $\frac{24}{100} \times 325 = 78$

Percentage of passing girls = $\frac{20}{100} \times 160 = 32$

Total passed = 78 + 32 = 110

Total failed = (325 + 160) − 110 = 375.

Choice (d)

Solution 44

Ratio of salary of 2010 and 2011 = $1\frac{1}{3} : 2$

$$= \frac{4}{3} : 2$$
$$= 2 : 3$$

Required percentage = $\frac{3-2}{2} \times 100 = 50\%$.

Choice (c)

Solution 45

Let the number of boys = B
And number of girls = G

$B + G = 60$ ... (1)

$1.2B + 1.3G = 76$ ... (2)

Multiplying equation (1) with 1.2

$1.2B + 1.2G = 72$ ... (3)

Subtracting equation (3) from (2)

$0.1G = 4$

$\therefore G = 40$

and $B = 60 - 40 = 20$.

Choice (a)

Solution 46

If the present value of machine is P, and it depreciates at the rate of $R\%$ per year then:

Value after n years = $P\left(1 - \frac{R}{100}\right)^n$

Value after 3 years = $P\left(1 - \frac{R}{100}\right)^3$

$$13824 = P\left(1 - \frac{4}{100}\right)^3$$

∴ $P = ₹\ 15625.$

Choice (c)

Solution 47

If the present population is P, and it increases at the rate of $R\%$ every year, then:

Population after n years = $P\left(1 + \frac{R}{100}\right)^n$

$$2P = P\left(1 + \frac{25}{100}\right)^n$$

$$\left(\frac{5}{4}\right)^n = 2$$

∴ n should be at least 4 to satisfy the condition. Hence the population will get double in 4th year.

Choice (c)

Solution 48

If the present population is P, and it increases at the rate of $R\%$ every year, then:

Population n years ago = $\dfrac{P}{\left(1 + \dfrac{R}{100}\right)^n}$

Population 2 years ago = $\dfrac{16000}{\left(1 + \dfrac{33\frac{1}{3}}{100}\right)^2}$

$$= \frac{16000}{\left(1 + \frac{1}{3}\right)^2} = 9000.$$

Choice (a)

Solution 49

Let the original price of share = ₹ 100

Price, if increased by 10% = $100 \times \dfrac{110}{100}$ = ₹ 110

Price, if decreased by 30% = $110 \times \dfrac{70}{100}$ = ₹ 77

Price, if increased by 20% = $77 \times \dfrac{120}{100}$ = ₹ 92.4

If the initial price is assumed as ₹ 100, then finally at the time of closing the price of share becomes ₹ 92.4. If the actual price of share at the time of closing is ₹ 1386, then:

Initial price = $\dfrac{1386 \times 100}{92.4}$ = ₹ 1500.

Choice (c)

Solution 50

Assuming the strength of hostel as 1000.

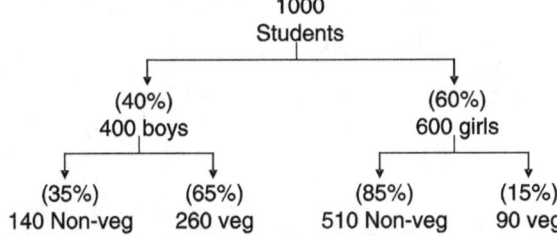

Required percentage = $\dfrac{510}{1000} \times 100 = 51\%$.

Choice (b)

Solution 51

Assuming the present salary of Raju as ₹ 100.
Present saving = ₹ 20
Present expenses = 100 − 20 = ₹ 80
New saving = 20 + (25% of 20) = 20 + $\dfrac{25}{100} \times 20$ = ₹ 25
New expenses = 100 − 25 = ₹ 75
Required percentage = $\dfrac{80-75}{80} \times 100 = 6.25\%$
Raju should reduce his present expenses by 6.25%.

Choice (a)

Solution 52

Let the score of A = 100
∴ Score of B = 90
∴ Score of C = 80

Required percentage = $\dfrac{90-80}{80} \times 100 = \dfrac{1}{8} \times 100 = 12.5\%$.

Choice (b)

Solution 53

Assuming present year's salary as ₹ 1000.
Present spending = 60% of 1000 = ₹ 600
Present saving = 40% of 1000 = ₹ 400

Next year's salary = $1000 \times \dfrac{125}{100}$ = ₹ 1250

Next year's spending = $600 \times \dfrac{120}{100}$ = ₹ 720

∴ Next year's saving = 1250 − 720 = ₹ 530

Percentage increase in saving in these 2 years = $\dfrac{530-400}{400} \times 100$

= 32.5%.

Choice (c)

Solution 54

If the present price of gold is ₹ P per gram and it increases by $R\%$ every year, then:

Price after n years = $P\left(1+\dfrac{R}{100}\right)^n$

Price after 4 years = $P\left(1+\dfrac{R}{100}\right)^4$

$$1250 = 512\left(1+\dfrac{R}{100}\right)^4$$

$$\left(1+\dfrac{R}{100}\right)^4 = \dfrac{625}{256}$$

$$1+\dfrac{R}{100} = \dfrac{5}{4}$$

∴ $R = 25\%$.

Choice (d)

Solution 55

Suppose if 100 votes are polled, then A must have got (54%) i.e., 54 votes and B must have got 46 votes. In this case A wins by a margin of 8 votes.

If 100 votes are polled ⇒ A wins by a margin of 8 votes

If x votes are polled ⇒ A wins by a margin of 112 votes

∴ $x = \dfrac{112 \times 100}{8} = 1400.$

Choice (b)

Solution 56

Suppose if 1000 votes are polled, out of which only 900 votes are valid.

Votes in favor of winning candidate = $\frac{52}{100} \times 900 = 468$

Votes in favor of other candidate = $\frac{48}{100} \times 900 = 432$

In this case the winning candidate wins by a margin of (468 − 432) i.e., 36 votes.

If the margin is of 36 votes ⇒ other candidate gets 432 votes

If the margin is of 160 votes ⇒ other candidate gets x votes

$\therefore x = \frac{160 \times 432}{36} = 1920$.

Choice (c)

Solution 57

As winning candidate gets is 60% of valid votes, hence other candidate is getting 40% of valid votes. Therefore the winning candidate wins by a margin of 20%.

20% ⇒ 1680 votes

100% ⇒ $\frac{1680 \times 100}{20} = 8400$

So, total votes polled = valid votes + invalid votes
= 8400 + 36
= 8436.

Choice (b)

Solution 58

Let salary of Prakash = ₹ P
And salary of Ramesh = ₹ R

$P + R = 24000$

As their savings are same:

$\frac{15P}{100} = \frac{45R}{100}$

$\therefore \frac{P}{R} = \frac{3}{1}$ or $P = 3R$

$\therefore 3R + R = 24000$

$R = ₹ 6000$
$P = ₹ 18000$.

Choice (c)

Solution 59

If the present value of car is P, and it depreciates at the rate of $R\%$ per year then:

Value after n years = $P\left(1 - \dfrac{R}{100}\right)^n$

Value of car after 3 years = $P\left(1 - \dfrac{R}{100}\right)^3$

$= 600000 \left(1 - \dfrac{20}{100}\right)^3$

$= ₹\ 307200.$

Choice (b)

Solution 60

If the present value of machine is P, and it depreciates at the rate of $R\%$ per year then:

Price n years ago = $\dfrac{P}{\left(1 - \dfrac{R}{100}\right)^n}$

Price 3 years ago = $\dfrac{6750}{\left(1 - \dfrac{25}{100}\right)^3}$

$= ₹\ 16000.$

Choice (a)

8

Profit and Loss

IMPORTANT POINTS

- **Cost Price**—The price at which an article is purchased is called its Cost Price (CP).
- **Selling Price**—The price at which an article is sold is called its Selling Price (SP).
- **Profit**—If the selling price is greater than cost price then the seller will get a profit.

  Profit (or Gain) = $SP - CP$
- **Loss**—If the selling price is less than cost price then the seller will face a loss.

  Loss = $CP - SP$
- **Percentage Profit**—Percentage profit is calculated on the base of cost price as follows:

  Profit % = $\dfrac{\text{Profit}}{\text{CP}} \times 100$
- **Percentage Loss**—Percentage loss is also calculated on the base of cost price as follows:

  Loss % = $\dfrac{\text{Loss}}{\text{CP}} \times 100$
- If an article is sold at a profit of $R\%$, then:

  $SP = (100 + R)\%$ of CP
- If an article is sold at a loss of $R\%$, then:

  $SP = (100 - R)\%$ of CP
- If two articles are purchased at the same price, but while selling one article is sold at $R\%$ profit and other at $R\%$ loss, then in the whole transaction there is 'no profit' and 'no loss'.
- If two articles are sold at the same price, but if first article is sold at $R\%$ profit and second article is sold at $R\%$ loss, then in the whole transaction there is always a 'loss'. Percentage loss is calculated as:

  Loss % = $\dfrac{R^2}{100}$
- Marked price (or List price) is the price that is indicated or marked on the product. This is the price at which a product is intended to be sold. However there can be some 'discount' on this price and as a result, the actual selling price of the product may be less than the marked price.

  Selling price = Marked price − Discount

- Percentage of discount on a article can be calculated as:

$$\text{Discount \%} = \frac{\text{Marked Price} - \text{Selling Price}}{\text{Marked Price}} \times 100$$

Or $\text{Discount \%} = \frac{\text{Discount}}{\text{Marked Price}} \times 100$.

SOLVED EXAMPLES

Example 1

Two items were sold at ₹ 900 each. The first was sold at 25% profit and second wad sold at 40% loss. Find the cost price of first and second item.

Solution

1. *Cost price of first item*
   To make a profit of 25%, an item worth ₹ 100 is sold for ₹ 125

   $100 \rightarrow 125$
   $x \rightarrow 900$

   $\therefore \quad x = \frac{900 \times 100}{125} = ₹ 720$

   Hence the cost price of first item must be ₹ 720 which is sold at ₹ 900 to make 25% profit.

2. *Cost price of second item*
   If an item worth ₹ 100 is sold for ₹ 60, there will be a loss of 40%.

   $100 \rightarrow 60$
   $x \rightarrow 900$

   $\therefore \quad x = \frac{900 \times 100}{60}$
   $= ₹ 1500$

   Hence the cost price of first item must be ₹ 1500 which is sold at ₹ 900 will make a loss of 40%.

Example 2

A shopkeeper gains 20% by selling an article for ₹ 60. Find his percentage of profit or loss if the same article is sold at:

1. ₹ 45
2. ₹ 75.

Solution

To make a profit of 20%, an article worth ₹ 100 is sold for ₹ 120

$$100 \rightarrow 120$$
$$x \rightarrow 60$$

$$\therefore x = \frac{60 \times 100}{120} = ₹\ 50$$

So, the cost price of article is ₹ 50.

1. Selling the article at the price is ₹ 45
   As $CP > SP$, there will be a loss.

   $$\text{Loss \%} = \frac{CP - SP}{CP} \times 100$$
   $$= \frac{50 - 45}{50} \times 100$$
   $$= 10\%.$$

2. Selling the article at the price is ₹ 75
   As $CP < SP$, there will be a profit.

   $$\text{Profit \%} = \frac{SP - CP}{CP} \times 100$$
   $$= \frac{75 - 50}{50} \times 100 = 50\%.$$

Example 3

P sells an article to Q at 25% profit, Q sells same to R at 20% profit.
1. By what percent the cost price of R is more than cost price of P?
2. If R purchased it for ₹ 900, then how much profit P earns?

Solution

Assuming the cost price of P as ₹ 100.

CP of P = ₹ 100

SP of $P = \frac{125}{100} \times 100 = ₹\ 125$ ($\because$ P sells the article at 25% profit)

CP of Q = ₹ 125

SP of $Q = \frac{120}{100} \times 125 = ₹\ 150$ ($\because$ Q sells the article at 20% profit)

$\therefore CP$ of R = ₹ 150

1. Percentage by which CP of R is more than CP of P

   Required percentage = $\frac{150 - 100}{100} \times 100 = 50\%.$

2. Profit earned by P

If the CP of P is assumed as ₹ 100, then R purchase it for ₹ 150, and P earns a profit of ₹ 25. In actual if R purchased it for ₹ 900, then:

Profit earned by $P = \dfrac{900 \times 25}{150} = ₹\ 150$.

Example 4

Two articles were sold such that there was a profit of 10% on first article and a loss of 10% on other article. Find the overall percentage of profit or loss made if:
1. Their cost price is same
2. Their selling price is same.

Solution

1. *If CP is same*
   If the cost price of two articles is same and out of it one is sold at R% profit and other at R% loss, then in that case there will be no profit and no loss.
2. *If SP is same*
   If two articles are sold at the same price, but if first article is sold at R% profit and second at R% loss, then in the whole transaction there is always a loss. Percentage loss is calculated as:

$$\text{Loss \%} = \dfrac{R^2}{100} = \dfrac{(10)^2}{100} = 1\%.$$

Example 5

A bookseller sells a book at two-third of its selling price and thus makes a loss of 20%. How much percentage of profit he will make if he sells the book at actual selling price?

Solution

Let the actual selling price = SP.

By selling the article at two-third of its actual SP, there is a loss of 20%

$$\dfrac{2}{3} \times SP = 20\% \text{ loss}$$

$$\dfrac{2}{3} \times SP = \dfrac{80}{100} \times CP$$

$$\therefore \quad \dfrac{SP}{CP} = \dfrac{6}{5}.$$

Therefore percentage of profit if sold for actual SP can be found as:

$$\text{Profit \%} = \dfrac{SP - CP}{CP} \times 100 = \dfrac{6-5}{5} \times 100 = 20\%.$$

Example 6

By selling 20 apples a fruit vendor gains the cost price of 5 apples. Find the gain percent.

Solution

Let the cost price of 1 apple = 1 CP
and the selling price of 1 apple = 1 SP

$$\text{Gain} = SP - CP$$
$$5\,CP = 20\,SP - 20\,CP$$
$$25\,CP = 20\,SP$$
$$\therefore \quad \frac{SP}{CP} = \frac{5}{4}.$$

Percentage gain can be found as:

$$\text{Gain \%} = \frac{SP - CP}{CP} \times 100$$
$$= \frac{5-4}{4} \times 100$$
$$= 25\%.$$

Example 7

A shopkeeper buys 6 toffees for a rupee. How many toffees for a rupee he should sell to make a profit of 20%?

Solution

Let the number of toffees the shopkeeper sell for a rupee be x.

SP of each toffee = $\frac{1}{x}$

CP of each toffee = $\frac{1}{6}$

$$\frac{SP - CP}{CP} \times 100 = \text{Profit \%}$$

$$\frac{\frac{1}{x} - \frac{1}{6}}{\frac{1}{6}} \times 100 = 20$$

$$\frac{6-x}{6x} \times 6 = \frac{1}{5}$$
$$30 - 5x = x$$
$$\therefore \qquad x = 5$$

So, the shopkeeper must sell 5 toffees for a rupee to make a profit of 20%.

Example 8

A man buys 12 oranges for ₹ 10 and sells them at 10 oranges for ₹ 12. Find his profit or loss percent.

Solution

In such problems, the buying and selling quantity is not equal, so the first task is to make it equal.

Buy $\Rightarrow$ 12 oranges for ₹ 10 $\Rightarrow$ 60 oranges for ₹ 50
Sell $\Rightarrow$ 10 oranges for ₹ 12 $\Rightarrow$ 60 oranges for ₹ 72

As 60 oranges are purchased for ₹ 50 but sold for ₹ 72, hence he will make profit.

Profit % $= \dfrac{SP - CP}{CP} \times 100$

$= \dfrac{72 - 50}{50} \times 100$

$= 44\%.$

Example 9

If the cost price of 10 eggs is same as selling price of 8 eggs. Find the profit or loss percent.

Solution

Let the CP of 1 egg = ₹ 1

$\therefore$ CP of 8 eggs = ₹ 8

and SP of 8 eggs = ₹ 10   ($\because$ SP of 8 eggs = CP of 10 eggs)

Profit % $= \dfrac{SP - CP}{CP} \times 100$

$= \dfrac{10 - 8}{8} \times 100$

$= 25\%.$

Example 10

Getting four successive discounts of 10% each on a trouser is equivalent to a single discount of what percent?

Solution

Let the original price of trouser be ₹ 1000

After applying four successive discounts of 10% each on the trouser, the cost of trouser will be:

Discounted price $= \dfrac{90}{100} \times \dfrac{90}{100} \times \dfrac{90}{100} \times \dfrac{90}{100} \times ₹\ 1000 = ₹\ 656.10$

Discount offered = 1000 − 656.10 = ₹ 343.9

Percentage of single discount = $\frac{343.9}{1000} \times 100$ = 34.39%

So, four successive discounts of 10% each is equivalent to a single discount of 34.39%.

Example 11

A trader marks his product 30% above the cost price, and offers a discount of 20% to the customer. If he finally earns a profit of ₹ 28, find:
1. Cost price of product
2. Marked price of product
3. Selling price of product.

Solution

Assuming the cost price of product, i.e. CP = ₹ 100

∴ The marked price, i.e. MP = ₹ 130

∴ The selling price, i.e. SP = $\frac{80}{100} \times 130$ = ₹ 104   (∵ 20% discount if offered)

So, the profit earned is ₹ 4.

1. Cost price of product
   Assumed value 100 → 4 (Profit earned)
   Actual value x → 28 (Profit earned)
   ∴ $x = \frac{100 \times 28}{4}$
   = ₹ 700
   So, actual CP of product = ₹ 700.

2. Marked price of product
   MP = 130% of CP
   = $\frac{130}{100} \times 700$
   = ₹ 910
   So, actual MP of product = ₹ 910.

3. Selling price of product
   SP = 80% of MP
   = $\frac{80}{100} \times 910$
   = ₹ 728
   So, actual SP of product = ₹ 728.

Example 12

By how much percent above the cost price the product should be marked so as to make a profit of 16% after allowing the customer a discount of 20%?

Solution

Assuming the cost price of product, *i.e.* $CP = ₹\ 100$

To make a profit of 16%, the selling price should be 116% of CP

∴ The selling price, *i.e.* $SP = \dfrac{116}{100} \times 100 = ₹\ 116$

$$\text{Discount \%} = \dfrac{\text{Marked Price - Selling price}}{\text{Marked Price}} \times 100$$

$$20 = \dfrac{MP - 116}{MP} \times 100$$

Solving the above equation;

∴ $MP = ₹\ 145$

So, the product should be marked 45% above the cost price.

EXERCISE

1. A trader brought an article for ₹ 200. If he wants a profit of 22%, then at what price must he sell it?
    (a) ₹ 122
    (b) ₹ 222
    (c) ₹ 244
    (d) ₹ 240

2. By selling a chair at ₹ 300, a shopkeeper makes a profit of 20%. Find the cost price of chair.
    (a) ₹ 248
    (b) ₹ 250
    (c) ₹ 240
    (d) ₹ 360

3. If the cost price of an article is 60% of its selling price, then the profit percentage is:
    (a) $33\tfrac{1}{3}\%$
    (b) 40%
    (c) 60%
    (d) $66\tfrac{2}{3}\%$

4. By selling an article for ₹ 100, a man gains ₹ 20. Then his gain % is:
    (a) 20%
    (b) 25%
    (c) $33\tfrac{1}{3}\%$
    (d) 40%

5. By selling an article for ₹ 150, a trader makes a loss ₹ 50. Then the loss % is:
    (a) 20%
    (b) 25%
    (c) $33\tfrac{1}{3}\%$
    (d) 40%

6. The ratio of cost price to selling price is 5:4, then there will be:
   (a) 25% profit
   (b) 20% profit
   (c) 25% loss
   (d) 20% loss

7. A man buys an old scooter for ₹ 5500 and spends ₹ 1700 on its repairs. If he sells the scooter for ₹ 7560, then what percentage of profit he makes?
   (a) 5%
   (b) 6.25%
   (c) 12%
   (d) 28.6%

8. A man gains 20% by selling an article for certain price. If he sells it at double the price, the percentage of profit will be:
   (a) 40%
   (b) 100%
   (c) 120%
   (d) 140%

9. By selling an article at certain price, a trader gains a profit of 40%. How much will be the percentage of loss if the same article is sold at half the price?
   (a) 20%
   (b) 30%
   (c) 40%
   (d) 60%

10. A trader purchased 160 watermelons for ₹ 2240. He spent ₹ 280 on transportation. If 20 watermelons were spoiled during transportation, then at what price he should sell each watermelon to make a profit of $33\frac{1}{3}\%$?
    (a) ₹ 18
    (b) ₹ 18.62
    (c) ₹ 21
    (d) ₹ 24

11. Raju sold a bicycle for ₹ 1275 and thus makes a loss of 15%. At what price he should sell the bicycle to make a profit of 15%?
    (a) ₹ 1657.50
    (b) ₹ 1725
    (c) ₹ 1466.25
    (d) ₹ 1500

12. A shopkeeper brought 9 pencils for ₹ 10, but sold them at the rate of 6 pencils for ₹ 7. The shopkeeper makes:
    (a) Profit of 5%
    (b) Loss of 5%
    (c) Profit of 2%
    (d) Loss of 2%

13. A vegetable vendor buys 6 lemons for ₹ 5 and sold at 5 lemons for ₹ 6. His gain percent is:
    (a) $16\frac{2}{3}\%$
    (b) 20%
    (c) 40%
    (d) 44%

14. Raman brought 18 kg of sugar for ₹ 360. He was forced to sell it at a loss which is as much as selling price of 4.5 kg. At what price did he sell each kg of sugar?
    (a) ₹ 12.50
    (b) ₹ 14
    (c) ₹ 15.25
    (d) ₹ 16

15. A shopkeeper sold a book at 10% loss. Had he sold it for ₹ 85 more, he would have made a profit of 7%. What is the cost price of book?
    (a) ₹ 500
    (b) ₹ 850
    (c) ₹ 615
    (d) ₹ 585

16. By selling an article at a certain price, a person incurs a loss of 30%. Instead if he sells for ₹ 128 more, then he incurs 10% loss. Find the cost price of article.
    (a) ₹ 620
    (b) ₹ 640
    (c) ₹ 680
    (d) ₹ 720

17. A shopkeeper sells an article for ₹ 60 at a profit of 20%. At what price should he sell it to gain 30%?
    (a) ₹ 63
    (b) ₹ 65
    (c) ₹ 68
    (d) ₹ 70

18. By selling an item at three-fourth of actual selling price, a trader incurs a loss of 10%. What will be the profit percent, if the trader sells the item at actual selling price?
    (a) 10%
    (b) 20%
    (c) 15%
    (d) 25%

19. A sells B a diamond at a profit of 30%. B sells it to C at a profit of 20%. What profit did A earn if C paid ₹ 1040 for the diamond?
    (a) ₹ 410
    (b) ₹ 200
    (c) ₹ 400
    (d) ₹ 140

20. The cost price of 11 articles is equal to selling price of 10 articles. What is the profit/loss percentage?
    (a) 10% Profit
    (b) 10% Loss
    (c) 11.11% Profit
    (d) 11.11% Loss

21. If the selling price of 20 articles is equal to the cost price of 16 articles, then the loss or gain percent is:
    (a) 20% gain
    (b) 25% gain
    (c) 20% loss
    (d) 25% loss

22. A trader buys some apples at a price of 10 apples for ₹ 8 and sold them at a price of 8 apples for ₹ 10. Find his profit or loss percent.
    (a) 45.5% loss
    (b) 56.25% loss
    (c) 45.5% profit
    (d) 56.25% profit

23. By selling 80 apples a man gains the selling price of 20 apples. Find the gain percentage.
    (a) 20%
    (b) 25%
    (c) $33\frac{1}{3}\%$
    (d) 40%

24. By selling 80 apples a man gains the cost price of 20 apples. Find the gain percentage.
    (a) 20%
    (b) 25%
    (c) $33\frac{1}{3}\%$
    (d) $66\frac{1}{3}\%$

25. The cost price of 20 oranges is same as selling price of 'n' oranges. If the profit is 25% then the value of n is:
    (a) 16
    (b) 18
    (c) 24
    (d) 25

26. The difference between the cost price and selling price of the article is ₹ 160. If the profit is 20%, the selling price is:
    (a) ₹ 640 (b) ₹ 800
    (c) ₹ 840 (d) ₹ 960

27. A trader sell the sugar to the customer at the cost price, but cheats him by using faulty weight, thus giving 800 gram sugar to customer instead of 1000 gram. Find the profit percent of trader.
    (a) 20% (b) 25%
    (c) 33% (d) 10%

28. By selling 25 bags, a shopkeeper gained an amount equal to selling price of 5 bags. Find the profit percent.
    (a) $16\frac{2}{3}\%$ (b) 20%
    (c) 25% (d) 30%

29. By selling 20 meters of cloth, a shopkeeper earns a profit equal to cost price of 5 meters of cloth. Find his profit percent.
    (a) 25% (b) 33.33%
    (c) 20% (d) 12.5%

30. A milk vendor sell the milk at the cost price but still earns a profit of 25% by mixing water in it. Find the percentage of water in the mixture.
    (a) $33\frac{1}{3}\%$ (b) 25%
    (c) 20% (d) 15%

31. A milk vendor bought 20 liters of milk at ₹ 15 per liter and mixes water to it such that the ratio of milk and water is 5:1. He sold the mixture at ₹ 20 per liter then how much percent of profit he makes?
    (a) 11.11% (b) 20%
    (c) 33.33% (d) 60%

32. A shopkeeper marks a product 30% over the cost price and then gives some discount. If he makes a profit of 4%, what is the percentage discount that he has offered on the marked price?
    (a) 20% (b) 10%
    (c) 16% (d) 26%

33. A shopkeeper marks cost of a machine 30% above the cost price and then gives a discount of 20%. If the profit of ₹ 12000 is made, find the selling price of machine.
    (a) ₹ 312000 (b) ₹ 300000
    (c) ₹ 212000 (d) ₹ 330000

34. A trader sells two articles at the same price but earns 12% profit on one article and incurs 12% loss on the other article. What is his overall profit or loss percentage?
    (a) 12% profit (b) 1.44% profit
    (c) 1.44% loss (d) No profit and no loss

35. A trader allows a discount of 10% on his articles but wants to make a profit of 8%. By how much percent above the cost price he should mark the article?
    (a) 8%   (b) 10%
    (c) 12%   (d) 20%

36. A retailer gets a discount of 20% from the wholesaler on the marked price and he offers a discount of 10% to the customer on the same marked price. Find the percentage of profit the retailer makes.
    (a) 10%   (b) 11.11%
    (c) 12.5%   (d) 15%

37. By selling an article at 80% of its marked price, a merchant makes a loss of 12%. What will be the percentage of profit or loss made by the merchant if he sells the article at 90% of its marked price?
    (a) 1% profit   (b) 1% loss
    (c) 2% loss   (d) No profit and no loss

38. A merchant who marked his goods 50% above the cost price, decided to offer a discount of 20%. What is the percentage profit that the merchant will make after offering the discount?
    (a) 20%   (b) 25%
    (c) 30%   (d) 40%

39. What is the maximum percentage discount that a merchant can offer on her marked price so that he ends up selling at no profit or loss, if he had initially marked his goods up by 50%?
    (a) $33\frac{1}{3}\%$ (b) 40%
    (c) 50%   (d) $66\frac{2}{3}\%$

40. A dealer sold a computer at a loss of 10%. Had he sold it for ₹ 3200 more, he would have earned a profit of 10%. Find the cost price of computer.
    (a) ₹ 16000   (b) ₹ 18000
    (c) ₹ 20000   (d) ₹ 28800

41. An article was sold at a price after giving two successive discounts of 50% and 20%. If the selling price of article was ₹ 64, then what was the marked price of article?
    (a) ₹ 120   (b) ₹ 160
    (c) ₹ 180   (d) ₹ 200

42. If after giving a discount of 20%, a profit of 20% was made on an article, then by what percent was the price marked up?
    (a) 40%   (b) 50%
    (c) 60%   (d) 80%

43. An article was marked up by 40% and after that a discount of 5% is given on it. If the article was sold at ₹ 798, the how much profit was earned by selling it?
    (a) ₹ 133   (b) ₹ 156
    (c) ₹ 198   (d) ₹ 243

44. A shopkeeper purchased certain number of eggs in two different lots. In the first lot he purchased 3 eggs for ₹ 1, and in second lot he purchased same number of eggs but at the rate of 2 eggs for ₹ 1. At what price should he sell each dozen of eggs to make a profit of 20%?
    (a) ₹ 2.20
    (b) ₹ 4.40
    (c) ₹ 5
    (d) ₹ 6

45. A shopkeeper marks an article 50% above the cost price. He sells the article by offering a discount of 16%. Find his profit percentage.
    (a) 26%
    (b) 30%
    (c) 34%
    (d) 36%

46. A dishonest dealer professes to sell his goods at cost price, but uses 900 grams instead of 1 kg of weight. Find his gain percentage.
    (a) 9.09%
    (b) 10%
    (c) 11.11%
    (d) 12.5%

47. A merchant purchased 25 kg of rice at ₹ 16 per kg and mixed it with another 15 kg of rice costing ₹ 10 per kg. At what rate per kg he should sell the mixture to gain 20%?
    (a) ₹ 12
    (b) ₹ 13.20
    (c) ₹ 14.50
    (d) ₹ 15

48. A fruit vendor purchased some oranges, out of which one-third was spoiled during transportation. Out of the remaining oranges half of them were sold at a profit of 20% and another half at a loss of 20%. Find the overall loss percentage.
    (a) 20%
    (b) $33\frac{1}{3}\%$
    (c) 30%
    (d) $66\frac{2}{3}\%$

49. A man brought 100 watermelons at a certain price, with the intension of selling each at a profit of 20%. But 20 watermelons got spoiled during transportation. If he sold remaining at the intended price, what was his profit or loss percentage?
    (a) 4% loss
    (b) 4% profit
    (c) 2% loss
    (d) 2% profit

50. Karan purchased some calculators. He sold one-third of them at 20% loss. Find the profit percentage at which rest of the calculators must be sold to realize an overall profit of 20%.
    (a) 30%
    (b) 40%
    (c) 50%
    (d) $66\frac{2}{3}\%$

51. A bakery owner use to mark the cost of cake ₹ 25 more than the cost of making. If the cost of making the cake is reduced by ₹ 25, accordingly he offered a discount of 25% on the marked price of cake. If he still makes a profit of 25%, what was his initial cost price?
    (a) ₹ 50
    (b) ₹ 75
    (c) ₹ 100
    (d) ₹ 125

52. A computer dealer marked the price of laptop 35% above the cost price. What should be the discount percentage, so that he makes a profit of 20%?
    (a) 10%
    (b) 11.11%
    (c) 15%
    (d) $16\frac{2}{3}\%$

53. A man gets back the amount he invested in buying 100 laptops by selling 80 of them. What is his profit percentage?
    (a) 20%
    (b) 25%
    (c) $33\frac{1}{3}\%$
    (d) 40%

54. If the discount and profit percentage are both 20%, then by what percent is the marked price above the cost price?
    (a) 20%
    (b) 40%
    (c) 50%
    (d) 60%

55. A trader buys an article 10% less than its value and sells it for 10% more than its value. His gain or loss percent is:
    (a) 20% profit
    (b) More than 20% profit
    (c) Less than 20% profit
    (d) No profit and No loss

56. A merchant sells two-third of the wheat stock at profit of 5% and the remaining wheat stock at a loss of 3%. If the total profit was ₹ 4900, then the value of the stock was:
    (a) ₹ 15000
    (b) ₹ 98000
    (c) ₹ 156000
    (d) ₹ 210000

57. By selling an air-conditioner at the marked price of ₹ 21000, a dealer gains 20%. During the off-season, the dealer offers a discount of 10% on the marked price. His gain percent during off-season is:
    (a) 6%
    (b) 8%
    (c) 10%
    (d) 12%

58. Even after reducing the marked price of a pen-drive by ₹ 50, a shopkeeper makes a profit of 15%. If the cost price of pen-drive is ₹ 500, what percentage of profit he can make if he had sold it at marked price?
    (a) 20%
    (b) 25%
    (c) 30%
    (d) 40%

59. Ashish buys an article at a discount of 20%. At what percentage above the cost price should he sell it to make a profit of 20% over the original marked price?
    (a) 20%
    (b) 25%
    (c) 40%
    (d) 50%

60. Ratan got 25% concession on the labeled price of a music system. He sold it for ₹ 4050 with 20% profit on the price he brought. What is the labeled price?
    (a) ₹ 4500
    (b) ₹ 4750
    (c) ₹ 5000
    (d) ₹ 5250

KEYS

1. (c)	2. (b)	3. (d)	4. (b)	5. (b)	6. (d)	7. (a)	8. (d)
9. (b)	10. (d)	11. (b)	12. (a)	13. (d)	14. (d)	15. (a)	16. (b)
17. (b)	18. (b)	19. (b)	20. (a)	21. (c)	22. (d)	23. (c)	24. (b)
25. (a)	26. (b)	27. (b)	28. (c)	29. (a)	30. (c)	31. (d)	32. (a)
33. (a)	34. (c)	35. (d)	36. (c)	37. (b)	38. (a)	39. (d)	40. (a)
41. (b)	42. (b)	43. (c)	44. (d)	45. (a)	46. (c)	47. (b)	48. (b)
49. (a)	50. (b)	51. (c)	52. (b)	53. (b)	54. (c)	55. (b)	56. (d)
57. (b)	58. (b)	59. (d)	60. (a)				

SOLUTIONS

Solution 1

$CP = ₹\ 200$

If profit expected is 22%, then:

$SP = 122\%$ of CP

$SP = \dfrac{122}{100} \times 200 = ₹\ 244.$

Choice (c)

Solution 2

$SP = ₹\ 300$

If profit made is 20%, then:

$SP = 120\%$ of CP

$SP = \dfrac{120}{100} \times CP$

$300 = \dfrac{120}{100} \times CP$

$\therefore \quad CP = \dfrac{300 \times 100}{120} = ₹\ 250.$

Choice (b)

Solution 3

$CP = 60\%$ of SP

$CP = \dfrac{60}{100} \times SP$

$$\therefore \quad \frac{CP}{SP} = \frac{3}{5}$$

Profit % = $\frac{SP-CP}{CP} \times 100 = \frac{5-3}{3} \times 100 = 66\frac{2}{3}\%$.

Choice (d)

Solution 4

$SP = ₹ 100$

Profit = ₹ 20

$\therefore \quad CP = 100 - 20 = ₹ 80$

Profit % = $\frac{SP-CP}{CP} \times 100 = \frac{20}{80} \times 100 = 25\%$.

Choice (b)

Solution 5

$SP = ₹ 150$

Loss = ₹ 50

$\therefore \quad CP = 150 + 50 = ₹ 200$

Loss % = $\frac{Loss}{CP} \times 100 = \frac{50}{200} \times 100 = 25\%$.

Choice (b)

Solution 6

$\frac{CP}{SP} = \frac{5}{4}$

As $CP > SP$, there will be loss.

Loss % = $\frac{Loss}{CP} \times 100 = \frac{1}{5} \times 100 = 20\%$.

Choice (d)

Solution 7

Total $CP = 5500 + 1700 = ₹ 7200$

$SP = ₹ 7560$

Profit % = $\frac{SP-CP}{CP} \times 100$

$= \frac{7560-7200}{7200} \times 100 = 5\%$.

Choice (a)

Solution 8

Let $CP = ₹\ 100$

As profit made is 20%, therefore $SP = ₹\ 120$

New $SP = 2 \times 120 = ₹\ 240$

Profit % $= \dfrac{SP-CP}{CP} \times 100 = \dfrac{240-100}{100} \times 100 = 140\%$.

Choice (d)

Solution 9

Let $\quad CP = ₹\ 100$

As profit made is 40%, therefore $SP = ₹\ 140$

New $\quad SP = \dfrac{1}{2} \times 140 = ₹\ 70$

Loss % $= \dfrac{CP-SP}{CP} \times 100 = \dfrac{100-70}{100} \times 100 = 30\%$.

Choice (b)

Solution 10

As 20 watermelons are spoiled out of 160, hence we will consider that the trader purchased only 140 watermelons.

CP of 1 watermelon $= \dfrac{2240 + 280}{140} = ₹\ 18$

As expected profit is $33\ \dfrac{1}{3}\%$, therefore:

$$SP = \dfrac{4}{3} \times CP$$

$$SP = \dfrac{4}{3} \times 18$$

SP of 1 watermelon $= ₹\ 24$.

Choice (d)

Solution 11

If he makes a loss of 15% in selling the bicycle, then:

$\quad SP = 85\%$ of CP

$\quad 1275 = \dfrac{85}{100} \times CP$

$\therefore \quad CP = ₹\ 1500$

To make a profit of 15%

$SP = 115\%$ of CP

$\therefore \quad SP = \dfrac{115}{100} \times 1500 = ₹\,1725.$

Choice (b)

Solution 12

Buy ⇒ 9 pencils for ₹ 10 ⇒ 18 pencils for ₹ 20
Sell ⇒ 6 pencils for ₹ 7 ⇒ 18 pencils for ₹ 21

As 18 pencils are purchased for ₹ 20 but sold for ₹ 21, hence he will make profit.

Profit % $= \dfrac{SP - CP}{CP} \times 100 = \dfrac{21 - 20}{20} \times 100 = 5\%$

Choice (a)

Solution 13

Buy ⇒ 6 lemons for ₹ 5 ⇒ 30 lemons for ₹ 25
Sell ⇒ 5 lemons for ₹ 6 ⇒ 30 lemons for ₹ 36

As 30 lemons are purchased for ₹ 25 but sold for ₹ 36, hence he will make profit.

Profit % $= \dfrac{SP - CP}{CP} \times 100$

$= \dfrac{36 - 25}{25} \times 100 = 44\%.$

Choice (d)

Solution 14

$\text{Loss} = CP - SP$
$4.5 SP = 18 CP - 18 SP$
$4.5 SP = 360 - 18 SP$
$22.5 SP = 360$
$\therefore \quad SP = ₹\,16.$

Choice (d)

Solution 15

Sold at 10% loss ⇒ $\dfrac{90}{100} \times CP$

Sold at 7% profit ⇒ $\dfrac{107}{100} \times CP$

(Sold at 10% loss) + ₹ 85 = (Sold at 7% profit)

Profit and Loss

$$\frac{90}{100} \times CP + 85 = \frac{107}{100} \times CP$$

$$\frac{17}{100} \times CP = 85$$

∴ $CP = ₹ 500.$

Choice (a)

Solution 16

Sold at 30% loss $\Rightarrow \frac{70}{100} \times CP$

Sold at 10% loss $\Rightarrow \frac{90}{100} \times CP$

(Sold at 30% loss) + ₹ 128 = (Sold at 10% loss)

$$\frac{70}{100} \times CP + 128 = \frac{90}{100} \times CP$$

$$\frac{20}{100} \times CP = 128$$

∴ $CP = ₹ 640.$

Choice (b)

Solution 17

If the shopkeeper makes a profit of 20%, then:

$SP = 120\%$ of CP

$SP = \frac{120}{100} \times CP$

$60 = \frac{120}{100} \times CP$

∴ $CP = ₹ 50$

To gain 30%, $SP = 130\%$ of CP

$SP = \frac{130}{100} \times CP = \frac{130}{100} \times 50 = ₹ 65.$

Choice (b)

Solution 18

$\frac{3}{4} \times SP = 10\%$ loss

$\frac{3}{4} \times SP = \frac{90}{100} \times CP$

∴ $\frac{SP}{CP} = \frac{6}{5}$

Profit % $= \dfrac{SP-CP}{CP} \times 100$

$= \dfrac{6-5}{5} \times 100 = 20\%.$

Choice (b)

Solution 19

Let the CP of A = ₹ 100
SP of A = ₹ 130 (∵ A sold to B at 30% profit)
CP of B = ₹ 130
SP of B = ₹ 156 (∵ B sold to C at 20% profit)
CP of C = ₹ 156
In actual C paid a cost price of ₹ 1040, the profit earned by A can be found as:
₹ 156 → ₹ 1040
₹ 30 → ₹ x
∴ $x = \dfrac{1040 \times 30}{156} = ₹ 200.$

Choice (b)

Solution 20

Let CP of 1 article = ₹ 1
∴ CP of 10 articles = ₹ 10
and SP of 10 articles = CP of 11 articles
= ₹ 11.

If 10 articles are purchased for ₹ 10 but sold for ₹ 11, then there will be profit.
Profit % $= \dfrac{SP-CP}{CP} \times 100$

$= \dfrac{11-10}{10} \times 100 = 10\%.$

Choice (a)

Solution 21

Let CP of 1 article = ₹ 1
∴ CP of 20 articles = ₹ 20
and SP of 20 articles = CP of 16 articles = ₹ 16.

If 20 articles are purchased for ₹ 20 but sold for ₹ 16, then there will be loss.

Loss% $= \dfrac{CP-SP}{CP} \times 100 = \dfrac{20-16}{20} \times 100 = 20\%.$

Choice (c)

Solution 22

Buy ⇒ 10 apples for ₹ 8 ⇒ 40 apples for ₹ 32
Sell ⇒ 8 apples for ₹ 10 ⇒ 40 apples for ₹ 50
As 40 apples are purchased for ₹ 32 but sold for ₹ 50, hence he will make profit.

Profit % $= \dfrac{SP-CP}{CP} \times 100$

$= \dfrac{50-32}{32} \times 100$

$= 56.25\%$.

Choice (d)

Solution 23

Gain $= SP - CP$
$20\ SP = 80\ SP - 80\ CP$
$80\ CP = 60\ SP$
$\dfrac{CP}{SP} = \dfrac{3}{4}$

Gain % $= \dfrac{SP-CP}{CP} \times 100$

$= \dfrac{4-3}{3} \times 100$

$= 33\tfrac{1}{3}\%$.

Choice (c)

Solution 24

Gain $= SP - CP$
$20CP = 80\ SP - 80\ CP$
$100\ CP = 80\ SP$
$\dfrac{CP}{SP} = \dfrac{4}{5}$

Gain % $= \dfrac{SP-CP}{CP} \times 100 = \dfrac{5-4}{4} \times 100 = 25\%$.

Choice (b)

Solution 25

If the cost price of 20 oranges is same as selling price of 'n' oranges and if there is a profit, then:
$n < 20$

Gain % $= \dfrac{SP-CP}{CP} \times 100$

$$\frac{20-n}{n} \times 100 = 25$$

$$20 - n = \frac{n}{4}$$

$$\therefore \quad n = 16.$$

Choice (a)

Solution 26

$$SP - CP = ₹\ 160$$

$$\text{Profit \%} = \frac{SP - CP}{CP} \times 100$$

$$20 = \frac{160}{CP} \times 100$$

$$\therefore \quad CP = \frac{160}{20} \times 100 = ₹\ 800.$$

Choice (b)

Solution 27

Let 1 gram cost ₹ 1

CP of 800 gram = ₹ 800

SP of 800 gram = ₹ 1000 (∵ Instead of 1000 gram, he gives only 800 gram to customer)

$$\text{Profit \%} = \frac{SP - CP}{CP} \times 100$$

$$= \frac{1000 - 800}{800} \times 100$$

$$= 25\%.$$

Choice (b)

Solution 28

$$\text{Gain} = SP - CP$$

$$5\ SP = 25\ SP - 25\ CP$$

$$25\ CP = 20\ SP$$

$$\frac{CP}{SP} = \frac{4}{5}$$

$$\text{Profit \%} = \frac{SP - CP}{CP} \times 100$$

$$= \frac{5-4}{4} \times 100 = 25\%.$$

Choice (c)

Solution 29

Profit = $SP - CP$
$5\ CP = 20\ SP - 20\ CP$
$25\ CP = 20\ SP$
$\dfrac{CP}{SP} = \dfrac{4}{5}$

Profit % $= \dfrac{SP - CP}{CP} \times 100$

$= \dfrac{5-4}{4} \times 100$

$= 25\%.$

Choice (a)

Solution 30

Let 100 liters of pure milk cost ₹ 100. By mixing 25 liters of water in it, the mixture can be sold for ₹ 125, thus earning a profit of 25%.

∴ Percentage of water in mixture = $\dfrac{25}{125} \times 100 = 20\%.$

Choice (c)

Solution 31

Cost price of 20 liters of pure milk = 20×15 = ₹ 300

Ratio of milk and water = $5x : x$

If $5x = 20$ liters

∴ $x = 4$ liters

So, water added in pure milk is 4 liters and the mixture formed will be 24 liters.

Selling price of 24 liters of mixtures = 24×20 = ₹ 480

Profit % $= \dfrac{SP - CP}{CP} \times 100$

$= \dfrac{480 - 300}{300} \times 100 = 60\%.$

Choice (d)

Solution 32

Let the CP = ₹ 100

So, MP = ₹ 130 (∵ Marked price is 30% above cost price)

If he makes a profit of 4%, it means ₹ 100 article he is selling for ₹ 104, therefore he is offering a discount of ₹ 26.

Discount % = $\dfrac{\text{Discount}}{\text{Marked Price}} \times 100$

$= \dfrac{26}{130} \times 100 = 20\%.$

Choice (a)

Solution 33

Let the *CP* of machine = ₹ 100

So, the *MP* of machine = ₹ 130 (∵ Marked price is 30% above cost price)

SP of machine = 80% of MP (∵ Discount of 20% is offered)

$= \dfrac{80}{100} \times 130 = 104.$

Therefore as per our assumption that *CP* of machine is ₹ 100 then *SP* will be ₹ 104, and hence the profit earned is ₹ 4. In actual the profit earned is ₹ 12000, so the actual selling price of machine can be found as:

$SP = 104 \rightarrow \text{Profit} = ₹ 4$

$SP = x \rightarrow \text{Profit} = ₹ 12000$

∴ $x = \dfrac{12000 \times 104}{4} = ₹ 312000.$

Choice(a)

Solution 34

If two articles are sold at the same price, making *R%* profit one and *R%* loss on other, then in the whole transaction there is always a loss. Percentage loss is calculated as:

Loss % $= \dfrac{R^2}{100} = \dfrac{12^2}{100} = 1.44.$

Choice (c)

Solution 35

Let the *CP* of article = ₹ 100

To make a profit of 8%, *SP* = ₹ 108

Discount % $= \dfrac{\text{Discount}}{\text{Marked Price}} \times 100$

$10 = \dfrac{MP - 108}{MP} \times 100$

∴ $MP = ₹ 120.$

So, the marked price should be 20% above the cost price.

Choice (d)

Solution 36

Let the marked price of article = ₹ 100

CP of retailer = 80% of MP (∵ He gets a discount of 20% on marked price)

$$= \frac{80}{100} \times 100$$
$$= ₹\ 80$$

SP of retailer = 90% of MP (∵ He gives a discount of 10% to the customer)

$$= \frac{90}{100} \times 100$$
$$= ₹\ 90$$

Profit % $= \dfrac{SP - CP}{CP} \times 100$

$$= \frac{90 - 80}{80} \times 100 = 12.5\%.$$

Choice (c)

Solution 37

Let the CP of article = ₹ 100

80% of MP = 12% of Loss

$$\frac{80}{100} \times MP = 88$$

∴ $MP = \dfrac{88 \times 100}{80} = ₹\ 110$

If the article is sold at 90% of marked price, then:

$$SP = 90\% \text{ of } MP$$
$$= \frac{90}{100} \times 110 = ₹\ 99.$$

If the article purchased at ₹ 100 and sold at ₹ 99, then the merchant will make a loss of 1%.

Choice (b)

Solution 38

Let   CP = ₹ 100
So,   MP = ₹ 150 (∵ Marked price is 50% above cost price)
      SP = 80% of MP (∵ He gives a discount of 20% on marked price)

$$= \frac{80}{100} \times 150 = ₹\ 120.$$

If ₹ 100 product is sold finally for ₹ 120, then the merchant will make a profit of 20%.

Choice (a)

Solution 39

Let $CP = ₹\ 100$

So, $MP = ₹\ 150$ (∵ Marked price is 50% above cost price)

To make no profit and no loss, the SP should be equal to CP i.e. ₹ 100. Assuming that the merchant can offer a maximum discount of $D\%$.

$D\%$ of $MP = SP$

$$\frac{D}{100} \times 150 = 100$$

∴ $D = 66\frac{2}{3}\%$.

Choice (d)

Solution 40

Sold at 10% loss $\Rightarrow \frac{90}{100} \times CP$

Sold at 10% profit $\Rightarrow \frac{110}{100} \times CP$

(Sold at 10% loss) + ₹ 3200 = (Sold at 10% profit)

$$\frac{90}{100} \times CP + 3200 = \frac{110}{100} \times CP$$

$$\frac{20}{100} \times CP = 3200$$

∴ $CP = ₹\ 16000$.

Choice (a)

Solution 41

Let the marked price = ₹ 100

SP after two successive discounts of 50% and 20% = $\frac{50}{100} \times \frac{80}{100} \times 100 = ₹\ 40$

₹ 100 → ₹ 40
₹ x → ₹ 64

∴ $x = \frac{64 \times 100}{40} = ₹\ 160$.

Choice (b)

Solution 42

Let the CP of article = ₹ 100

80% of MP = 20% of Profit

$$\frac{80}{100} \times MP = 120$$

∴ $MP = \dfrac{120 \times 100}{80} = ₹\,150$

Hence the article was marked 50% up.

Choice (b)

Solution 43

Let the *CP* of article = ₹ 100
So, the *MP* of article = ₹ 140 (∵ Marked price is 40% above cost price)

∴ $SP = 95\%$ of $MP = \dfrac{95}{100} \times 140 = ₹\,133$

∴ Profit earned = 133 − 100 = ₹ 33.

If the *CP* is assumed as ₹ 100, then the article is finally sold for ₹ 133 thus earning a profit of ₹ 33. In actual if the article is sold for ₹ 798, the profit earned can be found as:

₹ 133 → ₹ 33
₹ 798 → ₹ x

∴ $x = \dfrac{33 \times 798}{133} = ₹\,198$.

Choice (c)

Solution 44

Lot No. 1 ⇒ 3 eggs for ₹ 1 ⇒ 6 eggs for ₹ 2
Lot No. 2 ⇒ 2 eggs for ₹ 1 ⇒ 6 eggs for ₹ 3

∴ Lot No. 1 + Lot No. 2 ⇒ 12 eggs for ₹ 5

To make a profit of 20% on each dozen of eggs:

$SP = \dfrac{120}{100} \times CP = \dfrac{120}{100} \times 5 = ₹\,6.$

Choice (d)

Solution 45

Let $CP = ₹\,100$
So, $MP = ₹\,150$ (∵ Marked price is 50% above cost price)
  $SP = 84\%$ of MP (∵ He gives a discount of 16% on marked price)
    $= \dfrac{84}{100} \times 150 = ₹\,126.$

If ₹ 100 product is sold finally for ₹ 126, then the shopkeeper will make a profit of 26%.

Choice (a)

Solution 46

Let 1 gram cost ₹ 1
CP of 900 gram = ₹ 900
SP of 900 gram = ₹ 1000 (∵ Instead of 1000 gram, he gives only 900 gram to customer)

Profit % $= \dfrac{SP - CP}{CP} \times 100$

$= \dfrac{1000 - 900}{900} \times 100$

$= 11.11\%.$

Choice (c)

Solution 47

Average cost price of mixture $= \dfrac{25(16) + 15(10)}{25 + 15}$

$= ₹\ 11$

To earn a profit of 20%

$SP = 120\%$ of CP

$= \dfrac{120}{100} \times 11$

$= 13.2.$

Choice (b)

Solution 48

Assuming that the fruit vendor purchased 300 oranges for ₹ 300
Oranges Spoiled = 100
Oranges sold at 20% profit = 100
Oranges sold at 20% loss = 100

∴ Earning = (120% of 100) + (80% of 100)

$= \left(\dfrac{120}{100} \times 100\right) + \left(\dfrac{80}{100} \times 100\right)$

$= ₹\ 200.$

If originally he spent ₹ 300 to buy 300 oranges but finally got ₹ 200 on selling 200 oranges hence he will make loss.

Loss % $= \dfrac{CP - SP}{CP} \times 100$

$= \dfrac{300 - 200}{300} \times 100$

$= 33\frac{1}{3}\%.$

Choice (b)

Solution 49

Assuming the CP of each watermelon = ₹ 10
To make a profit of 20%, expected SP = ₹ 12
Total   CP = 100 × 10 = ₹ 1000
Total   SP = 80 × 12 = ₹ 960 (∵ 20 watermelons got spoiled)
As CP > SP, hence he will make a loss.

Loss % $= \dfrac{CP - SP}{CP} \times 100$

$= \dfrac{1000 - 960}{1000} \times 100 = 4\%$.

Choice (a)

Solution 50

Assuming Karan purchased 30 calculators at the rate of ₹ 100 per calculator.
CP of one-third calculators = 10 × 100 = ₹ 1000
CP of two-third calculators = 20 × 100 = ₹ 2000
Total CP = 1000 + 2000 = ₹ 3000
If he wants to make an overall profit of 20%, then:
Total   SP = 120% of Total CP

$= \dfrac{120}{100} \times 3000$

= ₹ 3600

One-third of calculators sold at 20% loss:
SP of one-third calculators = ₹ 800
So, to earn the expected profit, the remaining two-third calculators should be sold for:
SP of two-third calculators = 3600 – 800 = ₹ 2800

∴ Percentage profit on two-third of calculators = $\dfrac{2800 - 2000}{2000} \times 100 = 40\%$.

Choice (b)

Solution 51

Let the initial cost of making or CP_1 of cake = x
So, initial selling price or SP_1 of cake = $x + 25$
New cost of cake or $CP_2 = x - 25$

New selling price or $SP_2 = \dfrac{3}{4}(x + 25)$

As he makes a profit of 25% on new cost price and selling price, then:

$SP_2 = 125\%$ of CP_2

$\frac{3}{4}(x+25) = \frac{5}{4}(x-25)$

$3x + 75 = 5x - 125$

$\therefore \quad x = 100.$

Choice (c)

Solution 52

Let the CP of laptop = ₹ 100
So, the MP of laptop = ₹ 135 (∵ Marked price is 35% more than cost price)
To make a profit of 20%, his SP should be ₹ 120.

Discount % = $\frac{135-120}{135} \times 100 = 11.11\%.$

Choice (b)

Solution 53

Let CP of 100 laptops = ₹ 100
So, CP of 80 laptops = ₹ 80
∴ SP of 80 laptops = ₹ 100 (∵ By selling 80, he gets the price of 100 laptops)

If 80 laptops are purchased for ₹ 80 but sold for ₹ 100, then:

Profit % $= \frac{SP - CP}{CP} \times 100$

$= \frac{100-80}{80} \times 100 = 25\%.$

Choice (b)

Solution 54

Let the CP = ₹ 100
So, the SP = ₹ 120 (∵ Profit is 20%)

Discount % = $\frac{\text{Marked Price} - \text{Selling price}}{\text{Marked Price}} \times 100$

$20 = \frac{MP - 120}{MP} \times 100$

$\frac{MP}{5} = MP - 120$

$\therefore \quad MP = ₹ 150.$

Hence the marked price is 50% above the cost price.

Choice (c)

Solution 55

Let the value of article = ₹ 100
CP of trader = ₹ 90 (∵ He buys at 10% less)
SP of trader = ₹ 110 (∵ He sells at 10% more)

Profit % $= \dfrac{SP - CP}{CP} \times 100$

$= \dfrac{110 - 90}{90} \times 100$

$= 22.22\%.$

Choice (b)

Solution 56

Let the value of wheat stock = ₹ x

$\dfrac{2}{3}x$ is sold at a profit of 5% $\Rightarrow$ $\dfrac{5}{100}\left(\dfrac{2}{3}x\right)$

$\dfrac{1}{3}x$ is sold at a loss of 3% $\Rightarrow$ $\dfrac{3}{100}\left(\dfrac{1}{3}x\right)$

Profit on $\dfrac{2}{3}x$ stock – Loss on $\dfrac{1}{3}x$ stock = Overall Profit

$$\dfrac{5}{100}\left(\dfrac{2}{3}x\right) - \dfrac{3}{100}\left(\dfrac{1}{3}x\right) = 4900$$

$$\dfrac{10x}{300} - \dfrac{3x}{300} = 4900$$

∴ $\quad x = \dfrac{4900 \times 300}{7}$

$= ₹\ 210000.$

Choice (d)

Solution 57

Let the CP = ₹ 100
So, the MP = ₹ 120 (∵ His profit is 20% on marked price)

If he offers a discount of 10% during off-season, then:

$SP = 90\%$ of MP

$= \dfrac{90}{100} \times 120$

$= ₹\ 108.$

So, if he offers a discount of 10% during off season, still he makes a profit of 8%.

Choice (b)

Solution 58

CP of pen-drive = ₹ 500
SP of pen-drive = MP − 50

If the pen-drive is sold at ₹ 50 less than MP, still he makes 15% profit.

∴ SP = 115% of CP

$MP - 50 = \frac{115}{100} \times 500$

∴ MP = ₹ 625

If he sells at actual marked price, then:

Profit % $= \frac{625 - 500}{500} \times 100$

$= 25\%.$

Choice (b)

Solution 59

Let the original MP = ₹ 100
CP paid by Ashish = ₹ 80 (∵ He purchased at 20% discount)
SP taken by Ashish = ₹ 120 (∵ He want to earn 20% profit over MP)

Required percentage $= \frac{120 - 80}{80} \times 100$

$= 50\%.$

Choice (d)

Solution 60

Assuming the labeled price of music system = ₹ 100
CP paid by Ratan = ₹ 75 (∵ He purchased at 25% discount)
SP taken by Ratan = $\frac{120}{100} \times 75 = ₹ 90$ (∵ He has taken 20% profit on CP)

If the labeled price is assumed as ₹ 100, the music system is finally sold for ₹ 90. In actual if the music system is sold for ₹ 4050, then its actual labeled price can be found as:

100 → 90
 x → 4050

∴ $x = \frac{4050 \times 100}{90}$

$= ₹ 4500.$

Choice (a)

9

Partnership

When two or more people come together to do business by pooling their resources, then they are called partners, and the deal is known as partnership. The money put in by each of the partners is called his 'Investment' or 'Capital'.

TYPES OF PARTNERSHIP

1. *Simple Partnership*—In case of simple partnership the duration of investment is same. So the amounts of profit are divided according to the ratio among their capital respectively. Suppose, if three partners invested their money in the ratio of $A : B : C$, then the profit will be divided between them in the ratio of $A : B : C$.
2. *Compound Partnership*—In case of compound partnership the duration of investment is not constant. So the amount of profit is divided according to the product ratio among their capital and duration of investment respectively. Suppose, if three partners invested their money in the ratio of $A : B : C$, and duration of investment is $X : Y : Z$, then the profit will be divided in the ratio $AX : BY : CZ$ respectively.

TYPES OF PARTNERS

1. *Working Partners*—The partner who is involved in day to day activities of business or who works in the business or manages the business is known as a working partner. From the profit gained in the business, at first the remuneration (or salary) of working partner is paid, and then the remaining profit is distributed between all the partners.
2. *Sleeping Partners*—The partner who dose not work in the business, but invested his money in that business is known as sleeping partner. The sleeping partner gets his/her share after distributing the remuneration to the working partner from the total profit.

SOLVED EXAMPLES

Example 1

Three partners P, Q and R start a business by investing ₹ 50000, ₹ 70000 and ₹ 80000 respectively. Out of the total annual profit of ₹ 440000 how much share the person Q should get?

Solution

Ratio of their profit share = $P : Q : R = 5 : 7 : 8$

As the profit is divided in total of 20 parts i.e., 5 + 7 + 8

So, share of $Q = \frac{7}{20} \times 440000 = ₹ 154000$.

Example 2

Ajay started a business with ₹ 40000. Three months later, Vijay joined him with ₹ 50000. Find the ratio in which they should share the annual profit.

Solution

Ratio of profits of Ajay and Vijay = The ratio of the product of their investments and period of investment.

Ratio of profit share among Ajay and Vijay = $(40000 \times 12) : (50000 \times 9) = 16 : 15$.

Example 3

Sam and Robert started a business by investing 3 lakh and 4 lakh respectively. Sam being the working partner receives a salary of ₹ 3000 per month. If the annual profit made is ₹ 106000, find the total earning of Sam in the year.

Solution

Ratio of profit share of Sam and Robert = 3 : 4
Annual salary paid to Sam = $3000 \times 12 = 36000$
Remaining profit after paying salary to Sam = $106000 - 36000 = 70000$
Profit share of Sam = $\frac{3}{7} \times 70000 = 30000$
Total earning of Sam at the end of year = Salary + Profit share = $36000 + 30000 = ₹ 66000$.

Example 4

Amar started a business with ₹ 72000. After few months Bharat joins him with ₹ 96000. After how many months did Bharat joins Amar if profits are divided equally?

Solution

Suppose Bharat joins after x months, hence his money was invested for $(12 - x)$ months.

As the profit is divided equally:
$$72000 \times 12 = 96000 \times (12 - x)$$
$$72 = 8 \times (12 - x)$$
$$9 = 12 - x$$
$$x = 3$$

So, Bharat joined after 3 months.

Example 5

P started a business with ₹ 20000. After three months Q joined him with ₹ 40000. After some more months R joined them with ₹ 100000. Q received 18000 out of the total annual profit of ₹ 55000. How many months after P started the business did R joins?

Solution

Suppose R joins after x months, hence his money was invested for $(12 - x)$ months.

Ratio of profit share among P, Q and $R = (20000 \times 12) : (40000 \times 9) : (100000 \times 12 - x)$
$= 12 : 18 : 5 (12 - x)$

As Q received his share of ₹ 18000 out of ₹ 55000

$$\frac{18}{12 + 18 + 5(12 - x)} = \frac{18000}{55000}$$

$$\frac{18}{90 - 5x} = \frac{18}{55}$$

$$90 - 5x = 55$$

So, $x = 7$

R joins P in the business after 7 months.

EXERCISE

1. Three partners A, B and C invests ₹ 12000, ₹ 15000 and ₹ 18000 respectively. Find the share of A in an annual profit of ₹ 45000.
   (a) ₹ 6000
   (b) ₹ 8000
   (c) ₹ 12000
   (d) ₹ 15000

2. Ram and Shyam are partners in a business. Ram invests ₹ 35000 for 8 months and Shyam invests ₹ 42000 for 10 months. Out of a profit of ₹ 31570 Ram's share is:
   (a) ₹ 9475
   (b) ₹ 12628
   (c) ₹ 18040
   (d) ₹ 18942

3. Raj started a business with ₹ 20000. After 4 months, Sanjay joined him with ₹ 30000. At the beginning of fifth month, Raj added ₹ 10000. Find the ratio in which annual profit will be shared.
   (a) 3 : 4
   (b) 4 : 3
   (c) 3 : 5
   (d) 5 : 3

4. Karan started a business investing ₹ 9000. After five months, Sameer joined with a capital of ₹ 8000. If at the end of the year, they earn a profit of ₹ 6970, then what will be the share of Sameer in the profit?
   (a) ₹ 2380
   (b) ₹ 3690
   (c) ₹ 3860
   (d) ₹ 4270

5. Sanjay started a small scale business by investing ₹ 50000. After six months, Naresh joined him with a capital of ₹ 80000. After 3 years, they earned a profit of ₹ 24500. What will be Sanjay's share in the profit?

(a) ₹ 10150 (b) ₹ 10250
(c) ₹ 10500 (d) ₹ 12500

6. A and B started a partnership business investing some amount in the ratio of 3 : 5. C joined them after six months with an amount equal to that of B. In what proportion should the profit at the end of one year be distributed amount A, B and C?
   (a) 6 : 10 : 5 (b) 3 : 5 : 5
   (c) 3 : 5 : 2 (d) None of these

7. A, B and C start a business with investment of ₹ 36000, ₹ 40000 and ₹ 24000 respectively. After five months, A withdraws his investment and after five more months, C also withdraws his investment. What is the share of C in the total profit of ₹ 45000 at the end of year?
   (a) ₹ 10000 (b) ₹ 12000
   (c) ₹ 14000 (d) ₹ 15000

8. P and Q entered into partnership with capitals in the ratio 3 : 5. After 3 months, P withdrew one-third of his capital and Q withdrew one-fifth of his capital. The gain at the end of year was ₹ 156000. P's share in this profit is:
   (a) ₹ 54000 (b) ₹ 56000
   (c) ₹ 60000 (d) ₹ 64000

9. Kapil and Kailash started a business by making an investment of ₹ 9000 and ₹ 12000. After three months Karan joined them with an investment of ₹ 15000. In the business they made a half yearly profit of ₹ 5700. Find Karan's Share.
   (a) ₹ 2900 (b) ₹ 1900
   (c) ₹ 1700 (d) ₹ 1500

10. A started a business with ₹ 21000 and is joined afterwards by B with ₹ 36000. After how many months did B join if the profits at the end of the year are divided equally?
    (a) 7 (b) 5
    (c) 4 (d) 3

11. A starts a business with ₹ 3500 and after 5 months, B joins with A as his partner. After a year, the profit is divided in the ratio 2 : 3. What is B's contribution in the capital?
    (a) ₹ 4500 (b) ₹ 6000
    (c) ₹ 7500 (d) ₹ 9000

12. A started a business with ₹ 75000. He was joined afterwards by B with ₹ 60000. After how many months did B join, if the profits at the end of the year are divided between A and B in the ratio of 3 : 1?
    (a) 7 (b) 5
    (c) 4 (d) 3

13. P and Q started a business in partnership investing ₹ 20000 and ₹ 15000 respectively. After six months, R joined them with ₹ 20000. What will be Q's share in total profit of ₹ 75,000 earned at the end of 2 years from the starting of the business?
    (a) ₹ 45000 (b) ₹ 37500
    (c) ₹ 25000 (d) ₹ 22500

14. Ajay and Bharat entered in to a partnership investing ₹ 16000 and ₹ 12000 respectively. After three months Ajay withdraws ₹ 5000, while Bharat invested ₹ 5000 more, and a third partner Chetan joins them with a capital of ₹ 20000. By what percent the profit share of Bharat exceeds the profit share of Chetan?
    (a) 3%
    (b) 5%
    (c) 7 %
    (d) 8 %

15. P, Q, and R started a business with their investments in the ratio 1 : 3 : 5. After 4 months, P invested the same amount as before and Q as well as R withdrew half of their investments. The ratio of their profits at the end of the year is:
    (a) 5 : 6 : 10
    (b) 6 : 5 : 10
    (c) 10: 5 : 6
    (d) 4 : 3 : 5

16. A, B and C start a business. Twice of A's capital is equal to thrice of B's capital which is equal to four times C's capital. Find the share of C in the annual profit of ₹ 39000.
    (a) ₹ 6000
    (b) ₹ 9000
    (c) ₹ 12000
    (d) ₹ 15000

17. P, Q and R start a business together. P invests three times as Q invests, and Q invests two-third of what R invests. Out of the total profit of ₹ 9900, Q's share is:
    (a) ₹ 1800
    (b) ₹ 2200
    (c) ₹ 3300
    (d) ₹ 3500

18. A, B and C started their business by investing the capital in the ratio of $2/5 : 1/3 : 7/10$ respectively. After four months B invested double the capital, what he invested earlier. Find the share of B in the annual profit of ₹ 67600.
    (a) ₹ 16000
    (b) ₹ 22400
    (c) ₹ 28000
    (d) ₹ 32800

19. Three milkmen A, B, and C rented a grazing land. A grazed his 45 cows for 12 days, B grazed his 36 cows for 15 days and C grazed his 60 cows for 10 days. If B's share of rent was ₹ 540, what is the total rent?
    (a) ₹ 1680
    (b) ₹ 1560
    (c) ₹ 1440
    (d) ₹ 1420

20. A and B enters into a partnership with their investments in the ratio of 7 : 9. At the end of 8 months, A withdraws his capital. If they receive the profits in the ratio of 8 : 9, then for how many months B's capital was used?
    (a) 6
    (b) 7
    (c) 8
    (d) 9

21. Sai and Harsha invested ₹ x and ₹ y in a business for a period of 9 months and 12 months respectively. If the profits earning by Sai and Harsha at the end of year are equal, then x : y is:
    (a) 4 : 3
    (b) 3 : 4
    (c) 3 : 5
    (d) 2 : 3

22. P and Q enter into a partnership with investments of ₹ 54000 and ₹ 81000 respectively. P stayed in the entire year. If at the end of year the profit was distributed equally, then Q's money was invested for how many months?

(a) 6 (b) 8
(c) 9 (d) 10

23. A starts a business with an investment of ₹ 7200. After three months, B invests ₹ 9600 and joins the business. After few more months, C invests ₹ 10800 and joins the business. The ratio of profit at the end of year is 4 : 4 : 3. How many months after B joined did C join the business?
    (a) 2 (b) 3
    (c) 4 (d) 6

24. The ratio of profits of A, B and C is 4 : 5 : 6 and ratio of their time periods is 2 : 3 : 9, how much more did A invest than B in the business in terms of percentage?
    (a) 16.66 % (b) 20 %
    (c) 25 % (d) None of these

25. Ramesh, Suresh and Bhavesh invest ₹ 64000, ₹ 32000 and ₹ 48000 respectively in a business. Suresh stayed in the business for a period of 4 months more than that of Bhavesh. Bhavesh stayed for a period of four months more than Ramesh. For how many months did the business run if the ratio of shares of profit at the end of business is 2 : 3 : 3?
    (a) 14 (b) 10
    (c) 18 (d) 12

26. P, Q and R enter into a partnership with the ratio of capitals as 3 : 5 : 8. If at the end of year the ratio of their profits is 6 : 15 : 4, find the ratio of period of their investments.
    (a) 4 : 6 : 1 (b) 4 : 9 : 3
    (c) 3 : 6 : 2 (d) 2 : 9 : 1

27. John and Mack started a business by investing ₹ 70000 and ₹ 80000 respectively. As John is a working partner it wad decided that he will receive 10% of the total profit as his commission and the remaining profit will be shared on the ratio of their capital. If the annual profit made was ₹ 150000, how much John earns in that year?
    (a) ₹ 70000 (b) ₹ 75000
    (c) ₹ 78000 (d) ₹ 80000

28. Jai and Madhav invest ₹ 4 lakh and ₹ 5 lakh respectively in a business. Being a working partner Jai gets ₹ 10000 per month. If the annual profit is ₹ 3.9 lakh, then find the ratio of their earning.
    (a) 4 : 5 (b) 6 : 5
    (c) 8 : 5 (d) 5 : 4

29. Ajay and Vijay start a business with investments in the ratio of 3 : 5. At the end of year, a profit of ₹ 40000 is obtained. For running the business, Ajay was paid a salary equal to 20% of the total profit. What is the share of Vijay in the total profit?
    (a) ₹ 20000 (b) ₹ 22000
    (c) ₹ 24500 (d) ₹ 28000

30. Krishna and Kushal start a partnership firm with initial investment of ₹ 5000 and ₹ 60000 respectively. Govind invests ₹ 5000 at the end of every month and Kushal withdraws ₹ 5000 at the end of every month. In what ratio will they share their profits at the end of one year?
   (a) 1 : 1
   (b) 1 : 2
   (c) 1 : 6
   (d) 1 : 12

KEYS

1. (c)	2. (b)	3. (b)	4. (a)	5. (c)	6. (a)	7. (b)	8. (a)
9. (d)	10. (b)	11. (d)	12. (a)	13. (d)	14. (b)	15. (a)	16. (b)
17. (a)	18. (c)	19. (a)	20. (b)	21. (a)	22. (b)	23. (b)	24. (b)
25. (d)	26. (d)	27. (c)	28. (c)	29. (a)	30. (a)		

SOLUTIONS

Solution 1

The sharing of profit depends on the investment made.

Ratio of their profit share $= A : B : C = 4 : 5 : 6$

As the profit is divided in total of 15 parts i.e., $4 + 5 + 6$

So, share of $A = \frac{4}{15} \times 45000 = ₹\ 12000$.

Choice (c)

Solution 2

Ratio of profits of Ram and Shyam = The ratio of the product of their investments and period of investment.

Ratio of profit share among Ram and Shyam $= (35000 \times 8) : (42000 \times 10) = 2 : 3$

So, share of Ram $= \frac{2}{5} \times 31570 = ₹\ 12628$.

Choice (b)

Solution 3

Ratio of profits of Raj and Sanjay = The ratio of the product of their investments and period of investment.

Ratio of profit share among Raj and Sanjay = (20000 × 12 + 10000 × 8) : (30000 × 8) = 4 : 3.

Choice (b)

Solution 4

Ratio of profit share among Karan and Sameer = (9000 × 12) : (8000 × 7) = 27 : 14

So, share of Sameer = $\frac{14}{41} \times 6970$ = ₹ 2380.

Choice (a)

Solution 5

Ratio of profit share among Sanjay and Naresh = (50000 × 36) : (80000 × 30) = 3 : 4

So, share of Sanjay (after 3 years) = $\frac{3}{7} \times 24500$ = ₹ 10500.

Choice (c)

Solution 6

Ratio of profit shared between A, B and C = (3 × 12) : (5 × 12) : (5 × 6) = 6 : 10 : 5.

Choice (a)

Solution 7

Ratio of profit share among A, B and C = (36000 × 5) : (40000 × 12) : (24000 × 10) = 3 : 8 : 4

So, Share of C = $\frac{4}{15} \times 45000$ = ₹ 12000.

Choice (b)

Solution 8

Ratio of profit share among P and Q = (3 × 3) + (2 × 9) : (5 × 3) + (4 × 9)
= 9 + 18 : 15 + 36
= 27 : 51

So, Share of P = $\frac{27}{78} \times 156000$ = ₹ 54000.

Choice (a)

Solution 9

Ratio of profit share among Kapil, Kailash and Karan (in six months)
= (9000 × 6) : (12000 × 6) : (15000 × 3)
= 6 : 8 : 5

So, Share of Karan = $\frac{5}{19} \times 5700$ = ₹ 1500.

Choice (d)

Solution 10

Suppose B joins after x months, hence his money was invested for $(12 - x)$ months.
As the profit is divided equally:
$$21000 \times 12 = 36000 \times (12 - x)$$
$$21 = 3 \times (12 - x)$$
$$7 = 12 - x$$
$$x = 5$$

So, B joined after 5 months.

Choice (b)

Solution 11

Suppose B joins with a capital of ₹ x after 5 months, so he worked for 7 months.
As the profit is divided between A and B in the ratio of 2 : 3:
$$\frac{3500 \times 12}{x \times 7} = \frac{2}{3}$$
$$x = 9000.$$

Choice (d)

Solution 12

Suppose B joins after x months, hence his money was invested for $(12 - x)$ months.
As the profit is divided between A and B in the ratio of 3 : 1
$$\frac{75000 \times 12}{60000 \times (12 - x)} = \frac{3}{1}$$

Solving above equation, $x = 7$
So, B joined after 7 months.

Choice (a)

Solution 13

Ratio of profit share among P, Q and R (in twenty four months)
$= (20000 \times 24) : (15000 \times 24) : (20000 \times 18) = 4 : 3 : 3$

So, Share of $Q = \frac{3}{10} \times 75000$ = ₹ 22500.

Choice (d)

Solution 14

The ratio of profit sharing of Ajay, Bharat, and Chetan is as follows:

	Ajay	Bharat	Chetan
In first 3 months	(16000×3)	(12000×3)	0
In last 9 months	$+ (11000 \times 9)$	$+ (17000 \times 9)$	(20000×9)
Ratio	147000	189000	180000
	49	63	60

Share of Bharat exceeds share of Chetan by $\frac{63-60}{60} \times 100 = 5\%$.

Choice (b)

Solution 15

Let us assume the investments of P, Q and R as 20, 60 and 100 respectively which in the ratio of $1 : 3 : 5$.

	P	Q	R
In first 4 months	(20×4)	(60×4)	(100×4)
In last 8 months	$+ (40 \times 8)$	$+ (30 \times 8)$	$+ (50 \times 8)$
Ratio	400	480	800
	5	6	10

Choice (a)

Solution 16

$(2 \times A) = (3 \times B) = (4 \times C)$

Let us equate above equation to a number which is divisible by 2, 3 and 4, say 12.

$(2 \times A) = (3 \times B) = (4 \times C) = 12$

So, the ratio of profit share of A, B and C is $6 : 4 : 3$

So, C's Share $= \frac{3}{13} \times 39000 = ₹ 9000$.

Choice (b)

Solution 17

The ratio of investments of P, Q and R is $6 : 2 : 3$

So, Q's Share $= \frac{2}{11} \times 9900 = ₹ 1800$.

Choice (a)

Solution 18

Ratio of investment of A, B and C is $\frac{2}{5}, \frac{1}{3},$ and $\frac{7}{10}$

To convert this ratio to a integer, let us multiply it by LCM of 5, 3 and 10 *i.e.,* 30

So the ratio of investment of A, B and C will be 12 : 10 : 21

Ratio of profit share among A, B and C = $(12 \times 12) : (10 \times 4 + 30 \times 8) : (21 \times 12)$
$$= 144 : 280 : 252$$
$$= 36 : 70 : 63$$

So, Share of B = $\frac{70}{169} \times 67600$
$$= ₹\, 28000.$$

Choice (c)

Solution 19

Rent shared by A, B and C is in the ratio:
$$(45 \times 12)x : (36 \times 15)x : (60 \times 10)x$$
$$= 9x : 9x : 10x$$

If B's share of rent was ₹ 540 *i.e.,* $9x = 540$, so $x = 60$

Therefore total rent = $9x + 9x + 10x = 28x = 28 \times 60 = ₹\, 1680.$

Choice (a)

Solution 20

Assuming B's capital was used for x months

(A's investment × A's Duration)/(B's investment × B's Duration) = 8/9

$$\frac{7 \times 8}{9 \times x} = \frac{8}{9}$$

So, $x = 7$.

Choice (b)

Solution 21

As they are sharing equal profit:

(Sai's investment × Sai's Duration) = (Harsha's investment × Harsha's Duration)
$x \times 9 = y \times 12$

$$\frac{x}{y} = \frac{12}{9} = \frac{4}{3}.$$

Choice (a)

Solution 22

Suppose Q's money was invested for x months.

As the profit is divided equally:

$54000 \times 12 = 81000 \times x$

$x = \dfrac{54 \times 12}{81}$

$x = 8$

So, Q's money was invested for 8 months.

Choice (b)

Solution 23

The ratio of profit sharing of A, B and C is as follows:

A	B	C
(7200 × 12)	(9600 × 9)	(10800 × x)
8 :	8 :	x

As, $8 : 8 : x = 4 : 4 : 3$

So, $x = 6$

C joined the business 3 months after B joined.

Choice (b)

Solution 24

The ratio of investments of A, B, and C = $\dfrac{4}{2} : \dfrac{5}{3} : \dfrac{6}{9}$

$= 2 : \dfrac{5}{3} : \dfrac{2}{3}$

To convert the ratio to integer multiplying each term by 3.

So, ratio of investment of A, B and $C = 6 : 5 : 2$

A's investment is more than B by $\dfrac{6-5}{5} \times 100 = 20\%$.

Choice (b)

Solution 25

Let Ramesh stays in the business for x months

So, Bhavesh stays for $(x + 4)$ months

And, Suresh stays for $(x + 8)$ months

The ratio of profit sharing is as follows:

	Ramesh	Suresh	Bhavesh
	$64000 \times x$	$32000 \times (x+8)$	$48000 \times (x+4)$
	$4x$	$2(x+8)$	$3(x+4)$

As Suresh and Bhavesh share their profit equally,

$2(x+8) = 3(x+4)$

$x = 4$

So the business last for a maximum of $(x+8)$ i.e., for 12 months.

Choice (d)

Solution 26

The ratio of investments of P, Q and $R = \frac{6}{3} : \frac{15}{5} : \frac{4}{8} = 2 : 3 : \frac{1}{2}$

To convert the ratio to integer multiplying each term by 2.

So, ratio of investment of P, Q and $R = 4 : 6 : 1$.

Choice (a)

Solution 27

Commission (or salary) of John = 10% of Total profit
= 10% of 150000
= ₹ 15000

Remaining profit = 150000 – 15000 = ₹ 135000

John and Mack share this remaining profit in the ratio of 7 : 8

Profit Share of John = $\frac{7}{15} \times 135000$ = ₹ 63000.

Total earning of John = Commission + Profit Share = ₹ 15000 + ₹ 63000 = ₹ 78000.

Choice (c)

Solution 28

Jai's earning = Salary + Profit share

Madhav's earning = Profit share

Profit to be shared = Total profit – Salary of Jai
= 390000 – 120000
= ₹ 270000

Jai and Madhav share this remaining profit in the ratio of 4 : 5

Jai's earning = $(12 \times 10000) + \frac{4}{9} \times 270000$ = ₹ 240000

Madhav's earning = $\frac{5}{9} \times 270000$ = ₹ 150000

Ratio of Jai's and Madhav's earning = 240000 : 150000 = 8 : 5.

Choice (c)

Solution 29

Salary of Ajay = 20% of Total profit
= 20% of 40000
= ₹ 8000

Remaining profit to be shared between the partners = 40000 – 8000 = ₹ 32000

Share of Vijay = $\frac{5}{8} \times 32000$ = ₹ 20000.

Choice (a)

Solution 30

Investment and withdrawal of Krishna and Kushal in the partnership over a year is as follows:

	Krishna	Kushal
Jan.	5000	60000
Feb.	10000	55000
Mar.	15000	50000
.	.	.
.	.	.
.	.	.
Dec.	60000	5000

As Krishna is uniformly adding ₹ 5000 and Kushal is uniformly removing ₹ 5000, hence at the end of year investment of Krishna will be ₹ 60000, and Kushal's capital stays in the business as ₹ 5000. So, they will share their profit in the ratio of 1 : 1.

Choice (a)

10

Average

Average is a very simple but effective way of representing an entire group by a single value. Mathematically it is expressed as:

$$\text{Average} = \frac{\text{Sum of all the terms}}{\text{Number of terms}}$$

Suppose if there are 60 students in a class, instead of talking of height of each individual student, we can talk of average height of class. The average height of class of students is equal to sum of heights of all the students of class divided by number of students in a class. Average also called "mean" or mean value of all the values.

WEIGHTED AVERAGE

If the averages of two groups are given individually then we can find out the average of entire group combined together as weighted average. Suppose there are two sections in a class *i.e.*, section A and section B. The average height of students of section A is 140 cm, while the average height of students of section B is 150 cm. On the basis of this information, we cannot find the average height of entire class as we do not know the number of students in each section.

Now, if we are provided with the additional information that there are 30 students in section A and 20 students in section B, then we can find out the average height of entire class as follows:

$$\text{Average} = \frac{(140 \times 30) + (150 \times 20)}{30 + 20} = 144$$

This average height of 144 cm of the entire class is known as the "weighted average" of the class. The above average can also be calculated if the ratio of students in two sections (*i.e.*, 3:2 in this case) is given instead of actual number of students. Even if there are more than two groups of items to be combined, then also the weighted average can be calculated by same method.

POINTS TO NOTE

- If the average of a group increases by addition of a new term, then the value of that term is more than the average of group.
- If the average of a group decreases by subtracting a term, then the value of that term is more than the average of group.
- If the average of a group decreases by addition of a new term, then the value of that term is less than the average of group.

- If the average of a group increases by subtracting a term, then the value of that term is less than the average of group.
- If the value of each term is increased by x, then average of entire group increases by x.
- If the value of each term is decreased by x, then average of entire group decreases by x.
- If each term is multiplied by x, then the average of the group also gets multiplied by x.
- If each term is divided by x, then the average of the group also gets divided by x.

AVERAGE OF A SERIES

Let us consider first 10 natural numbers *i.e.*, 1, 2, 3, ..., 10.

The average of these numbers can be found as:

$$\text{Average} = \frac{\text{First term} + \text{Last term}}{2}$$

So, Average $= \frac{1+10}{2} = 5.5$

This method of finding average can be only applicable if the numbers are consecutive or in an arithmetic progression (increases or decreases by a common difference).

SOLVED EXAMPLES

Example 1

Find the average of first 100 even natural numbers.

Solution

The numbers are 2, 4, 6, ..., 200. As we can see that there is a common difference between any two consecutive terms, hence the average can be found as:

$$\text{Average} = \frac{\text{First term} + \text{Last term}}{2} = \frac{2+200}{2} = 101$$

Example 2

In an examination consisting of six subjects, a student scored 65, 68, 70, 72, 74 and 77 marks. Find the average score.

Solution

$$\text{Average} = \frac{\text{Sum of scores}}{\text{Number of subjects}}$$

$$= \frac{65+68+70+72+74+77}{6} = 71 \text{ marks}$$

Alternate Method:

The problem can be also solved using assumed average/mean also. Let us take 70 as the assumed mean, the actual average score will be,

$$= 70 + \frac{-5-2+0+2+4+7}{6}$$

$$= 70 + \frac{6}{6}$$

$$= 71 \text{ marks.}$$

Example 3

The average of nine observations is 40. If the average of first five observations is 35 and that of last five observations is 42, then how much is the reading of fifth observation?

Solution

Total of first five readings (*i.e.*, 1 to 5) = $35 \times 5 = 175$

Total of last five readings (*i.e.*, 5 to 9) = $42 \times 5 = 210$

Reading of 5th observation = (Total of first five + Total of last five) − Total of nine observations

Reading of 5th observation = $(175 + 210) - 40 \times 9 = 25$.

Example 4

The average weight of P, Q and R is 60 kg. The average weight of P and Q is 55 kg, while that of Q and R is 68 kg. Find the weight of Q.

Solution

Total weight of P, Q and R:

$P + Q + R = 60 \times 3 = 180$ kg

Total weight of P and Q:

$P + Q = 55 \times 2 = 110$ kg

Total weight of Q and R:

$Q + R = 68 \times 2 = 136$ kg

Weight of $Q = (P + Q) + (Q + R) - (P + Q + R)$
$= 110 + 136 - 180$
$= 66$ kg.

Example 5

A salesman of mobile company sales 55 handsets on the 6th day of a week and thus increases his average by 2. Find his average for first five days.

Solution

Let the average up to 5th day = A

Then average after 6 days = $A + 2$

Total sale of 5 days + Sale on 6th day = Total sale of 6 days

$\quad (5 \times A) + 55 = 6 \times (A + 2)$

$\quad A = 43$

So the average sale for first five days = 43.

Example 6

Five persons went to a restaurant for dinner. Four of them spent ₹ 80 each on their meals, and the fifth person spent ₹ 20 more than the average expenditure of all five. Find the total expenditure of dinner.

Solution

Let the average expenditure of 5 persons = A

So, amount spent by 5th person = $A + 20$

$$\frac{(80 \times 4) + (A + 20)}{5} = A$$

$A = 85$

Total expenditure of dinner = $85 \times 5 = ₹ 425$

Example 7

Three different qualities of oil costing ₹ 50, ₹ 60 and ₹ 40 a liter are mixed in the ratio of 4:7:9. Find the cost per liter of resulting mixture.

Solution

Average cost of mixture = $\dfrac{(50 \times 4) + (60 \times 7) + (40 \times 9)}{4 + 7 + 9} = ₹ 49$

Example 8

The average age of a group of 10 friends is 15 years. A new friend joins them and their average age increases to 16 years. What is the age of new friend?

Solution

As the new friend joins the group the average age increases by 1 year, hence he must be older than 15 years and he is able to add 1 year to each one.

Age of new friend = 15 + (11 × 1) = 26 years

Alternate Method:

Let the age of new friend = x years

$$\frac{(10 \times 15) + x}{11} = 16$$

So, x = 26 years

Example 9

The average age of 8 employees working on a certain project is 38 years. If one of the employee leaves the project, then average age of remaining employees increases by 2 years. Find the age of the employee who left.

Solution

As one of the employees leaves the group then average age of remaining 7 employees increases by 2 year, hence his age must be less than 38 years.

Age of employee who left = 38 − (7 × 2) = 24 years.

Alternate Method:

Let the age of employee who left = x years

$$\frac{(38 \times 8) - x}{7} = 40$$

So, x = 24 years.

EXERCISE

1. The average of the first five multiples of 7 is,
   - (a) 20
   - (b) 28
   - (c) 21
   - (d) 30

2. Find the average of the first 97 natural numbers.
   - (a) 47
   - (b) 48
   - (c) 37
   - (d) 49

3. The average of first 50 odd natural numbers is,
   - (a) 49
   - (b) 50
   - (c) 51
   - (d) 52

4. The average of 10 numbers is 7. If each number is multiplied by 12 then the average of the new set of numbers is,
   - (a) 19
   - (b) 82
   - (c) 7
   - (d) 84

5. The average of 7 consecutive numbers is n. If next 4 numbers are considered, the average of these 11 numbers will be:
   (a) n
   (b) n + 1
   (c) n + 2
   (d) n + 4

6. A student obtained 36, 38, 45, 37 and 44 marks in Algebra, Geometry, Physics, Chemistry and Biology. What are his average marks?
   (a) 39
   (b) 40
   (c) 40.5
   (d) 41.5

7. The average age of A, B and C is 45 years. If the average age of A and B be 42 years and that of B and C be 44 years, then the age of B is:
   (a) 37
   (b) 39
   (c) 41
   (d) 43

8. The average cost of 4 apples and 7 bananas is ₹ 16. The average cost of 7 apples and 4 bananas is ₹ 24. The cost of 1 apple and 1 banana is (in ₹):
   (a) 8
   (b) 11
   (c) 30
   (d) 40

9. The average of 10 numbers is 15. If each number is multiplied by 3 and added to 5, the average of new set of numbers is
   (a) 15
   (b) 40
   (c) 45
   (d) 50

10. A student was asked to find the arithmetic mean of the numbers 5, 20, 18, 12, 15, 8, 7, 25, and x. He found the mean to be 14. What should be the number in place of x?
    (a) 16
    (b) 17
    (c) 19
    (d) 21

11. A vegetable vendor has a sale of ₹ 435, ₹ 427, ₹ 455, ₹ 430 and ₹ 462 for 5 consecutive days. How much sale must he have in the sixth day so that he gets an average sale of ₹ 450?
    (a) 409
    (b) 419
    (c) 461
    (d) 491

12. The average monthly income of A and B is ₹ 12050. The average monthly income of B and C is ₹ 11250 and the average monthly income of A and C is ₹ 10200. The monthly income of A is:
    (a) ₹ 11000
    (b) ₹ 11200
    (c) ₹ 11350
    (d) ₹ 11700

13. Three years ago the average age of P, Q, and R was 27 years and that of Q and R 5 years ago was 20 years. P's present age is:
    (a) 48
    (b) 30
    (c) 35
    (d) 40

14. A family consists of two grandparents, two parents and three grandchildren. The average age of the grandparents is 70 years, that of the parents is 40 years and that of the grandchildren is 6 years. What is the average age of the family?

(a) 32 (b) 34
(c) 36 (d) 40

15. The average age of a family of six members is 22 years. If the age of youngest member be 7 years, what was the average age of family at the birth of youngest member?
    (a) 15 (b) 12
    (c) 18 (d) 21

16. The average age of a husband and his wife was 25 years at the time of their marriage. After three years they have a child one year old. The average age of the family now is:
    (a) 19 (b) 20
    (c) 21 (d) 22

17. A batsman has a certain average for 9 innings. In the 10th inning he scores 100 runs thereby increasing his average by 8 runs. His new average is:
    (a) 20 (b) 28
    (c) 32 (d) 24

18. The batting average for 30 innings of a cricketer is 75 runs. His highest score exceeds his lowest score by 122 runs. If these two innings are excluded, the average of the remaining 28 innings is 72 runs. The highest score of the player is:
    (a) 178 (b) 165
    (c) 162 (d) 156

19. In an aptitude test conducted for 60 students, the average score was 36 marks out of 50. If the score of two students who scored highest and least marks is excluded, then the average score of remaining 58 students remains as it was. If the difference between highest and least score is 20, then find the highest score.
    (a) 41 (b) 44
    (c) 46 (d) 47

20. The average weight of a class is unaffected, if two boys with average weight of 45 kg leaves the class and three girls with an average weight of 43 kg joins the class. Find the average weight of class.
    (a) 44 (b) 39
    (c) 40 (d) cannot be determined

21. If we take 4 numbers, the average of first 3 is 16 and that of the last 3 is 16. If the last number is 18, the first number is:
    (a) 18 (b) 20
    (c) 22 (d) 24

22. The average age of 24 students and the teacher is 15 years. When the teacher's age is excluded, the average age decreases by 1 year. What is the age of teacher?
    (a) 40 (b) 38
    (c) 39 (d) 42

23. The average age of 40 students in a group is 16 years. When teacher's age is included to it, the average increases by one. What is the teacher's age in years?

(a) 51 (b) 52
(c) 54 (d) 57

24. The average of five numbers is 27. If one number is excluded, the average becomes 25. The excluded number is:
    (a) 35 (b) 27
    (c) 23 (d) 21

25. The average weight of nine mangoes is 120 gram. If one mango out of it is replaced by another new mango, then the average weight increases by 5 gram. Find the weight of new mango.
    (a) 75 gram (b) 125 gram
    (c) 160 gram (d) 165 gram

26. The average weight of 50 oranges kept in a wooden box is 100 gram. If the weight of box is also included the average becomes 150 gram. Find the weight of wooden box.
    (a) 1.6 kg (b) 2.65 kg
    (c) 5.15 kg (d) 7.65 kg

27. The average weight of 5 boys is decreased by 3 kg when one of them weighing 75 kg is replaced by another student; find the weight of new student (in kg).
    (a) 60 (b) 65
    (c) 78 (d) 90

28. After replacing an old member by a new member, it was found that the average age of five members of a committee is the same as it was 4 years ago. What is the difference between the ages of the replaced and the new member?
    (a) 16 (b) 20
    (c) 24 (d) cannot be determined

29. The average weight of 8 persons increases by 1.5 kg when a new person comes in place of one of them weighing 60 kg. Find the weight of the new person (in kg).
    (a) 61.5 (b) 48
    (c) 72 (d) 78

30. A motorist covers one-fifth of a certain journey at the speed of 60 km/hr, half of the remaining journey at the speed of 40 km/hr and remaining at the speed of 30 km/hr. Find the average speed of whole journey (in km/hr).
    (a) 37.5 (b) 40
    (c) 43.33 (d) 50

31. A train travels 400 km at the speed of 80 km/hr, and then its speed is reduced by 20 km/hr every hour for the next 3 hrs. Find the average speed of train during entire journey (in km/hr).
    (a) 60 (b) 65
    (c) 50 (d) 45

32. The average salary of entire staff in a company is ₹ 3,200 per month. The average salary of engineers is ₹ 6,800 and that of labors is ₹ 2,000. If the numbers of engineers is 5, find the number of labors in the company.
   (a) 8
   (b) 5
   (c) 12
   (d) 15

33. The average salary of all the workers in a workshop is ₹ 6000. The average salary of 5 technicians is ₹ 12000 and the average salary of all the staff is ₹ 8000. The total number of workers in the workshop is
   (a) 5
   (b) 8
   (c) 10
   (d) 15

34. Mohanlal has three sons named Arjun, Bupen and Chetan. The average height of any two sons exceeds half the height of third son by 80 cm. Find the height of Bupen.
   (a) 80 cm
   (b) 120 cm
   (c) 160 cm
   (d) cannot be determined

35. A school has for sections that contain 10, 20, 30 and 40 students respectively. The pass percentage of these sections is 20%, 30%, 60% and 100% respectively. Find the passing percentage of entire school.
   (a) 56
   (b) 34
   (c) 76
   (d) 66

36. A certain number of trucks were required to transport 60 tons of iron from a company. However it was found that each truck could take 0.5 tons of cargo less and another four trucks were needed. How many trucks were initially planned to be used?
   (a) 10
   (b) 20
   (c) 15
   (d) 25

37. A library has an average of 240 visitors on every Saturday and 156 on other days. The average number of visitors per day in a month of 30 days beginning with a Saturday is
   (a) 198
   (b) 172
   (c) 170
   (d) 160

38. Sonu appeared for an exam and score an average of 75 marks per paper. If he had obtained 15 marks more in physiology paper and 20 marks more in political science paper, then his average marks per paper would have been 80 out of 100. For how many papers did Sonu appears?
   (a) 5
   (b) 6
   (c) 7
   (d) 8

KEYS

1. (c)	2. (d)	3. (b)	4. (d)	5. (c)	6. (b)	7. (a)	8. (d)
9. (d)	10. (a)	11. (d)	12. (a)	13. (d)	14. (b)	15. (c)	16. (a)
17. (b)	18. (a)	19. (c)	20. (b)	21. (a)	22. (c)	23. (d)	24. (a)
25. (d)	26. (b)	27. (a)	28. (b)	29. (c)	30. (a)	31. (b)	32. (d)
33. (c)	34. (c)	35. (d)	36. (b)	37. (c)	38. (c)		

SOLUTIONS

Solution 1

First five multiples are 7, 14, 21, 28, and 35. The average of these five numbers with a common difference between any two consecutive numbers will be the centre *i.e.,* 21.

Choice (c)

Solution 2

The numbers are 1, 2, 3, ..., 97.

$$\text{Average} = \frac{\text{First term + Last term}}{2} = \frac{1+97}{2} = 49.$$

Choice (d)

Solution 3

The numbers are 1, 3, 5,..., 99.

$$\text{Average} = \frac{\text{First term + Last term}}{2} = \frac{1+99}{2} = 50.$$

Choice (b)

Solution 4

If each number in a set of 10 numbers is multiplied by 12, then the average also gets multiplied by 12.

New average = $7 \times 12 = 84$.

Choice (d)

Solution 5

Let us assume the seven consecutive numbers as 1, 2, 3, 4, 5, 6, and 7. Here the average will be the number at the centre *i.e.,* 4. So, $n = 4$ in this case.

If we consider next four numbers the series will be 1, 2, 3, 4, 5, 6, 7, 8, 9, 10 and 11. Here the average will be the number at the centre *i.e.,* 6. This average is more than previous average by 2 *i.e.,* $n + 2$.

Choice (c)

Solution 6

$$\text{Average} = \frac{\text{Sum of scores}}{\text{Number of subjects}} = \frac{36+38+45+37+44}{5} = \frac{200}{5} = 40 \text{ marks}.$$

Alternate Method:

The problem can be also solved using assumed average/mean also. Let us take 38 as the assumed mean, the actual average score will be,

$$= 38 + \frac{-2+0+7-1+6}{5}$$

$$= 38 + \frac{10}{5}$$

$$= 40 \text{ marks.}$$

Choice (b)

Solution 7

Total age of A, B and C:

$$A + B + C = 45 \times 3 = 135 \text{ years.}$$

Total age of A and B:

$$A + B = 42 \times 2 = 84 \text{ years}$$

Total age of B and C:

$$B + C = 44 \times 2 = 88 \text{ years}$$

Age of $B = (A + B) + (B + C) - (A + B + C)$
$$= 84 + 88 - 135 = 37 \text{ years.}$$

Choice (a)

Solution 8

Total cost of 4 apple and 7 bananas will be:

$$4a + 7b = 16 \times 11 \qquad \ldots (1)$$

Total cost of 7 apple and 4 bananas will be:

$$7a + 4b = 24 \times 11 \qquad \ldots (2)$$

Adding (1) and (2),

$$11a + 11b = (16 + 24) \times 11$$

$$a + b = 40.$$

Choice (d)

Solution 9

If each number in a set of 10 numbers is multiplied by 3, then the average also gets multiplied by 3. Further if 5 is added to each number so the average is also increased by 5.
New average = $(15 \times 3) + 5 = 50$.

Choice (d)

Solution 10

If we arrange these numbers in ascending order it can be written as:

5, 7, 8, 12, 15, 18, 20, 25 and there is a number x.

$$\frac{5+7+8+12+15+18+20+25+x}{9} = 14$$

So, $x = 16$.

Choice (a)

Solution 11

Let the sale on sixth day is ₹ x

As the average of sale of six days should be ₹ 450, then the equation will be,

$$\frac{435+427+455+430+462+x}{6} = 450$$

So, $x = 491$.

Choice (d)

Solution 12

Total income of A and B is:

$A + B = 12050 \times 2 = 24100$

Total income of B and C is:

$B + C = 11250 \times 2 = 22500$

Total income of A and C is:

$A + C = 10200 \times 2 = 20400$

Adding the above equations:

$(A + B) + (B + C) + (A + C) = 67000$
$2A + 2B + 2C = 67000$
$A + B + C = 33500$

So income of A is

$(A + B + C) - (B + C) = 33500 - 22500 = 11000$.

Choice (a)

Solution 13

Total age of P, Q and R 3 years ago is:

$P + Q + R = 27 \times 3 = 81$

Total present age of P, Q and R is:

$P + Q + R = 81 + 9 = 90$ (∵ age of each person is increased by 3 years)

Total age of Q and R 5 years ago is:

$Q + R = 20 \times 2 = 40$

Total present age of Q and R is:

$Q + R = 40 + 10 = 50$ (∵ age of each person is increased by 5 years)

P's present age $= (P + Q + R) - (Q + R)$
$= 90 - 50 = 40$ years.

Choice (d)

Solution 14

In this problem we need to find the weighted average of the family:

Weighted average $= \dfrac{(70 \times 2) + (40 \times 2) + (6 \times 3)}{2 + 2 + 3} = 34$ years.

Choice (b)

Solution 15

Present total age of family members $= 22 \times 6 = 132$

Total age during birth of youngest member $= 132 - (6 \times 7) = 90$

Average age (of remaining 5 member) $= \dfrac{90}{5} = 18$.

Choice (c)

Solution 16

Total age of husband and wife during marriage $= 25 \times 2 = 50$

Total age of husband and wife now $= 50 + 6 = 56$

Total age of husband, wife and child now $= 56 + 1 = 57$

Average age now $= \dfrac{57}{3} = 19$.

Choice (a)

Solution 17

Let the old average be A, So new average will be $A + 8$

$$\dfrac{9A + 100}{10} = A + 8$$

$9A + 100 = 10A + 80$

$A = 20$

So, new average is 28.

Choice (b)

Solution 18

Total score of 30 innings = $30 \times 75 = 2250$
Total score of 28 innings = $28 \times 72 = 2016$
Highest score + lowest score = $2250 - 2016 = 234$ ... (1)
Highest score – lowest score = 122 ... (2)

Adding (1) and (2)

$2 \times$ Highest score = 356

So, Highest score = 178.

Choice (a)

Solution 19

Total score of 60 students = $60 \times 36 = 2160$
Total score of 58 students = $58 \times 36 = 2088$
Highest score + lowest score = $2160 - 2088 = 72$ ... (1)
Highest score – lowest score = 20 ... (2)

Adding (1) and (2)

$2 \times$ Highest score = 92

So, Highest score = 46.

Choice (c)

Solution 20

Total weight added by 3 girls = $43 \times 3 = 129$

Total weight subtracted by 2 boys = $45 \times 2 = 90$

Net addition = $129 - 90 = 39$

Due to addition of 39 in the total, and an extra girl the average is unaffected, hence the average is 39.

Choice (b)

Solution 21

Let the four numbers be a, b, c, and d.

Total of first three numbers:
$$a + b + c = 48$$

Total of last three numbers:
$$b + c + d = 48$$
$$b + c + 18 = 48$$
$$b + c = 30$$

So, the first number i.e., $a = 18$.

Choice (a)

Solution 22

As the teacher leaves the group then average age of student decreases by 1 year, hence teacher's age must be more than 15 years.

Age of teacher = $15 + (24 \times 1) = 39$ years.

Alternate Method:

Let the age of teacher = x

$$\frac{(25 \times 15) - x}{24} = 14$$

$$x = 39.$$

Choice (c)

Solution 23

As the teacher joins the group then average age of 40 student and a teacher increases by 1 year, hence teacher's age must be more than 16 years.

Age of teacher = $16 + (41 \times 1) = 57$ years.

Alternate Method:
Let the age of teacher = x

$$\frac{(40 \times 16) + x}{41} = 17$$

$$x = 57.$$

Choice (d)

Solution 24

As the number is excluded, the average of remaining four numbers is reduced by 2; hence the excluded number must be greater than 27.

Excluded number = 27 + (4 × 2)
= 35.

Alternate Method:

Let the number be x

$$\frac{(5 \times 27) - x}{4} = 25$$

$$x = 35.$$

Choice (a)

Solution 25

As one mango is replaced by a new mango, the average is increased by 5 gram; hence the weight of new mango is more than 120 gram.

Weight of new mango = 120 + (9 × 5) = 165.

Alternate Method:

Let the weight of new mango be x

$$\frac{(8 \times 120) + x}{9} = 125$$

$$x = 165.$$

Choice (d)

Solution 26

As the weight of wooden box is also included, the average weight is increased by 50 grams; hence wooden box is heavier than 100 gram.

Weight of wooden box = 100 + (51 × 50) = 2650 gram or 2.65 kg

Alternate Method

Let the weight of wooden box be x

$$\frac{(50 \times 100) + x}{51} = 150$$

$$x = 2650 \text{ gram or } 2.65 \text{ kg}.$$

Choice (b)

Solution 27

If a student in the existing group is replaced by another new student the average decreases by 3 kg, hence the weight of new student must be less than 75 kg.

Weight of new student = 75 – (5 × 3) = 60

Alternate Method:

Let the average weight be A

Let the weight of new student be N

$$\frac{(5 \times A) - 75 + N}{5} = A - 3$$

$5A - 75 + N = 5A - 15$

$N = 60$.

Choice (a)

Solution 28

Total increase in age of 5 members after 4 years = $5 \times 4 = 20$.

As Average age before 4 years is same as average age after 4 years hence total age of 5 members before 4 years will be same as after 4 year. This is only possible if the difference between the age of replaced member and new member is 20, or new member is 20 years younger than old member.

Choice (b)

Solution 29

As the average weight increases by 1.5 kg, hence the new person must be heavier than the existing person.

Weight of new person = $60 + (8 \times 1.5)$
= 72

Alternate Method
Let the average weight of 8 persons be A.
Let the weight of new person be N.

$$\frac{(8 \times A) - 60 + N}{8} = A + 1.5$$

$8A - 60 + N = 8A + 12$

$N = 72$.

Choice (c)

Solution 30

Let us assume total journey as $5x$ km.

x km at 60 km/hr

$2x$ km at 40 km/hr

$2x$ km at 30 km/hr

Average speed = $\dfrac{\text{Total distance covered}}{\text{Total time taken}}$

$= \dfrac{5x}{\dfrac{x}{60} + \dfrac{2x}{40} + \dfrac{2x}{30}}$

$= \dfrac{5}{16} \times 120$

$= 37.5$ km/hr.

Choice (a)

Solution 31

Speed for first 5 hrs = 80 km/hr

Speed for next 3 hrs = 60, 40 and 20 km/hr respectively

Average speed = $\dfrac{\text{Total distance covered}}{\text{Total time taken}}$

$= \dfrac{400 + 60 + 40 + 20}{5 + 1 + 1 + 1}$

$= \dfrac{520}{8}$

$= 65$ km/hr.

Choice (b)

Solution 32

Let the number of labors be x.
Total salary of engineers = 6800 × 5 = 34000
Total salary of labors = 2000 × x
Total salary of all staff = 3200 × (5 + x)
  3200 × (5 + x) = 34000 + (2000 × x)
  x = 15.

Choice (d)

Solution 33

Let the number of workers be x.
Total salary of technicians = 12000 × 5 = 60000
Total salary of workers = 6000 × x
Total salary of all staff = 8000 × (5 + x)
8000 × (5 + x) = 60000 + (6000 × x)
x = 10.

Choice (c)

Solution 34

As average height of any two sons exceeds half the height of third son, hence

$$\frac{A+B}{2} - \frac{C}{2} = \frac{A+C}{2} - \frac{B}{2} = \frac{B+C}{2} - \frac{A}{2} = 80 \text{ cm}$$

As any person can be replaced by any person, so we can conclude that all three sons are of equal height.

$$\frac{A+B}{2} - \frac{C}{2} = 80 \text{ cm}$$

$$\frac{B+B}{2} - \frac{B}{2} = 80 \text{ cm}$$

$$B = 160 \text{ cm}.$$

Choice (c)

Solution 35

Passed in 1st section = 20% of 10 = 2
Passed in 2nd section = 30% of 20 = 6
Passed in 3rd section = 60% of 30 = 18
Passed in 4th section = 100% of 40 = 40

Passing percentage of entire school = $\frac{\text{Total passed}}{\text{Total students in school}} \times 100$

$$= \frac{66}{100} \times 100$$

$$= 66\%.$$

Choice (d)

Solution 36

Number of trucks planned initially = x
(Average load carried by x trucks) − (Average load carried by $x + 4$ trucks) = 0.5 tons

$$\frac{60}{x} - \frac{60}{x+4} = 0.5$$

Solving the above equation, $x = 20$.

Choice (b)

Solution 37

In a month of 30 days beginning with Saturday, there will be 5 Saturdays.
Total visitors on 5 Saturdays = 240 × 5 = 1200
Total visitors on remaining 25 week days = 156 × 25 = 3900

Total visitors in the month = 1200 + 3900 = 5100
Average visitors per day in the month = 5100/30 = 170.

Choice (c)

Solution 38

Number of papers that Sonu appears = x
Total marks scored = $75x$

$$\frac{75x + 15 + 20}{x} = 80$$

$$75x + 35 = 80x$$

$$x = 7$$

Alternate Method
Total increased = 35
Average increased = 5

Number of papers = $\dfrac{\text{Increased Total}}{\text{Increased Average}} = \dfrac{35}{5} = 7.$

Choice (c)

11

Alligation or Mixture

RULE OF MIXTURE

Mixing of two or more items of different qualities produces a mixture. When two solutions of different qualities are thus mixed, the quality of resulting mixture lies in between the quality of superior and inferior solution. Similarly, if two types of products of different prices are mixed, then price of resulting mixture lie between the price of cheaper and dearer product. Here, the average quality is essentially the weighted average of two constituent items.

If three different items costing R_1, R_2, and R_3 are mixed in the ratio of a, b and c respectively then average price of resulting mixture can be found as:

Weighted average = $\dfrac{R_1(a) + R_2(b) + R_3(c)}{a+b+c}$

For example if three different qualities of milk costing ₹ 20, ₹ 24 and ₹ 30 per liter are mixed in the ratio of 2:3:5, then the cost of resulting mixture is found by the weighted average.

Weighted average = $\dfrac{20(2) + 24(3) + 30(5)}{2+3+5}$ = ₹ 26.20.

So, the cost of resulting mixture of three different qualities of milk is ₹ 26.20.

RULE OF ALLIGATION

It is the rule that enable us to know the ratio in which two ingredients at a given price (or quality) to be mixed, in order to get a mixture of desired price (or quality). In a descriptive manner, the rule of alligation can be written as:

$\dfrac{\text{Quantity of Cheaper}}{\text{Quantity of Dearer}} = \dfrac{\text{Rate of Dearer} - \text{Average Rate}}{\text{Average Rate} - \text{Rate of Cheaper}}$

The above formula can be pictorially represented as follows:

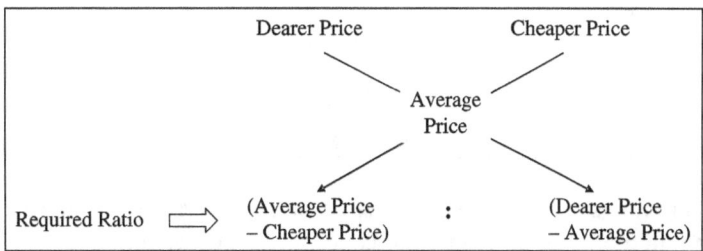

For example the cost price of petrol is ₹ 75 a liter, and the cost price of kerosene is ₹ 25 a liter. If we want to bring down the cost of petrol from ₹ 75 to ₹ 65 by adulterating it with kerosene, then the rule of alligation will help us to know the ratio in which these two fuels are to be mixed.

    Price of dearer fuel = ₹ 75

    Price of cheaper fuel = ₹ 25

    Desired price of resulting mixture = ₹ 65

Applying the rule of alligation as follows:

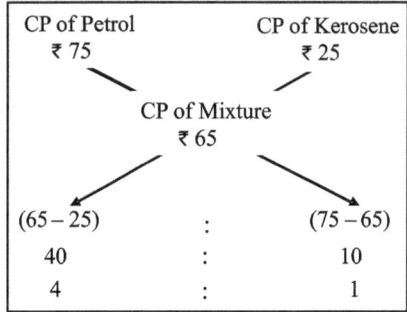

So, petrol and kerosene needs to be mixed in the ratio of 4:1. It means in every 1 liter, there will be 800 ml of pure petrol and 200 ml of kerosene.

Another example can be taken of mixing two different qualities of milk. Vessel *A* contains milk and water solution with 70% milk and 30% water, and vessel *B* contains milk and water solution with 40% milk and 60% water. If we want to form a mixture containing 50% milk and 50% water by mixing the solutions from these two vessels, then the rule of alligation will help us to know the ratio in which these two solutions are to be mixed.

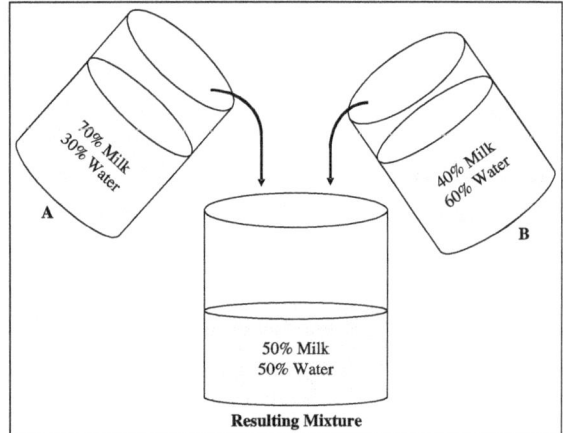

These types of problems can be solved in terms of concentration of any one *i.e.,* either in terms of concentration of milk or in terms of concentration of water.

Solving in Terms of Concentration of Milk

Concentration of milk in vessel $A = 70\%$
Concentration of milk in vessel $B = 40\%$
Required concentration of milk in mixture $= 50\%$

Applying the rule of alligation as follows:

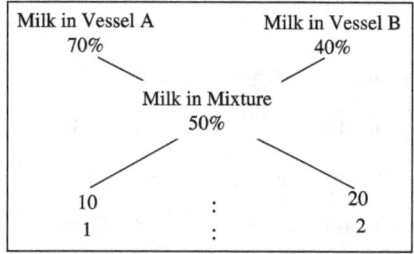

So, the solution from vessel A and vessel B are mixed in the ratio of 1:2 to get equal quantity of milk and water in the resulting mixture.

Solving in Terms of Concentration of Water

Concentration of water in vessel $A = 30\%$
Concentration of water in vessel $B = 60\%$
Required concentration of water in mixture $= 50\%$

Applying the rule of alligation as follows:

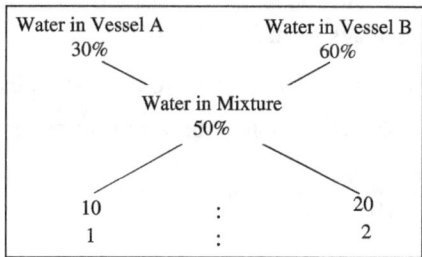

We get the same result as above, even if we solve in terms of concentration of water.

RULE OF DILUTION

If there is P liters of pure liquid initially, and it is replaced by Q liters of another liquid every time, then at the end of 'n' such operations, the concentration 'k' of the liquid in the solution is given by:

$$\left(\frac{P-Q}{P}\right)^n = k$$

This gives the concentration 'k' of the liquid as a proportion of the total volume of the solution. If the concentration has to be expressed in percentage, then it will be equal to 100 k.

SOLVED EXAMPLES

Example 1

2 liters of pure milk is added to 8 liters of a solution of milk and water containing 60% milk. Find the percentage of water in the resulting solution.

Solution

Milk content in 2 liter of 1st solution = 2 liter

Milk content in 10 liter of 2nd solution = $\frac{60}{100} \times 8 = 4.8$ liters

Milk content in the mixture of 2 solutions = 2 + 4.8 = 6.8 liters

Percentage concentration of milk in mixture = $\frac{6.8}{2+8} \times 100 = 68\%$

∴ Percentage of water in resulting solution = 100 − 68 = 32%.

Example 2

From a bottle completely filled with a mixture of wine and water, if 120 ml of wine from a bottle is replaced by 120 ml of water, the concentration of wine drops from 50% to 40%. Find the capacity of bottle.

Solution

As 120 ml of mixture of wine and water is replaced by 120 ml of pure water, the wine concentration in the mixture changes from 50% to 40%.

To reduce concentration by 10% ⇒ 120 ml mixture is to be replaced by water.

To reduce concentration by 50% ⇒ complete mixture is to be replaced by water.

∴ The capacity of bottle = $\frac{50 \times 120}{10} = 600$ ml.

Example 3

In what proportion should milk and water be mixed to reduce the price of milk from ₹ 20 per liter to ₹ 15 per liter?

Solution

Cost price of milk = ₹ 20 per liter

Cost price of water = ₹ 0 per liter

Required cost price of mixture = ₹ 15 per liter

Applying the rule of alligation as follows:

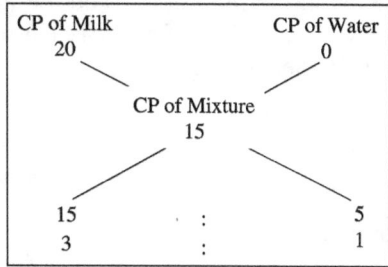

So, milk and water is to be mixed in the ratio of 15 : 5 or 3 : 1 to reduce the CP from ₹ 20 to ₹ 15.

Example 4

How many kilogram of rice costing ₹ 36 per kg must be mixed with 24 kg of rice costing ₹ 43 per kg so as to gain of 20% of profit by selling the mixture at ₹ 46.80 per kg?

Solution

To earn a profit of 20%:

SP of mixture = 120% of CP of mixture

$$46.80 = \frac{120}{100} \times CP \text{ of mixture}$$

$\therefore$ CP of mixture = $\frac{46.80 \times 100}{120}$ = ₹ 39.

Applying the rule of alligation as follows:

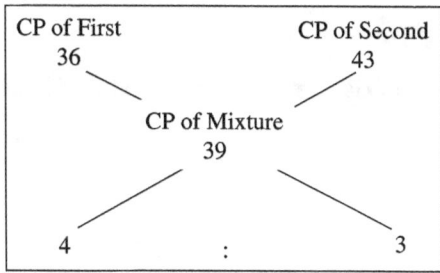

So, the first variety costing ₹ 36/kg and second variety costing ₹ 43/kg should be mixed in the ratio of 4:3.

As second variety of rice costing ₹ 43 a kg is taken 24 kg;

$\therefore 3x = 24$ kg $\Rightarrow x = 8$

Quantity of rice costing ₹ 43 per kg to be mixed = $4 \times 8 = 32$ kg.

Example 5

Two varieties of sugars are mixed in the ratio of 3:2 and the mixture is sold for ₹ 28.60 at 10% profit. If the cost price of second variety of sugar is ₹ 5 per kg more than that of first variety. Find the cost price of first variety of sugar.

Solution

To earn a profit of 10%:

SP of mixture = 110% of CP of mixture

$$28.60 = \frac{110}{100} \times CP \text{ of mixture}$$

$\therefore$ CP of mixture = $\frac{28.60 \times 100}{110}$ = ₹ 26

Let the CP of first variety of sugar = ₹ x

So, CP of second variety of sugar = ₹ $x + 5$

Applying the rule of alligation as follows:

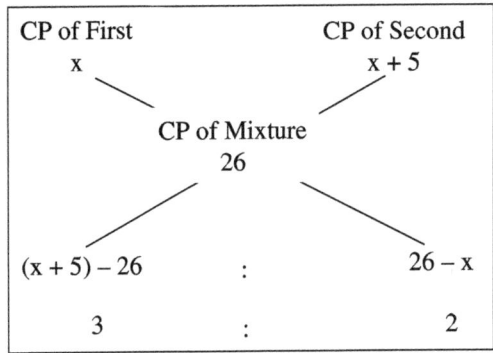

As the first and second variety of rice are mixed in the ratio of 3:2,

$$\frac{(x+5)-26}{26-x} = \frac{3}{2}$$

$\Rightarrow \frac{x-21}{26-x} = \frac{3}{2}$

$\Rightarrow 2(x-21) = 3(26-x)$

$\Rightarrow 2x - 42 = 78 - 3x$

$\Rightarrow 5x = 120$

$\therefore x = 24.$

So, the cost price of first variety of sugar is ₹ 24 per kg.

Example 6

Vessels P contain alcohol and water in the ratio of 2:3, while vessel Q contains alcohol and water in the ratio of 4:1. Find the ratio in which these two solutions are to be mixed to get a resulting mixture in which the ratio of alcohol to water is 3:1.

Solution

As the ratio of alcohol and water in P vessel is 2:3, so the content of alcohol in vessel P is $2/5^{th}$ of the total solution.

As the ratio of alcohol and water in Q vessel is 4:1, so the content of alcohol in vessel Q is $4/5^{th}$ of the total solution.

As the ratio of alcohol and water in resulting mixture should be 3:1, so the content of alcohol in the resulting mixture should be $3/4^{th}$ of the total solution.

Applying the rule of alligation as follows:

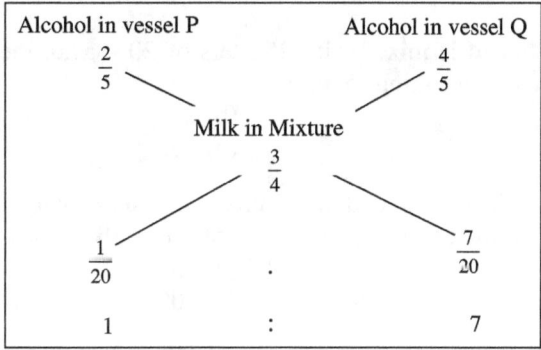

So, the solutions from the vessel P and vessel Q are mixed in the ratio of 1:7.

Example 7

A tank contains 50 liters of acid. 10 liters of acid is removed from the tank and is replaced by 10 liters of water. If this operation is repeated another two times, what is the percentage of acid left in tank?

Solution

If there is P liters of pure liquid initially, and it is replaced by Q liters of another liquid every time, then at the end of 'n' such operations, the concentration 'k' of the liquid in the solution is given by:

$$\left(\frac{P-Q}{P}\right)^n = k$$

$$\left(\frac{50-10}{50}\right)^3 = k$$

$$\left(\frac{4}{5}\right)^3 = k$$

∴ $k = \dfrac{64}{125}$.

Percentage of concentration = $100\,k = 100 \times \dfrac{64}{125} = 51.2\%$

So, percentage of acid left in the tank after 3 such operations is 51.2%.

EXERCISE

1. If two kinds of milks which cost ₹ 18 a liter and ₹ 24 a liter are mixed in the ratio of 3:2, then find the cost of the mixture per liter.
   (a) ₹ 20.4
   (b) ₹ 21.0
   (c) ₹ 20.8
   (d) ₹ 21.80

2. If 20 liters of 30% acid is mixed with 25 liters of 20% acid, then find the percentage concentration of acid in resulting solution.
   (a) 22.8
   (b) 25.2
   (c) 24.4
   (d) 23.6

3. A vessel contains 20 liters of a mixture of milk and water containing 60% milk. If 5 liters of pure milk is added to it, then find the percentage of milk in the new mixture.
   (a) 62%
   (b) 65%
   (c) 68%
   (d) 70%

4. A vessel is full of a mixture of milk and water, with 9% milk. 9 liters are withdrawn and then replaced with pure water. If the milk is now 6%, how much liters dose the vessel hold?
   (a) 25
   (b) 18
   (c) 40
   (d) 27

5. A liter of pure milk is added to 6 liters of a solution of milk and water containing 30% milk. Find the percentage of water in the resulting solution.
   (a) 55%
   (b) 50%
   (c) 60%
   (d) 65%

6. A milkman has 50 liters of pure milk. Find the quantity of water to be added in it so that he gets 20% profit by selling it at its cost price?
   (a) 10 liters
   (b) 12 liters
   (c) 15 liters
   (d) 20 liters

7. In what ratio must a grocer mix two varieties of pulses costing ₹ 16 per kg and ₹ 22 per kg respectively so as to get a mixture worth ₹ 20.50 per kg?
   (a) 1:1
   (b) 1:2
   (c) 1:3
   (d) 2:3

8. An investor invests a total sum of ₹ 42000 in two different schemes for a year. In the 1st scheme he earns an interest of 8% and in the 2nd scheme he earns an interest of 11%. The overall interest he received at the end of year is 10.5%. How much money he invested in 2nd scheme?
   (a) ₹ 24000
   (b) ₹ 28000
   (c) ₹ 30000
   (d) ₹ 35000

9. A total of ₹ 810 was collected from boys and girls of a class of 120 students. If each boy contributes ₹ 8 and each girl contributes ₹ 5, then find the number of boys and girls in the class.
   (a) 90, 30
   (b) 80, 40
   (c) 70, 50
   (d) 60, 60

10. In what proportion should milk and water be mixed to reduce the price of milk from ₹ 18 per liter to ₹ 16 per liter?
    (a) 8:1
    (b) 10:1
    (c) 6:1
    (d) None of these

11. There is 65 liters of solution of milk and water in which milk forms 75%. How much water must be added to this solution to make it solution in which milk forms 65%?
    (a) 5 liters
    (b) 6 liters
    (c) 8 liters
    (d) 10 liters

12. In 20 liters of sugar solution containing 300 gm of sugar per liter another sugar solution containing 120 gm of sugar per liter is mixed with it. The resulting solution contains 200 gm of sugar per liter. Find the quantity of second sugar solution.
    (a) 15 liters
    (b) 22 liters
    (c) 25 liters
    (d) 30 liters

13. In what ratio a trader must mix two varieties of tea worth ₹ 60 per kg and ₹ 72 per kg so that by selling the mixture at ₹ 80 per kg he may gain 25%?
    (a) 1:2
    (b) 2:1
    (c) 1:3
    (d) 2:3

14. How many kilogram of sugar costing ₹ 24 per kg must be mixed with 15 kg of sugar costing ₹ 28 per kg so as to gain of 10% of profit by selling the mixture at ₹ 27.50 per kg?
    (a) 36 kg
    (b) 45 kg
    (c) 48 kg
    (d) 60 kg

15. Two varieties of rice are mixed together in the ratio 2:3. The cost price of each kg of second variety is ₹ 5 more than the cost price of each kg of first variety of rice. If the cost price of mixture is ₹ 25, then find the cost price of first variety of rice.
    (a) ₹ 20
    (b) ₹ 22
    (c) ₹ 23
    (d) ₹ 24

16. A shopkeeper mixes two varieties of cooking oil in the ratio 2:3, which cost ₹ 20 per liter and ₹ 24 per liter respectively. Find the ratio in which two varieties of oil is to be mixed

if the cost price of second variety drops by ₹ 1 per liter and cost price of mixture remained the same.
(a) 1:3 (b) 1:4
(c) 1:2 (d) 2:1

17. Two vessels contain spirit and water mixed respectively in the ratio of 1:3 and 3:5. Find the ratio in which these are to be mixed to get a new mixture in which the ratio of spirit to water is 1:2.
(a) 2:1 (b) 1:2
(c) 3:1 (d) 1:3

18. There are two glasses having mixtures of wine and water. In glass 1 the ratio of wine and water is 1:2 and in glass 2 the ratio of wine and water is 4:1. Find the amount of mixture that should be taken from glass 1 in order to make 280 ml of mixture containing equal amount of water and wine.
(a) 180 ml (b) 140 ml
(c) 200 ml (d) None of these

19. Vessel A contains milk and water in the ratio of 1:4 while vessel B contains milk and water in the ratio of 3:1. How much liters of solution should be taken from vessel A to mix with solution from vessel B so as to form a resulting mixture of 44 liters containing equal amount of milk and water?
(a) 15 liters (b) 18 liters
(c) 20 liters (d) 24 liters

20. How many liters of mixture having acid and water in the proportion of 3:2 should be added to 60 liters of 75% acid solution such that a resultant mixture having $2/3^{rd}$ of acid is obtained?
(a) 60 liters (b) 75 liters
(c) 80 liters (d) 90 liters

21. A tank is filled with a mixture of acid and water in the ratio of 5:3. How much of the mixture must be drawn off from the tank and replaced with water so that the resulting mixture should have equal amount of acid and water?
(a) $1/3^{rd}$ (b) $1/4^{th}$
(c) $1/5^{th}$ (d) $1/6^{th}$

22. A vessel has 60 liters of solution of alcohol and water, having 80% alcohol. How many liters of the solution must be withdrawn from the vessel and replaced with water so that the vessel should have 60% alcohol solution?
(a) 10 (b) 15
(c) 20 (d) 24

23. Two vessels contain water and alcohol in the ratio of 1:2 and 2:3. The two solutions are mixed by taking 6 liters from first vessel and 30 liters from second vessel. Find the ratio of alcohol to water in the resulting solution.
(a) 5:7 (b) 5:9
(c) 7:11 (d) 5:13

24. From a tank containing only diesel, 6 liters are drawn and replaced with kerosene. Again 6 liters of the mixture is taken out and replaced with kerosene. The ratio of diesel to kerosene now is 9 : 16. How many liters of diesel was there initially?
    (a) 14 liters
    (b) 15 liters
    (c) 16 liters
    (d) 18 liters

25. From a vessel containing 300 liters of pure milk, 60 liters is taken out and was diluted with 60 liters of water. Again 60 liters of diluted milk is taken out and is replaced with water. How much is the concentration of milk after these two operations?
    (a) 64%
    (b) 70%
    (c) 75%
    (d) 78%

26. A can contains 500 ml of beer. 50 ml of beer is removed from the can and is replaced by 50 ml of water. If this operation is repeated another two times, what is the percentage of beer left in can at the end?
    (a) 65%
    (b) 68.5%
    (c) 72.9%
    (d) 81%

27. Milk and water are mixed in the ratio of 5 : 4 in a vessel. By adding 5 liters of water the vessel becomes full and the ratio of milk and water changes to 4 : 5. What is the capacity of vessel?
    (a) 20 liters
    (b) 22.5 liters
    (c) 24 liters
    (d) 25 liters

28. Alloy A contains copper and zinc in the ratio of 2:3, while alloy B contains copper and zinc in the ratio of 3:1. Equal weights of two alloys are melted and mixed to form a third alloy. Find the ratio of copper and zinc in the third alloy.
    (a) 12:17
    (b) 17:20
    (c) 23:17
    (d) 21:32

KEYS

1. (a)	2. (c)	3. (c)	4. (d)	5. (c)	6. (a)	7. (c)	8. (d)
9. (c)	10. (a)	11. (d)	12. (c)	13. (b)	14. (b)	15. (b)	16. (b)
17. (b)	18. (a)	19. (c)	20. (b)	21. (c)	22. (b)	23. (c)	24. (b)
25. (a)	26. (c)	27. (d)	28. (c)				

SOLUTIONS

Solution 1

Cost of mixture $= \dfrac{18(3) + 24(2)}{3+2}$

$= \dfrac{54+48}{5}$

$= ₹\ 20.4.$

Choice (a)

Solution 2

Acid content in 1st solution = 30% of 20 liters $= \dfrac{30}{100} \times 20 = 6$ liters

Acid content in 2nd solution = 20% of 25 liters $= \dfrac{20}{100} \times 25 = 5$ liters

Acid contents in the mixture of 2 solutions = 6 + 5 = 11 liters

Percentage concentration in resulting mixture $= \dfrac{11}{20+25} \times 100$

$= 24.4\%.$

Choice (c)

Solution 3

Quantity of pure milk in initial solution $= \dfrac{60}{100} \times 20 = 12$ liters

Quantity of pure milk after 5 liters is added = 12 + 5 = 17 liters

Percentage of milk in the new mixture $= \dfrac{17}{25} \times 100 = 68\%.$

Choice (c)

Solution 4

As 9 liters of solution is replaced by 9 liters of pure water, the milk concentration in the solution changes from 9% to 6%

To reduce concentration by 3% ⇒ 9 liters solution is to be replaced by water
To reduce concentration by 9% ⇒ complete solution is to be replaced by water

Amount of solution the vessel can hold $= \dfrac{9 \times 9}{3} = 27$ litres.

Choice (d)

Solution 5

Milk content in 1 liter of 1st solution = 1 liter

Milk content in 6 liter of 2nd solution = $\frac{30}{100} \times 6 = 1.8$ liters

Milk content in the mixture of 2 solutions = $1 + 1.8 = 2.8$ liters

Percentage concentration of milk in mixture = $\frac{2.8}{1+6} \times 100 = 40\%$

∴ Percentage of water in resulting solution = 60%.

Choice (c)

Solution 6

If the CP and SP of milk are same, and if he sells 50 liter, then he will not get any profit.

To earn 20% profit the milkman should sell = $1.2 \times 50 = 60$ liters

So, quantity of water to be added to make 20% profit = $60 - 50 = 10$ liters.

Choice (a)

Solution 7

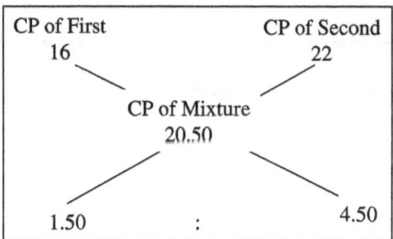

So, the two varieties of pulses should be mixed in the ratio of 1.50 : 4.50 or 1:3.

Choice (c)

Solution 8

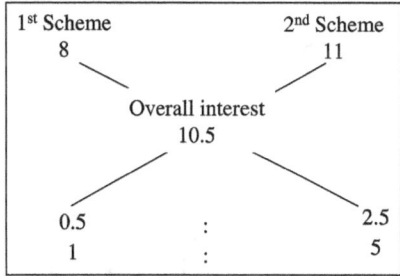

Ratio of Investment in 1st scheme and 2nd scheme is $x : 5x$.

$x + 5x = ₹\ 42000$

$6x = ₹\ 42000$

∴ $x = ₹\ 7000$

So, investment in 2nd scheme = $5 \times 7000 = ₹\ 35000$.

Choice (d)

Solution 9

Assuming the class is full of boys, total amount collected = $120 \times 8 = ₹\ 960$

Assuming the class is full of girls, total amount collected = $120 \times 5 = ₹\ 600$.

Ratio of boys to girls can be found by applying allegation rule as follows:

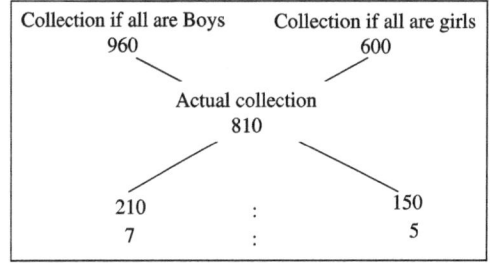

So, boys and girls are in the ratio of 7:5 in the class.

$7x + 5x = 120$

$12x = 120$

∴ $x = 10$

Boys = 70 and Girls = 50.

Choice (c)

Solution 10

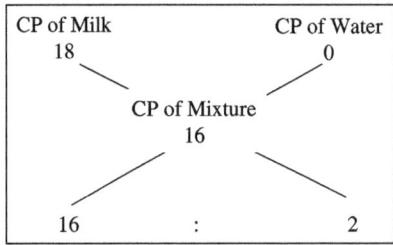

So, milk and water is to be mixed in the ratio of 16 : 2 or 8 : 1.

Choice (a)

Solution 11

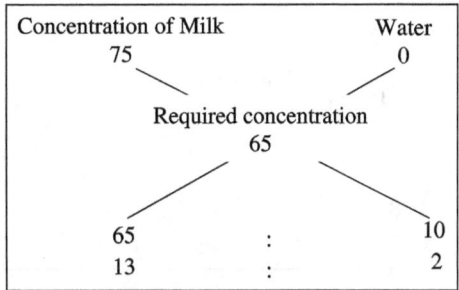

$13x = 65$ liters

$\therefore x = 5$

So, water to be added = $2 \times 5 = 10$ liters.

Choice (d)

Solution 12

The ratio in which two solutions are mixed can be found by the rule of alligation:

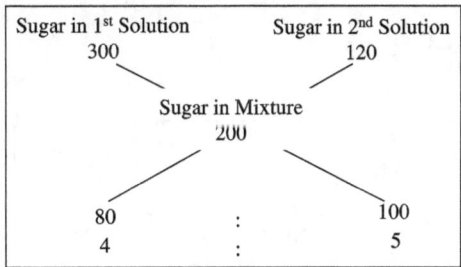

Quantity of 1st sugar solution = $4x = 20$ liters

$\therefore x = 5$

So, quantity of 2nd sugar solution = $5x = 5 \times 5 = 25$ liters.

Choice (c)

Solution 13

To earn a profit of 25%:

SP of mixture = 125% of CP of mixture

$80 = \frac{125}{100} \times CP$ of mixture

$\therefore CP$ of mixture = $\frac{80 \times 100}{125}$ = ₹ 64

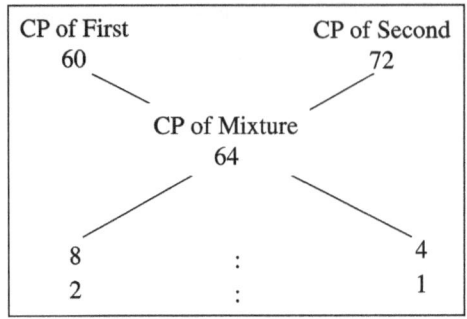

So, the ratio in which tea costing ₹ 60 per kg and ₹ 72 per kg should be mixed is 2:1.

Choice (b)

Solution 14

To earn a profit of 10%:

SP of mixture = 110% of CP of mixture

$$27.50 = \frac{110}{100} \times CP \text{ of mixture}$$

$\therefore$ CP of mixture = $\frac{27.50 \times 100}{110}$ = ₹ 25.

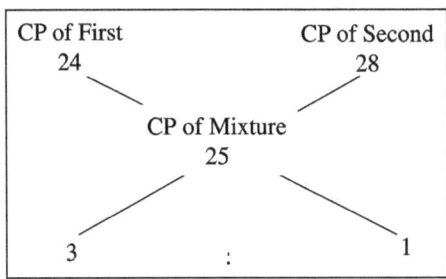

So, the first variety costing ₹ 24/kg and second variety costing ₹ 28/kg should be mixed in the ratio of 3:1.

Quantity of sugar costing ₹ 24 per kg = 3 × 15 = 45 kg.

Choice (b)

Solution 15

Let the CP of first variety of rice = ₹ x

So, CP of second variety of rice = ₹ $x + 5$

Applying the rule of alligation as follows:

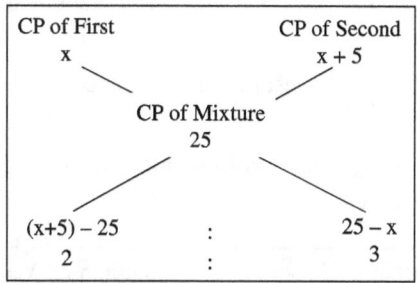

As the first and second variety of rice are mixed in the ratio of 2:3,

$$\frac{(x+5)-25}{25-x} = \frac{2}{3}$$

$\Rightarrow \frac{x-20}{25-x} = \frac{2}{3}$

$\Rightarrow 3(x-20) = 2(25-x)$

$\Rightarrow 3x - 60 = 50 - 2x$

$\Rightarrow 5x = 110$

$\therefore x = 22.$

Choice (b)

Solution 16

CP of mixture = $\frac{20(2) + 24(3)}{2+3} = \frac{40+72}{5} =$ ₹ 22.40

If the cost price of second variety of oil drops by ₹ 1 (new CP = ₹ 23 per liter), and the CP of mixture remained the same, the ratio of mixing can be found by rule of allegation as follows:

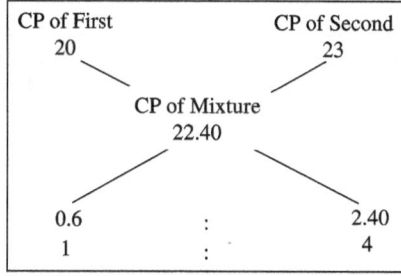

So, after the price of second variety of oil drops by ₹ 1, the ratio in which first and second variety of oils are mixed is 1:4.

Choice (b)

Solution 17

As the ratio of sprit and water in 1st vessel is 1:3, so the content of spirit in 1st vessel is 1/4th of the total solution.

As the ratio of sprit and water in 2nd vessel is 3:5, so the content of spirit in 2nd vessel is 3/8th of the total solution.

As the ratio of sprit and water in the resulting mixture is 1:2, so the content of spirit in mixture is 1/3rd of the total solution.

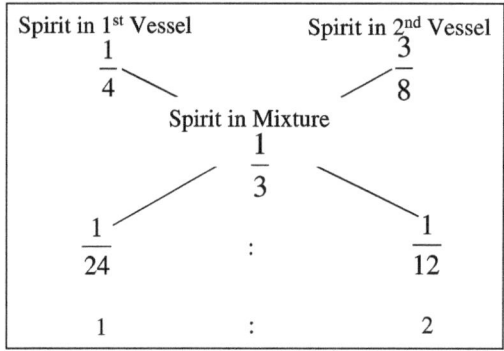

So, the solutions from the first and second vessel are mixed in the ratio of 1:2.

Choice (b)

Solution 18

As the ratio of wine and water in 1st glass is 1:2, so the content of wine in 1st glass is 1/3rd of the total solution.

As the ratio of wine and water in 2nd glass is 4:1, so the content of wine in 2nd glass is 4/5th of the total solution.

As the ratio of wine and water in resulting mixture should be 1:1, so the content of wine in the resulting mixture will be half of the total solution.

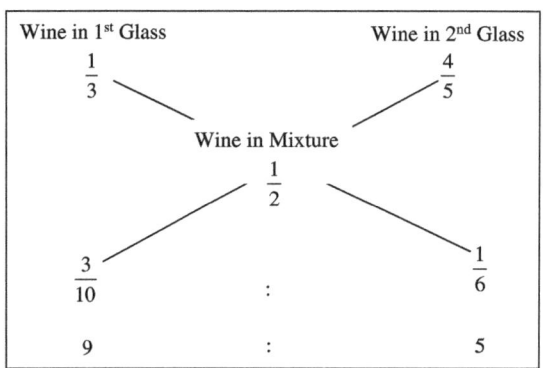

Solution taken from 1st glass = $9x$

Solution taken from 2nd glass = $5x$

$9x + 5x = 280$ ml

$14x = 280$

∴ $x = 20$

Therefore, solution taken from first glass = 9×20
= 180 ml.

Choice (a)

Solution 19

As the ratio of milk and water in A vessel is 1:4, so the content of milk in vessel A is 1/5th of the total solution.

As the ratio of milk and water in B vessel is 3:1, so the content of milk in vessel B is 3/4th of the total solution.

As the ratio of milk and water in resulting mixture should be 1:1, so the content of milk in the resulting mixture will be half of the total solution.

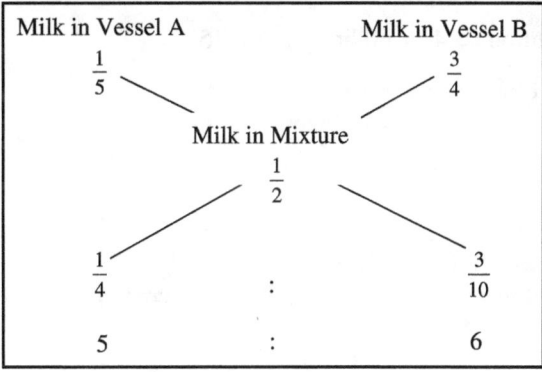

Solution from vessel A + Solution from vessel B = 44 liters

$5x + 6x = 44$ liters

$11x = 44$

∴ $x = 4$

So, solution to be taken from vessel A = 5×4
= 20 liters.

Choice (c)

Solution 20

Acid in first solution = $\frac{3}{5}$ (∵ Acid and water is in the ratio of 3:2)

Acid in second solution = $\frac{3}{4}$ (∵ 75% is given)

Acid in resulting solution = $\frac{2}{3}$

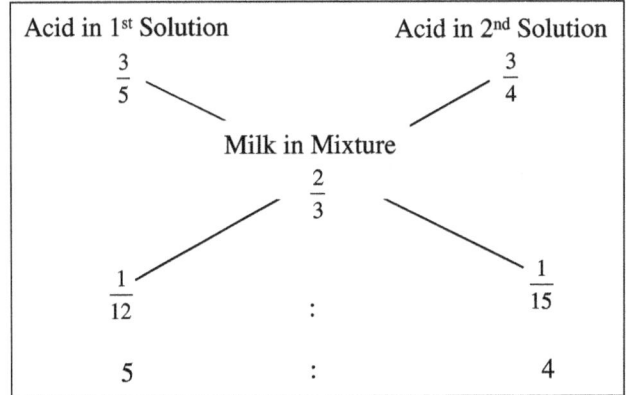

Quantity of second solution ⇒ $4x = 60$ liters ∴ $x = 15$

∴ Quantity of first solution ⇒ $5x = 5 \times 15$
= 75 liters.

Choice (b)

Solution 21

As the ratio of acid and water in the tank is 5:3, so the content of acid in the tank is $5/8^{th}$ of the total solution.

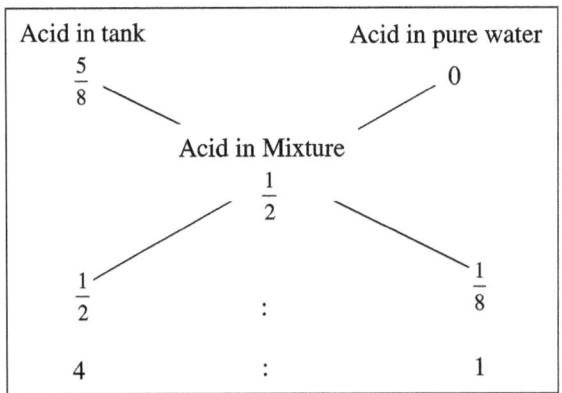

So, to make equal volume of acid and water in the tank, the solution and water should be mixed in the ratio of 4:1, or 1/5th part of the solution is to be replaced with water.

Choice (c)

Solution 22

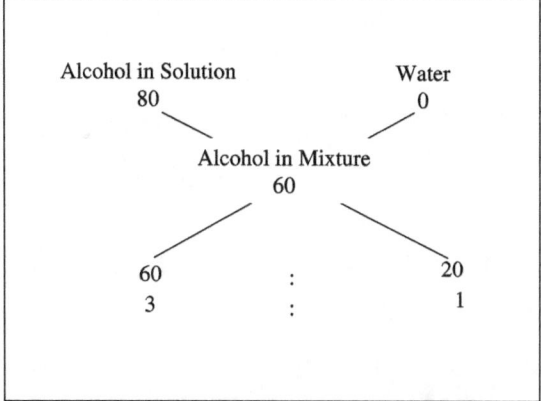

So, to reduce the concentration of alcohol from 80% to 60%, alcohol solution and pure water should be mixed in the ratio of 3:1, or 1/4th part of solution is to be replaced with water.

Quantity of solution to be replaced with water = $\frac{1}{4} \times 60$ liters

= 15 liters.

Choice (b)

Solution 23

Alcohol from first vessel = $\frac{1}{3} \times 6 = 2$ liters

Water from first vessel = $\frac{2}{3} \times 6 = 4$ liters

Alcohol from second vessel = $\frac{2}{5} \times 30 = 12$ liters

Water from second vessel = $\frac{3}{5} \times 30 = 18$ liters

Total alcohol in mixture = 2 + 12 = 14 liters

Total water in mixture = 4 + 18 = 22 liters

Ratio of alcohol to water in resulting solution = 14 : 22
= 7 : 11.

Choice (c)

Solution 24

If there is P liters of pure liquid initially, and it is replaced by Q liters of another liquid every time, then at the end of 'n' such operations, the concentration 'k' of the liquid in the solution is given by:

$$\left(\frac{P-Q}{P}\right)^n = k$$

$$\Rightarrow \left(\frac{P-6}{P}\right)^2 = \frac{9}{9+16}$$

$$\Rightarrow \left(\frac{P-6}{P}\right)^2 = \frac{9}{25}$$

$$\Rightarrow \frac{P-6}{P} = \frac{3}{5}$$

$$\Rightarrow 5(P-6) = 3P$$

$$\Rightarrow 5P - 30 = 3P$$

$$\Rightarrow 2P = 30$$

$$\therefore P = 15.$$

Choice (b)

Solution 25

If there is P liters of pure liquid initially, and it is replaced by Q liters of another liquid every time, then at the end of 'n' such operations, the concentration 'k' of the liquid in the solution is given by:

$$\left(\frac{P-Q}{P}\right)^n = k$$

$$\left(\frac{300-60}{300}\right)^2 = k$$

$$\left(\frac{4}{5}\right)^2 = k$$

$$\therefore k = \frac{16}{25}$$

Percentage of concentration $= 100\,k$

$$= 100 \times \frac{16}{25} = 64\%.$$

Choice (a)

Solution 26

If there is P liters of pure liquid initially, and it is replaced by Q liters of another liquid every time, then at the end of 'n' such operations, the concentration 'k' of the liquid in the solution is given by:

$$k = \left(\frac{P-Q}{P}\right)^n$$

$$k = \left(\frac{500-50}{500}\right)^3 = \left(\frac{9}{10}\right)^3 = 0.729$$

Percentage of concentration = 100 k
= 100 × 0.729
= 72.9%.

Choice (c)

Solution 27

Let the initial volume of milk and water in the vessel be $5x$ and $4x$ respectively.

After adding 5 liters of water to it the vessel becomes full;

So the capacity of vessel = $(5x + 4x + 5)$ liters

$$\frac{5x}{4x+5} = \frac{4}{5}$$

$\Rightarrow 25x = 16x + 20$

$\Rightarrow 9x = 20$

$\therefore x = \frac{20}{9}$

So, capacity of vessel = $5x + 4x + 5$
= $9x + 5$
= $9 \times \frac{20}{9} + 5$
= 25 liters.

Choice (d)

Solution 28

Let x kg of each alloy is taken for melting.

Copper in alloy A = $\frac{2x}{5}$

Copper in alloy B = $\frac{3x}{4}$

Portion of copper in third alloy $= \dfrac{\dfrac{2x}{5}+\dfrac{3x}{4}}{2x}$

$= \dfrac{\dfrac{8x+15x}{20}}{2x}$

$= \dfrac{23x}{20} \times \dfrac{1}{2x}$

$= \dfrac{23}{40}$

∴ Portion of zinc in third alloy $= 1 - \dfrac{23}{40}$

$= \dfrac{17}{40}$

So, the ratio of copper and zinc in third alloy is 23:17.

Choice (c)

12

Time and Work

INTRODUCTION

If a person can do a particular work in 'n' days, then in a day he is able to $1/n^{th}$ of work. This is considered by assuming the total work as one unit. Instead of this if we consider a total work as 'n' units which can be finished in 'n' days then the person can do one unit of work per day.

Let us assume that there is a job to make 50 wooden chairs. But there is only one carpenter available for this job. It is obvious that he cannot make all 50 chairs in a day, and his capacity is to make only 5 chairs in a day. Now the question is in how many days he will finish the total work (making 50 chairs)? He will take 10 days.

Following are the parameters involved in these problems:

Making 50 chairs $\Rightarrow$ Total Work $\Rightarrow$ W units
5 chairs per day $\Rightarrow$ Rate of doing work $\Rightarrow$ R units/day
10 days $\Rightarrow$ Number of days required $\Rightarrow$ N days

So, the relation between these variables is as follows:

Number of days required = $\dfrac{\text{Total work}}{\text{Rate of doing work}}$ i.e., $N = \dfrac{W}{R}$

or

Rate of doing work = $\dfrac{\text{Total work}}{\text{Number of days}}$ i.e., $R = \dfrac{W}{N}$

or

Total work = Number of days × Rate of doing work

i.e., $W = N \times R$

From the above relation we can conclude that rate of doing work and number of days required are inversely proportional. It means if we double the rate, the number of days required will be half.

Suppose if A is thrice as efficient as B, then the rate of doing work by them will be in the ratio of 3 : 1, and time taken by them to complete the work will be in the ratio of 1 : 3.

VARIATION

Following points are important in variation problems on time and work:

- If the time is constant, then work and men are directly proportional to each other *i.e.,* if work increases, then the number of men required to complete the work in same duration increases proportionately and vice-versa.
- If work is constant, Men and days are inversely proportional *i.e.,* if the number of men increases, the number of days required to complete the same work decreases in inverse proportion and vice-versa.
- If the number of working men is constant, then work and days are directly proportional *i.e.,* if work increases, the number of days required to complete the work with same working men proportionately increases and vice-versa.

SOLVED EXAMPLES

Example 1

A and B can complete a piece of work in 10 days and 15 days respectively. In how many days the work can be finished if both *A* and *B* work together?

Solution

Let us tabulate the case as follows:

	A	B	A+B
N	10 days	15 days	
R			
W			

Selecting the total work as LCM of 10 and 15, or any number which is divisible by both 10 and 15. So assuming total work as 30 units.

	A	B	A+B
N	10 days	15 days	
R			
W = 30 units			

Therefore rate of doing work of *A* is 3 units/day while that of *B* will be 2 units/day. If both work together they can do 3 + 2 = 5 units of work in a day.

	A	B	A+B
N	10 days	15 days	6 days
R	3	2	5
W = 30 units			

If total 30 units of work is done at the rate of 5 units per day (working together), then the work can be finished in 6 days.

Example 2

Two painters A and B can paint a building individually in 20 and 30 days respectively. With the help of C they finished the painting work in 10 days. In how many days C alone can paint the entire building?

Solution

Let us tabulate the case as follows:

	A	B	C	A + B + C
N	20 days	30 days		10 days
R				
W				

Selecting the total work as LCM of 20, 30 and 10.

	A	B	C	A + B + C
N	20 days	30 days		10 days
R				
W = 60 units				

Therefore the rate of doing work of A will be 3 units per day and B will be 2 units per day. If they work with C i.e., all three works together then their rate of working will be 6 units per day.

	A	B	C	A + B + C
N	20 days	30 days		10 days
R	3	2		6
W = 60 units				

It means C can do 1 unit per day; hence he can finish the painting of entire building in 60 days.

	A	B	C	A + B + C
N	20 days	30 days	60 days	10 days
R	3	2	1	6
W = 60 units				

Example 3

P and Q can finish a work individually in 12 and 15 days respectively. If P started the work alone and worked for 4 days and left; then Q alone can finish the remaining work in how many days?

Solution

Let us tabulate the case as follows:

	P	Q
N	12 days	15 days
R		
W		

Selecting the total work as LCM of 12 and 15 *i.e.*, 60. So rate of working of P and Q becomes 5 and 4 units/day respectively.

	P	Q
N	12 days	15 days
R	5	4
W = 60 units		

If P started the work and is working for 4 days, then:

P in 4 days = 5 × 4 = 20 units

Remaining work = 60 – 20 = 40 units

Time required by Q to finish remaining work = 40/4 = 10 days.

Example 4

A can finish a job in 16 days. He started the work and after 4 days, B joined him. They completed the job in 4 more days. Find the number of days in which B alone can complete the job.

Solution

Let us tabulate the case as follows:

	A	B	A+B
N	16 days	?	
R			
W			

To proceed further in this problem, at first we need to assume some value of total work (*i.e.*, W) as any number which is a multiple of 16.

	A	B	A+B
N	16 days	?	
R	5		
W = 80 units			

If we assume total work as 80 units, the rate of working of A is 5 units/day. If A started the work and is working for 4 days, then:

A in 4 days = 5 × 4 = 20 units

Remaining work = 80 – 20 = 60 units

This remaining work (of 60 units) is done by both A and B together in 4 days.
∴ Rate of A + B = 60/4 = 15 units/day

	A	B	A+B
N	16 days	8 days	
R	5	10	15
W = 80 units			

So rate of B will be 10 units/day, and hence he can finish the entire work alone in 8 days.

Example 5

A and B together can complete a job in 8 days and 16 days respectively. If they work on alternate days, then in how many days the job can be finished if:

1. A starts the work
2. B starts the work.

Solution

Let us tabulate the case as follows:

	A	B
N	8 days	16 days
R		
W		

Assuming the total work as 16 units, hence rate of working of A and B will be 2 units/day and 1 unit/day respectively.

	A	B
N	8 days	16 days
R	2	1
W = 16		

(i) If A Starts the Work

In 2 days   – 3 units
In 10 days   – 15 units

On 11th day it's a turn of A ($\because$ A is working on all odd number of days). A will do 1 units of work, for which time required is half day, therefore the work will be finished in 10½ days.

Hence the work can be finished in 10½ days.

(ii) If B Starts the Work

In 2 days   - 3 units
In 10 days - 15 units

On 11th day it's a turn of B ($\because$ B is working on all odd number of days). B will do 1 units of work on 11th day and the work is finished.

Hence the work can be finished in 11 days.

Example 6

Bharat is twice as good a workman as Chetan, and Amar is 50% more efficient than Bharat. If together they can finish a work in 15 days, then in how many days Bharat alone can finish it?

Solution

Let us tabulate the case as follows:

	A	B	C	A + B + C
N				15 days
R				
W				

As it is said that B is twice as good workman as C, it means if C can do 1 unit of work in a day then B is able to do 2 units of work in a day. If A is 50% more efficient than B, then A is able to do 3 units of work per day.

	A	B	C	A + B + C
N				15 days
R	3	2	1	6
W				

So, together they are able to do 6 units of work per day. So the total work will be 15 × 6 = 90 units.

	A	B	C	A + B + C
N		45 days		15 days
R	3	2	1	6
W = 90 units				

So B alone can finish it in 45 days.

Example 7

A and B can do a piece of work in 24 days; B and C can do it in 30 days; A and C can do it in 60 days. In how many days can A alone finish it?

Solution

Let us tabulate the case as follows:

	A	A + B	B + C	A + C
N	?	24 days	30 days	60 days
R				
W				

Taking the total work as LCM of 24, 30 and 60 i.e., 120 units. Therefore the rate of doing work of A and B, B and C and A and C will be 5, 4, and 2 units/day respectively.

	A	A + B	B + C	A + C
N	?	24 days	30 days	60 days
R		5	4	2
W = 120 units				

If we add the rate of A and B and A and C it will be 5 + 2 = 7 units/day.

	A	A + B	B + C	A + C	2A + B + C
N	?	20 days	30 days	40 days	
R		5	4	2	7
W = 120 units					

So, the rate of $A = \dfrac{(2A + B + C) - (B + C)}{2} = \dfrac{7 - 4}{2} = 1.5$ units/day

	A	A + B	B + C	A + C	2A + B + C
N	80 days	20 days	30 days	40 days	
R	1.5	5	4	2	7
W = 120 units					

Therefore A alone can finish the work in 120/1.5 = 80 days.

Example 8

20 men take 10 days to complete a job working 12 hours a day. Find the number of men required to complete a job, twice as large, in 40 days working 8 hours a day.

Solution

Assuming that 1 man working for 1 hour is able to do 1 unit of work

Units of work done by 20 men in 10 day working 12 hrs/day:

$20 \times 10 \times 12 = 2400$ units

Amount of work expected from x men in 40 days working 8 hrs/day = 4800 units

$\therefore x \times 40 \times 8 = 4800$ units

$\therefore \quad x = \dfrac{4800}{40 \times 8} = 15.$

Example 9

6 men and 8 women can complete a job in 10 days. 8 men and 22 women can complete it in 5 days. Find the time taken by 34 women to complete the same job.

Solution

$(6m + 8w) \times 10 \text{ days} = \text{Job}$ ... (1)
$(8m + 22w) \times 5 \text{ days} = \text{Job}$ ... (2)
$34w \times x \text{ days} = \text{Job}$ ... (3)

Equating equation (1) and (2)

$(6m + 8w) \times 10 = (8m + 22w) \times 5$
$60m + 80w = 40m + 110w$
$20m = 30w$
$2m = 3w$

Equating equation (1) and (3)

$(6m + 8w) \times 10 = 34w \times x$
$(9w + 8w) \times 10 = 34w \times x$ $\quad (\because 6m = 9w)$

$\therefore x = \dfrac{17 \times 10}{34} = 5$ days.

EXERCISE

1. Ajay can do a work in 12 days while Anand can do the same work in 8 days. Both of them finish the work together and get ₹ 6500. What is the share of Ajay?
   (a) ₹ 2500
   (b) ₹ 2600
   (c) ₹ 2700
   (d) ₹ 3000

2. A man can do a piece of work in 20 days, but with the help of his son; he can do it in 12 days. In what time can the son do it alone?
   (a) 30 days
   (b) 28 days
   (c) 26 days
   (d) 25 days

3. Rohan and Sohan can do a piece of work in 10 days and Rohan alone can do it in 12 days. In how many days can Sohan do it alone?
   (a) 60 days
   (b) 30 days
   (c) 50 days
   (d) 45 days

4. A can do a piece of work in 10 days and B can do the same work in 20 days. With the help of C, they finished the work in 5 days. How long will it take for C alone to finish the work?
   (a) 20 days
   (b) 10 days
   (c) 35 days
   (d) 15 days

5. P can do a piece of work in 20 days. He works at it for 5 days and then Q finishes it in 10 more days. In how many days will P and Q together finish the work?
   (a) 6 days
   (b) 8 days
   (c) 10 days
   (d) 12 days

6. Anil and Sunil undertake to do a piece of work for ₹ 200. Anil alone can do it in 24 days while Sunil alone do it in 30 days. With the help of Pradeep, they finished the work in 12 days. How much should Pradeep get for his work?
   (a) ₹ 20
   (b) ₹ 100
   (c) ₹ 180
   (d) ₹ 50

7. John and Thomas together can complete a project in 45 days and receives ₹ 13,500. If John is three times as efficient as Thomas, what is the amount of money he earns in 10 days?
   (a) ₹ 2000
   (b) ₹ 2250
   (c) ₹ 2500
   (d) ₹ 2750

8. In 8 days, P can do as much work as Q can do it in 12 days. To do a certain job both together take 36 days. In how many days can P, working alone, complete the job?
   (a) 45 days
   (b) 50 days
   (c) 60 days
   (d) 90 days

9. A can do as much work in 2 days as B can do in 3 days and B can do as much in 4 days as C in 5 days. A piece of work takes 20 days if all work together. How long would B take to do all the work by himself?
   (a) 82 days
   (b) 44 days
   (c) 66 days
   (d) 50 days

10. A is 25% more efficient than B. How much time will they take working together to complete a job which A alone could have done in 90 days?
    (a) 75 days
    (b) 60 days
    (c) 55 days
    (d) 50 days

11. A machine of type A which has to produce 1500 parts, can do so in 30 hours. The machine breaks down after 10 hours. Another machine of type B completes the remaining work in 10 hours. In 30 hours how many parts can both of them together produce?
    (a) 3000
    (b) 4500
    (c) 6000
    (d) 2500

12. A does 40% of a work in 20 days. He then calls in B and they together finish the remaining work in 10 days. How long B alone would take to do the whole work?
    (a) 40 days
    (b) 30 days
    (c) 28 days
    (d) 25 days

13. P and Q can complete a job working individually in 30 and 45 days respectively. If Q joins P after some days and the whole work is completed in 20 days from the beginning, after how many days did Q join P?
    (a) 5 days
    (b) 14 days
    (c) 15 days
    (d) 10 days

14. Pranay and Raju are working on an assignment. Pranay takes 8 hrs to type 32 pages on a computer, while Raju takes 6 hrs to type 36 pages. How much time will they take, working together on two different computers to type an assignment of 200 pages?
    (a) 30 hrs
    (b) 25 hrs
    (c) 20 hrs
    (d) 15 hrs

15. Manoj and Nandu together can complete a work in 12 days. Manoj alone can complete it in 20 days. If Nandu does the work only for half a day daily, then in how many days they together will complete the work?
    (a) 10 days
    (b) 12 days
    (c) 15 days
    (d) 18 days

16. Abhay, Bharat and Chandra can complete a job together in 15 days, whereas Bharat and Chandra can complete the same work together in 30 days. After Abhay has worked for 5 days and stopped, Bharat took up and worked for 15 days. Chandra completed the remaining work in 30 days. In how many days can each complete the work alone?
    (a) 30; 45; 90
    (b) 30; 90; 45
    (c) 45; 30; 90
    (d) 45; 90; 30

17. P, Q and R can do a project in 30, 15 and 20 days respectively. They all together started the work on project. P leaves 4 days before completion of project and Q leaves 1 day before completion of project. In how many days will the project be completed?
    (a) 9 days
    (b) 10 days
    (c) 11 days
    (d) 8 days

18. P and Q can complete a piece of work in 20 days, Q and R in 15 days, and P and R in 12 days. In how many days respectively can P, Q and R competes the work if they work individually?
    (a) 30; 60; 20
    (b) 45; 60; 180
    (c) 30; 45; 90
    (d) 45; 60; 20

19. P and Q can individually complete the work in 15 days and 25 days respectively. In how many days can P and Q complete the work, if they work on alternate days with P beginning the work?
    (a) 18 days
    (b) 18½ days
    (c) 18⅗ days
    (d) 19 days

20. Sam can type a report in 12 hours, whereas Raj can type the same report in 18 hours. If they work alternately for 2 hrs each, starting with Sam, in how much time will they complete the work?
    (a) 14 1/3 hrs
    (b) 14½ hrs
    (c) 14 hrs
    (d) 7 hrs

21. A, B and C can complete a certain work in 8, 16 and 12 days respectively. If they work in rotation with one day each in the order of A, B, and C, in how many days will the work be completed?
    (a) 10 2/3
    (b) 10½
    (c) 11
    (d) 11 3/5

22. A mountain is 30 m high. A mountaineer climbs 3 m in one minute and comes down by 1 m every next minute. In what time dose the mountaineer can reach the peak of mountain?
    (a) 28 2/3 min
    (b) 30 min
    (c) 29 1/3 min
    (d) None of these

23. A and B together can do a piece of work in 18 days. A having worked for 10 days, B finishes the remaining work in 30 days. In how many days shall B finish the whole work alone?
    (a) 40 days
    (b) 45 days
    (c) 50 days
    (d) 60 days

24. Twenty women can do a work in sixteen days. Sixteen men can complete the same work in fifteen days. What is the ratio between the capacity of a man and a woman?
    (a) 2 : 3
    (b) 4 : 3
    (c) 4 : 5
    (d) 1 : 1

25. 5 men and 2 boys working together can do four times as much work as a man and a boy. Working capacities of a man and a boy are in the ratio
    (a) 2 : 1
    (b) 3 : 1
    (c) 3 : 2
    (d) 4 : 1

26. 18 men take 20 days to complete a job working 12 hours a day. Find the number of days that 15 men will take to complete it if they work 9 hours a day.
    (a) 26 days
    (b) 28 days
    (c) 30 days
    (d) 32 days

27. 30 men can produce 1500 bolts in 24 days working 6 hours a day. In how many days can 18 men produce 1800 bolts working 8 hours a day?
    (a) 36
    (b) 63
    (c) 18
    (d) 45

28. A certain number of men can complete a piece of work in 30 days. If there were 5 men more, the work would have finished in 10 days less. How many men were originally there?
    (a) 15
    (b) 12
    (c) 10
    (d) 8

29. 20 workers can finish a piece of work in 30 days. After how many days should 5 workers leave the job so that the work is completed in 35 days?
    (a) 5 days (b) 10 days
    (c) 15 days (d) 20 days

30. 60 men can do a piece of work in 30 days. After every 10 days, 10 men leave. In how many days will the work be completed?
    (a) 45 (b) 40
    (c) 50 (d) 55

31. 6 men or 8 women can level a field in 42 days. In how many days can 9 men and 2 women complete the same work?
    (a) 24 days (b) 12 days
    (c) 21 days (d) 30 days

32. 10 men or 6 women can do a piece of work in 20 days. In what time can 3 men and 3 women do the work?
    (a) 20 days (b) 22 days
    (c) 24 days (d) 25 days

33. 3 men and 6 women can do a piece of work in 12 days; 5 men and 6 women can do the same work in 9 days. In how many days can 3 men and 3 women complete the work?
    (a) 16 (b) 9
    (c) 12 (d) 8

34. A work can be finished by 1 man and 3 boys together in 10 days, which one woman can complete in 30 days. How many women should accompany 3 men and 9 boys to complete the same work in 2 days?
    (a) 2 (b) 3
    (c) 4 (d) 6

35. 2 men and 3 women together can complete a work in 30 days. It takes 90 days for one man alone to complete the same work. How many days will be required for one woman alone to complete the same work?
    (a) 90 days (b) 135 days
    (c) 180 days (d) 270 days

36. A labor was engaged for 30 days on the condition that he would receive ₹ 30 each day he worked and would loose ₹ 12 for each day he was absent. If he gets ₹ 564, for how many days he was absent?
    (a) 8 (b) 6
    (c) 4 (d) 7

37. 4 boys and 6 girls can do a software project in 8 days, while 3 boys and 7 girls can make it in 10 days. In how many days can 10 girls alone make it?
    (a) 20 days (b) 30 days
    (c) 40 days (d) 45 days

38. A group of painters are employed to paint a building. After half the building is painted, double the number of painters joins the original group. The painting work is finished 6 days earlier than scheduled. What is the total number of days the initial group of painters would have taken to paint the complete building?
    (a) 16 days
    (b) 18 days
    (c) 20 days
    (d) 21 days

39. A contractor needs 80 workers to make 20 km road in 84 days. How many workers dose he need to make 30 km road in 63 days?
    (a) 100
    (b) 120
    (c) 150
    (d) 160

40. The work done by a man in 3 days is equal to the work done by four women in 2 days. How many men are needed to do a piece of work in 48 days which 72 women can do in 16 days?
    (a) 9
    (b) 10
    (c) 12
    (d) 15

KEYS

1. (b)	2. (a)	3. (a)	4. (a)	5. (b)	6. (a)	7. (b)	8. (c)
9. (c)	10. (d)	11. (b)	12. (d)	13. (a)	14. (c)	15. (c)	16. (b)
17. (d)	18. (a)	19. (c)	20. (c)	21. (c)	22. (a)	23. (b)	24. (b)
25. (a)	26. (d)	27. (a)	28. (c)	29. (c)	30. (b)	31. (a)	32. (d)
33. (a)	34. (d)	35. (d)	36. (a)	37. (c)	38. (b)	39. (d)	40. (a)

SOLUTIONS

Solution 1

Let us tabulate the case as follows:

	Ajay	Anand	Ajay + Anand
N	12 days	8 days	
R			
W			

Taking total work as LCM of 12 and 8 *i.e.*, 24 units. Therefore rate of working of Ajay will be 2 units/day while that of Anand will be 3 units/day. So together they are able to do 5 units/day.

	Ajay	Anand	Ajay + Anand
N	12 days	8 days	
R	2	3	5
W = 24 units			

If they start and finish the work together, then amount of work done depends on their rate of working.

Amount of work done by Ajay = $\frac{2}{5}$ of total work

Amount of work done by Anand = $\frac{3}{5}$ of total work

∴ Share of Ajay = $\frac{2}{5} \times 6500$ = ₹ 2600.

Choice (b)

Solution 2

Let us tabulate the case as follows:

	Man	Son	Man + Son
N	20 days	?	12 days
R			
W			

Taking total work as LCM of 20 and 12 i.e., 60 units. Therefore rate of working of Man will be 3 units/day while that of Man and Son together will be 5 units/day. So the Son alone can do 2 unit/day.

	Man	Son	Man + Son
N	20 days		12 days
R	3	2	5
W = 60 units			

So, number of days taken by Son to finish the work alone = 60/2 = 30 days.

Choice (a)

Solution 3

Let us tabulate the case as follows:

	R	S	R + S
N	12 days	?	10 days
R			
W			

Taking total work as LCM of 12 and 10 i.e., 60 units. Therefore rate of working of Rohan will be 5 units/day while that of Rohan and Sohan together will be 6 units/day. So the Sohan alone can do 1 unit/day.

	R	S	R + S
N	12 days		10 days
R	5	1	6
W = 60 units			

So, number of days taken by Sohan to finish the work alone = 60/1 = 60 days.

Choice (a)

Solution 4

Let us tabulate the case as follows:

	A	B	C	A + B + C
N	10 days	20 days		5 days
R				
W				

Selecting the total work as LCM of 10, 20 and 5 i.e., 60 units

	A	B	C	A + B + C
N	10 days	20 days		5 days
R				
W = 60 units				

Therefore the rate of doing work of A will be 6 units per day and B will be 3 units per day. If they work with C i.e., all three works together then their rate of working will be 12 units per day.

	A	B	C	A + B + C
N	10 days	20 days		5 days
R	6	3		12
W = 60 units				

It means C can do 3 units per day; hence he can finish the work alone in 20 days.

	A	B	C	A + B + C
N	10 days	20 days	20 days	5 days
R	6	3	3	12
W = 60 units				

Choice (a)

Solution 5

Let us tabulate the case as follows:

	P	Q	P + Q
N	20 days		
R			
W			

Assuming the total work as any number which is divisible by 20; say 60 units. Therefore rate of working of P will be 3 units/day.

	P	Q	P + Q
N	20 days		
R	3		
W = 60 units			

Work done by P in 5 days = 3 × 5 = 15 units

Remaining work of 45 units is done by Q in 10 days.
Rate of Q = 45/10 = 4.5 units/day

	P	Q	P + Q
N	20 days		8 days
R	3	4.5	7.5
W = 60 units			

P and Q can together do it in 60/7.5 = 8 days.

Choice (b)

Solution 6

Let us tabulate the case as follows:

	A	S	P	A + S + P
N	24 days	30 days		12 days
R				
W				

Taking total work as LCM of 24, 30 and 12 *i.e.*, 120 units. Therefore rate of working of Anil will be 5 units/day; Sunil will be 4 units/day while that Anil, Sunil and Pradeep together will be 10 units/day. So the Pradeep alone can do 1 unit/day.

	A	S	P	A + S + P
N	24 days	30 days		12 days
R	5	4	1	10
W = 120 units				

If they start and finish the work together, then amount of work done depends on their rate of working.

Amount of work done by Anil = $\frac{5}{10}$ of total work

Amount of work done by Sunil = $\frac{4}{10}$ of total work

Amount of work done by Pradeep = $\frac{1}{10}$ of total work

$\therefore$ Share of Pradeep = $\frac{1}{10} \times 200$ = ₹ 20.

Choice (a)

Solution 7

Let us tabulate the case as follows:

	J	T	J + T
N			45 days
R			
W			

If John is thrice as efficient as Thomas, means if Thomas can do 1 unit of work in a day, then John will do 3 units of work per day. Together they are able to do 4 units of work in a day. Therefore total work done by then in 45 days will be 45 × 4 = 180 units.

	J	T	J + T
N			45 days
R	3	1	4
W = 180 units			

Total earning of John in 45 days = $\frac{3}{4} \times 13500$ = ₹ 10125

Earning of John in 10 days = $\frac{10125}{45} \times 10$ = ₹ 2250.

Choice (b)

Solution 8

$\dfrac{\text{Time taken by } P}{\text{Time taken by } Q} = \dfrac{8}{12} = \dfrac{2}{3}$

$\dfrac{\text{Rate of } P}{\text{Rate of } Q} = \dfrac{3 \text{ units/day}}{2 \text{ units/day}}$ ($\because$ Rate and time are inversely proportional)

Together they are able to do 5 units/day. Therefore total work done by them in 36 days will be 36 × 5 = 180 units.

	P	Q	P + Q
N			36 days
R	3	2	5
W = 180 units			

Time taken by P alone to complete the job = 180/3 = 60 days.

Choice (c)

Solution 9

Comparison between *A* and *B*:

$$\frac{\text{Time taken by } A}{\text{Time taken by } B} = \frac{2}{3}$$

$$\frac{\text{Rate of } A}{\text{Rate of } B} = \frac{3 \text{ units/day}}{2 \text{ units/day}} \quad (\because \text{ Rate and time are inversely proportional})$$

Comparison between *B* and *C*:

$$\frac{\text{Time taken by } B}{\text{Time taken by } C} = \frac{4}{5}$$

$$\frac{\text{Rate of } B}{\text{Rate of } C} = \frac{5 \text{ units/day}}{4 \text{ units/day}} \quad (\because \text{ Rate and time are inversely proportional})$$

Ratio of rate of working of *A*, *B* and *C* is:

A	:	B	:	C
3	:	2		
		5	:	4
15	:	10	:	8

Together they are able to do 33 units/day. Therefore total work done by them in 20 days will be 20 × 33 = 660 units.

Let us tabulate the case as follows:

	A	B	C	A + B + C
N				20
R	15	10	8	33
W = 660 units				

Time taken by *B* alone to finish the complete work = 660/10 = 66 days.

Choice (c)

Solution 10

If A is 25% more efficient then B then the ratio of their rate of working will be:

$$\frac{\text{Rate of } A}{\text{Rate of } B} = \frac{5}{4}$$

Let us tabulate the case as follows:

	A	B	A + B
N	90 days		
R	5	4	
W			

Total work will be 90 × 5 = 450 units.

	A	B	A + B
N	90 days		50 days
R	5	4	9
W = 450 units			

So, working together the work can be finished in 450/9 = 50 days.

Choice (d)

Solution 11

Let us tabulate the case as follows:

	A	B	A + B
N	30 hrs		
R	50		
W = 1500 parts			

Parts produced by machine A in 10 hrs = 50 × 10 = 500

Remaining 1000 parts are produced by machine B in 10 hrs.

∴ Rate of machine $B = \frac{1000}{10} = 100$ parts/hr

	A	B	A + B
N	30 hrs		
R	50	100	
W = 1500 parts			

Machine A and B together can produce 50 + 100 = 150 parts per hr.

Parts produced by both machines together in 30 hrs = 150 × 30 = 4500.

Choice (b)

Solution 12

A can do 40% work $\Rightarrow$ 20 days

A can do 60% work $\Rightarrow \dfrac{20 \times 60}{40} = 30$ days

Let us tabulate the case for remaining 60% of work as follows:

	A	B	A + B
N	30 days		10 days
R			
60% of W			

Let us take 60% of work as 30 units. So, the rate of working of A will be 1 unit/day while that of A and B together will be 3 units per day. It means B alone can do 2 units/day.

	A	B	A + B
N	30 days	15 days	10 days
R	1	2	3
60% of W = 30 units			

B can do 60% work $\Rightarrow$ 15 days

B can do 100% work $\Rightarrow \dfrac{15 \times 100}{60} = 25$ days.

Choice (d)

Solution 13

Let us tabulate the case as follows:

	P	Q
N	30 days	45 days
R		
W		

Let us take total work as LCM of 30 and 45 i.e., 90 units. So P can do 3 units per day and Q will be able to do 2 units per day.

	P	Q
N	30 days	45 days
R	3	2
W = 90 units		

P is the only person who is working for all 20 days.

∴ Units of work done by P in 20 days = 3 × 20 = 60 units

Remaining work = 90 – 60 = 30 units.

These 30 units of remaining work is carried out by Q alone.

Time taken by $Q = \dfrac{30 \text{ units}}{2 \text{ units/day}} = 15$ days.

So, Q joined P after 5 days.

Choice (a)

Solution 14

Typing rate of Pranay $= \dfrac{32}{8} = 4$ pages/hr

Typing rate of Raju $= \dfrac{36}{6} = 6$ pages/hr

Together they can type $6 + 4 = 10$ pages/hr

Time taken to type 200 pages $= \dfrac{200}{10} = 20$ hrs.

Choice (c)

Solution 15

Let us tabulate the case as follows:

	M	N	M + N
N	20 days		12 days
R			
W			

Taking total work as LCM of 20 and 12 *i.e.*, 60 units. So rate of working of Manoj will be 3 units/day, while that of Manoj and Nandu together will be 5 units/day. It means Nandu is able to do 2 units/day.

	M	N	M + N
N	20 days		12 days
R	3	2	5
W = 60 units			

If Nandu works for half a day daily, so he delivers only 1 unit of work per day.

Units of work done by Manoj and Nandu together $= 3 + 1 = 4$ units/day

Time required to complete the work $= \dfrac{60}{4} = 15$ days.

Choice (c)

Solution 16

Let us tabulate the case as follows:

	A	B	C	B + C	A + B + C
N				30 days	15 days
R					
W					

Assuming total work as 30 units, so Bharat and Chandra can co 1 unit/day, while all three working together can do 2 units/day. Therefore Abhay alone can do 1 unit/day.

	A	B	C	B + C	A + B + C
N				30 days	15 days
R	1			1	2
W = 30 units					

Work done by Abhay in 5 days = 1 × 5 = 5 units

Bharat worked ⇒ 15 days ⎫ Bhart + Chandra ⇒ 15 days
Chandra worked ⇒ 30 days ⎭ Chandra ⇒ 15 days

Work done by Bharat and Chandra in 15 days = 15 units

Remaining work = 30 − (5 + 15) = 10 units

This remaining work is carried out by Chandra in last 15 days.

Rate of Chandra = $\frac{10}{15} = \frac{2}{3}$ units/day

∴ Rate of Bharat = $1 - \frac{2}{3} = \frac{1}{3}$ units/day

	A	B	C	B + C	A + B + C
N				30 days	15 days
R	1	1/3	2/3	1	2
W = 30 units					

Days taken by Abhay to finish the work alone = $\frac{30}{1}$ = 30 days

Days taken by Bharat to finish the work alone = $\frac{30}{1/3}$ = 90 days

Days taken by Chandra to finish the work alone = $\frac{30}{2/3}$ = 45 days.

Choice (b)

Solution 17

Let us tabulate the case as follows:

	P	Q	R
N	30 days	15 days	20 days
R			
W			

Assuming the total work as 60 units. So rate of P will be 2 units/day, Q will be 4 units/day and R will be 3 units/day.

	P	Q	R
N	30 days	15 days	20 days
R	2	4	3
W = 60 units			

Let N number of days required to complete the project.

$2(N-4) + 4(N-1) + 3N = 60$ units

$\therefore N = 8$ days.

Choice (d)

Solution 18

Let us tabulate the case as follows:

	P	Q	R	P+Q	Q+R	P+R
N				20 days	15 days	12 days
R						
W						

Taking the total work as LCM of 20, 15 and 12 i.e., 60 units. Therefore the rate of doing work of P and Q, Q and R and P and R will be 3, 4, and 5 units/day respectively.

	P	Q	R	P+Q	Q+R	P+R
N				20 days	15 days	12 days
R				3	4	5
W = 60 units						

Total working rate of P, Q and R = $\dfrac{(P+Q)+(Q+R)+(P+R)}{2} = \dfrac{3+4+5}{2} = 6$ units/day

	P	Q	R	P+Q	Q+R	P+R	P+Q+R
N				20 days	15 days	12 days	
R				3	4	5	6
W = 60 units							

Working rate of $P = (P + Q + R) - (Q + R) = 6 - 4 = 2$ units/day
Working rate of $Q = (P + Q + R) - (P + R) = 6 - 5 = 1$ unit/day
Working rate of $R = (P + Q + R) - (P + Q) = 6 - 3 = 3$ units/day

	P	Q	R	P + Q	Q + R	P + R	P + Q + R
N				20 days	15 days	12 days	
R	2	1	3	3	4	5	6
W = 60 units							

Days required by P to finish the work individually = $\dfrac{60}{2}$ = 30 days

Days required by Q to finish the work individually = $\dfrac{60}{1}$ = 60 days

Days required by R to finish the work individually = $\dfrac{60}{3}$ = 20 days.

Choice (a)

Solution 19

Let us tabulate the case as follows:

	P	Q
N	15 days	25 days
R		
W		

Assuming the total work as 75 units, hence rate of working of P and Q will be 5 units/day and 3 unit/day respectively.

	P	Q
N	15 days	25 days
R	5	3
W = 75 units		

If P begins the work on the first day he will do 5 units while on the next day Q will do 3 units, so in every 2 days 8 units of work can be completed.

In 2 days — 8 units
In 18 days — 72 units

On 19th day it's a turn of P ($\because$ P is working on all odd number of days). P can do 3 units of work in $3/5$ day.

Hence work can be finished in $18\, 3/5$ days.

Choice (c)

Solution 20

Let us tabulate the case as follows:

	S	R
N	12 hrs	18 hrs
R		
W		

Assuming the total work as 36 units, hence rate of working of Sam and Raj will be 3 units/hr and 2 unit/hr respectively.

	S	R
N	12 hrs	18 hrs
R	3	2
W = 36 units		

If Sam begins the work, then in first 2 hrs he will do 6 units while in the next 2 hrs Raj will do 4 units, so in every 4 hrs 10 units of work can be completed.

In 4 hrs   - 10 units
In 12 hrs - 30 units

In the next 2 hrs Sam will do 6 units of remaining work. Hence the work can be completed in 14 hrs.

Choice (c)

Solution 21

Let us tabulate the case as follows:

	A	B	C
N	8 days	16 days	12 days
R			
W			

Assuming total work as LCM of 8, 16 and 12 *i.e.,* 48 units. So the rate of working of A, B and C is 6, 3 and 4 units/day respectively.

	A	B	C
N	8 days	16 days	12 days
R	6	3	4
W = 48 units			

If they are working in rotation in the order of *A*, *B* and *C* with each person working one day, then in 3 days they will do 13 units of work.

In 3 days   - 13 units
In 9 days   - 39 units
In 10 days   - 45 units   (∵ A is working)
In 11 days   - 48 units   (∵ B is working)

Hence the work can be completed in 11 days.

Choice (c)

Solution 22

He is going up (by 3 m) in every odd minute and comes down (by 1 m) in every even minute.

Distance climbed in 2 min   - 2 m
Distance climbed in 28 min   - 28 m

In 29th min it's a turn to go up, and the peak is close to him by 2 m. So he will take two-third of a minute to climb these 2 m. Hence he will reach the peak in $28\frac{2}{3}$ min.

Choice (a)

Solution 23

Assuming the rate of working of A as 'a' units/day while that of B as 'b' units/day. Also taking total work as any number which is a multiple of 18.
Let us tabulate the case as follows:

	A	B	A + B
N			18 days
R	a	b	5
W = 90 units			

$a + b = 5$ ... (1)

$10a + 30b = 90$ ... (2)

Solving equation (1) and (2),

$a = 3$ and $b = 2$

	A	B	A + B
N			18 days
R	3	2	5
W = 90 units			

Days required by B alone = $\frac{90}{2}$ = 45 days.

Choice (b)

Solution 24

$20w \times 16d = \text{work}$ ... (1)
$16m \times 15d = \text{work}$ ... (2)

Equating (1) and (2)

$20w \times 16d = 16m \times 15d$

$\dfrac{m}{w} = \dfrac{4}{3}.$

Choice (b)

Solution 25

$m + b = \text{work}$ ... (1)
$5m + 2b = 4 \times \text{work}$ ... (2)

$\therefore 5m + 2b = 4(m + b)$

$5m + 2b = 4m + 4b$

$m = 2b$

$\dfrac{m}{b} = \dfrac{2}{1}.$

Choice (a)

Solution 26

Assuming that 1 man working for 1 hour is able to do 1 unit of work.

Units of work done by 18 men in 20 days working 12 hrs/day:

$18 \times 20 \times 12 = 4320$ units

Amount of work expected from 15 men in x days working 9 hrs/day = 4320 units

$\therefore 15 \times x \times 9 = 4320$ units

$\therefore x = \dfrac{4320}{15 \times 9} = 32$ days.

Choice (d)

Solution 27

$30m \times 24d \times 6h = 1500$ bolts

$1m \times 1d \times 1h = \dfrac{1500}{30 \times 24 \times 6}$ bolts ... (1)

$18m \times x\, d \times 8h = 1800$ bolts

$1m \times 1d \times 1h = \dfrac{1800}{18 \times x \times 8}$ bolts ... (2)

Equating (1) and (2)

$\dfrac{1500}{30 \times 24 \times 6} = \dfrac{1800}{18 \times x \times 8}$

$x = 36$ days.

Choice (a)

Solution 28

Let there be x number of men originally.

x men × 30 days = work ... (1)

$(x + 5)$ men × 20 days = work ... (2)

Equating (1) and (2)

$x \times 30 = (x + 5) \times 20$

∴ $x = 10$ men.

Choice (c)

Solution 29

Assuming that 1 man working for 1 day is able to do 1 unit of work

Units of work done by 20 men in 30 days:

$20 \times 30 = 600$ units

Let 5 men leaves the job after x days, then:

$20x + 15(35 - x) = 600$ units

∴ $x = 15$ days.

Choice (c)

Solution 30

Assuming that 1 man working for 1 day is able to do 1 unit of work

Units of work done by 60 men in 30 days:

$60 \times 30 = 1800$ units

If 10 men leave the work after every 10 days from the start, then:

60 men × 10 days = 600 units

50 men × 10 days = 500 units

40 men × 10 days = 400 units
30 men × 10 days = 300 units

Hence to finish 1800 units now 40 days are required.

Choice (b)

Solution 31

$6m = 8w$ or $3m = 4w$

$8w \times 42d$ = level a field ... (1)

$(9m + 2w) \times x\,d$ = level a field ... (2)

Equating (1) and (2)

$(9m + 2w) \times x\,d = 8w \times 42d$

$(12w + 2w) \times x = 8w \times 42$

$\therefore x = \dfrac{8 \times 42}{14} = 24$ days.

Choice (a)

Solution 32

$10m = 6w$ or $5m = 3w$

$10m \times 20d$ = work ... (1)

$(3m + 3w) \times x\,d$ = work ... (2)

Equating (1) and (2)

$(3m + 3w) \times x\,d = 10m \times 20d$

$(3m + 5m) \times x = 10m \times 20$

$\therefore x = \dfrac{10 \times 20}{8} = 25$ days.

Choice (d)

Solution 33

$(3m + 6w) \times 12$ days = work ... (1)

$(5m + 6w) \times 9$ days = work ... (2)

$(3m + 3w) \times x$ days = work ... (3)

Equating equation (1) and (2)

$(3m + 6w) \times 12 = (5m + 6w) \times 9$

$36m + 72w = 45m + 54w$

$18w = 9m$

$2w = 1m$

Equating equation (1) and (3)

$(3m + 6w) \times 12 = (3m + 3w) \times x$

$(6w + 6w) \times 12 = (6w + 3w) \times x$ ($\because$ 3m = 6w)

$\therefore x = \dfrac{12 \times 12}{9} = 16$ days.

Choice (a)

Solution 34

$(1m + 3b) \times 10$ days = work ... (1)

$1w \times 30$ days = work ... (2)

$[(3m + 9b) + xw] \times 2$ days = work ... (3)

Equating equation (1) and (2)

$(1m + 3b) \times 10 = 1w \times 30$

$10m + 30b = 30w$

$\therefore 1m + 3b = 3w$

So, $3m + 9b = 9w$

Equating equation (2) and (3)

$1w \times 30 = [(3m + 9b) + xw] \times 2$

$1w \times 30 = (9 + x)w \times 2$

$15 = 9 + x$

$\therefore x = 6$ women.

Choice (d)

Solution 35

$(2m + 3w) \times 30$ days = work ... (1)

$1m \times 90$ days = work ... (2)

$1w \times x$ days = work ... (3)

Equating equation (1) and (2)

$(2m + 3w) \times 30 = 1m \times 90$

$60m + 90w = 90m$

$90w = 30m$

$3w = 1m$

Equating equation (2) and (3)

$1m \times 90 = 1w \times x$

$3w \times 90 = 1w \times x$

$\therefore x = 270$ days.

Choice (d)

Solution 36

If the labor is absent for 1 day his loss = ₹ 30 + ₹ 12 = ₹ 42

(₹ 30 × 30 days) − (₹ 42 × x days) = 564

$\therefore \quad x = \dfrac{900 - 564}{42}$

= 8 days.

Choice (a)

Solution 37

$(4b + 6g) \times 8$ days = Project ... (1)

$(3b + 7g) \times 10$ days = Project ... (2)

$10g \times x$ days = Project ... (3)

Equating equation (1) and (2)

$(4b + 6g) \times 8 = (3b + 7g) \times 10$

$32b + 48g = 30b + 70g$

$2b = 22g$

$b = 11g$

Equating equation (1) and (3)

$10g \times x = (4b + 6g) \times 8$

$10g \times x = (44g + 6g) \times 8 \ (\because 4b = 44g)$

$\therefore \quad x = \dfrac{50 \times 8}{10}$

= 40 days.

Choice (c)

Solution 38

Let x number of painters can paint half the building in d number of days.

$x \times d = (x + 2x) \times (d - 6)$

$x \times d = 3x \times (d - 6)$

$$xd = 3xd - 18x$$
$$2xd = 18x$$
$$\therefore \quad d = 9 \text{ days.}$$

Initial group can paint half the building in 9 days, so the complete building can be painted in 18 days.

Choice (b)

Solution 39

$$80m \times 84 \text{ days} = 20 \text{ km road}$$

$$1m \times 1d = \frac{20}{80 \times 84} \text{ km road} \quad \ldots (1)$$

$$x\,m \times 63 \text{ days} = 30 \text{ km road}$$

$$1m \times 1d = \frac{30}{x \times 63} \quad \ldots (2)$$

Equating (1) and (2)

$$\frac{20}{80 \times 84} = \frac{30}{x \times 63}$$

$$\therefore x = 160 \text{ men}$$

Choice (d)

Solution 40

$$1m \times 3 \text{ days} = 4w \times 2 \text{ days}$$
$$\therefore \quad 3m = 8w$$
$$xm \times 48 \text{ days} = 72w \times 16 \text{ days}$$
$$xm \times 48 \text{ days} = 27m \times 16 \text{ days} \ (\because 72w = 27m)$$
$$\therefore \quad x = \frac{27 \times 16}{48} = 9 \text{ men.}$$

Choice (a)

13
Pipes and Cistern

The approach for solving questions on pipes and cistern is almost similar to time and work. There are pipes (or taps) filling (or emptying) tanks with water. The time taken by different taps (to fill or empty the tank) may be different. Hence these problems can be dealt in the same manner as foregoing problems on time and work have been dealt with. In the problems of pipes and cistern there is an involvement of negative work if there is a leakage in the cistern (tank).

Following are the parameters involved in these problems:

C = Capacity of tank (in liters)

R = Rate of filling or emptying (in liters/min or liters/hr)

N = Time required to fill/empty the tank (in min or hrs)

So, the relation between these variables is as follows:

Rate of filling the pipe = Capacity of tank/Time required to fill the tank

$$\boxed{R = \frac{C}{N}}$$

SOLVED EXAMPLES

Example 1

A filling pipe P can fill an empty tank in 30 min, while the leak L at the bottom of tank can empty the full tank in 45 min. If both pipes are opened simultaneously, how long will it take to fill the empty tank?

Solution

Let us tabulate the case as follows:

	P	L	P – L
N	30 min	45 min	
R			
C			

Selecting the capacity of tank as LCM of 30 and 45, or any number which is divisible by both 30 and 45. So selecting capacity of tank as 90 liters.

	P	L	P – L
N	30 min	45 min	
R			
C = 90 liters			

Therefore rate of filling pipe P is 3 liters/min while that of emptying pipe will be 2 liters/min. Also if both are opened (as mentioned in the problem) net storage in tank is 1 liter per min.

	P	L	P – L
N	30 min	45 min	90 min
R	3	2	1
C = 90 liters			

Hence 90 min are required to fill the tank.

Example 2

Pipe A can fill an empty tank in 24 min, pipe B can fill it in 36 min and pipe C can empty it in 72 min. If all of them are opened together find the time taken to fill the empty tank.

Solution

Let us tabulate the case as follows:

	A	B	C	A + B – C
N	24 min	36 min	72 min	
R				
C				

Selecting the capacity of tank as LCM of 24, 36 and 72.

	A	B	C	A + B – C
N	24 min	36 min	72 min	
R				
C = 72 liters				

Therefore the rate of filling of pipe A and pipe B will be 3 liters/min and 2 liters/min respectively. Pipe C can empty the tank at the rate of 1 liter/min.

	A	B	C	A + B – C
N	24 min	36 min	72 min	18 min
R	3	2	1	4
C = 72				

Hence time taken to fill the empty tank will be 18 min.

Example 3

A tank is filled in 5 hours by three pipes P, Q and R. The pipe R is twice as fast as Q and Q is twice as fast as P. How much time will pipe P alone take to fill the tank?

Solution

Whenever the efficiency of pipe (or taps) is given, we should express it in terms of rate of doing work. Rate of Q is double the rate of P and Rate of R is double the rate of Q.

	P	Q	R	P + Q + R
N				5 hrs
R	1	2	4	
C				

Total rate of P, Q and R will be 7 liters/hr. Therefore the capacity of tank will be a product of N and R i.e., 35 liters.

	P	Q	R	P + Q + R
N				5 hrs
R	1	2	4	7
C = 35 liters				

So, the time required to fill the tank by pipe P alone found out as 35 min.

	P	Q	R	P + Q + R
N	35 min			5 hrs
R	1	2	4	7
C = 35 liters				

Example 4

Two pipes can fill a tank in 20 and 24 minutes respectively and a leak pipe can empty the tank at the rate 3 liters/min. All the three pipes opened together can fill the tank in 15 min. How much is the capacity of tank?

Solution

Let us tabulate the case as follows:

	Pipe 1	Pipe 2	Leak	Pipe 1 + Pipe 2 – Leak
N	20 min	24 min		15 min
R			3	
C				

Assuming the capacity of tank as x liters. Therefore the rate of filling of pipe 1 and pipe 2 will be $\frac{x}{20}$ and $\frac{x}{24}$ liters/min respectively. If all three pipes are opened the rate will be $\frac{x}{15}$ liters/min.

	Pipe 1	Pipe 2	Leak	Pipe 1 + Pipe 2 – Leak
N	20 min	24 min		15 min
R	$\frac{x}{20}$	$\frac{x}{24}$	3	$\frac{x}{15}$

C = x liters

$$\frac{x}{20} + \frac{x}{24} - 3 = \frac{x}{15}$$

$$\frac{x}{20} + \frac{x}{24} - \frac{x}{15} = 3$$

$$\frac{6x + 5x - 8x}{120} = 3$$

So, $x = 120$ liters.

Example 5

Two pipes A and B can fill a tank in 24 min and 32 min respectively. If both the pipes are opened simultaneously, after how much time B should be closed so that the tank is full in 18 minutes?

Solution

Let us tabulate the case as follows:

	A	B
N	24 min	32 min
R		
C		

Assuming the capacity of tank as 96 liters, hence rate of filling of pipe A and B will be 4 liters/min and 3 liters/min respectively.

	A	B
N	24 min	32 min
R	4	3

C = 96 liters

As time in which tank should be filled is 18 min, so working time of pipe A is complete 18 min.

Pipe A in 18 min = 18 × 4 = 72 liters

Remaining part of 24 liters is filled by pipe B

Time required by pipe B to add 24 liters = 24/3 = 8 min

Hence, pipe B should be closed after 8 min to fill the tank in a total of 18 min.

Example 6

An inlet pipe can fill a tank full of water in 20 min, while an outlet pipe can empty it in 30 min. If the inlet pipe is opened first, then after how much time outlet pipe should be opened so that the tank will be full in 30 min?

Solution

Let us tabulate the case as follows:

	Inlet	Outlet
N	20 min	30 min
R		
C		

Assuming the capacity of tank as 60 liters, hence rate of filling of inlet pipe will be 3 liter/min, while rate of emptying of outlet pipe will be 2 liters/min.

	Inlet	Outlet
N	20 min	30 min
R	3	2
C = 60 liters		

If the outlet is not opened, the tank will be full in 20 min, but if we want to fill the same tank in 30 min then outlet pipe needs to be opened for some duration. If inlet pipe is kept open for 30 min then:

Inlet pipe in 30 min = 30 × 3 = 90 liters

As capacity of tank is 60 liters, hence this extra 30 liters need to be drained out.

Time required to drain 30 liters of water = 30/2 = 15 min.

So the outlet pipe should be kept open in last 15 min, hence it should be opened 15 min after opening the inlet pipe.

EXERCISE

1. An empty tank can be filled by two pipes individually in 30 min and 60 min respectively. There is a leak pipe which can empty a full tank in 45 min. If all the three pipes are opened, how much time dose it take to fill an empty tank?
   (a) 36 min
   (b) 18 min
   (c) 30 min
   (d) 24 min

2. A pipe can fill a tank in 16 hours. Due to a leak in the bottom, it is filled in 24 hours. If the tank is full, how much time will the leak take to empty it?
   (a) 32 hrs
   (b) 48 hrs
   (c) 20 hrs
   (d) 52 hrs

3. A pump can fill a tank in 6 hrs. Because of a leak in the tank, it took 7 hours to fill the tank. The leak can drain out all the water of tank in how much time?
   (a) 21 hrs
   (b) 35 hrs
   (c) 42 hrs
   (d) 48 hrs

4. Two pipes can fill a tank in 5 hours and 6 hours respectively. A third pipe empties the full tank in 10 hours. If all the three pipes operate simultaneously, in how much time the tank will be filled?
   (a) 3 hrs 15 min
   (b) 3 hrs 40 min
   (c) 4 hrs 20 min
   (d) 4 hrs 45 min

5. Three taps can fill an empty cistern in 12, 18 and 24 min. Three min after the first tap was opened; the second tap was also opened. After three more min, the third tap was opened and the first two taps were shut. Find the time taken to fill the cistern after closing the first two taps.
   (a) 18 min
   (b) 15 min
   (c) 12 min
   (d) 8 min

6. The filling rate of pipe P is twice the filling rate of pipe Q. If together they can fill the tank in 36 min, then the slower pipe can fill the tank alone in how much time?
   (a) 54 min
   (b) 108 min
   (c) 72 min
   (d) 96 min

7. Filling rate of tap B is 40% more than filling rate of tap A. If tap A alone can fill the tank in 21 min, then tap B can fill the tank alone in how much time?
   (a) 15 min
   (b) 35 min
   (c) 14 min
   (d) 28 min

8. A tank can be filled by a tap A in 20 minutes and by another tap B in 60 min. Both taps are kept open for 10 min and then the first tap A is shut off. After this, the remaining tank will be completely filled in how much time?
   (a) 20 min
   (b) 30 min
   (c) 40 min
   (d) 45 min

9. 12 buckets of water fill a tank when the capacity of each bucket is 13.5 liters. How many buckets will be needed to fill the same tank, if the capacity of each bucket is 9 liters?
   (a) 8
   (b) 16
   (c) 15
   (d) 18

10. A tap can fill a tank in 6 hours. After half the tank is filled, two more similar taps are opened. What is the total time taken to fill the complete tank?
    (a) 5 hrs
    (b) 3 hrs 30 min
    (c) 4 hrs
    (d) 4 hrs 30 min

11. Bucket P has double the capacity as bucket Q. It takes 45 turns for bucket P to fill the empty drum. How many turns it will take for both the buckets P and Q having each turn together to fill the empty drum?
   (a) 20
   (b) 30
   (c) 35
   (d) 40

12. A pipe can fill an empty tank in 3 hours less than another pipe, which can empty a full tank. If both the pipes are opened at the same time, the tank will be filled in 6 hours. In how much time can the second pipe empty the full tank?
   (a) 6 hours
   (b) 3 hours
   (c) 4 hours
   (d) 5 hours

13. Two pipes A and B fill a tank in 15 hours and 20 hours respectively while a third pipe C can empty the full tank in 25 hours. All the three pipes are opened in the beginning, after 10 hrs, C is closed. In how much time, will the tank be full?
   (a) 10 hrs
   (b) 12 hrs
   (c) 14 hrs
   (d) 16 hrs

14. Two pipes A and B and can fill a cistern in 12 minutes and 15 minutes respectively, but a third pipe C can empty the full tank in 6 min. A and B are kept open for 5 min in the beginning and then C is also opened. In what time is the cistern emptied?
   (a) 30 min
   (b) 36 min
   (c) 45 min
   (d) 50 min

15. Two pipes A and B can fill a tank in 6 hours and 4 hours respectively. If they are opened on alternate hours and if pipe A is opened first, in how many hours, the tank will be full?
   (a) 4 ½ hrs
   (b) 5 hrs
   (c) 5 ½ hrs
   (d) None of these

16. A pipe can fill a tank in 4 hours, while a leak which is at one-fourth the height of the tank can empty up to that part in 2 hours. If both are operated simultaneously and initially the tank is full, then when it will be one-fourth full?
   (a) 2 hours
   (b) 2 hours and 20 min
   (c) 1 hour and 30 min
   (d) 6 hours

17. Two pipes P and Q can fill a tank in 12 and 18 hours respectively. Both the pipes were opened at 10 a.m. and the tank was full at 6 p.m. What could be the maximum possible duration for which one of the pipes must have been closed during that interval?
   (a) 4 hours
   (b) 2 hours and 30 min
   (c) 2 hours
   (d) 1 hour and 20 min

18. P and Q are filling pipes which can fill a tank in 15 and 20 min respectively. R is emptying pipe which can empty the full tank in 30 min. All three pipes are opened continuously one after the other in the order of P, Q and R, each being kept opened for 2 min until the tank is filled. After how much time will the tank be full?
   (a) 30 min
   (b) 32 min and 40 sec
   (c) 36 min
   (d) None of these

19. Three pipes P, Q and R can fill a tank in 12, 15 and 20 min respectively. If pipe P is kept open and pipe Q and R are opened 1 min each alternately, then in how much time the tank will be full?
    (a) 6 min
    (b) $6\frac{2}{3}$ min
    (c) 7 min
    (d) $7\frac{1}{2}$ min

20. Two pipes can fill a tank in 14 and 16 hours respectively. The pipes are opened simultaneously and it is found that due to leakage in the bottom of the tank it takes 32 min extra for the tank to be filled up. When the tank is full, in what time will the leak empty it?
    (a) 114 hours
    (b) 112 hours
    (c) 100 hours
    (d) 80 hours

21. A tap can fill a tank in 16 minutes and another can empty it in 8 minutes. If the tank is already half-full and both taps are opened together, then tank will be:
    (a) empty in 8 min
    (b) empty in 16 min
    (c) full in 8 min
    (d) full in 16 min

22. Pipe A can fill 12 liters per min and pipe B can fill 6 liters per min. Pipe C can empty a drum in 10 min. If all the three pipes are opened, the drum is filled in 15 min. What is the capacity of drum?
    (a) 105 liters
    (b) 108 liters
    (c) 120 liters
    (d) 116 liters

23. A large tanker can be filled by two pipes A and B in 30 minutes and 20 minutes respectively. How many minutes will it take to fill the tanker from empty state if B is used for half the time and pipe A and B fill it together for the other half?
    (a) 7.5 min
    (b) 15 min
    (c) 20 min
    (d) 22.5 min

24. Pipe A can fill a tank in 20 min. Pipe A and B both are opened and after 6 min pipe A is closed, and pipe B takes 15 min to fill the tank. In how many minutes can pipe B fill the tank individually?
    (a) 34
    (b) 28
    (c) 30
    (d) 33

25. A tank is full of water. A drain pipe which can empty the full tank in 60 min is opened. 18 min later another pipe which can fill the empty tank in 30 min is opened. After how much time, in total, is the tank full again?
    (a) 18 min
    (b) 20 min
    (c) 36 min
    (d) 40 min

26. Three pipes P, Q and R can fill a tank in 6 hrs. If all are opened for 2 hrs and then R is closed, then P and Q can fill the remaining part of tank in 8 hours. In how many hours R alone can fill the tank?

(a) 10 (b) 16
(c) 12 (d) 14

27. Two pipes A and B can fill a cistern in 12 minutes and 15 min respectively. If both the pipes are opened together, then after how much time B should be closed so that the tank is full in 8 minutes?
(a) 4 min (b) 5 min
(c) 6 min (d) 7 min

KEYS

1. (a)   2. (b)   3. (c)   4. (a)   5. (d)   6. (b)   7. (a)   8. (a)
9. (d)   10. (c) 11. (b) 12. (a) 13. (b) 14. (c) 15. (b) 16. (d)
17. (c) 18. (b) 19. (c) 20. (b) 21. (a) 22. (b) 23. (b) 24. (c)
25. (c) 26. (c) 27. (b)

SOLUTIONS

Solution 1

	P_1	P_2	L	$P_1 + P_2 - L$
N	30 min	60 min	45 min	
R				
C = 180 liters				

Taking capacity of tank as 180 liters, which is the LCM of 30, 60 and 45. Therefore the rate of filling of P_1 and P_2 will be 6 liters/min and 3 liters/min respectively, while the rate of leaking will be 4 liters/min. As 9 liters in coming inside the tank and 4 liters is going outside, hence net volume of water stored in the tank will be 5 liters every min.

	P_1	P_2	L	$P_1 + P_2 - L$
N	30 min	60 min	45 min	36 min
R	6	3	4	5
C = 180 liters				

To fill 180 liters it will require 180/5 = 36 min.

Choice (a)

Solution 2

	P	L	P − L
N	16 hrs		24 hrs
R			
C = 48 liters			

Taking capacity of tank as 48 liters, which is the LCM of 16 and 24. Rate of filling pipe will be 3 liters/hr, and if leak is also opened the rate of filling will be 2 liters/hr. Therefore the rate of leaking is 1 liter per hr.

	P	L	P − L
N	16 hrs		24 hrs
R	3	1	2
C = 48 liters			

Hence time required by the leak to empty the full tank will be 48 hrs.

Choice (b)

Solution 3

	Pump	Leak	P − L
N	6 hrs		7 hrs
R			
C = 42 liters			

Taking capacity of tank as 42 liters, which is the LCM of 6 and 7. Rate of filling pump will be 7 liters/hr, and if leak is also opened the rate of filling will be 6 liters/hr. Therefore the rate of leaking is 1 liter per hr.

	Pump	Leak	P − L
N	6 hrs		7 hrs
R	7	1	6
C = 42 liters			

Hence the leak will drain out full tank in 42 hrs.

Choice (c)

Solution 4

	P_1	P_2	P_3	$P_1 + P_2 - P_3$
N	5 hrs	6 hrs	10 hrs	
R				
C = 30 liters				

Taking capacity of tank as 30 liters, which is the LCM of 5, 6 and 10. Therefore the rate of filling of P_1 and P_2 will be 6 liters/hr and 5 liters/hr respectively, while the rate of outlet pipe P_3 will be 3 liters/hr. As 11 liters in coming inside the tank and 3 liters is going outside, hence net volume of water stored in the tank will be 8 liters every hr.

	P_1	P_2	P_3	$P_1 + P_2 - P_3$
N	5 hrs	6 hrs	10 hrs	30/8 hrs
R	6	5	3	8
C = 30 liters				

To fill 30 liters it will require $30/8 = 3\frac{3}{4}$ hrs = 3hrs and 15 min.

Choice (a)

Solution 5

	T_1	T_2	T_3
N	12 min	18 min	24 min
R			
C = 72 liters			

Assuming capacity of tank as 72 liters, therefore the rate of filling by three taps will be 6, 4 and 3 liters/min respectively.

	T_1	T_2	T_3
N	12 min	18 min	24 min
R	6	4	3
C = 72 liters			

T_1 in 3 min = $6 \times 3 = 18$ liters

$T_1 + T_2$ in next 3 min = $(6 + 4) \times 3 = 30$ liters

Net stored in tank in these 6 min = $18 + 30 = 48$ liters

Remaining tank to be filled by T_3 as T_1 and T_2 are shut off = $72 - 48 = 24$ liters

Time taken to fill the cistern by third tap = $24/3 = 8$ min.

Choice (d)

Solution 6

	P	Q	P + Q
N			36 min
R	2	1	3
C			

Assuming the filling rate of pipe Q as 1 liter/min, so rate of P will be 2 liter/min. If both are opened together rate of filling will be 3 liter/min.

Capacity of tank = 3 liter/min × 36 min = 108 liters

	P	Q	P + Q
N			36 min
R	2	1	3
C = 108 liters			

Time required to fill by slower pipe alone = 108 min.

Choice (b)

Solution 7

	A	B
N	21 min	
R	10	14
C = 210 liters		

Assuming the filling rate of tap A as 10 liter/min, so rate of tap B will be 14 liter/min.

Capacity of tank = 10 liter/min × 21 min = 210 liters

Time required by tap B alone to fill the tank = 210/14 = 15 min.

Choice (a)

Solution 8

	A	B
N	20 min	60 min
R		
C = 60 liters		

Assuming capacity of tank as 60 liters, so the rate of filling by tap A and B will be 3 liters/min and 1 liter/min respectively.

	A	B
N	20 min	60 min
R	3	1
C = 60 liters		

Tap $A + B$ in 10 min = (3 + 1) × 10 = 40 liters

Remaining tank to be filled = 60 − 40 = 20 liters

Tap *B* can fill the remaining tank of 20 liters in 20 min.

Choice (a)

Solution 9

Capacity of tank = Number of buckets × Capacity of each bucket

Capacity of tank = 12 × 13.5 = 162 liters

Number of buckets needed to fill the tank by a bucket of 9 liters = 162/9 = 18.

Choice (d)

Solution 10

Let us assume the capacity of tank as 6 liters. So tap can fill it at the rate of 1 liter/hr.

Half tank (3 liters) is full in 3 hrs.

After this two more similar taps are opened.

Time required to fill remaining half tank = 3 liters/(1 + 1 + 1) = 1 hr

Total time taken = time to fill first half tank + time to fill remaining half tank = 3 hrs + 1 hr.

Choice (c)

Solution 11

	P	Q
N	45 turns	
R	2	1
C		

Assuming capacity of bucket *P* and *Q* as 2 liters and 1 liter respectively. Therefore the capacity of drum will be 45 × 2 = 90 liters.

If both the buckets are turned together, then number of turns = 90 liters/(2 + 1) = 30 turns.

Choice (b)

Solution 12

	P_1	P_2	$P_1 - P_2$
N	$n-3$	n	6 hrs
R	$1/n-3$	$1/n$	1/6
C = 1 liter			

Rate of filling of P_1 − Rate of filling of P_2 = 1/6

$$\frac{1}{n-3} - \frac{1}{n} = \frac{1}{6}$$

∴ n = 6.

Choice (a)

Solution 13

	A	B	C
N	15 hrs	20 hrs	25 hrs
R	20	15	12

C = 300 liters

Assuming capacity of tank as 300 liters, so rate of filling of pipe A and B will be 20 and 15 liters/hr, while the rate of emptying by pipe C will be 12 liters/hr. If all three pipes are opened in the beginning, 35 liters of water is added and 12 liters of water will be drained out every hr.

Therefore in 10 hrs, water collected in tank = (20 + 15 − 12) × 10 = 230 liters

Remaining tank to be filled = 300 − 230 = 70 liters

Time required to fill this 70 liters by pipe A and B = 70/(20 + 15) = 2 hrs

Therefore total time required = 10 hrs + 2 hrs = 12 hrs.

Choice (b)

Solution 14

	A	B	C
N	12 min	15 min	6 min
R	5	4	10

C = 60 liters

Assuming capacity of tank as 60 liters, so rate of filling of pipe A and B will be 5 and 4 liters/min, while the rate of emptying by pipe C will be 10 liters/min.

Pipe A and B together in 5 min = (5 + 4) × 5 = 45 liters

After this pipe C is also opened, so water coming in the tank is 9 liters/min and going out is 10 liters/min. Therefore, net water drained out from tank is 1 liter/min.

To empty 45 liters collected in first 5 min it will take 45 min.

Choice (c)

Solution 15

	A	B
N	6 hrs	4 hrs
R	2	3
C = 12 liters		

If the capacity of tank is assumed as 12 liters, so rate filling of pipe A and B will be 2 and 3 liters/hr respectively.

In 2 hrs 5 liters is filled.

In 4 hrs 10 liters is filled

In 5th hr its turn of pipe A which can add 2 liters and hence the tank will be full.

Choice (b)

Solution 16

As the pipe can fill the full tank in 4 hrs, so the upper three fourth part it can fill in 3 hrs. Let us do the calculation for the upper three fourth part of tank. The leak can empty the upper three fourth part in 2 hrs as mentioned.

	P	L
N	3 hrs	2 hrs
R	2	3
C of ¾ part = 6 liters		

When the tank is full and both are opened, then 2 liter/hr is added while 3 liters/hr is taken out. So 1 liters is taken out every hr. To take out complete 6 liters out it will take 6 hrs.

Choice (d)

Solution 17

	P	Q
N	12 hrs	18 hrs
R	3	2
C = 36 liters		

If the capacity of tank is assumed as 36 liters, the rate of filling of pipe P and Q will be 3 and 2 liters/hr respectively.

Duration for 10 a.m. to 6 p.m. = 8 hrs

If both pipes are opened for 8 hrs, the water added = (3 + 2) × 8 = 40 liters

But as 36 liters is filled, hence one of the pipes was closed and this extra 4 liter was not added.

As maximum duration of closing is to be found out, so the pipe of slower rate will be considered.

Duration of closure = 4 liters/2 liter per hr = 2 hrs.

Choice (c)

Solution 18

	P	Q	R
N	15 min	20 min	30 min
R	4	3	2

C = 60 liters

P and Q are the inlet pipe with rate of filling 4 and 3 liters/min while R is an outlet pipe with rate of emptying 2 liters/min. As they are opened in rotation in the order of P, Q and R for a duration of 2 min each, then:

Water collected in the tank in 6 min (1 cycle) = 10 liters

Water collected in the tank in 30 min (or 5 cycles) = 50 liters

Again its turn of pipe P, Water collected in 32 min = 50 liters + (4 × 2) = 58 liters

Remaining tank of 2 liters can be filled by pipe Q in next $2/3^{rd}$ of a min or 40 sec.

Choice (b)

Solution 19

	P	Q	R
N	12 min	15 min	20 min
R	5	4	3

C = 60 liters

If the capacity of tank is assumed as 60 liters, then rate of filling of pipe P, Q and R will be 5, 4 and 3 liters/hr respectively.

Water added by $P + Q$ in 1st min = 9 liters
Water added by $P + R$ in 2nd min = 8 liters
Water added in 2 min = 9 + 8 = 17 liters
Water added in 6 min = 51 liters

Again, Water added by $P + Q$ in 7th min = 9 liters

Hence tank will be full in 7 min.

Choice (c)

Solution 20

	P_1	P_2	L	$P_1 + P_2$	$P_1 + P_2 - L$
N	14 hrs	16 hrs		7 hrs and 28 min	
R	8	7		15	
C = 112 liters					

Assuming capacity of tank as 112 liters as LCM of 14 and 16. Rate of P_1 and P_2 will be 8 and 7 liters/hr, so if both are opened the tank should be full in $112/15 = 7\frac{7}{15}$ hrs or 7 hrs and 28 min. But due to leak extra 32 min are required; hence total time required because of leak is 8 hrs.

	P_1	P_2	L	$P_1 + P_2$	$P_1 + P_2 - L$
N	14 hrs	16 hrs		7 hrs and 28 min	8 hrs
R	8	7		15	14
C = 112 liters					

From the above table it can be seen that the rate of leaking is 1 liter/hr, so the leak can empty the full tank in 112 hours.

Choice (b)

Solution 21

	Inlet Tap	Outlet Tap
N	16 min	8 min
R	1	2
C = 16 liters		

As the rate of outlet tap is more than inlet tap, hence tank will become empty. If both are opened then the rate of emptying will be 1 liter/min. Time required to empty half tank *i.e.,* 8 liters will be 8 min.

Choice (a)

Solution 22

	A	B	C	A + B − C
N			10 min	15 min
R	12	6		
C = x liters				

Assuming the capacity of drum as x liters, so rate of emptying of pipe C will be $\frac{x}{10}$.

Rate of filling the drum will be $\dfrac{x}{15}$.

	A	B	C	A + B − C
N			10 min	15 min
R	12	6	$\dfrac{x}{10}$	$\dfrac{x}{15}$

C = x liters

Rate of A + Rate of B − Rate of C = Filling rate of drum

$12 + 6 - \dfrac{x}{10} = \dfrac{x}{15}$

∴ x = 108 liters.

Choice (b)

Solution 23

	A	B
N	30 min	20 min
R	2	3

C = 60 liters

Let us assume total 2*t* min are required.

Pipe B working for half the time + Pipes A and B working for remaining half time = tanker capacity.

(3 liters/min × *t*) + (5 liters/min × *t*) = 60 liters

Solving the equation, *t* = 15/2 min

Therefore total time, 2*t* = 15 min.

Choice (b)

Solution 24

	A	B
N	20 min	
R		
C		

Let us assume the capacity of tank as any number which is a multiple of 20, say 60 liters. Therefore rate of A will be 3 liters/min.

Pipes and Cistern 345

	A	B
N	20 min	
R	3	
C = 60 liters		

Working time of A = 6 min
Working time of B = 6 min + 15 min = 21 min
Water added by pipe A in 6 min = 18 liters

Therefore remaining 42 liters of water is added by pipe B in 21 min

Rate of pipe B = 42/21 = 2 liters/min

	A	B
N	20 min	30 min
R	3	2
C = 60 liters		

Hence pipe B can fill the tank alone in 30 min.

Choice (c)

Solution 25

	Inlet Pipe	Outlet Pipe
N	30 min	60 min
R	2	1
C = 60 liters		

Water leaked out in 18 min = 18 liters

If both inlet and outlet pipe is opened then rate of filling will be 1 liter/min.

So, the tank will be again full in next 18 min.

Therefore, total time taken = 18 + 18 = 36 min.

Choice (c)

Solution 26

Let us tabulate the case as follows:

	P + Q	R	P + Q + R
N			6 hrs
R			
C			

Let us assume the capacity of tank as any number which is a multiple of 6, say 60 liters. Therefore rate of filling by all the three pipes together will be 10 liters/min.

	P + Q	R	P + Q + R
N			6 hrs
R			10
C = 60 liters			

Water added by P + Q + R in 2 hrs = 20 liters

After R is closed, remaining tank filled by P + Q = 40 liters in 8 hrs

Rate of P + Q = 40/8 = 5 liters/hr

Therefore rate of pipe R alone = 5 liters/hr.

	P + Q	R	P + Q + R
N		12 hrs	6 hrs
R	5	5	10
C = 60 liters			

Hence R alone can fill the rank in 12 hrs.

Choice (c)

Solution 27

	A	B
N	12 min	15 min
R	5	4
C = 60 liters		

As pipe A is open for complete 8 min, water added by pipe A = 8 × 5 = 40 liters

Water added by pipe B (remaining part) = 20 liters

Time required by pipe B to add 20 liters = 20/4 = 5 min

As they are opened together, pipe B should be closed after 5 min, so that 60 liters of tank will be filled in a total span of 8 min.

Choice (b)

14
Chain Rule

DIRECT PROPORTION

There exists a direct proportion between the variables if on the increase (or decrease) of one, the other increases (or decreases) to the same extent. For example:
- Men and work are directly proportional *i.e.,* more men, more work.
- Time and work are directly proportional *i.e.,* more time, more work.
- Cost and number of items are directly proportional *i.e.,* more cost, more number of items.

In case of direct proportion, the variables which are directly proportional are written on either side of "equal to", which indicates that a change in one variable will affect the another variable by same proportion.

INDIRECT PROPORTION

There exists an indirect proportion between the variables if on the increase of one variable, the other decreases to the same extent or vice-versa. For example:
- Men and time required to do a work are inversely proportional *i.e.,* more the number of men, less time required.
- Men and days of food provision are inversely proportional *i.e.,* more the number of men, the same food will last for less days.
- Speed and time are inversely proportional *i.e.,* more speed, less the time taken to cover a certain distance.

In case of indirect proportion, the variables which are inversely proportional are written on same side of "equal to", which indicates that a change in one variable will affect the another variable by same proportion.

SOLVED EXAMPLES

Example 1

If $3\frac{1}{2}$ kg of mangoes cost ₹ 84, then find what is the cost of $5\frac{1}{2}$ kg mangoes?

Solution

As more mangoes, more cost (direct proportion), so these variables will be written on either side of "equal to".

3½ kg mangoes = ₹ 84

1 kg of mangoes = $\dfrac{84}{3\frac{1}{2}} = \dfrac{84}{7/2}$ = ₹ 24

So the cost of 5½ kg of mangoes can be found as:

5½ kg mangoes = $\dfrac{11}{2} \times 24$ = ₹ 132.

Example 2

If 20 men can finish a work in 15 days working for 8 hrs a day, then how many days will be required by 24 men working 5 hrs a day to finish the same amount of work?

Solution

As more men, less time (inversely proportional), so these variables are written on same side of "equal to". The problem can still be simplified by writing all inputs given (men, days and hrs) on left hand side of "equal to" and the output (work) on right hand side.

$20 \text{ m} \times 15 \text{ d} \times 8 \text{ hrs} = \text{work}$ ... (1)

$24 \text{ m} \times x \text{ d} \times 5 \text{ hrs} = \text{work}$ ... (2)

Equating left hand sides of equation (1) and (2),

$24 \times x \times 5 = 20 \times 15 \times 8$

∴ $x = \dfrac{20 \times 15 \times 8}{24 \times 5}$

= 20 days.

Example 3

A garrison of 1200 men is provisioned for 15 days at the rate of 3 kg per day per man. How many days can the same provisions last for 1800 men at 5 kg per day per man?

Solution

Let the provision last for x days for 1800 men at the rate of 5 kg per day per man.

$1200 \text{ m} \times 15 \text{ d} \times 3 \text{ kg} = \text{Total food}$ ... (1)

$1800 \text{ m} \times x \text{ d} \times 5 \text{ kg} = \text{Total food}$ ... (2)

Equating left hand sides of equation (1) and (2)

$1800 \times x \times 5 = 1200 \times 15 \times 3$

∴ $x = \dfrac{1200 \times 15 \times 3}{1800 \times 5}$

= 6 days.

Example 4

If 6 machines working for 3 days and 8 hrs a day can make 3600 boxes, then how many boxes will be made by 4 machines working in 5 days and working for 6 hrs a day?

Solution

In this problem the input is machine, days and hrs; while the output is the number boxes produced.

$$6 \text{ m} \times 3 \text{ d} \times 8 \text{ hrs} = 3600 \text{ boxes}$$

Number of boxes produced by 1 machine in 1 day by working for 1 hr can be found as:

$$1 \text{ m} \times 1 \text{ d} \times 1 \text{ hr} = \frac{3600}{6 \times 3 \times 8}$$
$$= 25 \text{ boxes}$$

So, the number of boxes produced by 4 machines in 5 days by working for 6 hrs can be found as:

$$4 \text{ m} \times 5 \text{ d} \times 6 \text{ hrs} = 25 \times (4 \times 5 \times 6)$$
$$= 3000 \text{ boxes.}$$

Example 5

If 8 workers working for 3 days and 5 hrs a day can dig a trench 2 m wide, 1 m deep and 40 m long. How many men are required to dig a trench 3 m wide, 2 m deep and 30 m long by working 9 hrs a day in 2 days?

Solution

In this problem the input is men, days and hrs; while the output is the volume of trench that they are digging.

$$8 \text{ m} \times 3 \text{ d} \times 5 \text{ hrs} = \text{Trench of volume } 2 \times 1 \times 40 \text{ m}^3$$
$$8 \text{ m} \times 3 \text{ d} \times 5 \text{ hrs} = 80 \text{ m}^3$$

So, the input required to dig 1 m^3 of trench $= \dfrac{8 \times 3 \times 5}{80}$ ... (1)

$$x \text{ m} \times 2 \text{ d} \times 9 \text{ hrs} = \text{Trench of volume } 3 \times 2 \times 30 \text{ m}^3$$
$$x \text{ m} \times 2 \text{ d} \times 9 \text{ hrs} = 180 \text{ m}^3$$

So, the input required to dig 1 m^3 of trench $= \dfrac{x \times 2 \times 9}{180}$ ... (2)

Equating equation (1) and (2)

$$\frac{x \times 2 \times 9}{180} = \frac{8 \times 3 \times 5}{80}$$

$$\therefore \quad x = \frac{8 \times 3 \times 5 \times 180}{80 \times 2 \times 9}$$
$$= 15 \text{ men.}$$

Example 6

A power station has a sufficient stock of diesel to run 20 similar engines continuously for 30 days. After some days should 5 engines were shut down, such that the stock of diesel should now last for a total of 35 days. After how many days 5 engines were shut down?

Solution

Here the consumption of diesel directly depends on the number of engines running and the days for which they are running.

$\quad$ 20 e × 30 days = Stock of diesel $\hfill$ ... (1)

Let 5 engines be shut off after x days. So, 20 engines will run for x days and then 15 engines will run for remaining $(35 - x)$ days.

$\quad$ [20 e × x days] + [15 e × (35 − x)] = Stock of diesel $\hfill$ ... (2)

Equating equation (1) and (2)

$\quad\quad [20 \times x] + [15 \times (35 - x)] = 20 \times 30$

$\quad\quad\quad 20x + 525 - 15x = 600$

$\quad\quad\quad\quad\quad 5x = 75$

$\therefore \quad\quad\quad\quad\quad x = 15$ days

So, 5 engines were shut down after 15 days.

Example 7

The cost of grass to feed 20 cows and 30 goats for 30 days is ₹ 720. If 30 goats eat double the grass eaten by 20 cows, what will be the cost of grass eaten by 50 goats in 45 days?

Solution

Grass consumed by 30 goats is double the grass consumed by 20 cows.

$\quad \therefore$ 30 Goats = 40 Cows $\quad$ or $\quad$ 3 G = 4 C

$\quad$ (20 C + 30 G) × 30 days = ₹ 720 of grass

$\quad$ (15 G + 30 G) × 30 days = ₹ 720 of grass ($\because$ 20 C = 15 G)

$\quad$ 45 G × 30 days = ₹ 720 of grass

Grass consumed by one goat in one day can be found as:

$\quad$ 1 G × 1 day = ₹ $\dfrac{720}{45 \times 30}$ of grass

So, grass consumed by 50 goats in 45 days can be found as:

$\quad$ 50 G × 45 days = ₹ $\dfrac{720}{45 \times 30}$ × 50 × 45 = ₹ 1200 of grass.

50 goats will eat grass of ₹ 1200 in 45 days.

Chain Rule

EXERCISE

1. If 4 men can load a truck in 3 hrs, then 6 men can load the same truck in how many hours?
   - (a) 3 hrs
   - (b) 2 hrs
   - (c) 1½ hrs
   - (d) 1 hr

2. If a 2.5 kg of apples costs ₹ 75, then what will the cost of 3.5 kg apples?
   - (a) ₹ 90
   - (b) ₹ 100
   - (c) ₹ 105
   - (d) ₹ 120

3. Rohan can type 3 pages in 25 minutes. How many pages he can type in 2½ hours?
   - (a) 24
   - (b) 22
   - (c) 20
   - (d) 18

4. A group of workers can do a piece of work in 20 days. Twice the number of such workers can do thrice of that work in how many days?
   - (a) 10 days
   - (b) 20 days
   - (c) 25 days
   - (d) 30 days

5. Ajay can type 21 pages in the same time in which Vijay can type 15 pages. If Vijay types 100 pages then, how many pages Ajay can type in the same time?
   - (a) 140
   - (b) 150
   - (c) 165
   - (d) 170

6. If 4 liters of oil is sufficient to light 80 lamps simultaneously for 5 hrs, then 6 liters of oil can light how many lamps simultaneously for 8 hrs?
   - (a) 60
   - (b) 75
   - (c) 100
   - (d) 120

7. If 5 identical machines running at the constant rate can produce a 1200 toys per hour. At this rate, how many toys could 8 such machines produce in 40 minutes?
   - (a) 800
   - (b) 960
   - (c) 1200
   - (d) 1280

8. A 7.5 m long uniform steel pipe weighs 30 kg, then what will be the weight of 10 m long such pipe?
   - (a) 35 kg
   - (b) 37.5 kg
   - (c) 40 kg
   - (d) 45 kg

9. In a beverage factory, a certain quantity of juice can be filled in 200 bottles each of capacity 750 ml. In how many bottles of 500 ml capacity the same quantity of juice can be filled?
   - (a) 300
   - (b) 320
   - (c) 350
   - (d) 380

10. 8 examiners can valuate a certain number of answer books in 6 hrs and can declare the result. If the result is to be declared in 4 hrs, then how many extra examiners are needed?
    - (a) 10
    - (b) 11
    - (c) 12
    - (d) 14

11. 8 tailors can stitch 64 shirts in 4 days. At the same rate, how many shirts would be stitched by 16 tailors in 16 days?
    (a) 256
    (b) 360
    (c) 420
    (d) 512

12. A worker starts a job on 1st February of 2011 completes $4/7$ of a job on the last day of the month. At this rate, how many more days will it takes him to finish the job?
    (a) 14
    (b) 21
    (c) 35
    (d) 49

13. Two boilers of same capacity consume 100 kg of coal in 5 hrs. If two more boilers of same capacity are installed then 160 kg of coal will last for how many hours?
    (a) 4 hrs
    (b) 4½ hrs
    (c) 5 hrs
    (d) 5½ hrs

14. If 20 men can build wall 160 m long in 10 days working 8 hrs a day. What length of a similar wall can be built by 25 men in 4 days, working 4 hrs a day?
    (a) 40 m
    (b) 60 m
    (c) 80 m
    (d) 90 m

15. A certain number of men can finish a piece of work in 60 days. If however, there are 5 men less, it would have taken 10 days more for the work to be finished. How many men were there originally?
    (a) 22
    (b) 25
    (c) 30
    (d) 35

16. A private firm for a certain project hires 20 engineers and 40 technicians for 10 days whose total wages amount to ₹ 140000. What would be the cost of hiring 10 engineers and 30 technicians for 15 days if the cost of hiring 5 technicians is same as the cost of hiring 1 engineer?
    (a) ₹ 90000
    (b) ₹ 115000
    (c) ₹ 120000
    (d) ₹ 150000

17. 20 workers can reap 100 acres of land in 20 days working 5 hours a day. How many more acres of land can 30 workers working 8 hours a day reap in 15 days?
    (a) 75
    (b) 80
    (c) 90
    (d) 100

18. If 45 men can do a certain work in 30 days. After 10 days, 25 men left the job, then how many more days are required to finish the remaining work?
    (a) 25
    (b) 30
    (c) 45
    (d) 50

19. 1 man can load 1 box in a truck in 5 minutes and a truck can hold 20 boxes. How many trucks are completely loaded by 6 men in 2½ hour?
    (a) 6
    (b) 7
    (c) 8
    (d) 9

20. A hostel of 630 boys has a provision for 24 days when consumption is 2 kg per day per boy. For how many days are the provisions sufficient for 360 girls at the rate of 1.5 kg per day per girl?
    (a) 42 (b) 48
    (c) 56 (d) 60

21. A physics teacher teaches 25% of the syllabus in 20 days with 2 hrs of lecture per day. To complete the remaining syllabus in 30 more days, how much time the lecture should be conducted per day?
    (a) 3½ (b) 4
    (c) 4½ (d) 5

22. 30 carpenters can make 120 tables in 8 days working 10 hours/day. If 10 carpenters leave the work after 4 days, then how many hours per day should the rest of the carpenters work to finish the work on time?
    (a) 12 (b) 13
    (c) 14 (d) 15

23. A garrison of 100 men had a provision of 30 days. After 5 days, 25 more men arrived, then the remaining food will last for how many days?
    (a) 15 (b) 18
    (c) 20 (d) 25

24. There is a provision for a garrison of 500 men for 40 days. After some days, 200 men left the garrison. If the entire provision lasted 60 days, after how many days did the 200 men leave?
    (a) 10 (b) 12
    (c) 15 (d) 20

25. A camp had provision of food for 50 boys for 15 days. After 3 days, 10 boys returned back to their home. The number of days for which the remaining food will last, is:
    (a) 10 (b) 12
    (c) 15 (d) 20

26. A tank 2 m long, 3 m wide and 6 m deep can be filled by 3 pumps of same capacity working continuously for 5 hrs. In how much time the same tank can be filled if one pump fails after an hour from the start?
    (a) 6 hrs (b) 7 hrs
    (c) 8 hrs (d) 9 hrs

27. A team of 40 employees can complete a project in 12 days, working 5 hours a day. In how many days will 30 employees, working 8 hours a day, complete the project?
    (a) 8   (b) 9
    (c) 10 (d) 12

28. A full charge battery operated toy car can make 8 rounds of a circular track of radius 15 m. How many rounds the same toy car can make if it's a circular track of 20 m radius?
    (a) 4½   (b) 5
    (c) 10⅔ (d) 6

29. An air pump fills 40% of air in a hot-air balloon in 10 min. In how much time 5 such hot-air balloons can be filled by single air pump?
    (a) 1 hr 50 min
    (b) 2 hr 5 min
    (c) 2 hr 15 min
    (d) 2 hr 20 min

30. In a dairy farm 15 cows eat as much as 10 buffalos. If 300 cows can consume certain quantity of grass in 15 days, then how many buffalos can consume double the grass in 25 days?
    (a) 250
    (b) 300
    (c) 360
    (d) 240

KEYS

1. (b)	2. (c)	3. (d)	4. (d)	5. (a)	6. (b)	7. (d)	8. (c)
9. (a)	10. (c)	11. (d)	12. (b)	13. (a)	14. (a)	15. (d)	16. (c)
17. (b)	18. (c)	19. (d)	20. (c)	21. (b)	22. (d)	23. (c)	24. (a)
25. (c)	26. (b)	27. (c)	28. (d)	29. (b)	30. (d)		

SOLUTIONS

Solution 1

$\quad$ 4 m × 3 hrs = Loading a truck $\quad$ ... (1)

$\quad$ 6 m × x hrs = Loading a truck $\quad$ ... (2)

Equating equation (1) and (2)

$\quad$ 6 × x = 4 × 3

∴ $\quad x = \dfrac{4 \times 3}{6} = 2$ hrs.

Choice (b)

Solution 2

$\quad$ 2.5 kg apples = ₹ 75

$\quad$ 1 kg of apples = $\dfrac{75}{2.5}$ = ₹ 30

$\quad$ 3.5 kg apples = 3.5 × 30 = ₹ 105.

Choice (c)

Solution 3

$25 \text{ min} \Rightarrow 3 \text{ pages}$

$150 \text{ min} \Rightarrow x \text{ pages}$

$\therefore \quad x = \dfrac{150 \times 3}{25} = 18 \text{ pages.}$

Choice (d)

Solution 4

Let the number of workers in the initial group be x.

$x \times 20 \text{ days} = \text{work}$ ... (1)

$2x \times d \text{ days} = 3(\text{work})$ ... (2)

$\therefore \quad 2x \times d = 3 \times (x \times 20)$

$\therefore \quad d = \dfrac{3 \times 20x}{2x} = 30 \text{ days.}$

Choice (d)

Solution 5

15 pages of Vijay = 21 pages of Ajay

$\therefore$ 5 pages of Vijay = 7 pages of Ajay

Multiplying both the sides of above equation with 20.

100 pages of Vijay = 140 pages of Ajay.

Choice (a)

Solution 6

4 liters $\Rightarrow$ 80 lamps × 5 hrs

Oil required to light 1 lamp for 1 hr = $\dfrac{4}{80 \times 5}$ liters ... (1)

6 liters $\Rightarrow$ x lamps × 8 hrs

Oil required to light 1 lamp for 1 hr = $\dfrac{6}{x \times 8}$ liters ... (2)

Equating equation (1) and (2)

$\dfrac{4}{80 \times 5} = \dfrac{6}{x \times 8}$

$\therefore \quad x = 75$

Choice (b)

Solution 7

5 machines × 60 min = 1200 toys

5 machines × 40 min = $\frac{2}{3} \times 1200 = 800$ toys

1 machine × 40 min = $\frac{800}{5} = 160$ toys

8 machine × 40 min = 160 × 8 = 1280 toys

Choice (d)

Solution 8

7.5 m long pipe $\Rightarrow$ 30 kg

10 m long pipe $\Rightarrow$ x kg

$\therefore \quad x = \frac{10 \times 30}{7.5} = 40$ kg.

Choice (c)

Solution 9

$\quad$ 200 bottles × 750 ml = Total juice $\quad$ ... (1)

$\quad$ x bottles × 500 ml = Total juice $\quad$ ... (2)

Equating equation (1) and (2)

$\quad x \times 500 = 200 \times 750$

$\therefore \quad x = \frac{200 \times 750}{500}$

$\quad = 300.$

Choice (a)

Solution 10

8 examiners × 6 hrs = Answer books $\quad$ ... (1)

x examiners × 4 hrs = Answer books $\quad$ ... (2)

Equating equation (1) and (2)

$\quad x \times 4 = 8 \times 6$

$\therefore \quad x = \frac{8 \times 6}{4}$

$\quad = 12.$

Choice (c)

Solution 11

8 tailors × 4 days = 64 shirts

1 tailor × 1 day = $\dfrac{64}{8 \times 4}$ = 2 shirts

16 tailors × 1 days = 16 × 2 = 32 shirts

16 tailors × 16 days = 16 × 32 = 512 shirts.

Choice (d)

Solution 12

In the month of February 2011 there are 28 days.

$\dfrac{4}{7}$ of work ⇒ 28 days

∴ Complete work = $\dfrac{28}{4/7}$ = 49 days

Days required to finish remaining work = 49 − 28 = 21.

Choice (b)

Solution 13

100 kg coal ⇒ 2 boilers × 5 hrs

Coal required to run 1 boiler for 1 hr = $\dfrac{100}{2 \times 5}$ kg ... (1)

160 kg coal ⇒ 4 boilers × x hrs

Coal required to run 1 boiler for 1 hr = $\dfrac{160}{4 \times x}$ kg ... (2)

Equating equation (1) and (2)

$\dfrac{100}{2 \times 5} = \dfrac{160}{4 \times x}$

∴ x = 4 hrs.

Choice (a)

Solution 14

20 m × 10 d × 8 hrs = 160 m wall

Length of wall built by 1 man working for 1 hr in 1 day:

1 m × 1 d × 1 hr = $\dfrac{160}{20 \times 10 \times 8} = \dfrac{1}{10}$ m

Length of wall built by 25 men working for 4 hrs/day in 4 days:

$$25 \text{ m} \times 4d \times 4 \text{ hr} = \frac{1}{10} \times 25 \times 4 \times 4 = 40 \text{ m}.$$

Choice (a)

Solution 15

Let there be x number of men initially.

x m × 60 days = work ... (1)
$(x - 5) \times 70$ days = work ... (2)

Equating equation (1) and (2)

$x \times 60 = (x - 5) \times 70$
$60x = 70x - 350$
∴ $x = 35$.

Choice (d)

Solution 16

5 Technicians = 1 Engineer

$(20\,E + 40\,T) \times 10$ days = ₹ 140000
$(20\,E + 8\,E) \times 10$ days = ₹ 140000 (∵ 5 T = 1 E)

$$E = \frac{140000}{10 \times 28} = ₹\,500$$

∴ $T = 500 / 5 = ₹ 100$.

So the wage of engineer is ₹ 500 per day, while a technician is paid ₹ 100 per day.

$(10\,E + 30\,T) \times 15$ days = $(10 \times 500 + 30 \times 100) \times 15$
$\phantom{(10\,E + 30\,T) \times 15 \text{ days }}= (5000 + 3000) \times 15$
$\phantom{(10\,E + 30\,T) \times 15 \text{ days }}= 8000 \times 15$
$\phantom{(10\,E + 30\,T) \times 15 \text{ days }}= 120000.$

Choice (c)

Solution 17

20 m × 20 d × 5 hrs = 100 acre of land

Acres of land reaped by 1 man working for 1 hr in 1 day:

$$1 \text{ m} \times 1 \text{ d} \times 1 \text{ hr} = \frac{100}{20 \times 20 \times 5}$$
$$\phantom{1 \text{ m} \times 1 \text{ d} \times 1 \text{ hr} } = \frac{1}{20} \text{ acre}$$

Acres of land reaped by 30 men working for 8 hrs/day in 15 days:

$$30 \text{ m} \times 15 \text{ d} \times 8 \text{ hr} = \frac{1}{20} \times 30 \times 15 \times 8 = 180 \text{ acre}$$

Extra work = 180 − 100 = 80 acre of land.

Choice (b)

Solution 18

$$45 \text{ m} \times 30 \text{ d} = \text{work} \qquad \ldots (1)$$
$$(45 \text{ m} \times 10 \text{ d}) + (20 \text{ m} \times x \text{ d}) = \text{work} \qquad \ldots (2)$$

Equating equation (1) and (2)

$$(45 \text{ m} \times 10 \text{ d}) + (20 \text{ m} \times x \text{ d}) = 45 \text{ m} \times 30 \text{ d}$$
$$450 + 20x = 1350$$
$$\therefore \quad x = \frac{1350 - 450}{20} = 45 \text{ days.}$$

So, after 25 men left the job 45 more days are required to finish the remaining work.

Choice (c)

Solution 19

$$1 \text{ m} \times 5 \text{ min} = 1 \text{ box}$$

Number of boxes loaded by 1 man in 1 min:

$$1 \text{ m} \times 1 \text{ min} = \frac{1}{5} \text{ box}$$

Number of boxes loaded by 6 men in 2½ hrs (150 min):

$$6 \text{ m} \times 150 \text{ min} = \frac{1}{5} \times 6 \times 150 = 180 \text{ boxes}$$

Number of trucks loaded = $\frac{180}{20} = 9$.

Choice (d)

Solution 20

$$630 \times 24 \text{ d} \times 2 \text{ kg} = \text{Provision of food} \qquad \ldots (1)$$
$$360 \times x \text{ d} \times 1.5 \text{ kg} = \text{Provision of food} \qquad \ldots (2)$$

Equating equation (1) and (2)

$$360 \times x \times 1.5 = 630 \times 24 \times 2$$
$$\therefore \quad x = \frac{630 \times 24 \times 2}{360 \times 1.5} = 56 \text{ days.}$$

Choice (c)

Solution 21

In 40 hrs $\Rightarrow$ 25% syllabus
In x hrs $\Rightarrow$ 75% syllabus

$\therefore \quad x = \dfrac{75 \times 40}{25} = 120$ hrs

To complete the syllabus in next 30 days, duration of lecture = $\dfrac{120}{30} = 4$ hrs/day.

Choice (b)

Solution 22

$30\ m \times 8\ d \times 10\ hrs = 120$ tables ... (1)
$(30\ m \times 4\ d \times 10\ hrs) + (20\ m \times 4\ d \times x\ hrs) = 120$ tables ... (2)

Equating equation (1) and (2)

$(30 \times 4 \times 10) + (20 \times 4 \times x) = 30 \times 8 \times 10$

$1200 + 80x = 2400$

$\therefore \quad x = \dfrac{2400 - 1200}{80}$

$= 15$ hrs/day.

Choice (d)

Solution 23

$100\ m \times 30$ days = Provision of food ... (1)
$(100\ m \times 5$ days$) + (125 \times x$ days$) =$ Provision of food ... (2)

Equating equation (1) and (2)

$(100 \times 5) + (125 \times x) = 100 \times 30$

$500 + 125x = 3000$

$\therefore \quad x = \dfrac{3000 - 500}{125}$

$= 20$ days.

Choice (c)

Solution 24

Let us assume that 200 men left after x days.

$500\ m \times 40$ days = Provision ... (1)
$[500\ m \times x$ days$] + [300\ m \times (60 - x)$ days$] =$ Provision ... (2)

Equating equation (1) and (2)

$$[500 \times x] + [300 \times (60 - x)] = 500 \times 40$$
$$500x + 18000 - 300x = 20000$$
$$200x = 2000$$
$$\therefore \quad x = 10 \text{ days.}$$

Choice (a)

Solution 25

$$50 \text{ b} \times 15 \text{ days} = \text{Provision} \quad \ldots (1)$$
$$(50 \text{ b} \times 3 \text{ days}) + (40 \text{ b} \times x \text{ days}) = \text{Provision} \quad \ldots (2)$$

Equating equation (1) and (2)

$$(50 \times 3) + (40 \times x) = 50 \times 15$$
$$150 + 40x = 750$$
$$\therefore \quad x = \frac{750 - 150}{40} = 15 \text{ days.}$$

Choice (c)

Solution 26

Volume of tank = $2 \text{ m} \times 3 \text{ m} \times 6 \text{ m} = 36 \text{ m}^3$
3 pumps × 5 hrs = 36 m^3 ... (1)
(3 pumps × 1 hr) + (2 pumps × x hrs) = 36 m^3 ... (2)

Equating equation (1) and (2)

$$(3 \times 1) + (2 \times x) = 3 \times 5$$
$$3 + 2x = 15$$
$$\therefore \quad x = 6 \text{ hrs}$$

Total time taken to fill the tank = 1 + 6 = 7 hrs.

Choice (b)

Solution 27

40 m × 12 days × 5 hrs = Project ... (1)
30 m × x days × 8 hrs = Project ... (2)

Equating equation (1) and (2)

$$30 \times x \times 6 = 40 \times 12 \times 5$$
$$\therefore \quad x = \frac{40 \times 12 \times 5}{30 \times 8} = 10 \text{ days.}$$

Choice (c)

Solution 28

Let us assume that car makes x rounds of a track of 20 m radius.

Run of toy car on 15 m radius track $\Rightarrow (2\pi \times 15) \times 8$ ... (1)

Run of toy car on 20 m radius track $\Rightarrow (2\pi \times 20) \times x$ ... (2)

Equating equation (1) and (2)

$$(2\pi \times 20) \times x = (2\pi \times 15) \times 8$$

$\therefore \quad x = \dfrac{15 \times 8}{20} = 6 \text{ rounds.}$

Choice (d)

Solution 29

In 10 min $\Rightarrow$ 40% Air filled
In x min $\Rightarrow$ 100% Air filled

$\therefore \quad x = \dfrac{100 \times 10}{40} = 25 \text{ min}$

If one balloon can be filled in 25 min, so 5 such balloons can be filled in 125 min.

Choice (b)

Solution 30

15 Cows = 10 Buffalos or 3 Cows = 2 Buffalos

300 Cows × 15 days = Grass ... (1)

x Buffalos × 25 days = 2 × Grass ... (2)

x Buffalos × 25 days = 2 × (300 Cows × 15 days)

x Buffalos × 25 days = 2 × (200 Buffalos × 15 days)

$\therefore \quad x = \dfrac{2 \times 200 \times 15}{25}$

$= 240.$

Choice (d)

15

Time and Distance

BASIC FORMULAE

The problems in this topic encompass only three variables *i.e.*, speed, time and distance. The relation between these variables is expressed as:

$$\text{Speed} = \frac{\text{Distance}}{\text{Time}}$$

From the above relation we can say that:

- There is an inverse relation between speed and time if distance is constant. $\left(\text{Speed} \, \alpha \, \frac{1}{\text{Time}}\right)$
- There is a direct variation between distance and speed if the time of journey remains constant. (Distance α Speed)
- There is a direct variation between distance and time if speed during the journey remains constant. (Distance α Time)

Distance is normally measured in kilometers, meters or miles; time in hours or seconds and speed in km/hr (also denoted by kmph), miles/hr (also denoted by mph) or meters/sec (also denoted by m/s). To convert the speed from km/hr to m/s or vice-versa following conversion is to be used:

$$\text{km/hr} \times \frac{5}{18} = \text{m/s}$$

$$\text{m/s} \times \frac{18}{5} = \text{km/hr.}$$

AVERAGE SPEED

The most important point to note here is that the average speed is NOT always equal to the average of the given speeds. Average speed of a moving body traveling at different speeds is calculated as follows:

$$\text{Average speed} = \frac{\text{Total distance covered}}{\text{Total time taken}}$$

Suppose if a body travels from one point to other at the speed of m, and returned back at the speed of n, then the average speed during the entire journey is calculated as:

$$\text{Average speed} = \frac{2mn}{m+n}$$

Please note that the average speed is not dependent upon the distance between two points.

RELATIVE SPEED

The speed of one moving body in relation to another moving body is called the relative speed of these two bodies, *i.e.,* it is the speed of one moving body as observed from the second moving body. If two moving bodies are moving in same direction, the relative speed is equal to the difference between the speeds of two bodies. If two moving bodies are moving in opposite direction, the relative speed is equal to the sum of the speeds of two bodies.

Going in same direction ⇒ Difference of speeds

Going in opposite direction ⇒ Sum of speeds.

RACES

When two persons *A* and *B* are running a race, they can start the race at the same time or one of them may start a race little later than the other. As per the second case, suppose if *B* starts the race 10 seconds after *A* starts, then we say *A* has a 'start' of 10 seconds.

It may be also possible that these competitors may start at the same point or one person is ahead of other right from the beginning. As per the second case, suppose if *B* is starting from the start point, while *A* is starting from 10 meters ahead of *B* (start point), then we say A has got a 'start' of 10 meters.

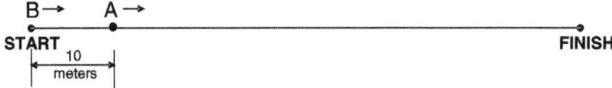

In a race if *B* wins and by that time *A* is 20 meters behind the finish line, then it can be said that *B* beats *A* by 20 meters. From the figure below we can say that *B* beats *C* by 30 meters, but we can't always say that *A* beats *C* by 10 meters, because by the time *A* reaches the finishing line the distance between *A* and *C* may vary if they are not running at same speeds.

If suppose *B* finishes the race and *A* requires further 10 seconds to reach the finishing line (*i.e.,* to cover 20 meters), then it can be also said as *B* beats *A* by 10 seconds.

SOLVED EXAMPLES

Example 1
A cyclist is moving at the speed of 2 m/s. How much kilometers he will cover in 2½ hour?

Solution

Speed = 2 m/s × $\dfrac{18}{5}$ = $\dfrac{36}{5}$ km/hr

Time = 2½ hr = $\dfrac{5}{2}$ hr

Distance = Speed × Time = $\dfrac{36}{5} \times \dfrac{5}{2}$ = 18 km.

Example 2
A person can cover a certain distance in 9 hrs traveling at a speed of 60 km/hr. At what speed he should travel to cover the distance in 6 hrs?

Solution

Distance = Speed × Time = 60 × 9 = 540 km

540 = Speed × 6

Speed = $\dfrac{540}{6}$ = 90 km/hr.

Example 3
A car travels for 9 hours. If it covers first half of the journey at the speed of 30 km/hr and remaining at the speed of 45 km/hr, find the total distance covered by the car.

Solution

Let the total distance be 2d km.

$$\xleftarrow{\hspace{3cm}} \underset{30}{\overset{d}{\longrightarrow}} \underset{45}{\overset{d}{\longrightarrow}} \xrightarrow{\hspace{3cm}}$$

Time to run first half + Time to run remaining half = 9 hrs

$\dfrac{d}{30} + \dfrac{d}{45} = 9$

$\dfrac{3d + 2d}{90} = 9$

$$d = \frac{90 \times 9}{5}$$
$$= 162 \text{ km}$$

So, total distance covered by car = $2d$ = 324 km.

Example 4

Walking at $\frac{3}{4}$ of its usual speed, a man is 15 min late. Find the usual time to cover the journey.

Solution

We know that the distance walked by the person is fixed, say it is D km.

Distance = Speed × Time
$$D = S \times T \qquad \ldots (1)$$
$$D = \frac{3}{4} S \times \left(T + \frac{15}{60}\right) \qquad \ldots (2)$$

As the L.H.S. of both the equations is same, we can equate the R.H.S.

$$S \times T = \frac{3}{4} S \times \left(T + \frac{15}{60}\right)$$

$$T = \frac{3}{4}\left(T + \frac{1}{4}\right)$$

$$4T = 3T + \frac{3}{4}$$

$$T = \frac{3}{4} \text{ hr or 45 min.}$$

Alternative Method:

	S_{old}		S_{new}
Speed ratio	4x	:	3x
Time ratio	3x	:	4x

($\because$ Speed & time are inversely proportional)

As new time taken is 15 min more than usual time taken, hence $4x - 3x$ = 15 min, or x = 15 min.

Usual time taken = $3x = 3 \times 15$ = 45 min.

Example 5

A man travels from city A to city B at the speed of 90 km/hr and returns back at the speed of 60 km/hr. What is his average speed during the entire journey?

Solution

$$\frac{2mn}{m+n} = \frac{2 \times 90 \times 60}{90 + 60} = 72 \text{ km/hr.}$$

Example 6

A car travels from P to Q at a uniform speed of 80 km/hr and a distance from Q to R at a uniform speed of 120 km/hr. What is the average speed for the entire journey if the ratio of distance between PQ and QR is 2 : 3?

Solution

Distance between $PQ = 2x$
Distance between $QR = 3x$

Time required to cover $PQ = \dfrac{2x}{80}$

Time required to cover $QR = \dfrac{3x}{120}$

$$\begin{aligned}
\text{Average speed} &= \dfrac{\text{Total distance covered}}{\text{Total time taken}} \\
&= \dfrac{2x+3x}{\dfrac{2x}{80}+\dfrac{3x}{120}} \\
&= \dfrac{5x}{\dfrac{6x+6x}{240}} \\
&= \dfrac{5}{12} \times 240 \\
&= 100 \text{ km/hr.}
\end{aligned}$$

Example 7

Distance between Nagpur and Hyderabad is 500 km. Car A starts from Nagpur towards Hyderabad at 7:00 a.m. at the speed of 60 km/hr; while Car B starts from Hyderabad towards Nagpur at 8:00 a.m. at the speed of 50 km/hr. If they are traveling at uniform speed, at what time will they meet?

Solution

Distance covered by Car A in 1 hr (7:00 a.m. to 8:00 a.m.) = 60 km
Distance between two cars at 8:00 a.m. = 500 − 60 = 440 km

Time required after 8:00 a.m. = $\dfrac{\text{Distance}}{\text{Relative Speed}} = \dfrac{440}{60+50} = 4$ hrs

So, the cars will meet 4 hrs past 8:00 a.m. *i.e.,* at 12 noon.

Example 8

A thief is spotted by a policeman from a distance of 160 m. The policeman immediately starts chasing the thief at the speed of 5 m/s, while the thief also runs at the speed of 3 m/s. How far the thief can run before he is caught?

Solution

Time required by policeman to catch the thief = $\dfrac{\text{Distance}}{\text{Realtive speed}} = \dfrac{160}{5-3} = 80$ seconds

Distance covered by thief in 80 seconds = Speed × Time = $3 \times 80 = 240$ meters.

Example 9

In a kilometer race between A and B, B has a start of 100 m. At the end A beats B by 100 m or 20 sec. What is the ratio of speeds of A and B?

Solution

Distance covered by A on the race track = 1000 m

Distance covered by B on the race track = 800 m (∵ Start of 100 m & lost the race by 100 m)

Time required by A to run 1000 m = Time required by B to run 800 m

$$\dfrac{1000}{S_A} = \dfrac{800}{S_B}$$

$$\dfrac{S_A}{S_B} = \dfrac{5}{4}.$$

Example 10

In a race of 1500 m, P beats Q by 50 sec. In the same race Q beats R by 40 sec. If P beats R by 450 m, then in how much time Q completes the race?

Solution

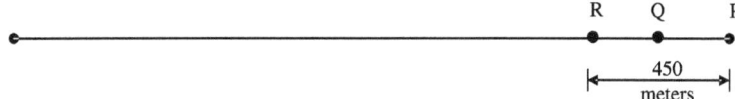

Time taken by P to run the race = t sec.

Time taken by Q to run the race = $(t + 50)$ sec.

Time taken by R to run the race = $(t + 90)$ sec.

So, we can say that R requires 90 sec to cover 450 meters.

$$S_R = \dfrac{450}{90} = 5 \text{ m/s.}$$

Time required by R to run complete race = $\dfrac{1500}{5} = 300$ sec.

As Q finishes the race 40 sec earlier than R, time required by Q to complete the race will be 260 sec.

EXERCISE

1. A train covers a distance of 550 meters in 1 minute whereas a bus covers a distance of 33 km in 45 minutes. The speed ratio of train and bus is:
   (a) 4 : 3
   (b) 3 : 4
   (c) 3 : 5
   (d) 5 : 3

2. Driving at the speed of 45 km/hr a car reaches a destination in 40 min. If it runs at the speed of 60 km/hr, in how much time it can reach the destination?
   (a) 15 min
   (b) 30 min
   (c) 45 min
   (d) 60 min

3. An airplane covers a certain distance at a speed of 350 km/hr in 6 hours. To cover the same distance in 4 hours, it must travel at a speed of:
   (a) 525 km/hr
   (b) 625 km/hr
   (c) 700 km/hr
   (d) 1050 km/hr

4. Raju can cover 12 km in 40 min. The distance covered by him in 1½ hrs is:
   (a) 21 km
   (b) 25 km
   (c) 27 km
   (d) 30 km

5. The ratio between the speeds of two trains is 4 : 7. If the first train runs 320 km in 4 hours, then the speed of the second train is:
   (a) 70 km/hr
   (b) 105 km/hr
   (c) 126 km/hr
   (d) 140 km/hr

6. If a person walks at 12 km/hr instead of 10 km/hr, he would have walked 10 km more. The actual distance traveled by him is:
   (a) 50 km
   (b) 60 km
   (c) 66 km
   (d) 70 km

7. A person saves 180 min when he increases his speed from 25 km/hr to 30 km/hr to cover a certain distance. Find the distance.
   (a) 500 km
   (b) 420 km
   (c) 250 km
   (d) 450 km

8. Rahul and Rajesh run same distance at the speed of 12 km/hr and 15 km/hr respectively. If Rahul takes 40 min more than Rajesh, then how much distance each of them run?
   (a) 15 km
   (b) 30 km
   (c) 40 km
   (d) 60 km

9. A man in a train notices that he can count 31 electricity poles in one minute. If they are known to be 30 meters apart, then at what speed is the train traveling?
   (a) 30 km/hr
   (b) 45 km/hr
   (c) 50 km/hr
   (d) 54 km/hr

10. A farmer walks towards city from his village at the speed of 15 km/hr and returns back at a speed of 10 km/hr. If he takes 5 hours in going and coming, the distance between his village and the city is:

(a) 20 km (b) 30 km
(c) 40 km (d) 45 km

11. Akshay can cover a certain distance in 50 min, by covering two-third of the distance at 4 km/hr and rest at 3 km/hr. The total distance is:
    (a) 3 km (b) 3.5 km
    (c) 4 km (d) 4.5 km

12. A car reaches from city A to city B in 10 hours. It travels first half of the journey at the speed of 80 km/hr and second half at the speed of 120 km/hr. Find the distance between city A and city B.
    (a) 240 km (b) 480 km
    (c) 720 km (d) 960 km

13. A person has to cover a distance of 6 km in 45 minutes. If he covers one-half of the distance in two-thirds of the total time; then to cover the remaining distance in the remaining time, his speed must be:
    (a) 6 km/hr (b) 8 km/hr
    (c) 12 km/hr (d) 15 km/hr

14. If a man travels at the speed of 30 km/hr, he will reach his destination on time. He covers half the journey in four-fifth time. How much should be his speed in the remaining half of journey, so that he reaches his destination on time?
    (a) 45 km/hr (b) 50 km/hr
    (c) 60 km/hr (d) 75 km/hr

15. A villager traveled a distance of 50 km in 10 hours. He traveled partly on foot at the speed of 4 km/hr and partly on bicycle at the speed of 8 km/hr. The distance traveled on foot is:
    (a) 24 km (b) 30 km
    (c) 36 km (d) 40 km

16. A bus covered a distance of 160 km in 4 hrs, covering a part of it at 30 km/hr and the remaining at 70 km/hr. For how much time did the bus travel at 70 km/hr?
    (a) ½ hr (b) 1 hr
    (c) 1½ hr (d) 2 hrs

17. The distance between Karan's house and his friend's house is 12 km. He walked at the speed of 4 km/hr and after every 4 km he took rest for 10 min. How much time did it take Karan to reach his friend's house?
    (a) 3 hrs (b) $3\frac{1}{2}$ hrs
    (c) $3\frac{2}{3}$ hrs (d) 4 hrs

18. A car takes 2 hrs more to cover a distance of 480 km when its speed is reduced by 8 km/hr. Find its usual speed.
    (a) 48 km/hr (b) 55 km/hr
    (c) 60 km/hr (d) 64 km/hr

19. Walking at 5/6th of usual speed a man is 20 min late. The usual time to cover the same distance is:
    (a) 1 hr
    (b) 1½ hr
    (c) 1⅓ hr
    (d) 1⅔ hr

20. Traveling at 4/5th of usual speed Amit is 15 min late. What is the usual time to cover the same distance?
    (a) 1 hour
    (b) 75 min
    (b) 30 min
    (d) 45 min

21. If a person increases his speed by 1 km/hr he reaches his office in 3/4th of the time he normally takes and if he decreases his speed by 1 km/hr, he reaches his office 2 hrs late. What distance dose the person travels to his office?
    (a) 10 kms
    (b) 8 kms
    (c) 12 kms
    (d) 9 kms

22. If a man drives his car at the speed of 50 km/hr, he will reach office 20 min late; but if he drives at 75 km/hr, he will reach office 10 min early. Find the distance between house and office.
    (a) 60 km
    (b) 70 km
    (c) 75 km
    (d) 90 km

23. Chintu walks from his house to school at the rate of 4 km/hr; he reaches the school 10 min earlier than the scheduled time. However, if he walks at the rate of 3 km/hr, he reaches 10 min late. The distance of the school from his house is:
    (a) 3 km
    (b) 4 km
    (c) 6 km
    (d) 8 km

24. A man gets late by 20 min if he covers the distance between house and office at 50 km/hr. If he increases his speed by 10 km/hr, he reaches office 10 min early. Find the distance between house and office.
    (a) 140 km
    (b) 160 km
    (c) 150 km
    (d) 180 km

25. If a student walks from his house to school at the speed of 10 km/hr, he reaches school 15 min late. On the next day he walks at the speed of a 15 km/hr, still he reaches 5 min late. At what speed should he walk so that he reaches school on correct time?
    (a) 16 km/hr
    (b) 18.5 km/hr
    (c) 20 km/hr
    (d) 21 km/hr

26. Speed of Krishna while going away from city is 60 km/hr and his speed while coming towards the city is 40 km/hr. If the total time of journey cannot exceed 8 hours, how far can he go so that he returns back to city within 8 hours?
    (a) 192 km
    (b) 202 km
    (c) 186 km
    (d) 156 km

27. Speed of a train excluding stoppages is 90 km/hr, while including stoppages is 75 km/hr. For how many minutes dose the train stops per hour?
    (a) 10 min
    (b) 15 min
    (c) 30 min
    (d) 45 min

28. The average speed for an entire journey is 60 km/hr without considering stoppages. When stoppages are considered the average speed becomes 48 km/hr. How many minutes per hour on an average were the stoppages?
    (a) 10 min
    (b) 12 min
    (c) 16 min
    (d) 18 min

29. Jatin traveled a certain distance at 30 km/hr and returned back at 60 km/hr using same route. Find the average speed of Jatin.
    (a) 40 km/hr
    (b) 45 km/hr
    (c) 48 km/hr
    (d) 50 km/hr

30. A bus travels X km at 60 km/hr and then travels another $2X$ km at 40 km/hr. Find average speed over entire distance.
    (a) 45 km/hr
    (b) 56 km/hr
    (c) 50 km/hr
    (d) 48 km/hr

31. A person travels from A to B at a speed of 40 km/hr and returns by increasing his speed by 50%. What is his average speed for the round trip?
    (a) 45 km/hr
    (b) 42 km/hr
    (c) 50 km/hr
    (d) 48 km/hr

32. A car travels 200 km at a speed of 40 km/hr. It then increases its speed by 10 km/hr every hour for another 5 hours and comes to rest. Find the average speed for the entire journey.
    (a) 45 km/hr
    (b) 55 km/hr
    (c) 60 km/hr
    (d) 65 km/hr

33. P is twice as fast as Q, and Q is thrice as fast as R. The journey covered by R in 120 min will be covered by Q in:
    (a) 360 min
    (b) 60 min
    (c) 40 min
    (d) 30 min

34. Two persons A and B move towards each other from city P and city Q respectively. They meet 50 km away from city Q. If the ratio of speeds of A and B is 4 : 1, find the distance between city P and city Q.
    (a) 200 km
    (b) 125 km
    (c) 150 km
    (d) 250 km

35. Two trains $T1$ and $T2$ start from stations A and B respectively and go towards B and A at 10 am and 11 am respectively. The speed of $T1$ and $T2$ are 10 km/hr and 15 km/hr respectively. At what time will they meet if A and B are 160 km apart?
    (a) 4 pm
    (b) 5 pm
    (c) 6 pm
    (d) 7 pm

36. The distance between two cities A and B is 330 Km. A train starts from A at 8 a.m. and travel towards B at 60 km/hr. Another train starts from B at 9 a.m and travels towards A at 75 Km/hr. At what time do they meet?
    (a) 10 a.m.
    (b) 10:30 a.m.
    (c) 11 a.m.
    (d) 11:30 a.m.

37. A man wants to catch a bus which is 210 m ahead of him. The bus also started at the same time. If the speed of bus is 3 m/s and the man runs at 36 km/hr, in how much time can he catch the bus?
    (a) 30 sec
    (b) 7/11 sec
    (c) 21 sec
    (d) 15 sec

38. A passenger train left the station at 6 a.m. and travels with the uniform speed of 60 km/hr. After 4 hrs an express train also leaves from the same station and travels in the same direction as that of passenger train with the uniform speed of 80 km/hr. At what time express train will be able to overtake the passenger train?
    (a) 6 p.m.
    (b) 9 p.m.
    (c) 10 p.m.
    (d) 11 p.m.

39. An artillery gun was fired twice at an interval of 24 seconds. A jeep driver who is traveling towards the gun heard the sound after an interval of 22 seconds. If the sound is traveling at the speed of 330 m/s, find the speed of jeep.
    (a) 11 m/s
    (b) 22 m/s
    (c) 24 m/s
    (d) 30 m/s

40. An express train traveled at an average speed of 60 km/hr, stopping for 5 minutes after every 60 km. How long did it take to reach its destination 540 km from the starting point?
    (a) 9 hrs
    (b) 9 hrs 40 min
    (c) 9 hrs 45 min
    (d) 10 hrs

41. In covering a distance of 30 km, Binu takes 2 hours more than Rajan. If Binu doubles his speed, then he would take 1 hour less than Rajan. Find Binu's speed.
    (a) 5 km/hr
    (b) 5.5 km/hr
    (c) 6 km/hr
    (d) 6.5 km/hr

42. Sameer wants to reach the Railway station at 11:30 a.m. The station is 10 km away from his home. If Sameer walks at the speed of 4 km/hr at what time shall he start from his home?
    (a) 8:30 a.m.
    (b) 9:00 a.m.
    (c) 9:30 a.m.
    (d) 10:00 a.m.

43. Sita and Rita are 81 meters apart from the two ends A and B of a road. They start traveling towards each other at the same time. If Sita runs at double the speed of Rita, then how much distance Sita needs to run to meet Rita?
    (a) 27 m
    (b) 40.2 m
    (c) 54 m
    (d) 60 m

44. A overtakes B at 6 a.m. on the way when both are traveling towards a city. A reaches city at 9 a.m. and starts for return journey after one hour. On the way back he meets B at 11 a.m. At what time B reaches city?
   (a) 1:00 p.m.
   (b) 1:30 p.m.
   (c) 2:00 p.m.
   (d) 2:30 p.m.

45. A beats B by 125 m in a kilometer race. Find B's speed if A's speed is 16 m/s.
   (a) 21 m/s
   (b) 18 m/s
   (c) 14 m/s
   (d) 7 m/s

46. In a km race P beats Q by 100 m and R by 190 m. In a race of 500 m, by how many meters would Q beat R?
   (a) 90 m
   (b) 50 m
   (c) 45 m
   (d) 100 m

47. Rama is 4/3 times as fast as Parth. If Parth has a head start of 50 m, what should be the length of race track such that both of them reach the finishing point at same time?
   (a) 90 m
   (b) 200 m
   (c) 50 m
   (d) 150 m

48. L, M and N participate in a 100 m race. L beats M by 20 m and M beats N by 10 m. By how many meters dose L beats N?
   (a) 30 m
   (b) 28 m
   (c) 22 m
   (d) 25 m

49. In a race Sam gives Abhay a start of 350 m and still beats him by 50 m. If Sam's speed is 1.25 times Abhay's speed, how much is the length of race?
   (a) 1 km
   (b) 1.5 km
   (c) 2 km
   (d) 4 km

50. Bharat runs $1\frac{2}{3}$ times as fast as Chetan. In a race if Bharat beats Chetan by 40 meters, find the length of race.
   (a) 80 m
   (b) 90 m
   (c) 100 m
   (d) 120 m

KEYS

1. (b)	2. (b)	3. (a)	4. (c)	5. (d)	6. (a)	7. (d)	8. (c)
9. (d)	10. (b)	11. (a)	12. (d)	13. (c)	14. (d)	15. (b)	16. (b)
17. (b)	18. (a)	19. (d)	20. (a)	21. (c)	22. (c)	23. (b)	24. (c)
25. (c)	26. (a)	27. (a)	28. (b)	29. (a)	30. (a)	31. (d)	32. (b)
33. (c)	34. (d)	35. (b)	36. (c)	37. (a)	38. (c)	39. (d)	40. (b)
41. (a)	42. (b)	43. (c)	44. (b)	45. (c)	46. (b)	47. (b)	48. (b)
49. (c)	50. (c)						

SOLUTIONS

Solution 1

Speed of train:

$$S_t = \frac{550}{60} = \frac{55}{6} \text{ m/s} \times \frac{18}{5} = 33 \text{ km/hr}$$

Speed of bus:

$$S_b = \frac{33}{45/60} = \frac{33 \times 60}{45} = 44 \text{ km/hr}$$

$S_t : S_b = 3 : 4$.

Choice (b)

Solution 2

Distance covered by car:

$$D = S \times T = 45 \times \frac{40}{60} = 30 \text{ km}$$

Time required to cover this distance at the speed of 60 km/hr:

$$T = \frac{D}{S} = \frac{30}{60} = \frac{1}{2} \text{ hr or 30 min.}$$

Choice (b)

Solution 3

Distance covered by Airplane:

$$D = S \times T = 350 \times 6 = 2100 \text{ km}$$

Required speed to cover the distance in 4 hrs:

$$S = \frac{D}{T} = \frac{2100}{4} = 525 \text{ km/hr.}$$

Choice (a)

Solution 4

Speed of Raju:

$$S = \frac{D}{T} = \frac{12}{40/60}$$

$$= \frac{12 \times 60}{40} = 18 \text{ km/hr}$$

Distance covered by Raju in 1½ hrs:

$$D = S \times T = 18 \times 1½ = 18 \times \frac{3}{2} = 27 \text{ km.}$$

Choice (c)

Solution 5

Speed of 1st train:

$$S_1 = \frac{D}{T} = \frac{320}{4} = 80 \text{ km/hr}$$

As the speed ratio of two trains is 4 : 7

$$\frac{S_1}{S_2} = \frac{4}{7}$$

$$\frac{80}{S_2} = \frac{4}{7}$$

$$S_2 = \frac{80 \times 7}{4} = 140 \text{ km/hr.}$$

Choice (d)

Solution 6

If a person walks at 12 km/hr instead of 10 km/hr:

Extra distance covered by person in 1 hr = 2 km.
1 hr →   2 km extra
x hrs →   10 km extra

$$x = \frac{10 \times 1}{2} = 5 \text{ hrs}$$

So if he is walking at 10 km/hr, actual distance covered:

$$D = S \times T = 10 \times 5 = 50 \text{ km.}$$

Choice (a)

Solution 7

Let the distance be D km

Time required at the speed of 25 km/hr = $\frac{D}{25}$ hrs

Time required at the speed of 30 km/hr = $\frac{D}{30}$ hrs

As the time required is 180 min more with speed of 25 km/hr compared to 30 km/hr:

$$\frac{D}{25} - \frac{D}{30} = \frac{180}{60}$$

$$\frac{30D - 25D}{750} = 3$$

$$D = \frac{3 \times 750}{5} = 450 \text{ km.}$$

Choice (d)

Solution 8

Let the distance be D km

Time required by Rahul = $\frac{D}{12}$ hrs

Time required by Rajesh = $\frac{D}{15}$ hrs

As Rahul takes 40 min more than Rajesh:

$$\frac{D}{12} - \frac{D}{15} = \frac{40}{60}$$

$$\frac{5D - 4D}{60} = \frac{2}{3}$$

$$D = \frac{2}{3} \times 60$$

$$= 40 \text{ km.}$$

Choice (c)

Solution 9

There will be 30 spaces between 31 poles.

    1 space = 30 m.

Total distance between first and last pole = $30 \times 30 = 900$ m or 0.9 km

Speed of train:

$$S = \frac{D}{T}$$

$$= \frac{0.9}{1/60}$$

$$= 54 \text{ km/hr.}$$

Choice (d)

Solution 10

Let the distance between village and city be D km

Time to go = $\dfrac{D}{15}$ hrs

Time to return = $\dfrac{D}{10}$ hrs

$\dfrac{D}{15} + \dfrac{D}{10} = 5$ hrs

$\dfrac{2D + 3D}{30} = 5$

$D = \dfrac{5 \times 30}{5} = 30$ km.

Choice (b)

Solution 11

Let the distance traveled be $3D$ km.

He travels $2D$ km at the speed of 4 km/hr and D km at the speed of 3 km/hr.

$\dfrac{2D}{4} + \dfrac{D}{3} = \dfrac{50}{60}$

$\dfrac{6D + 4D}{12} = \dfrac{5}{6}$

$D = \dfrac{5}{6} \times \dfrac{12}{10} = 1$

Total distance traveled = $3D = 3$ km.

Choice (a)

Solution 12

Let the distance between city A and city B be $2D$ km.

Time required to travel first half = $\dfrac{D}{80}$ hrs

Time required to travel second half = $\dfrac{D}{120}$ hrs

$\dfrac{D}{80} + \dfrac{D}{120} = 10$ hrs

$\dfrac{3D + 2D}{240} = 10$

$D = \dfrac{10 \times 240}{5} = 480$ km

So, distance between city A and city $B = 2D = 960$ km.

Choice (d)

Solution 13

He covers half the journey *i.e.*, 3 km in two-third time *i.e.*, $(\frac{2}{3}\times 45)$ in 30 min. It means 15 min are left with him.

```
    3 km           3 km
●————————————+————————————●
    30 min          15 min
```

Required speed = $\dfrac{\text{Remaining Distance}}{\text{Remaining Time}} = \dfrac{3}{15/60} = 12$ km/hr.

Choice (c)

Solution 14

$S = \dfrac{D}{T} = 30$ km/hr

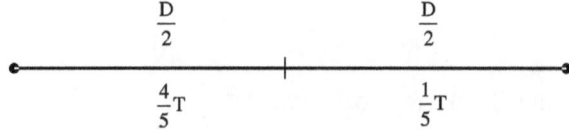

Required speed in remaining journey = $\dfrac{D/2}{T/5}$

$= \dfrac{D}{T} \times \dfrac{5}{2}$

$= 30 \times \dfrac{5}{2} = 75$ km/hr.

Choice (d)

Solution 15

Let the distance traveled on foot = x km.

Time required to travel by foot = $\dfrac{x}{4}$ hrs

Time required to travel by bicycle = $\dfrac{(50-x)}{8}$ hrs

$\dfrac{x}{4} + \dfrac{(50-x)}{8} = 10$ hrs

$\dfrac{2x + 50 - x}{8} = 10$

$x + 50 = 80$

So, $x = 30$ km.

Choice (b)

Solution 16

Let the distance traveled by bus at 70 km/hr = x km.
So, distance traveled by bus at 30 km/hr = $(160 - x)$ km.
Time required to travel at speed of 70 km/hr = $\frac{x}{70}$ hrs
Time required to travel at speed of 30 km/hr = $\frac{(160-x)}{30}$ hrs

$$\frac{x}{70} + \frac{(160-x)}{30} = 4 \text{ hrs}$$

Solving above equation, $x = 70$ km.

Time for which bus traveled at the speed of 70 km/hr:

$$T = \frac{D}{S} = \frac{70}{70} = 1 \text{ hr.}$$

Choice (b)

Solution 17

In traveling 12 km Karan will take rest for 3 times.
Time spent in taking rest = $3 \times 10 = 30$ min or ½ hr
Time spent in traveling = $\frac{12}{4} = 3$ hrs
Total time required = Travel time + Rest time = $3 + ½ = 3½$ hrs.

Choice (b)

Solution 18

Let the usual speed be S km/hr.

$$\frac{480}{S-8} - \frac{480}{S} = 2 \text{ hrs}$$

Going with options, S should be 48 km/hr.

Choice (a)

Solution 19

	S_{old}		S_{new}
Speed ratio	$6x$	:	$5x$
Time ratio	$5x$	:	$6x$	(∵ Speed & time are inversely proportional)

As new time taken is 20 min more than usual time taken, hence $6x - 5x = 20$ min, or $x = 20$ min.

Usual time taken = $5x = 5 \times 20 = 100$ min or $1⅔$ hr.

Choice (d)

Solution 20

	S_{old}		S_{new}
Speed ratio	$5x$	:	$4x$
Time ratio	$4x$	:	$5x$

($\because$ Speed & time are inversely proportional)

As new time taken is 15 min more than usual time taken, hence $5x - 4x = 15$ min, or $x = 15$ min.

Usual time taken $= 4x = 4 \times 15 = 60$ min or 1 hr.

Choice (a)

Solution 21

$$D = S \times T \qquad \text{... (1)}$$
$$D = (S+1) \times \frac{3}{4}T \qquad \text{... (2)}$$
$$D = (S-1) \times (T+2) \qquad \text{... (3)}$$

Equating the R.H.S. of (1) and (2):

$$S \times T = (S+1) \times \frac{3}{4}T$$
$$S = 3 \text{ km/hr}$$

Equating the R.H.S. of (1) and (3):

$$S \times T = (S-1) \times (T+2)$$
$$3 \times T = (3-1) \times (T+2)$$
$$T = 4 \text{ hrs}$$
$$D = S \times T = 3 \times 4 = 12 \text{ km.}$$

Choice (c)

Solution 22

If $S_1 = 50$ km/hr,

Time required i.e., $T_1 = T + 20$ min

If $S_2 = 75$ km/hr,

Time required i.e., $T_2 = T - 10$ min

So, difference of time $T_1 - T_2 = (T + 20) - (T - 10) = 30$ min

	S_1		S_2
Speed ratio	50	:	75
	2	:	3
	T_1		T_2
Time ratio	$3x$	:	$2x$

($\because$ Speed & time are inversely proportional)

As the difference between the timing is 30 min, hence $3x - 2x = 30$ min, or $x = 30$ min.

$$\begin{array}{ccc} & T_1 & T_2 \\ \text{Time ratio} & 3x & : \quad 2x \\ & \downarrow & \downarrow \\ & 90 \text{ min} & 60 \text{ min} \end{array}$$

$D = S \times T = 50 \times \dfrac{90}{60}$ or $75 \times \dfrac{60}{60} = 75$ km.

Choice (c)

Solution 23

If $S_1 = 4$ km/hr,

Time required *i.e.*, $T_1 = T - 10$ min

If $S_2 = 3$ km/hr,

Time required *i.e.*, $T_2 = T + 10$ min

So, difference of time $T_2 - T_1 = (T + 10) - (T - 10) = 20$ min

$$\begin{array}{ccc} & S_1 & S_2 \\ \text{Speed ratio} & 4 & : \quad 3 \\ & T_1 & T_2 \\ \text{Time ratio} & 3x & : \quad 4x \quad (\because \text{Speed \& time are inversely proportional}) \end{array}$$

As the difference between the timing is 20 min, hence $4x - 3x = 20$ min, or $x = 20$ min.

$$\begin{array}{ccc} & T_1 & T_2 \\ \text{Time ratio} & 3x & : \quad 4x \\ & \downarrow & \downarrow \\ & 60 \text{ min} & 80 \text{ min} \end{array}$$

$D = S \times T = 4 \times \dfrac{60}{60}$ or $3 \times \dfrac{80}{60} = 4$ km.

Choice (b)

Solution 24

If $S_1 = 50$ km/hr,

Time required *i.e.*, $T_1 = T + 20$ min

If $S_2 = 60$ km/hr,

Time required *i.e.*, $T_2 = T - 10$ min

So, difference of time $T_1 - T_2 = (T + 20) - (T - 10) = 30$ min

$$\begin{array}{ccc} & S_1 & S_2 \\ \text{Speed ratio} & 5 & : & 6 \\ & T_1 & T_2 \\ \text{Time ratio} & 6x & : & 5x \end{array}$$ (∵ Speed & time are inversely proportional)

As the difference between the timing is 30 min, hence $6x - 5x = 30$ min, or $x = 30$ min.

$$\begin{array}{ccc} & T_1 & T_2 \\ \text{Time ratio} & 6x & : & 5x \\ & \downarrow & & \downarrow \\ & 180 \text{ min} & & 150 \text{ min} \end{array}$$

$D = S \times T = 50 \times \dfrac{180}{60}$ or $60 \times \dfrac{150}{60} = 150$ km.

Choice (c)

Solution 25

$D = S \times T$

$D = 10 \times (T + 15 \text{ min})$ ... (1)

$D = 15 \times (T + 5 \text{ min})$ ... (2)

Equating the R.H.S. of (1) and (2):

$10 \times (T + 15 \text{ min}) = 15 \times (T + 5 \text{ min})$

$10T + 150 \text{ min} = 15T + 75 \text{ min}$

$5T = 75 \text{ min}$

$T = 15$ min (This is the correct time required)

Substituting value of T in equation (1):

$D = 10 \times \dfrac{(15+15) \text{ min}}{60} = 5$ km.

Required speed to reach on time = $\dfrac{5 \text{ km}}{15 \text{ min}/60} = 20$ km/hr.

Choice (c)

Solution 26

$D = S \times T$

Assuming that Krishna spends x hrs while going away from city.

$D = 60 \times x$ ... (1)

$D = 40 \times (8 - x)$ ... (2)

Equating the R.H.S. of (1) and (2):

$60 \times x = 40 \times (8 - x)$

$x = \dfrac{16}{5}$ hrs

Substituting value of x in equation (1):

$D = 60 \times \dfrac{16}{5} = 192$ km.

Choice (a)

Solution 27

Let us assume that the train is traveling a distance of 75 km.

75 km

Time required to travel with stoppages = $\dfrac{\text{Distance}}{75} = \dfrac{75}{75} = 1$ hr or 60 min.

Time required to travel without stoppages = $\dfrac{\text{Distance}}{90} = \dfrac{75}{90} = \dfrac{5}{6}$ hr or 50 min

So, the stoppage time is 10 min every hour.

Choice (a)

Solution 28

Let us assume that the train is traveling a distance of 48 km.

48 km

Time required to travel with stoppages = $\dfrac{\text{Distance}}{48} = \dfrac{48}{48} = 1$ hr or 60 min.

Time required to travel without stoppages = $\dfrac{\text{Distance}}{60} = \dfrac{48}{60} = \dfrac{4}{5}$ hr or 48 min

So, the stoppage time is 12 min every hour.

Choice (b)

Solution 29

Average speed = $\dfrac{2mn}{m+n} = \dfrac{2 \times 30 \times 60}{30+60} = 40$ km/hr.

Choice (a)

Solution 30

Average speed = $\dfrac{\text{Total distance covered}}{\text{Total time taken}}$

$= \dfrac{x+2x}{\dfrac{x}{60}+\dfrac{2x}{40}}$

$= \dfrac{3x}{\dfrac{2x+6x}{120}}$

$= \dfrac{3}{8} \times 120 = 45$ km/hr.

Choice (a)

Solution 31

Speed while going = 40 km/hr

Speed while returning = $1.5 \times 40 = 60$ km/hr

Average speed $= \dfrac{2mn}{m+n}$

$= \dfrac{2 \times 40 \times 60}{40+60} = 48$ km/hr.

Choice (d)

Solution 32

Average speed = $\dfrac{\text{Total distance covered}}{\text{Total time taken}}$

$= \dfrac{200+50+60+70+80+90}{5+1+1+1+1+1}$

$= \dfrac{550}{10} = 55$ km/hr.

Choice (b)

Solution 33

	P	Q	R
Speed ratio	6	3	1
		↓	↓
		40 min	120 min

If speed of Q is thrice the speed of R, the Q can cover the journey in one-third the time in which R can cover.

Choice (c)

Solution 34

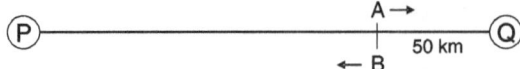

Ratio of distance covered by A and B will be same as the ratio of their speeds i.e., 4 : 1. If B covers 50 km prom point Q, so A will cover 200 km from point P. Hence distance between P and Q will be 250 km.

Choice (d)

Solution 35

The two trains meet x hrs after 10 a.m.

Distance covered by T1 in x hrs + Distance covered by T2 in $(x - 1)$ hrs = 160 km

$$10x + 15(x - 1) = 160$$
$$10x + 15x - 15 = 160$$
$$x = \frac{175}{25} = 7$$

So, they will meet 7 hrs past 10 a.m. *i.e.,* 5 p.m.

Choice (b)

Solution 36

The two trains meet x hrs after 8 a.m.

Distance covered by 1st train in x hrs + Distance covered by 2nd train in $(x - 1)$ hrs = 330 km

$$60x + 75(x - 1) = 330$$
$$60x + 75x - 75 = 330$$
$$x = \frac{405}{135} = 3$$

So, they will meet 3 hrs past 8 a.m. *i.e.,* 11 a.m.

Choice (c)

Solution 37

Speed of Bus = 3 m/s

Speed of Man = 36 km/hr × $\frac{5}{18}$ = 10 m/s

$$\text{Time} = \frac{\text{Distance}}{\text{Relative speed}}$$

$$= \frac{210}{10-3} = 30 \text{ sec.}$$

Choice (a)

Solution 38

The express train is able to overtake passenger train x hrs after 6 a.m.

Distance covered by Express train in $(x-4)$ hrs = Distance covered by Passenger train in x hrs

$$80 \times (x-4) = 60 \times x$$
$$80x - 320 = 60x$$
$$20x = 320$$
$$x = 16$$

So, the express train will overtake the passenger train 16 hrs past 6 a.m. *i.e.*, 10 p.m.

Choice (c)

Solution 39

Distance traveled by jeep in 22 sec = Distance that sound can travel in 2 sec.
$$x \times 22 = 330 \times 2$$
$$x = 30 \text{ m/s.}$$

Choice (d)

Solution 40

In traveling 540 km the train will halt for a total of $\frac{540}{60} - 1 = 8$ times.

Time spent in stoppage = $5 \times 8 = 40$ min

Time spent in traveling = $\frac{540}{60} = 9$ hrs

Total time required = Travel time + stoppage time = 9 hrs 40 min.

Choice (b)

Solution 41

Speed of Binu = b km/hr
Speed of Rajan = r km/hr

$$\frac{30}{b} - \frac{30}{r} = 2 \text{ hrs} \qquad \qquad \ldots (1)$$

$$\frac{30}{r} - \frac{30}{2b} = 1 \text{ hrs} \qquad \qquad \ldots (2)$$

388 Quantitative Aptitude

Adding equation (1) and (2)

$$\frac{30}{b} - \frac{30}{2b} = 3 \text{ hrs}$$

$$\frac{60 - 30}{2b} = 3$$

$$b = 5 \text{ km/hr.}$$

Choice (a)

Solution 42

Time required in reaching the station:

$$T = \frac{D}{S} = \frac{10}{4} = 2½ \text{ hrs}$$

So, he needs to leave 2½ hrs prior to 11:30 a.m. *i.e.*, at 9:00 a.m.

Choice (b)

Solution 43

The ratio of distance covered by Sita and Rita will be same as the ratio of their speeds. If speed of Sita is double the speed of Rita, so she will cover double the distance as compared to Rita.

Distance covered by Sita + Distance covered by Rita = 81 m
2 × (Distance covered by Rita) + Distance covered by Rita = 81 m
3 × (Distance covered by Rita) = 81 m
Distance covered by Rita = 27 m
So, Distance covered by Sita = 54 m.

Choice (c)

Solution 44

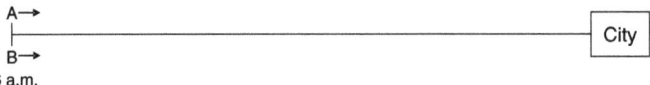

On the return journey A meets B at 11 a.m. So the distance that A can cover in further 2 hrs, B has covered it in 5 hrs, or distance which A can cover in 1 hr, B can cover in 2½ hrs.

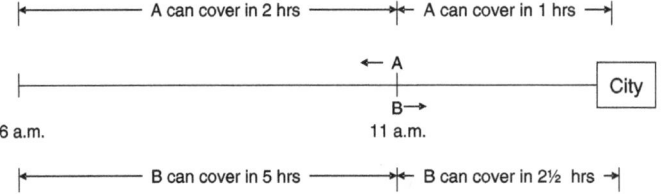

So, B will reach city 2½ hrs past 11 a.m. *i.e.*, at 1:30 p.m.

Choice (b)

Solution 45

The time in which A runs 1000 m is same as time in which B runs 875 m.

$$T_A = T_B$$
$$\frac{1000}{16} = \frac{875}{S_B}$$
$$S_B = \frac{875 \times 16}{1000} = 14 \text{ m/s.}$$

Choice (c)

Solution 46

When P covers 1000 m, at that time Q covers 900 m and R covers 810 m.

$P : Q : R = 1000 : 900 : 810$

When Q runs 900 m → R runs 810 m
When Q runs 500 m → R runs x m

$$x = \frac{810 \times 500}{900} = 450 \text{ m}$$

So Q beats R by 50 m.

Choice (b)

Solution 47

Let the length of race track be L meters.

$$S_R = \frac{4}{3} S_P$$
$$\frac{S_R}{S_P} = \frac{4}{3}$$

Time in which Rama runs L meters = Time in which Parth runs $(L - 50)$ meters

$$T_R = T_P$$
$$\frac{L}{4} = \frac{L-50}{3}$$
$$3L = 4(L - 50)$$
$$L = 200 \text{ m.}$$

Choice (b)

Solution 48

When L runs 100 m, at that time M runs 80 m.

$L : M = 10 : 8$

When M runs 100 m, at that time N runs 90 m.

$M : N = 10 : 9$

Finding the common ratio:

L	:	M	:	N
10	:	8		
		10	:	9
100	:	80	:	72

So, L beats N by 28 m.

Choice (b)

Solution 49

Let the length of race be L meters.

$S_S = 1.25 \times S_A$

$S_S = \frac{5}{4} \times S_A$

$\frac{S_S}{S_A} = \frac{5}{4}$

As Abhay has a start of 350 m, and also he lost the race by 50 meters, hence he runs 400 m less than Sam.

Time in which Sam runs L meters = Time in which Abhay runs (L – 400) meters.

$\frac{L}{5} = \frac{L - 400}{4}$

$4L = 5L - 2000$

$L = 2000$ m or 2 km.

Choice (c)

Solution 50

Let the length of race be L meters.

$S_B = 1\frac{2}{3} \times S_C$

$S_B = \frac{5}{3} \times S_C$

$\frac{S_B}{S_C} = \frac{5}{3}$

Time in which Bharat runs L meters = Time in which Chetan runs $(L - 40)$ meters.

$$\frac{L}{5} = \frac{L-40}{3}$$

$3L = 5(L - 40)$

$L = 100$ m.

Choice (c)

16

Problem on Trains

SPEED CONVERSIONS

To convert the speed from km/hr to m/s following relation is to be used:

$$\text{Km/hr} \times \frac{5}{18} = \text{m/s}$$

To convert the speed from m/s to km/hr following relation is to be used:

$$\text{m/s} \times \frac{18}{5} = \text{Km/hr.}$$

RELATIVE SPEED

The speed of one train in relation to another train is called the relative speed of these two trains, *i.e.,* it is the speed of one moving train as observed from the second moving train. If two trains are moving in same direction, the relative speed is equal to the difference between the speeds of two trains. If two trains are moving in opposite direction, the relative speed is equal to the sum of the speeds of two trains.

Going in same direction $\Rightarrow$ Difference between the speeds of two trains
Going in opposite direction $\Rightarrow$ Sum of the speeds of two trains

Time Taken to Cross Pole or Standing Man

Time taken by a train of length L meters to pass a pole or standing man or a signal post is equal to the time taken by the train to cover L meters.

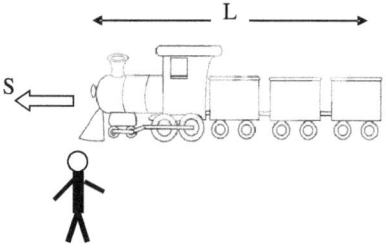

Train crossing a man

$$\text{Time taken} = \frac{\text{Length of Train}}{\text{Speed of Train}} = \frac{L}{S}$$

Time Taken to Cross Platform or Bridge

Time taken by a train of length L meters to pass a platform or bridge or tunnel P meters is equal to the time taken by the train to cover $(L + P)$ meters. In this case length of platform or bridge or tunnel is taken into consideration.

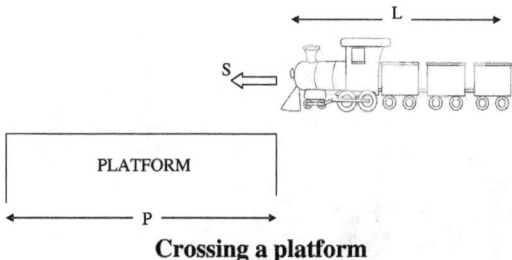

Crossing a platform

Time taken = $\dfrac{\text{Length of Train} + \text{Length of Platform}}{\text{Speed of Train}} = \dfrac{L+P}{S}$

Time Taken to Overtake or Cross a Running Man

Time taken by a train of length L meters to overtake or cross a running man or cyclist is equal to the length of train by relative speed.

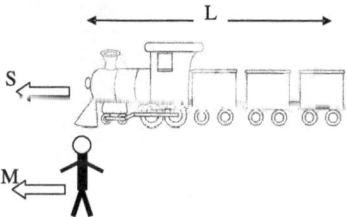

Overtaking the running man

Time to overtake = $\dfrac{\text{Length of Train}}{\text{Relative Speed}} = \dfrac{L}{S-M}$

Crossing the man running in opposite direction

Time to cross = $\dfrac{\text{Length of Train}}{\text{Relative Speed}} = \dfrac{L}{S+M}$

Time Taken a Train to Overtake or Cross another Train

Time taken by a train of length L_1 meters long to overtake or cross another train L_2 meters long is equal to sum of the lengths of train by their relative speed.

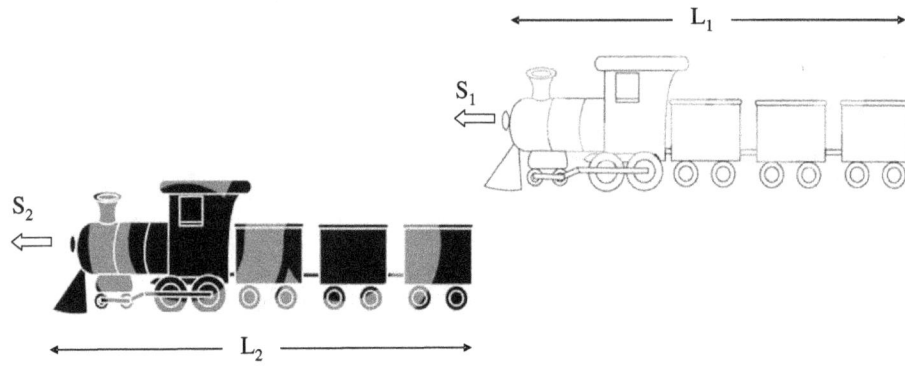

Overtaking another train

Time to overtake = $\dfrac{\text{Length of Train 1 + Length of Train 2}}{\text{Relative Speed}} = \dfrac{L_1 + L_2}{S_1 - S_2}$

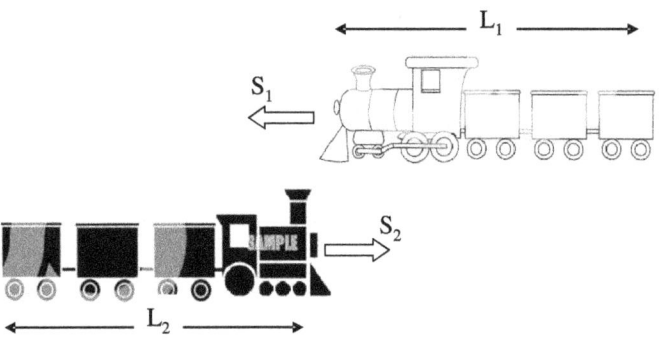

Crossing another train in opposite direction

Time to cross = $\dfrac{\text{Length of Train 1 + Length of Train 2}}{\text{Relative Speed}} = \dfrac{L_1 + L_2}{S_1 + S_2}$.

FINDING SPEED RATIO

If two trains $T1$ and $T2$ start at the same time from two points P and Q towards each other and after crossing they take x and y hours in reaching Q and P respectively, then:

$$\dfrac{\text{Speed of } T1}{\text{Speed of } T2} = \dfrac{\sqrt{y}}{\sqrt{x}}.$$

SOLVED EXAMPLES

Example 1
Find the time taken by a train 200 m long, running at the speed of 90 km/hr to cross a signal pole.

Solution

Speed of train = $90 \times \frac{5}{18} = 25$ m/s

Distance moved in passing a signal pole = 200 m

Time to cross signal pole = $\frac{D}{S} = \frac{200}{25} = 8$ sec.

Example 2
Find the time taken by a train 200 m long, running at the speed of 60 km/hr to pass through a 350 m long tunnel.

Solution

Speed of train = $60 \times \frac{5}{18} = \frac{50}{3}$ m/s

Total distance covered in passing the tunnel = 200 + 350 = 550 m

Time to pass through tunnel = $\frac{D}{S} = \frac{200+350}{50/3} = 33$ sec.

Example 3
A passenger train running with a uniform speed crosses a bridge 140 m long in 30 sec, and a tunnel 180 m long in 34 sec. Find the speed and length of train.

Solution

If 140 m is crossed in 30 sec and 180 m in 34 sec, it means to cross the extra length of 40 m (*i.e.*, 180 m – 140 m) 4 more seconds are required.

Speed of train = $\frac{40}{4} = 10$ m/s

∴ Speed of train in km/hr = $10 \times \frac{18}{5} = 36$ km/hr

If time taken to cross bridge 140 m long is 30 sec, then:

$$\frac{\text{Length of Train} + \text{Length of Bridge}}{\text{Speed of Train}} = 30 \text{ sec.}$$

$$\frac{\text{Length of Train} + 140}{10} = 30 \text{ sec.}$$

∴ Length of train = $(30 \times 10) - 140 = 160$ m.

Example 4

A man is standing on a railway bridge which is 240 m long. He finds that a train crosses the bridge in 25 seconds but himself in 10 seconds. Find the length of the train and its speed.

Solution

Let the length of train be L meters, and the speed be S m/s.

As the train crosses a man in 10 sec:

$$10 \text{ sec} = \frac{L}{S}$$

$\therefore L = 10S$

As the train crosses the bridge in 25 sec:

$$25 \text{ sec} = \frac{L+240}{S}$$

$25S = L + 240$
$25S = 10S + 240$
$15S = 240$

$\therefore$ Speed = 16 m/s

and Length = $10 \times 16 = 160$ m.

Example 5

A man sitting in a passenger train which is traveling at 54 km/hr observes that a goods train, traveling in opposite direction, takes 15 seconds to pass him. If the goods train is 300 m long, find its speed.

Solution

Speed of passenger train = $54 \times \frac{5}{18} = 15$ m/s

As the passenger train is running at the speed of 15 m/s means the man is also traveling at the same speed. If goods train crosses the man sitting in passenger train in 15 sec, then:

$$15 \text{ sec} = \frac{\text{Length of goods train}}{\text{Relative speed}}$$

$$15 \text{ sec} = \frac{300}{15 + S_G}$$

$225 + 15S_G = 300$
$15S_G = 75$

$\therefore \quad S_G = 5$ m/s

Speed of goods train = $5 \times \frac{18}{5} = 18$ km/hr.

Example 6

Two trains 120 meters and 180 meters long are running in the same direction on parallel tracks with speeds of 36 km/hr and 54 km/hr. In how much time will the faster train overtakes the slower train?

Solution

Speed of slower train = $36 \times \frac{5}{18} = 10$ m/s

Speed of faster train = $54 \times \frac{5}{18} = 15$ m/s

Time to overtake = $\frac{\text{Sum of Lengths}}{\text{Relative speed}}$

$= \frac{120 + 180}{15 - 10}$

$= 60$ sec.

Example 7

A train running at 72 km/hr completely crosses another train having half its length and running in opposite direction at 90 km/hr, in 10 seconds. If the faster train passes a tunnel in 30 sec., then find the length of the tunnel.

Solution

Let the length of faster train = L

$\therefore$ Length of slower train = $2L$

Speed of slower train = $72 \times \frac{5}{18} = 20$ m/s

Speed of faster train = $90 \times \frac{5}{18} = 25$ m/s

Time to cross = $\frac{\text{Sum of Lengths}}{\text{Relative speed}}$

10 sec = $\frac{2L + L}{20 + 25}$

10 sec = $\frac{3L}{45}$

$\therefore L = 150$ m

If the time taken by this faster train to pass the tunnel is 30 sec, then:

30 sec = $\frac{150 + \text{Length of tunnel}}{25}$

Length of tunnel = 600 m.

Example 8

Two trains running in opposite directions cross a man standing on the platform in 30 seconds and 22 seconds respectively and they cross each other in 25 seconds. Find the ratio of their speeds.

Solution

Let the length and speed of first train be L_1 and S_1 respectively.

Let the length and speed of second train be L_2 and S_2 respectively.

First train crosses the man in 30 sec:

$$\frac{L_1}{S_1} = 30 \text{ sec}$$

∴ $L_1 = 30 S_1$

Second train crosses the man in 22 sec:

$$\frac{L_2}{S_2} = 22 \text{ sec}$$

∴ $L_2 = 22 S_2$

As the two trains cross each other in 25 sec.

$$\frac{L_1 + L_2}{S_1 + S_2} = 25 \text{ sec}$$

$30S_1 + 22S_2 = 25S_1 + 25S_2$

$5S_1 = 3S_2$

$$\frac{S_1}{S_2} = \frac{3}{5}$$

∴ The speeds of two trains are in the ratio of 3 : 5.

EXERCISE

1. A train 150 m long is running at the speed of 54 km/hr. Find the time taken by it to pass an electric pole.
   (a) 5 sec (b) 10 sec
   (c) 15 sec (d) 20 sec

2. In how much time a train 280 m long, running with a speed of 63 km/hr will pass a tree?
   (a) 10 sec (b) 12 sec
   (c) 14 sec (d) 16 sec

3. A train running at the speed of 90 km/hr crosses a tree in 8 seconds. Find the length of the train.
   (a) 120 m
   (b) 150 m
   (c) 180 m
   (d) 200 m

4. A train running at the speed of 45 km/hr crosses a standing man in 20 sec. Find the length of train.
   (a) 150 m
   (b) 180 m
   (c) 250 m
   (d) 300 m

5. A farmer standing near the railway track observes that a goods train of 25 wagons crosses him in 30 seconds. Find the speed of goods train if length of each wagon is 8 m.
   (a) 24 km/hr
   (b) 36 km/hr
   (c) 40 km/hr
   (d) 45 km/hr

6. How long does a train 112 m long running at the speed of 72 km/hr take to cross a bridge 128 m in length?
   (a) 8 sec
   (b) 10 sec
   (c) 12 sec
   (d) 14 sec

7. A train 160 m long passes a pole in 8 seconds. How long will it take to pass a tunnel 120 m long?
   (a) 10 sec
   (b) 12 sec
   (c) 14 sec
   (d) 15 sec

8. A train 220 m long is running at 54 km/hr. If it crosses a tunnel in 1 minute, find the length of the tunnel.
   (a) 540 m
   (b) 580 m
   (c) 620 m
   (d) 680 m

9. Find the length of a bridge which a train 170 m long running at 45 km/hr crosses in half a minute.
   (a) 205 m
   (b) 195 m
   (c) 175 m
   (d) 145 m

10. A person standing on a platform observes that a train crosses him in 16 sec and the platform in 30 sec. If the length of platform is 350 m, then what is the speed of the train?
    (a) 45 km/hr
    (b) 60 km/hr
    (c) 70 km/hr
    (d) 90 km/hr

11. A passenger train running with a uniform speed crosses a tunnel 110 m long in 15 sec, and the other tunnel 160 m long in 20 sec. Find the speed of train.
    (a) 18 km/hr
    (b) 36 km/hr
    (c) 40 km/hr
    (d) 50 km/hr

12. A train 150 m long is running with a speed of 60 km/hr. In what time will it overtake a cyclist who is traveling at 6 km/hr in the same direction as that of the train?
    (a) 10 sec
    (b) 12 sec
    (c) 14 sec
    (d) 15 sec

13. A train 110 m long is running with a speed of 27 km/hr. In what time will it pass a dog running at 9 km/hr in the direction opposite to that in which the train is going?
    (a) 10 sec (b) 11 sec
    (c) 11.5 sec (d) 13 sec

14. A 200 m long train crosses a platform in 45 seconds while it crosses a signal pole in 18 seconds. What is the length of the platform?
    (a) 250 m (b) 300 m
    (c) 360 m (d) 450 m

15. A super fast train of 100 m covers a distance of 120 km in 1½ hour. In what will it cross a bridge which is double the length of train?
    (a) 10 sec (b) 11.5 sec
    (c) 13.5 sec (d) 15 sec

16. Two trains travel in opposite directions at 36 km/hr and 45 km/hr. A man sitting in slower train observes that the faster train crosses him in 8 seconds. Find the length of the faster train.
    (a) 200 m (b) 180 m
    (c) 160 m (d) 150 m

17. A man sitting near the window of a passenger train observes that a goods train running in the same direction on a parallel track passes him in a minute. If the speeds of passenger train and goods train are 60 km/hr and 90 km/hr respectively, then what is the length of goods train?
    (a) 300 m (b) 400 m
    (c) 450 m (d) 500 m

18. Two trains A and B of length 100 m and 150 m respectively enter a tunnel 200 m long simultaneously from the opposite ends. If the speeds of train A and train B are 54 km/hr and 90 km/hr respectively, then which train will come out of the tunnel at first?
    (a) Train A (b) Train B
    (c) Both together (d) Cannot be determined

19. Two trains of length 200 m and 250 m respectively running in same direction enter a tunnel 300 m long. If the speeds of shorter and longer trains are 72 km/hr and 90 km/hr respectively, then the difference in the timing between them to exit the tunnel is:
    (a) 2 sec (b) 3 sec
    (c) 4 sec (d) 5 sec

20. Two trains have length of 150 m and 200 m. They are running on parallel tracks towards each other. Find the total distance traveled by the trains from the time they start to cross each other to the time they completely cross each other.
    (a) 150 m (b) 200 m
    (c) 350 m (d) 700 m

21. Two trains are running in opposite directions with the same speed. If the length of each train is 140 m and they cross each other in 10 seconds, then the speed of each train (in km/hr) is:
    (a) 45.8 (b) 48.6
    (c) 50.4 (d) 52.5

22. Two goods train each 150 m long, are running in opposite directions on parallel tracks. Their speeds are 45 km/hr and 27 km/hr respectively. Find the time taken by the slower train to pass the engine driver of the faster one.
    (a) 30 sec
    (b) 15 sec
    (c) 10 sec
    (d) 7.5 sec

23. A train 120 m long moving at a speed of 54 km/hr crosses a train 130 m long coming from opposite direction in 10 seconds. Find the speed of the second train.
    (a) 30 km/hr
    (b) 36 km/hr
    (c) 45 km/hr
    (d) 50 km/hr

24. Two trains 150 meters and 170 meters long are running in the same direction on parallel tracks with speeds of 45 km/hr and 63 km/hr. In how much time will the faster train overtakes the slower train?
    (a) 7.3 sec
    (b) 24 sec
    (c) 36 sec
    (d) 64 sec

25. A train running at 48 km/hr completely crosses another train having half its length and running in opposite direction at 42 km/hr, in 15 seconds. If the faster train passes a tunnel in a minute, then find the length of the tunnel.
    (a) 400 m
    (b) 500 m
    (c) 550 m
    (d) 600 m

26. A train running at a uniform speed takes 18 seconds to cross a bridge 162 m long and 15 seconds to completely pass through a tunnel 120 m long. The length of the train is:
    (a) 90 m
    (b) 110 m
    (c) 120 m
    (d) 210 m

27. A man is standing on a railway bridge which is 180 m long. He finds that a train crosses the bridge in 20 seconds but himself in 8 seconds. Find the length of the train and its speed.
    (a) 120 m, 15 m/s
    (b) 150 m, 12 m/s
    (c) 180 m, 10 m/s
    (d) Cannot be determined

28. A man sitting in a passenger train which is traveling at 60 km/hr observes that a goods train, traveling in opposite direction, takes 9 seconds to pass him. If the goods train is 240 m long, find its speed.
    (a) 24 km/hr
    (b) 36 km/hr
    (c) 42 km/hr
    (d) 45 km/hr

29. Two trains of equal length are running on parallel tracks in the same direction at 48 km/hr and 60 km/hr. The faster train overtakes the slower train in 45 seconds. The length of each train is:
    (a) 75 m
    (b) 80 m
    (c) 90 m
    (d) 150 m

30. Two trains running in opposite directions cross a man standing on the platform in 40 seconds and 30 seconds respectively and they cross each other in 34 seconds. The ratio of their speeds is:

(a) 2 : 3 (b) 2 : 5
(c) 3 : 5 (d) 4 : 7

31. A train overtakes two persons who are running at the speed of 1 m/s and 2 m/s in the same direction in 12 and 15 seconds respectively. Find the length of train.
    (a) 60 m (b) 75 m
    (c) 90 m (d) 100 m

32. A train 180 m long passes a signal pole in 18 seconds and another train of the same length traveling in opposite direction in 8 seconds. The speed of the second train is:
    (a) 90 km/hr (b) 108 km/hr
    (c) 198 km/hr (d) 126 km/hr

33. A train takes 2 min to overtake a cyclist traveling at 18 km/hr and 1½ min to overtake another cyclist traveling at 9 km/hr. Find the speed of the train.
    (a) 25/2 m/s (b) 25/3 m/s
    (c) 15/2 m/s (d) 20/3 m/s

34. Train A crosses a pole in 20 sec and also another train B of length 180 m in 20 sec. Find the speed of train B.
    (a) 8 m/s (b) 9 m/s
    (c) 10 m/s (d) 12 m/s

35. A train 200 m long crosses a pole in 10 sec. Another train of same length crosses a bridge of same length in 25 sec. What is the difference in distance covered by the two trains in 2 hours?
    (a) 14.4 km (b) 18.5 km
    (c) 28.8 km (d) 30.4 km

36. Two trains of same length cross each other in 20 sec if run in same direction, and in 8 sec if run in opposite direction. Find the ratio of their speeds.
    (a) 5 : 4 (b) 5 : 3
    (c) 7 : 3 (d) 7 : 5

37. Two, trains, one from Mumbai to Nagpur and the other from Nagpur to Mumbai, start simultaneously. After they meet, the trains reach their destinations after 5 hr 20 min and 12 hrs respectively. The ratio of their speeds is:
    (a) 3 : 2 (b) 3 : 5
    (c) 1 : 2 (d) 1 : 3

38. A train running at certain speed crosses a pole in 10 sec. To find the speed of train, how much data in the following two statements is sufficient?
    I. Length of train is 150 m
    II. It overtakes a cyclist running in 12 sec.
    (a) Only I (b) Only II
    (c) Both I and II needed (d) Both I and II are not sufficient

39. Two train T1 and T2 of length in the ratio of 8 : 5 are running in opposite direction. To find out the speed of train T2, how much data in the following two statements is sufficient?
   I. Speed of train T1 is 90 km/hr
   II. They took 30 sec to cross each other
   (a) Only I
   (b) Only II
   (c) Both I and II needed
   (d) Both I and II are not sufficient

40. A train of length 200 m crosses a platform in 30 sec. To find the speed of train, how much data in the following two statements is sufficient?
   I. Length of platform is twice the length of train
   II. If the platform had been 100 m more, then train would have taken 5 more seconds to cross the platform.
   (a) Only I
   (b) Only II
   (c) Both I and II needed
   (d) Either of the statements is individually sufficient

KEYS

1. (b)	2. (d)	3. (d)	4. (c)	5. (a)	6. (c)	7. (c)	8. (d)
9. (a)	10. (d)	11. (b)	12. (a)	13. (b)	14. (b)	15. (c)	16. (b)
17. (d)	18. (b)	19. (b)	20. (c)	21. (c)	22. (d)	23. (b)	24. (d)
25. (c)	26. (a)	27. (a)	28. (b)	29. (a)	30. (a)	31. (a)	32. (d)
33.(a)	34. (b)	35. (c)	36. (c)	37. (a)	38. (a)	39. (d)	40. (d)

SOLUTIONS

Solution 1

Speed of train = $54 \times \frac{5}{18} = 15$ m/s

Time to cross pole = $\frac{D}{S} = \frac{150}{15} = 10$ sec.

Choice (b)

Solution 2

Speed of train = $63 \times \frac{5}{18} = \frac{35}{2}$ m/s

Time to cross tree = $\frac{D}{S} = \frac{280}{35/2} = \frac{280 \times 2}{35} = 16$ sec.

Choice (d)

Solution 3

Speed of train = $90 \times \dfrac{5}{18}$ = 25 m/s

Length of train = $S \times T$
$= 25 \times 8 = 200$ m.

Choice (d)

Solution 4

Speed of train = $45 \times \dfrac{5}{18} = \dfrac{25}{2}$ m/s

Length of train = $S \times T$
$= \dfrac{25}{2} \times 20 = 250$ m.

Choice (c)

Solution 5

Length of train = Number of wagons × Length of each wagon = $25 \times 8 = 200$ m

Speed of train $= \dfrac{D}{T} = \dfrac{200}{30} = \dfrac{20}{3}$ m/s

Speed in km/hr = $\dfrac{20}{3} \times \dfrac{18}{5} = 24$ km/hr.

Choice (a)

Solution 6

Speed of train = $72 \times \dfrac{5}{18} = 20$ m/s

Time required to cross the bridge = $\dfrac{112 + 128}{20}$

$= \dfrac{240}{20} = 12$ sec.

Choice (c)

Solution 7

Speed of train $= \dfrac{D}{T} = \dfrac{160}{8} = 20$ m/s

Time required to cross tunnel = $\dfrac{160 + 120}{20}$

$= 14$ sec.

Choice (c)

Solution 8

Speed of train = $54 \times \frac{5}{18}$ = 15 m/s

Time required to cross tunnel = $\frac{220 + \text{Length of Tunnel}}{15 \text{ m/s}}$

60 sec. = $\frac{220 + \text{Length of Tunnel}}{15 \text{ m/s}}$

∴ Length of tunnel = $(60 \times 15) - 220 = 680$ m.

Choice (d)

Solution 9

Speed of train = $45 \times \frac{5}{18} = \frac{25}{2}$ m/s

Time required to cross bridge = $\frac{170 + \text{Length of Bridge}}{25/2}$

30 sec = $\frac{170 + \text{Length of Bridge}}{25/2}$

∴ Length of bridge = $\left(30 \times \frac{25}{2}\right) - 170$

   = 375 − 170 = 205 m.

Choice (a)

Solution 10

A person is crossed in 16 sec, and a platform (of length 350 m) in 30 sec.

Hence to cover 350 m, the train requires 14 sec (*i.e.*, 30 sec − 16 sec)

Speed of train = $\frac{350}{14}$ = 25 m/s

Speed of train in km/hr = $25 \times \frac{18}{5}$ = 90 km/hr.

Choice (d)

Solution 11

If 110 m is crossed in 15 sec and 160 m in 20 sec, it means to cross the extra length of 50 m (*i.e.*, 160 m − 110 m) 5 more seconds are required.

Speed of train = $\frac{50}{5}$ = 10 m/s

Speed of train in km/hr = $10 \times \frac{18}{5}$ = 36 km/hr.

Choice (b)

Solution 12

Speed of train = $60 \times \frac{5}{18} = \frac{50}{3}$ m/s

Speed of cyclist = $6 \times \frac{5}{18} = \frac{5}{3}$ m/s

Time to overtake the cyclist = $\frac{\text{Length of Train}}{\text{Relative Speed}}$

$= \frac{150}{\frac{50}{3} - \frac{5}{3}}$

$= \frac{150 \times 3}{45}$

$= 10$ sec.

Choice (a)

Solution 13

Speed of train = $27 \times \frac{5}{18} = \frac{15}{2}$ m/s

Speed of dog = $9 \times \frac{5}{18} = \frac{5}{2}$ m/s

Time = $\frac{\text{Length of Train}}{\text{Relative Speed}}$

$= \frac{110}{\frac{15}{2} + \frac{5}{2}}$

$= \frac{110}{20/2}$

$= 11$ sec.

Choice (b)

Solution 14

Speed of train = $\frac{200}{18} = \frac{100}{9}$ m/s

Time required to cross platform = $\frac{200 + \text{Length of Platform}}{100/9}$

45 sec = $\frac{200 + \text{Length of Platform}}{100/9}$

∴ Length of Platform = $\left(45 \times \frac{100}{9}\right) - 200 = 300$ m.

Choice (b)

Solution 15

Speed of train = $\dfrac{120 \text{ km}}{1\frac{1}{2} \text{ hr}}$ = 80 km/hr

Speed of train in m/s = $80 \times \dfrac{5}{18} = \dfrac{200}{9}$ m/s

Length of bridge = $2 \times 100 = 200$ m

Time required to cross a bridge = $\dfrac{100 + 200}{200/9}$

$= \dfrac{300 \times 9}{200}$

$= 13.5$ sec.

Choice (c)

Solution 16

Speed of slower train = $36 \times \dfrac{5}{18} = 10$ m/s

Speed of faster train = $45 \times \dfrac{5}{18}$

$= \dfrac{25}{2}$ m/s

As the faster train crosses the person in 8 sec, so the equation will be:

Time to cross = $\dfrac{\text{Length of Faster train}}{\text{Relative speed}}$

8 sec = $\dfrac{\text{Length of Faster train}}{10 + \dfrac{25}{2}}$

$\therefore$ Length of faster train = $8 \times \dfrac{45}{2}$

$= 180$ m.

Choice (b)

Solution 17

Speed of passenger train = $60 \times \dfrac{5}{18} = \dfrac{50}{3}$ m/s

Speed of goods train = $90 \times \dfrac{5}{18} = 25$ m/s

As the goods train passes the person sitting near the window in 60 sec, so the equation will be:

Time to pass = $\dfrac{\text{Length of goods train}}{\text{Relative speed}}$

$$60 \text{ sec} = \frac{\text{Length of goods train}}{25 - \frac{50}{3}}$$

∴ Length of goods train $= 60 \times \frac{25}{3}$

$= 500$ m.

Choice (d)

Solution 18

Speed of train $A = 54 \times \frac{5}{18} = 15$ m/s

Speed of train $B = 90 \times \frac{5}{18} = 25$ m/s

Time required by train A to exit tunnel $= \frac{100 + 200}{15}$

$= 20$ sec

Time required by train B to exit tunnel $= \frac{150 + 200}{25}$

$= 14$ sec.

Hence train B will come out of the tunnel at first.

Choice (b)

Solution 19

Speed of shorter train $= 72 \times \frac{5}{18} = 20$ m/s

Speed of longer train $= 90 \times \frac{5}{18} = 25$ m/s

Time required by shorter train to exit tunnel $= \frac{200 + 300}{20}$

$= 25$ sec.

Time required by longer train to exit tunnel $= \frac{250 + 300}{25}$

$= 22$ sec.

Hence longer train will exit the tunnel at first and after 3 sec the shorter train will exit.

Choice (b)

Solution 20

Total distance traveled by the trains from the time they start to cross each other to the time they completely cross each other will be sum of the lengths of two trains *i.e.,* 350 m.

Choice (c)

Solution 21

Time to cross = $\dfrac{140 + 140}{S_1 + S_2}$

10 sec = $\dfrac{280}{2 \times S_1}$ ($\because S_1 = S_2$)

$\therefore S_1 = 14$ m/s

Speed of each train = $14 \times \dfrac{18}{5} = 50.4$ km/hr.

Choice (c)

Solution 22

Speed of slower train = $27 \times \dfrac{5}{18} = \dfrac{15}{2}$ m/s

Speed of faster train = $45 \times \dfrac{5}{18} = \dfrac{25}{2}$ m/s

Time to pass the engine driver of faster train = $\dfrac{\text{Length of Slower train}}{\text{Relative speed}}$

$= \dfrac{150}{\dfrac{15}{2} + \dfrac{25}{2}}$

$= \dfrac{150 \times 2}{40}$

$= 7.5$ sec.

Choice (d)

Solution 23

Speed of first train = $54 \times \dfrac{5}{18} = 15$ m/s

Time to cross = $\dfrac{120+130}{15+S_2}$

10 sec = $\dfrac{120+130}{15+S_2}$

$150 + 10 S_2 = 250$

$\therefore \quad S_2 = 10$ m/s

Speed of second train = $10 \times \dfrac{18}{5}$

$= 36$ km/hr.

Choice (b)

Solution 24

Speed of slower train = $45 \times \frac{5}{18} = \frac{25}{2}$ m/s

Speed of faster train = $63 \times \frac{5}{18} = \frac{35}{2}$ m/s

Time to overtake = $\frac{\text{Sum of Lengths}}{\text{Relative speed}}$

$$= \frac{150+170}{\frac{35}{2} - \frac{25}{2}} = \frac{320}{10/2} = 64 \text{ sec.}$$

Choice (d)

Solution 25

Speed of faster train = $48 \times \frac{5}{18} = \frac{40}{3}$ m/s

Speed of slower train = $42 \times \frac{5}{18} = \frac{35}{3}$ m/s

Time to cross = $\frac{\text{Sum of Lengths}}{\text{Relative speed}}$

15 sec = $\frac{2L+L}{\frac{40}{3} + \frac{35}{3}}$

15 sec = $\frac{3L}{75/3}$

∴ $L = 125$ m

So length of faster train = $2L = 250$ m

If the time taken by this faster train to pass the tunnel is 1 minute, then:

$$60 \text{ sec} = \frac{250 + \text{Length of tunnel}}{40/3}$$

Length of tunnel = $\left(60 \times \frac{40}{3}\right) - 250$

$= 550$ m.

Choice (c)

Solution 26

If 162 m is crossed in 18 sec and 120 m in 15 sec, it means to cross the extra length of 42 m (*i.e.,* 162 m – 120 m) 3 more seconds are required.

Speed of train = $\frac{42}{3} = 14$ m/s

As time required to cross 120 m long tunnel is 15 sec., so the equation is:

$$15 \text{ sec.} = \frac{\text{Length of Train} + 120}{14}$$

Length of train = $(15 \times 14) - 120 = 90$ m.

Choice (a)

Solution 27

As the train crosses a man in 8 sec:

$$8 \text{ sec.} = \frac{L}{S}$$

∴ $L = 8S$

As the train crosses the bridge in 20 sec:

$$20 \text{ sec} = \frac{L+180}{S}$$

$$20S = L + 180$$
$$20S = 8S + 180$$
$$12S = 180$$

∴ $S = 15$ m/s

So, $L = 8 \times 15$
     $= 120$ m.

Choice (a)

Solution 28

Speed of passenger train = $60 \times \frac{5}{18} = \frac{50}{3}$ m/s

If goods train crosses the man sitting in passenger train in 9 sec., then:

$$9 \text{ sec.} = \frac{\text{Length of goods train}}{\text{Relative speed}}$$

$$9 \text{ sec.} = \frac{240 \text{ m}}{\frac{50}{3} + S_G}$$

∴ $S_G = 10$ m/s

Speed of goods train = $10 \times \frac{18}{5}$
                     $= 36$ km/hr.

Choice (b)

Solution 29

Speed of slower train $= 48 \times \dfrac{5}{18}$

$= \dfrac{40}{3}$ m/s

Speed of faster train $= 60 \times \dfrac{5}{18}$

$= \dfrac{50}{3}$ m/s

As the faster train overtakes the slower train of same length in 45 sec.

$$45 \text{ sec.} = \dfrac{L+L}{\text{Relative speed}}$$

$$45 \text{ sec.} = \dfrac{2L}{\dfrac{50}{3} - \dfrac{40}{3}}$$

$\therefore \quad L = 75$ m.

Choice (a)

Solution 30

Let the length and speed of first train be L_1 and S_1 respectively.

Let the length and speed of second train be L_2 and S_2 respectively.

First train crosses the man in 40 sec:

$\dfrac{L_1}{S_1} = 40$ sec $\qquad \therefore L_1 = 40\, S_1$

Second train crosses the man in 30 sec:

$\dfrac{L_2}{S_2} = 30$ sec $\qquad \therefore L_2 = 30\, S_2$

As the two trains cross each other in 34 sec:

$\dfrac{L_1 + L_2}{S_1 + S_2} = 34$ sec

$40 S_1 + 30 S_2 = 34 S_1 + 34 S_2$

$6 S_1 = 4 S_2$

$\dfrac{S_1}{S_2} = \dfrac{2}{3}.$

Choice (a)

Solution 31

Let the length and speed of train be L and S respectively.

It overtakes the first man running at 1 m/s in 12 sec:

$\dfrac{L}{S-1} = 12$ sec $\qquad \therefore L = 12S - 12$

It overtakes the second man running at 2 m/s in 15 sec:

$\dfrac{L}{S-2} = 15$ sec $\qquad \therefore L = 15S - 30$

$12S - 12 = 15S - 30 \qquad \therefore S = 6$ m/s

So, $\qquad L = 60$ m.

Choice (a)

Solution 32

As the train crosses the signal pole in 18 seconds:

Speed of train $= \dfrac{180}{18} = 10$ m/s

As the first train crosses the second train (of equal length) coming in opposite direction in 8 seconds:

$\dfrac{180+180}{10+S_2} = 8$ sec $\qquad \therefore S_2 = 35$ m/s

Speed of second train $= 35 \times \dfrac{18}{5} = 126$ km/hr.

Choice (d)

Solution 33

Let the length and speed of train be L and S respectively.

Speed of first cyclist $= 18 \times \dfrac{5}{18} = 5$ m/s

Speed of second cyclist $= 9 \times \dfrac{5}{18} = \dfrac{5}{2}$ m/s

It overtakes the first cyclist running at 5 m/s in 120 sec:

$\dfrac{L}{S-5} = 120$ sec $\qquad \therefore L = 120S - 600$

It overtakes the second cyclist running at $\dfrac{5}{2}$ m/s in 90 sec:

$$\frac{L}{S-\frac{5}{2}} = 90 \text{ sec} \qquad \therefore L = 90S - 225$$

$$120S - 600 = 90S - 225$$

$$\therefore S = \frac{25}{2} \text{ m/s.}$$

Choice (a)

Solution 34

Let the length and speed of train A be L_A and S_A

Let the speed of train B be S_B

As train A crosses the pole in 20 sec:

$$\frac{L_A}{S_A} = 20 \text{ sec}$$

$$\therefore \quad L_A = 20S_A$$

As train A crosses another train B (180 m long) also in 20 sec, it means the train B is coming in opposite direction.

$$\frac{L_A + 180}{S_A + S_B} = 20 \text{ sec}$$

$$L_A + 180 = 20S_A + 20S_B$$

$$20S_A + 180 = 20S_A + 20S_B$$

$$\therefore \qquad S_B = 9 \text{ m/s.}$$

Choice (b)

Solution 35

Speed of first train = $\frac{200}{10}$ = 20 m/s

Speed of second train = $\frac{200+200}{25}$ = 16 m/s

Difference of distance covered in 1 sec = 4 m

Difference of distance covered in 1 hr = 4×3600
= 14400 m

Difference of distance covered in 2 hrs = 2×14400
= 28800 m
= 28.8 km.

Choice (c)

Solution 36

If both the trains run in same direction:

$$\frac{L+L}{S_1 - S_2} = 20 \text{ sec}$$

$\therefore 2L = 20S_1 - 20S_2$

If both the trains run in opposite direction:

$$\frac{L+L}{S_1 + S_2} = 8 \text{ sec}$$

$\therefore$
$$2L = 8S_1 + 8S_2$$
$$20S_1 - 20S_2 = 8S_1 + 8S_2$$
$$12S_1 = 28S_2$$
$$\frac{S_1}{S_2} = \frac{7}{3}.$$

Choice (c)

Solution 37

Both trains meet at point P, and after that train 1 takes 16/3 hrs (5 hr & 20 min) to reach Mumbai, while train 2 takes 12 hrs to reach Nagpur.

$$\frac{\text{Speed of Train 1}}{\text{Speed of Train 2}} = \frac{\sqrt{12}}{\sqrt{16/3}}$$

$$= \sqrt{\frac{12 \times 3}{16}}$$

$$= \frac{3}{2}.$$

Choice (a)

Solution 38

As it crosses the pole in 10 sec:

$$\frac{L}{S} = 10 \text{ sec}$$

If the length is known, speed of train can be found out. So, statement I alone is sufficient.

It over takes the cyclist in 12 sec, but here we do not know the speed of cyclist as well as length of train is not mentioned in statement II, hence it's not sufficient.

Choice (a)

Solution 39

Length of train 1 = $8x$
Length of train 2 = $5x$

In statement I only speed of first train is mentioned by which we cannot find out the speed of second train.

In statement II only time taken to cross each other is given by which we can not determine the speed of any train.

If we combine the data of both the statements, then speed of first train and time to cross each other is known to us.

$$\frac{T_1 \text{ Length} + T_2 \text{ Length}}{\text{Relative speed}} = \text{Time to cross each other}$$

$$\frac{8x + 5x}{25 \text{ m/s} + S_2} = 30 \text{ sec}$$

As actual length of the trains is not known to us, hence even by combining the data of both the statements we cannot find out the speed of second train.

Choice (d)

Solution 40

If a train (of length 200 m) crosses a platform in 30 sec, then speed of train can be found as:

$$\text{Speed} = \frac{\text{Length of Train} + \text{Length of Platform}}{\text{Time}}$$

Statement I gives us the length of platform (*i.e.,* 2 × 200), hence speed of the train can be found out.

As per statement II if length of platform is 100 m more, the train will take 5 seconds more. It means 100 m can be covered in 5 seconds. Hence speed of train can be determined.

Choice (d)

17

Boats and Streams

IMPORTANT FORMULAE

If the boat is moving with a certain speed in still (stationary) water, then it is called '*speed of boat in still water*' and is denoted by b.

In case of river or stream, water is not stationary and is flowing, then it is called '*speed of water current*' and is denoted by w.

If the boat is moving against the direction of stream (or water current), then the speed of water reduces the speed of boat, which is called as '*upstream speed*' and is denoted by u.

If the boat is moving along the direction of stream (or water current), then the speed of water increases the speed of boat, which is called as '*downstream speed*' and is denoted by d.

Upstream speed can be found as:

$u = b - w$

Downstream speed can be found as:

$d = b + w$

Speed of boat in still water can be found as:

$b = \frac{1}{2}(d + u)$

Speed of water current can be found as:

$w = \frac{1}{2}(d - u)$.

SOLVED EXAMPLES

Example 1

A boat travels 45 km upstream in 9 hrs and 42 km downstream in 6 hrs. Find the speed of boat in still water and speed of water current.

Solution

Upstream speed, $u = \frac{45}{9} = 5$ km/hr

Downstream speed, $d = \dfrac{42}{6} = 7$ km/hr

Speed of boat in still water can be found as:

$$b = \dfrac{1}{2}(d+u) = \dfrac{1}{2}(7+5) = 6 \text{ km/hr}$$

Speed of water current can be found as:

$$w = \dfrac{1}{2}(d-u) = \dfrac{1}{2}(7-5) = 1 \text{ km/hr.}$$

Example 2

A man can row at 10 km/hr in still water. If it takes a total of 5 hrs for him to go to a place 24 km away and return, then how much is the speed of water current?

Solution

Let the speed of water current be w km/hr.
Upstream speed, $u = 10 - w$
Downstream speed, $d = 10 + w$

Time to travel upstream + Time to travel downstream = 5 hrs

$$\dfrac{24}{10-w} + \dfrac{24}{10+w} = 5$$

$$\dfrac{480}{100-w^2} = 5$$

$$480 = 500 - 5w^2$$

$$w^2 = 4$$

$\therefore \qquad w = 2$ km/hr.

Example 3

The speed of a boat in still water is 6 km/hr. If the time required by the boat to cover 32 km downstream or 16 km upstream is same, then how much is the speed of stream?

Solution

Let the speed of stream be w km/hr.
Speed of boat in still water, $b = 6$ km/hr

Time to go 32 km downstream = Time to go 16 km upstream

$$\dfrac{32}{b+w} = \dfrac{16}{b-w}$$

$$\dfrac{32}{6+w} = \dfrac{16}{6-w}$$

$$192 - 32w = 96 + 16w$$
$$48w = 96$$
∴ $$w = 2 \text{ km/hr}.$$

Example 4

A boat covers a certain distance downstream in 3 hrs, while it returns back in 4 hrs. If the speed of the stream be 3 km/hr, what is the speed of the boat in still water?

Solution

Speed of stream, $w = 3$ km/hr

Let the distance traveled by boat is x km, and its speed in still water be b km/hr.

As the boat travels a distance of x km downstream in 3 hr,

∴ $\dfrac{x}{b+w} = 3$ hr or $x = 3(b + w)$ ... (1)

As the boat travels a distance of x km upstream in 4 hrs,

∴ $\dfrac{x}{b-w} = 4$ hrs or $x = 4(b - w)$ ... (2)

Equating equation (1) and (2),

$$3(b + w) = 4(b - w)$$
$$3b + 3w = 4b - 4w$$
∴ $$b = 7w$$
$$= 7 \times 3$$
$$= 21 \text{ km/hr}.$$

Example 5

A boat travels 22 km upstream in 38 min and returns back the same distance in 28 min. How much is the average speed of boat for the entire journey?

Solution

Average speed = $\dfrac{\text{Total distance traveled}}{\text{Total time taken}}$

$= \dfrac{22 + 22}{\dfrac{38}{60} + \dfrac{28}{60}}$

$= \dfrac{44}{66/60}$

$= 40$ km/hr.

EXERCISE

1. A man can row with a speed of 15 km/hr in still water. If the stream flows at 3 km/hr then his speed in downstream is:
   (a) 9 km/hr
   (b) 12 km/hr
   (c) 18 km/hr
   (d) 20 km/hr

2. A man can row upstream at 12 km/hr and downstream at 22 km/hr, then the speed of current is:
   (a) 5 km/hr
   (b) 10 km/hr
   (c) 17 km/hr
   (d) 20 km/hr

3. A man can swim down stream at 12 km/hr and upstream at 6 km/hr. Find the speed of man in still water in km/hr.
   (a) 6
   (b) 3
   (c) 9
   (d) 7.5

4. A man swims downstream 30 km and upstream 18 km taking 3 hours each time what is the speed of the man in still water?
   (a) 2 km/hr
   (b) 6 km/hr
   (c) 7 km/hr
   (d) 8 km/hr

5. A boatman goes 7 km against the current of the stream in 1 hour and goes 6 km along the current in 40 minutes. How long will it take to go 20 km in stationary water?
   (a) 2 hrs
   (b) 2½ hrs
   (c) 3 hrs
   (d) 3½ hrs

6. A man can row a distance of 5 km in 30 min with the help of tide. The direction of tide is reverses with the same speed. Now he travels further 15 km in 5 hrs. How much time would he have saved if the direction of tide had not changed?
   (a) 4 hrs
   (b) 3½ hrs
   (c) 6 hrs
   (d) 7½ hrs

7. Two boats travel in opposite direction of river, one upstream and other down stream. The speed of each boat is 15 km/hr and the speed of water current is 3 km/hr. If the length of river is 150 km, then find the time taken by the boats to meet.
   (a) 5 hrs
   (b) 7.5 hrs
   (c) 4 hrs
   (d) 6 hrs

8. A man can row 6 km/hr in still water. When the river is running at 1.2 km/hr, it takes him 1 hour to row to a place and back. How far the place?
   (a) 2 km
   (b) 2.88 km
   (c) 3 km
   (d) 3.12 km

9. A man can row 8 km/hr in still water. When the water is flowing at the speed of 2 km/hr, it takes him 2 hrs to row to a place and back. How far the place?
   (a) 5.75 km
   (b) 6 km
   (c) 6.25 km
   (d) 7.5 km

10. In one hour, a boat goes 11 km along the stream and 5 km against the stream. The speed of the boat in still water (in km/hr) is:
    (a) 4   (b) 5
    (c) 8   (d) 10

11. The current of a stream runs at the rate of 4 km/hr. A boat goes 6 km and back to the starting point in 2 hours, then find the speed of boat in still water.
    (a) 6 km/hr   (b) 8 km/hr
    (c) 12 km/hr   (d) 14 km/hr

12. The current of a stream flows at 1 km/hr. A boat goes 35 km upstream and back to the starting point in 12 hours. The speed of the boat in still water is:
    (a) 6 km/hr   (b) 8 km/hr
    (c) 10 km/hr   (d) 12 km/hr

13. A man can row 22 km/hr in still water. It takes him thrice as long to row up as to row down the river. Find the rate of stream.
    (a) 4 km/hr   (b) 9 km/hr
    (c) 11 km/hr   (d) 16 km/hr

14. A motorboat, whose speed in 9 km/hr in still water goes 40 km downstream and comes back in a total of 10 hours. The speed of the stream (in km/hr) is:
    (a) 2½ km/hr   (b) 3 km/hr
    (c) 4 km/hr   (d) 6 km/hr

15. A boat running upstream takes 18 hrs to cover a certain distance, while it takes 6 hrs to cover the same distance running downstream. What is the ratio between the speed of the boat (in still water) and speed of the water current respectively?
    (a) 3 : 1   (b) 4 : 1
    (c) 3 : 2   (d) 2 : 1

16. A boat takes 2 hrs less to travel 48 km downstream than to travel the same distance upstream. If the speed of the boat in still water is 10 km/hr, the speed of the stream is:
    (a) 1 km/hr   (b) 2 km/hr
    (c) 3 km/hr   (d) 5 km/hr

17. A boat covers a certain distance downstream in 1 hr, while it returns back in 1½ hrs. If the speed of the stream be 4 km/hr, what is the speed of the boat in still water?
    (a) 12 km/hr   (b) 15 km/hr
    (c) 18 km/hr   (d) 20 km/hr

18. Speed of motorboat in still water is 10 km/hr. If it can travel 55 km downstream and 45 km upstream in the same time, the speed of stream is:
    (a) 1 km/hr   (b) 1.5 km/hr
    (c) 2 km/hr   (d) 3 km/hr

19. A boat can travel 12 km in 1 hr in still water and takes 20 min extra if it travels against the stream. How much time the boat will take to row 45 km along the steam and return back to the starting point?
    (a) 4 hrs
    (b) 5 hrs
    (c) 6 hrs
    (d) 8 hrs

20. In a given time, the distance traveled by a boat upstream and downstream is in the ratio of 2 : 5. If the speed of boat in still water is 14 km/hr, how much is the speed of stream?
    (a) 3 km/hr
    (b) 5 km/hr
    (c) 6 km/hr
    (d) 8 km/hr

21. A boat travels 25 km upstream in 45 min and returns back the same distance in 30 min. How much is the average speed of boat for the entire journey?
    (a) 25 km/hr
    (b) 30 km/hr
    (c) 40 km/hr
    (d) 45 km/hr

22. Two points in a river are 24 km apart. A boat takes 9 hrs to make a round trip between two points. If the water is still, the boat can make a round trip between two points in 8 hrs. How much is the speed of stream?
    (a) 2 km/hr
    (b) 2½ km/hr
    (c) 3 km/hr
    (d) 4 km/hr

23. Speed of the boat in still water is 6 km/hr and the speed of stream is 1.5 km/hr. If the boat travels a distance of 135 km from the starting point and again returns back the same distance, then how much time it will take for the round trip?
    (a) 31 hrs
    (b) 35 hrs
    (c) 42 hrs
    (d) 48 hrs

24. A man rows 5/6th of a kilometer upstream in 25 min and returns in 10 min. Find the speed of water current.
    (a) 1 km/hr
    (b) 1.5 km/hr
    (c) 2 km/hr
    (d) 2.5 km/hr

KEYS

1. (c)	2. (a)	3. (c)	4. (d)	5. (b)	6. (b)	7. (a)	8. (b)
9. (d)	10. (c)	11. (b)	12. (a)	13. (c)	14. (b)	15. (b)	16. (b)
17. (d)	18. (a)	19. (d)	20. (c)	21. (c)	22. (a)	23. (d)	24. (b)

SOLUTIONS

Solution 1

$b = 15$ km/hr
$w = 3$ km/hr

Downstream speed, $d = b + w$
$ = 15 + 3$
$ = 18$ km/hr.

Choice (c)

Solution 2

$u = 12$ km/hr
$d = 22$ km/hr

Speed of water current, $w = \dfrac{1}{2}(d - u)$
$ = \dfrac{1}{2}(22 - 12) = 5$ km/hr.

Choice (a)

Solution 3

$u = 6$ km/hr
$d = 12$ km/hr

Speed in still water, $b = \dfrac{1}{2}(d + u)$
$ = \dfrac{1}{2}(12 + 6) = 9$ km/hr.

Choice (c)

Solution 4

Downstream speed, $d = \dfrac{30}{3} = 10$ km/hr

Upstream speed, $u = \dfrac{18}{3} = 6$ km/hr

Speed in still water, $b = \dfrac{1}{2}(d + u)$
$ = \dfrac{1}{2}(10 + 6)$
$ = 8$ km/hr.

Choice (d)

Solution 5

Upstream speed, $u = \frac{7}{1} = 7$ km/hr

Downstream speed, $d = \frac{6}{40/60} = 9$ km/hr

Speed in still water, $b = \frac{1}{2}(d + u)$

$\qquad = \frac{1}{2}(9 + 7) = 8$ km/hr.

Time required to travel 20 km in stationary water $= \dfrac{\text{Distance}}{\text{Speed in still water}}$

$\qquad = \dfrac{20}{8}$

$\qquad = 2\frac{1}{2}$ hrs.

Choice (b)

Solution 6

As 5 km he travels in 30 min with the help of tide, hence further 15 km he can travel in 1½ hrs if direction of tide remains same.

But, as the direction of tide reverses, he travels 15 km in 5 hrs, which means he is requiring 3½ hrs extra.

So, if the direction of tide is not reversed, he would have saved 3½ hrs.

Choice (b)

Solution 7

$b = 15$ km/hr
$w = 3$ km/hr

Speed of boat going upstream, $u = b - w$
$\qquad\qquad = 15 - 3$
$\qquad\qquad = 12$ km/hr

Speed of boat going downstream, $d = b + w$
$\qquad\qquad = 15 + 3$
$\qquad\qquad = 18$ km/hr

Time required to meet $= \dfrac{\text{Distance}}{\text{Relative Speed}}$

$\qquad = \dfrac{150}{12+18} = 5$ hrs.

Choice (a)

Solution 8

$b = 6$ km/hr
$w = 1.2$ km/hr

Upstream speed, $u = 6 - 1.2 = 4.8$ km/hr

Downstream speed, $d = 6 + 1.2 = 7.2$ km/hr

Let the place is x km far from the starting point.

Time taken to go upstream + Time taken to return downstream = 1 hr

$$\frac{x}{4.8} + \frac{x}{7.2} = 1 \text{ hr}$$

$$\frac{2x + 3x}{14.4} = 1$$

$\therefore \quad x = \frac{14.4}{5}$

$= 2.88$ km.

Choice (b)

Solution 9

$b = 8$ km/hr
$w = 2$ km/hr

Upstream speed, $u = 8 - 2 = 6$ km/hr

Downstream speed, $d = 8 + 2 = 10$ km/hr

Let the place is x km far from the starting point.

Time taken to go upstream + Time taken to return downstream = 2 hrs

$$\frac{x}{6} + \frac{x}{10} = 2 \text{ hrs}$$

$$\frac{5x + 3x}{30} = 2$$

$\therefore x = \frac{60}{8} = 7.5$ km.

Choice (d)

Solution 10

Upstream speed, $u = \frac{5}{1} = 5$ km/hr

Downstream speed, $d = \frac{11}{1} = 11$ km/hr

Speed in still water, $b = \frac{1}{2}(d+u) = \frac{1}{2}(11+5) = 8$ km/hr.

Choice (c)

Solution 11

$w = 4$ km/hr

Time taken to go 6 km upstream + Time taken to return 6 km downstream = 2 hrs

$$\frac{6}{b-4} + \frac{6}{b+4} = 2$$

$$\frac{12b}{b^2 - 16} = 2$$

$6b = b^2 - 16$

$b^2 - 6b - 16 = 0$

$b^2 - 8b + 2b - 16 = 0$

$(b-8)(b+2) = 0$

$\therefore b = 8$ or -2

So, speed of boat in still water is 8 km/hr.

Choice (b)

Solution 12

$w = 1$ km/hr

Time taken to go 35 km upstream + Time taken to return 35 km downstream = 12 hrs

$$\frac{35}{b+1} + \frac{35}{b-1} = 12$$

$$\frac{70b}{b^2 - 1} = 12$$

$70b = 12b^2 - 12$

$6b^2 - 35b - 6 = 0$

$6b^2 - 36b + b - 6 = 0$

$6b(b-6) + 1(b-6) = 0$

$(b-6)(6b+1) = 0$

$\therefore b = 6$ or $-1/6$

So, speed of boat in still water is 6 km/hr.

Choice (a)

Solution 13

$b = 22$ km/hr

Time to go upstream = 3 × Time to go downstream

$$\frac{\text{Time to go upstream}}{\text{Time to go downstream}} = \frac{3}{1}$$

$$\frac{\text{Upstream speed}}{\text{Downstream speed}} = \frac{1}{3} \quad (\because \text{Speed and time are inversely proportional})$$

$$\frac{22-w}{22+w} = \frac{1}{3}$$

$66 - 3w = 22 + w$

$4w = 44$

$\therefore w = 11$ km/hr

So, rate of stream is 11 km/hr.

Choice (c)

Solution 14

$b = 9$ km/hr

Time taken to go 40 km upstream + Time taken to return 40 km downstream = 10 hrs

$$\frac{40}{9-w} + \frac{40}{9+w} = 10$$

$$\frac{720}{81-w^2} = 10$$

$720 = 810 - 10w^2$

$w^2 = 9$

$\therefore w = 3$ km/hr

So, speed of stream is 3 km/hr.

Choice (b)

Solution 15

$$\frac{T_{\text{Upstream}}}{T_{\text{Downstream}}} = \frac{18}{6} = \frac{3}{1}$$

$$\frac{S_{\text{Upstream}}}{S_{\text{Downstream}}} \Rightarrow \frac{u}{d} = \frac{1}{3} \quad (\because \text{Speed and time are inversely proportional})$$

Speed in still water, $b = \frac{1}{2}(d+u)$

$= \frac{1}{2}(3+1)$

$= 4$

Speed of water current, $w = \frac{1}{2}(d-u)$

$= \frac{1}{2}(3-1) = 1$

Ratio of speed of boat to speed in still water = 4 : 1.

Choice (b)

Solution 16

$b = 10$ km/hr

Time taken to go 48 km upstream – Time taken to go 48 km downstream = 2 hrs

$$\frac{48}{10-w} - \frac{48}{10+w} = 2$$

$$\frac{96w}{100-w^2} = 2$$

$96w = 200 - 2w^2$

$w^2 + 48w - 100 = 0$

$w^2 + 50w - 2w - 100 = 0$

$(w+50)(w-2) = 0$

$\therefore b = -50$ or 2

So, speed of stream is 2 km/hr.

Choice (b)

Solution 17

$w = 4$ km/hr

Let the distance traveled by boat is x km, and its speed in still water be b km/hr.

As the boat travels a distance of x km upstream in 1 hr,

$\therefore \frac{x}{b+w} = 1$ hr or $x = b+w$ ... (1)

As the boat travels a distance of x km downstream in 1½ hrs,

$\therefore \frac{x}{b-w} = 1½$ hrs or $x = \frac{3}{2}(b-w)$ ... (2)

Equating equation (1) and (2),

$$b + w = \frac{3}{2}(b - w)$$

$$2b + 2w = 3b - 3w$$

$$\therefore b = 5w = 5 \times 4 = 20 \text{ km/hr.}$$

Choice (d)

Solution 18

$b = 10$ km/hr

Time to go 55 km downstream = Time to go 45 km upstream

$$\frac{55}{b+w} = \frac{45}{b-w}$$

$$\frac{55}{10+w} = \frac{45}{10-w}$$

$$550 - 55w = 450 + 45w$$

$$100w = 100$$

$$\therefore w = 1 \text{ km/hr.}$$

Choice (a)

Solution 19

$b = 12$ km/hr

Upstream speed, $u \Rightarrow b - w = \dfrac{12 \text{ km}}{80/60} = 9$ km/hr

$\therefore w = 3$ km/hr

Time required to make round trip $= \dfrac{45 \text{ km}}{b+w} + \dfrac{45 \text{ km}}{b-w}$

$$= \frac{45 \text{ km}}{12+3} + \frac{45 \text{ km}}{12-3}$$

$$= 8 \text{ hrs.}$$

Choice (d)

Solution 20

Speed of boat in still water, $b = 14$ km/hr

Let the speed of stream $= w$ km/hr

The ratio of distance traveled in upstream and downstream is 2:5,

$$\frac{D_{\text{Upstream}}}{D_{\text{Downstream}}} = \frac{2}{5}$$

Therefore the ratio of speed in downstream and upstream will be:

$$\frac{S_{\text{Upstream}}}{S_{\text{Downstream}}} = \frac{2}{5} \quad (\because \text{Speed is directly proportional to distance})$$

$$\frac{b-w}{b+w} = \frac{2}{5}$$

$$\frac{14-w}{14+w} = \frac{2}{5}$$

$\therefore \quad w = 6$ km/hr.

Choice (c)

Solution 21

Average speed = $\dfrac{\text{Total distance traveled}}{\text{Total time taken}}$

$$= \frac{25+25}{\frac{45}{60}+\frac{30}{60}} = \frac{50}{75/60} = 40 \text{ km/hr.}$$

Choice (c)

Solution 22

If the water is still, the boat can make a round trip in 8 hrs. So, the speed of boat in still water can be found as:

$$b = \frac{24+24}{8} = 6 \text{ km/hr}$$

Time to go 24 km upstream + Time to return 24 km downstream = 9 hrs

$$\frac{24}{b-w} + \frac{24}{b+w} = 9$$

$$\frac{24}{6-w} + \frac{24}{6+w} = 9$$

$$\frac{288}{36-w^2} = 9$$

$$36 - w^2 = 32$$

$$w^2 = 4$$

$\therefore \quad w = 2$ km/hr.

Choice (a)

Solution 23

$b = 6$ km/hr
$w = 1.5$ km/hr

Time taken for round trip = Time to go upstream + Time to return downstream

$$= \frac{135}{6-1.5} + \frac{135}{6+1.5}$$
$$= 30 + 18$$
$$= 48 \text{ hrs.}$$

Choice (d)

Solution 24

Upstream speed, $u = \dfrac{5/6}{25/60} = \dfrac{5}{6} \times \dfrac{60}{25} = 2$ km/hr

Downstream speed, $d = \dfrac{5/6}{10/60} = \dfrac{5}{6} \times \dfrac{60}{10} = 5$ km/hr

Speed of water current $= \dfrac{1}{2}(d - u)$

$$= \dfrac{1}{2}(5 - 2)$$
$$= 1.5 \text{ km/hr.}$$

Choice (b)

18

Permutation and Combination

COMBINATION

These are the number of ways in which selection of some or all the items can be made out of the given items.

$^nC_r \Rightarrow$ Number of ways of selecting 'r' items out of 'n' items.

The number of combinations of n things taking r at a time is denoted as ^nC_r and read as '^nC_r'. In combination the order in which items are taken are not important. For example, the combination of three items X, Y and Z taken two at a time are XY, YZ and XZ. Here, XY and YX are not considered separately because the order in which X and Y are taken is not important but it is only required that a combination including X and Y be counted.

Mathematically combination is given as:

$$^nC_r = \frac{n!}{(n-r)!r!}$$

Suppose the task is to select any three vowels out of five English vowels *i.e.*, A, E, I, O, and U. So number of selection of three vowels out of five can be done as follows:

$$^5C_3 = \frac{5!}{(5-3)!3!} = \frac{5!}{2!\ 3!} = 10 \text{ ways}$$

The ways are: AEI, AIO, AEO, EIO, IOU, EOU, EIU, AUE, AUI, and AUO.

DIFFERENT ARRANGEMENTS

If suppose three persons A, B and C are sitting in a row, then the number of ways in which they arrange themselves in that row are as follows:

- 1st way   ⇒   A   B   C
- 2nd way   ⇒   A   C   B
- 3rd way   ⇒   B   A   C
- 4th way   ⇒   B   C   A
- 5th way   ⇒   C   A   B
- 6th way   ⇒   C   B   A

The total number of ways are 6 (or 3!). If there 'r' number of persons sitting in a row, then number of different arrangements possible are '$r!$'. In a similar way 10 letters can be sealed in 10 envelopes in 10! Ways.

PERMUTATION

Permutation is an extension of combination. In combination we are only restricted up to the number of ways of selection, but in permutation after selection we do further different arrangements also.

^nP_r $\Rightarrow$ Number of ways of selecting 'r' items out of 'n' items and then '$r!$' arrangements.
  $\Rightarrow$ Ways of section × Arrangements

The number of permutations of n things taking r at a time is denoted as ^nP_r and read as '^nP_r'. In permutation the order in which items are taken is important. For example, the permutation of three items X, Y and Z taken two at a time are XY, YZ and XZ. Here, XY and YX are counted separately as two different permutations.

Mathematically permutation is given as:

$$^nP_r = {}^nC_r \times r!$$
$$= \frac{n!}{(n-r)!\,r!} \times r!$$
$$= \frac{n!}{(n-r)!}$$

Suppose the task is to form all possible three letter words from five English vowels i.e., A, E, I, O, and U such that each letter is distinct. So here we need to select at first 3 letters out of 5 and then arrange them in 3! Ways. It can be solved as follows:

Number of 3 letter words = Selection of 3 out of 5 × Arrangements

$$^5P_3 = {}^5C_3 \times 3! = \frac{5!}{2!\,3!} \times 3!$$
$$= 60$$

The same example can also be solved without using expression of permutation. As three distinct letters are to be selected out of five, so first letter can be selected in 5 ways, second letter can be selected in 4 ways, and the third letter can be selected in remaining 3 ways.

$5 \times 4 \times 3 = 60$

If the repetition of letters is allowed, then obviously the number of words formed is more that 60 and the problem can be solved as follows:

$5 \times 5 \times 5 = 125$

POINTS TO NOTE

- *The number of combination (or selection) of 'n' dissimilar things taken 'r' at a time is ^nC_r*

  For example: Out of 7 rainbow colors, if we want to select any 3 colors, it can be done in $^7C_3$ number of ways. If all seven colors need to be selected then it can be done in $^7C_7$ ways i.e., in only 1 way.

- *The number of permutations (or arrangements) of 'n' dissimilar things taken 'r' at a time is ^nP_r*

  For example: If we want to design a tri-colored flag from seven rainbow colors, then the first task is to select any 3 colors out of 7 and then arranging them in 3! Ways, which can be done in $^7P_3$ number of ways.

- *The number of permutations (or arrangements) of 'n' dissimilar things all at a time is ^nP_n or n!*

  For example: If we want to find out the number of ways of arranging the letters of a 9 letters word 'EDUCATION' which has all dissimilar letters can be done in $^9P_9$ or 9! Ways.

- *The number of ways of arranging 'n' distinct items in a row of which 'p' of the things are exactly alike of one kind, 'q' of then are exactly alike of another kind, 'r' of them are exactly alike of a third kind and rest all distinct is n!/p!q!r!*

  For example: If we want to find out the number of ways of arranging the letters of a 9 letters word 'ASSISTANT' which has some similar letters (like 3 times 'S', 2 times 'I', and 2 times 'T') can be done as follows:

  Number of arrangements = $\dfrac{9!}{3!\,2!\,2!}$

- *The number of ways of selecting one or more items from n given items is $2^n - 1$*

  For example: A question paper consists of 10 questions of true or false type, in how many ways the entire paper can be solved such that at least one question is marked as true?

  As every question can be solved in 2 ways (*i.e.,* either to mark true or false), hence the entire paper can be solved in 2^{10} ways. So, here exist one of the possibility that all the questions are marked as false and if we eliminate that possibility, then resulting number of ways are $2^{10} - 1$.

- *The number of ways in which a group of '(a + b + c)' things can be arranged (or splited) in to three small subgroups of size 'a', 'b' and 'c' respectively is (a + b + c)!/a!b!c!*

  For example: The number of ways of dividing 120 students in three groups of 30, 40 and 50 students can be done as follows:

  Number of ways = $\dfrac{120!}{30!\,40!\,50!}$

- *The number of ways of diving 3P items into three equal groups of P each when group has distinct identity is $(3P)!/(P!)^3$*

  For example: 15 distinct books can be divided equally among 3 boys in $\dfrac{15!}{(5!)^3}$ ways.

- *The number of ways of diving 3P items into three equal groups of P each when groups are identical (or not having distinct identity) is $(3P)!/3!\,(P!)^3$*

  For example: 15 distinct books can be divided equally in to 3 parcels in $\dfrac{15!}{3!\,(5!)^3}$ ways.

- *The number of ways of arranging 'n' distinct items in a row is n!*

  For example: 3 persons A, B and C can be seated in a row in 3! number of ways.

- The number of circular arrangements of 'n' distinct items is $(n-1)!$ if there is a difference between clockwise and anticlockwise arrangement

  For example: 3 persons A, B and C can be seated on a circular table in 2! Ways. An important point to be noted here rotation of the persons or items cannot be treated as a separate arrangement.

- The number of circular arrangements of 'n' distinct items is $(n-1)!/2$, if there is a no difference between clockwise and anticlockwise arrangement.

  For example: Number of different garlands that can be designed by arrangement of 10 different flowers are $(10-1)!/2$, *i.e.*, $9!/2$.

SOLVED EXAMPLES

Example 1

In how many ways can three colors are selected simultaneously from a shade-card containing 12 different colors?

Solution

As the task is to select any 3 colors out of 12 colors available on shade-card, which can be done in $^{12}C_3$ number of ways.

$$^{12}C_3 = \frac{12!}{9!\,3!} = \frac{12 \times 11 \times 10}{3!} = 220 \text{ ways.}$$

Exmaple-2

In how many ways can 4 persons be seated on 6 different chairs in a row for a photo session?

Solution

This is a problem of permutation. As 4 persons need only 4 chairs to sit, hence at first any 4 chairs to be selected out of 6, this can be done in $^6C_4$ number of ways. On the selected 4 chairs, 4 persons can arrange themselves in 4! ways.

$$^6P_4 = {}^6C_4 \times 4! = \frac{6!}{2!\,4!} \times 4! = 360 \text{ ways.}$$

Example 3

How many seven letter words can be formed by rearranging the letters of the word INCLUDE, such that:

1. Each word should begin with L.
2. Each word should begin with L and end with D.

3. Vowels should be always together.
4. No two vowels should be together.

Solution

1. Each word should begin with L.
   As the word INCLUDE has 7 letters, so total number of words that can be formed by rearranging letters are 7! or 5040. If each word should begin with L, then remaining 6 letters be arranged at 6 places in 6! or 720 ways.

   L _ _ _ _ _ _ = 6! or 720 words

2. Each word should begin with L and end with D.
   If each word should begin with L, and end with D then remaining 5 letters be arranged at 5 places in 5! or 120 ways.

   L _ _ _ _ _ D = 5! or 120 words

3. Vowels should be always together
   In the word INCLUDE, there are three vowels i.e., I, U and E. Let us treat these three vowels as one single unit, so there will be total 5 units.

   I U   E N C L D
    1   2 3 4 5

   These 5 units can be arranged in 5! ways, also the 3 vowels can be arranged among themselves in 3! ways.

   ∴ Total number of words = 5! × 3! = 720 words.

4. No two vowels should be together.
   The 4 consonants i.e., N, C, L and D can be arranged in 4! (or $^4P_4$) number of ways.

   _ N _ C _ L _ D _

   Now there are 5 vacant places as shown above where if we place vowels, then there will be at least one consonant between any two vowels. So, out of these 5 places we need to select any 3 places and arrange there these 3 vowels (i.e., I, U and E)

   Total number of words = Arrangement of consonants × Arrangement of vowels
   $$= {}^4P_4 \times {}^5P_3$$
   $$= 4! \times \frac{5!}{2!}$$
   $$= 1440 \text{ words.}$$

Example 4

How many six digit numbers can be formed using the digits 0, 1, 2, 3, 4, and 5 such that:
1. Repetition of digit is not allowed
2. Repetition of digit is allowed
3. Odd digits should occupy odd places only
4. Repetition of digit is not allowed and the number must be divisible by 5.

Solution

1. **Repetition of digit is not allowed**

   The first digit can be selected in 5 ways (as any digit can come there except zero), the second digit in 5 ways (as zero can come, but the selected first digit should not repeat), the third, fourth, fifth and sixth digit in remaining 4, 3, 2 and 1 way respectively.

   $5 \times 5 \times 4 \times 3 \times 2 \times 1 = 600$ numbers

2. **Repetition of digit is allowed**

   In this case except first digit, every digit can be selected in 6 ways. Only the first digit is selected in 5 ways (as zero should not appear at first place).

   $5 \times 6 \times 6 \times 6 \times 6 \times 6 = 38880$ numbers

3. **Odd digits should occupy odd places only**

   There are 3 odd digits and 3 odd places, so these three digits can be arranged in 3 odd places in 3! Ways. The remaining three digits can be arranged at 3 even places in another 3! Ways.

   Total possible numbers = Arrangement of odd numbers × Arrangement of even numbers

   $= 3! \times 3!$
   $= 36$

4. **Repetition of digit is not allowed and the number must be divisible by 5.**

   If the number needs to be divisible by 5, the unit place should be either 0 or 5. The possible numbers that can be formed by taking unit place as zero, without repetition of digits is as follows:

   $\overline{5} \times \overline{4} \times \overline{3} \times \overline{2} \times \overline{1} \times \dfrac{0}{1} = 120$ numbers

   The possible numbers that can be formed by taking unit place as 5, without repetition of digits is as follows:

   $\overline{4} \times \overline{4} \times \overline{3} \times \overline{2} \times \overline{1} \times \dfrac{5}{1} = 96$ numbers

   Hence total possible numbers which are divisible by 5 (without repetition of digits) = 216

Example 5

From 10 persons waiting in a queue, in how many ways can a selection of 4 be made so that:
1. A specified person is always included
2. A specified person is always excluded

Solution

1. **A specified person is always included**

   If one specified person is to be always included, then we need to select only 3 persons out of remaining 9 persons.

   Number of ways = $^9C_3 = \dfrac{9!}{6!\,3!} = \dfrac{9 \times 8 \times 7}{3!} = 84$ ways

2. A specified person is always excluded

   If one specified person is to be always excluded, then we need to select all 4 persons out of remaining 9 persons.

   Number of ways = $^9C_4 = \dfrac{9!}{5!\,4!} = \dfrac{9\times 8\times 7\times 6}{4!} = 126$ ways.

Example 6

Find the number of ways of forming a committee of 10 members, out of 7 men and 6 women, such that there should be:
1. Equal number of men and women
2. Majority of men in the committee
3. Majority of women in the committee.

Solution

1. *Equal number of men and women*

   Here we need to select 5 men and 5 women out of 7 men and 6 women which can be done as follows:

   Number of ways = $^7C_5 \times {}^6C_5 = 21 \times 6 = 126$ ways.

2. *Majority of men in committee*

   Total number of ways = (7 men and 3 women) or (6 men and 4 women)
   $$= ({}^7C_7 \times {}^6C_3) + ({}^7C_6 \times {}^6C_4)$$
   $$= (1 \times 20) + (7 \times 15)$$
   $$= 125 \text{ ways}$$

3. *Majority of women in committee*

   Total number of ways = (6 women and 4 men)
   $$= {}^6C_6 \times {}^7C_4$$
   $$= 1 \times 35 = 35 \text{ ways.}$$

Example 7

Rahul has 5 friends whom he can to invite for a dinner.
1. In how many ways he can invite at least 2 of them?
2. If all 5 friends are invited, in how many ways they can be arranged on a circular table including Rahul?

Solution

1. *Inviting at least 2 friends*

   Total number of ways = Inviting 2 friends or 3 friends or 4 friends or all 5 friends
   $$= {}^5C_2 + {}^5C_3 + {}^5C_4 + {}^5C_5$$
   $$= 10 + 10 + 5 + 1 = 26 \text{ ways}$$

2. *Arrangement on a circular table*
   In this case there is a difference between clockwise and anticlockwise arrangement or these are counted as a separate arrangement. As there are 6 persons (including Rahul), they can be arranged on a circular table in 5! Ways or 120 ways.

EXERCISE

1. In how many ways one can enter a hexagonal room having door on each wall, such that he exits from different door?
   (a) 6
   (b) 5
   (c) 11
   (d) 30

2. How many three digit numbers are there such that each digit is distinct?
   (a) 648
   (b) 720
   (c) 600
   (d) 270

3. How many triangles can be drawn using vertices of a hexagon?
   (a) 20
   (b) 18
   (c) 10
   (d) 3

4. How many diagonals are there in a regular octagon?
   (a) 28
   (b) 20
   (c) 16
   (d) 8

5. If $^nC_4 = {}^nC_6$, then $^{12}C_n$ is:
   (a) 144
   (b) 121
   (c) 100
   (d) 66

6. In how many seven letter words can be formed by arranging the letters of the word TITANIC?
   (a) 7!
   (b) 5!
   (c) 7!/4!
   (d) 7!/2! 2!

7. In how many ways can 5 men and 2 women sit in a row such that the two women should never sit together?
   (a) 5! (6 × 5)
   (b) 5! × 2!
   (c) 5! × 6!
   (d) 6!

8. In how many ways 3 boys and 3 girls can be seated in a row such that boys and girls sit alternately?
   (a) 2 × 6!
   (b) 3! × 3!
   (c) 2 × 3! × 3!
   (d) 2 × 3!

9. In how many ways 200 students can be divided into 4 sections of 30, 45, 50 and 75 each?
   (a) 200!/4!
   (b) 30! × 45! × 50! × 75!
   (c) $\dfrac{200!}{30!\,45!\,50!\,75!}$
   (d) $\dfrac{30!\,45!\,50!\,75!}{4!}$

10. How many different words can be formed using the letters of the word URGENT that begin with *U* and end with *T*?
    (a) 24 (b) 48
    (c) 50 (d) 60

11. In how many ways can the letters of the word GENIUS be arranged in a row such that the vowels are always together?
    (a) 720 (b) 144
    (c) 120 (d) 24

12. In how many ways can the letters of the word ARTICLE be arranged in a row such that the vowels are always together?
    (a) 5040 (b) 720
    (c) 360 (d) 120

13. In how many different ways can the letters of the word OPTICAL be arranged in a row so that the vowels never come together?
    (a) 720 (b) 1440
    (c) 4680 (d) 5040

14. How many different words can be formed using all the letters of the word INSTITUTE?
    (a) 9!/3!2! (b) 9!/3!
    (c) 5! (d) 9!/3!6!

15. In how many different ways can the letters of the word MISTAKE be arranged in such a way that the vowels occupy only the odd positions?
    (a) 7! (b) 7!/3! 4!
    (c) 3! × 4! (d) 7!/3!

16. In how many ways can a group of 5 boys and 3 girls be made out of a total of 7 boys and 5 girls?
    (a) 120 (b) 210
    (c) 525 (d) 720

17. Out of 5 consonants and 3 vowels, how many words of 3 consonants and 2 vowels can be formed?
    (a) 30 (b) 360
    (c) 720 (d) 3600

18. From a group of 5 boys and 8 girls, 6 students are to be selected to form a committee such that there should be a majority of boys. In how many ways can it be done?
    (a) 140 (b) 148
    (c) 152 (d) 160

19. Out of 6 mechanical engineers and 4 electrical engineers, a team of 4 engineers is to be formed for a particular project. In how many different ways can they be selected such that at least one electrical engineer and one mechanical engineer should be there?
    (a) 28 (b) 36
    (c) 90 (d) 210

20. A boy attempts a multiple choice question paper consisting of 10 questions and each question having 4 choices. The number of ways in which he can attempt the entire paper if he is marking the answers at random is
    (a) $^{10}P_4$ (b) 40
    (c) 4^{10} (d) 10^4

21. In how many ways can 5 letters be posted into 3 letter boxes?
    (a) 3^5 (b) 5^3
    (b) $^5P_3$ (d) $^5C_3$

22. If 8 students are participating in a running race, in how many ways first 3 prizes can be won?
    (a) 3! (b) $8 \times 7 \times 6$
    (c) $^8P_3$ (d) $^8C_3$

23. Raman attempts a true or false question paper which contains 10 questions at random. The number of ways in which he could have answered one or more questions is:
    (a) 3^{10} (b) $3^{10}-1$
    (b) 2^{10} (d) $2^{10}-1$

24. How many numbers between 50000 and 70000 can be formed using the integers from 3 to 9 when any digit can occur any number of times?
    (a) 5012 (b) 2506
    (c) 2401 (d) 4802

25. How many four digit numbers can be formed using the digits 0, 1, 2, 3, 4, 5 and 6 without repetition of digits such that the number is divisible by 5?
    (a) 120 (b) 150
    (c) 220 (d) 720

26. A number plate should have four digits. If the first digit is 7, the second digit is an even natural number and the last two digits are in ascending order, then find the total number of different number plates possible.
    (a) 225 (b) 144
    (c) 180 (d) 135

27. There are 4 books of physics, 6 books of chemistry and 3 books of English. The number of ways of selecting 4 books in which at least two are English books is:
    (a) 71 (b) 145
    (c) 139 (d) 75

28. In how many ways can 6 different physics books, 5 different chemistry books and 4 different biology books be arranged on a shelf such that books belonging to same subject are always together?
    (a) 3! (b) $6! \times 5! \times 4!$
    (c) $3! \times 3!$ (d) $3! \times 6! \times 5! \times 4!$

29. In how many ways can 4 letters be selected from the letters of the word ADDRESS?
    (a) 10 (b) 18
    (c) 35 (d) 45

30. In how many ways 8 persons can be arranged on two round tables consisting of 4 chairs each?
    (a) 720
    (b) 1260
    (c) 2520
    (d) 5040

31. Find the number of ways of arranging 25 colored beads in a necklace.
    (a) 24!
    (b) 24!/2
    (c) 25!/2
    (d) 24!/12!

32. In how many ways can 4 boys and 4 girls sit around a circular table so that no two boys are sitting together?
    (a) 3! 3!
    (b) 7!
    (c) 3! 4!
    (d) 8!/2!

33. An advertising board is to be designed with five vertical stripes using some or all of the colors red, yellow and orange. In how many ways the board can be designed such that no two adjacent strips have same color?
    (a) 6
    (b) 15
    (c) 18
    (d) 48

34. If 8 different varieties of ice-creams are available at an ice-cream parlor, then the number of ways of selecting at least one of them is:
    (a) 2^8
    (b) 2^8-1
    (c) 2^7
    (d) 8!

35. In a chess tournament 'n' number of players participated. If each player plays with every other player exactly once and total 105 games were played, then find the value of n.
    (a) 15
    (b) 18
    (c) 20
    (d) 25

KEYS

1. (d)	2. (a)	3. (a)	4. (b)	5. (d)	6. (d)	7. (a)	8. (c)
9. (c)	10. (a)	11. (b)	12. (c)	13. (b)	14. (a)	15. (c)	16. (b)
17. (d)	18. (b)	19. (a)	20. (c)	21. (a)	22. (b)	23. (b)	24. (d)
25. (c)	26. (c)	27. (b)	28. (d)	29. (b)	30. (c)	31. (b)	32. (c)
33. (d)	34. (b)	35. (a)					

SOLUTIONS

Solution 1

To enter the hexagonal room there are 6 ways (or doors), but to exit there are 5 ways (or doors).

Enter Exit

Number of ways to enter and exit = $^6C_1 \times {}^5C_1 = 6 \times 5 = 30$ ways.

Choice (d)

Solution 2

Total digits available with us are 10 *i.e.*, from 0, 1, 2, 3, ..., 9.

The first digit can be selected in 9 ways (as any digit can come there except zero), the second digit in 9 ways (as zero can come, but the selected first digit should not repeat), the third digit can be selected in remaining 8 ways.

$9 \times 9 \times 8 = 648$ numbers

Choice (a)

Solution 3

A hexagon has 6 vertices. To form a triangle we need to join 3 points, so the number of triangles that can be formed are:

Triangles = Number of ways of selecting 3 points out of 6

$$= {}^6C_3 = \frac{6!}{3!\,3!} = 20.$$

Choice (a)

Solution 4

An octagon has 8 vertices or we can consider as 8 non-collinear points. Number of lines that can be drawn by joining these points are $^8C_2$ or 28 lines. But out of these 28 lines 8 are the edges of octagon; hence the number of diagonals are 20.

Choice (b)

Solution 5

If $^nC_4 = {}^nC_6$, then n will be equal to $4 + 6 = 10$

$\therefore \quad {}^{12}C_{10} = \frac{12!}{2!\,10!} = 66.$

Choice (d)

Solution 6

The seven letter word TITANIC has two similar letters (like 2 times 'T', and 2 times 'I') and if these similar letters interchange their position, it cannot be treated as a separate arrangement.

∴ Number of arrangements = $\dfrac{7!}{2!\,2!}$.

Choice (d)

Solution 7

5 men can be arranged in 5! (or $^5P_5$) number of ways.

$$\_\_ M_1 \_\_ M_2 \_\_ M_3 \_\_ M_4 \_\_ M_5 \_\_$$

Now there are 6 vacant places as shown above where if we place women, then there will be at least one man between any two women. So, out of these 6 places we need to select any 2 places and arrange there these 2 women.

Total number of ways = Arrangement of men × Arrangement of women
$$= {}^5P_5 \times {}^6P_2$$
$$= 5! \times \dfrac{6!}{4!}$$
$$= 5!\,(6 \times 5).$$

Choice (a)

Solution 8

If we assume that boys are sitting at odd places and girls are sitting at even places, then 3 boys can be arranged on 3 odd places in 3! Ways, similarly 3 girls can be arranged on 3 even places in 3! Ways. So, the number of ways = 3! × 3!

As another possibility exist that boys can be in even place and girls can be in odd place, then the total number of ways get doubled.

∴ Total number of ways = 2 × 3! × 3!

Choice (c)

Solution 9

The number of ways in which a group of $(a + b + c)$ things can be arranged (or splited) in to three small subgroups of size 'a', 'b' and 'c' respectively is $(a + b + c)!/a!b!c!$. As here we are splitting a group of 200 students in to four small subgroups, so the number of ways will be:

Number of ways = $\dfrac{200!}{30!\,45!\,50!\,75!}$.

Choice (c)

Solution 10

If each word should begin with U, and end with T then remaining 4 letters be arranged at 4 places in 4! or 24 ways.

$\underline{U}\ \_\ \_\ \_\ \_\ \underline{T}$ = 4! or 24 words.

Choice (a)

Solution 11

In the word GENIUS, there are three vowels *i.e.*, E, I and U. Let us treat these three vowels as one single unit, so there will be total 4 units.

$\underline{E\ I\ U}\ \underline{G}\ \underline{N}\ \underline{S}$
$\quad 1 \quad\ \ 2\ \ 3\ \ 4$

These 4 units can be arranged in 4! ways, also the 3 vowels can be arranged among themselves in 3! ways.

∴ Total number of words = $4! \times 3! = 144$ words.

Choice (b)

Solution 12

In the word ARTICLE, there are three vowels *i.e.*, A, I and E. Let us treat these three vowels as one single unit, so there will be total 5 units.

$\underline{A\ I\ E}\ \underline{R}\ \underline{T}\ \underline{C}\ \underline{L}$
$\quad 1 \quad\ \ 2\ \ 3\ \ 4\ \ 5$

These 5 units can be arranged in 5! ways, also the 3 vowels can be arranged among themselves in 3! ways.

∴ Total number of words = $5! \times 3! = 360$ words.

Choice (c)

Solution 13

The 4 consonants *i.e.*, P, T, C and L can be arranged in 4! (or $^4P_4$) number of ways.

$\_\ P\ \_\ T\ \_\ C\ \_\ L\ \_$

Now there are 5 vacant places as shown above where if we place vowels, then there will be at least one consonant between any two vowels. So, out of these 5 places we need to select any 3 places and arrange there these 3 vowels (*i.e.*, O, I and A)

Total number of words = Arrangement of consonants × Arrangement of vowels
$$= {}^4P_4 \times {}^5P_3$$
$$= 4! \times \frac{5!}{2!} = 1440 \text{ words.}$$

Choice (b)

Solution 14

The nine letter word INSTITUTE has some similar letters (like 2 times 'I', and 3 times 'T') and if these similar letters interchange their position, it cannot be treated as a separate arrangement.

∴ Number of arrangements = $\dfrac{9!}{3!\,2!}$.

Choice (a)

Solution 15

In a 7 letter word MISTAKE there are 3 vowels (*i.e.*, *I*, *A* and *E*) and 3 odd places. The 3 vowels can be arranged 3! ways and 4 consonants can be arranged at 4 even places in 4! ways.

Number of arrangements = 3! × 4!

Choice (c)

Solution 16

5 boys can be selected out of 7 boys in $^7C_5$ ways.

3 girls can be selected out of 5 girls in $^5C_3$ ways.

Number of ways of making a group of 5 boys and 3 girls = $^7C_5 \times {}^5C_3$

= 21 × 10

= 210 ways.

Choice (b)

Solution 17

3 consonants can be selected out of 5 consonants in $^5C_3$ ways.

2 vowels can be selected out of 3 vowels in $^3C_2$ ways.

Number of words formed = $(^5C_3 \times {}^3C_2) \times 5!$ (∵ 5 selected letters arranged in 5! Ways)
= 3600.

Choice (d)

Solution 18

Total number of ways = (5 boys and 1 girl) or (4 boys and 2 girls)
= $(^5C_5 \times {}^8C_1) + (^5C_4 \times {}^8C_2)$
= (1 × 8) + (5 × 28)
= 148 ways.

Choice (b)

Solution 19

If one mechanical engineer and one electrical engineer have to be there in the team of four engineers, then the remaining two vacant places can be filled as follows:

Number of ways = (both mechanical) or (both electrical) or (1 electrical and 1 mechanical)
$$= (^5C_2) + (^3C_2) + (^5C_1 \times {}^3C_1)$$
$$= 10 + 3 + 15$$
$$= 28.$$

Choice (a)

Solution 20

As every question can be answered in 4 ways, hence the entire paper of 10 questions can be answered in 4^{10} ways.

Choice (c)

Solution 21

As every letter can be posted in 3 ways or in 3 letter boxes, hence 5 letters can be posted in 3^5 ways.

Choice (a)

Solution 22

The 1st prize can be won by any of the 8 students, 2nd prize can be won by any of the remaining 7 students and third prize can be won by any of the remaining 6 students, hence number of ways are as follows:

$$\frac{1^{st} \text{ Prize}}{8} \times \frac{2^{nd} \text{ Prize}}{7} \times \frac{3^{rd} \text{ Prize}}{6}.$$

Choice (b)

Solution 23

To deal with any question Raman has three ways as follows:
- 1st way – Not to attempt the question and proceed to next question
- 2nd way – To mark option as true
- 3rd way – To mark option as false

Total number of ways in which he can deal with these 10 questions are 3^{10} ways. In these number of ways it also includes a way in which he will not attempt any of the question. So if this way is eliminated the remaining number of ways in which he could have answered one or more questions is $3^{10}-1$.

Choice (b)

Solution 24

As the number should be between 50000 and 70000, the first digit needs to be either 5 or 6, and the remaining 4 digits can be selected in 7 ways each.

$$\frac{5}{} \times \frac{}{7} \times \frac{}{7} \times \frac{}{7} \times \frac{}{7} = 2401 \text{ numbers}$$

$$\frac{6}{} \times \frac{}{7} \times \frac{}{7} \times \frac{}{7} \times \frac{}{7} = 2401 \text{ numbers}$$

Possible number between 50000 to 60000 which can be formed using digits 3 to 9 = 4802.

Choice (d)

Solution 25

If the number is divisible by 5, the unit place should be either 0 or 5.

$$\frac{}{6} \times \frac{}{5} \times \frac{}{4} \times \frac{0}{} = 120 \text{ numbers}$$

$$\frac{}{6} \times \frac{}{5} \times \frac{}{5} \times \frac{5}{} = 100 \text{ numbers}$$

Total possible numbers are 220.

Choice (c)

Solution 26

First digit is 7. Number of ways to select it = 1

Second digit is an even natural number (*i.e.,* 2, 4, 6 or 8). Number of ways to select it = 4

If the last two digits are in ascending order, then from 10 available digits we need to select every time two digits such that the next digit is always greater than its previous digit, which can be done in $^{10}C_2$ ways.

Possible number plates $= 1 \times 4 \times {}^{10}C_2$
$= 180.$

Choice (c)

Solution 27

Total number of ways = (2 English and 2 Other) or (3 English and 1 Other)
$= ({}^3C_2 \times {}^{10}C_2) + ({}^3C_3 \times {}^{10}C_1)$
$= (3 \times 45) + (1 \times 10)$
$= 145.$

Choice (b)

Solution 28

As the books belonging to same subject are always together, hence we can treat 6 physics books as one single unit, 5 chemistry books as second unit and 4 biology books as third unit.

$$\underbrace{P1\ P2\ P3\ P4\ P5\ P6}_{1\ \text{unit}} \times \underbrace{C1\ C2\ C3\ C4\ C5}_{1\ \text{unit}} \times \underbrace{B1\ B2\ B3\ B4}_{1\ \text{unit}}$$

The 3 units can be arranged in 3! ways, while 6 physics books, 5 chemistry books and 4 biology books can be arranged among themselves in 6!, 5! and 4! ways respectively.

∴ Number of ways = 3! × 6! × 5! × 4!

Choice (d)

Solution 29

The word ADDRESS has 5 distinct letters A, R, E, D (2 times) and S (2 times). The number of ways in which 4 letters can be selected is as follows:

All 4 distinct letters $\Rightarrow {}^5C_4 = 5$ ways
2 similar and 2 distinct $\Rightarrow {}^2C_1 \times {}^4C_2 = 12$ ways
2 similar and 2 similar $\Rightarrow {}^2C_2 = 1$ way

∴ Total number of ways = 5 + 12 + 1
= 18 ways.

Choice (b)

Solution 30

The group of 8 persons can be divided in to two groups of 4 persons each in $\dfrac{8!}{4!\ 4!}$ ways.

Now on every circular table 4 persons can be arranged in 3! Ways.

Number of arrangements = $\dfrac{8!}{4!\ 4!} \times 3! \times 3!$
= 2520 ways.

Choice (c)

Solution 31

In this case there is no difference between clockwise and anticlockwise arrangement and these are not counted as a separate arrangement, as the necklace can be taken and turned back to back. Therefore the number of circular arrangement will be exactly half *i.e.,* 24!/2.

Choice (b)

Solution 32

Four girls can be arranged on a circular table in 3! Ways. Now there are four vacant places for 4 boys between them as shown.

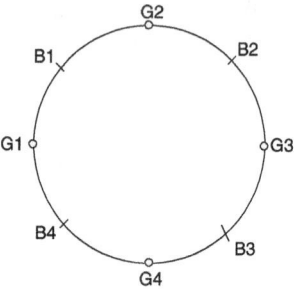

These 4 boys can be arranged in 4! Ways as their rotation is permitted. This will be considered as two separate rings in which if one ring is fixed and other is rotated, it will be counted as a separate arrangement.

∴ Arrangements possible = 3! 4!

Choice (c)

Solution 33

The color for first strip can be selected in 3 ways, while the color for remaining 4 strips can be selected in 2 ways each.

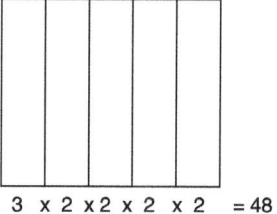

3 x 2 x 2 x 2 x 2 = 48

Choice (d)

Solution 34

Each variety of ice-cream can be deal in 2 ways *i.e.,* whether to select or not to select, hence total number of ways will be 2^8. In these number of ways it also includes a way in which none of the 8 varieties are selected, and if this is excluded the remaining number of ways are 2^8-1.

Choice (b)

Solution 35

The number of ways in which every time two different players can be selected out of 'n' players to count one game is $^nC_2$.

$$^nC_2 = 105$$

$$\frac{n!}{(n-2)!\,2!} = 105$$

$$\frac{n \times (n-1)}{2!} = 105$$

$$n \times (n-1) = 210$$

∴ $\quad n = 15.$

Choice (a)

19
Probability

INTRODUCTION

The word probability means chance or in a broad sense it is expressed as the possibility that a particular event may occur. Mathematically probability of any event 'E' is expressed as:

$$P(E) = \frac{\text{Favourable occurences}}{\text{Total possible occurences}} \text{ such that } 0 \leq P(E) \leq 1$$

The exact output of a random experiment cannot be predicted in advance, hence expressed as probability. The total possible occurrences are the all possible outcomes of an experiment. For example:

1. If a coin is tossed the total possible occurrences are 2 *i.e.*, {H, T}, if two coins are tossed then total possible occurrences are 2^2 *i.e.*, {HH, HT, TH, TT}. In fact the total possible outcomes for 'n' number of coins tossed together or a single coin tossed n times are 2^n.
2. If a dice is rolled the total possible occurrences are 6 *i.e.*, {1, 2, 3, 4, 5, 6}, if two dice are rolled together then total possible occurrences will be 6^2. In fact the total possible outcomes for 'n' number of dice rolled together or a single dice rolled n times are 6^n.
3. If 'n' number of cards is drawn from a well shuffled pack of 52 playing cards, then total possible occurrences will be $^{52}C_n$.

EVENTS

Events are defined as collection of one or more occurrences. For example we roll a dice we can define following 6 events as:

    Getting 1,   Getting 2,   Getting 3
    Getting 4,   Getting 5,   Getting 6

Equally likely events

Two events are said to be equally likely if their chance of happening is exactly same. For example if a dice is rolled, the possibility of any number appearing from 1 to 6 is equal. So in this trail we can say that six events are equally likely.

Compound events

When two or more events are in relation with each other, then they are known as compound events. For example if a coin is tossed two times, the event of getting head first time and tail in second time are compound events.

Mutually exclusive events

The events are said to be mutually exclusive if occurrence or non occurrence of one event affects the occurrence or non occurrence of any other event. For example if a dice is rolled, then the probability of getting an odd number or an even number are mutually exclusive. If odd number appears, even number wont appear and vice-versa. Hence occurrence of one event is affecting the non occurrence of other event.

Independent events

The events are said to be independent if occurrence or non occurrence of one event do not affects the occurrence or non occurrence of any other event. For example if two coins are tossed together then the face which appears on first coin is independent (or unaffected) of the face which appears on second coin.

ADDITION THEOREM ON PROBABILITY

If there are two sets A and B, then the number of elements in $A \cup B$ is given as:

$n(A \cup B) = n(A) + n(B) - n(A \cap B)$

A similar relation exists in probability theory expressed as:

$P(A \cup B) = P(A) + P(B) - P(A \cap B)$

If the events are mutually exclusive:

Then $P(A \cup B) = P(A) + P(B)$, because $P(A \cap B)$ is zero.

If the events are independent:

Then $P(A \cap B) = P(A) \times P(B)$

BIASED AND UNBIASED EXPERIMENTS

When we roll a dice the possibility of any number appearing is equal, hence we say this dice as an unbiased (or fair) dice. In a similar way if one or more number will turn up more frequently as compared to remaining numbers on the dice, then we call it as biased (or unfair) dice.

Please note that normally the problems appearing in competitive exams are of unbiased experiments. Hence unless it is specified in the problem, a coin or dice is to be treated as unbiased (or fair).

CLASSIFICATION OF PLAYING CARDS

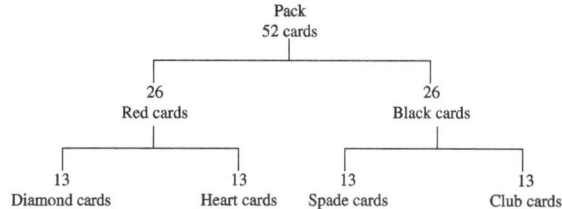

So there are four suits in a pack *i.e.,* Diamond, Heart, Spade and Club. In every suit of 13 cards there are 4 honor cards and 9 numbered cards.

Honor cards – *A, K, Q, J* out of which *K, Q* and *J* are called as face cards.

Numbered cards – Cards from 2 to 10 are called as numbered cards.

SOLVED EXAMPLES

Example 1

If 5 coins are tossed together, then find the probability of getting:
1. Exact 2 heads
2. At least 2 heads
3. At most 2 heads

Solution

1. Probability of getting exact 2 heads

    If 5 coins are tossed together total possible occurrences will be 2^5. The number of ways of getting exact 2 heads out of 5 heads will be $^5C_2$.

    $$P(\text{exact 2 heads}) = \frac{^5C_2}{2^5} = \frac{10}{32} = \frac{5}{16}$$

2. Probability of getting at least 2 heads

    In this case the number of heads can be 2, 3, 4 or all 5. So, the probability can be found as follows:

    $$P(\text{at least 2 heads}) = \frac{^5C_2}{2^5} + \frac{^5C_3}{2^5} + \frac{^5C_4}{2^5} + \frac{^5C_5}{2^5}$$

    $$= \frac{10}{32} + \frac{10}{32} + \frac{5}{32} + \frac{1}{32}$$

    $$= \frac{13}{16}$$

    Alternative Method

    As the sum of all the possibilities is equal to 1, therefore we can also eliminate the unwanted possibilities from 1 to get the required result.

    $P(\text{at least 2 heads}) = 1 - \{P(\text{No head}) \text{ or } P(\text{Exact 1 head})\}$

    $$= 1 - \left\{\frac{^5C_0}{2^5} + \frac{^5C_1}{2^5}\right\}$$

    $$= 1 - \left\{\frac{1}{32} + \frac{5}{32}\right\} = \frac{13}{16}$$

3. Probability of getting at most 2 heads
   In this case the number of heads can be 0, 1 or 2. So, the probability can be found as follows:

   $$P(\text{at most 2 heads}) = \frac{^5C_0}{2^5} + \frac{^5C_1}{2^5} + \frac{^5C_2}{2^5}$$

   $$= \frac{1}{32} + \frac{5}{32} + \frac{10}{32}$$

   $$= \frac{1}{2}.$$

Example 2

If two dice are rolled together then:
1. What is the probability that both dice shows a same number?
2. What is the probability that first dice shows a greater number than second dice?
3. What is the probability that sum of the score is greater than 4?
4. What is the probability that product of score is 12?

Solution

1. Probability that both dice shows a same number
   In this case 6 occurrences or combinations are favoring us out of 36 *i.e.*, (1, 1), (2, 2), (3, 3), (4, 4), (5, 5) and (6, 6)

   $$P = \frac{6}{36} = \frac{1}{6}$$

2. Probability that first dice shows greater number than second dice

   Total possibilities = 36

   Possibilities of getting same number = 6

   Remaining possibility (unequal number) = 36 − 6 = 30

   Half of these possibilities which give unequal numbers will have greater number on first dice and the other half will have greater number on second dice.

   $$P = \frac{15}{36} = \frac{5}{12}$$

3. Probability that sum of the score is greater than 4
   Following are the possibilities (or combinations) that will give sum as 4 or less than 4.
   Sum as 4 ⇒ (1, 3), (3, 1), (2, 2)
   Sum as 3 ⇒ (1, 2), (2, 1)
   Sum as 2 ⇒ (1, 1)
   $P(\text{sum greater than 4}) = 1 - P(\text{sum equal to or less than 4})$

   $$= 1 - \frac{6}{36} = \frac{30}{36} = \frac{5}{6}.$$

4. Probability that product of score is 12
   Following are the possibilities (or combinations) that will give the product of score on two dice as 12.
   Product as $12 \Rightarrow (2, 6), (3, 4), (4, 3)$ and $(6, 2)$
   $$P = \frac{4}{36} = \frac{1}{9}.$$

Example 3

Two balls are picked one after other from a bag containing 4 red and 6 green balls. Find the probability that first ball is red and second is green if:
1. First ball is replaced back
2. First ball is not replaced back.

Solution

1. First ball is replaced back
   $$P = \frac{4}{10} \times \frac{6}{10} = \frac{6}{25}.$$
2. First ball is not replaced
   $$P = \frac{4}{10} \times \frac{6}{9} = \frac{4}{15}.$$

Example 4

Probability that A dose the work is 1/3. Probability that B dose the work is 3/4. What is the probability that:
1. The work gets done
2. The work is not done.

Solution

The probability of A and B doing the work is:
$$P(A) = \frac{1}{3}, \ P(B) = \frac{3}{4}$$

Similarly the probability of A and B not doing the work is:
$$P(\overline{A}) = \frac{2}{3}, \ P(\overline{B}) = \frac{1}{4}$$

1. The work gets done
   P (work gets done) $= 1 - P$(both not doing the work)
   $$= 1 - \frac{2}{3} \times \frac{1}{4}$$
   $$= \frac{5}{6}.$$

2. The work is not done
   P (work is not done) = P (A and B both not doing the work)
   $$= \frac{2}{3} \times \frac{1}{4}$$
   $$= \frac{1}{6}.$$

Example 5

The odds against an event P are 3 to 4 and odds in favor of another event Q which is independent of former event P is 2 to 5. What is the probability that:
1. Exactly one of them occurs
2. At least one of them occurs.

Solution

There are 3 possibilities against event P and 4 possibilities in favor of event P.

$$\therefore P(P) = \frac{4}{7} \text{ and } P(\bar{P}) = \frac{3}{7}$$

Similarly there are 2 possibilities in favor of event Q and 5 possibilities against event Q.

$$\therefore P(Q) = \frac{2}{7} \text{ and } P(\bar{Q}) = \frac{5}{7}.$$

1. Probability that exactly one of them occurs
   This probability can be found as: Event P occurs and Q doesn't occur or event Q occurs and P doesn't occur.
   P (exactly one occurs) = {P(P) × P($\bar{Q}$)} or { P($\bar{P}$) × P(Q)}
   $$= \frac{4}{7} \times \frac{5}{7} + \frac{3}{7} \times \frac{2}{7}$$
   $$= \frac{26}{49}.$$

2. Probability that at least one of them occurs
   P (at least one occurs) = 1 – P (both doesn't occur)
   = 1 – P($\bar{P}$) × P($\bar{Q}$)
   $$= 1 - \frac{3}{7} \times \frac{5}{7} = 1 - \frac{15}{49} = \frac{34}{49}.$$

Example 6

If a card is drawn at random from a pack of 52 cards, find the probability that it is:
1. A red colored king
2. A numbered card

3. A black honor
4. Either a spade or a queen.

Solution

1. $P \text{ (red king)} = \dfrac{2}{52} = \dfrac{1}{26}$

2. $P \text{ (numbered card)} = \dfrac{36}{52} = \dfrac{9}{13}$

3. $P \text{ (black honor)} = \dfrac{8}{52} = \dfrac{2}{13}$

4. $P \text{ (either spade or queen)} = \dfrac{13+4-1}{52} = \dfrac{4}{13}$

$\because P(A \cup B) = P(A) + P(B) - P(A \cap B).$

EXERCISE

1. What is the probability that any single digit natural number selected at random is a multiple of 3?
   (a) 1/3
   (b) 2/3
   (c) 1/6
   (d) 1/9

2. If a coin is tossed for 5 times, what is the probability of getting head exactly once?
   (a) 1/2
   (b) 5/32
   (c) 1/32
   (d) 27/32

3. If a coin is tossed 3 times, what is the probability of getting tail at most once?
   (a) 1/3
   (b) 1/2
   (c) 2/3
   (d) 1/4

4. The probability of getting at least one head when 4 coins are tossed together is:
   (a) 1/16
   (b) 15/16
   (c) 3/16
   (d) 7/16

5. If 4 coins are tossed together, what is the probability of getting 2 heads and 2 tails?
   (a) 3/8
   (b) 6/11
   (c) 2/5
   (d) 4/5

6. If an unbiased coin is tossed four times, then probability that same face dose not show up in two consecutive trails is:
   (a) 1/8
   (b) 1/16
   (c) 3/16
   (d) 3/8

7. 6 dice are thrown simultaneously, what is the probability that all dice shows different faces?
   (a) $1/6^6$
   (b) $6!/6^6$
   (c) $6/6^6$
   (d) $5/6^6$

8. Two dice are thrown simultaneously, what is the probability that the sum obtained is less than 9?
   (a) 1/3
   (b) 21/36
   (c) 5/36
   (d) 13/18

9. When 3 dice are thrown simultaneously, what is the probability that the first dice shows a prime number, second dice shows an odd number and third dice shows an odd prime number?
   (a) 11/36
   (b) $21/6^3$
   (c) 1/12
   (d) $1/6^3$

10. Two dice are thrown simultaneously. What is the probability of getting two numbers whose product is an odd number?
    (a) 1/2
    (b) 1/3
    (c) 1/4
    (d) 1/5

11. Two dice are rolled together. What is the probability that the sum of the number on the two faces is divisible by 4 or 6?
    (a) 5/36
    (b) 1/9
    (c) 1/18
    (d) 1/12

12. Two letters are selected randomly from English alphabets. What is the probability that one is a consonant and other is a vowel?
    (a) 10/67
    (b) 21/65
    (c) 44/65
    (d) 2/13

13. A carton has 12 soft drink bottles in which 3 bottles are empty. If 4 bottles are taken out at random what is the probability of getting at least one filled bottle?
    (a) 3/10
    (b) 0
    (c) 7/10
    (d) 1

14. A basket contains 10 oranges in which three are rotten. If two oranges are selected from the basket, what is the probability that both of them are not rotten?
    (a) 2/5
    (b) 9/15
    (c) 7/15
    (d) 8/15

15. What is the probability that a leap year selected at random contains 53 Sundays?
    (a) 1/7
    (b) 2/7
    (c) 1/366
    (d) 1/365

16. In a family there are four children. What is the probability that it contains at least one male child?
    (a) 15/16
    (b) 1/8
    (c) 7/8
    (d) 1/16

17. There are 20 tokens numbered from 1 to 20. If one token is drawn at random then what is the probability that the token has a number which is a multiple of 2 or 3?
    (a) 4/5
    (b) 2/5
    (c) 11/20
    (d) 13/20

18. Three natural numbers are selected from first 10 natural numbers. The probability that their product is an odd number?
    (a) 1/10
    (b) 1/2
    (c) 1/12
    (d) 3/10

19. A box contains 10 glassware pieces with 3 defective in it, it is opened for examination. The probability that 6th draw contains the last broken piece is:
    (a) 1/12
    (b) 17/60
    (c) 7/12
    (d) 27/60

20. A committee of 3 members is to be formed from a group of 3 men and 5 women. What is the probability that all the committee members are women?
    (a) 1/8
    (b) 1/56
    (c) 5/28
    (d) 3/28

21. From a box containing six bulbs, of which exactly one half are good. Two bulbs are chosen at random to fit in 2 bulb holders in a room. The probability that room gets lighted is:
    (a) 1/5
    (b) 2/15
    (c) 4/15
    (d) 4/5

22. If two cards are drawn at random from the pack of 52 cards, what is the probability that one of these is diamond and other is a heart?
    (a) 13/102
    (b) 13/51
    (c) 1/2
    (d) 15/102

23. If two cards are drawn at random from the pack of 52 cards, what is the probability that both are diamond or both are heart?
    (a) 15/102
    (b) 7/51
    (c) 2/17
    (d) 15/51

24. A dice has 2 faces painted blue, 2 faces painted green and remaining 2 faces painted white. If the dice is rolled 3 times, what is the probability that same color appears every time?
    (a) 1/3
    (b) 1/9
    (c) 2/3
    (d) 2/9

25. A bag contains 5 white balls and 4 green balls. If two balls are drawn at random, what is the probability that both of them are of same color?
    (a) 1/9
    (b) 2/9
    (c) 4/9
    (d) 5/9

26. Out of two bags, first bag contains 3 red and 4 white balls, while second bag contains 5 red and 2 white balls. If one bag is selected at random and a ball is drawn out of it, what is the probability that it will be red colored?
    (a) 4/7
    (b) 5/7
    (c) 3/7
    (d) 6/7

27. A bag contains 5 red, 4 white and 3 yellow balls. If three balls are selected one after other from the bag without replacement, then what is the probability that first ball is red, second ball is white and third ball is yellow?
   (a) 1/4
   (b) 1/22
   (c) $\dfrac{^5C_1 \times {}^4C_1 \times {}^3C_1}{^{12}C_3}$
   (d) $\dfrac{^{12}C_1}{^{12}C_3}$

28. In a box, there are 8 red, 5 blue and 3 green balls. Two balls are picked up randomly. What is the probability that at least one of them is red?
   (a) 7/30
   (b) 1/15
   (c) 23/30
   (d) 19/120

29. If the letters of the word ARTICLE are arranged at random, then what is the probability that all the 3 vowels will be together?
   (a) 1/7!
   (b) 1/7
   (c) 5!/7!
   (d) 3!/7!

30. Four persons A, B, C and D went to a restaurant and occupied a circular table consisting of 4 chairs. What is the probability that A and D will be sitting opposite to each other?
   (a) 1/3
   (b) 1/4
   (c) 1/3!
   (d) 3/4

31. Six persons are seated in a row. Probability that two particular persons A and B are seated at the ends is:
   (a) 1/6
   (b) 1/3
   (c) 1/15
   (d) 1/24

32. If A and B are two mutually exclusive events such that $P(A) = 3 \times P(B)$, then $P(A \cup B)$ is:
   (a) 0
   (b) 1
   (c) 1/3
   (d) 2/3

33. If A and B are independent events such that $P(A) = 0.25$, $P(B) = 0.4$
   (a) 0.65
   (b) 0.1
   (c) 0.5
   (d) 0.55

34. A speaks the truth is 60% of the cases while B speaks in 80% of the cases. What is the probability that they will contradict each other in stating the same fact?
   (a) 7/10
   (b) 11/25
   (c) 1/10
   (d) 8/25

35. The odds against Ajay in solving a problem are 5:7 and the odds in favor of Vijay solving the same problem are 4:3. The probability that exactly one of them can solve the problem is:
   (a) 17/84
   (b) 23/84
   (c) 41/84
   (d) 53/84

36. A card is drawn from a pack of 52 cards. The probability of getting a queen of diamond or a king of heart is:
   (a) 1/13
   (b) 1/26
   (c) 2/13
   (d) 1/52

37. Two cards are drawn at random from a pack of 52 cards. What is the probability that both the cards drawn are black colored face card?
   (a) $^6C_2/^{52}C_2$
   (b) $8/^{52}C_2$
   (c) $^8C_2/^{52}C_2$
   (d) $6/^{52}C_2$

38. When 4 cards are drawn in succession from the pack of 52 cards with replacement, what is the probability that all the cards are from different suits?
   (a) 1/13
   (b) 1/256
   (c) 4/13
   (d) 1/64

39. Two cards are drawn from a pack one after the other without replacement. What is the probability that the first card is a diamond and the second is a black?
   (a) 1/8
   (b) 3/51
   (c) 13/102
   (d) 13/204

40. A card is drawn randomly from a pack of 52 cards. The probability that it is either a diamond or red honor is:
   (a) 21/52
   (b) 17/52
   (c) 8/13
   (d) 4/13

41. A card is drawn from the pack of 52 cards. What is the probability that the card is a numbered card or a red colored card?
   (a) 3/13
   (b) 2/13
   (c) 11/13
   (d) 4/13

42. A biased dice is such that an even number appears two times as frequently as an odd number. If the dice is rolled twice, then probability of getting both the times odd number is:
   (a) 5/9
   (b) 1/9
   (c) 8/9
   (d) 4/9

KEYS

1. (a)	2. (b)	3. (b)	4. (b)	5. (a)	6. (a)	7. (b)	8. (d)
9. (c)	10. (c)	11. (b)	12. (b)	13. (d)	14. (c)	15. (b)	16. (a)
17. (d)	18. (c)	19. (a)	20. (c)	21. (d)	22. (a)	23. (c)	24. (b)
25. (c)	26. (a)	27. (b)	28. (c)	29. (b)	30. (a)	31. (c)	32. (b)
33. (d)	34. (b)	35. (c)	36. (b)	37. (a)	38. (b)	39. (c)	40. (b)
41. (c)	42. (b)						

SOLUTIONS

Solution 1

There are 9 single digit natural numbers. Out of these the numbers which are multiples of 3 are 3, 6, and 9.

$$\therefore P = \frac{3}{9} = \frac{1}{3}.$$

Choice (a)

Solution 2

If the coin is tossed 5 times, total possible occurrences are 2^5. The favorable number of occurrences *i.e.*, the number of ways of getting head exactly 1 time out of 5 is $^5C_1$.

$$\therefore P = \frac{^5C_1}{2^5} = \frac{5}{32}.$$

Choice (b)

Solution 3

P (tail at most once) $= P$ (no tail) or P (exact 1 time tail)

$$= \frac{^3C_0}{2^3} + \frac{^3C_1}{2^3} = \frac{1}{8} + \frac{3}{8} = \frac{1}{2}.$$

Choice (b)

Solution 4

P (at least one head) $= 1 - P$ (no head)

$$= 1 - \frac{^4C_0}{2^4} = 1 - \frac{1}{16} = \frac{15}{16}.$$

Choice (b)

Solution 5

If we need 2 head and 2 tail to appear $\Rightarrow H H T T$

These 2 heads and 2 tails can be arranged in a total of $\frac{4!}{2!\,2!}$ ways *i.e.*, 6 ways

$$P \text{ (2H and 2T)} = \frac{6}{2^4} = \frac{3}{8}.$$

Choice (a)

Solution 6

If a coin is tossed 4 times then total possible occurrences are 2^4. Out of these only two occurrences will favor *i.e.,* {H T H T} or {T H T H}

$\therefore \quad P = \dfrac{2}{2^4} = \dfrac{1}{8}.$

Choice (a)

Solution 7

There are 6 faces on each dice and 6 such dice. The number of ways in which each dice shows a different face is 6!

$\therefore \quad P = \dfrac{6!}{6^6}.$

Choice (b)

Solution 8

Let us first find out all the possibilities which give us sum 9 or more than 9.
Sum 9 $\Rightarrow$ (4, 5), (5, 4), (6, 3), (3, 6)
Sum 10 $\Rightarrow$ (5, 5), (4, 6), (6, 4)
Sum 11 $\Rightarrow$ (6, 5), (5, 6)
Sum 12 $\Rightarrow$ (6, 6)
P (sum is less than 9) $= 1 - P$ (sum is 9 or more than 9) $= 1 - \dfrac{10}{6^2} = \dfrac{26}{36}$ or $\dfrac{13}{18}.$

Choice (d)

Solution 9

Favorable cases in which first dice shows a prime number $\Rightarrow$ 2, 3 and 5
Favorable cases in which second dice shows an odd number $\Rightarrow$ 1, 3 and 5
Favorable cases in which third dice shows an odd prime number $\Rightarrow$ 1 and 3

$\therefore \quad P = \dfrac{3}{6} \times \dfrac{3}{6} \times \dfrac{2}{6} = \dfrac{1}{12}.$

Choice (c)

Solution 10

For the product of numbers to be odd, both the dice must show an odd number ($\because$ odd $\times$ odd = odd).

$\therefore \quad P = \dfrac{3}{6} \times \dfrac{3}{6} = \dfrac{1}{4}.$

Choice (c)

Solution 11

The sum of numbers which are divisible by 4 $\Rightarrow$ 4, 8 and 12.
The sum of numbers which are divisible by 6 $\Rightarrow$ 6 and 12.

$$P \text{ (sum divisible by 4 or 6)} = \frac{3+2-1}{6^2} = \frac{1}{9}.$$

Choice (b)

Solution 12

The total possible occurrences or number of ways of selecting 2 alphabets out of 26 is $^{26}C_2$
Number of ways of getting 1 consonant out of 21 consonants = $^{21}C_1$
Number of ways of getting 1 vowel out of 5 vowels = $^{5}C_1$

$$\therefore P = \frac{^{21}C_1 \times {^5C_1}}{^{26}C_2} = \frac{21 \times 5}{13 \times 25} = \frac{21}{65}.$$

Choice (b)

Solution 13

P (at least 1 filled bottle) = 1

Because in case if all 3 empty bottles comes in the selection of 4 bottles, still 1 filled bottle will be there, hence the chances are 100%.

Choice (d)

Solution 14

The total possible occurrences or number of ways of selecting 2 Oranges out of 10 is $^{10}C_2$

Favorable number of ways of getting two oranges which are not rotten = $^{7}C_2$

$$\therefore P = \frac{^{7}C_2}{^{10}C_2} = \frac{21}{45} = \frac{7}{15}.$$

Choice (c)

Solution 15

An ordinary year (of 365 days) consists of 52 weeks and 1 odd day. Probability that this odd day is Sunday is 1/7.

In a similar way leap year (of 366 days) consists of 52 weeks and 2 odd days. Probability that out of these two odd days, one day will be Sunday is 2/7.

Choice (b)

Solution 16

Every child can be either a male or female, so if there are 4 children the total possible occurrences will be 2^4.

P (at least one male child) $= 1 - P$ (all female child)
$$= 1 - \frac{1}{2^4} = \frac{15}{16}.$$

Choice (a)

Solution 17

The total possible occurrences or number of ways of selecting 1 token out of 20 is $^{20}C_1$
Favorable number which are multiple of $2 \Rightarrow 2, 4, 6, 8, 10, 12, 14, 16, 18$ and 20.
Favorable number which are multiple of $3 \Rightarrow 3, 6, 9, 12, 15$ and 18.

$$\therefore \quad P = \frac{10+6-3}{20} = \frac{13}{20}.$$

Choice (d)

Solution 18

For the product to be odd, it is necessary that all the three numbers should be odd. In first 10 natural numbers there are 5 odd numbers.
So, the total possible occurrences or number of ways of selecting 3 numbers out of 10 is $^{10}C_3$
Similarly the number of ways of getting 3 odd numbers out of 5 is $^5C_3$,

$$\therefore \quad P = \frac{^5C_3}{^{10}C_3} = \frac{10}{120} = \frac{1}{12}$$

Choice (c)

Solution 19

Good pieces $= 7$
Broken pieces $= 3$

If the 6th draw contains last broken pieces, it means first 5 draws contains 3 good pieces and 2 broken pieces. Also, at the time of 6th draw there are 4 good pieces and 1 broken piece.

1st 5 draws   6th draw

$$\therefore P = \frac{^7C_3 \times {}^3C_2}{^{10}C_5} \times \frac{1}{5} = \frac{5}{12} \times \frac{1}{5} = \frac{1}{12}.$$

Choice (a)

Solution 20

The total possible occurrences or number of ways of selecting 3 members out of 8 is $^8C_3$

$\therefore$ P (all women) = $\dfrac{^5C_3}{^8C_3} = \dfrac{10}{56} = \dfrac{5}{28}$.

Choice (c)

Solution 21

Number of good bulbs = 3
Number of defective bulbs = 3

The room gets lighted if at least one bulb is good. The total possible occurrences or number of ways of selecting 2 bulbs out of 6 is $^6C_2$.

$\therefore$ P (at least one good bulb) = $1 - P$ (all are defective bulbs)

$$= 1 - \dfrac{^3C_2}{^6C_2} = 1 - \dfrac{3}{15} = \dfrac{4}{5}.$$

Choice (d)

Solution 22

The total possible occurrences or number of ways of selecting 2 cards out of 52 is $^{52}C_2$

P (1 diamond and 1 heart) = $\dfrac{^{13}C_1 \times {}^{13}C_1}{^{52}C_2} = \dfrac{13 \times 13}{26 \times 51} = \dfrac{13}{102}$.

Choice (a)

Solution 23

The total possible occurrences or number of ways of selecting 2 cards out of 52 is $^{52}C_2$

P (both diamond or both heart) = $\dfrac{^{13}C_2 + {}^{13}C_2}{^{52}C_2} = \dfrac{2 \times (13 \times 6)}{26 \times 51} = \dfrac{2}{17}$.

Choice (c)

Solution 24

P (same color appear) = P (3 times blue) or P (3 times green) or P (3 times white)

$$= \left(\dfrac{2}{6} \times \dfrac{2}{6} \times \dfrac{2}{6}\right) + \left(\dfrac{2}{6} \times \dfrac{2}{6} \times \dfrac{2}{6}\right) + \left(\dfrac{2}{6} \times \dfrac{2}{6} \times \dfrac{2}{6}\right) = \dfrac{1}{9}.$$

Choice (b)

Solution 25

Number of white balls = 5
Number of green balls = 4

The total possible occurrences or number of ways of selecting 2 balls out of 9 is $^9C_2$

P (both are of same color) = $\dfrac{^5C_2 + {^4C_2}}{^9C_2} = \dfrac{10+6}{36} = \dfrac{4}{9}.$

Choice (c)

Solution 26

In bag-1 $\Rightarrow$ 3 red balls and 4 white balls
In bag-2 $\Rightarrow$ 5 red balls and 2 white balls

P (getting a red colored ball) = P (selecting any one bag) $\times P$ (getting red ball from selected bag)

$$= \dfrac{1}{2} \times \left(\dfrac{3}{7} + \dfrac{5}{7}\right)$$
$$= \dfrac{4}{7}.$$

Choice (a)

Solution 27

Number of red balls = 5
Number of white balls = 4
Number of yellow balls = 3

$\therefore P$ (1st red, 2nd white and 3rd yellow) = $\dfrac{5}{12} \times \dfrac{4}{11} \times \dfrac{3}{10} = \dfrac{1}{22}.$

Choice (b)

Solution 28

Number of red balls = 8
Number of blue balls = 5
Number of green balls = 3

The total possible occurrences or number of ways of selecting 2 balls out of 16 is $^{16}C_2$

$\therefore P$ (at least 1 red color ball) = $1 - P$ (both ball other than red)

$$= 1 - \dfrac{^8C_2}{^{16}C_2} = 1 - \dfrac{28}{120} = \dfrac{23}{30}.$$

Choice (c)

Solution 29

Total possible occurrences or the number of ways in which letters of the word ARTICLE be permuted are 7! ways.

Number of ways in which all the three vowels (*i.e.*, A, I and E) will be together can be found as follows:

$$\underset{1}{\underline{AIE}}\ \underset{2}{\underline{R}}\ \underset{3}{\underline{T}}\ \underset{4}{\underline{C}}\ \underset{5}{\underline{L}}$$

5 units can be arranged in 5! ways and the 3 vowels can be arranged among themselves in further 3! ways. Therefore favorable number of occurrences are $3! \times 5!$

$$P = \frac{3 \times 5!}{7!} = \frac{1}{7}.$$

Choice (b)

Solution 30

Four persons can occupy four chairs on a circular table in 3! or 6 ways. Out of these 6 ways, in 2 ways *A* and *D* are opposite to each other.

$$\therefore \quad P = \frac{2}{6} = \frac{1}{3}.$$

Choice (a)

Solution 31

Six persons can be arranged in a row in 6! number of ways. Out of these if two persons A and B are fixed at the end then in between 4 persons can be arranged in 4! number of ways.

$$P = \frac{4!\ 2!}{6!} = \frac{1}{15}.$$

Choice (c)

Solution 32

Given $\quad P(A) = 3 \times P(B)$
$\quad P(A) + P(B) = 1$
$3 \times P(B) + P(B) = 1$
$\quad 4 \times P(B) = 1$

$\therefore \qquad P(B) = \frac{1}{4}$ and $\quad P(A) = \frac{3}{4}$

If *A* and *B* are mutually exclusive events:

$$P(A \cup B) = P(A) + P(B) = \frac{1}{4} + \frac{3}{4} = 1.$$

Choice (b)

Solution 33

If A and B are independent events:

$P(A \cup B) = P(A) + P(B) - P(A \cap B)$
$= 0.25 + 0.4 - (0.25 \times 0.4)$
$= 0.65 - 0.1$
$= 0.55.$

Choice (d)

Solution 34

The probability that A and B are speaking the truth is:

$P(A) = \dfrac{3}{5}$ and $P(B) = \dfrac{4}{5}$

The probability that A and B not speaking the truth is:

$P(\overline{A}) = 1 - \dfrac{3}{5} = \dfrac{2}{5}$ and $P(\overline{B}) = 1 - \dfrac{4}{5} = \dfrac{1}{5}$

A and B will contradict each other in stating the same fact when exactly one of them is speaking truth.

P (A and B will contradict) = $\{P(A)$ and $P(\overline{B})\}$ or $\{P(\overline{A})$ and $P(B)\}$

$= \dfrac{3}{5} \times \dfrac{1}{5} + \dfrac{2}{5} \times \dfrac{4}{5} = \dfrac{11}{25}.$

Choice (b)

Solution 35

There are 5 possibilities against Ajay solving the problem and 7 possibilities in favor of Ajay solving the problem.

$\therefore P(A) = \dfrac{7}{12}$ and $P(\overline{A}) = \dfrac{5}{12}$

Similarly there are 4 possibilities in favor of Vijay solving the problem and 3 possibilities against Vijay solving the problem.

$\therefore P(V) = \dfrac{4}{7}$ and $P(\overline{V}) = \dfrac{3}{7}$

Probability that exactly one of them solves the problem can be found as follows:

$P = \{P(A) \times P(\overline{V})\}$ or $\{P(V) \times P(\overline{A})\}$

$= \dfrac{7}{12} \times \dfrac{3}{7} + \dfrac{4}{7} \times \dfrac{5}{12} = \dfrac{41}{84}.$

Choice (c)

Solution 36

In a pack of 52 cards there is 1 queen of diamond and 1 king of heart, so out of 52 cards 2 cards are favoring us.

$$\therefore \ P = \frac{1+1}{52} = \frac{1}{26}.$$

Choice (b)

Solution 37

The total possible occurrences or number of ways to select 2 cards out of 52 is $^{52}C_2$.

There are 6 black colored face cards which are favoring us, and the number of ways of getting any two cards out of it is $^6C_2$.

$$\therefore \ P = \frac{^6C_2}{^{52}C_2}.$$

Choice (a)

Solution 38

If 4 cards are drawn in succession and not simultaneously then it becomes 4 independent events.

$$P = P(1 \text{ Heart}) \text{ and } P(1 \text{ Diamond}) \text{ and } P(1 \text{ Club}) \text{ and } P(1 \text{ Spade})$$
$$= \frac{13}{52} \times \frac{13}{52} \times \frac{13}{52} \times \frac{13}{52}$$
$$= \frac{1}{256}.$$

Choice (b)

Solution 39

1st Diamond 2nd Black

$$P = \frac{13}{52} \times \frac{26}{51} \quad (\because \text{The first card is not replaced back})$$
$$= \frac{13}{102}.$$

Choice (c)

Solution 40

In a pack of 52 cards there are 13 diamonds and 8 red honor cards, so out of 52 cards 21 cards are favoring us. But there are some common cards *i.e.,* 4 honor diamond cards which are counted twice, hence need to be eliminated.

$\therefore \quad P = \dfrac{13+8-4}{52}$

$= \dfrac{17}{52}.$

Choice (b)

Solution 41

In a pack of 52 cards there are 36 numbered cards and 26 red colored cards. But there are some common cards like half the numbered cards are red in color. Similarly out of 26 red color cards 18 are numbered cards.

$\therefore \quad P = \dfrac{36+26-18}{52}$

$= \dfrac{11}{13}.$

Choice (c)

Solution 42

$P(E) = 2 \times P(O)$
$P(E) + P(O) = 1$
$2 \times P(O) + P(O) = 1$
$\therefore P(O) = \dfrac{1}{3}$ and $P(E) = \dfrac{2}{3}$

$P \text{ (both times odd)} = \dfrac{1}{3} \times \dfrac{1}{3}$

$= \dfrac{1}{9}.$

Choice (b)

20

Clocks

Whenever we consider a clock, immediately a 360° circle comes to our mind. Let's take a dial of a clock which is divided into 12 equal parts.

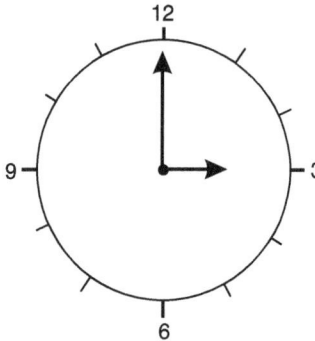

As the 360° circle is divided into 12 equal parts, each part will be 30°. If the minute hand is moving ahead by 30°, we say it has gone ahead by 5 min. As 30° is covered by minute hand in 5 min, therefore it can cover 6° in 1min. We can also say that the circumference of the clock is divided in to 60 equal parts, so each part is 6°.

From the figure we can see that the clock is showing a time of sharp 3'O clock. After an hour (or 60 min) the clock will indicate 4'O clock. It means the hour hand of clock is moving ahead by 30° in 60 min. So, it can cover ½° in 1 min. As minute hand runs at a speed of 6° per min while hour hand at as speed of ½° per min, hence minute hand gains 5½° over hour hand every min.

Minute hand can overtake the hour hand if it gains complete 360° over hour hand. If 1 min is required to gain 5½° over hour hand, hence to gain 360°, it will require $65\frac{5}{11}$ min. So, we can say that the minute hand of the clock overtakes the hour hand after every $65\frac{5}{11}$ min.

The hour and the minute hand of clock move in relation to each other continuously. If the time shown by clock is known, the angle between hands can be calculated. Similarly, if the angle between two hands is known, the time shown by the clock can be found out

POINTS TO NOTE

- Speed of seconds hand = 360° per min.
- Speed of minute hand = 6° per min.

- Speed of hour hand = ½° per min.
- Relative speed of hour and minute hand = 5½° per min.
- Gap between minute and hour hand increases/reduces by 5½° every min.
- Minute and Hour hands will coincide 11 times in 12 hrs.
- Minute and Hour hand will be opposite 11 times in 12 hrs.
- Minute and Hour hands will make any angle (up to 180°) 22 times in 12 hrs.
- Actual time in the clock + Time seen in mirror image = 12 hrs
- Minute and hour hands will coincide after every $65\frac{5}{11}$ min.

SOLVED EXAMPLES

Example 1

What is the angle between the minute hand and hour hand of a clock at 4:20?

Solution

Consider the time as sharp 4'O clock. The angle between hour and minute hand at this time is 120°.

In the next 20 min
Angle covered by minute hand = 20 × 6 = 120°
Angle covered by hour hand = 20 × ½ = 10°

Minute hand will try to coincide, but hour hand will move ahead by 10°, hence the angle between them will be 10°.

Example 2

At what time between 7 and 8'O clock the minute and hour hands of clocks coincide?

Solution

Consider the time as sharp 7'O clock. The angle between hour and minute hand at this time is 210°. We just want to calculate the time when this 210° becomes 0°. As minute hand runs at a speed of 6° per min while hour hand at as speed of ½° per min, hence minute hand gains 5½° over hour hand every min. It also means that the gap between minute and hour hand is reduced by 5½° ever min.

5½° gap reduced in → 1 min
210° gap reduced in → x min

$$x = \frac{210}{5\frac{1}{2}} = \frac{210}{11/2} = 38\frac{2}{11} \text{ min.}$$

Hence the hands will coincide at $7 : 38\frac{2}{11}$.

Example 3

At what time between 9 and 10'O clock the minute and hour hands of clocks will be opposite?

Solution

Consider the time as sharp 9'O clock. The angle between hour and minute hand at this time is 90°. To make the hands opposite the angle between them should be 180°, so we want to calculate the time when this gap is further increased by 90°. The gap between minute and hour hand is increased by 5½° ever min.

5½° gap increases in → 1 min
90° gap increases in → x min

$$x = \frac{90}{5\frac{1}{2}} = \frac{90}{11/2} = 16\frac{4}{11} \text{ min}.$$

Hence the hands will coincide at $9:16\frac{4}{11}$.

Example 4

A clock loses 5 min every hour and other gains 5 min every hour. If they are set at 10 a.m. on Monday, then when will they be 12 hrs apart?

Solution

As one clock loses 5 min and other gains 5 min every hour, so they will differ by 10 min every hr.

For 10 min difference → 1 hr required
For 12 hrs (720 min) difference → x hrs required

$$x = \frac{720}{10} = 72 \text{ hrs (or 3 days)}$$

So, they will be 12 hrs apart after 3 days *i.e.,* 10 a.m. on Thursday.

Example 5

A clock which loses uniformly was observed to be 5 min fast at 10:00 a.m. on Sunday. On the subsequent Tuesday at 10:00 a.m. the clock was 7 min slow. When did the clock show correct time?

Solution

Sunday 10:00 a.m. → 5 min faster than correct time
Tuesday 10:00 a.m. → 7 min slower than correct time

The duration from Sunday 10:00 a.m. to Tuesday 10:00 a.m. is of 48 hrs. The clock which was running faster before 48 hrs has lost those 5 min and now becomes slower by 7 more min.

Hence the clock has lost total 12 min in this span of 48 hrs. The clock will show the correct time, the moment it looses these 5 min by which it was faster.

To loose 12 min → 48 hrs required
To loose 5 min → x hrs required

$$x = \frac{48 \times 5}{12} = 20 \text{ hrs}$$

The clock will show correct time 20 hrs after Sunday 10:00 a.m. *i.e.*, on Monday 6:00 a.m.

Example 6

A clock is set right at 6:00 a.m. The clock gains 10 min in 24 hrs. What will be the true time when clock indicates 11:00 a.m. on the following day?

Solution

Time from 6:00 a.m. to 11:00 a.m. on following day = 29 hrs

24 hrs and 10 min of this clock = 24 hrs of correct clock

$24\frac{1}{6}$ hrs of this clock → 24 hrs in actual

29 hrs of this clock → x hrs in actual

$$x = \frac{24 \times 29}{24\frac{1}{6}}$$

$$x = 24 \times 29 \times \frac{6}{145} = 28 \text{ hrs and } 48 \text{ min in actual.}$$

So, the correct time will be 28 hrs and 48 min past 6:00 a.m. *i.e.*, 10:48 a.m. on the following day.

Example 7

The minute hand of a clock overtakes the hour hand after every 65 min of correct time. How much time the clock gain or lose in a day?

Solution

Minute and hour hands of a normal clock will coincide (or overlaps) after every $65\frac{5}{11}$ min.

As the minute and hour hands of this clock coincides after every 65 min, hence this clock is running faster than a normal clock.

Time gained = $\left(65\frac{5}{11} - 65\right) = \frac{5}{11}$ min in every 65 min of run of a normal clock

In 65 min run → $\frac{5}{11}$ min gain

In 24 hrs run → x min gain

$$x = \frac{24 \times 60 \times 5}{65 \times 11}$$

$$= 10\frac{10}{143} \text{ min}$$

So, the clock will gain $10\frac{10}{143}$ min in 24 hrs.

EXERCISE

1. What is the angle covered by minute hand in 25 min?
   (a) 120°   (b) 150°
   (c) 160°   (d) 180°

2. What is the angle covered by hour hand in 36 min?
   (a) 6°   (b) 12°
   (c) 18°   (d) 24°

3. By how many degrees the hour hand will lag behind the minute hand of a clock in a span of 10 min?
   (a) 52°   (b) 55°
   (c) 56°   (d) 58°

4. If the seconds hand covers 900°, then how many degrees hour hand move in the same time?
   (a) $1\frac{1}{4}$ (b) $1\frac{1}{2}$
   (c) $2\frac{1}{2}$ (d) $2\frac{3}{4}$

5. A clock shows 6'O clock in the morning. Through how many degrees the hour hand of clock will rotate when it is 2'O clock in the afternoon?
   (a) 120°   (b) 180°
   (c) 220°   (d) 240°

6. What is the angle between the minute hand and hour hand of a clock at 6:50?
   (a) 90°   (b) 95°
   (c) 120°   (d) 145°

7. What is the angle between the minute hand and hour hand of a clock at 8:30?
   (a) 75°   (b) 80°
   (c) 65°   (d) 60°

8. If the minute hand is pointing towards south direction at 4:30, then in which direction hour hand will point?
   (a) South-West   (b) South-East
   (c) North-West   (d) North-East

9. If the reflection of a wall clock in a mirror shows the time as 3 hrs and 20 min, then what is the actual time in the clock?
   (a) 7:40
   (b) 7:50
   (c) 8:40
   (d) 8:20

10. If the actual time in the clock is 10:10, then what time can be seen in its mirror reflection?
    (a) 1:40
    (b) 1:50
    (c) 2:40
    (d) 2:50

11. How many times are the hands of the clock at right angle in a day?
    (a) 22
    (b) 24
    (c) 44
    (d) 48

12. How many times will the minute and hour hands of a clock are opposite to each other between 1 p.m. to 9 p.m. of a day?
    (a) 6
    (b) 7
    (c) 8
    (d) 9

13. How many times the minute hand of the clock will be opposite to hour hand from 4 p.m. on Monday to 10:00 a.m. on subsequent Wednesday?
    (a) 46
    (b) 44
    (c) 40
    (d) 38

14. How many times the minute and hour hand of the clock will coincide from 9 a.m. on Sunday to 2:00 p.m. on subsequent Tuesday?
    (a) 46
    (b) 47
    (c) 48
    (d) 49

15. At what time between 2'O clock and 3'O clock, will minute and hour hands of clock coincide?
    (a) 2:10
    (b) $2:10\frac{2}{11}$
    (c) $2:10\frac{10}{11}$
    (d) $2:11\frac{5}{11}$

16. At what time between 4'O clock and 5'O clock, will minute and hour hands of clock coincide?
    (a) $4:21\frac{9}{11}$
    (b) $4:20\frac{9}{11}$
    (c) $4:22\frac{9}{11}$
    (d) $4:22\frac{10}{11}$

17. At what time between 12:00 noon and 1:00 p.m. the minute and hour hands of clock will be opposite?
    (a) $12:30\frac{9}{11}$
    (b) $12:32\frac{8}{11}$
    (c) 12:30
    (d) $12:31\frac{2}{11}$

18. At what time between 4:00 to 4:30, minute and hour hand will be making an angle of 60°?
    (a) $4:10\frac{2}{11}$
    (b) $4:10\frac{10}{11}$
    (c) $4:11\frac{10}{11}$
    (d) $4:12\frac{10}{11}$

19. At what time between 5:30 to 6:00, minute and hour hand will be making an angle of 90°?
    (a) 5:45
    (b) $5:42\frac{10}{11}$
    (c) $5:44\frac{8}{11}$
    (d) $5:43\frac{7}{11}$

20. A clock which was gaining time uniformly was observed to be 3 min slow at 7 a.m. on a Friday. On a subsequent Sunday at 4 a.m., the clock was 12 min fast. When did the clock show correct time?
    (a) Friday 4:00 p.m.
    (b) Saturday 2:00 a.m.
    (c) Saturday 4:00 p.m.
    (d) Sunday 12:00 midnight

21. A clock which was gaining time uniformly was observed to be 8 min slow at 6 a.m. on a Sunday. On a subsequent Tuesday at 12:00 noon, the clock was 10 min fast. When did the clock show correct time?
    (a) Sunday 8:00 p.m.
    (b) Monday 6:00 a.m.
    (c) Monday 8:00 a.m.
    (d) Tuesday 2:00 a.m.

22. A clock which loses time uniformly was observed to be 3 min fast at 3:00 p.m. on Tuesday. On the subsequent Thursday at 10 p.m., the clock was 8 min slow. When did the clock show correct time?
    (a) Tuesday 11:00 p.m.
    (b) Wednesday 3:00 a.m.
    (c) Wednesday 6:00 a.m.
    (d) Thursday 2:00 a.m.

23. A clock loses 2 min every hour and other clock gains 1 min in every 2 hrs. If both these clocks are set at 12:00 noon on Monday, then after how much hours the difference between the timing of these clocks will be 6 hrs?
    (a) 120 hrs
    (b) 132 hrs
    (c) 144 hrs
    (d) 156 hrs

24. If the minute and hour hands of clock overlaps in every 64 min of correct time, then how much time the dose the clock gain or lose in 12 hrs?
    (a) $16\frac{4}{11}$ min gain
    (b) $32\frac{8}{11}$ min gain
    (c) $16\frac{4}{11}$ min loss
    (d) $32\frac{8}{11}$ min loss

25. If the minute and hour hands of clock overlaps in every 66 min of correct time, then how much time the dose the clock gain or lose in a day?
    (a) $10\frac{59}{121}$ min gain
    (b) $11\frac{109}{121}$ min gain
    (c) $10\frac{59}{121}$ min loss
    (d) $11\frac{109}{121}$ min loss

26. The number of minutes from 4'O clock to now is five times the number of minutes from now to 8'O clock. Find the present time.
    (a) 6:20
    (b) 6:40
    (c) 7:20
    (d) 7:30

27. The number of minutes from present time to 6'O clock is four times the number of minutes from 3'O clock to the time 15 min ago. The present time is:
    (a) 3:51
    (b) 4: 15
    (c) 4:45
    (d) 5:25

28. A clock which looses time uniformly was 10 min fast at 8:00 a.m. After 2 hrs, the timing of this clock exactly matches with the actual timing. When this clock shows 3:30 on the same day, then what is the actual time?
    (a) 4:00 p.m.
    (b) 4:30 p.m.
    (c) 4:40 p.m.
    (d) 5:00 p.m.

KEYS

1. (b)	2. (c)	3. (b)	4. (a)	5. (d)	6. (b)	7. (a)	8. (b)
9. (c)	10. (b)	11. (c)	12. (b)	13. (d)	14. (c)	15. (c)	16. (a)
17. (b)	18. (b)	19. (d)	20. (a)	21. (b)	22. (c)	23. (c)	24. (a)
25. (d)	26. (c)	27. (a)	28. (a)				

SOLUTIONS

Solution 1

As speed of minute hand is 6° per min, hence angle covered = 6 × 25 = 150°

Choice (b)

Solution 2

As speed of hour hand is ½° per min, hence angle covered = ½ × 36 = 18°

Choice (c)

Solution 3

Angle covered by minute hand in 10 min = 6 × 10 = 60°
Angle covered by hour hand in 10 min = ½ × 10 = 5°
Hour hand will lag behind minutes hand by 55°.

Choice (b)

Solution 4

Speed of seconds hand = 360° per min.

Time taken by seconds hand to cover 900° = $\frac{900}{360} = \frac{5}{2}$ min.

Angle covered by hour hand in $\frac{5}{2}$ min = $\frac{1}{2} \times \frac{5}{2} = \frac{5}{4}$ or $1\frac{1}{4}°$.

Choice (a)

Solution 5

From 6:00 a.m. in morning to 2:00 p.m. in afternoon it's duration of 8 hrs.

As hour hand moves 30° in every hour, so in 8 hrs it will cover 240°.

Choice (d)

Solution 6

Consider the time as sharp 6'O clock. The angle between hour and minute hand at this time is 180°.

In the next 50 min:
Angle covered by minute hand = 50 × 6 = 300° (or 180° + 120° ahead)
Angle covered by hour hand = 50 × ½ = 25°
Angle at 6:50 = 120° − 25° = 95°.

Choice (b)

Solution 7

Consider the time as sharp 8'O clock. The angle between hour and minute hand at this time is 240°.

In the next 30 min:
Angle covered by minute hand = 30 × 6 = 180°
Angle covered by hour hand = 30 × ½ = 15°
Angle at 8:30 = (240° − 180°) + 15° = 75°.

Choice (a)

Solution 8

Hour hand will point in South-East direction.

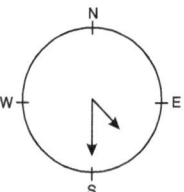

Choice (b)

Solution 9

Actual time in the clock + Time seen in mirror image = 12 hrs

Actual time in the clock + 3:20 = 12

Actual time in the clock = 12 – 3:20 = 8:40.

Choice (c)

Solution 10

Actual time in the clock + Time seen in mirror image = 12 hrs
10:10 + Time seen in mirror image = 12
Time seen in mirror image = 12 – 10:10 = 1:50.

Choice (b)

Solution 11

In 12 hrs of span any angle (up to 180°) minute and hour hand will make 22 times.

So, in a day of 24 hrs minute and hour hands will be 90° for 44 times.

Choice (c)

Solution 12

From 1:00 to 2:00, 1 time
From 2:00 to 3:00, 1 time
From 3:00 to 4:00, 1 time
From 4:00 to 5:00, 1 time
From 5:00 to 7:00, 1 time (at 6'O clock)
From 7:00 to 8:00, 1 time
From 8:00 to 9:00, 1 time

Hence minute and hour hand will be opposite (180°) for 7 times.

Choice (b)

Solution 13

Monday 4 p.m. to Tuesday 4 p.m. → 24 hrs, hence 22 times opposite

Tuesday 4 p.m. to Wednesday 4 a.m. → 12 hrs, hence 11 times opposite

On Wednesday:
       From 4 a.m. to 5 a.m., 1 time
       From 5 a.m. to 7 a.m., 1 time (at 6' O clock)
       From 7 a.m. to 8 a.m., 1 time
       From 8 a.m. to 9 a.m., 1 time

From 9 a.m. to 10 a.m., 1 time
Total = 22 + 11 + 5 =38 times.

Choice (d)

Solution 14

Sunday 9 a.m. to Monday 9 a.m. → 24 hrs, hence 22 times
Monday 9 a.m. to Tuesday 9 a.m. → 24 hrs, hence 22 times

On Tuesday:
From 9 a.m. to 10 a.m., 1 time
From 10 a.m. to 11 a.m., 1 time
From 11 a.m. to 1 p.m., 1 time (at 12:00 noon)
From 1 p.m. to 2 p.m., 1 time
Total = 22 + 22 + 4 =48 times.

Choice (c)

Solution 15

Consider the time as sharp 2'O clock. The angle between hour and minute hand at this time is 60°. We just want to calculate the time when this 60° becomes 0°. As minute hand runs at a speed of 6° per min while hour hand at as speed of ½° per min, hence minute hand gains 5½° over hour hand every min. It also means that the gap between minute and hour hand is reduced by 5½° ever min.

5½° gap reduced in → 1 min
60° gap reduced in → x min

$$x = \frac{60}{5\frac{1}{2}} = \frac{60}{11/2} = 10\frac{10}{11} \text{ min}$$

Hence the hands will coincide at $2:10\frac{10}{11}$.

Choice (c)

Solution 16

Consider the time as sharp 4'O clock. The angle between hour and minute hand at this time is 120°. We just want to calculate the time when this 120° becomes 0°. The gap between minute and hour hand is reduces by 5½° ever min.

5½° gap reduced in → 1min
120° gap reduced in → x min

$$x = \frac{120}{5\frac{1}{2}} = \frac{120}{11/2} = 21\frac{9}{11} \text{ min}$$

Hence the hands will coincide at $4:21\frac{9}{11}$

Choice (a)

Solution 17

Consider the time as sharp 12'O clock. At this time the minute and hour hands will coincide. So the gap between them is 0°. We want to calculate the time when this gap becomes 180° (to make the hands opposite). As the minute hand gains 5½° over hour hand every min, hence the gap between minute and hour hand increases by 5½° ever min.

5½° gap increases in → 1min
180° gap increases in → x min

$$x = \frac{180}{5\frac{1}{2}} = \frac{180}{11/2} = 32\frac{8}{11} \text{ min}$$

Hence the hands will be opposite at $12:32\frac{8}{11}$.

Choice (b)

Solution 18

Consider the time as sharp 4'O clock. The angle between hour and minute hand at this time is 120°. We just want to calculate the time when this 120° reduces to 60°. The gap between minute and hour hand is reduces by 5½° ever min.

5½° gap reduced in → 1min
60° gap reduced in → x min

$$x = \frac{60}{5\frac{1}{2}} = \frac{60}{11/2} = 10\frac{10}{11} \text{ min}$$

Hence the angle between minute and hour hands will be 60° at $4:10\frac{10}{11}$

Choice (b)

Solution 19

Consider the time as sharp 5'O clock. The angle between hour and minute hand at this time is 150°. At first this 150° will be reduced to 0°, then the gap further increases by 90°. So, we want to calculate the time required by minute hand to gain 240° (150° + 90°) over hour hand.

5½° gain in → 1 min
240° gain in → x min

$$x = \frac{240}{5\frac{1}{2}}$$
$$= \frac{240}{11/2} = 43\frac{7}{11} \text{ min}$$

Hence between 5:30 to 6:00, the hands will make right angle at $5:43\frac{7}{11}$.

Choice (d)

Solution 20

Friday 7:00 a.m. → 3 min slower than correct time.
Sunday 4:00 a.m. → 12 min faster than correct time.

The duration from Friday 7:00 a.m. to Sunday 4:00 a.m. is of 45 hrs. The clock which was running slower before 45 hrs has gained those 3 min and now becomes faster by 12 more min. Hence the clock has gained total 15 min in this span of 45 hrs. The clock will show the correct time, the moment it gains these 3 min by which it was slower.

To gain 15 min → 45 hrs required.
To gain 3 min → x hrs required.

$$x = \frac{45 \times 3}{15} = 9 \text{ hrs.}$$

The clock will show correct time 9 hrs after Friday 7:00 a.m. *i.e.,* on Friday 4:00 p.m.

Choice (a)

Solution 21

Sunday 6:00 a.m. → 8 min slower than correct time.
Tuesday 12:00 noon → 10 min faster than correct time.

The duration from Sunday 6:00 a.m. to Tuesday 12:00 noon is of 54 hrs. The clock which was running slower before 54 hrs has gained those 8 min and now becomes faster by 10 more min. Hence the clock has gained total 18 min in this span of 54 hrs. The clock will show the correct time, the moment it gains these 8 min by which it was slower.

To gain 18 min → 54 hrs required.
To gain 8 min → x hrs required.

$$x = \frac{54 \times 8}{18}$$
$$= 24 \text{ hrs.}$$

The clock will show correct time 24 hrs after Sunday 6:00 a.m. *i.e.,* on Monday 6:00 a.m.

Choice (b)

Solution 22

Tuesday 3:00 p.m. → 3 min faster than correct time.
Thursday 10:00 p.m. → 8 min slower than correct time.

The duration from Tuesday 3:00 p.m. to Thursday 10:00 p.m. is of 55 hrs. The clock which was running faster before 54 hrs has lost those 3 min and now becomes slower by 8 more min. Hence the clock has lost total 11 min in this span of 55 hrs. The clock will show the correct time, the moment it looses these 3 min by which it was faster.

To loose 11 min → 55 hrs required
To loose 3 min → x hrs required

$$x = \frac{55 \times 3}{11} = 15 \text{ hrs.}$$

The clock will show correct time 15 hrs after Tuesday 3:00 p.m. *i.e.*, on Wednesday 6:00 a.m.

Choice (c)

Solution 23

As one clock loses 2 min every hr and other gains 1 min every 2 hrs (½ min every hr) or so they will differ by 2½ min every hr.

For 2½ min difference → 1 hr required
For 6 hrs (360 min) difference → x hrs required

$$x = \frac{360}{2\frac{1}{2}} = \frac{360}{5/2} = 144 \text{ hrs.}$$

So, they will be 6 hrs apart after 144 hrs.

Choice (c)

Solution 24

Minute and hour hands of a normal clock will coincide (or overlaps) after every $65\frac{5}{11}$ min.

As the minute and hour hands of this clock coincides after every 64 min, hence this clock is running faster than a normal clock.

Time gained = $65\frac{5}{11} - 64 = 1\frac{5}{11}$ min in every 64 min of run of a normal clock

In 64 min run → $1\frac{5}{11}$ min gain

In 12 hrs run → x min gain

$$x = \frac{12 \times 60 \times 1\frac{5}{11}}{64} = \frac{12 \times 60 \times 16}{64 \times 11}$$

$$x = 16\frac{4}{11}$$

So, the clock will gain $16\frac{4}{11}$ min in 12 hrs.

Choice (a)

Solution 25

Minute and hour hands of a normal clock will coincide (or overlaps) after every $65\frac{5}{11}$ min.

As the minute and hour hands of this clock coincides after every 66 min, hence this clock is running slower than a normal clock.

Time lost = $66 - 65\frac{5}{11} = \frac{6}{11}$ min in every 66 min of run of a normal clock.

In 66 min run → $\frac{6}{11}$ min loss

In 24 hrs run → x min loss

$$x = \frac{24 \times 60 \times 6}{66 \times 11} = \frac{1440}{121} = 11\frac{109}{121} \text{ min}$$

So, the clock will loose $11\frac{109}{121}$ min in 24 hrs.

Choice (d)

Solution 26

$X = 5Y$
$X + Y = 240$ min
$\Rightarrow 5Y + Y = 240$ min
$\Rightarrow 6Y = 240$ min
$\Rightarrow Y = 40$ min.

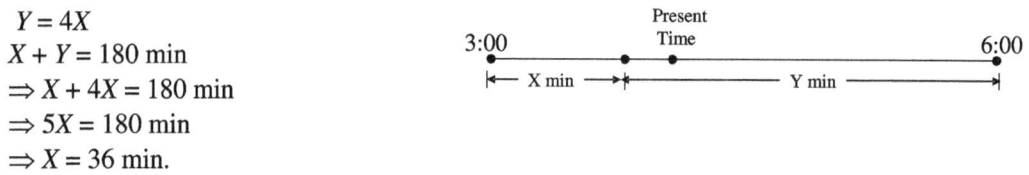

So, present time is 8:00 − 40 min = 7:20.

Choice (c)

Solution 27

$Y = 4X$
$X + Y = 180$ min
$\Rightarrow X + 4X = 180$ min
$\Rightarrow 5X = 180$ min
$\Rightarrow X = 36$ min.

∴ Present time = 3:00 + 36 min + 15 min = 3:51.

Choice (a)

Solution 28

In 2 hrs, the clock has lost 10 min. It means it is loosing 5 min in every hour.

From 10:00 a.m. to 4:00 p.m. it's a span of 6 hrs in which it will loose a total of 30 min. So, if the actual time is 4:00, the clock will show 30 min less *i.e.,* 3:30.

Choice (a)

21

Calendar

If it's an aptitude question on this topic, you may be given a date and will be asked to find out the week day or you may be given a month/year and will be asked which month/year calendar is matching to it. The week day can be obtained by finding the number of 'odd days' in the given period. In a given period, the number of days more than the complete weeks are called odd days.

For example if 1st of any particular month is Monday, then which day it will be on 25th of that month?

1st – Monday
25th – ?

Well, here the 1st of that month is our reference date. After the reference date till 25th there are 24 days. Let us find out the number of odd days in these 24 days by diving 24 with 7, and getting the remainder as follows:

$$\begin{array}{r} 3 \\ 7\overline{)24} \\ \underline{21} \\ 3 \end{array}$$

As the remainder (odd days) is 3, we need to count 3 days after the reference date *i.e.*, Monday, so it will be Thursday on 25th of that month.

1st – Monday
25th – Thursday

How this works? 21 days are merged into 3 weeks, and the leftover extra days (odd days) are 3. So, if 1st is Monday, the next three Mondays will appear on 8th, 15th and 22nd. Counting 3 days after 22nd will give the correct day on 25th.

LEAP AND NON-LEAP YEAR

Year consisting of 365 days is said to be a Non-leap year, while a Leap year consist of 366 days. The extra day in this Leap year is in the month of February (29 days). The way to identify the year as leap or non-leap is as follows:

1. Every non century year which is divisible by 4 is a leap year. For example 1992, 1996, 2004, etc.
2. Every century year which is divisible by 400 is a leap year. For example 400, 800, 1200, 1600, 2000, etc.

3. A non century year which is NOT divisible by 4 or a century year which is NOT divisible by 400 is a non-leap year. For example 1900, 1962, 1998, 2006, 2100 are non-leap years.

CALENDAR FROM THE PAST

It is assumed that 1st January 1 A.D. was a Monday, and with this as a reference the calendar is formed. If we go one day previous to this *i.e.,* Sunday as reference day, we can include 1st Jan of 1 A.D. in our count. Now, the task is to find out how many odd days are there in a span of first 100 years.

Sunday (Reference day)
    1st Jan 1 A.D.   – Monday
    31st Dec 100 A.D.   – ?

First 100 years = 76 ordinary years + 24 leap years
                  = 76 odd days + 48 odd days
                  = 124 odd days
                  = 5 odd days.

So, in a span of 100 years there are 5 odd days and therefore 31st Dec. 100 A.D. will be Friday (5 days after the reference day *i.e.,* Sunday).

Let us take the number of odd days in a span of every 100 years as follows:

- 1st Jan 1 A.D. to 31st Dec 100 A.D.   ⇒ 5 odd days
- 1st Jan 101 A.D. to 31st Dec 200 A.D. ⇒ 5 odd days
- 1st Jan 201 A.D. to 31st Dec 300 A.D. ⇒ 5 odd days
- 1st Jan 301 A.D. to 31st Dec 400 A.D. ⇒ 6 odd days   (∵ 400 is a leap year)

So in a span of first 400 years there are 5 + 5 + 5 + 6 = 21 odd days, resulting in zero odd days (as 21 is divisible by 7). It means the last day after every 400 years will be the reference day *i.e.,* Sunday.

POINTS TO NOTE

- Ordinary year = 365 days   ⇒ 52 weeks + 1 odd day
- Leap year = 366 days   ⇒ 52 weeks + 2 odd days
- Number of odd days in first 100 years   ⇒ 5 odd days
- Number of odd days in first 200 years   ⇒ 3 odd days
- Number of odd days in first 300 years   ⇒ 1 odd day
- Number of odd days in first 400 years   ⇒ 0 odd days
- Number of odd days in every 400 years starting from 1 A.D. will be zero.
    1ST JAN. 1 A.D. TO 31ST DEC 400 A.D.   ⇒ 0 ODD DAYS
    1ST JAN. 401 A.D. TO 31ST DEC 800 A.D.   ⇒ 0 ODD DAYS
    1ST JAN. 801 A.D. TO 31ST DEC 1200 A.D.   ⇒ 0 ODD DAYS
    1ST JAN. 1201 A.D. TO 31ST DEC 1600 A.D. ⇒ 0 ODD DAYS
    1ST JAN. 1601 A.D. TO 31ST DEC 2000 A.D. ⇒ 0 ODD DAYS

- The last day of every century leap-year *i.e.*, after every 400 years will be always Sunday.

  31st Dec. 400 A.D. $\Rightarrow$ Sunday
  31st Dec. 800 A.D. $\Rightarrow$ Sunday
  31st Dec. 1200 A.D. $\Rightarrow$ Sunday
  31st Dec. 1600 A.D. $\Rightarrow$ Sunday
  31st Dec. 2000 A.D. $\Rightarrow$ Sunday.

SOLVED EXAMPLES

Example 1

If 21st March 2010 it was Sunday, then which day will be on 26th August of the same year?

Solution

21st March 2010   –   Sunday (Reference day)
26th August 2010   –   ?

Let us find out the number of odd days from 21st March to 26th August as follows:

	Days	Odd days
March	10	3
April	30	2
May	31	3
June	30	2
July	31	3
August	26	5

Total odd days = 3 + 2 + 3 + 2 + 3 + 5 = 18 $\Rightarrow$ 4 odd days.

So, 26th August 2010 will be 4 days after Sunday *i.e.*, Thursday.

Example 2

Rohan's birthday comes on 20th of April. In the year 2006 his birthday was on Thursday, then on which days his birthday will fall in the year:

1. 2007
2. 2008
3. 2009

Solution

1. **2007**
   20th April 2006 – Thursday (Reference day)
   From 20th April 2006 to 20th April 2007 $\Rightarrow$ 365 days (excluding reference day *i.e.*, Thursday)
   365 days $\Rightarrow$ 52 weeks + 1 odd days
   20th April 2007 – Friday.

2. **2008**
   20th April 2007 – Friday (Reference day)
   From 20th April 2007 to 20th April 2008 $\Rightarrow$ 366 days (excluding reference day *i.e.*, Friday)
   366 days $\Rightarrow$ 52 weeks + 2 odd days
   20th April 2008 – Sunday.

3. **2009**
   20th April 2008 – Sunday (Reference day)
   From 20th April 2008 to 20th April 2009 $\Rightarrow$ 365 days (excluding reference day *i.e.*, Sunday)
   365 days $\Rightarrow$ 52 weeks + 1 odd days
   20th April 2009 – Monday.

Example 3

If 1st February 2008 it was Friday, then which day of the week will be on 25th September of 2011?

Solution

1st February 2008 – Friday (Reference day)
25th September 2011 – ?

Let us find out the number of odd days after 1st February till 25th September of 2008 as follows:

	Days	Odd Days
February	28	0
March	31	3
April	30	2
May	31	3
June	30	2
July	31	3
August	31	3
September	25	4

Total odd days = 0 + 3 + 2 + 3 + 2 + 3 + 3 + 4 = 20 $\Rightarrow$ 6 odd days.

So, 25th September 2008 will be 6 days after Friday *i.e.*, Thursday.

25th September 2008 – Thursday
25th September 2009 – Friday

25th September 2010 – Saturday
25th September 2011 – Sunday.

Example 4

Which day of the week was 31st January 1901?

Solution

31st December 1600 – Sunday (Reference day)

If we go ahead by 300 years there will be 5 + 5 + 5 = 15 odd days ⇒ 1 odd day
31st December 1900 – Monday (New reference day)

In next 31 days there are 3 odd days, so 31st January 1901 will be 3 days after Monday *i.e.*, Thursday.

Example 5

On which dates of August 2009, did Sundays fall?

Solution

31st December 2000 – Sunday (Reference day)

Next 8 years = 6 ordinary years + 2 leap years
= 6 odd days + 4 odd days
= 10 odd days
= 3 odd days.

So, 31st December 2008 will be 3 days after Sunday *i.e.*, Wednesday (new reference day).

Let us find out the number of odd days from 1st January 2009 to 31st July 2009 as follows:

	Days	*Odd days*
January	31	3
February	28	0
March	31	3
April	30	2
May	31	3
June	30	2
July	31	3

Total odd days = 3 + 0 + 3 + 2 + 3 + 2 + 3 = 16 ⇒ 2 odd days.

31st July 2009 will be 2 days after Wednesday *i.e.*, Friday.

In the month of August Sundays will fall on – 2nd, 9th, 16th, 23rd and 30th.

Example 6

In a non-leap year the calendar for the month of January is exactly same for which month in the same year?

Solution

Consider January, if we add all the odd days month wise then at end of September sum of odd days will be zero.

Month	Jan.	Feb.	Mar	Apr.	May	Jun.	Jul.	Aug.	Sep.	Oct.	Nov.	Dec.
Odd Days	3	0	3	2	3	2	3	3	2	3	2	3

So, 1st day of October will be exactly same as 1st day of January, also both months have 31 days.

In a non-leap year January has same calendar as October.

EXERCISE

1. Which of the following is not a leap year?
   (a) 1596
   (b) 1600
   (c) 1660
   (d) 1700

2. After 1496 which will be the next leap year?
   (a) 1500
   (b) 1600
   (c) 1504
   (d) 1508

3. How many odd days are there in a leap year?
   (a) 1
   (b) 2
   (c) 3
   (d) 4

4. If the first day of an ordinary year is Monday, then the last day of that year is:
   (a) Sunday
   (b) Monday
   (c) Tuesday
   (d) Wednesday

5. If the year 2004 starts with Thursday, then on which day of the week will that year end?
   (a) Thursday
   (b) Friday
   (c) Saturday
   (d) Sunday

6. If today it's Friday. After 57 days it will be:
   (a) Saturday
   (b) Sunday
   (c) Monday
   (d) Tuesday

7. If today it's Sunday. After 100 days it will be:
   (a) Saturday
   (b) Sunday
   (c) Monday
   (d) Tuesday

Calendar

8. Which of the following year has same calendar as 1749?
   (a) 1751 (b) 1754
   (c) 1755 (d) 1757

9. Which of the following year has same calendar as 2007?
   (a) 2014 (b) 2016
   (c) 2018 (d) 2019

10. In a leap year which month has same calendar as January?
    (a) April (b) July
    (c) August (d) Both (a) and (b)

11. If the first and last day of the year is Monday, then which day will be on 25th May?
    (a) Thursday (b) Friday
    (c) Saturday (d) Sunday

12. If a year starts on Saturday, then what can be the maximum possible number of Mondays in that year?
    (a) 51 (b) 52
    (c) 53 (d) 54

13. If 1st January 2009 it was Thursday, then which day of the week lies on 1st January 2008?
    (a) Sunday (b) Monday
    (c) Tuesday (d) Wednesday

14. If 7th March, 2005 is Monday, what was the day of the week on 7th March, 2004?
    (a) Saturday (b) Sunday
    (c) Monday (d) Tuesday

15. If 15th March 2010 it is Monday, then which day will be on 5th January of 2009?
    (a) Saturday (b) Sunday
    (c) Monday (d) Tuesday

16. If 16th December in a year is a Tuesday, then what is the day of a week on 1st of March in that year?
    (a) Saturday (b) Sunday
    (c) Monday (d) Tuesday

17. If 10th June 2011 it is Friday, then which day will be on 10th November 2014?
    (a) Saturday (b) Sunday
    (c) Monday (d) Tuesday

18. If 1st January 2000 it was Saturday, then what day of the week will be on 1st January 2100?
    (a) Saturday (b) Sunday
    (c) Thursday (d) Friday

19. If 9th May of 2005 is Monday, then 9th May of 2045 will be which day?
    (a) Saturday (b) Sunday
    (c) Monday (d) Tuesday

20. If 29th February of 2008 is Friday, then 29th February of 2012 will be which day?
    (a) Saturday (b) Sunday
    (c) Monday (d) Wednesday

21. Which day of the week was 15th August 1947?
    (a) Friday (b) Saturday
    (c) Monday (d) Tuesday

22. Which day of the week was 27th October 1983?
    (a) Thursday (b) Friday
    (c) Saturday (d) Sunday

23. On which dates of April, 2001 did Mondays fall?
    (a) 1st, 8th, 15th, 22nd, 29th (b) 2nd, 9th, 16th, 23rd, 30th
    (c) 3rd, 10th, 17th, 24th (d) 4th, 11th, 18th, 25th

24. On which dates of September, 1872 did Sundays fall?
    (a) 1st, 8th, 15th, 22nd, 29th (b) 2nd, 9th, 16th, 23rd, 30th
    (c) 3rd, 10th, 17th, 24th (d) 4th, 11th, 18th, 25th

KEYS

1. (d)	2. (c)	3. (b)	4. (b)	5. (b)	6. (a)	7. (d)	8. (c)
9. (c)	10. (d)	11. (b)	12. (b)	13. (c)	14. (b)	15. (c)	16. (a)
17. (c)	18. (d)	19. (d)	20. (d)	21. (a)	22. (a)	23. (b)	24. (a)

SOLUTIONS

Solution 1

If it's a non century year, it must be divisible by 4. As 1596 and 1660 are both divisible by 4 they are leap years.

If it's a century year (in multiple of 100), it must be divisible by 400. As 1700 is not divisible by 400 it is not a leap years.

Choice (d)

Solution 2

After every 3 years, the fourth year is a leap year, but the year 1500 being a century year is not divisible by 400, hence it's not a leap year. The next leap year after 1496 will be directly 1504.

Choice (c)

Solution 3

A leap year contains 366 days $\Rightarrow$ 52 weeks + 2 odd days.

Choice (b)

Solution 4

Ordinary year contains 365 days.

1st January   –   Monday (Reference day)
31st December –   ?

After the reference date there are 364 days $\Rightarrow$ 0 odd days.

Hence the last day of the year will be same as first day *i.e.*, Monday.

Choice (b)

Solution 5

2004 is a leap year which contains 366 days.

1st January   –   Thursday (Reference day)
31st December –   ?

After the reference date there are 365 days $\Rightarrow$ 1 odd day.

Hence the last day of the year will be one day after Thursday *i.e.*, Friday.

Choice (b)

Solution 6

Today   –   Friday (Reference day).
57 days $\Rightarrow$ 8 weeks + 1 odd day.

Hence it will be one day after Friday *i.e.*, Saturday.

Choice (a)

Solution 7

Today   –   Sunday (Reference day).

100 days $\Rightarrow$ 14 weeks + 2 odd day.

Hence it will be two days after Sunday *i.e.,* Tuesday.

Choice (d)

Solution 8

The calendar will be same if the number of odd days between the two years is zero.

(a) 1751

1751 – 1749 = 2 years.

2 years are both ordinary years ⇒ 2 odd days

Hence calendar does not match.

(b) 1754

1754 – 1749 = 5 years

= 4 ordinary years + 1 leap year

= 4 odd days + 2 odd days

= 6 odd days.

Hence calendar does not match.

(c) 1755

1755 – 1749 = 6 years = 5 ordinary years + 1 leap year

= 5 odd days + 2 odd days

= 7 odd days

= 0 odd days.

Hence calendar of 1755 will be exactly same as calendar of 1749.

Choice (c)

Solution 9

The calendar will be same if the number of odd days between the two years is zero.

(a) 2014

2014 – 2007 = 7 years = 6 ordinary years + 1 leap year

= 6 odd days + 2 odd days

= 8 odd days.

Hence calendar does not match.

(b) 2016

2016 – 2007 = 9 years

= 8 ordinary years + 1 leap year

= 8 odd days + 2 odd days

= 10 odd days

= 3 odd days.

Hence calendar does not match.

(c) 2018

2018 – 2007 = 11 years
= 8 ordinary years + 3 leap year
= 8 odd days + 6 odd days
= 14 odd days
= 0 odd days.

Hence calendar of 2018 will be exactly same as calendar of 2007.

Choice (c)

Solution 10

From January let us add all the odd days month wise as follows:

Month	Jan	Feb	Mar	Apr	May	Jun	Jul	Aug	Sep	Oct	Nov	Dec
Odd Days	3	1	3	2	3	2	3	3	2	3	2	3

Till end of March the number of odd days are $3 + 1 + 3 = 7 \Rightarrow 0$ odd days.

Hence Calendar of January is same as April.

Till end of Jun the number of odd days are $3 + 1 + 3 + 2 + 3 + 2 = 14 \Rightarrow 0$ odd days.

Hence Calendar of January is same as July also.

Choice (d)

Solution 11

If the year starts and ends with Monday *i.e.,* same day, it's not a leap year.

1st January – Monday (Reference day)
25th May – ?

Let us find out the number of odd days after 1st January to 25th May as follows:

	Days	Odd days
January	30	2
February	28	0
March	31	3
April	30	2
May	25	4

Total odd days = $2 + 0 + 3 + 2 + 4 = 11 \Rightarrow 4$ odd days.

The day of 25th May will be 4 days after Monday *i.e.,* Friday.

Choice (b)

Solution 12

If the year is an ordinary year ⇒ It will start and end on Saturday, so 53 Saturdays and other week days are 52.

If the year is a leap year ⇒ It will start on Saturday but will end on Sunday, so 53 Saturdays and Sundays, while other week days are 52.

In any case number of Mondays are 52.

Choice (b)

Solution 13

1st January 2009 – Thursday (Reference day)
1st January 2008 – ?

From 1st January 2008 to 1st January 2009 ⇒ 366 days (excluding reference day *i.e.,* Thursday)
366 days ⇒ 52 weeks + 2 odd days

So, 1st January 2008 will be 2 days prior to Thursday *i.e.,* Tuesday.

Choice (c)

Solution 14

7th March 2005 – Monday (Reference day)
7th March 2004 – ?

From 7th March 2004 to 7th March 2005 ⇒ 365 days (excluding reference day *i.e.,* Monday)
365 days ⇒ 52 weeks + 1 odd days

So, 7th March 2004 will be 1 days prior to Monday *i.e.,* Sunday.

Choice (b)

Solution 15

Let us first move from 15th March 2010 (Monday) to 5th January 2010 by calculating the number of odd days.

	Days	Odd Days
March	14	0
February	28	0
January	27	6

So, 5th January 2010 will be 6 days prior to Monday *i.e.,* Tuesday (new reference).

5th January 2010 – Tuesday (new reference)
5th January 2009 – Monday.

Choice (c)

Solution 16

16th December   –   Tuesday (Reference day)
1st March   –   ?

Let us first move from 16th December (Monday) to 1st March by calculating the number of odd days.

	Days	Odd Days
Dec	15	1
Nov	30	2
Oct	31	3
Sep	30	2
Aug	31	3
Jul	31	3
Jun	30	2
May	31	3
Apr	30	2
Mar	31	3

Total odd days = 24 $\Rightarrow$ 3 odd days.

So, 1st March will be 3 days prior to Tuesday *i.e.*, Saturday.

Choice (a)

Solution 17

10th June 2011   –   Friday (Reference day).
10th Nov 2014   –   ?

Let us first move from 10th June 2011 (Friday) to 10th Nov. 2011 by calculating the odd days.

	Days	Odd Days
Jun.	20	6
Jul.	31	3
Aug.	31	3
Sep.	30	2
Oct.	31	3
Nov.	10	3

Total odd days = 20 $\Rightarrow$ 6 odd days.

So, 10th Nov. 2011 will be six days after Friday *i.e.*, on Thursday.

10th Nov. 2011 – Thursday
10th Nov. 2012 – Saturday   ($\because$ 2012 is a leap year)
10th Nov. 2013 – Sunday
10th Nov. 2014 – Monday.

Choice (c)

Solution 18

1st January 2000 — Saturday (Reference day)
1st January 2100 — ?

From 1st January 2000 to 1st January 2100 $\Rightarrow$ 100 years

In 100 years = 75 ordinary years + 25 leap years ($\because$ 2000 is leap year)
= 75 odd days + 50 odd days
= 125 odd days
= 6 odd days.

Hence 1st January 2100 will be 6 days after Saturday *i.e.*, Friday.

Choice (d)

Solution 19

9th May 2005 — Monday (Reference day)
9th May 2045 — ?

From 9th May 2005 to 9th May 2045 $\Rightarrow$ 40 years

In 40 years = 30 ordinary years + 10 leap years
= 30 odd days + 20 odd days
= 50 odd days
= 1 odd day.

Hence 9th May 2045 will be one day after Monday *i.e.*, Tuesday.

Choice (d)

Solution 20

29th Feb. 2008 — Friday (Reference day)
29th Feb. 2012 — ?

From 29th Feb. 2008 to 29th Feb. 2012 $\Rightarrow$ 4 years

In 4 years = 3 ordinary year + 1 leap year
= 3 odd days + 2 odd days
= 5 odd days.

Hence 29th Feb 2012 will be 5 days after Friday *i.e.*, Wednesday.

Choice (d)

Solution 21

31st December 1600 — Sunday (Reference day)

If we go ahead by 300 years there will be 5 + 5 + 5 = 15 odd days $\Rightarrow$ 1 odd day

31st December 1900 – Monday (New reference day).

Let us now find out the day on 31st December 1946.

From 31st December 1900 to 31st December 1946 = 46 years.

Next 46 years = 35 ordinary years + 11 leap years.
= 35 odd days + 22 odd days
= 57 odd days
= 1 odd day.

So, 31st December 1946 will be 1 day after Monday *i.e.*, Tuesday (New reference day).

Let us find out the number of odd days from 1st January 1947 to 15th August 1947 as follows:

	Days	*Odd Days*
January	31	3
February	28	0
March	31	3
April	30	2
May	31	3
June	30	2
July	31	3
August	15	1

Total odd days = 17 $\Rightarrow$ 3 odd days.

15th August 1947 will be 3 days after Tuesday *i.e.*, Friday.

Choice (a)

Solution 22

31st December 1600 – Sunday (Reference day)

If we go ahead by 300 years there will be 5 + 5 + 5 = 15 odd days $\Rightarrow$ 1 odd day

31st December 1900 – Monday (New reference day).

Let us now find out the day on 31st December 1982.

From 31st December 1900 to 31st December 1982 = 82 years

Next 82 years = 62 ordinary years + 20 leap years
= 62 odd days + 40 odd days
= 102 odd days
= 4 odd days.

So, 31st December 1982 will be 4 days after Monday *i.e.*, Friday (New reference day).

Let us find out the number of odd days from 1st January 1983 to 27th October 1983 as follows:

	Days	Odd Days
January	31	3
February	28	0
March	31	3
April	30	2
May	31	3
June	30	2
July	31	3
August	31	3
September	30	2
October	27	6

Total odd days = 27 $\Rightarrow$ 6 odd days.

27th September 1983 will be 6 days after Friday i.e., Thursday.

Choice (a)

Solution 23

31st December 2000 – Sunday (Reference day)

Let us find out the number of odd days from 1st January 2001 to 31st March 2001 as follows:

	Days	Odd Days
January	31	3
February	28	0
March	31	3

Total odd days = 6.

31st March 2001 will be 6 days after Sunday i.e., Saturday.

So in the month of April, 2001 Mondays will fall on 2nd, 9th, 16th, 23rd and 30th.

Choice (b)

Solution 24

31st December 1600 – Sunday (Reference day)

If we go ahead by 200 years there will be 5 + 5 = 10 odd days $\Rightarrow$ 3 odd days

31st December 1800 – Wednesday (New reference day)

Let us now find out the day on 31st December 1871.

From 31st December 1800 to 31st December 1871 = 71 years

Next 71 years = 54 ordinary years + 17 leap years
= 54 odd days + 34 odd days
= 88 odd days
= 4 odd days.

So, 31st December 1871 will be 4 days after Wednesday *i.e.,* Sunday (New reference day).

Let us find out the number of odd days from 1st January 1872 to 31st August 1872 as follows:

	Days	*Odd Days*
January	31	3
February	29	1
March	31	3
April	30	2
May	31	3
June	30	2
July	31	3
August	31	3

Total odd days = 20 $\Rightarrow$ 6 odd days.

31st August 1872 will be 6 days after Sunday *i.e.,* Saturday.

So in the month of September, 1872 Sunday will fall on 1st, 8th, 15th, 22nd, and 29th.

Choice (a)

22

Simple and Compound Interest

BASIC CONCEPTS

When someone lends money to someone else, the borrower usually pays a fee to the lender. This fee is called 'interest'. This interest can be either simple or it can be compound. Let us have a look at the basic terminologies in this topic as mentioned below:

- *Principal:* The money borrowed or lent out for a certain period is called principal or the sum. It is denoted by 'P'.
- *Interest:* Money paid by the borrower for using lenders money is called interest. It is denoted by 'I'.
- *Time:* This is the duration for which money is borrowed. It is denoted by 'n' which is normally in years.
- *Rate of Interest:* This is the rate at which interest is calculated on the principal. It is denoted by 'r' and is expressed in percentage per annum.
- *Amount:* This is the total money which a borrower needs to pay to the lender. It is the total of principal and interest. It is denoted by 'A'.

SIMPLE INTEREST

When the interest is calculated every year (or in every period) on the original principal, such interest is called simple interest. Here rate of interest is charged on the original principal only.

Simple Interest = $\dfrac{P n r}{100}$

For example: A sum of ₹ 1000 deposited under the scheme of simple interest at the rate of 10% p.a. over a period of 4 years. The money grows over a period of time as follows:

	1st Year	2nd Year	3rd Year	4th Year
Simple Interest	100	100	100	100
Amount (Principal + SI)	1100	1200	1300	1400

The simple interest for 1 year = $\dfrac{P n r}{100} = \dfrac{1000 \times 1 \times 10}{100}$ = ₹ 100

This flat interest of ₹ 100 every year will be getting on the original principal. Hence the amount at the end of 4 years will be ₹ 1400.

COMPOUND INTEREST

When the interest is calculated every year (or in every period) on the previous accumulated amount, such interest is called compound interest. Here rate of interest is charged on the original principal as well as previous year's interest also.

In other words, the amount at the end of first year (*i.e.*, principal + interest of 1st year) will become principal for the second year. The amount at the end of second year (*i.e.*, principal for 2nd year + interest of 2nd year) will become principal for third year and so on.

For example: A sum of ₹ 1000 deposited under the scheme of compound interest at the rate of 10% p.a. over a period of 4 years. The money grows over a period of time as follows:

	1st Year	2nd Year	3rd Year	4th Year
Compound Interest	100	110	121	133.1
Amount (Principal + CI)	1100	1210	1331	1464.1

Here the interest for the first year is ₹ 100 (which is 10% of ₹ 1000); hence the amount becomes ₹ 1100 at the end of first year. In the second year the interest of 10% is charged on this amount of ₹ 1100, which will be ₹ 110, hence the amount at the end of second year is ₹ 1210 (*i.e.*, 1100 + 110). In the third year the interest of 10% is charged on this amount of ₹ 1210, which will be ₹ 121, hence the amount at the end of third year is ₹ 1331 (*i.e.*, 1210 + 121). In the fourth year the interest of 10% is charged on this amount of ₹ 1331, which will be ₹ 133.1, hence the amount at the end of fourth year is ₹ 1464.1 (*i.e.*, 1331 + 133.1).

Following points can be concluded by looking at these calculations on SI and CI:
1. The interest in the very first year or first period is always same whether it is simple interest or compound interest.
2. Simple interest is constant over a period of time, while compound interest grows.
3. The amount in simple interest over a period of time follows an arithmetic progression (AP), and the amount in compound interest over a period of time follows a geometric progression (GP).

IMPORTANT FORMULAE

1. Amount on simple interest after n years at the rate of r% p.a. is:

   Amount on SI $= P\left(1+\dfrac{nr}{100}\right)$

2. Amount on compound interest, after n years at the rate of r% p.a. is:

   Amount on CI at annual compounding $= P\left(1+\dfrac{r}{100}\right)^n$

   Amount on CI at half-yearly compounding $= P\left(1+\dfrac{r/2}{100}\right)^{2n}$

   Amount on CI at quarterly compounding $= P\left(1+\dfrac{r/4}{100}\right)^{4n}$

   Amount on CI at every moment compounding $= P \cdot e^{\frac{nr}{100}}$

3. The present value of ₹ x due n years hence under simple interest is given as:

$$\text{Present value} = \frac{x}{\left(1 + \frac{nr}{100}\right)}.$$

4. The present value of ₹ x due n years hence under compound interest is given as:

$$\text{Present value} = \frac{x}{\left(1 + \frac{r}{100}\right)^n}.$$

5. Repayment of a sum of P borrowed at $r\%$ per annum under compound interest in n equal installments is given as:

$$\text{Each installment} = \frac{P \cdot r}{100\left[1 - \left(\frac{100}{100+r}\right)^n\right]}.$$

SOLVED EXAMPLES

Example 1

What sum of money will obtain a simple interest of ₹ 27648 in 2¼ years at the rate of 8% p.a.?

Solution

$$SI = ₹\ 27648$$
$$n = 9/4$$
$$r = 8$$
$$SI = \frac{Pnr}{100}$$
$$27648 = \frac{P \times 9 \times 8}{4 \times 100}$$
$$\therefore\quad P = \frac{27648 \times 4 \times 100}{9 \times 8}$$
$$= ₹\ 153600.$$

Alternate Method

Let the principal, $P = ₹\ 100$

At the rate of 8% p.a. the interest in 2¼ years $= 8 + 8 + 2 = ₹\ 18$

$$100 \to 18$$
$$x \to 27648$$

∴ $x = \dfrac{27648 \times 100}{18}$

$= ₹\ 153600.$

Example 2

If the simple interest on a sum of money for 2 years at 5% per annum is ₹ 1500, what is the compound interest on the same at the same rate and for the same time period?

Solution

$SI = ₹\ 1500$

$n = 2$

$r = 5\%$

$SI = \dfrac{Pnr}{100}$

$1500 = \dfrac{P \times 2 \times 5}{100}$

∴ $P = \dfrac{1500 \times 100}{2 \times 5} = ₹\ 15000.$

Calculation of compound interest

Amount on CI $= P\left(1+\dfrac{r}{100}\right)^n = 15000\left(1+\dfrac{5}{100}\right)^2 = 16537.5.$

Interest earned on compound interest = 16537.5 – 15000 = ₹ 1537.5.

Alternate Method

Calculation of compound interest:

	1ˢᵗ year		2ⁿᵈ year
CI	750	5% →	787.5
Amount	15750		16537.5

Total interest earned on compound interest = 750 + 787.5 = ₹ 1537.5.

Example 3

A sum of ₹ 20000 is deposited under the scheme of compound interest at the rate of 12% p.a. Find the interest earned in 1 year if the compounding is done:
1. Yearly
2. Half yearly

Solution

1. Interest earned on yearly compounding

   $P = ₹ 20000$

   $r = 12\%$ p.a.

   $n = 1$ year

Amount on yearly compounding $= P\left(1 + \dfrac{r}{100}\right)^n$

$= 20000\left(1 + \dfrac{12}{100}\right)^1$

$= 22400.$

So, interest earned $= 22400 - 20000 = ₹ 2400.$

Alternate Method

   $P = ₹ 20000$

   $r = 12\%$ p.a.

   $n = 1$ year

CI for 1 year $= 1.2 \times 20000 = ₹ 2400.$

	1 year
CI	2400
Amount	22400

So, interest earned $= ₹ 2400.$

2. Interest earned on half yearly compounding

   $P = ₹ 20000$

   $r = 12\%$ p.a.

   $n = 1$ year.

Amount on half yearly compounding $= P\left(1 + \dfrac{r/2}{100}\right)^{2n}$

$= 20000\left(1 + \dfrac{6}{100}\right)^2$

$= 22472.$

So, interest earned $= 22472 - 20000 = ₹ 2472.$

Alternate Method

   $P = ₹ 20000$

   $r = 6\%$ for 6 months period

$n = 2$ periods

	6 months		12 months
CI	1200	6% ↗	1272
Amount	21200		22472

So, interest earned $= 1200 + 1272 = ₹ 2472$.

Example 4

A sum of money deposited at compound interest becomes double in 3½ years. In how many years from the beginning it will become 8 times itself?

Solution

If the sum doubles:

$$P\left(1+\frac{r}{100}\right)^n = 2P$$

$$\left(1+\frac{r}{100}\right)^{7/2} = 2.$$

If sum becomes 8 times:

$$P\left(1+\frac{r}{100}\right)^n = 8P$$

$$\left(1+\frac{r}{100}\right)^n = 2^3$$

$$\left(1+\frac{r}{100}\right)^n = \left[\left(1+\frac{r}{100}\right)^{\frac{7}{2}}\right]^3$$

$$\left(1+\frac{r}{100}\right)^n = \left(1+\frac{r}{100}\right)^{\frac{21}{2}}$$

$$\therefore \quad n = \frac{21}{2} = 10½ \text{ years.}$$

Alternate Method

$P \xrightarrow{CI=P} 2P$ in 3½ years

$2P \xrightarrow{CI=2P} 4P$ in 3½ years (∵ Sum doubles in every 3½ years)

$4P \xrightarrow{CI=4P} 8P$ in 3½ years (∵ Sum doubles in every 3½ years)

Total time required = 3½ + 3½ + 3½ = 10½ years.

Example 5

In what time will ₹ 3125 becomes ₹ 7776 at 20% per annum compounded annually?

Solution

$$P\left(1+\frac{r}{100}\right)^n = \text{Amount}$$

$$3125\left(1+\frac{20}{100}\right)^n = 7776$$

$$\left(1+\frac{1}{5}\right)^n = \frac{7776}{3125}$$

$$\left(\frac{6}{5}\right)^n = \left(\frac{6}{5}\right)^5$$

∴ $n = 5$ years.

Example 6

Find the present worth of ₹ 1749.6 due in 2 years at 8% per annum compound interest.

Solution

Present worth of ₹ x due in 2 years at r% p.a. compound interest is given as:

Present worth $= \dfrac{x}{\left(1+\dfrac{r}{100}\right)^n}$

$= \dfrac{1749.6}{\left(1+\dfrac{8}{100}\right)^2} = ₹\ 1500.$

Alternate Method

Let the present worth = ₹ 100

Amount after 2 years at 8% p.a. compound interest will be:

	1ˢᵗ Year	2ⁿᵈ Year
CI	8 8% ↗	8.64
Amount	108	116.64

$100 \to 116.64$

$x \to 1749.6$

∴ $x = \dfrac{1749.6 \times 100}{116.64} = ₹\ 1500$

Example 7

A man borrowed ₹ 25000 at 10% p.a. He repaid ₹ 15000 at the end of 1st year. What amount should he pay at the end of the 2nd year to completely discharge the loan, compound interest being reckoned annually?

Solution

The calculation of compound interest is as follows:

	1st Year	2nd Year
CI	2500	1250
Loan Amount	27500	13750
Repaid	−15000	
Remaining loan	12500	

So, he should repay ₹ 13750 at the end of second year to completely discharge the loan.

Example 8

What annual installment will discharge a debt of ₹ 972 due in 3 years at 8% p.a. simple interest?

Solution

Let each installment be ₹ 100.

	1st	2nd	3rd
Installment	100	100	100
SI		8	16
Total	= 100 +	108 +	116
	= 324		

$100 \to 324$
$x \to 972$

$\therefore \quad x = \dfrac{972 \times 100}{324}$

$= 300$

So, each installment = ₹ 300.

Example 9

What annual installment will discharge a debt of ₹ 72820 due in 3 years at 10% per annum compound interest?

Solution

Let each installment be ₹ 100.

	1st	2nd	3rd
Installment	100	100	100
CI		10	21
Total =	100 +	110 +	121
=	331		

$100 \rightarrow 331$
$x \rightarrow 72820$

$\therefore \quad x = \dfrac{72820 \times 100}{331} = 22{,}000$

So, each installment = ₹ 22,000.

EXERCISE

1. At the rate of 12.5% p.a., a sum of ₹ 7200 will earn how much simple interest in 2½ years?
   (a) ₹ 2100
   (b) ₹ 2250
   (c) ₹ 2400
   (d) ₹ 2520

2. What will be the simple interest earned on a sum of ₹ 4400, in 5 months at the rate of 9% p.a.?
   (a) ₹ 165
   (b) ₹ 210
   (c) ₹ 254
   (d) ₹ 396

3. The simple interest on ₹ 12000 from 1st January 2010 to 27th May 2010 at the rate of 8% p.a. will be:
   (a) ₹ 225.6
   (b) ₹ 312.5
   (c) ₹ 384
   (d) ₹ 480

4. What sum of money will fetch a simple interest of ₹ 7800 in 3¼ years at the rate of 8% p.a.?
   (a) ₹ 24000
   (b) ₹ 30000
   (c) ₹ 36000
   (d) ₹ 39000

5. Ajay lent ₹ 8000 to Bharat for 2 years and ₹ 4500 to Chetan for 4 years on simple interest at the same rate of interest and received ₹ 2380 in all from both of them as interest. The rate of interest per annum is:
   (a) 5%
   (b) 6%
   (c) 7%
   (d) 8%

6. A certain sum amounts to ₹ 17700 in 3 years and ₹ 20400 in 6 years under simple interest. Find the sum and rate of interest

(a) ₹ 14000, 6% (b) ₹ 15000, 6%
(c) ₹ 16400, 7% (d) ₹ 16000, 8%

7. Vijay took a loan at 8% per annum simple interest for a period of 5 years. At the end of 5 years he paid 19600 to clear his loan. How much loan did he take?
   (a) ₹ 13000 (b) ₹ 14000
   (c) ₹ 15400 (d) ₹ 16000

8. A sum of money lent on compound interest at 10% p.a. compounded annually yields an interest of ₹ 6615 in 2 years. Find the sum.
   (a) ₹ 25000 (b) ₹ 28600
   (c) ₹ 30500 (d) ₹ 31500

9. In what time ₹ 3000 amounts to ₹ 3630 at 10% p.a. compound interest, compounded annually?
   (a) 1½ years (b) 2 years
   (c) 2¼ years (d) 3 years

10. Dheeraj invested an amount of ₹ 15000 in a fixed deposit scheme for 1½ years at compound interest of 20% p.a. compounded half yearly. How much amount he will get on maturity of fixed deposit?
    (a) ₹ 19965 (b) ₹ 20145
    (c) ₹ 19800 (d) ₹ 20600

11. The compound interest on a certain sum for 2 years is ₹ 2520 and simple interest on the same sum of money at same rate of interest for 2 years is ₹ 2400. Find the sum and rate of interest.
    (a) ₹ 12000, 10% (b) ₹ 18000, 6%
    (c) ₹ 13600, 12% (d) ₹ 24000, 5%

12. In 5 years a sum of money doubles itself under simple interest. In how many years the sum becomes 3 times itself?
    (a) 7½ (b) 9
    (c) 10 (d) 15

13. An amount of ₹ 2040 is due after 6 years under simple interest at 6% p.a. Find its present value.
    (a) ₹ 1400 (b) ₹ 1500
    (c) ₹ 1640 (d) ₹ 1760

14. The compound interest on a certain sum for 2 years is ₹ 3870, and simple interest is 3600. Find the rate of interest.
    (a) 8% (b) 12%
    (c) 15% (d) 18%

15. A sum of money lent at compound interest amounts to ₹ 2500 in 2 years and to ₹ 2650 in 3 years. Find the interest rate.
    (a) 6% (b) 8%
    (c) 12% (d) 15%

16. Find the difference between simple interest and compound interest on ₹ 18000 at 20% p.a. for 2 years.
    (a) ₹ 720
    (b) ₹ 750
    (c) ₹ 840
    (d) ₹ 900

17. A sum earns an interest equal to 9/16 times the principal in 2 years. Find the rate of interest, if compounded annually?
    (a) 12%
    (b) 16%
    (c) 20%
    (d) 25%

18. What sum will amount to ₹ 7320.50 at the end of one year at 40% p.a. compound interest, if interest is compounded quarterly?
    (a) ₹ 5000
    (b) ₹ 5200
    (c) ₹ 5850
    (d) ₹ 6500

19. There is 50% increase in an amount in 4 years at simple interest. What will be the compound interest on ₹ 24000 in 2 years at same rate?
    (a) ₹ 3600
    (b) ₹ 4540
    (c) ₹ 5405
    (d) ₹ 6375

20. What will be the difference between the amount on ₹ 8000 for 1 year at 8% p.a. compounded yearly and half-yearly?
    (a) ₹ 12.8
    (b) ₹ 51.2
    (c) ₹ 58.4
    (d) ₹ 64

21. The compound interest on a certain sum of money for 2 years at 5% p.a. is ₹ 2255. The simple interest on the same sum for double the time period and at half the rate of interest per annum is:
    (a) ₹ 1800
    (b) ₹ 2000
    (c) ₹ 2200
    (d) ₹ 2500

22. Find the effective annual rate of interest corresponding to a nominal rate of 40% p.a. and the interest is compounded quarterly.
    (a) 44.44%
    (b) 46.41%
    (c) 47.20%
    (b) 48.24%

23. Find the difference between the interest earned on ₹ 12000 at 20% p.a. for 1 year, when the interest is compounded yearly and half yearly.
    (a) ₹ 120
    (b) ₹ 240
    (c) ₹ 280
    (d) ₹ 320

24. A sum of ₹ 700 deposited at compound interest becomes double after 2½ years. After 10 years it will become:
    (a) ₹ 7000
    (b) ₹ 3500
    (c) ₹ 6300
    (d) ₹ 11200

25. Ram invested a sum of money at compound interest for 2 years at 20% p.a. compounded annually. Shyam also invested the same sum of money at compound interest for 2 years

at 20% p.a. but compounded half-yearly. If Shyam receives an interest of ₹ 723 more than Ram at the end of 2 years, find the sum of money each of them has invested.
(a) ₹27500
(b) ₹ 30000
(c) ₹34000
(d) ₹ 38600

26. Ratanlal invested ₹ 60000 for 3 years, interest being compounded annually. If the rate of interest is 10%, 15% and 20% respectively for 1st, 2nd and 3rd years, then find the interest earned by Ratanlal.
(a) ₹26400
(b) ₹ 27320
(c) ₹29650
(d) ₹ 31080

27. The difference between simple and compound interest on a certain principal after 2 years at the rate of 10% p.a. is ₹ 44.50. Find the principal.
(a) ₹3550
(b) ₹ 4450
(c) ₹4500
(d) ₹ 5050

28. A man borrows ₹ 20000 at 8% compound interest. At the end of first year and second year he pays ₹ 10000 each as a part of repayment. How much dose he still owe after two such installments?
(a) ₹ 800
(b) ₹ 2420
(c) ₹ 2528
(d) ₹ 3200

29. A man borrowed ₹ 25000 from a bank at 20% compound interest. At the end of every year he paid ₹ 8000. At the end of third year, if he wants to clear his loan then how much should he pay?
(a) ₹ 12400
(b) ₹ 16040
(c) ₹ 20800
(d) ₹ 22080

30. If the simple interest on a sum of money at 5% per annum for 3 years is ₹ 1800, find the compound interest on the same sum for the same period at the same rate.
(a) ₹ 1870.50
(b) ₹ 1875.25
(c) ₹ 1891.50
(d) ₹ 1951

31. In what time will ₹ 4096 becomes ₹ 6561 at 12.5% per annum compounded annually?
(a) 3 years
(b) 3½ years
(c) 4 years
(d) 5 years

32. The difference in compound interest earned on a certain sum, for which interest is compounded annually, in first and second year is ₹ 80. If the rate of interest becomes thrice the original rate, then the difference in amount would be:
(a) ₹ 120
(b) ₹ 160
(c) ₹ 240
(d) ₹ 720

33. Rajesh borrowed ₹ 21000 at the rate of 10% p.a. compound interest. If the amount has to be repaid in two equal installments, find the value of each installment.
(a) ₹ 11000
(b) ₹ 11500
(c) ₹ 12100
(d) ₹ 12500

34. What would ₹ 4000 amount to in 10 years at 10% rate of interest, if the interest is compounded every moment? (given e = 2.71)
    (a) ₹ 8800
    (b) ₹ 9680
    (c) ₹ 10000
    (d) ₹ 10840

35. What annual installment will discharge a debt of ₹ 1650 due in 3 years at 10% p.a. simple interest?
    (a) ₹ 500
    (b) ₹ 525
    (c) ₹ 650
    (d) ₹ 700

36. What annual installment will discharge a debt of ₹ 3150 due in 2 years at the rate of 10% p.a. compound interest?
    (a) ₹ 1745
    (b) ₹ 1500
    (c) ₹ 1850
    (d) ₹ 1900

KEYS

1. (b)	2. (a)	3. (c)	4. (b)	5. (c)	6. (b)	7. (b)	8. (d)
9. (b)	10. (a)	11. (a)	12. (c)	13. (b)	14. (c)	15. (a)	16. (a)
17. (d)	18. (a)	19. (d)	20. (a)	21. (c)	22. (b)	23. (a)	24. (d)
25. (b)	26. (d)	27. (b)	28. (c)	29. (d)	30. (c)	31. (c)	32. (d)
33. (c)	34. (d)	35. (a)	36. (b)				

SOLUTIONS

Solution 1

Let Principal, P = ₹ 1000

At the rate of 12.5% p.a. the interest in 2½ years = 125 + 125 + 62.5
$$= ₹ 312.5$$

$1000 \to 312.5$

$7200 \to x$

$\therefore \quad x = \dfrac{7200 \times 312.5}{1000}$

$\quad = ₹ 2250.$

Choice (b)

Solution 2

Simple interest in 1 year on ₹ 4400 at 9% p.a. = $4400 \times \dfrac{9}{100}$ = ₹ 396

12 months → 396
5 months → x

∴ $x = \dfrac{396 \times 5}{12}$ = ₹ 165.

Choice (a)

Solution 3

Number of days from 1st January 2010 to 27th May 2010 = 146 days

Simple interest in 1 year (365 days) on ₹ 12000 at 8% p.a. = $12000 \times \dfrac{8}{100}$ = ₹ 960

365 days → 960
146 days → x

∴ $x = \dfrac{960 \times 146}{365}$ = ₹ 384.

Choice (c)

Solution 4

Let Principal, P = ₹ 100

At the rate of 8% p.a. the interest in 3¼ years = 8 + 8 + 8 + 2 = ₹ 26.

100 → 26
x → 7800

∴ $x = \dfrac{7800 \times 100}{26}$ = ₹ 30000.

Choice (b)

Solution 5

SI from Bharat in 2 years + SI from Chetan in 4 years = ₹ 2380

$$\dfrac{8000 \times 2 \times r}{100} + \dfrac{4500 \times 4 \times r}{100} = 2380$$

$$160r + 180r = 2380$$

∴ $r = 7\%$.

Choice (c)

Solution 6

$P + 3SI = 17700$ ... (1)

$P + 6SI = 20400$ ... (2)

Subtracting equation (1) from equation (2)

$3SI = 20400 - 17700$

$3SI = 2700$

∴ $SI = 900.$

Substituting the value of SI in equation (1)

$P + 3(900) = 17700$

∴ $P = 15000$

On a principal of ₹ 15000, one year's simple interest is ₹ 900, so rate of interest is:

$r = \dfrac{900}{15000} \times 100 = 6\%.$

Choice (b)

Solution 7

Let Vijay take a loan of ₹ 100. At the rate of 8% p.a. simple interest the amount at the end of 5 years will be:

Amount after 5 years = Loan taken + 5 years SI
= 100 + 5 (8)
= 140.

$100 \rightarrow 140$

$x \rightarrow 19600$

∴ $x = \dfrac{19600 \times 100}{140}$

= ₹ 14000.

Choice (b)

Solution 8

Let the principal, P = ₹ 100

Calculation of compound interest at the rate of 10% p.a. is as follows:

	1st Year		2nd Year
CI	10	10% ↗	11
Amount	110		121

Interest earn on ₹ 100 in 2 years at 10% p.a. = 10 + 11 = ₹ 21.

$$100 \to 21$$
$$x \to 6615$$

∴ $x = \dfrac{6615 \times 100}{21}$

= ₹ 31500.

Choice (d)

Solution 9

$$P\left(1+\dfrac{r}{100}\right)^n = \text{Amount}$$

$$3000\left(1+\dfrac{10}{100}\right)^n = 3630$$

$$\left(\dfrac{11}{10}\right)^n = \dfrac{121}{100}$$

$$\left(\dfrac{11}{10}\right)^n = \left(\dfrac{11}{10}\right)^2$$

∴ $n = 2$ years.

Choice (b)

Solution 10

Rate of interest = 20% p.a.

As the compounding is done half yearly, so $r = 10\%$ for every six months

Calculation of compound interest on ₹ 15000 at the rate of 10% for six months is as follows:

	6 months	12 months	18 months
CI	1500	1650	1815
Amount	16500	18150	19965

So, he will receive an amount of ₹ 19965 on maturity of fixed deposit.

Choice (a)

Solution 11

If the simple interest for 2 years is ₹ 2400, then for 1 year it must be ₹ 1200. Also, the simple and compound interest for the 1st year (or period) is always same and it start deviating from next year (or next period).

Simple Interest = 1200 in 1st year + 1200 in 2nd year
Compound Interest = 1200 in 1st year + (1200 + 120) in 2nd year

₹ 120 of extra interest received in 2nd year is the interest on 1st year's interest. So the rate of interest can be found as:

$$r = \frac{120}{1200} \times 100 = 10\%$$

Simple Interest $= \frac{Pnr}{100}$

$$2400 = \frac{P \times 2 \times 10}{100}$$

∴ $\quad P = ₹\ 12000.$

Choice (a)

Solution 12

If a principal of P is becoming an amount of $2P$ after 5 years, hence the *SI* received in these 5 years is P.

Simple interest = Amount − Principal
$\qquad\qquad\quad = 2P - P = P.$

$$\frac{Pnr}{100} = SI$$

$$\frac{P \times 5 \times r}{100} = P$$

∴ $\quad r = 20\%.$

If a principal of P will become an amount of $3P$, hence the *SI* on this principal is $2P$.

Simple interest = Amount − Principal
$\qquad\qquad\quad = 3P - P = 2P.$

$$\frac{Pnr}{100} = SI$$

$$\frac{P \times n \times 20}{100} = 2P$$

∴ $\quad n = 10$ years.

Alternate Method:

$P \xrightarrow{SI = P} 2P \quad$ in 5 years
$2P \xrightarrow{SI = P} 3P \quad$ in 5 years $\quad (\because SI$ of P is received in every 5 years)

Total time required = 5 + 5 = 10 years.

Choice (c)

Solution 13

Let the present value = ₹ 100

After 6 years at the rate of 6% p.a. simple interest it will amount to:

Amount = Principal + 6 years SI
= 100 + 6(6) = 136.

100 → 136
x → 2040

$\therefore x = \dfrac{2040 \times 100}{136} = ₹ 1500.$

Alternate Method

The present value of ₹ x due n years hence under simple interest is given as:

$$\text{Present value} = \dfrac{x}{\left(1 + \dfrac{nr}{100}\right)}$$

$$= \dfrac{2040}{\left(1 + \dfrac{6 \times 6}{100}\right)} = ₹ 1500.$$

Choice (b)

Solution 14

If the simple interest for 2 years is ₹ 3600, then for 1 year it must be ₹ 1800. Also, the simple and compound interest for the 1st year (or period) is always same and it start deviating from next year (or next period).

Simple Interest = 1800 in 1st year + 1800 in 2nd year
Compound Interest = 1800 in 1st year + (1800 + 270) in 2nd year

₹ 270 of extra interest received in 2nd year is the interest on 1st year's interest. So the rate of interest can be found as:

$r = \dfrac{270}{1800} \times 100 = 15\%.$

Choice (c)

Solution 15

Amount in 2 years = ₹ 2500

Amount in 3 years = ₹ 2500 + ₹ 150

$\therefore$ Rate of interest = $\dfrac{150}{2500} \times 100 = 6\%.$

Choice (a)

Solution 16

Let the principal, P = ₹ 100

At the rate of 20% p.a. the simple interest for 2 years is:
  SI = 20 + 20
  = ₹ 40

At the rate of 20% p.a. the compound interest for 2 years is:
  CI = 20 + (20 + 4)
  = ₹ 44

Difference between compound and simple interest = 44 – 40
  = ₹ 4

100 → Difference is ₹ 4
18000 → Difference is ₹ x

∴ $x = \dfrac{18000 \times 4}{100}$
  = ₹ 720.

Choice (a)

Solution 17

$CI = \dfrac{9}{16} P$

Amount = Principal + CI
  $= P + \dfrac{9}{16} P$
  $= \dfrac{25}{16} P$

$P\left(1 + \dfrac{r}{100}\right)^n =$ Amount on CI

$P\left(1 + \dfrac{r}{100}\right)^2 = \dfrac{25}{16} P$

$1 + \dfrac{r}{100} = \dfrac{5}{4}$

$\dfrac{r}{100} = \dfrac{1}{4}$

∴ $r = 25\%.$

Choice (d)

Solution 18

$$P\left(1+\frac{r/4}{100}\right)^{4n} = \text{Amount after quarterly compounding}$$

$$P\left(1+\frac{40/4}{100}\right)^{4} = 7320.50$$

$$P\left(1+\frac{1}{10}\right)^{4} = 7320.5$$

$$P\left(\frac{11}{10}\right)^{4} = 7320.5$$

$$P = \frac{7320.5 \times 10000}{14641} = ₹\,5000.$$

Choice (a)

Solution 19

If there is 50% increase in amount means a principal of ₹ 100 becomes an amount of ₹ 150 in 4 years.

∴ SI of 4 years = Amount − Principal = 150 − 100 = ₹ 50

SI of 1 year = $\frac{50}{4}$ = 12.5

So, rate of interest $r = \frac{12.5}{100} \times 100 = 12.5\%$

Amount on CI if principal is 24000 is:

$$\text{Amount} = P\left(1+\frac{r}{100}\right)^{n}$$

$$= 24000\left(1+\frac{12.5}{100}\right)^{2}$$

$$= ₹\,30375.$$

∴ CI = 30375 − 24000 = ₹ 6375.

Choice (d)

Solution 20

P = 8000
n = 1 years
r = 8%

Amount on yearly compounding $= P\left(1+\dfrac{r}{100}\right)^n$

$= 8000\left(1+\dfrac{8}{100}\right)^1$

$= 8640$

Amount on half yearly compounding $= P\left(1+\dfrac{r/2}{100}\right)^{2n}$

$= 8000\left(1+\dfrac{4}{100}\right)^2$

$= 8652.8.$

Difference $= 8652.8 - 8640 = ₹ 12.8.$

Choice (a)

Solution 21

Let the principal, $P = ₹ 1000$

At the rate of 5% p.a. the compound interest for 2 years will be:

CI for 1st year $= ₹ 50$

CI for 2nd year $= 50 + \dfrac{5}{100} \times 50 = 52.5$

$\therefore$ CI of 2 years $= 50 + 52.5 = ₹ 102.5$

$1000 \rightarrow 102.5$
$x \rightarrow 2255$

$\therefore$ $x = \dfrac{2255 \times 1000}{102.5} = ₹ 22000$

So, original principal $= ₹ 22000$

Simple interest on ₹ 22000 at 2.5% rate of interest for a period of 4 years is:

$SI = \dfrac{Pnr}{100}$

$= \dfrac{22000 \times 4 \times 2.5}{100} = ₹ 2200.$

Choice (c)

Solution 22

Assuming a principal, $P = ₹ 1000$

Given rate of interest, $r = 10\%$ per quarter.

	3 months	6 months	9 months	12 months
Compound Interest	100	→ 110	→ 121	→ 133.1
Amount (Principal + CI)	1100 →	1210 →	1331 →	1464.1

As the original principal of ₹ 1000 will become a final amount of ₹ 1464.1, therefore the effective rate of interest is 46.41%.

Choice (b)

Solution 23

P = 12000
n = 1 years
r = 20%

Amount on yearly compounding $= P\left(1+\dfrac{r}{100}\right)^n$

$= 12000\left(1+\dfrac{20}{100}\right)^1$

$= 14400$

∴ Interest earned in yearly compounding = 14400 − 12000 = ₹ 2400

Amount on half yearly compounding $= P\left(1+\dfrac{r/2}{100}\right)^{2n}$

$= 12000\left(1+\dfrac{10}{100}\right)^2 = 14520.$

∴ Interest earned in half yearly compounding = 14520 − 12000 = ₹ 2520.

Difference = 2520 − 2400 = ₹ 120.

Choice (a)

Solution 24

P	$\xrightarrow{CI=P}$	2P	in 2½ years	
2P	$\xrightarrow{CI=2P}$	4P	in 2½ years	(∵ Sum doubles in every 2½ years)
4P	$\xrightarrow{CI=4P}$	8P	in 2½ years	(∵ Sum doubles in every 2½ years)
8P	$\xrightarrow{CI=8P}$	16P	in 2½ years	(∵ Sum doubles in every 2½ years)

Hence in 10 years the sum will become 16 times itself.

∴ Amount = 16 × 700
= ₹ 11200.

Choice (d)

Solution 25

Assuming the principal invested, $P = ₹\ 1000$

Rate of interest, $r = 20\%$ p.a. or 10% for every six months

Growth of principal invested by Ram under compound interest at annual compounding is as follows:

	1 year	2 year
CI	200	240
Amount	1200	1440

Growth of principal invested by Shyam under compound interest at half yearly compounding is as follows:

	6 months	12 months	18 months	24 months
CI	100	110	121	133.1
Amount	1100	1210	1331	1464.1

Additional amount received by Shyam as compared to Ram = $1464.1 - 1440 = ₹\ 24.1$

$1000 \rightarrow 24.1$

$x \rightarrow 723$

$\therefore x = \dfrac{723 \times 1000}{24.1} = ₹\ 30000.$

Choice (b)

Solution 26

$P = ₹\ 60000$

	1st Year (10%)	2nd Year (15%)	3rd Year (20%)
CI	6000	9900	15180
Amount	66000	75900	91080

$\therefore$ Total interest earned = $6000 + 9900 + 15180 = ₹\ 31080.$

Choice (d)

Solution 27

Assuming the principal, $P = ₹\ 100$

At the rate of 10% p.a. the simple interest and compound interest for 2 years is:

$SI = 10 + 10 = ₹\ 20$

$CI = 10 + 11 = ₹\ 21$

Difference = 21 − 20 = ₹ 1

$$100 \rightarrow 1$$
$$x \rightarrow 44.5$$

∴ x = 44.5 × 100
   = ₹ 4450.

Choice (b)

Solution 28

The calculation of compound interest is as follows:

	1st Year	*2nd Year*
CI	1600	928
Loan Amount	21600	12528
Repaid	−10000	−10000
Remaining loan	11600	2528

So, after paying two installments of ₹ 10000 each he still owe ₹ 2528 at the end of second year.

Choice (c)

Solution 29

The calculation of compound interest is as follows:

	1st Year	*2nd Year*	*3rd Year*
CI	5000	4400	3680
Loan Amount	30000	26400	22080
Repaid	−8000	−8000	
Remaining loan	22000	18400	

So, at the end of 3rd year he should pay ₹ 22080 to clear his loan.

Choice (d)

Solution 30

$$\frac{P n r}{100} = \text{Simple Interest}$$

$$\frac{P \times 3 \times 5}{100} = 1800$$

∴   P = ₹ 12000

Amount on CI = $P\left(1+\frac{r}{100}\right)^n$

$= 12000\left(1+\frac{5}{100}\right)^3$

= ₹ 13891.5.

∴ Compound interest earned = 13891.5 − 12000
= ₹ 1891.5.

Choice (c)

Solution 31

$P\left(1+\frac{r}{100}\right)^n$ = Amount

$4096\left(1+\frac{12.5}{100}\right)^n = 6561$

$\left(1+\frac{1}{8}\right)^n = \frac{6561}{4096}$

$\left(\frac{9}{8}\right)^n = \left(\frac{9}{8}\right)^4$

∴ n = 4 years.

Choice (c)

Solution 32

Assuming the principal, $P = 100$ and rate of interest, $r = 10\%$
CI in 1st year = ₹ 10
CI in 2nd year = 10 + 1 = ₹ 11

Difference in CI in 1st and second year = 11 − 10 = ₹ 1

Suppose the principal $P = 100$ and rate of interest is thrice, r = 30%
CI in 1st year = ₹ 30
CI in 2nd year = 30 + 9 = ₹ 39

Difference in CI in 1st and second year = 39 − 30 = ₹ 9.

So, the difference is 9 times the previous difference. Hence if the previous difference is ₹ 80, the new difference will be:

New difference = 9 × 80 = ₹ 720.

Choice (d)

Solution 33

If an amount of P is borrowed at the rate of $r\%$ per annum compound interest, then equal number of installments for n years is calculated as:

Each installment $= \dfrac{P \cdot r}{100\left[1-\left(\dfrac{100}{100+r}\right)^n\right]} = \dfrac{21000\times 10}{100\left[1-\left(\dfrac{100}{100+10}\right)^2\right]} = ₹\,12100.$

Choice (c)

Solution 34

If the interest is compounded every moment, then:

Amount on $CI = P \cdot e^{\frac{nr}{100}} = 4000 \times (2.71)^{\frac{10\times 10}{100}} = 4000 \times 2.71 = ₹\,10840.$

Choice (d)

Solution 35

Let each installment be ₹ 100.

	1st	2nd	3rd
Installment	100	100	100
SI		10	20
Total =	100 +	110 +	120
=	330		

$100 \to 330$
$x \to 1650$

$\therefore \quad x = \dfrac{1650 \times 100}{330} = 500.$

Choice (a)

Solution 36

Let each installment be ₹ 100.

	1st	2nd
Installment	100	100
CI		10
Total =	100 +	110
=	210	

$100 \to 210$
$x \to 3150$

$\therefore \quad x = \dfrac{3150 \times 100}{210} = 1500.$

Choice (b)

23
Stocks and Shares

SHARES OR STOCK

A limited company raises capital by dividing it into small units, called *shares* or *stock*. For each investment, the company issues a 'share-certificate', showing the value of each share and the number of shares held by a person. The person who buys shares or stock of a particular company is called a share holder or stock holder of that company.

FACE VALUE

The capital required is divided into small units called shares. The value of a share or stock printed on the share-certificate is called its *Face Value* or *Par Value*. In India, the generally accepted value for such a unit is ₹ 10 or ₹ 100.

MARKET VALUE

The shares of a public limited company are sold and bought in the open market through brokers at stock-exchanges and depending on the demand for share, the price fluctuates. The rate at which a share is brought or sold in the market is the *Market Value* of share. A share or stock is said to be:
- At premium or above par, if its market value is more than its face value.
- At par, if its market value is the same as its face value.
- At discount or below par, if its market value is less than its face value.

DIVIDEND

The people who are holding the shares are called shareholders. The annual profit distributed among share holders is called dividend. The dividend is expressed as a percentage of the face value. Whenever any company quotes a dividend percentage figure, it goes without saying that it is percentage of face value:

$$\% \text{ of dividend} = \frac{\text{Dividend Amount}}{\text{Face Value}} \times 100$$

Dividend is always calculated on the face value (or par value) and is irrespective of the price at which the share was purchased (market value).

BROKERAGE

The broker's commission is called brokerage.
- When stock is purchased, broker adds his commission to the cost price.
- When stock is sold, broker subtracts his commission from the selling price.

POINTS TO NOTE

1. Face value of share always remains constant.
2. Market value of share changes from time to time.
3. Dividend is always paid on the face value of share.
4. A 7% stock at a premium of 10% means:
   Face value = ₹ 100
   Market Value = ₹ 110
   Annual dividend = 7% of ₹ 100 = ₹ 7.
5. A 4% stock at a discount of 5% means:
   Face value = ₹ 100
   Market Value = ₹ 95
   Annual dividend = 4% of ₹ 100 = ₹ 4.

SOLVED EXAMPLES

Example 1

Find the total investment made if:
1. 120 shares of ₹ 100 face value are purchased at a premium of 10%
2. 150 shares of ₹ 100 face value are purchased at a discount of 15%

Solution

1. Market value = ₹ 110
   Investment = Number of shares × Market value of each share
   $\qquad$ = 120 × 110
   $\qquad$ = ₹ 13200
2. Market value = ₹ 85
   Investment = Number of shares × Market value of each share
   $\qquad$ = 150 × 85
   $\qquad$ = ₹ 12750.

Example 2

Find the annual income of a person who invested ₹ 72150 in a 7% stock at of 11% premium.

Solution

Market value of each share = 100 + 11 = ₹ 111

Number of shares = $\dfrac{\text{Investment}}{\text{Market Value of each share}}$

$= \dfrac{72150}{111}$

$= 650$

Income from each share = 7% of Face value

$= \dfrac{7}{100} \times 100 = ₹ 7$

Total annual income = 650 × 7 = ₹ 4550.

Example 3

Mohan invested ₹ 38000 in a 4% stock at 20% discount. Find the yield percent at the end of year.

Solution

Market value of each share = 100 – 20 = ₹ 80

Number of shares = $\dfrac{\text{Investment}}{\text{Market Value of each share}}$

$= \dfrac{38000}{80} = 475$

Total annual income = 475 × 4 = ₹ 1900

Annual yield = $\dfrac{\text{Income}}{\text{Investment}} \times 100$

$= \dfrac{1900}{38000} \times 100 = 5\%.$

Example 4

Govind invests in a 9% stock at 25% discount. He gets a dividend of ₹ 4500 at the end of year. How much did he invest?

Solution

Dividend = 9% of face value = 9% of ₹ 100 = ₹ 9

To earn ₹ 9, number of shares = 1

To earn ₹ 4500, number of shares = $\dfrac{4500}{9} = 500$

Market value of each share = 100 − 25 = ₹ 75

Investment = Number of shares × Market value of each share = 500 × 75 = ₹ 37500.

Example 5

Which is the better investment 6% stock at 20% discount or 8% stock at 25% premium?

Solution

Case 1

Market value of share at 20% discount = 100 − 20 = ₹ 80
Dividend = 6% of ₹ 100 = ₹ 6
By investing ₹ 80, income is ₹ 6
Returns in case-1 = $\frac{6}{80} \times 100 = 7.5\%$

Case 2

Market value of share at 25% premium = 100 + 25 = ₹ 125
Dividend = 8% of ₹ 100 = ₹ 8
By investing ₹ 125, income is ₹ 8
Returns in case-2 = $\frac{8}{125} \times 100$
$= 6.4\%$.

As percentage returns in case-1 is more than percentage returns in case-2, hence 6% stock at 20% discount is better investment.

Example 6

Lala invests some money partly in 9% stock at 90 and partly in 12% stock at 112. To obtain equal dividends from both in what ratio he must invest the money?

Solution

Investment in 9% stock at 90 = ₹ x

Investment in 12% stock at 112 = ₹ y

As the dividends are equal:

$$\left(\frac{x}{90}\right) \times 9 = \left(\frac{y}{112}\right) \times 12$$

$$\frac{x}{y} = \frac{90}{9} \times \frac{12}{112}$$

$$\frac{x}{y} = \frac{15}{14}$$

So, Lala should invest his money in the ratio of 15 : 14.

EXERCISE

1. The cost price of ₹ 100 stock at 5% discount with brokerage of 0.5% is:
   (a) ₹ 94.5
   (b) ₹ 95.5
   (c) ₹ 99.5
   (d) ₹ 100.5

2. The amount obtained on selling a 14% stock at ₹ 103.25, brokerage being 0.25% is:
   (a) ₹ 99.75
   (b) ₹ 100.25
   (c) ₹ 103
   (d) ₹ 103.5

3. How many shares of market value ₹ 40 each can be purchased for ₹ 15990 when brokerage being 2.5%?
   (a) 390
   (b) 410
   (c) 400
   (d) 415

4. Anand invested ₹ 15000 in a 6% stock at par. Find his annual income.
   (a) ₹ 450
   (b) ₹ 500
   (c) ₹ 600
   (d) ₹ 900

5. Ratan invested ₹ 41000 in a 4% stock at 2.5% premium. How much annual income dose he earn?
   (a) ₹ 400
   (b) ₹ 1000
   (c) ₹ 1600
   (d) ₹ 1640

6. A man invested ₹ 17250 in shares of a company of face value ₹ 100 at 15% premium. If the company declares 6% dividend at the end of the year, then how much annual income the man gets?
   (a) ₹ 600
   (b) ₹ 750
   (c) ₹ 900
   (d) ₹ 1035

7. An investor invested ₹ 19000 in ₹ 100 shares quoted at ₹ 95. If the rate of dividend be 11%, his annual income is:
   (a) ₹ 2200
   (b) ₹ 2090
   (c) ₹ 1100
   (d) ₹ 1045

8. Find the annual income of a person who invested ₹ 10550 in a 4% stock at 5.5% premium.
   (a) ₹ 200
   (b) ₹ 400
   (c) ₹ 800
   (d) ₹ 1200

9. Find the annual income of a person who invested ₹ 39000 in a 7% stock at 2.5% discount.
   (a) ₹ 700
   (b) ₹ 2800
   (c) ₹ 2730
   (d) ₹ 3900

10. Sanjay invests ₹ 49350 in a 4% stock at 5% premium and the same amount in a 6% stock at 6% discount. What is total annual income at the end of year?
    (a) ₹ 4935
    (b) ₹ 5030
    (c) ₹ 6720
    (d) ₹ 9950

11. By investing ₹ 21000 in 9% stock, Dhanraj earns an income of ₹ 1400. The market value of ₹ 100 stock is then quoted at:
    (a) ₹ 85
    (b) ₹ 109
    (c) ₹ 115
    (d) ₹ 135

12. The market value of a 6% stock, in which an income of ₹ 750 is earned by investing ₹ 11250, is:
    (a) ₹ 90
    (b) ₹ 94
    (c) ₹ 105
    (d) ₹ 115

13. A man invested ₹ 1710 in a stock at 95 to obtain an income of ₹ 162. The dividend from the stock is:
    (a) 8%
    (b) 9%
    (c) 9.5%
    (d) 10%

14. A man bought 50 shares of ₹ 100 at 10% discount, the rate of dividend being 4.5%. The rate of interest obtained is:
    (a) 4%
    (b) 5%
    (c) 6%
    (d) 9%

15. A man invests in a 18% stock at 144. The interest obtained by him is:
    (a) 8%
    (b) 12%
    (c) 12.5%
    (d) 16%

16. Ajay invested ₹ 26000 in a 6½% stock at 30% premium. Find the yield percent at the end of year.
    (a) 6½%
    (b) 6%
    (c) 5 ½%
    (d) 5%

17. In order to obtain an income of ₹ 920 from 8% stock at ₹ 80, one must make an investment of:
    (a) ₹ 8000
    (b) ₹ 9000
    (c) ₹ 9200
    (d) ₹ 10000

18. In order to obtain an income of ₹ 3000 from 6% stock at ₹ 75, one must make an investment of:
    (a) ₹ 30000
    (b) ₹ 37500
    (c) ₹ 80000
    (d) ₹ 60000

19. John invests in a 5% stock at 10% premium. He gets a dividend of ₹ 3500 at the end of year. How much is his investment?
    (a) ₹ 35000
    (b) ₹ 64000
    (c) ₹ 75000
    (d) ₹ 77000

20. A man invests in a 8% stock at 12% discount. He gets a dividend of ₹ 4800 at the end of year. How much is his investment?
    (a) ₹ 48000
    (b) ₹ 52400
    (c) ₹ 52800
    (d) ₹ 56800

21. Which is the better investment 6% stock at 125 or 4% stock at 100?
    (a) 6% @ ₹ 125
    (b) 4% @ ₹ 100
    (c) Both are equally good
    (d) Cannot be determined

22. Which is the better investment 7% stock at 112 or 6% stock at 96?
    (a) 7% @ ₹ 112
    (b) 6% @ ₹ 96
    (c) Both are equally good
    (d) Cannot be determined

23. Which is the better investment 4% stock at 120 or 5% stock at 125?
    (a) 4% @ ₹ 120
    (b) 5% @ ₹ 125
    (c) Both are equally good
    (d) Cannot be determined

24. Prakash invested ₹ 26500 in 15% stock at ₹ 106. Pranay invested ₹ 30600 in 12% stock at ₹ 102. Who will earn the greater annual income?
    (a) Prakash
    (b) Pranay
    (c) Same income for both
    (d) Cannot be determined

25. Madanlal invests a part of ₹ 30000 in 10% stock at ₹ 150 and the remaining amount in 12% stock at ₹ 120. If his total dividend per annum is ₹ 2700, how much does he invest in 10% stock at ₹ 150?
    (a) ₹ 6000
    (b) ₹ 9000
    (c) ₹ 12000
    (d) ₹ 15000

26. A man invests some money partly in 10% stock at 95 and partly in 15% stock at 120. To obtain equal dividends from both he must invest the money in the ratio of:
    (a) 5 : 6
    (b) 2 : 3
    (c) 19 : 24
    (d) 19 : 16

KEYS

1. (b)	2. (c)	3. (a)	4. (d)	5. (c)	6. (c)	7. (a)	8. (b)
9. (b)	10. (b)	11. (d)	12. (a)	13. (b)	14. (b)	15. (c)	16. (d)
17. (c)	18. (b)	19. (d)	20. (c)	21. (a)	22. (c)	23. (b)	24. (a)
25. (b)	26. (d)						

SOLUTIONS

Solution 1
Cost price = 100 – 5 + 0.5 = ₹ 95.5.
Choice (b)

Solution 2
Selling price = 103.25 – 0.25 = ₹ 103.
Choice (c)

Solution 3
Cost price of each share = 40 + 2.5% of 40
= ₹ 41

Number of shares = $\frac{15990}{41}$ = 390.

Choice (a)

Solution 4
At par means purchased at face value.
Number of shares = $\frac{15000}{100}$ = 150

Annual income = 150 × 6 = ₹ 900.
Choice (d)

Solution 5
If the face value is 100, then 2.5% premium means the market value = ₹ 102.50

Number of shares = $\frac{41000}{102.50}$ = 400.

Since this is a 4% stock, so it will yield an interest of ₹ 4 on face value of ₹ 100

Total annual income = 400 × 4 = ₹ 1600.
Choice (c)

Solution 6
Number of shares = $\frac{17250}{115}$ = 150

Face value = 150 × 100 = ₹ 15000

Annual Income = $\frac{6}{100} \times 15000$ = ₹ 900.

Choice (c)

Solution 7

Number of Shares = $\frac{19000}{95}$ = 200

Face value = 200 × 100 = ₹ 20000

Annual income = $\frac{11}{100} \times 20000$ = ₹ 2200.

Choice (a)

Solution 8

Number of shares = $\frac{10550}{105.50}$ = 100

Dividend paid is ₹ 4 (on face value of ₹ 100)

Annual income = 100 × 4 = ₹ 400.

Choice (b)

Solution 9

Number of shares = $\frac{39000}{97.50}$ = 400

Dividend paid is ₹ 7 (on face value of ₹ 100)

Annual income = 400 × 7 = ₹ 2800.

Choice (b)

Solution 10

Number of shares at 5% premium = $\frac{49350}{105}$ = 470

Income (₹ 4 dividend) = 470 × 4 = ₹ 1880

Number of shares at 6% discount = $\frac{49350}{94}$ = 525

Income (₹ 6 dividend) = 525 × 6 = ₹ 3150

Total income = 1880 + 3150 = ₹ 5030.

Choice (b)

Solution 11

To earn ₹ 1400, investment made is ₹ 21000

To earn ₹ 9, investment required = $\dfrac{21000}{1400} \times 9$ = ₹ 135

So, the market value of ₹ 100 stock is 135.

Choice (d)

Solution 12

To earn ₹ 750, investment made is ₹ 11250

To earn ₹ 6, investment required = $\dfrac{11250}{750} \times 6$ = ₹ 90

So, the market value of ₹ 100 stock is 90.

Choice (a)

Solution 13

Shares purchased = $\dfrac{1710}{95}$ = 18

Income from 18 shares ⇒ ₹ 162

Income from 1 share = $\dfrac{162}{18}$ = ₹ 9

Hence dividend is 9%.

Choice (b)

Solution 14

Investment = 50 × (100 − 10) = ₹ 4500

Face value = 50 × 100 = ₹ 5000

Dividend of 4.5% on Face value = $\dfrac{4.5}{100} \times 5000$ = ₹ 225

Interest obtained = $\dfrac{225}{4500} \times 100$ = 5%.

Choice (b)

Solution 15

By investing ₹ 144, income earned is ₹ 18

By investing ₹ 100, income earned = $\dfrac{18}{144} \times 100$ = 12.5%.

Choice (c)

Solution 16

Number of shares with Ajay = $\dfrac{26000}{130}$ = 200

Dividend paid is ₹ 6.50 (on face value of ₹ 100)

Income of Ajay = 200 × 6.50 = ₹ 1300

Yield percent = $\dfrac{\text{Income}}{\text{Investment}} \times 100$

$= \dfrac{1300}{26000} \times 100$

= 5%.

Choice (d)

Solution 17

Dividend is 8% of face value (₹ 100) ⇒ ₹ 8

To obtain ₹ 8, investment = ₹ 80.

To obtain ₹ 920, investment = $\dfrac{80}{8} \times 920$ = ₹ 9200.

Choice (c)

Solution 18

Dividend is 6% of face value (₹ 100) ⇒ ₹ 6

To obtain ₹ 6, investment = ₹ 75

To obtain ₹ 3000, investment = $\dfrac{75}{6} \times 3000$ = ₹ 37500.

Choice (b)

Solution 19

For a dividend of ₹ 5, number of shares required = 1

For a dividend of ₹ 3500, number of shares = $\dfrac{3500}{5}$ = 700

Cost of each share = ₹ 110

Investment = Number of shares × Cost of each share = 700 × 110
= ₹ 77000.

Choice (d)

Solution 20

For a dividend of ₹ 8, number of shares required = 1

For a dividend of ₹ 4800, number of shares = $\frac{4800}{8}$ = 600

Cost of each share = ₹ 88

Investment = Number of shares × Cost of each share = 600 × 88 = ₹ 52800.

Choice (c)

Solution 21

By investing ₹ 125, income is ₹ 6

Hence returns = $\frac{6}{125} \times 100$ = 4.8%

By investing ₹ 100, income is ₹ 4

Hence returns = $\frac{4}{100} \times 100$ = 4%

So, 6% stock at 125 is a better investment as they are giving more returns.

Choice (a)

Solution 22

By investing ₹ 112, income is ₹ 7

Hence returns = $\frac{7}{112} \times 100$ = 6.25%

By investing ₹ 96, income is ₹ 6

Hence returns = $\frac{6}{96} \times 100$ = 6.25%

As they are giving equal returns both are equally good.

Choice (c)

Solution 23

By investing ₹ 120, income is ₹ 4.

Hence returns = $\frac{4}{120} \times 100$ = 3.33%.

By investing ₹ 125, income is ₹ 5.

Hence returns = $\frac{5}{125} \times 100$ = 4%.

So, 5% stock at 125 is a better investment as they are giving more returns.

Choice (b)

Solution 24

Number of shares with Prakash = $\dfrac{26500}{106}$ = 250.

Dividend paid is ₹ 15 (on face value of ₹ 100)

Annual income of Prakash = 250 × 15 = ₹ 3750.

Number of shares with Pranay = $\dfrac{30600}{102}$ = 300.

Dividend paid is ₹ 12 (on face value of ₹ 100).
Annual income of Pranay = 300 × 12 = ₹ 3600.

So, Prakash will earn more than Pranay.

Choice (a)

Solution 25

Let Madanlal invests ₹ x in 10% stock at ₹ 150.

So, he invests (30000 − x) in 12% stock at ₹ 120.

$$\left(\dfrac{x}{150}\right) \times 10 + \left(\dfrac{30000-x}{120}\right) \times 12 = 2700$$

$$\dfrac{x}{15} + \dfrac{30000-x}{10} = 2700$$

$$\dfrac{2x + 90000 - 3x}{30} = 2700$$

$$x = 9000.$$

Choice (b)

Solution 26

He invests ₹ x in 10% stock at ₹ 95, and ₹ y in 15% stock at 120. As the dividends from both the investments is same:

$$\dfrac{x}{95} \times 10 = \dfrac{y}{120} \times 15$$

$$\dfrac{x}{y} = \dfrac{19}{16}.$$

Choice (d)

24

Heights and Distances

INTRODUCTION

The height of any vertically standing building, tower or a wall with respect to an observer standing on a horizontal ground at some distance from it forms a triangle with a line joining the observer and the top of building, tower or wall, which is a right angle triangle. The branch of mathematics which deals with the ratios between the sides of a right-angled triangle is trigonometry.

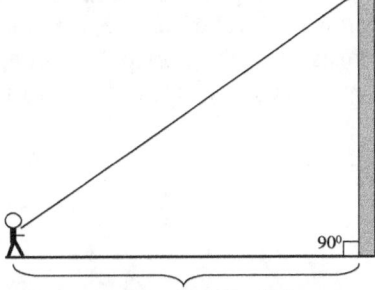

Distance between Building & observer

TRIGONOMETRIC RELATIONS

$$\sin\theta = \frac{\text{Opposite Side}}{\text{Hypotenuse}}$$

$$\cos\theta = \frac{\text{Adjecent Side}}{\text{Hypotenuse}}$$

$$\tan\theta = \frac{\text{Opposite Side}}{\text{Adjecent Side}}$$

$$\text{cosec}\theta = \frac{1}{\sin\theta}$$

$$\sec\theta = \frac{1}{\cos\theta}$$

$$\cot\theta = \frac{1}{\tan\theta}$$

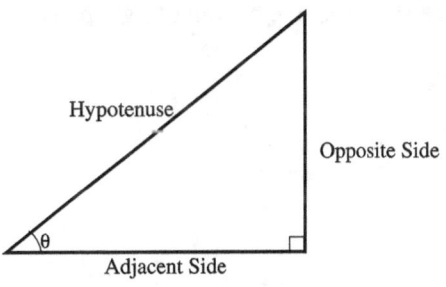

VALUES OF TRIGONOMETRIC RATIOS

θ	$0°$	$30°$	$45°$	$60°$	$90°$
$\sin\theta$	0	$\frac{1}{2}$	$\frac{1}{\sqrt{2}}$	$\frac{\sqrt{3}}{2}$	1
$\cos\theta$	1	$\frac{\sqrt{3}}{2}$	$\frac{1}{\sqrt{2}}$	$\frac{1}{2}$	0
$\tan\theta$	0	$\frac{1}{\sqrt{3}}$	1	$\sqrt{3}$	∞

ANGLE OF ELEVATION

If the observer from a point O is looking at an object A, placed above the level of his eye, then the angle which the line of sight makes with the horizontal through O is called the angle of elevation of object A as seen from O.

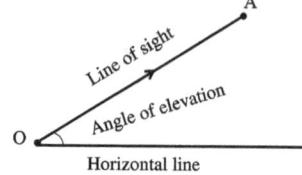

ANGLE OF DEPRESSION

If the observer from a point O is looking at an object A, placed below the level of his eye, then the angle which the line of sight makes with the horizontal through O is called the angle of depression of object A as seen from O.

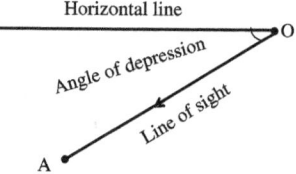

SOLVED EXAMPLES

Example 1

From a lighthouse 150 m high a ship is observed with an angle of depression of 30°. How far is the ship from the bottom of light house?

Solution

$$\tan 30° = \frac{150}{d}$$

$$\frac{1}{\sqrt{3}} = \frac{150}{d}$$

$$\therefore \quad d = 150\sqrt{3} \text{ m}$$

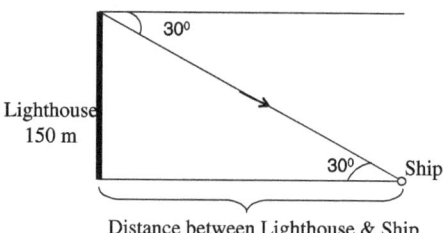

Hence the ship is $150\sqrt{3}$ meters far from bottom of light house.

Example 2

Two towers are separated by a distance of 600 m. A man stood at the mid point of the road joining their bases. If his angle of elevation towards the top of 1st tower is 30° and 2nd tower is 60°, then find the difference between heights of two towers.

Solution

Let the two towers be of height A and B respectively.

The angle of elevation towards tower A is 30° while towards tower B is 60°.

$$\tan 30° = \frac{A}{300}$$

∴ $A = 300 \times \frac{1}{\sqrt{3}} = 100\sqrt{3}$ m

$$\tan 60° = \frac{A}{300}$$

∴ $A = 300 \times \sqrt{3} = 300\sqrt{3}$ m

Difference between heights $= 300\sqrt{3} - 100\sqrt{3}$
$= 200\sqrt{3}$.

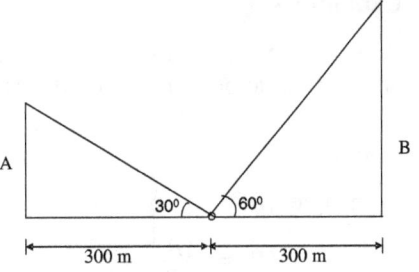

Example 3

A security guard standing on the top of an observation tower observes a jeep coming towards him. If it takes 2 min for the angle of depression to change from 30° to 60° how soon will it reach near the observation tower?

Solution

In triangle ABC,

$$\tan 60° = \frac{AB}{BC}$$

∴ $AB = \sqrt{3}\, BC$ ... (1)

In triangle ABD,

$$\tan 30° = \frac{AB}{BD}$$

∴ $AB = \frac{BD}{\sqrt{3}}$ ... (2)

Equating equation (1) and (2)

$$\frac{BD}{\sqrt{3}} = \sqrt{3}\, BC$$

$$BD = 3BC$$

$$BC + CD = 3BC$$

$$2BC = CD$$

∴ $BC = \frac{CD}{2}$

As time required in covering the distance CD is 2 min, so distance BC can be covered in its half time i.e. in 1 min. So the jeep will reach at the observation tower in 1 min.

Example 4

A solider observes a flag with an angle of elevation of 45°. After walking 18 m towards it, the angle of elevation changes to 60°. At what height above the ground the flag was hosted?

Solution

In triangle ABC,

$$\tan 60° = \frac{AB}{BC}$$

$\therefore \quad AB = \sqrt{3}\, BC \quad \ldots (1)$

In triangle ABD,

$$\tan 45° = \frac{AB}{BD}$$

$\therefore \quad AB = BD \quad \ldots (2)$

Equating equation (1) and (2),

$$\sqrt{3}\, BC = BD$$
$$\sqrt{3}\, BC = BC + 18 \text{ m}$$
$$BC(\sqrt{3} - 1) = 18$$

$\therefore \quad BC = \dfrac{18}{0.732} = 24.6 \text{ m}$

So, the flag was hosted 24.6 m above the ground.

EXERCISE

1. A person standing 60 m away from the foot of a tower observes the top of a tower to be at an angle of elevation of 60°. Find the height of tower.
   (a) 20 m
   (b) $20\sqrt{3}$ m
   (c) $60\sqrt{3}$ m
   (d) $\dfrac{60}{\sqrt{3}}$

2. If the length of shadow is $\sqrt{3}$ times its height of a pole, then the angle of elevation of sun is:
   (a) 30°
   (b) 45°
   (c) 60°
   (d) cannot be determined

3. At an instant of time if the length of shadow of a tree is equal to its height, then the angle of elevation of sun is:
   (a) 30°
   (b) 45°
   (c) 60°
   (d) cannot be determined

4. A ladder is placed against a wall. It makes an angle of 30° with the ground. Its top end which is resting on wall is 10 m above the foot of wall. Find the length of ladder.
   (a) 15 m
   (b) 20 m
   (c) $10\sqrt{3}$ m
   (d) $20\sqrt{3}$ m

5. A pole 6 m high is standing vertically in a ground. A rope is tied from the top end of the pole to a point on the ground, such that the rope makes an angle of 60° with ground. Find the length of rope.
   (a) $6\sqrt{3}$ m
   (b) $4\sqrt{3}$ m
   (c) $\dfrac{12}{\sqrt{3}}$ m
   (d) $12\sqrt{3}$ m

6. A pole 5 m high is fixed on the top of a tower. The angle of elevation of the top of the pole observed from a point 'A' on the ground is 60° and the angle of depression of the point 'A' from the top of the tower is 45°. Find the height of the tower.
   (a) 10 m
   (b) $5\sqrt{3}$ m
   (c) $\dfrac{5}{\sqrt{3}}$ m
   (d) $\dfrac{5}{\sqrt{3}-1}$ m

7. The angle of elevation of the top of tower from a certain place is 30°. If the observer moves 50 m towards the tower, the angle of elevation towards the top of tower changes to 60°. Find the height of tower.
   (a) 25 m
   (b) $25\sqrt{3}$ m
   (c) $50\sqrt{3}$ m
   (d) 50 m

8. Two persons A and B are standing on the either side of a tower. The angle of elevation of the top of the tower as observed by A is 30° and by B is 45°. If the tower is 100 m high, the distance between A and B is:
   (a) 200 m
   (b) $200\sqrt{3}$ m
   (c) $100\sqrt{3}$ m
   (d) $100(1 + \sqrt{3})$ m

9. From the top of a lighthouse two ships are observed with angle of depression of 30° and 60° on the same side of lighthouse. If the height of light house is 120 m, the distance between the ships is:
   (a) 120 m
   (b) $120\sqrt{3}$ m
   (c) $\dfrac{240}{\sqrt{3}}$ m
   (d) $240\sqrt{3}$ m

10. The horizontal distance between two towers is 140 m. The angle of elevation of the top of the first tower when seen from the top of the second tower is 30°. If the height of the second tower is 60 m, find the height of the first tower in meters.
    (a) $60\sqrt{3}$
    (b) $140\sqrt{3}$
    (c) $\dfrac{140}{\sqrt{3}}$
    (d) $60 + \dfrac{140}{\sqrt{3}}$

11. Two towers are separated by a distance of 600 m. At a point mid-way between them, the angles of elevation of the towers are 30° and 45°. Find the ratio of their heights.
    (a) 1 : 1
    (b) 1 : $\sqrt{3}$
    (c) 2 : $\sqrt{3}$
    (d) 1 : 2$\sqrt{3}$

12. A man on the top of a vertical light house observes a boat is coming directly towards it. If it takes 10 minutes for the angle of depression to change from 30° to 60° how soon will it reach the light house?
    (a) 5 min
    (b) 5$\sqrt{3}$ min
    (c) 10$\sqrt{3}$ min
    (d) 15 min

13. Ajay is standing at a point P on a level ground such that the distance between the point P and the bottom of a building is $\sqrt{3}$ times the height of the building. If Vijay, who looks towards Ajay from the top of the building, then his angle of depression is:
    (a) 15°
    (b) 30°
    (c) 45°
    (d) 60°

14. An airplane flying horizontally at a height of 1.5 km above the ground is observed at an angle of elevation of 60°. After 15 seconds, its angle of elevation from the same point is becomes 30°. Find the speed of the airplane in km/hr.
    (a) 160/$\sqrt{3}$
    (b) 120$\sqrt{3}$
    (c) 160
    (d) 240$\sqrt{3}$

KEYS

1. (c)	2. (a)	3. (b)	4. (b)	5. (b)	6. (d)	7. (b)	8. (d)
9. (c)	10.(d)	11.(b)	12.(a)	13.(b)	14.(d)		

SOLUTIONS

Solution 1

$\tan 60° = \dfrac{\text{Tower Height}}{60 \text{ m}}$

∴ Tower Height = 60$\sqrt{3}$

Choice (c)

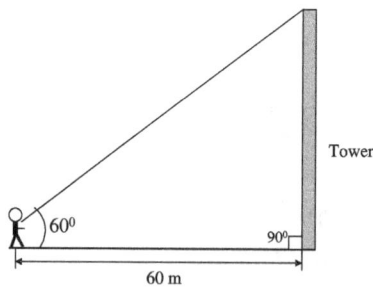

Solution 2

Here θ is the angle of elevation of sun.

$$\tan \theta = \frac{L}{L\sqrt{3}}$$

$$\theta = \tan^{-1} \frac{1}{\sqrt{3}}$$

∴ $\theta = 30°$.

Choice (a)

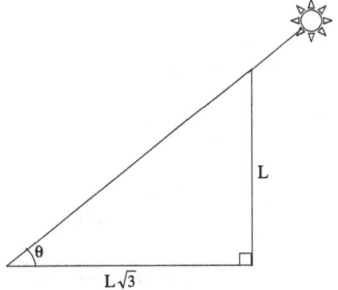

Solution 3

If the length of shadow is equal to height of tree, then it will be an isosceles right angle triangle.

In this case the angle of elevation will be 45°.

Choice (b)

Solution 4

$$\sin 30° = \frac{10 \text{ m}}{\text{Length of ladder}}$$

∴ Length of ladder $= \dfrac{10}{\frac{1}{2}}$

$= 20$ m.

Choice (b)

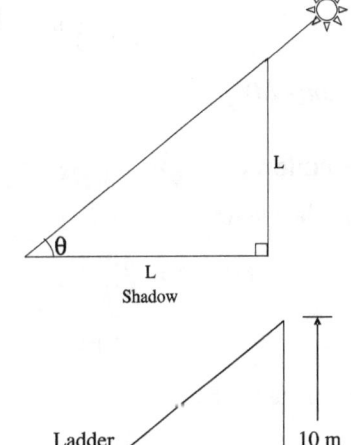

Solution 5

$$\sin 60° = \frac{6 \text{ m}}{\text{Length of rope}}$$

∴ Length of rope $= \dfrac{6}{\sqrt{3}/2}$

$= \dfrac{12}{\sqrt{3}}$

$= 4\sqrt{3}$ m.

Choice (b)

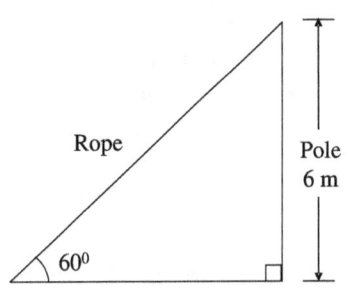

Solution 6

$$\tan 45° = \frac{T}{AB}$$

∴ Tower length = AB

$$\tan 60° = \frac{T+5}{AB}$$

$$\sqrt{3} = \frac{T+5}{AB}$$

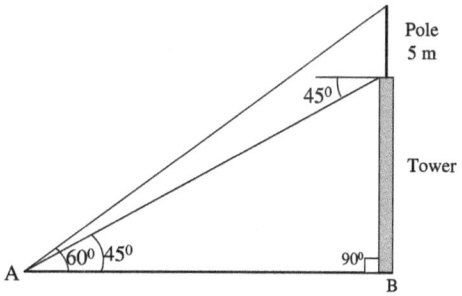

$$\sqrt{3} = \frac{T+5}{T}$$

∴ $T = \dfrac{5}{\sqrt{3}-1}$ m.

Choice (d)

Solution 7

In triangle ABC,

$$\tan 60° = \frac{AB}{BC}$$

∴ $AB = \sqrt{3}\ BC$ ... (1)

In triangle ABD,

$$\tan 30° = \frac{AB}{BD}$$

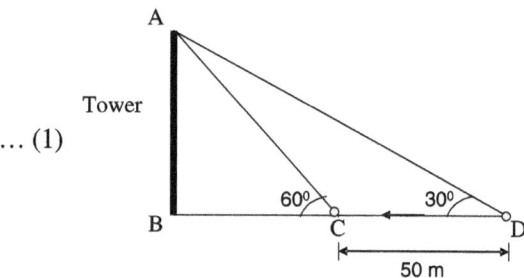

∴ $AB = \dfrac{BD}{\sqrt{3}}$ ... (2)

Equating equation (1) and (2)

$$\frac{BD}{\sqrt{3}} = \sqrt{3}\ BC$$

$$BD = 3BC$$

$$BC + CD = 3BC$$

$$2BC = CD$$

∴ $BC = \dfrac{50}{2} = 25$ m.

So, Height of tower i.e. $AB = \sqrt{3}\ BC$
$= 25\sqrt{3}$.

Choice (b)

Solution 8

$\tan 30° = \dfrac{CD}{AC}$

∴ $AC = 100\sqrt{3}$ ... (1)

$\tan 45° = \dfrac{CD}{BC}$

∴ $BC = 100$ ... (2)

$AB = AC + BC$

$= 100 + 100\sqrt{3}$

$= 100(1 + \sqrt{3})$

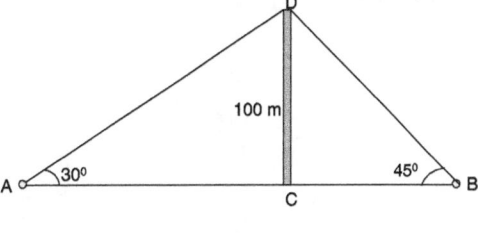

Choice (d)

Solution 9

$\tan 60° = \dfrac{AB}{BS1}$

∴ $BS1 = \dfrac{120}{\sqrt{3}}$ ... (1)

$\tan 30° = \dfrac{AB}{BS2}$

∴ $BS2 = 120\sqrt{3}$ ... (2)

Distance between two ships $= BS2 - BS1$

$= 120\sqrt{3} - \dfrac{120}{\sqrt{3}}$

$= \dfrac{240}{\sqrt{3}}$ m.

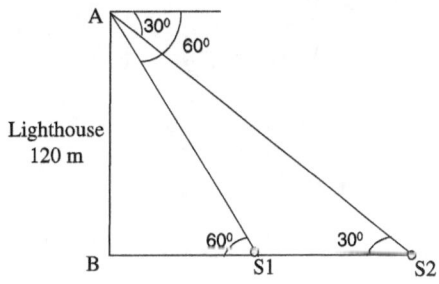

Choice (c)

Solution 10

$\tan 30° = \dfrac{x}{140}$

∴ $x = \dfrac{140}{\sqrt{3}}$

Height of first tower $= 60 + \dfrac{140}{\sqrt{3}}$

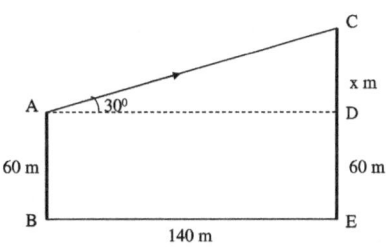

Choice (d)

Solution 11

$$\tan 30° = \frac{A}{300}$$

∴ $A = \frac{300}{\sqrt{3}}$

$$\tan 45° = \frac{B}{300}$$

∴ $B = 300$

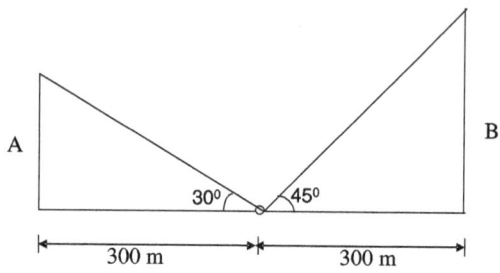

Ratio of their heights will be:

$$\frac{A}{B} = \frac{1}{\sqrt{3}}$$

Choice (b)

Solution 12

In triangle *ABC*,

$$\tan 60° = \frac{AB}{BC}$$

∴ $AB = \sqrt{3}\, BC$ ... (1)

In triangle *ABD*,

$$\tan 30° = \frac{AB}{BD}$$

∴ $AB = \frac{BD}{\sqrt{3}}$ ... (2)

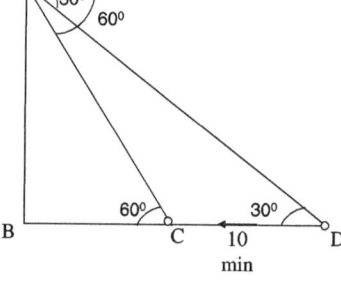

Equating equation (1) and (2)

$$\frac{BD}{\sqrt{3}} = \sqrt{3}\, BC$$

$$BD = 3BC$$
$$BC + CD = 3BC$$
$$2BC = CD$$

∴ $BC = \frac{CD}{2}$

As time required in covering the distance *CD* by the boat is 10 min, so distance *BC* can be covered in its half time i.e. in 5 min. So the boat will reach at the lighthouse in 5 min.

Choice (a)

Solution 13

$$\tan\theta = \frac{h}{h\sqrt{3}}$$

∴ $\theta = \tan^{-1}\frac{1}{\sqrt{3}}$

$\theta = 30°$

Choice (b)

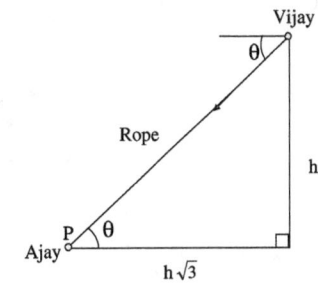

Solution 14

In triangle ABC,

$\tan 60° = \frac{BC}{AC}$

∴ $AC = \frac{1.5}{\sqrt{3}}$

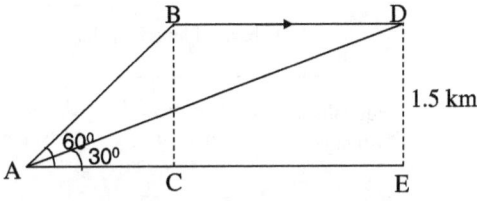

In triangle AED,

$\tan 30° = \frac{DE}{AE}$

∴ $AE = 1.5\sqrt{3}$

Distance traveled by plane i.e. $CE = AE - AC$

$= 1.5\sqrt{3} - \frac{1.5}{\sqrt{3}}$

$= \sqrt{3}$

Speed of the plane $= \frac{\sqrt{3}}{15}$ km/sec

$= \frac{\sqrt{3}}{15} \times 60 \times 60$

$= 240\sqrt{3}$ km/hr.

Choice (d)

25

Perimeter and Area

TRIANGLES

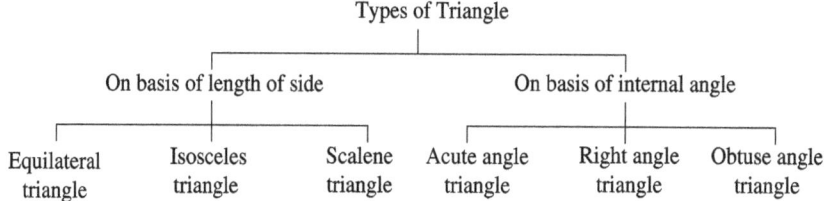

Important points to note

- Sum of any two sides is always greater than third side.
- The difference of any two sides is always less than the third side.
- If a, b and c are the three sides of a triangle and c is the largest side, then:

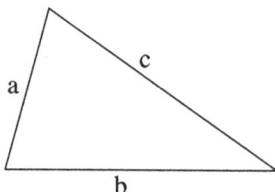

  If $c^2 < a^2 + b^2$, the triangle is acute angle triangle.
  If $c^2 = a^2 + b^2$, the triangle is right angle triangle (also called Pythagoras theorem).
  If $c^2 > a^2 + b^2$, the triangle is obtuse angle triangle.
- *Altitude (or Height):* The perpendicular drawn from a vertex to opposite side is called altitude of triangle. There are three altitudes in a triangle.
- *Orthocenter:* The point of intersection of the three altitudes is called as the orthocenter.
- *Median:* The line joining a vertex to the mid-point of opposite side is called median of a triangle. There are three medians in a triangle. A median bisects the area of triangle.
- *Centroid:* The point of intersection of three medians of a triangle is called the centroid. A centroid divides each median in the ratio 2 : 1 (vertex : base).
- *Incentre:* The point of intersection of three internal angles bisectors of a triangle is called incentre. The incentre is equidistant from all the three edges of the triangle. The distance between incentre to any edge is called inradius. By taking incentre as centre and inradius as the radius in compass, a circle can be drawn inside the triangle.

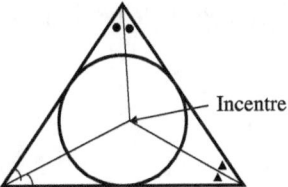

- *Circumcentre:* The point of intersection of the perpendicular bisectors of the sides of triangle is called circumcentre. The circumcentre is equidistant from the three vertices of triangle. The distance between circumcentre to any vertex is called circumradius. By taking circumcentre as centre and circumradius as the radius in compass, a circle can be drawn outside the triangle.

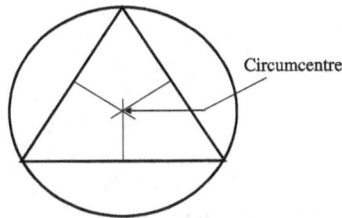

Area of Triangle

- When the measurement of three sides a, b and c is given,

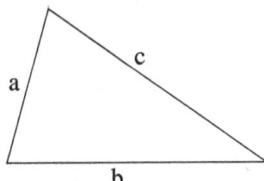

$$\text{Area} = \sqrt{s(s-a)(s-b)(s-c)}$$

Where $s = \dfrac{a+b+c}{2}$

- When base and altitude to that base is given,

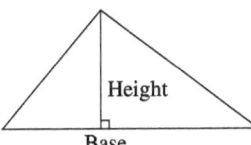

$$\text{Area} = \dfrac{1}{2} \times \text{Base} \times \text{Height}$$

- If length of two sides and the included angle between them is given,

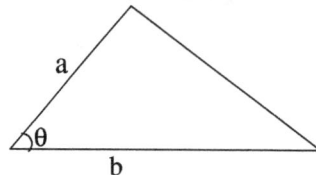

$$\text{Area} = \frac{1}{2} \times a \times b \times \sin\theta$$

- For an equilateral triangle,

$$\text{Area} = \frac{\sqrt{3}}{4} \times (\text{side})^2$$

$$\text{Height} = \frac{\sqrt{3}}{2} \times \text{side}$$

- For a right angled triangle,

$$\text{Area} = \frac{1}{2} \times \text{Product of perpendicular sides.}$$

QUADRILATERALS

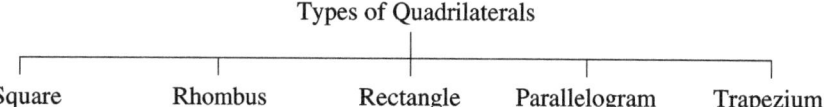

Square

If all the four sides and internal angles are equal, the quadrilateral is a square.

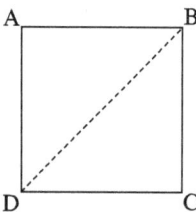

$\text{Area} = \text{Side}^2$

$\text{Area} = \frac{1}{2} \times \text{diagonal}^2$

$\text{Diagonal} = \sqrt{2} \times \text{side}$

$\text{Perimeter} = 4 \times \text{side}$

Rhombus

If all the four sides are equal, with two opposite angles acute and other two opposite angle obtuse will be a rhombus. In a rhombus the diagonals are perpendicular bisectors.

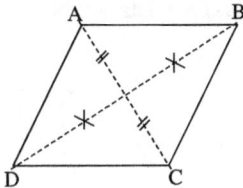

Area = $\frac{1}{2}$ × Product of diagonals

Perimeter = 4 × side.

Rectangle

If adjacent sides are unequal but opposite sides are parallel and equal with each internal angle as 90°, then it will be a rectangle. The diagonals are equal and bisect each other.

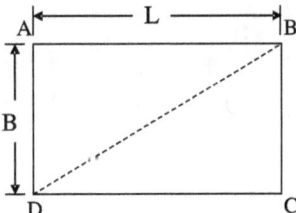

Area = $L \times B$
Perimeter = $2(L + B)$
Diagonal = $\sqrt{L^2 + B^2}$.

Parallelogram

If opposite sides are parallel and equal, with two opposite angles acute and other two opposite angle obtuse will be a parallelogram. The diagonals are unequal but bisect each other.

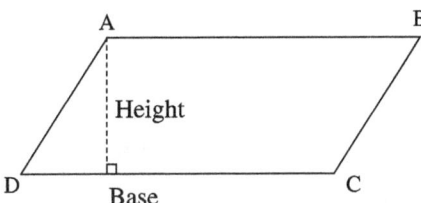

Area = Base × Height
Area = Product of two adjacent sides × Sine of included angle.

Trapezium

If two opposite sides are parallel while other two opposite sides are non parallel, then it will be a trapezium.

$$\text{Area} = \frac{1}{2} \times (\text{Sum of parallel sides}) \times \text{Distance between them}$$
$$= \frac{1}{2} \times (a + b) \times h.$$

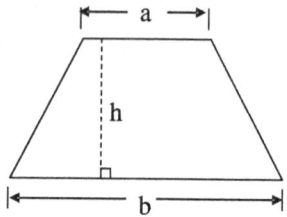

CIRCLE

Area of a Circle

Area of circle = πr^2
Circumference = $2\pi r$.

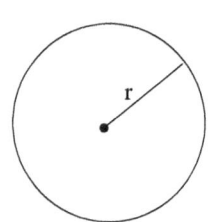

Area of Sector

Area of sector = $\frac{\theta}{360} \pi r^2$

Length of arc = $\frac{\theta}{360} 2\pi r$.

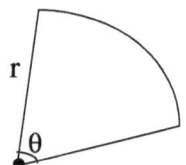

Area of Ring

Area of ring = $\pi(R^2 - r^2)$.

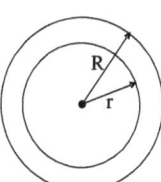

SOLVED EXAMPLES

Example 1

If the largest side and shortest side of a right angle triangle are 41 cm and 9 cm, then what will be the area of triangle?

Solution

The third side of triangle can be found by Pythagoras theorem:

$$9^2 + x^2 = 41^2$$
$$x^2 = 1681 - 81$$
∴ $\qquad x = 40$ cm.

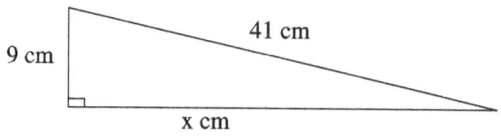

Area of triangle = $\frac{1}{2}$ × Product of perpendicular sides

= $\frac{1}{2}$ × 9 × 40 = 180 cm².

Example 2

How much will be the area of an isosceles triangle of perimeter 72 cm, if each of the equal sides is 6 cm more that its base?

Solution

Let the length of base = x cm

∴ Each equal side = $x + 6$ cm

Perimeter of triangle can be found as:

$x + (x + 6) + (x + 6) = 72$

$3x + 12 = 72$

∴ $x = \dfrac{72 - 12}{3}$

= 20 cm.

The height of triangle can be found by Pythagoras theorem:

$10^2 + h^2 = 26^2$

$h^2 = 676 - 100$

∴ $h = 24$ cm

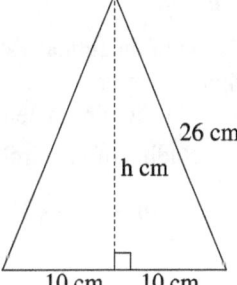

Area of triangle = $\frac{1}{2}$ × base × height

= $\frac{1}{2}$ × 20 × 24

= 240 cm².

Example 3

If the area of an equilateral triangle is $16\sqrt{3}$ cm², then how much is the length of its altitude?

Solution

$\dfrac{\sqrt{3}}{4}$ × (Side)² = Area of equilateral triangle

$\dfrac{\sqrt{3}}{4}$ × (Side)² = $16\sqrt{3}$

$$(\text{Side})^2 = 16\sqrt{3} \times \frac{4}{\sqrt{3}}$$

∴ Side = 8 cm

$$\text{Height} = \frac{\sqrt{3}}{2} \times \text{side}$$
$$= \frac{\sqrt{3}}{2} \times 8$$
$$= 4\sqrt{3} \text{ cm.}$$

Example 4

An equilateral triangle is of side 32 cm. Find the radius of the circle which can be drawn:
1. Inside the triangle
2. Outside the triangle

Solution

In case of an equilateral triangle the altitude, median and angle bisector is same. Hence orthocenter, centroid, incentre and circumcentre are also same.

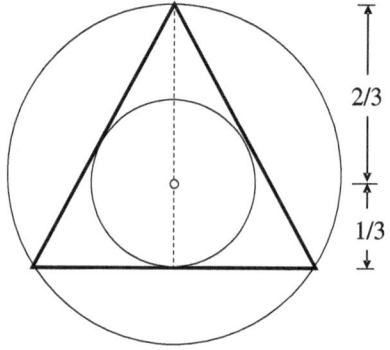

1. Radius of the circle drawn inside triangle

$$\text{Inradius} = \frac{1}{3} \times \text{Height of equilateral triangle}$$
$$= \frac{1}{3} \times \frac{\sqrt{3}}{2} \times 32$$
$$= \frac{16}{\sqrt{3}} \text{ cm}$$

2. Radius of the circle drawn outside triangle

$$\text{Circumradius} = \frac{2}{3} \times \text{Height of equilateral triangle}$$
$$= \frac{2}{3} \times \frac{\sqrt{3}}{2} \times 32$$
$$= \frac{32}{\sqrt{3}} \text{ cm.}$$

Example 5

A path of uniform width of 2 m runs around and outside a square plot of side 70 m. If the path is to be covered with tiles at the rate of ₹ 70 per sq. m, find the total cost of work.

Solution

Area of path = $(74)^2 - (70)^2$
= 576 sq. m.

Cost of work = Area × Rate per sq. m.
= 576 × 70
= ₹ 40320.

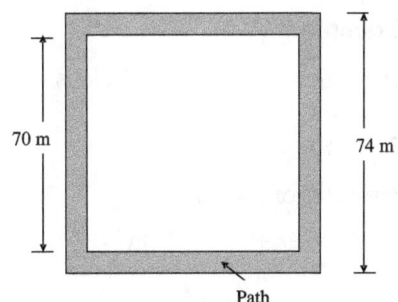

Example 6

A cow is tied to one of the corner of a square field of side 12 m with a rope length of 7 m. How much area of the square field the cow cannot graze?

Solution

Area of square field = $(12)^2$ = 144 sq. m.

Area of field cow can graze = $\dfrac{90}{360} \times \pi \times (7)^2$
= 38.5 sq. m.

Area of field cow cannot graze = 144 − 38.5
= 105.5 sq. m.

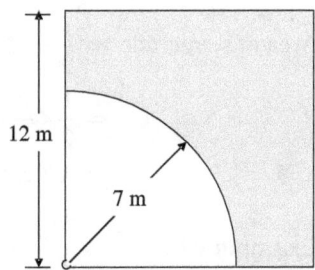

Example 7

If the length and breadth of a rectangle are increased by 2 cm, its area increases by 58 cm². If its length increases by 1 cm, its area increases by 12 cm². Find the length of rectangle.

Solution

Length of rectangle = L cm
Breadth of rectangle = B cm

As length is increased by 1 cm, area increases by 12 cm²,

$(L + 1) \times B = LB + 12$
$LB + B = LB + 12$
∴ $B = 12$ cm

As length and breadth are increased by 2 cm, area increases by 58 cm²,

$(L + 2) \times (B + 2) = LB + 58$
$LB + 2B + 2L + 4 = LB + 58$
$24 + 2L + 4 = 58$
∴ $L = 15$ cm

So, length of rectangle is 15 cm.

Example 8

The perimeter of a semi circle is 72 cm. How much will be its area?

Solution

Perimeter of a semicircle:
$$2r + \pi r = 72 \text{ cm}$$
$$2r + \frac{22}{7}r = 72$$
$$14r + 22r = 72 \times 7$$
$$\therefore \quad r = \frac{72 \times 7}{36} = 14$$

Area of semicircle $= \frac{1}{2} \times \pi r^2$
$$= \frac{1}{2} \times \frac{22}{7} \times (14)^2$$
$$= 308 \text{ cm}^2.$$

Example 9

How many revolutions are made by a wheel of diameter 28 cm to cover a distance of 616 m?

Solution

Distance covered in 1 revolution = Circumference of wheel = πd
$$= \frac{22}{7} \times 28 = 88 \text{ cm}.$$

Number of revolutions $= \frac{616 \text{ m}}{88 \text{ cm}} = \frac{616 \times 100}{88} = 700.$

Example 10

One of the diagonal of rhombus is 24 cm long and its area is 216 sq. cm. Find the perimeter of rhombus.

Solution

$\frac{1}{2} \times$ Product of diagonals = Area of rhombus
$$\frac{1}{2} \times 24 \times d_2 = 216$$
$$\therefore \quad d_2 = 18 \text{ cm}$$

As the diagonals of rhombus are perpendicular bisectors,
$$x^2 = 9^2 + 12^2$$
$$x^2 = 81 + 144$$
$$x^2 = 225$$
∴ $x = 15$ cm.

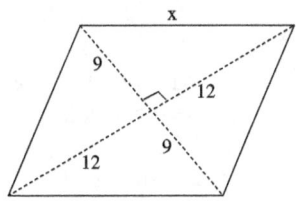

Perimeter of rhombus = 4 × Side
= 4 × 15
= 60 cm.

Example 11

Two adjacent sides of a parallelogram have lengths of 6 cm and 10 cm. If the angle between the adjacent sides is 30° then find the area of parallelogram.

Solution

Area of parallelogram = Product of two adjacent sides × Sine of included angle
= 6 × 10 × sin 30°
= 6 × 10 × $\frac{1}{2}$
= 30 cm².

Example 12

The parallel sides of a trapezium of area 33 sq. cm are 7 cm and 15 cm. Find the length of non parallel sides if they are equal in length.

Solution

$\frac{1}{2}$ × (Sum of parallel sides) × Distance between them = Area of trapezium

$\frac{1}{2}$ × (7 + 15) × H = 33

∴ $H = 3$ cm

Length of non parallel side can be found by Pythagoras theorem:
$$L^2 = 3^2 + 4^2$$
$$L^2 = 25$$
∴ $L = 5$ cm.

So, the length of non parallel sides is 5 cm.

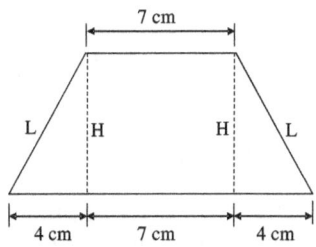

EXERCISE

1. The base of a triangle is 20 cm and height is 15 cm. Find the height of another triangle of double the area having base 30 cm.
   (a) 15 cm
   (b) 18 cm
   (c) 20 cm
   (d) 25 cm

2. The area of right-angled triangle is 2.5 times its base. What is its height?
   (a) 5 cm
   (b) 8 cm
   (c) 10 cm
   (d) 15 cm

3. The perimeter of a triangle is 60 cm and its sides are in the ratio 3 : 4 : 5. The area of the triangle is:
   (a) 120 cm^2
   (b) 150 cm^2
   (c) 180 cm^2
   (d) 225 cm^2

4. The hypotenuse and the longest perpendicular side of a right-angled triangle are in the ratio of 41 : 40. If the shortest side is 18 cm, then area of triangle in sq. cm is:
   (a) 640
   (b) 720
   (c) 960
   (d) 1440

5. If the area of an equilateral triangle is $36\sqrt{3}$ sq. cm, then its perimeter is:
   (a) 30 cm
   (b) $36\sqrt{3}$ cm
   (c) 36 cm
   (d) $18\sqrt{3}$ cm

6. If the height of an equilateral triangle is $15\sqrt{3}$, then its area is:
   (a) 225 cm^2
   (b) $225\sqrt{3}$ cm^2
   (c) 325 cm^2
   (d) $325\sqrt{3}$ cm^2

7. The area of a square of side 20 cm is equal to area of a triangle with base 20 cm. How much is the altitude of triangle?
   (a) $10\sqrt{3}$ cm
   (b) 20 cm
   (c) $20\sqrt{3}$ cm
   (d) 40 cm

8. A square and equilateral triangle has equal perimeters. If the diagonal of square is $9\sqrt{2}$ cm, then area of triangle is:
   (a) $18\sqrt{2}$ cm^2
   (b) 36 cm^2
   (c) $36\sqrt{2}$ cm^2
   (d) $36\sqrt{3}$ cm^2

9. If every side of the triangle is doubled, then area of new triangle is how much times the area of original triangle?
   (a) $\sqrt{2}$
   (b) 2
   (c) $\sqrt{3}$
   (d) 4

10. The difference between length and breadth of a rectangle is 13 cm. If the perimeter is 74 cm, then its area is:
    (a) 80 cm²
    (b) 150 cm²
    (c) 240 cm²
    (d) 300 cm²

11. The length of rectangular metal sheet is 8 cm more than its breadth. If the area of the sheet is 660 cm², then its length is:
    (a) 22 cm
    (b) 25 cm
    (c) 30 cm
    (d) 36 cm

12. The breadth of a rectangle is 70% of its length. If the perimeter is 306 cm, then its area is:
    (a) 5040 cm²
    (b) 5670 cm²
    (c) 5840 cm²
    (d) 6320 cm²

13. A conference room 24 m long and 15 m wide is to be renovated by fitting new tiles on the floor. If each square tile of 20 cm side is used, then how many such tiles are required?
    (a) 8000
    (b) 9000
    (c) 10000
    (d) 12000

14. The length of a rectangle is 40% more than its breadth. If the length is 16 cm more than its breadth, then area of the rectangle is:
    (a) 2160 cm²
    (b) 2240 cm²
    (c) 2620 cm²
    (d) 2600 cm²

15. The ratio of length and breadth of a rectangular park is 5 : 3. A man running along the boundary of the park at the speed of 2 m/s completes one round in 4 min. Then the are of the park (in sq. m) is:
    (a) 13500
    (b) 13800
    (c) 14600
    (d) 16200

16. The sides of a rectangular plot are in the ratio of 4 : 5. If the area of the plot is 180 sq. m then the cost of fencing the plot at the rate of ₹ 50 per meter is:
    (a) ₹ 2500
    (b) ₹ 2700
    (c) ₹ 3000
    (d) ₹ 3600

17. The length of a rectangular room is double its width. If the length of diagonal of that room is $6\sqrt{5}$ m, then how much is the perimeter of room?
    (a) $24\sqrt{5}$ cm
    (b) 32 cm
    (c) 36 cm
    (d) $36\sqrt{5}$ cm

18. The diagonal of a rectangle is 25 cm and its area is 168 sq. cm. How much is the perimeter of rectangle?
    (a) 60 cm
    (b) 62 cm
    (c) 68 cm
    (d) 70 cm

19. The length of a rectangular marble slab is 8 cm more than its breadth. If the length is increased by 10 cm and breadth is decreased by 4 cm, the area remains the same. Find the breadth of the slab.
    (a) 9 cm
    (b) 10 cm
    (c) 12 cm
    (d) 14 cm

20. What is the cost of making 1 meter broad path around a rectangular garden of perimeter 240 m at the rate of ₹ 20 per sq. m?
    (a) ₹ 4880
    (b) ₹ 4800
    (c) ₹ 3600
    (d) ₹ 4840

21. How many rectangular tiles of 30 cm × 50 cm are required to cover a square room of side 3 meters?
    (a) 45
    (b) 50
    (c) 60
    (d) 75

22. The perimeter of a square is 60 cm. The area of a rectangle is 5 cm^2 less than area of the square. If the length of rectangle is 20 cm, then its perimeter is:
    (a) 52 cm
    (b) 56 cm
    (c) 58 cm
    (d) 62 cm

23. The cost of fencing a square shaped park at ₹ 40 per meter is ₹ 5600. How much will be the cost of making a jogging track 2.5 m wide along the fencing inside the field at ₹ 50 per square meter?
    (a) ₹ 8437.50
    (b) ₹ 14500
    (c) ₹ 16250
    (d) ₹ 18650

24. A runner running diagonally in a square ground at the speed of 2 m/s reaches the opposite corner in 45 sec. How much is the area of ground?
    (a) ₹ 4050 m^2
    (b) ₹ 8100 m^2
    (c) ₹ 8500 m^2
    (d) ₹ 9600 m^2

25. The diagonal of a square is $6\sqrt{2}$ cm. Find the area of another square which can be formed inside this square by joining the mid points of its edges.
    (a) 9 cm^2
    (b) 18 cm^2
    (c) $18\sqrt{2}$ cm^2
    (d) $36\sqrt{2}$ cm^2

26. If the side of a square is increased by 3 cm, its area is increased by 81 sq. cm. How much is the side of square?
    (a) 10 cm
    (b) 12 cm
    (c) 13 cm
    (d) 16 cm

27. The area of a rhombus is 210 cm^2. The length of one of its diagonal is 15 cm. The length of other diagonal is:
    (a) 25 cm
    (b) 28 cm
    (c) 30 cm
    (d) 35 cm

28. One of the diagonal of rhombus is thrice the other diagonal. If the area of rhombus is 54 cm² then sum of diagonals is:
    (a) 18 cm
    (b) 20 cm
    (c) 24 cm
    (d) 28 cm

29. If each side of rhombus is 10 cm and one of its diagonal is 16 cm long, then its area will be:
    (a) 96 sq. cm
    (b) 108 sq. cm
    (c) 112 sq. cm
    (d) 120 sq. cm

30. One side of parallelogram is 15 cm and its distance from opposite side is 8 cm, then area of parallelogram is:
    (a) 60 sq. cm
    (b) 72 sq. cm
    (c) 100 sq. cm
    (d) 120 sq. cm

31. Two parallel sides of a trapezium are 4 cm and 6 cm respectively. If the area of the trapezium is 15 cm², then how much is the perpendicular distance between two parallel sides?
    (a) 2 cm
    (b) 2.5 cm
    (c) 3 cm
    (d) 4 cm

32. Two parallel sides of a trapezium are 8 cm and 14 cm. If the perpendicular distance between them is 4 cm, and the non parallel sides are equal in length, then the perimeter of the trapezium is:
    (a) 26 cm
    (b) 30 cm
    (c) 32 cm
    (d) 36 cm

33. A circle has same circumference as that of a perimeter of a square of side 22 cm. What is the area of the circle?
    (a) 512 sq. cm
    (b) 616 sq. cm
    (c) 914 sq. cm
    (d) 1256 sq. cm

34. If the circumference and area of the circle are numerically equal, then the diameter of the circle is equal to:
    (a) π
    (b) $\pi/2$
    (c) 2
    (d) 4

35. The difference between circumference and diameter of circle is 30 cm. The area of the circle is:
    (a) 154 sq. cm
    (b) 186 sq. cm
    (c) 216 sq. cm
    (d) 324 sq. cm

36. A pipe can be bent in the shape of a circle of radius 21 cm. If it is bent in the shape of a square, the each side of square will be:
    (a) 21 cm
    (b) 25 cm
    (c) 28 cm
    (d) 33 cm

37. A man runs along the boundary of a circular field at the speed of 2 m/s and completes one round in 44 seconds. Find the area of field.
    (a) 626 sq. m.
    (b) 616 sq. m
    (c) 576 sq. m.
    (d) 729 sq. m

38. The ratio of areas of two circles is 9 :16, then the ratio of their circumference will be:
    (a) 2 : 3
    (b) 3 : 4
    (c) 4 : 3
    (d) 3 : 8

39. A wheel of radius 35 cm will make how many revolutions in a travel of 11 km?
    (a) 3500
    (b) 4000
    (c) 5000
    (d) 7000

40. What will be the area of a semi-circle whose perimeter is 36 cm?
    (a) 77 sq. cm
    (b) 154 sq. cm
    (c) 158 sq. cm
    (d) 161 sq. cm

41. Find the area of the largest circle that can be drawn inside a rectangle with sides 28 cm and 35 cm.
    (a) 454 sq. cm
    (b) 586 sq. cm
    (c) 616 sq. cm
    (d) 724 sq. cm

42. A square is inscribed in a circle. If the diameter of the circle is $10\sqrt{2}$ cm, then area of square is:
    (a) 100 sq. cm
    (b) 121 sq. cm
    (c) 169 sq. cm
    (d) 144 sq. cm

43. A circle has a radius of 21 cm with centre O. AOB represents a sector where $\angle AOB = 60°$. Find the area of the sector AOB.
    (a) 121 sq. cm
    (b) 231 sq. cm
    (c) 462 sq. cm
    (d) 1386 sq. cm.

44. How much is the area enclosed by a ring if the radius of inner circle and outer circle is 6 cm and 8 cm respectively?
    (a) 64 sq. cm
    (b) 88 sq. cm.
    (c) 96.5 sq. cm
    (d) 112 sq. cm

45. If each side of an equilateral triangle is decreased by 40%, then its area is decreased by:
    (a) 36%
    (b) 40%
    (c) 64%
    (d) 80%

46. If the diameter of a circle is doubled, its area will be how much times the original area?
    (a) 2
    (b) 3
    (c) 4
    (d) 8

47. Two goats are tied to two opposite corners of a square plot of 15 m long side with rope length of 7 m. Find the area not grazed by the goats in the plot.
    (a) 148 sq. m.
    (b) 77 sq. m.
    (c) 186.5 sq. m
    (d) 225 sq. m.

48. An equilateral triangle has a side of 18 cm. The circle which can be drawn inside the triangle will have radius of:
    (a) 3 cm
    (b) 6 cm
    (c) $3\sqrt{3}$ cm
    (d) $6\sqrt{3}$ cm

49. The perimeter of a sector of a circle of radius 21 cm is 64 cm. How much will be the area of sector?
    (a) 221 sq. cm
    (b) 227 sq. cm
    (c) 231 sq. cm
    (d) 242 sq. cm

50. What should be the length of a pendulum which swings through an angle of 60° and describes an arc of 33 cm in length?
    (a) 31.5 cm
    (b) 27 cm
    (c) 34.5 cm
    (d) 42 cm

51. A largest possible circle is drawn inside a rectangle. If the length of rectangle is twice the diameter of this circle, then what will be the ratio between area of rectangle and area of circle?
    (a) 15 : 11
    (b) 25 : 22
    (c) 20 : 11
    (d) 28 : 11

52. Three circles of radius 2 cm, 3 cm and 4 cm are placed in such a way that each circle touches the other two. Find the area of a triangle which can be formed by joining their centers.
    (a) $8\sqrt{2}$ sq. cm
    (b) $6\sqrt{6}$ sq. cm
    (c) $10\sqrt{3}$ sq. cm
    (d) $12\sqrt{3}$ sq. cm

53. The area of largest triangle that can be inscribed in a semicircle of radius 5 cm is:
    (a) 10 sq. cm.
    (b) 25 sq. cm
    (c) 30 sq. cm.
    (d) 50 sq. cm

54. The wheel of a motorcycle, 70 cm in diameter, makes 25 revolutions in every 6 sec. Find the speed of motorcycle in km/hr.
    (a) 22 km/hr
    (b) 33 km/hr
    (c) 55 km/hr
    (d) 77 km/hr

KEYS

1. (c)	2. (a)	3. (b)	4. (b)	5. (c)	6. (b)	7. (d)	8. (d)
9. (d)	10. (d)	11. (c)	12. (b)	13. (b)	14. (b)	15. (a)	16. (b)
17. (c)	18. (b)	19. (c)	20. (a)	21. (c)	22. (d)	23. (c)	24. (a)
25. (b)	26. (b)	27. (b)	28. (c)	29. (a)	30. (d)	31. (c)	32. (c)
33. (b)	34. (d)	35. (a)	36. (d)	37. (b)	38. (b)	39. (c)	40. (a)
41. (c)	42. (a)	43. (b)	44. (b)	45. (c)	46. (c)	47. (a)	48. (c)
49. (c)	50. (a)	51. (d)	52. (b)	53. (b)	54. (b)		

SOLUTIONS

Solution 1

Area of 1st triangle $= \dfrac{1}{2} \times b \times h$

$= \dfrac{1}{2} \times 20 \times 15$

$= 150 \text{ cm}^2$

Area of 2nd triangle $= 2 \times 150$

$\dfrac{1}{2} \times b \times h = 300$

$\dfrac{1}{2} \times 30 \times h = 300$

$\therefore \qquad h = 20 \text{ cm.}$

Choice ©

Solution 2

$\dfrac{1}{2} \times b \times h = $ Area of triangle

$\dfrac{1}{2} \times b \times h = 2.5 \times b$

$\therefore \qquad h = 5 \text{ cm}$

Choice (a)

Solution 3

$3x + 4x + 5x = 60$

$12x = 60$

$\therefore \qquad x = 5$

So the sides of the triangle are 15 cm, 20 cm, and 25 cm.

Semi-perimeter of triangle, $S = \dfrac{15 + 20 + 25}{2} = 30$

$\therefore$ Area $= \sqrt{S(S-a)(S-b)(S-c)}$

$= \sqrt{30(30-15)(30-20)(30-25)}$

$= \sqrt{22500}$

$= 150 \text{ sq. cm.}$

Choice (b)

Solution 4

Let the longest perpendicular side = $40x$

So, the hypotenuse = $41x$

$$(\text{Shortest side})^2 = (41x)^2 - (40x)^2$$
$$18^2 = 1681x^2 - 1600x^2$$
$$324 = 81x^2$$
$$\therefore \quad x^2 = 4 \text{ or } x = 2.$$

Area of triangle = $\frac{1}{2} \times$ Product of perpendicular sides

$$= \frac{1}{2} \times 18 \times 80 = 720 \text{ cm}^2.$$

Choice (b)

Solution 5

For an equilateral triangle:

$$\frac{\sqrt{3}}{4} \times (\text{side})^2 = \text{Area}$$

$$\frac{\sqrt{3}}{4} \times (\text{side})^2 = 36\sqrt{3}$$

$$(\text{side})^2 = 144$$

$$\therefore \quad \text{Side} = 12 \text{ cm}$$

So perimeter of equilateral triangle = $3 \times 12 = 36$ cm.

Choice (c)

Solution 6

For an equilateral triangle:

$$\frac{\sqrt{3}}{2} \times \text{side} = \text{Height}$$

$$\frac{\sqrt{3}}{2} \times \text{side} = 15\sqrt{3}$$

$$\therefore \quad \text{Side} = 30 \text{ cm}.$$

$$\text{Area} = \frac{\sqrt{3}}{4} \times (\text{side})^2$$

$$= \frac{\sqrt{3}}{4} \times (30)^2$$

$$= 225\sqrt{3} \text{ sq. cm.}$$

Choice (b)

Solution 7

Area of square = $(20)^2$ = 400 sq. cm

$\frac{1}{2} \times b \times h$ = Area of triangle

$\frac{1}{2} \times 20 \times h = 400$

∴ $h = 40$ cm.

Choice (d)

Solution 8

In a square, the diagonal is $\sqrt{2}$ times its side.

∴ Side of square = 9 cm

Perimeter of square = 4 × 9 = 36 cm

Perimeter of equilateral triangle = Perimeter of square

     3 × Side = 36

∴ Side of triangle = 12 cm

Area of triangle = $\frac{\sqrt{3}}{4} \times (\text{side})^2 = \frac{\sqrt{3}}{4} \times (12)^2$

           = $36\sqrt{3}$ sq. cm.

Choice (d)

Solution 9

Assuming the triangle as an equilateral triangle.

Assuming Side = 2 cm

∴ Original Area = $\frac{\sqrt{3}}{4} \times (\text{side})^2 = \frac{\sqrt{3}}{4} \times (2)^2$

             = $\sqrt{3}$ sq. cm.

New side = 4 cm

∴ New Area = $\frac{\sqrt{3}}{4} \times (\text{side})^2$

         = $\frac{\sqrt{3}}{4} \times (4)^2 = 4\sqrt{3}$ sq. cm.

Hence if each side is doubled, the new area of bigger triangle is 4 times the area of smaller triangle.

Choice (d)

Solution 10

$L - B = 13$ ... (1)

$2(L + B) = 74 \Rightarrow L + B = 37$ ... (2)

Adding (1) and (2)

$2L = 50$

$\therefore L = 25$ and $B = 12$

Area $= L \times B = 25 \times 12 = 300$ sq. cm.

Choice (d)

Solution 11

$L = B + 8 \Rightarrow B = L - 8$

$L \times B = 660 \text{ cm}^2$

$L(L - 8) = 660$

$L^2 - 8L - 660 = 0$

$L^2 - 30L + 22L - 660 = 0$

$(L - 30)(L + 22) = 0$

$\therefore L = 30$ or -22.

So, the length of rectangular metal sheet is 30 cm.

Choice (c)

Solution 12

$B = \dfrac{70}{100} L$

$\dfrac{B}{L} = \dfrac{7x}{10x}$

Perimeter = 306 cm

$2(L + B) = 306$

$2(10x + 7x) = 306$

$34x = 306$

$\therefore \quad x = 9$

$\therefore L = 90$ cm and $B = 63$ cm

Area $= L \times B = 90 \times 63 = 5670$ sq. cm.

Choice (b)

Solution 13

Number of tiles required = $\dfrac{\text{Area of room}}{\text{Area of each tile}}$

$= \dfrac{2400 \times 1500}{20 \times 20}$

$= 9000.$

Choice (b)

Solution 14

$$L = \dfrac{140}{100} B$$

$$\dfrac{L}{B} = \dfrac{7x}{5x}$$

$L - B = 16$ cm

$7x - 5x = 16$ cm

$2x = 16$

∴ $x = 8$

∴ $L = 56$ cm and $B = 40$ cm

Area $= L \times B = 56 \times 40 = 2240$ sq. cm.

Choice (b)

Solution 15

$$\dfrac{L}{B} = \dfrac{5x}{3x}$$

Perimeter $= 2(L + B) = 2(5x + 3x) = 16x.$

Distance covered in one round = Speed × Time
$= 2$ m/s × (4×60) sec.
$= 480$ m.

Perimeter $= 480$ m

$16x = 480$

∴ $x = 30$

∴ $L = 150$ m and $B = 90$ m

Area $= L \times B = 150 \times 90 = 13500$ sq. m.

Choice (a)

Solution 16

$L = 5x$ and $B = 4x$

$L \times B = $ Area

$5x \times 4x = 180$

$20x^2 = 180$

∴ $\quad x = 3$

∴ $\quad L = 15$ m and $B = 12$ m

Perimeter $= 2(L + B)$
$= 2(15 + 12)$
$= 54$ m.

Cost of fencing $= 54 \times 50$
$= ₹\, 2700$.

Choice (b)

Solution 17

$(x)^2 + (2x)^2 = (6\sqrt{5})^2$

$x^2 + 4x^2 = 180$

$x^2 = 36$

∴ $\quad x = 6$

∴ $L = 12$ m and $B = 6$ m

Perimeter $= 2(L + B)$
$= 2(12 + 6)$
$= 36$ m.

Choice (c)

Solution 18

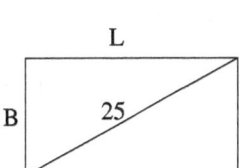

By Pythagoras theorem

$L^2 + B^2 = 25^2$

$L^2 + B^2 = 625$.

Area $= 168$ sq. cm

$L \times B = 168$ ... (1)

$(L + B)^2 = L^2 + B^2 + 2LB$

$(L + B)^2 = 625 + 2(168)$

$L + B = 31$ ... (2)

From equation (1) and (2)

$$L = 24 \text{ and } B = 7$$

∴   Perimeter = 2 (24 + 7) = 62 cm.

Choice (b)

Solution 19

$$L = B + 8$$
$$(L + 10)(B - 4) = LB \quad (\because \text{Area remains same})$$
$$LB + 10B - 4L - 40 = LB$$
$$10B - 4L = 40$$
$$10B - 4(B + 8) = 40$$
$$6B = 72$$

∴ $B = 12$ cm.

Choice (c)

Solution 20

Perimeter of garden = 240 m

∴ $2(L + B) = 240.$

Area of path = $(L + 2)(B + 2) - LB$
$= LB + 2L + 2B + 4 - LB$
$= 2(L + B) + 4$
$= 240 + 4 = 244$ sq. m.

Cost = 244 × 20 = ₹ 4880.

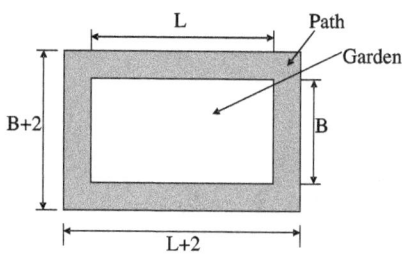

Choice (a)

Solution 21

Number of tiles required = $\dfrac{\text{Area of room}}{\text{Area of each tile}} = \dfrac{300 \times 300}{30 \times 50} = 60.$

Choice (c)

Solution 22

Perimeter of square = 60 cm

$$4 \times \text{Side} = 60$$

∴   Side = 15 cm.

Area of square = $(15)^2 = 225$ cm^2

∴ Area of rectangle = $225 - 5 = 220$ cm^2
$L \times B = 220$
$20 \times B = 220$
∴ $B = 11$.

Perimeter of rectangle = $2(L + B) = 2(20 + 11) = 62$ cm.

Choice (d)

Solution 23

Perimeter of square park = $\dfrac{5600}{40} = 140$ m

Side of park = $\dfrac{140}{4} = 35$ m

Area of jogging track = $(35)^2 - (30)^2$
$= 1225 - 900$
$= 325$ sq. m.

Cost = $325 \times 50 = ₹ 16250$.

Choice (c)

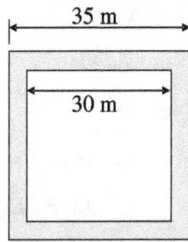

Solution 24

Length of diagonal = speed × time
$= 2$ m/s × 45 sec.
$= 90$ m.

Area of ground = $\dfrac{1}{2} \times$ (diagonal)^2
$= \dfrac{1}{2} \times (90)^2$
$= 4050$ m^2.

Choice (a)

Solution 25

In a square:

Diagonal = $\sqrt{2} \times$ Side
$6\sqrt{2} = \sqrt{2} \times$ Side
∴ Side = 6 cm.

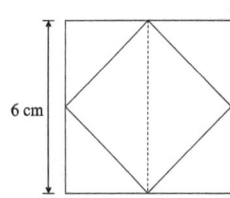

Area of internal square $= \dfrac{1}{2} \times$ (diagonal)^2

$\qquad\qquad\qquad\qquad\quad = \dfrac{1}{2} \times (6)^2$

$\qquad\qquad\qquad\qquad\quad = 18$ sq. cm.

Choice (b)

Solution 26

Let side of square $= x$ cm

$\therefore$ Area $= x^2$

New side $= x + 3$

New area $= (x + 3)^2$.

As new area of square is more than previous area by 81 cm^2,

$\qquad\qquad (x + 3)^2 = x^2 + 81$

$\qquad x^2 + 6x + 9 = x^2 + 81$

$\qquad\qquad\qquad 6x = 72$

$\therefore \qquad\qquad\qquad x = 12.$

So side of the square is 12 cm.

Choice (b)

Solution 27

$\dfrac{1}{2} \times$ Product of diagonals = Area of rhombus

$\qquad\qquad \dfrac{1}{2} \times 15 \times d_2 = 210$

$\qquad\qquad\qquad d_2 = \dfrac{210 \times 2}{15} = 28$ cm.

Choice (b)

Solution 28

$\dfrac{1}{2} \times$ Product of diagonals = Area of rhombus

$\qquad\qquad \dfrac{1}{2} \times x \times 3x = 54$

$$x^2 = \frac{54 \times 2}{3}$$
$$x^2 = 36$$
$$\therefore \qquad x = 6$$

Sum of diagonals $= x + 3x$
$\qquad\qquad\qquad = 4x = 4(6) = 24$ cm.

Choice (c)

Solution 29

The diagonals of rhombus are perpendicular bisectors.

So, there will be four right-angled triangles inside the rhombus.

By Pythagoras theorem:
$$x^2 = 10^2 - 8^2$$
$$x^2 = 36$$
$$\therefore \qquad x = 6.$$

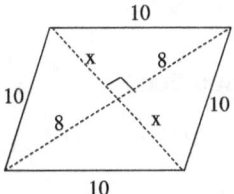

Area of rhombus $= \dfrac{1}{2} \times$ Product of diagonals
$\qquad\qquad\qquad = \dfrac{1}{2} \times 16 \times 12 = 96$ sq. cm.

Choice (a)

Solution 30

Area of parallelogram = Base × Height
$\qquad\qquad\qquad = 15 \times 8 = 120$ sq. cm.

Choice (d)

Solution 31

The perpendicular distance between two parallel sides is also called the height of trapezium.

$\dfrac{1}{2} \times$ (Sum of parallel sides) × Height = Area of trapezium

$\dfrac{1}{2} \times (4 + 6) \times$ Height $= 15$

$\therefore$ Height $= 3$ cm.

Choice (c)

Solution 32

In triangle ADE,

$$(AD)^2 = 4^2 + 3^2$$
$$(AD)^2 = 25$$
∴ $\quad AD = 5$ cm

So, $\quad BC = 5$ cm.

Perimeter $= AD + AB + BC + CD$
$= 5 + 8 + 5 + 14 = 32$ cm.

Choice (c)

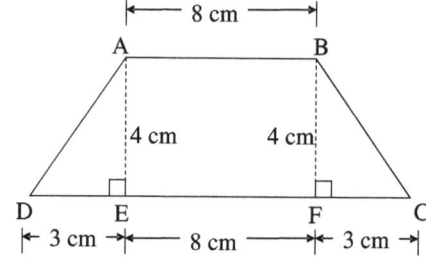

Solution 33

Perimeter of square $= 4 \times 22 = 88$ cm

$2\pi r =$ Circumference of circle

$$2 \times \frac{22}{7} \times r = 88$$

∴ $\quad r = \dfrac{88 \times 7}{44}$
$= 14$ cm.

Area of circle $= \pi r^2$
$= \dfrac{22}{7} \times (14)^2$
$= 616$ sq. cm.

Choice (b)

Solution 34

Area of circle = Circumference
$$\pi r^2 = 2\pi r$$
∴ $\quad r = 2$

So, diameter $= 4$.

Choice (d)

Solution 35

Circumference $-$ Diameter $= 30$ cm
$$2\pi r - 2r = 30$$

$$2r(\pi - 1) = 30$$
$$2r\left(\frac{22}{7} - 1\right) = 30$$
$$2r \times \frac{15}{7} = 30$$
$$\therefore \quad r = \frac{30 \times 7}{2 \times 15} = 7 \text{ cm}$$

Area of circle $= \pi r^2$
$$= \frac{22}{7} \times (7)^2$$
$$= 154 \text{ sq. cm.}$$

Choice (a)

Solution 36

Circumference of circle $= 2\pi r$
$$= 2 \times \frac{22}{7} \times 21 = 132 \text{ cm}$$

Perimeter of square = 132 cm

4 × Side of square = 132

$\therefore$ Side of square $= \dfrac{132}{4} = 33$ cm.

Choice (d)

Solution 37

Distance covered in 1 round = speed × time
$$= 2 \text{ m/s} \times 44 \text{ sec.} = 88 \text{ m.}$$

$2\pi r$ = Circumference of field
$$2 \times \frac{22}{7} \times r = 88 \text{ m}$$
$$\therefore \quad r = \frac{88 \times 7}{44} = 14 \text{ cm}$$

Area of circle $= \pi r^2$
$$= \frac{22}{7} \times (14)^2 = 616 \text{ sq. cm.}$$

Choice (b)

Solution 38

Ratio of Area = $\dfrac{9}{16}$

$\dfrac{\pi r_1^2}{\pi r_2^2} = \dfrac{9}{16}$

$\dfrac{r_1}{r_2} = \dfrac{3}{4}$

Ratio of circumference = $\dfrac{2\pi r_1}{2\pi r_2} = \dfrac{3}{4}$.

Choice (b)

Solution 39

Distance covered in 1 revolution = Circumference of wheel
$= 2\pi r$
$= 2 \times \dfrac{22}{7} \times 35 = 220$ cm.

Number of revolutions = $\dfrac{11 \ km}{220 \ cm}$

$= \dfrac{11 \times 1000 \times 100}{220}$

$= 5000.$

Choice (c)

Solution 40

$2r + \pi r$ = Perimeter of semicircle

$r(2 + \pi) = 36$ cm

$r\left(2 + \dfrac{22}{7}\right) = 36$

$r \times \dfrac{36}{7} = 36$

∴ $r = 7$ cm.

Area = $\dfrac{\pi r^2}{2} = \dfrac{\pi (7)^2}{2} = 77$ sq. cm.

Choice (a)

Solution 41

The largest circle that can be drawn inside the rectangle will be of diameter 28 cm.

Area of circle $= \pi r^2$
$= \dfrac{22}{7} \times (14)^2$
$= 616$ sq. cm.

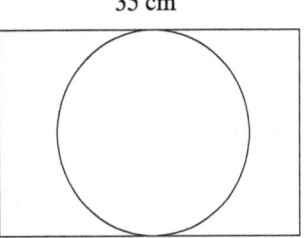

Choice (c)

Solution 42

The diameter of the circle is also the diagonal of inscribed square.

Diagonal of square $= \sqrt{2} \times$ Side of square

$10\sqrt{2} = \sqrt{2} \times$ Side of square

$\therefore$ Side of square $= 10$ cm

Area of square $= (10)^2 = 100$ sq. cm.

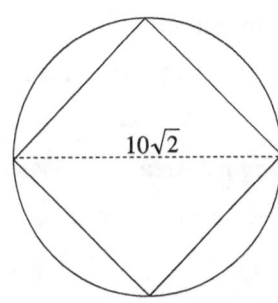

Choice (a)

Solution 43

Area of sector $AOB = \dfrac{\theta}{360} \pi r^2$

$= \dfrac{60}{360} \times \dfrac{22}{7} \times 21^2 = 231$ sq. cm.

Choice (b)

Solution 44

Area of ring $= \pi(R^2 - r^2)$

$= \dfrac{22}{7}(8^2 - 6^2) = 88$ sq. cm.

Choice (b)

Solution 45

Let original side $= 10$ cm

Original Area $= \dfrac{\sqrt{3}}{4} \times (10)^2 = 25\sqrt{3}$ sq. cm

Reduced length of side = 6 cm ($\because$ Reduced by 40%)

New Area = $\dfrac{\sqrt{3}}{4} \times (6)^2 = 9\sqrt{3}$ sq. cm.

Percentage decrease = $\dfrac{25\sqrt{3} - 9\sqrt{3}}{25\sqrt{3}} \times 100$

$= \dfrac{16\sqrt{3}}{25\sqrt{3}} \times 100$

$= 64\%$.

Choice (c)

Solution 46

Let original diameter = 2 cm

$\therefore r = 1$ cm

Original Area = $\pi r^2 = \pi$ sq. cm

New diameter = 4 cm

$\therefore r = 2$ cm

New Area = $\pi r^2 = 4\pi$ sq. cm.

Hence if diameter is doubled, the area of circle will be 4 times the original area.

Choice (c)

Solution 47

Area not grazed by the goats = Area of plot − Area grazed by the goats

$= (15)^2 - 2\left(\dfrac{90}{360} \times \pi \times (7)^2\right)$

$= 225 - 77$

$= 148$ sq. m.

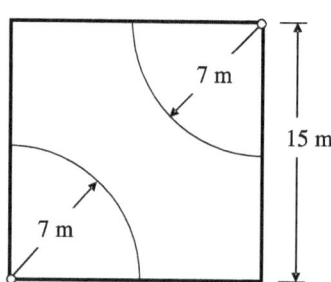

Choice (a)

Solution 48

In case of an equilateral triangle the altitude, median and angle bisector is same. Hence ortho-center, centroid, in centre and circum centre are also same.

Height $= \dfrac{\sqrt{3}}{2} \times$ Side

$= \dfrac{\sqrt{3}}{2} \times 18 = 9\sqrt{3}$ cm

Inradius $= \dfrac{1}{3} \times$ Height

$= \dfrac{1}{3} \times 9\sqrt{3}$

$= 3\sqrt{3}$ cm.

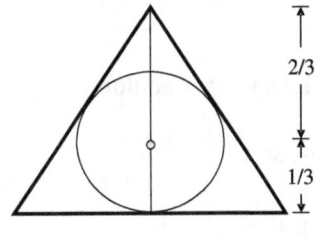

Choice (c)

Solution 49

2 × Radius + Length of arc = Perimeter of sector

2 × 21 + Length of arc = 64

∴ Length of arc = 22 cm.

Circumference of circle = $2\pi r$

$= 2 \times \dfrac{22}{7} \times 21$

$= 132.$

$\dfrac{\text{Length of arc}}{\text{Circumference}} = \dfrac{22}{132}$

$= \dfrac{1}{6}$

Hence area of sector = $\dfrac{1}{6}$ times Area of Circle.

Area of sector $= \dfrac{1}{6} \times \pi r^2$

$= \dfrac{1}{6} \times \dfrac{22}{7} \times 21^2$

$= 231$ sq. cm.

Choice (c)

Solution 50

Length of Arc = $\dfrac{\theta}{360} 2\pi r$

$33 \text{ cm} = \dfrac{60}{360} \times 2 \times \dfrac{22}{7} \times$ Length of pendulum

$\therefore$ Length of pendulum = $\dfrac{33 \times 6 \times 7}{2 \times 22} = 31.5$ cm.

Choice (a)

Solution 51

Area of rectangle = $L \times B = 4 \times 2 = 8$ cm^2

Area of circle = $\pi r^2 = \dfrac{22}{7} \times (1)^2 = \dfrac{22}{7}$ cm^2

Ratio = $\dfrac{8}{22/7} = \dfrac{28}{11}$.

Choice (d)

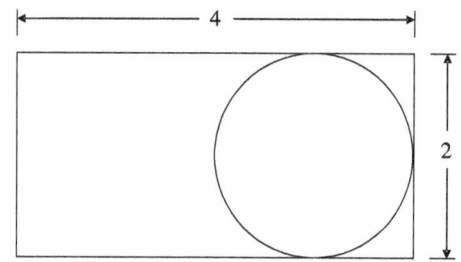

Solution 52

The sides of triangle are 5 cm, 6 cm and 7 cm respectively.

$S = \dfrac{5+6+7}{2} = 9$ cm

$\therefore$ Area = $\sqrt{S(S-a)(S-b)(S-c)}$

$= \sqrt{9(9-5)(9-6)(9-7)}$

$= \sqrt{216} = 6\sqrt{6}$ sq. cm.

Choice (b)

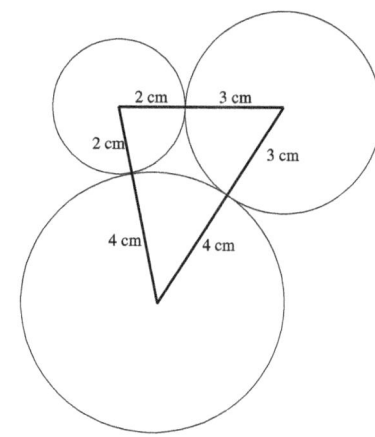

Solution 53

The largest triangle that can be inscribed in a semicircle is a right angle triangle with diameter as the hypotenuse.

As per Pythagoras theorem:

$x^2 + x^2 = 10^2$

$2x^2 = 100$

$\therefore \qquad x = \sqrt{50}$ cm.

Area of triangle = $\frac{1}{2} \times$ Product of perpendicular sides

$= \frac{1}{2} \times \sqrt{50} \times \sqrt{50}$

= 25 sq. cm.

Choice (b)

Solution 54

Circumference = $2\pi r$

$= 2 \times \frac{22}{7} \times 35$

= 220 cm.

Speed = $\frac{220 \times 25}{6 \times 100}$

$= \frac{55}{6}$ m/s

Speed in km/hr = $\frac{55}{6} \times \frac{18}{5}$

= 33 km/hr.

Choice (h)

26

Volume and Surface Area

Solids are three-dimensional objects which, in addition to area, have volume also. For solids two types of surface areas are defined as follows:
1. Lateral/Curved surface area
2. Total surface area.

As the name itself indicates, lateral surface area is the area of lateral surface or side of the solid. The total surface area includes the areas of the top and the bottom surfaces also along with lateral surface area. In solids like cylinders, cone and sphere, the lateral surface area is usually referred to as 'curved surface area'. The surface areas and volume for different types of solids are mentioned as follows.

PRISM

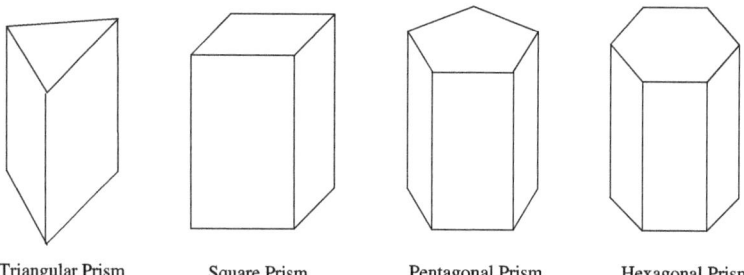

Triangular Prism   Square Prism   Pentagonal Prism   Hexagonal Prism

- Lateral surface area = Perimeter of base × Height
- Total surface area = Lateral surface area + 2 × Area of base
- Volume = Area of base × Height.

PYRAMID

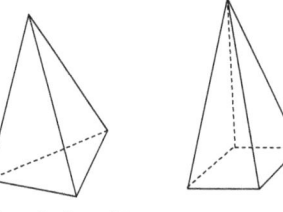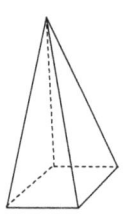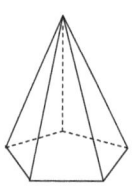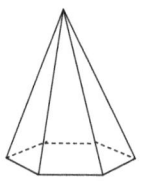

Triangular Pyramid   Square Pyramid   Pentagonal Pyramid   Hexagonal Pyramid

- Lateral surface area = ½ × Perimeter of base × Slant height
- Total surface area = Lateral surface area + Area of base
- Volume = ⅓ × Area of base × Height

CUBOID

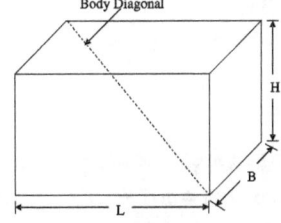

- Volume = $L \times B \times H$
- Surface area = $2(LB + BH + LH)$
- Length of body diagonal = $\sqrt{L^2 + B^2 + H^2}$

CUBE

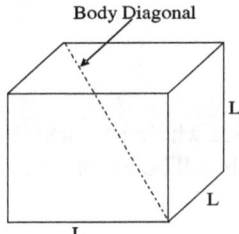

- Volume = L^3
- Surface area = $6L^2$
- Length of body diagonal = $L\sqrt{3}$.

CYLINDER

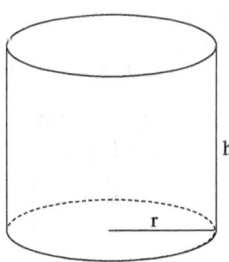

- Curved surface area = $2\pi rh$
- Total surface area = $2\pi r^2 + 2\pi rh = 2\pi r(r + h)$
- Volume = $\pi r^2 h$

CONE

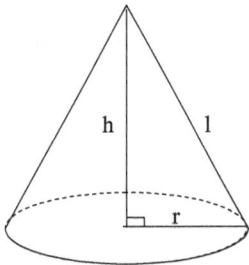

- Slant height, $l = \sqrt{r^2 + h^2}$
- Curved surface area = πrl
- Total surface area = $\pi rl + \pi r^2$
- Volume = $\dfrac{1}{3}\pi r^2 h$.

SPHERE

- Surface area = $4\pi r^2$
- Volume = $\dfrac{4}{3}\pi r^3$.

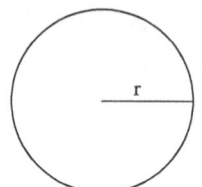

HEMISPHERE

- Curved surface area = $2\pi r^2$
- Total surface area = $\pi r^2 + 2\pi r^2 = 3\pi r^2$
- Volume = $\dfrac{2}{3}\pi r^3$.

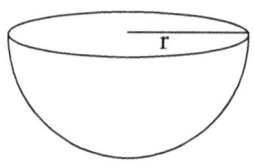

SOLVED EXAMPLES

Example 1

A triangular prism whose base and top is an equilateral triangle with length of side 4 cm is 8 cm long. How much will be its total surface area?

Solution

Height of prism = 8 cm
Side of base = 4 cm

∴ Perimeter of base = 3 × 4 = 12 cm

Total surface area = Top area + Bottom area + Lateral surface area
$$= (2 \times \text{Top area}) + (\text{Perimeter} \times \text{Height})$$
$$= \left(2 \times \dfrac{\sqrt{3}}{4} \times 4^2\right) + (12 \times 8)$$
$$= (8\sqrt{3} + 96) \text{ sq. cm.}$$

Example 2

Find the height of a pentagonal pyramid whose areas of base is 30 cm² and volume is 80 cm³.

Solution

Area of base = 30 cm²

Volume = 80 cm³

Volume of pyramid = $\dfrac{1}{3}$ × Area of base × Height

$80 = \dfrac{1}{3} \times 30 \times \text{Height}$

∴ Height = 8 cm.

Example 3

The total surface area of a cuboid is 214 sq. cm. The areas of two of its faces are 42 sq. cm and 35 sq. cm. How much is the length of longest side of cuboid?

Solution

Let the length, breadth and height of cuboid be L, B and H respectively.

$L \times B = 42$ sq. cm ... (1)

$L \times H = 35$ sq. cm ... (2)

Total surface area = 214 sq. cm

∴ Area of three perpendicular faces = $\dfrac{214}{2}$

= 107 sq. cm

$(L \times B) + (L \times H) + (B \times H) = 107$ sq. cm

$42 + 35 + (B \times H) = 107$ sq. cm

$B \times H = 30$ sq. cm

∴ $B \times H = 30$ ... (3)

Diving equation (1) by equation (3)

$\dfrac{L \times B}{B \times H} = \dfrac{42}{30} \Rightarrow \dfrac{L}{H} = \dfrac{7x}{5x}$

Substituting in equation (2)

$L \times H = 35$ sq. cm

$7x \times 5x = 35$

∴ $x = 1$.

So, Longest side $\Rightarrow L = 7x = 7$ cm.

Example 4

A swimming pool 50 m long and 30 m wide is 1 m deep at the shallow end and 3 m deep at the deep end. Find the volume of pool.

Solution

Volume of pool = $50 \times 30 \times \left(\dfrac{1+3}{2}\right) = 3000 \text{ m}^3$.

Example 5

A rectangular swimming pool of 25 m × 15 m × 3 m is full of water. The tank is emptied through a drain pipe of cross section area 60 cm^2 in 5 hrs. Find the speed of water flow.

Solution

Let the velocity of water flow be V m/hr.

Volume of swimming pool = 25 × 15 × 3 = 1125 m^3

$$\text{Time required to empty} = \frac{\text{Volume of tank}}{\text{Area of outlet} \times \text{Velocity of flow}}$$

$$5 \text{ hrs} = \frac{1125}{\frac{60}{10^4} \times V}$$

$$\therefore V = \frac{1125 \times 10^4}{60 \times 5} = 37500 \text{ m/hr} = 37.5 \text{ km/hr}.$$

Example 6

How much is the cost of painting the walls of a cubical room along with its ceiling at the cost of ₹ 40 per sq. m, if its volume is 64 cu. m?

Solution

(Side)^3 = Volume of room
(Side)^3 = 64 cu. m
∴ Side = 4 m.

Surface area of 4 walls and ceiling = 5 × (Side)^2 = 5 × 4^2 = 80 sq. m.

Cost of painting = Surface area × rate per sq. m
= 80 × 40 = ₹ 3200.

Example 7

Three metal cubes whose edges are in the ratio 3 : 4 : 5 are melted and one bigger cube is formed. If the diagonal of bigger cube is $12\sqrt{3}$, then how much is the surface area of smallest cube?

Solution

Let the edges of three cubes be 3x, 4x and 5x cm respectively.

Diagonal of a cube = $\sqrt{3}$ × side
$12\sqrt{3} = \sqrt{3}$ × side
∴ Side of bigger cube = 12 cm.

Sum of the volume of three small cubes = Volume of single bigger cube

$$(3x)^3 + (4x)^3 + (5x)^3 = (12)^3$$
$$\Rightarrow \quad 27x^3 + 64x^3 + 125x^3 = 1728$$
$$\Rightarrow \quad 216x^3 = 1728$$
$$\Rightarrow \quad x^3 = 8$$
$$\Rightarrow \quad x = 2.$$

∴ Side of smallest cube = $3x = 3(2) = 6$ cm

Surface area of smallest cube = $6 \times$ (side of smallest cube)^2 = $6 \times 6^2 = 216$ cm^2.

Example 8

The sum of radius of base and the height of a solid cylinder is 21 cm. If the total surface area of cylinder is 924 sq. cm, then find the volume of cylinder.

Solution

Let the radius of base = r cm and height of cylinder = h cm

Given:
$$r + h = 21 \text{ cm}$$
$$2\pi r^2 + 2\pi rh = \text{Total surface area}$$
$$2\pi r (r + h) = 924 \text{ sq. cm}$$
$$2 \times \frac{22}{7} \times r \times 21 = 924$$

∴
$$r = \frac{924 \times 7}{2 \times 22 \times 21} = 7 \text{ cm}$$

∴
$$h = 21 - 7 = 14 \text{ cm}$$

Volume of cylinder = $\pi r^2 h = \frac{22}{7} \times 7^2 \times 14 = 2156$ cu. cm.

Example 9

A metal pipe has an external diameter of 1.6 cm and thickness of 1 mm. If each cubic cm of metal weighs 10 gm, how much a pipe 70 cm long weigh?

Solution

$D_o = 1.6$ cm ∴ $R_o = 0.8$ cm
$D_i = 1.6 - 2 = 1.4$ cm. ∴ $R_i = 0.7$ cm

Cross section area = $\pi R_o^2 - \pi R_i^2$
$= 0.64\pi - 0.49\pi = 0.15\pi$
$= \frac{3.3}{7}$ sq. cm.

Volume of 70 cm long pipe = $\dfrac{3.3}{7} \times 70 = 33$ cm^3

Weight = $33 \times 10 = 330$ gm.

Example 10

The slant height of a right circular cone is 10 cm and its height is 8 cm. Find the area of its curved surface.

Solution

The slant height, height and base radius of a right circular cone form a right angled triangle.

Radius of base, $r = \sqrt{l^2 - h^2} = \sqrt{10^2 - 8^2} = 6$ cm

Curved surface area of cone = $\pi r l = \pi \times 6 \times 10 = 60\pi$ cm^2.

Example 11

If the radius and height of a right circular cone are increased by 20%, then by how much percent its volume will increase?

Solution

Original cone ⇒ Assuming Radius of base = 10 cm and height of cone = 10 cm

∴ Original Volume = $\dfrac{1}{3}\pi r^2 h = \dfrac{\pi}{3}(10)^2 \times 10 = \dfrac{\pi}{3} \times 1000$ cu. cm

New cone ⇒ 20% increased radius of base = 12 cm and height of cone = 12 cm

∴ New Volume = $\dfrac{1}{3}\pi r^2 h = \dfrac{\pi}{3}(12)^2 \times 12 = \dfrac{\pi}{3} \times 1728$ cu. cm

Percentage increase in volume = $\dfrac{1728 - 1000}{1000} \times 100$

= 72.8%.

Example 12

A solid metal sphere of radius 3 cm is melted and recast into a cone with radius of base 2 cm. How much will be the height of cone?

Solution

Volume of sphere = $\dfrac{4}{3}\pi r^3 = \dfrac{4}{3}\pi \times 3^3 = 36\pi$ cu. cm

Volume of cone = Volume of sphere

$$\frac{1}{3}\pi r^2 h = 36\pi$$

$$\frac{1}{3}\pi \times 2^2 \times h = 36\pi$$

$$\therefore h = \frac{36 \times 3}{2^2} = 27 \text{ cm}$$

So, the height of cone = 27 cm.

Example 13

Find the difference between the total surface area and curved surface area of a hemisphere of 7 cm diameter.

Solution

Total surface area of hemisphere = $3\pi r^2$
Curved surface area of hemisphere = $2\pi r^2$

Difference = $3\pi r^2 - 2\pi r^2 = \pi r^2$
$= \frac{22}{7} \times 7^2 = 154$ sq. cm.

EXERCISE

1. Find the surface area of a 4 cm × 6 cm × 12 cm brick.
   (a) 144 sq. cm
   (b) 216 sq. cm
   (c) 264 sq. cm
   (d) 288 sq. cm

2. Find the total surface area of a square prism of base edge 4 cm and height 5 cm.
   (a) 80 sq. cm
   (b) 96 sq. cm
   (c) 112 sq. cm
   (d) 160 sq. cm

3. Find the lateral surface area of a hexagonal prism of base edge 6 cm and height 10 cm.
   (a) 60 sq. cm
   (b) 180 sq. cm
   (c) 360 sq. cm
   (d) 420 sq. cm

4. The volume of a pentagonal prism of base area 25 sq. cm and height 12 cm is:
   (a) 150 cu. cm
   (b) 250 cu. cm
   (c) 300 cu. cm
   (d) 500 cu. cm

5. Find the lateral surface area of a hexagonal pyramid, whose side of base is 6 cm and slant height is 15 cm.
   (a) 90 cm^2
   (b) 180 cm^2
   (c) 270 cm^2
   (d) 540 cm^2

6. Find the volume of a square pyramid with perimeter of base as 12 cm and height as 4 cm.
   (a) 8 cm^3
   (b) 12 cm^3
   (c) 16 cm^3
   (d) 20 cm^3

7. A rectangular tank 4 m long and 3 m wide is filled with water up to a height of 2 m. The total area of wet surface is:
   (a) 24 sq. m
   (b) 28 sq. m
   (c) 40 sq. m
   (d) 52 sq. m

8. A swimming pool is 100 ft long and 60 ft wide. It is 3 ft deep at the shallow end of the length and 7 ft deep at the deep end of the length. Find the volume of pool.
   (a) 18000 cu. feet
   (b) 30000 cu. feet
   (c) 42000 cu. feet
   (d) 60000 cu. feet

9. The edges of a rectangular cardboard box are in the ratio of 4 : 3 : 2 and its surface area is 208 sq. cm. How much is the volume of box?
   (a) 104 cu. cm
   (b) 128 cu. cm
   (c) 176 cu. cm
   (d) 192 cu. cm

10. The weight of 1 cubic cm of wood is 1.2 gm. If the weight of a wooden block of 30 cm wide and 10 cm thick is 14.4 kg, then the length of block is:
    (a) 32 cm
    (b) 36 cm
    (c) 40 cm
    (d) 48 cm

11. What is the measure of a longest stick that can be placed in a rectangular box of dimensions 12 cm × 9 cm × 8 cm?
    (a) 12 cm
    (b) 16 cm
    (c) 17 cm
    (d) 21 cm

12. How many bricks, each measuring 10 cm × 8 cm × 6 cm will be needed to build a wall 15 m long, 10 m high and 16 cm wide?
    (a) 20000
    (b) 36000
    (c) 40000
    (d) 50000

13. A rectangular swimming pool of dimensions 20 m × 12 m is 3 m deep. How long it will take to fill with water flowing through a pipe of cross section area 40 cm^2 at 6 km/hr?
    (a) 3 hrs
    (b) 12 hrs
    (c) 18 hrs
    (d) 30 hrs

14. A rectangular hall is 15 m long and 10 m wide. If the sum of the areas of floor and ceiling is equal to the sum of the areas of four walls, then how much is the volume of hall?
    (a) 600 cu. m
    (b) 720 cu. m
    (c) 900 cu. m
    (d) 960 cu. m

15. If the areas of the three adjacent faces of a rectangular block are in the ratio of 12 : 4 : 3 and its volume is 96 cu. cm; the length of longest side is:
    (a) 6 cm
    (b) 8 cm
    (c) 12 cm
    (d) 24 cm

16. If the areas of three adjacent faces of a cuboid are 120 cm², 96 cm² and 80 cm² respectively, then how much is the volume of cuboid?
    (a) 960 cu. cm
    (b) 1040 cu. cm
    (c) 1184 cu. cm
    (d) 1260 cu. cm

17. The areas of two adjacent faces of a cuboid are 60 cm² and 40 cm². If the volume of the cuboid is 480 cm³, then how much is the difference between the longest and shortest side of cuboid?
    (a) 4 cm
    (b) 5 cm
    (c) 7 cm
    (d) 8 cm

18. A rectangular sheet has a length of 12 cm and a breadth of 10 cm. If four squares each of side 2 cm are cut from four corners of a rectangle and the resulting sheet is folded to form a tray, then how much will be the volume of tray?
    (a) 48 cu. cm
    (b) 96 cu. cm
    (c) 192 cu. cm
    (d) 240 cu. cm

19. A pit of size 10 m × 5 m is dug to a depth of 2.75 m in a rectangular farm of dimensions 70 m × 40 m. If the earth dug out is uniformly spread in the remaining part of farm, then find the rise in level of farm.
    (a) 2 cm
    (b) 5 cm
    (c) 10 cm
    (d) 25 cm

20. The perimeter of one face of cube is 24 cm, then the volume of cube is:
    (a) 216 cu. cm
    (b) 512 cu. cm
    (c) 576 cu. cm
    (d) 604 cu. cm

21. Find the length of the longest stick that can be kept in a cubical box of volume 512 cu. cm.
    (a) $6\sqrt{2}$
    (b) $6\sqrt{3}$
    (c) $8\sqrt{2}$
    (d) $8\sqrt{3}$

22. What is the volume of a cube whose body diagonal measures $4\sqrt{3}$ cm?
    (a) 8 cm³
    (b) 16 cm³
    (c) 27 cm³
    (d) 64 cm³

23. How many small cubical boxes of 12 cm edge can be put in a bigger cubical box of edge 1.2 m?
    (a) 10
    (b) 100
    (c) 1000
    (d) 10000

24. How many small cubes of 4 cm edge can be cut from a bigger cube of 12 cm edge?
    (a) 6
    (b) 9
    (c) 18
    (d) 27

25. A rectangular block of 45 cm × 20 cm × 10 cm is cut in to exact number of equal cubes. The least possible number of cubes will be:

(a) 36   (b) 50
(c) 60   (d) 72

26. Three cubes of copper whose edges are 3 cm, 4 cm and 5 cm respectively are melted to form a bigger cube. The edge of bigger cube will be:
    (a) 6 cm   (b) 8 cm
    (c) 10 cm   (d) 12 cm

27. The cost of painting the whole surface area of a cube at the rate of 25 paisa per sq. cm is ₹ 96. How much is the volume of cube?
    (a) 192 cu. cm   (b) 216 cu. cm
    (c) 343 cu. cm   (d) 512 cu. cm

28. If the volume of two cubes are in the ratio of 64 : 27, then the ratio of their surface area is:
    (a) 4:3   (b) 16:9
    (c) 64:27   (d) 27:64

29. If each edge of cube is reduced to half, then the volume of new cube is how much times the volume of original cube?
    (a) $\dfrac{1}{2}$ (b) $\dfrac{1}{4}$
    (c) $\dfrac{1}{8}$ (d) $\dfrac{1}{16}$

30. A cylindrical jar of radius 7 cm is filled with milk up to a height of 10 cm. The total area of wet surface is:
    (a) 440 sq. cm   (b) 594 sq. cm
    (c) 616 sq. cm   (d) 632 sq. cm

31. The volume of a right circular cylinder whose curved surface area is 220 cm^2 and circumference of base is 44 cm, is:
    (a) 660 cu. cm   (b) 770 cu. cm
    (c) 880 cu. cm   (d) 1100 cu. cm

32. If the volume of a right circular cylinder with its height equal to diameter is 2156 cm^3, then the radius of cylinder is equal to:
    (a) 3.5 cm   (b) 5 cm
    (c) 7 cm   (d) 14 cm

33. The height of a right circular cylinder is 5 cm and its curved surface area is 110 cm^2. The base area of cylinder is:
    (a) 38.5 cm^2 (b) 66 cm^2
    (c) 77 cm^2 (d) 88 cm^2

34. A closed cylindrical tin can for soft drink is 6.5 cm long with base diameter 7 cm. If the sheet metal cost 1 paisa per cm^2, then how much will be the cost of material used for making 300 such tin cans?

(a) ₹ 300 (b) ₹ 440
(c) ₹ 600 (d) ₹ 660

35. The ratio of total surface area to curved surface area of a cylinder whose height and diameter are equal is:
    (a) 1 : 1 (b) 2 : 1
    (c) 3 : 1 (d) 3 : 2

36. The curved surface area of a cylindrical vessel is 440 cm^2 and its volume is 1540 cm^3. Find the ratio of its diameter to height.
    (a) 7 : 3 (b) 7 : 4
    (c) 7 : 5 (d) 7 : 6

37. Two cylinders A and B are formed from the same sheet material. Cylinder B is having half the radius and double the height as that of cylinder A. Find the ratio of volume cylinder A and B.
    (a) 1 : 2 (b) 2 : 1
    (c) 1 : 1 (d) 4 : 1

38. A cylindrical vessel of diameter 28 cm is full of milk. If 770 ml of milk is drawn off, then the level of milk in the vessel will drop by:
    (a) 1.25 cm (b) 3.5 cm
    (c) 4 cm (d) 7 cm

39. A cylindrical tin can of 6 cm diameter is having a capacity to hold 396 ml of soft drink. How much is the height of tin can?
    (a) 10 cm (b) 12 cm
    (c) 14 cm (d) 16 cm

40. A copper wire is stretched in such a way that its length becomes nine times of original length. The ratio of radius of original wire to radius stretched wire is:
    (a) 2 : 1 (b) 3 : 1
    (c) 6 : 1 (d) 9 : 1

41. The largest possible right circular cylinder is cut out from a wooden cube of edge 7 cm. Find the volume of wood get wasted after cutting the cylinder.
    (a) 63.5 cu. cm (b) 70 cu. cm
    (c) 73.5 cu. cm (d) 78.5 cu. cm

42. The radius of a roller is 0.5 m and its length is 3.5 m. If it takes 200 revolutions to move once over a level field, find the area of the field.
    (a) 800 sq. m (b) 950 sq. m
    (c) 1050 sq. m (d) 1100 sq. m

43. A hollow alloy pipe has an external diameter of 8 cm and thickness of 1 cm. If each cubic cm of alloy weighs 10 gm, then how much will be the weight of pipe 100 cm long?
    (a) 1.1 kg (b) 2.2 kg
    (c) 11 kg (d) 22 kg

44. The radius of base and height of cone are 3 cm and 4 cm respectively, whereas the radius of base and height of cylinder are 4 cm and 3 cm respectively. The ratio of volume of cone to that of cylinder is:
    (a) 1 : 2
    (b) 1 : 3
    (c) 1 : 4
    (d) 2 : 3

45. The curved surface area (in cm^2) of right circular cone of height 12 cm and base diameter 18 cm is:
    (a) 108π
    (b) 120π
    (c) 135π
    (d) 150π

46. The radius and height of a right circular cone are in the ratio of 8 : 15. If its volume is 2560π cm^3, what is its slant height?
    (a) 17 cm
    (b) 20 cm
    (c) 28 cm
    (d) 34 cm

47. If the radius of base of a right circular cone is doubled and its height is reduced to half, then its volume will be how much times the original volume?
    (a) ½ times
    (b) 2 times
    (c) 4 times
    (d) no change in volume

48. If the volume of two cones are in the ratio of 1 : 3, and their diameters are in the ratio of 2 : 3, then the ratio of their height is:
    (a) 1 : 2
    (b) 2 : 3
    (c) 1 : 4
    (d) 3 : 4

49. A cylinder with base radius 2 cm and height 8 cm is melted to form a cone of height 6 cm. The base radius of cone will be:
    (a) 2 cm
    (b) 3 cm
    (c) 4 cm
    (d) 6 cm

50. If the volume of a sphere is divided by its surface area, the result is 7 cm. The diameter of the sphere is:
    (a) 14 cm
    (b) 21 cm
    (c) 42 cm
    (d) 70 cm

51. Spheres *A* and *B* have their radii 6 cm and 2 cm respectively. The ratio of surface area of *A* to surface area of B is:
    (a) 3 : 1
    (b) 6 : 1
    (c) 9 : 1
    (d) 9 : 4

52. The volume of two spheres are in the ratio of 125 : 27. The ratio of their surface area is:
    (a) 5 : 3
    (b) 3 : 5
    (c) 25 : 9
    (d) 9 : 25

53. Three spheres of radius 3 cm, 4 cm and 5 cm are melted to form a single big sphere. The diameter of this single big sphere will be:
    (a) 12 cm
    (b) 14 cm
    (c) 16 cm
    (d) 18 cm

54. A metallic cone of diameter 48 cm and height 18 cm is melted into identical spheres each of radius 2 cm. How many such spheres can be made?
    (a) 224
    (b) 272
    (c) 324
    (d) 346

55. A rectangular steel sheet of 88 mm × 49 mm with thickness of 9 mm is melted to form a sphere. The radius of the sphere is:
    (a) 14 mm
    (b) 21 mm
    (c) 22 mm
    (d) 28 mm

56. What is the maximum number of spherical balls of radius 2 cm can be packed in a box of size 48 cm × 40 cm × 8 cm?
    (a) 120
    (b) 180
    (c) 200
    (d) 240

57. A cylindrical vessel of 8 cm radius contains water. If a solid metal sphere of 6 cm radius is completely immersed in the vessel, then water level will rise by:
    (a) 3 cm
    (b) 4 cm
    (c) 4.5 cm
    (d) 6.5 cm

58. A wooden sphere of 12 cm diameter is carved to obtain the largest possible cone. The percentage of wood wasted is:
    (a) 25%
    (b) 50%
    (c) 60%
    (d) 75%

59. If the total surface area of a solid hemisphere is 462 cm^2, then its diameter is:
    (a) 7 cm
    (b) 8 cm
    (c) 12 cm
    (d) 14 cm

60. A hemisphere and a cone have equal base diameter. If their heights are also equal, then the ratio of their curved surface area will be:
    (a) 1 : 1
    (b) 2 : 1
    (c) $\sqrt{2}$: 1
    (d) $\sqrt{3}$: 1

KEYS

1. (d)	2. (c)	3. (c)	4. (c)	5. (c)	6. (b)	7. (c)	8. (b)
9. (d)	10. (c)	11. (c)	12. (d)	13. (d)	14. (c)	15. (b)	16. (a)
17. (c)	18. (b)	19. (b)	20. (a)	21. (d)	22. (d)	23. (c)	24. (d)
25. (d)	26. (a)	27. (d)	28. (b)	29. (c)	30. (b)	31. (b)	32. (c)
33. (a)	34. (d)	35. (d)	36. (c)	37. (b)	38. (a)	39. (c)	40. (b)
41. (c)	42. (d)	43. (d)	44. (c)	45. (c)	46. (d)	47. (b)	48. (d)
49. (c)	50. (c)	51. (c)	52. (c)	53. (a)	54. (c)	55. (b)	56. (d)
57. (c)	58. (d)	59. (d)	60. (c)				

SOLUTIONS

Solution 1

Surface area of brick = $2[(4 \times 6) + (4 \times 12) + (6 \times 12)]$
  = $2[24 + 48 + 72]$
  = 288 sq. cm.

Choice (d)

Solution 2

Perimeter of base = $4 \times$ Side of base
  = $4 \times 4 = 16$ cm

Total surface area = Lateral surface area + Top Area + Bottom area
  = $(16 \times 5) + 4^2 + 4^2$
  = $80 + 16 + 16$
  = 112 sq. cm.

Choice (c)

Solution 3

Perimeter of base = $6 \times$ Side of base
  = 6×6
  = 36 cm

Lateral surface area = Perimeter of base × Height
  = 36×10
  = 360 sq. cm.

Choice (c)

Solution 4

Volume of prism = Area of base × Height
  = 25×12
  = 300 sq. cm.

Choice (c)

Solution 5

Lateral surface area of pyramid = ½ × Perimeter of base × Slant height
  = ½ × $(6 \times 6) \times 15$
  = 270 sq. cm.

Choice (c)

Solution 6

Perimeter of square base = 4 × side

12 cm = 4 × side

∴ Side = 3 cm.

Volume of pyramid = $\frac{1}{3}$ × Area of base × Height
$= \frac{1}{3} \times 3^2 \times 4$
= 12 cu. cm.

Choice (b)

Solution 7

Area of wet surface = (4 × 3) + 2 (2 × 3) + 2 (2 × 4)
= 12 + 12 + 16
= 40 sq. m.

Choice (c)

Solution 8

Volume of pool = $100 \times 60 \times \left(\frac{3+7}{2}\right)$

= 30000 cu. feet.

Choice (b)

Solution 9

Let the length, breadth and height of box be $4x$, $3x$ and $2x$ respectively.

Surface area of box = 208 sq. cm

$2[(4x \times 3x) + (3x \times 2x) + (4x \times 2x)] = 208$

$\Rightarrow 2[12x^2 + 6x^2 + 8x^2] = 208$
$\Rightarrow 26x^2 = 104$
$\Rightarrow x^2 = 4$

∴ $x = 2$

Volume of box = $4x \times 3x \times 2x$
= $24x^3$
= 24×2^3
= 192 cu. cm.

Choice (d)

Solution 10

$$\text{Volume of wooden block} = \frac{\text{Total weight}}{\text{Weight per cm}^3}$$

$$= \frac{14.4 \times 10^3}{1.2} = 12000 \text{ cu. cm}$$

$L \times B \times H = \text{Volume}$

$L \times 30 \times 10 = 12000$

$\therefore \quad L = \frac{12000}{30 \times 10} = 40 \text{ cm.}$

Choice (c)

Solution 11

Longest stick in a rectangular box will be the body diagonal of cuboid.

$$\text{Length} = \sqrt{L^2 + B^2 + H^2}$$
$$= \sqrt{12^2 + 9^2 + 8^2}$$
$$= \sqrt{144 + 81 + 64}$$
$$= \sqrt{289} = 17.$$

Choice (c)

Solution 12

$$\text{Number of bricks} = \frac{\text{Volume of wall}}{\text{Volume of each brick}}$$

$$= \frac{(15 \times 10^2) \times (10 \times 10^2) \times 16}{10 \times 8 \times 6} = 50000.$$

Choice (d)

Solution 13

Volume of swimming pool $= 20 \times 12 \times 3 = 720 \text{ m}^3$

$$\text{Time required to fill} = \frac{\text{Volume of tank}}{\text{Area of inlet} \times \text{Velocity of flow}}$$

$$= \frac{720}{\frac{40}{10^4} \times (6 \times 10^3)} = 30 \text{ hrs.}$$

Choice (d)

Solution 14

Let the height of the hall be h meters.

Area of four walls = Area of floor + Area of ceiling

$\Rightarrow 2(15 \times h) + 2(10 \times h) = (15 \times 10) + (15 \times 10)$
$\Rightarrow 30h + 20h = 300$
$\Rightarrow 50h = 300$
$\Rightarrow h = 6$ m.

$\therefore$ Volume of hall $= L \times B \times H$
$= 15 \times 10 \times 6$
$= 900$ cu. m.

Choice (c)

Solution 15

Let $L \times B = 12x$, $L \times H = 4x$ and $B \times H = 3x$

$12x \times 4x \times 3x = (L \times B \times H)^2$
$144x^3 = (\text{Volume})^2$
$144x^3 = 96 \times 96$
$\therefore x^3 = 64$
$x = 4$.

So, $L \times B = 48$ cm, $L \times H = 16$ cm, $B \times H = 12$ cm

Longest side $\Rightarrow L = \dfrac{\text{Volume}}{B \times H}$

$= \dfrac{96}{12} = 8$ cm.

Choice (b)

Solution 16

Let the length, breadth and height of cuboid be L, B and H respectively.

Volume $= L \times B \times H$

$= \sqrt{(L \times B \times H)^2}$

$= \sqrt{LB \times BH \times LH}$

$= \sqrt{120 \times 96 \times 80}$

$= 960$ cm^3.

Choice (a)

Solution 17

Let the length, breadth and height of cuboid be L, B and H respectively.

$(L \times B) \times (L \times H) \times (B \times H) = (L \times B \times H)^2$

$\Rightarrow (L \times B) \times 60 \times 40 = (480)^2$

$\Rightarrow L \times B = 96$

Longest side $\Rightarrow L = \dfrac{\text{Volume}}{B \times H} = \dfrac{480}{40} = 12$ cm

Shortest side $\Rightarrow H = \dfrac{\text{Volume}}{L \times B} = \dfrac{480}{96} = 5$ cm

Difference = 12 – 5 = 7 cm.

Choice (c)

Solution 18

Length of sheet after folding = 12 – (2 + 2) = 8 cm
Breadth of sheet after folding = 10 – (2 + 2) = 6 cm
Volume of tray = 8 × 6 × 2
= 96 cu. cm.

Choice (b)

Solution 19

Volume of earth dug out = $10 \times 5 \times 2.75$ m^3

Area of spread = $(70 \times 40) - (10 \times 5) = 2750$ m^2

Rise in level can be found as:

$2750 \times h = 10 \times 5 \times 2.75$ m^3

$\therefore h = \dfrac{10 \times 5 \times 2.75}{2750}$

= 0.05 m
= 5 cm.

Choice (b)

Solution 20

4 × side = Perimeter of square face
4 × side = 24 cm

$\therefore$ Side = 6 cm

Volume of cube = $6^3 = 216$ cm^3.

Choice (a)

Solution 21

Let the length of each edge of cube is L cm.

$L^3 = 512$

$\therefore L = 8$

Length of longest stick in the cube $= L\sqrt{3} = 8\sqrt{3}$.

Choice (d)

Solution 22

Let the length of each edge of cube is L cm.

Body diagonal $= L\sqrt{3}$

$\Rightarrow 4\sqrt{3} = L\sqrt{3}$

$\therefore L = 4$ cm

Volume of cube $= L^3 = 4^3 = 64$ cm^3.

Choice (d)

Solution 23

Number of boxes $= \dfrac{\text{Volume of bigger box}}{\text{Volume of each smaller box}}$

$= \dfrac{1.2 \times 1.2 \times 1.2 \times 10^6}{12 \times 12 \times 12} = 1000.$

Choice (c)

Solution 24

Number of cubes $= \dfrac{\text{Volume of bigger cube}}{\text{Volume of each smaller cube}}$

$= \dfrac{12 \times 12 \times 12}{4 \times 4 \times 4} = 27.$

Choice (d)

Solution 25

Size of rectangular block $= 45$ cm $\times$ 20 cm $\times$ 10 cm

Length of edge of cube $=$ HCF of 45, 20 and 10 $= 5$ cm

Number of cubes $= \dfrac{\text{Volume of block}}{\text{Volume of each smaller cube}} = \dfrac{45 \times 20 \times 10}{5 \times 5 \times 5} = 72.$

Choice (d)

Solution 26

Let the length of edge of bigger cube be L cm.

Volume of bigger cube = Sum of volume of smaller cubes
$$L^3 = 3^3 + 4^3 + 5^3$$
$\Rightarrow L^3 = 27 + 64 + 125$
$\Rightarrow L^3 = 216$
$\Rightarrow L = 6$ cm.

Choice (a)

Solution 27

Let the length of edge of cube be L cm.

Total surface area = $6L^2$

Total surface area × Rate per sq. cm = Cost of painting
$$6L^2 \times 0.25 = 96$$
$\Rightarrow 6L^2 = 384$
$\Rightarrow L^2 = 64$
$\Rightarrow L = 8$ cm

∴ Volume of cube = $8^3 = 512$ cu. cm.

Choice (d)

Solution 28

Let the length of two cubes be a cm and b cm respectively.
$$\frac{a^3}{b^3} = \frac{64}{27}$$
$\Rightarrow \quad \frac{a}{b} = \frac{4}{3}$

Ratio of surface area
$$\frac{a^2}{b^2} = \frac{16}{9}.$$

Choice (b)

Solution 29

Assuming that length of edge of original cube as 2 cm.
Volume of original cube = $2^3 = 8$ cm^3
Length of edge of reduced cube = 1 cm

Volume of reduced cube = $1^3 = 1$ cm^3

So, volume of new cube is $1/8^{th}$ the volume of original cube.

Choice (c)

Solution 30

Total wet area = base area + curved surface area
$$= \pi r^2 + 2\pi rh$$
$$= \pi r (r + 2h)$$
$$= \frac{22}{7} \times 7 \times (7 + 2 \times 10)$$
$$= 22 \times 27$$
$$= 594 \text{ sq. cm.}$$

Choice (b)

Solution 31

Let the height and radius of cylinder be h and r cm respectively.

$$2\pi r = \text{Circumference}$$
$$2 \times \frac{22}{7} \times r = 44 \text{ cm}$$

∴ $r = 7$ cm.

$$2\pi rh = \text{Curved surface area}$$
$$44 \times h = 220$$

∴ $h = 5$ cm.

Volume $= \pi r^2 h = \frac{22}{7} \times 7^2 \times 5$

$= 770$ cu. cm.

Choice (b)

Solution 32

Let the height and radius of cylinder be h and r cm respectively.

Given: $h = 2r$

$\pi r^2 h = $ Volume

$\Rightarrow \frac{22}{7} \times r^2 \times 2r = 2156$

$\Rightarrow \frac{44}{7} \times r^3 = 2156$

$\Rightarrow r^3 = \dfrac{2156 \times 7}{44}$

$\Rightarrow r^3 = 343$

$\Rightarrow r = 7$ cm.

Choice (c)

Solution 33

Let the height and radius of cylinder be h and r cm respectively.

$2\pi rh$ = Curved surface area

$2 \times \dfrac{22}{7} \times r \times 5 = 110$

$\therefore r = \dfrac{110 \times 7}{2 \times 22 \times 5} = 3.5$ cm

Base area $= \pi r^2 = \dfrac{22}{7} \times \left(\dfrac{7}{2}\right)^2 = 38.5$ sq. cm.

Choice (a)

Solution 34

Total surface area = Base area + Top area + Curved surface area

$= \pi r^2 + \pi r^2 + 2\pi rh = 2\pi r(r+h)$

$= 2 \times \dfrac{22}{7} \times \dfrac{7}{2} \times \left(\dfrac{7}{2} + 6.5\right) = 220$ cm^2.

Cost of material for 1 can = Total surface area × Rate per cm^2

$= 220 \times \dfrac{1}{100} = ₹\, 2.20$.

Cost of material for 300 cans = $300 \times 2.20 = ₹\, 660$.

Choice (d)

Solution 35

Let the height and radius of cylinder be h and r cm respectively.

Given: $h = 2r$

$\dfrac{\text{Total surface area}}{\text{Curved surface area}} = \dfrac{2\pi r^2 + 2\pi rh}{2\pi rh}$

$= \dfrac{2\pi r^2 + 2\pi r(2r)}{2\pi r(2r)} = \dfrac{2\pi r^2 + 4\pi r^2}{4\pi r^2} = \dfrac{6\pi r^2}{4\pi r^2} = \dfrac{3}{2}$.

Choice (d)

Solution 36

Volume $\Rightarrow \pi r^2 h = 1540$ cm^3
Curved surface area $\Rightarrow 2\pi rh = 440$ cm^2

$$\frac{\pi r^2 h}{2\pi rh} = \frac{1540}{440}$$

$$\Rightarrow \frac{r}{2} = \frac{7}{2}$$

$\therefore r = 7$ cm and $d = 14$ cm.

Substituting the value of r as 7 cm, $h = 10$ cm.

Required ratio $\Rightarrow \dfrac{d}{h} = \dfrac{14}{10} = \dfrac{7}{5}$.

Choice (c)

Solution 37

Cylinder $A \Rightarrow$ Radius $= r$ cm and Height $= h$ cm.

Cylinder $B \Rightarrow$ Radius $= \dfrac{r}{2}$ cm and Height $= 2h$ cm.

Ratio of volume $= \dfrac{\pi r^2 h}{\pi \left(\dfrac{r}{2}\right)^2 2h} = \dfrac{\pi r^2 h}{\dfrac{1}{2}\times \pi r^2 h} = \dfrac{2}{1}$.

Choice (b)

Solution 38

$d = 28$ cm, $\therefore r = 14$ cm

Let the drop in level be h cm.

$\pi r^2 h = 770$ ml

$$\frac{22}{7} \times 14^2 \times h = 770$$

$\therefore h = \dfrac{770 \times 7}{22 \times 14^2} = 1.25$ cm.

Choice (a)

Solution 39

$d = 6$ cm, $\therefore r = 3$ cm

Volume = 396 ml

$$\pi r^2 h = 396$$

$$\frac{22}{7} \times 3^2 \times h = 396$$

$$\therefore h = \frac{396 \times 7}{22 \times 9} = 14 \text{ cm.}$$

Choice (c)

Solution 40

Original wire $\Rightarrow$ Radius = R_O cm and Length = L cm
Stretched wire $\Rightarrow$ Radius = R_S cm and Length = $9L$ cm

Volume of original wire = Volume of stretched wire

$$\pi R_O^2 L = \pi R_S^2 \times 9L$$

$$\frac{R_O^2}{R_S^2} = \frac{9}{1} \Rightarrow \frac{R_O}{R_S} = \frac{3}{1}.$$

Choice (b)

Solution 41

Edge of cube = 7 cm
Volume of cube = 7^3 = 343 cm^3

Diameter of cylinder = 7 cm, Height of cylinder = 7 cm
Volume of cylinder = $\pi r^2 h$ = 269.5 cm^3
Volume of wood wasted = 343 – 269.5 = 73.5 cm^3.

Choice (c)

Solution 42

Area of field leveled in 1 revolution of roller = Curved surface area of roller

$$= 2\pi r h$$

$$= 2 \times \frac{22}{7} \times \left(\frac{1}{2}\right)^2 \times 3.5$$

$$= \frac{11}{2} \text{ sq. m}$$

Area of field = $\frac{11}{2}$ × 200 revolutions = 1100 sq. m.

Choice (d)

Solution 43

$D_o = 8$ cm $\therefore R_o = 4$ cm

$D_i = 8 - 2 = 6$ cm. $\therefore R_i = 3$ cm

Cross section area = $\pi R_o^2 - \pi R_i^2$
$= 16\pi - 9\pi$
$= 7\pi$
$= 22$ sq. cm

Volume of 100 cm long pipe $= 22 \times 100$
$= 2200$ cm^3

Weight $= 2200 \times 10$
$= 22000$ gm $= 22$ kg.

Choice (d)

Solution 44

Cone $\Rightarrow r = 3$ cm, $h = 4$ cm

Cylinder $\Rightarrow r = 4$ cm, $h = 3$ cm

Volume of cone = $\frac{1}{3}\pi r^2 h = \frac{1}{3} \times \pi \times 3^2 \times 4 = 12\pi$ cm^3

Volume of cylinder = $\pi r^2 h = \pi \times 4^2 \times 3 = 48\pi$ cm^3

Required ratio = $\frac{12\pi}{48\pi} = \frac{1}{4}$.

Choice (c)

Solution 45

Diameter, $d = 18$ cm $\quad \therefore r = 9$ cm

Height, $h = 12$ cm

Slant height, $l = \sqrt{r^2 + h^2}$
$= \sqrt{9^2 + 12^2}$
$= \sqrt{225}$
$= 15$.

Curved surface area = $\pi r l$
$= \pi \times 9 \times 15$
$= 135\pi$ sq. cm.

Choice (c)

Solution 46

$$\frac{r}{h} = \frac{8x}{15x}$$

$$\frac{1}{3}\pi r^2 h = \text{Volume of cone}$$

$$\Rightarrow \frac{1}{3} \times \pi \times (8x)^2 \times 15x = 2560\pi$$

$$\Rightarrow 320\pi x^3 = 2560\pi$$
$$\Rightarrow x^3 = 8 \Rightarrow x = 2$$

$\therefore r = 16$ cm and $h = 30$ cm

Slant height, $l = \sqrt{r^2 + h^2} = \sqrt{16^2 + 30^2} = \sqrt{1156} = 34$ cm.

Choice (d)

Solution 47

Original cone $\Rightarrow$ Radius = r, height = h

New cone $\quad\Rightarrow$ Radius = $2r$, height = $\dfrac{h}{2}$

Volume of original cone = $\dfrac{1}{3}\pi r^2 h$

Volume of new cone = $\dfrac{1}{3}\pi \times (2r)^2 \times \dfrac{h}{2} = 2 \times \left(\dfrac{1}{3}\pi r^2 h\right)$.

So, volume of new cone is 2 times the volume of original cone.

Choice (b)

Solution 48

Ratio of diameter

$$\Rightarrow \quad \frac{d_1}{d_2} = \frac{r_1}{r_2} = \frac{2}{3}$$

Ratio of volume

$$\Rightarrow \frac{r_1^2 h_1}{r_2^2 h_2} = \frac{v_1}{v_2}$$

$$\frac{2^2 h_1}{3^2 h_2} = \frac{1}{3}$$

$$\frac{h_1}{h_2} = \frac{3}{4}.$$

Choice (d)

Solution 49

Cylinder
$\Rightarrow r = 2$ cm, $h = 8$ cm

Cone
$\Rightarrow r = ?$, $h = 6$ cm

Volume of cylinder $= \pi \times 2^2 \times 8$
$= 32\pi$ cm^3

Volume of cone $= \dfrac{1}{3}\pi \times r^2 \times 6$
$= 2\pi r^2$ cm^3

Volume of cone = Volume of cylinder

$2\pi r^2 = 32\pi$
$\Rightarrow r^2 = 16$
$\Rightarrow r = 4$ cm.

Choice (c)

Solution 50

$\dfrac{\text{Volume of sphere}}{\text{Surface area of sphere}} = 7$ cm

$\Rightarrow \qquad \dfrac{\frac{4}{3}\pi r^3}{4\pi r^2} = 7$ cm

$\Rightarrow \qquad \dfrac{r}{3} = 7$ cm

$\Rightarrow \qquad r = 21$ cm

∴ Diameter, $d = 42$ cm.

Choice (c)

Solution 51

$R_A = 6$ cm, $R_B = 2$ cm

$\dfrac{\text{Surface area of sphere A}}{\text{Surface area of sphere B}} = \dfrac{4\pi R_A^2}{4\pi R_B^2}$

$= \dfrac{6^2}{2^2} = \dfrac{9}{1}.$

Choice (c)

Solution 52

Ratio of volume = $\dfrac{125}{27}$

$$\dfrac{\dfrac{4}{3}\pi \times r_1^3}{\dfrac{4}{3}\pi \times r_2^3} = \dfrac{125}{27}$$

$\therefore \qquad \dfrac{r_1}{r_2} = \dfrac{5}{3}$

Ratio of surface area = $\dfrac{4\pi r_1^2}{4\pi r_2^2}$

$$= \dfrac{4\pi \times 5^2}{4\pi \times 3^2} = \dfrac{25}{9}.$$

Choice (c)

Solution 53

Let the radius of bigger sphere = R cm

Volume of single big sphere = Sum of volume of three small spheres

$$\dfrac{4}{3}\pi R^3 = \dfrac{4}{3}\pi \times 3^3 + \dfrac{4}{3}\pi \times 4^3 + \dfrac{4}{3}\pi \times 5^3$$

$\Rightarrow \qquad \dfrac{4}{3}\pi R^3 = \dfrac{4}{3}\pi \times (27 + 64 + 125)$

$\Rightarrow \qquad \dfrac{4}{3}\pi R^3 = \dfrac{4}{3}\pi \times (216)$

$\Rightarrow \qquad \dfrac{4}{3}\pi R^3 = \dfrac{4}{3}\pi \times 6^3$

$\therefore \qquad R = 6$ cm

So, diameter of single big sphere = 12 cm.

Choice (a)

Solution 54

Cone
$\Rightarrow d = 48$ cm, $r = 24$ cm, $h = 18$ cm

Sphere
$\Rightarrow r = 2$ cm

Number of spheres = $\dfrac{\text{Volume of cone}}{\text{Volume of each sphere}}$

$= \dfrac{\frac{1}{3}\pi \times (24)^2 \times 18}{\frac{4}{3}\pi \times (2)^3} = 324.$

Choice (c)

Solution 55

Volume of sphere = Volume of Sheet

$\dfrac{4}{3}\pi \times r^3 = 88 \times 49 \times 9$

$\Rightarrow \quad r^3 = \dfrac{88 \times 49 \times 9 \times 3 \times 7}{22 \times 4}$

$\Rightarrow \quad r^3 = 7^3 \times 3^3$

$\therefore \quad r = 21$ cm.

Choice (b)

Solution 56

Number of ball along length = $\dfrac{\text{Length of box}}{\text{Diameter of ball}} = \dfrac{48}{4} = 12$ balls

Number of ball along breadth = $\dfrac{\text{Breadth of box}}{\text{Diameter of ball}} = \dfrac{40}{4} = 10$ balls

Number of balls in one layer = $12 \times 10 = 120$ balls

Number of layers = $\dfrac{\text{Height of box}}{\text{Diameter of ball}} = \dfrac{8}{4} = 2$ layers

$\therefore$ Total number of balls in the box = $120 \times 2 = 240$ balls.

Choice (d)

Solution 57

Let the rise in water level inside the cylinder = h cm

$\pi \times 8^2 \times h$ = Volume of sphere dropped

$\pi \times 8^2 \times h = \dfrac{4}{3}\pi \times 6^3$

$\therefore \quad h = 4.5$ cm.

Choice (c)

Solution 58

Radius of sphere = 6 cm

Volume of sphere = $\frac{4}{3}\pi \times 6^3 = 288\pi$ cm^3

The largest cone that can be carved from a sphere of radius 6 cm, will have radius as well as its height as 6 cm.

Radius of cone = Height of cone = 6 cm

Volume of cone = $\frac{1}{3}\pi \times 6^2 \times 6 = 72\pi$ cm^3

Percentage of wood wasted = $\frac{288\pi - 72\pi}{288\pi} \times 100 = 75\%$.

Choice (d)

Solution 59

Total surface area = 462 sq. cm

$3\pi r^2 = 462$

$\Rightarrow \qquad r^2 = \frac{462 \times 7}{3 \times 22}$

$\Rightarrow \qquad r^2 = 49$

$\Rightarrow \qquad r = 7$ cm

∴ Diameter = 14 cm.

Choice (d)

Solution 60

Hemisphere
$\Rightarrow$ Radius = r, Height = r

Cone
$\Rightarrow$ Radius = r, Height = r

Slant height of cone, $l = \sqrt{r^2 + h^2} = \sqrt{r^2 + r^2} = r\sqrt{2}$

$\dfrac{\text{Curved surface area of Hemisphere}}{\text{Curved surface area of cone}} = \dfrac{2\pi r^2}{\pi r l} = \dfrac{2r^2}{r^2\sqrt{2}} = \dfrac{\sqrt{2}}{1}$.

Choice (c)

27

Number Series

INTRODUCTION

In a given series of numbers, it is required to identify the pattern in which the series is formed. After the identification of pattern, the task may be to find out the odd number, or wrong number or missing number in the series. Under this type of questions there are large varieties of patterns that are possible, which can be categorized as follows:

1. Difference series
2. Product series
3. Squares and cubes series
4. Miscellaneous series
5. Combination series.

DIFFERENCE SERIES

In these series of numbers, there is a common difference between any two consecutive terms, and hence it will be called as an arithmetic progression. For example:

5, 9, 13, 17, 21, 25, 29
    +4 +4 +4 +4 +4 +4

The difference between the terms can be increasing. For example:

2, 4, 8, 14, 22, 32, 44
   +2 +4 +6 +8 +10 +12

The difference between the terms can be decreasing. For example:

70, 60, 51, 43, 36, 30, 25
   -10 -9 -8 -7 -6 -5

PRODUCT SERIES

In these series of numbers, the terms are obtained by the process of multiplication. If the multiplying number is constant, it will be called as geometric progression. For example:

3, 9, 27, 81, 243, 729, 2187

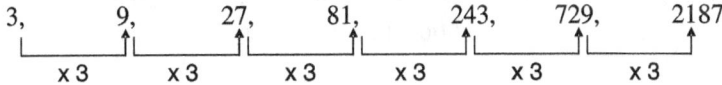

The multiplication factor can be increasing. For example:

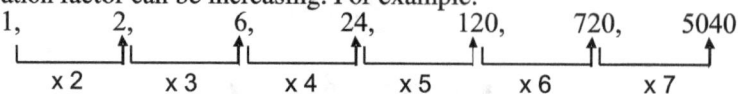

The multiplication factor can be decreasing. For example:

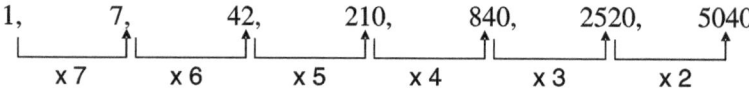

SQUARES AND CUBES SERIES

There can be series where all the terms are related to the square of numbers or cube of numbers. With square or cube of number as the basis, there can be many variations in pattern, few of which are mentioned below:

Example 1

$$1,\quad 4,\quad 9,\quad 16,\quad 25,\quad 36$$
$$\downarrow\quad \downarrow\quad \downarrow\quad \downarrow\quad \downarrow\quad \downarrow$$
$$1^2\quad 2^2\quad 3^2\quad 4^2\quad 5^2\quad 6^2$$

Example 2

$$1,\quad 8,\quad 27,\quad 64,\quad 125,\quad 216$$
$$\downarrow\quad \downarrow\quad \downarrow\quad \downarrow\quad \downarrow\quad \downarrow$$
$$1^3\quad 2^3\quad 3^3\quad 4^3\quad 5^3\quad 6^3$$

Example 3

$$2,\quad 5,\quad 10,\quad 17,\quad 26,\quad 37$$

Where the terms are $1^2 + 1, 2^2 + 1, 3^2 + 1, 4^2 + 1, \ldots$

Example 4

$$0,\quad 6,\quad 24,\quad 60,\quad 120,\quad 210$$

Where the terms are $1^3 - 1, 2^3 - 2, 3^3 - 3, 4^3 - 4, \ldots$

MISCELLANEOUS SERIES

There are series which do not come under the above discussed pattern, but is having its own specific pattern, which needs to be identified. Few examples of such miscellaneous series pattern are mentioned below.

Example 1

2, 3, 5, 7, 11, 13, 17

All the terms are prime numbers.

Example 2

2, 6, 12, 20, 30, 42

Here the pattern followed is $1 \times 2, 2 \times 3, 3 \times 4, 4 \times 5, 5 \times 6,\ldots\ldots$

Example 3

3, 35, 99, 195, 323, 483

Here the pattern followed is $1 \times 3, 5 \times 7, 9 \times 11, 13 \times 15, 17 \times 19, \ldots..$

Example 4

0, 5, 10, 15, 30, 35, 70, 75

Here addition of 5 and multiplication by 2 is done alternately to get the next term.

COMBINATION SERIES

A number series which has more than one type of operation performed or more than one series combined together is a combination series. The series that are combined can be two series of same type or could be different types of series as discussed. Let us look at some examples.

Example 1

2, 5, 4, 10, 8, 15, 16, 20

Here the $1^{st}, 3^{rd}, 5^{th}$ ... term are in geometric progression 2, 4, 8, 16. The $2^{nd}, 4^{th}, 6^{th}$ ...... term are multiples of 5 i.e. 5, 10, 15, 20.

Example 2

1, 5, 8, 10, 27, 20, 64, 35

Here the terms in odd position are cubes i.e. $1^3, 2^3, 3^3,\ldots.$ The terms in even position are 5, 10, 20, 35 in which the difference between the terms is increasing with 5.

Example 3

6, 7, 12, 14, 18, 21, 24, 28

Here the terms in the odd position are multiples of 6, while the terms in the even position are multiples of 7.

Example 4

4, 6, 9, 12, 25, 24, 49, 42

Here the terms in the odd position are square of odd number i.e. $1^2, 3^2, 5^2....$, while the terms in the even position are 6, 12, 24, 42 in which the difference between the terms is increasing with 6.

EXERCISE

Directions: Find the odd man out.

1. 2, 3, 5, 7, 9, 11, 13
   - (a) 2
   - (b) 5
   - (c) 9
   - (d) 11

2. 2, 3, 5, 7, 11, 13, 17, 19
   - (a) 2
   - (b) 5
   - (c) 11
   - (d) 19

3. 4, 8, 12, 16, 18, 20, 24, 28
   - (a) 4
   - (b) 18
   - (c) 20
   - (d) 28

4. 24, 30, 40, 48, 54, 60, 72, 78
   - (a) 30
   - (b) 40
   - (c) 54
   - (d) 72

5. 4, 8, 16, 32, 64, 96, 128, 256
   - (a) 16
   - (b) 64
   - (c) 96
   - (d) 128

6. 16, 25, 36, 49, 64, 72, 81
   - (a) 25
   - (b) 36
   - (c) 64
   - (d) 72

7. 8, 27, 64, 81, 125, 216, 343
   - (a) 8
   - (b) 81
   - (c) 125
   - (d) 343

8. 28, 37, 46, 55, 62, 73, 82, 91
   - (a) 37
   - (b) 55
   - (c) 62
   - (d) 91

9. 2, 5, 10, 17, 21, 26, 37, 50, 65
   - (a) 10
   - (b) 21
   - (c) 26
   - (d) 65

10. 12, 23, 34, 45, 55, 67, 78, 89
    - (a) 23
    - (b) 45
    - (c) 55
    - (d) 78

11. 0, 7, 26, 63, 124, 195, 215
    - (a) 0
    - (b) 7
    - (c) 124
    - (d) 195

12. 4, 8, 14, 19, 24, 29, 34, 39
    (a) 8 (b) 19
    (c) 29 (d) 39

13. 1.21, 1.44, 1.69, 1.96, 2.25, 2.56, 2.84
    (a) 1.44 (b) 1.96
    (c) 2.25 (d) 2.84

14. 132, 242, 275, 326, 484, 594, 671
    (a) 132 (b) 275
    (c) 326 (d) 594

15. 123, 235, 347, 426, 549, 617, 728
    (a) 123 (b) 347
    (c) 426 (d) 728

Directions: Find out the wrong number in each sequence.

16. 2, 6, 12, 20, 25, 30, 42, 56, 72
    (a) 12 (b) 25
    (c) 42 (d) 72

17. 3, 15, 35, 63, 99, 117, 143
    (a) 3 (b) 63
    (c) 99 (d) 117

18. 5, 2, 7, 4, 9, 8, 11, 16, 13, 20, 15
    (a) 2 (b) 9
    (c) 11 (d) 20

19. 1, 5, 14, 30, 42, 55, 91, 140
    (a) 5 (b) 30
    (c) 42 (d) 140

20. 5, 50, 25, 100, 250, 125, 1250, 625, 6250
    (a) 50 (b) 100
    (c) 1250 (d) 625

21. 2, 5, 11, 23, 47, 95, 180, 361, 723
    (a) 5 (b) 47
    (c) 180 (d) 723

22. 1, 4, 27, 16, 125, 36, 49, 64
    (a) 4 (b) 27
    (c) 125 (d) 49

23. 1, 1, 2, 6, 24, 120, 600, 4200
    (a) 1 (b) 2
    (c) 120 (d) 600

24. 100, 98, 95, 90, 83, 72, 59, 42, 30
    (a) 99 (b) 95
    (c) 61 (d) 30

25. 5, 10, 20, 25, 40, 45, 90, 95, 190, 195
    (a) 40 (b) 45
    (c) 190 (d) 195

26. 2, 6, 3, 9, 4.5, 14, 7, 21, 10.5
    (a) 9 (b) 4.5
    (c) 14 (d) 10.5

27. 5, 1, 10, 9, 20, 25, 40, 49, 80, 90, 160
    (a) 1 (b) 20
    (c) 49 (d) 90

28. 100, 75, 25, 0, −50, −75, −125, −175
    (a) 25 (b) 0
    (c) −75 (d) −175

29. 2, 3, 4, 9, 8, 30, 16, 81, 32, 243
    (a) 2 (b) 30
    (c) 81 (d) 32

30. 15625, 10000, 3125, 5000, 625, 2500, 125, 1250, 100
    (a) 3125 (b) 5000
    (c) 125 (d) 100

Directions: Insert the missing number

31. 5, −10, 20, −40, 80, ___, 320, −640
    (a) 120 (b) −120
    (c) 160 (d) −160

32. 1, 4, 9, 16, ___, 36, 49, 64, 81
    (a) 20 (b) 24
    (c) 25 (d) 28

33. 1, 8, 27, ___, 125, 216, 343
    (a) 64 (b) 81
    (c) 100 (d) 121

34. 5, 15, 45, 135, ___, 1215, 3645
    (a) 270 (b) 405
    (c) 825 (d) 915

35. 23, 29, 31, 37, 41, 43, ___
    (a) 45 (b) 47
    (c) 51 (d) 53

36. 4, 9, 25, 49, 121, 169, ___
    (a) 196
    (b) 225
    (c) 256
    (d) 289

37. 2, 8, 26, 80, 242, ___
    (a) 343
    (b) 441
    (c) 624
    (d) 728

38. 1, 2, 6, 12, 36, ___, 216
    (a) 49
    (b) 72
    (c) 96
    (d) 120

39. 5, 11, 23, 47, 95, ___
    (a) 159
    (b) 167
    (c) 177
    (d) 191

40. 50, 49, 47, 44, 40, 35, ___
    (a) 32
    (b) 30
    (c) 29
    (d) 28

41. 100, 80, 90, 70, 80, 60, ___
    (a) 70
    (b) 50
    (c) 40
    (d) 30

42. 5, 6, 10, 12, 15, 18, 20, ___
    (a) 22
    (b) 24
    (c) 25
    (d) 30

43. 0, 8, 24, 48, 80, ___
    (a) 90
    (b) 96
    (c) 112
    (d) 120

44. 5, 15, 35, 75, 155, ___
    (a) 275
    (b) 295
    (c) 305
    (d) 315

45. 100, 150, 250, 450, 850, ___
    (a) 1250
    (b) 1350
    (c) 1550
    (d) 1650

KEYS

1. (c)	2. (a)	3. (b)	4. (b)	5. (c)	6. (d)	7. (b)	8. (c)
9. (b)	10. (c)	11. (d)	12. (a)	13. (d)	14. (c)	15. (d)	16. (b)
17. (d)	18. (d)	19. (c)	20. (b)	21. (c)	22. (d)	23. (d)	24. (d)
25. (a)	26. (c)	27. (d)	28. (d)	29. (b)	30. (d)	31. (d)	32. (c)
33. (a)	34. (b)	35. (b)	36. (d)	37. (d)	38. (b)	39. (d)	40. (c)
41. (a)	42. (b)	43. (d)	44. (d)	45. (d)			

SOLUTIONS

Solution 1

Each of the numbers except 9 is a prime number.

Choice (c)

Solution 2

Each of the numbers except 2 is odd prime numbers.

Choice (a)

Solution 3

Each of the numbers except 18 is a multiple of 4.

Choice (b)

Solution 4

Each of the numbers except 40 is a multiple of 6.

Choice (b)

Solution 5

Each of the numbers except 96 is a power of 2.

Choice (c)

Solution 6

Each of the numbers except 72 is perfect square.

Choice (d)

Solution 7

Each of the numbers except 81 is a perfect cube.

Choice (b)

Solution 8

The sum of digits of every number is 10, except the number 62.

Choice (c)

Solution 9

The numbers are in the pattern of $x^2 + 1$, where $x = 1, 2, 3, 4, 5$...... and so on. All the numbers are following this pattern except 21.

Choice (b)

Solution 10

Each number except 55 is having its digit as consecutive numbers.

Choice (c)

Solution 11

The numbers are in the pattern of $x^3 - 1$, where $x = 1, 2, 3, 4$ .... and so on. All the numbers are following the pattern except 195.

Choice (d)

Solution 12

The numbers are in the pattern of $5x - 1$, where $x = 1, 2, 3, 4$ ... and so on. All the numbers are following this pattern except 8.

Choice (a)

Solution 13

Each number if multiplied by 100 is a perfect square, except 2.84.

Choice (d)

Solution 14

In each number the sum of 1st and 3rd digit is equal to the middle digit, except 326.

Choice (c)

Solution 15

In each number the sum if 1st and 2nd digit is equal to the last digit, except 728.

Choice (d)

Solution 16

The numbers are $1 \times 2, 2 \times 3, 3 \times 4, 4 \times 5, 5 \times 6, 6 \times 7, 7 \times 8, 8 \times 9$. In this pattern the number 25 is wrongly inserted.

Choice (b)

Solution 17

The numbers are 1 × 3, 3 × 5, 5 × 7, 7 × 9, 9 × 11, and 11 × 13. In this pattern the number 117 is wrongly inserted.

Choice (d)

Solution 18

The numbers in the odd position are odd 5, 7, 9, 11, 13, 15; while the numbers in the even position are all powers of 2 i.e. 2, 4, 8, 16 in which the number 20 is the wrong term.

Choice (d)

Solution 19

The numbers in the series follows a pattern 1^2, $1^2 + 2^2$, $1^2 + 2^2 + 3^2$, ... and so on, in which the number 42 is wrongly inserted.

Choice (c)

Solution 20

The terms are alternately multiplied by 10 and divided by 2. However, 100 dose not satisfy it.

Choice (b)

Solution 21

Every number is doubled and 1 is added to it to get the next number. So, 180 is wrong.

Choice (c)

Solution 22

These are the consecutive numbers from 1 to 8. Cube of odd numbers in odd position is taken, while the even numbers in even position are squared. As for the number 7 cube should be taken i.e. 343 should appear instead of 49.

Choice (d)

Solution 23

To get the next number, we need to go on multiplying with 1, 2, 3, 4, 5, 6, and 7. So, 600 is the wrong number in this pattern.

Choice (d)

Solution 24

If we go on subtracting the prime numbers 2, 3, 5, 7, 11… and so on, we get the next number. So, 30 is wrong.

Choice (d)

Solution 25

The terms are alternately added by 5 and doubled. However, 40 dose not satisfy it.

Choice (a)

Solution 26

The terms are alternately multiplied by 3 and divided by 2. However, 14 dose not satisfy it.

Choice (c)

Solution 27

This is a combination of two series in which first series is 5, 10, 20, 40 …… in this every term is doubled to get the next term. Second series is $1^2, 3^2, 5^2, 7^2$ ….. in which 81 i.e. 9^2 should appear instead of 90.

Choice (d)

Solution 28

The numbers 50 and 25 are alternately subtracted to get the next term. The number -175 is not following this pattern.

Choice (d)

Solution 29

There is a combination of two series in which first series is of powers of 2, while second series is of powers of 3. Here 30 is the wrong term.

Choice (b)

Solution 30

This is a combination of two series in which first series is $5^6, 5^5, 5^3$ …… and so on. In the second series 10000, 5000, 2500….. and so on every term is half of its previous term. So, 100 is the wrong number.

Choice (d)

Solution 31

Every term is multiplied by –2 to get the next term. So after 80, the next term will be -160.

Choice (d)

Solution 32

The numbers in series are $1^2, 2^2, 3^2, \ldots$ and so on. Square of 5 is missing in this series.

Choice (c)

Solution 33

The numbers in series are $1^3, 2^3, 3^3, \ldots$ and so on. Cube of 4 is missing in this series.

Choice (a)

Solution 34

The number series is a geometric progression with a common ratio as 3. So, after 135 the next term will be 405.

Choice (b)

Solution 35

These are the prime numbers in continuation. The next prime number after 43 will be 47.

Choice (b)

Solution 36

The series is a square of prime numbers i.e. $2^2, 3^2, 5^2, 7^2, 11^2\ldots$ and so on. Hence after 13^2 i.e.169 the next term will be 17^2 i.e. 289.

Choice (d)

Solution 37

The pattern is 1 subtracted from increasing powers of 3. So, the sixth term after 242 will be $3^6 - 1$ i.e. 728.

Choice (d)

Solution 38

The numbers are alternately multiplied by 2 and 3 to get the next number. Hence 36 will be multiplied by 2 to get the next term. The missing term will be 72.

Choice (b)

Solution 39

Each number is double of its previous term plus 1. So after 95, the next term will be 191.

Choice (d)

Solution 40

The numbers 1, 2, 3, 4, 5 and 6 are subtracted from successive terms. So, if 6 is subtracted from 35, the next term will be 29.

Choice (c)

Solution 41

The number 20 is subtracted and 10 is added alternately. So, the missing term is 70.

Choice (a)

Solution 42

This is a combination of two series in which one is a multiple of 5, while other is a multiple of 6 (5, 10, 15, 20 and 6, 12, 18). So the missing term is a multiple of 6 i.e. 24.

Choice (b)

Solution 43

The pattern is $(1^2 - 1)$, $(3^2 - 1)$, $(5^2 - 1)$,…. and so on. Hence the missing term will be $11^2 - 1$ i.e. 120.

Choice (d)

Solution 44

Each term is doubled and 5 is added to it to get the next term. So after 155, the next term will be 315.

Choice (d)

Solution 45

Each term is doubled and 50 is subtracted to it to get the next term. So after 850, the next term will be 1650.

Choice (d)

28
Data Interpretation

EXERCISE

Directions (Questions 1 to 5): The following table shows the sale of soft drink for a period of six months. Study the data provided in the table and answer the questions that follow.

Different flavors of drinks sold by a soft drink company in six months
(Numbers in thousand liters)

Month	Flavor of Soft drink			
	Apple	Orange	Mango	Cola
January	20	30	25	15
February	22	34	28	18
March	30	36	32	22
April	25	40	50	35
May	38	45	64	43
June	40	55	60	57

1. The total sale of all six months is maximum for which flavor?
   (a) Apple
   (b) Orange
   (c) Mango
   (d) Cola

2. In the month of April, the sale of Apple flavor is what percent of sale of orange flavor?
   (a) 25%
   (b) 40%
   (c) 60%
   (d) 62.5%

3. Which flavor of soft drink does not have continuous increase in sale from January to June?
   (a) Apple
   (b) Orange
   (c) Mango
   (d) Cola

4. How much is the percentage increase in sale of Mango flavor from January to June?
   (a) 40%
   (b) 60%
   (c) 120%
   (d) 140%

5. How much is the difference between the number of liters of cola flavor sold in March and May?
   (a) 19000 liters
   (b) 21000 liters
   (c) 23000 liters
   (d) 25000 liters

Data Interpretation

Directions (Questions 6 to10): The following table shows the price of mobile handsets of Just-connect company for different models from 2006 to 2010. Study the data provided in the table and answer the questions that follow.

Price of different models of handsets of Just-connect Company in five years (Price in Indian Rupees)

Model No.	2006	2007	2008	2009	2010
J-1100	10,000	9,200	8,400	7,000	5,300
J-1300	15,500	15,000	12,200	11,800	9,300
J-1500	16,400	12,000	11,300	9,400	7,500
J-1700	18,000	17,600	16,600	16,200	15,400
J-1900	20,000	17,300	14,500	13,200	13,000

6. Which handset model has maximum percentage decrease in price from 2006 to 2010?
   (a) J-1100
   (b) J-1300
   (c) J-1500
   (d) J-1900

7. For which model there is maximum drop in price between 2008 and 2009?
   (a) J-1100
   (b) J-1300
   (c) J-1500
   (d) J-1900

8. For the model no. J-1700, maximum reduction in price is in which duration?
   (a) 2006–07
   (b) 2007–08
   (c) 2008–09
   (d) 2009–10

9. The price of model J-1500 in the year 2010 is what percent of price of model J-1100 in the year 2006?
   (a) 40%
   (b) 45%
   (c) 60%
   (d) 75%

10. What was the average price of all models during the year 2008?
    (a) ₹ 12600
    (b) ₹ 12750
    (c) ₹ 12800
    (d) ₹ 13000

Directions (Questions 11 to15): The following table shows the marks scored by students in six different subjects. Study the data provided in the table and answer the questions that follow.

Marks scored by students in six different subjects

Name of Student	English (Out of 50)	History (Out of 100)	Physics (Out of 50)	Chemistry (Out of 50)	Biology (Out of 50)	Maths (Out of 100)
Ajay	22	46	28	42	34	88
Bharat	32	45	38	25	36	92
Chetan	42	84	44	25	25	46
Deepak	30	64	46	28	37	63
Eshant	35	44	18	26	42	75
Farhan	44	59	25	35	41	86

11. How much is the overall percentage of Eshant?
    (a) 45%
    (b) 60%
    (c) 70%
    (d) 80%

12. The average marks obtained by all six students in maths is:
    (a) 67.5
    (b) 72
    (c) 75
    (d) 78.5

13. The aggregate score of Bharat is how much more than aggregate score of Deepak?
    (a) 0
    (b) 6
    (c) 8
    (d) 12

14. How many students obtained more than 50% in all the subjects?
    (a) 1
    (b) 2
    (c) 3
    (d) 4

15. In which subject the students have performed the best?
    (a) English
    (b) Physics
    (c) Biology
    (d) Maths

Directions (Questions 16 to 20): The following table shows the number of students appeared and qualified the written test conducted for fresh engineering graduates by a public sector company. Study the data provided in the table and answer the questions that follow.

Candidates appeared and qualified from different branches of engineering in last 5 years

Year	Mechanical		Electrical		Computer		Electronics	
	Appear	Qualify	Appear	Qualify	Appear	Qualify	Appear	Qualify
2007	380	160	290	136	300	120	320	150
2008	390	175	270	195	340	160	340	195
2009	415	215	310	170	350	135	370	165
2010	440	275	340	195	420	175	410	215
2011	500	370	375	210	400	210	450	325

16. The percentage of students qualified from electrical branch is highest in which year?
    (a) 2008
    (b) 2009
    (c) 2010
    (d) 2011

17. For which branch of engineering, the percentage of students qualified are highest in the year 2011?
    (a) Mechanical
    (b) Electrical
    (c) Computer
    (d) Electronics

18. The number of students qualified from computer branch is what percent of students qualified from electronics branch in the year 2007?
    (a) 40%
    (b) 60%
    (c) 75%
    (d) 80%

19. For which branch the average number of candidates appeared over years is minimum?
    (a) Mechanical
    (b) Electrical
    (c) Computer
    (d) Electronics

20. What is the approximate percentage of total number of candidates qualified to the total number of candidates appeared during the year 2010?
    (a) 45%
    (b) 51%
    (c) 53%
    (d) 55%

Directions (Questions 21 to 25): The following table shows the arrival and departure timing of different flights between Mumbai and Delhi. The flights shown in the data fly only between Mumbai and Delhi. Study the data provided in the table considering that each flight makes only one round trip in 24 hrs and answer the questions that follow.

Flight schedule for direct flights between Mumbai and Delhi
(IST stands for Indian Standard Time)

Flight	Mumbai Departure IST	Delhi Arrival IST	Delhi Departure IST	Mumbai Arrival IST
Jet	9:15	11:30	18:45	21:00
Spice	14:10	15:50	19:10	21:00
Indigo	6:20	8:20	15:30	17:45
Deccan	17:00	19:30	7:30	10:00
Kingfisher	12:00	13:45	21:00	23:00

21. For how many flights travel time for Delhi to Mumbai is more than Mumbai to Delhi?
    (a) 1
    (b) 2
    (c) 3
    (d) 4

22. Which flight takes minimum time to travel from Mumbai to Delhi?
    (a) Spice
    (b) Indigo
    (c) Deccan
    (d) Kingfisher

23. Which flight takes maximum time to travel from Delhi to Mumbai?
    (a) Jet
    (b) Indigo
    (c) Deccan
    (d) Kingfisher

24. If a person arrives in Mumbai by Deccan airways and immediately want to return to Delhi, then which flight he should prefer?
    (a) Spice
    (b) Indigo
    (c) Deccan
    (d) Kingfisher

25. The halting time at Mumbai airport for Kingfisher flight is how much more than halting time at Delhi Airport?
    (a) 3 hrs
    (b) 4 hrs 15 min
    (c) 5 hrs
    (d) 5 hrs 45 min

Directions (Questions 26 to 30): The following bar graph shows the production of cloth by a textile mill in a year. Study the data provided in the graph and answer the questions based on it.

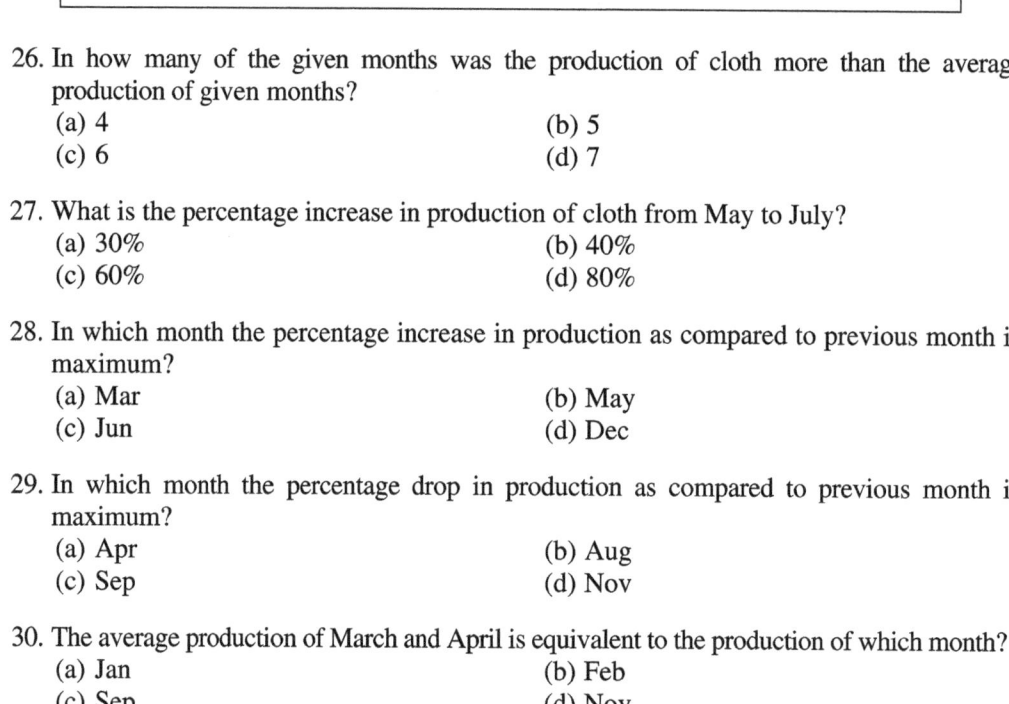

26. In how many of the given months was the production of cloth more than the average production of given months?
    (a) 4
    (b) 5
    (c) 6
    (d) 7

27. What is the percentage increase in production of cloth from May to July?
    (a) 30%
    (b) 40%
    (c) 60%
    (d) 80%

28. In which month the percentage increase in production as compared to previous month is maximum?
    (a) Mar
    (b) May
    (c) Jun
    (d) Dec

29. In which month the percentage drop in production as compared to previous month is maximum?
    (a) Apr
    (b) Aug
    (c) Sep
    (d) Nov

30. The average production of March and April is equivalent to the production of which month?
    (a) Jan
    (b) Feb
    (c) Sep
    (d) Nov

Directions (Questions 31 to 35): The following bar graph shows the income and expenditure of a company from the year 2005 to 2010. Study the data provided in the graph and answer the questions that follow.

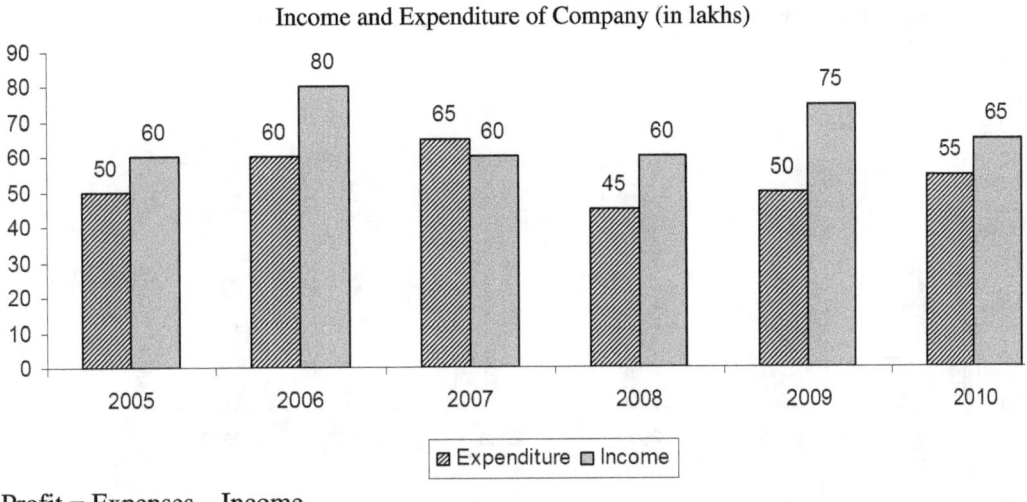

Profit = Expenses − Income

Percentage Profit = $\dfrac{\text{Profit}}{\text{Expenses}} \times 100$

31. For how many years the income was more than average for the given number of years?
    (a) 1
    (b) 2
    (c) 3
    (d) 4

32. In which year, the company's profit percent is highest?
    (a) 2006
    (b) 2008
    (c) 2009
    (d) 2010

33. What is the difference between average expenditure in first two years and its next two years?
    (a) 3 lakhs
    (b) 3.5 lakhs
    (c) 4.2 lakhs
    (d) None of these

34. In how many years the profit was more than 25% of the expenditure?
    (a) 1
    (b) 2
    (c) 3
    (d) 4

35. What is the ratio of total income to total expenditure in 2007 and 2008?
    (a) 11 : 12
    (b) 12 : 11
    (c) 5 : 6
    (d) 6 : 5

Directions (Questions 36 to 40): A company Digital World Pvt. Ltd. sales three different types of products—CD, DVD, Pen drive. The sale of these three products over a period of 6 years has been expressed in the bar graph provided below. Study the graph and answer the questions based on it.

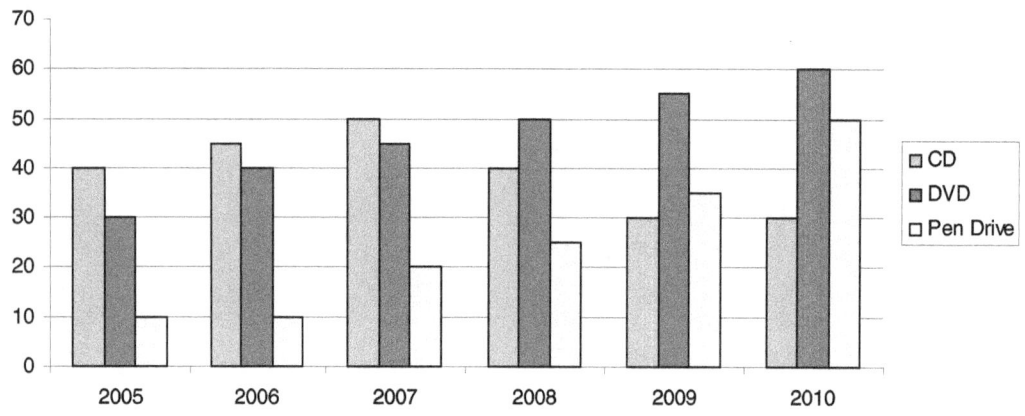

Sale of 3 different products by Digital World Pvt. Ltd. over the years (in thousands)

36. In which year the percentage rise in sale as compared to previous year is maximum for DVD?
    (a) 2006 (b) 2007
    (c) 2008 (d) 2009

37. For which product was the average annual sale was maximum in the given period?
    (a) CD (b) DVD
    (c) Pen drive (d) Cannot be determined

38. The total sale of Pen drives in 2007 and 2008 is what percent of total sale of CDs during the same period?
    (a) 40% (b) 45%
    (c) 50% (d) 60%

39. How much is the percentage decrease in sale of CDs from 2007 to 2010?
    (a) 30% (b) 40%
    (c) 45% (d) 60%

40. For how many years the sale of pen drives was more than its average sale for the given years?
    (a) 1 (b) 2
    (c) 3 (d) 4

Directions (Questions 41 to 45): A petroleum company makes different types of fuels – Petrol, Diesel, and CNG. The production of these three fuels over a period of 5 months from a refinery has been expressed in the bar graph provided below. Study the graph and answer the questions based on it.

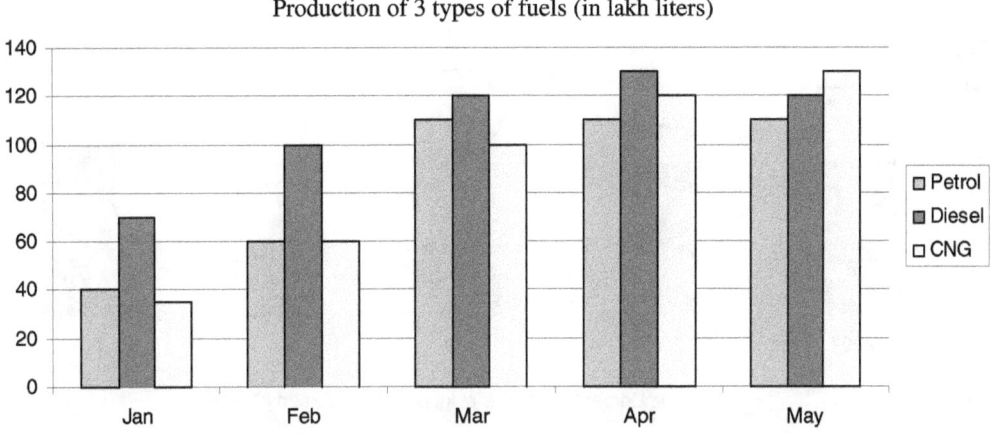

Production of 3 types of fuels (in lakh liters)

41. In which month the percentage rise in production of CNG as compared to previous month is maximum?
    (a) Feb
    (b) Mar
    (c) Apr
    (d) May

42. In which month the average production of petrol and CNG is equal to the production of Diesel?
    (a) Feb
    (b) Mar
    (c) Apr
    (d) May

43. From Jan to March the percentage increase in production of which fuel is maximum?
    (a) Petrol
    (b) Diesel
    (c) CNG
    (d) Cannot be determined

44. The production of CNG in the month of March is what percent of total production of petrol in first 2 months?
    (a) 80%
    (b) 90%
    (c) 100%
    (d) 120%

45. For how many months the production of diesel was more than its average production during the given months?
    (a) 1
    (b) 2
    (c) 3
    (d) 4

Directions (Questions 46 to 50): The following bar graph shows the total income of Precision Automation Ltd. from domestic market and through foreign trade. Study the data provided in the graph and answer the questions that follow.

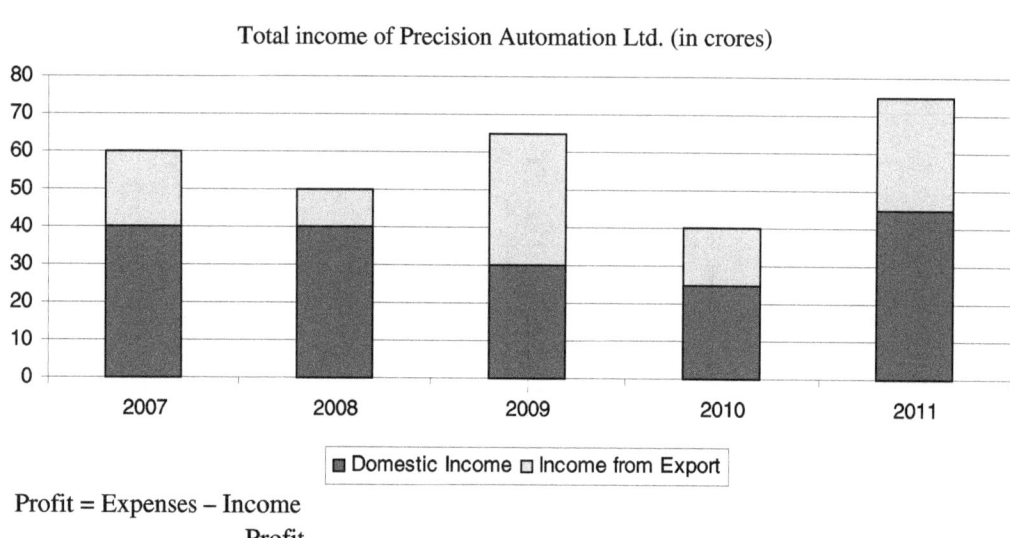

Total income of Precision Automation Ltd. (in crores)

■ Domestic Income □ Income from Export

Profit = Expenses − Income

Percentage Profit = $\dfrac{\text{Profit}}{\text{Expenses}} \times 100$

46. How much is the average income of the company over the given years through export?
    (a) 20 crores
    (b) 22 crores
    (c) 23 crores
    (d) 25 crores

47. In which year the income through export is more than domestic income?
    (a) 2007
    (b) 2009
    (c) 2010
    (d) 2011

48. If the percentage of profit made by the company in 2007 is 25%, then how much was the expenditure in 2007?
    (a) 40 crores
    (b) 45 crores
    (c) 48 crores
    (d) 50 crores

49. The average domestic income in 2010 and 2011 is equal to the income through export in which year?
    (a) 2007
    (b) 2009
    (c) 2010
    (d) 2011

50. What is the ratio of domestic income to income through export in the given years?
    (a) 13 : 9
    (b) 13 : 10
    (c) 15 : 8
    (d) 18 : 11

Directions (Questions 51 to 55): The following bar graph shows the total percentage sale of five different models of Laptops by a company in Indian market in 2010 and 2011. Study the data provided in the graph and answer the questions that follow.

Percentage share of laptop models in 2010 and 2011

Ratio of total sale of Laptops by the company in 2010 and 2011 = 2 : 3

51. In the year 2010, the total number of laptops sold are 12800 then how many laptops of model 'E' are sold?
    (a) 3640
    (b) 3720
    (c) 3840
    (d) 3900

52. For how many models among A, B, C, D and E the number of units sold decreased from 2010 to 2011?
    (a) 0
    (b) 1
    (c) 2
    (d) Cannot be determined

53. If the number of units of model 'C' sold in 2011 are 4500, then how many units of model 'A' are sold in the same year?
    (a) 7500
    (b) 8000
    (c) 8200
    (d) 8500

54. If the revenue from sale of model 'A' and model 'C' is equal in 2010, then what is the ratio of selling price of model 'A' and model 'C'?
    (a) 4 : 5
    (b) 5 : 4
    (c) 3 : 4
    (d) 5 : 3

55. In 2011 the sale of model 'D' is what percent of total sale of 'A' and 'C'?
    (a) 60%
    (b) 70%
    (c) 75%
    (d) 80%

Directions (Questions 55 to 60): The price of share of *ABC* Exports Ltd. in stock market over a period of one year is shown in the line graph. Study the graph and answer the questions based on it.

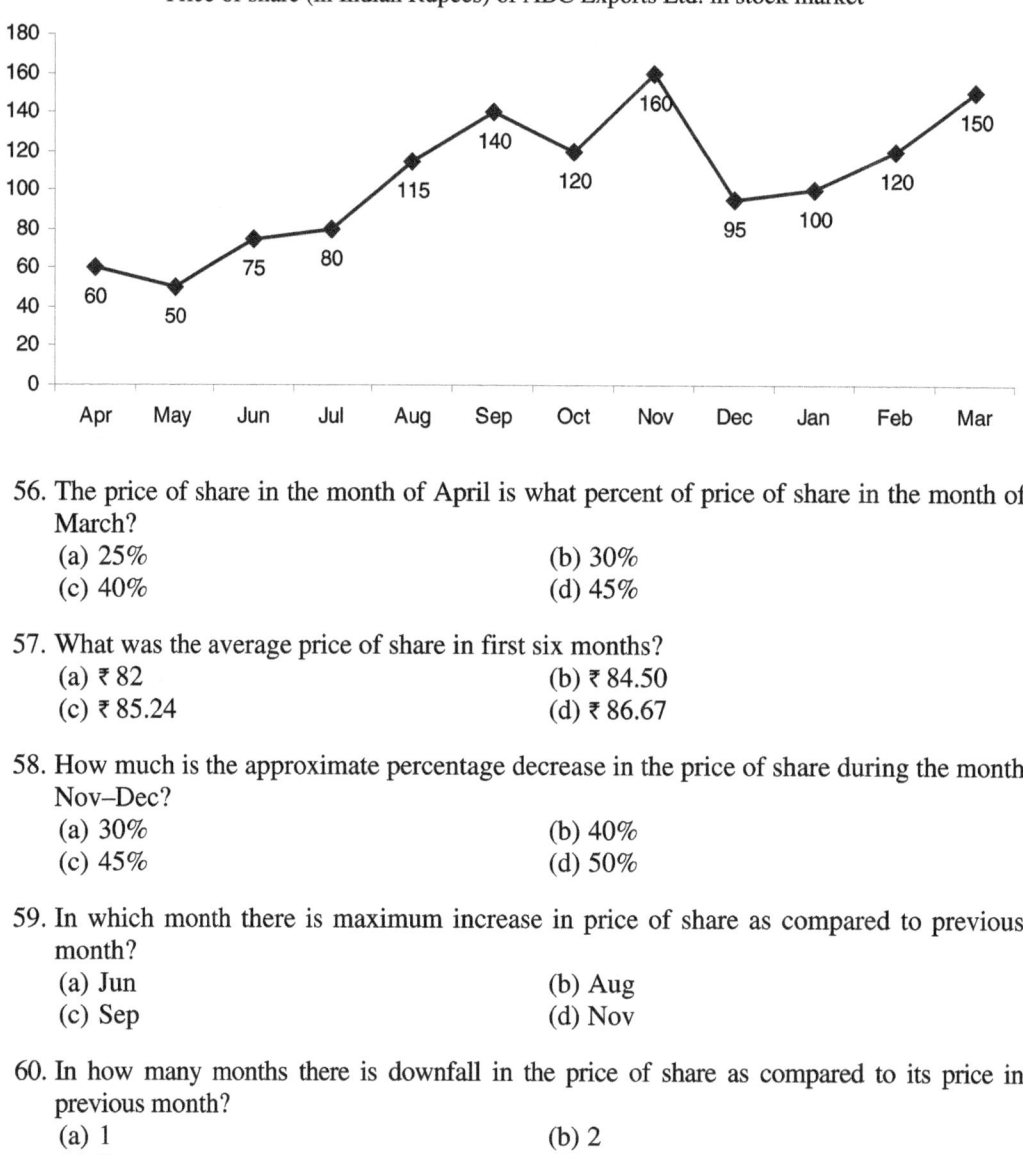

Price of share (in Indian Rupees) of ABC Exports Ltd. in stock market

56. The price of share in the month of April is what percent of price of share in the month of March?
    (a) 25%   (b) 30%
    (c) 40%   (d) 45%

57. What was the average price of share in first six months?
    (a) ₹ 82   (b) ₹ 84.50
    (c) ₹ 85.24   (d) ₹ 86.67

58. How much is the approximate percentage decrease in the price of share during the month Nov–Dec?
    (a) 30%   (b) 40%
    (c) 45%   (d) 50%

59. In which month there is maximum increase in price of share as compared to previous month?
    (a) Jun   (b) Aug
    (c) Sep   (d) Nov

60. In how many months there is downfall in the price of share as compared to its price in previous month?
    (a) 1   (b) 2
    (c) 3   (d) 4

Directions (Questions 61 to 65): Following line graph shows the annual percentage profit earned by a company during the period 2000 to 2005. Study the line graph and answer the questions based on it.

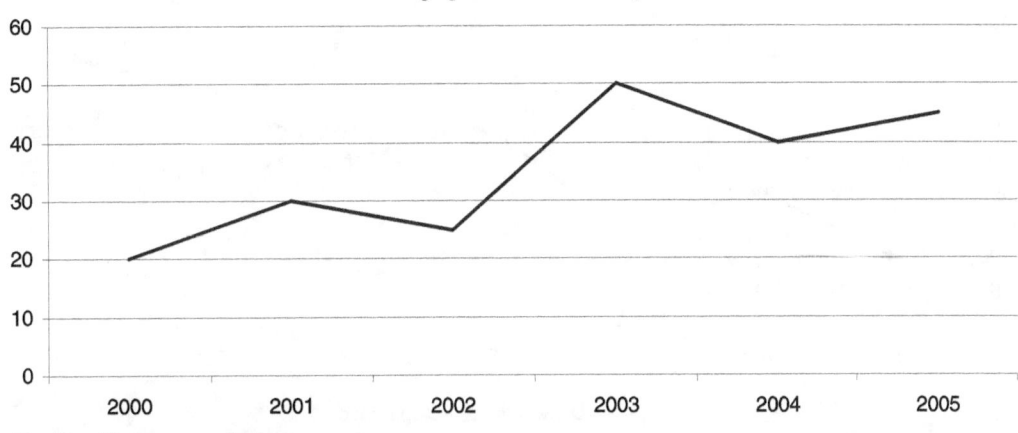

Percentage profit earned over years

Profit = Expenses − Income

Percentage Profit = $\dfrac{\text{Profit}}{\text{Expenses}} \times 100$

61. The income in the year 2000 was 48 crores, then how much was the expenditure?
    (a) 30 crores
    (b) 36 crores
    (c) 40 crores
    (d) 45 crores

62. During which year the ratio of percentage profit earned to that of previous year is minimum?
    (a) 2001
    (b) 2002
    (c) 2004
    (d) 2005

63. If the expenditure of company in the year 2003 and 2004 is same then what is the ratio of income in these two years?
    (a) 3 : 2
    (b) 5 : 4
    (c) 15 : 8
    (d) 15 : 14

64. If the expenditure in the year 2005 was 60 crores, then how much was the income in that year?
    (a) 70 crores
    (b) 75 crores
    (c) 85 crores
    (d) 87 crores

65. In which year the expenditure of the company was minimum?
    (a) 2000
    (b) 2002
    (c) 2003
    (d) Cannot be determined

Directions (Questions 66 to 70): Following line graph shows the tons of iron delivered and dispatched to/from a scrap yard in a week. Study the line graph and answer the questions based on it.

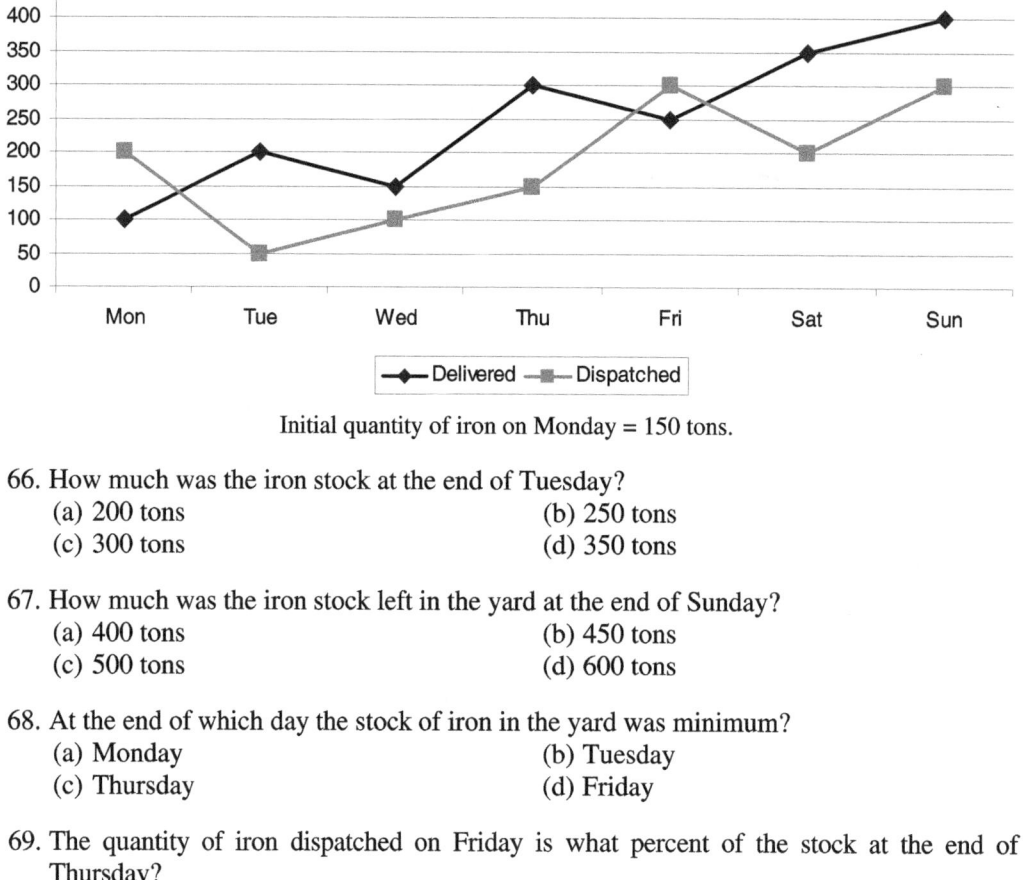

Tons of iron delivered and dispatched from a scrap yard

Initial quantity of iron on Monday = 150 tons.

66. How much was the iron stock at the end of Tuesday?
    (a) 200 tons (b) 250 tons
    (c) 300 tons (d) 350 tons

67. How much was the iron stock left in the yard at the end of Sunday?
    (a) 400 tons (b) 450 tons
    (c) 500 tons (d) 600 tons

68. At the end of which day the stock of iron in the yard was minimum?
    (a) Monday   (b) Tuesday
    (c) Thursday (d) Friday

69. The quantity of iron dispatched on Friday is what percent of the stock at the end of Thursday?
    (a) 60% (b) 70%
    (c) 75% (d) 80%

70. The ratio of total iron delivered to total iron dispatched from the yard during the week is:
    (a) 25 : 23 (b) 30 : 23
    (c) 35 : 29 (d) 35 : 26

Directions (Questions 71 to 75): Following line graph shows the production of inverters by three different companies from 2005 to 2011. Study the line graph and answer the questions based on it.

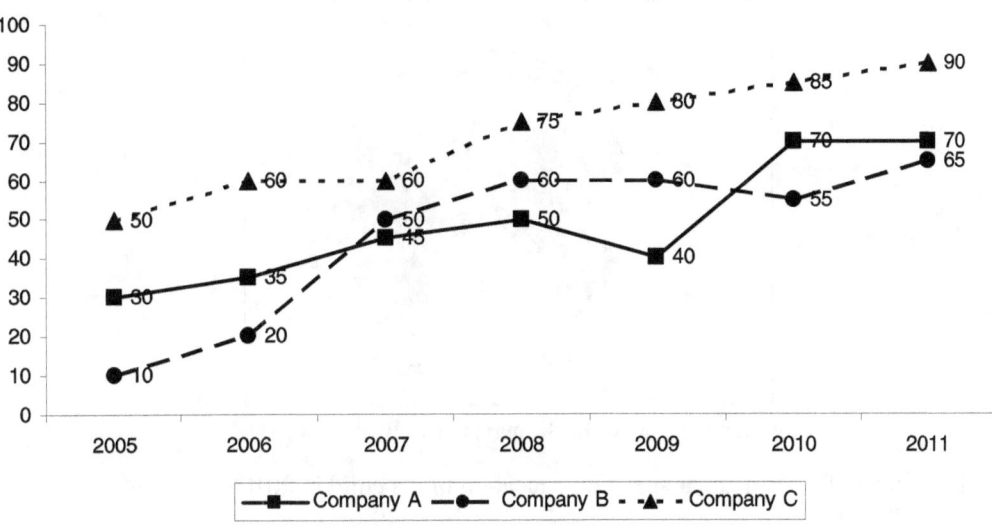

71. In how many years the average production of inverters by company B and C equals to production of inverters by company A?
    (a) 1
    (b) 2
    (c) 3
    (d) None of these

72. What is the difference between average production of Inverters by companies in 2010 and 2009?
    (a) 5000
    (b) 8000
    (c) 10000
    (d) 12000

73. In which year the difference between production of inverters by company B and company C is minimum?
    (a) 2007
    (b) 2008
    (c) 2009
    (d) 2011

74. In 2005 the ratio of cost of producing an inverter by companies A and B is 2 : 3. What is the ratio of total cost of production of company A and B?
    (a) 2 : 1
    (b) 3 : 1
    (c) 4 : 1
    (d) 4 : 3

75. In how many years the production of company C is more than average annual production over the given years?
    (a) 1
    (b) 2
    (c) 3
    (d) 4

Directions (Questions 76 to 80): Following pie chart shows the distribution of salary of Mr. Kumar in the year 2010. Study the pie chart and answer the questions based on it.

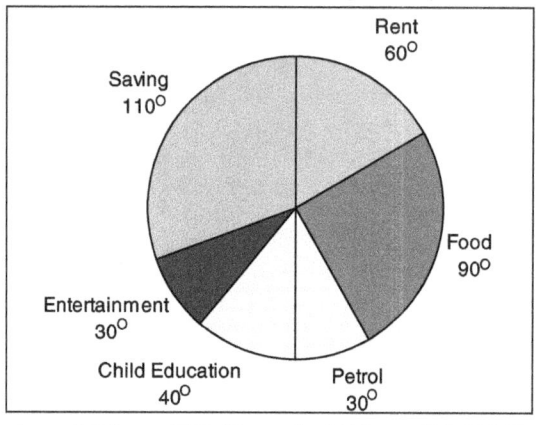

Distribution of Mr. Kumar's salary in the year 2010

Annual Salary of Mr. Kumar in 2010 was ₹ 3,60,000

76. How much did Mr. Kumar spend on education of his child in 2010?
    (a) ₹ 20000
    (b) ₹ 36000
    (c) ₹ 40000
    (d) ₹ 60000

77. Mr. Kumar's total expenditure on petrol and entertainment is what percent of expenditure on food?
    (a) 33.33%
    (b) 45%
    (c) 66.67%
    (d) 70%

78. What percent of total salary Mr. Kumar is spending on rent?
    (a) 16.67%
    (b) 20%
    (c) 30%
    (d) 60%

79. In the year 2011 the salary of Mr. Kumar remains same as 2010, but the rent is increased by 20%. How much additional money he need to spend on rent?
    (a) ₹ 6000
    (b) ₹ 12000
    (c) ₹ 16000
    (d) ₹ 20000

80. Expenses of Mr. Kumar in 2010 and 2011 on food is in the ratio of 3 : 4. If his salary remains constant in both the years, then what percent of salary he will be spending on food in 2011?
    (a) 30%
    (b) 33.33%
    (c) 40%
    (d) 45%

Directions (Questions 81 to 85): Following pie chart shows the distribution of different models of bikes manufactured by Alpha Motorcycles Ltd in 2011. Study the pie chart and answer the questions based on it.

Different models of bikes manufactured by Alpha Motorcycles Ltd. in 2011

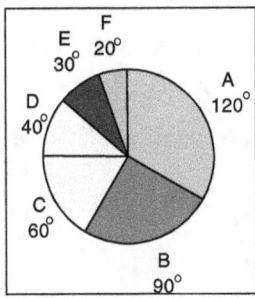

Total number of bikes manufactured in the year 2011 are 64,800

81. How many model *C* bikes were manufactured by the company in 2011?
    (a) 9600
    (b) 10800
    (c) 11200
    (d) 12400

82. By what percent model *B* bikes are manufactured more than model *C* bikes?
    (a) 15%
    (b) 30%
    (c) 33.33%
    (d) 45%

83. If the ratio of selling price of model *A* to model *F* is 1 : 3, then find the ratio of revenue obtained from the two models if all the manufactured bikes are sold.
    (a) 2 : 1
    (b) 1 : 2
    (c) 1 : 3
    (d) 3 : 1

84. If only 60% of the model *D* bikes are sold out of the total manufactured, then how many bikes of model D are not sold?
    (a) 1800
    (b) 2460
    (c) 2880
    (d) 3240

85. Total number of model A and model E bikes manufactured by the company is same as:
    (a) *B* and *D*
    (b) *B* and *C*
    (c) *C* and *D*
    (d) *B* and *E*

Directions (Questions 86 to 90): Following pie charts shows the sale of cell phone of different companies in 2 consecutive years 2010 and 2011 in a town. Study the pie chart and answer the questions based on it.

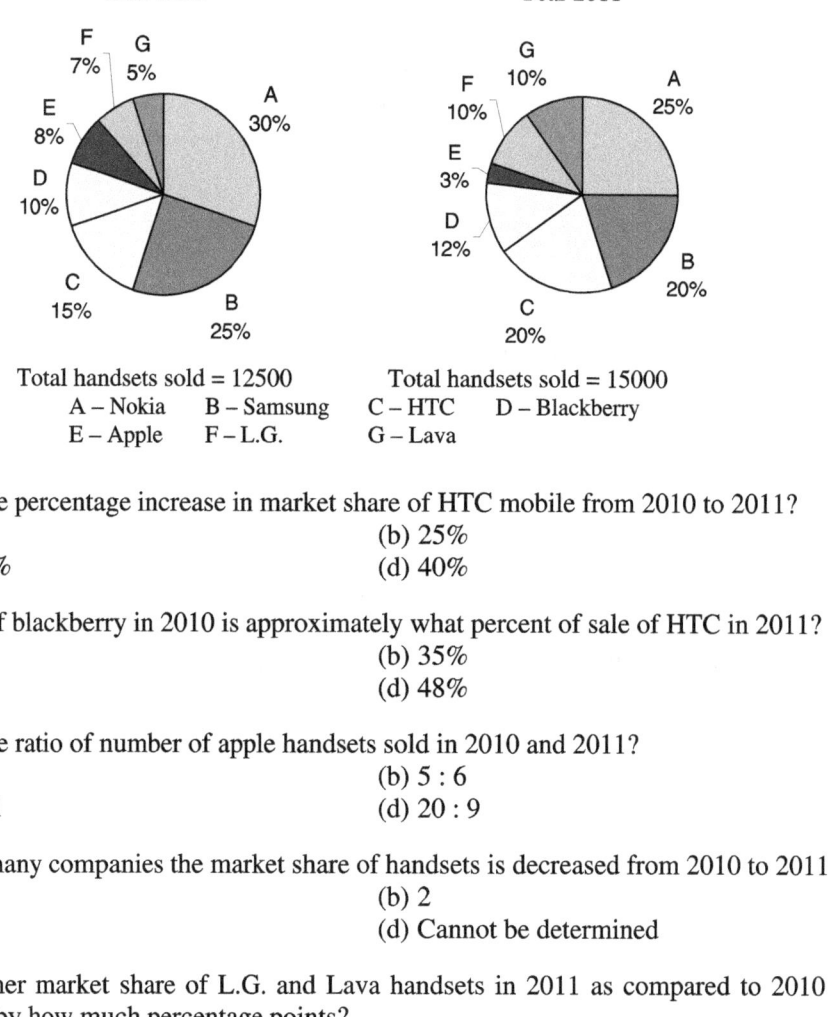

Year 2010   Year 2011

Total handsets sold = 12500   Total handsets sold = 15000
A – Nokia   B – Samsung   C – HTC   D – Blackberry
E – Apple   F – L.G.   G – Lava

86. What is the percentage increase in market share of HTC mobile from 2010 to 2011?
   (a) 5%   (b) 25%
   (c) 33.33%   (d) 40%

87. The sale of blackberry in 2010 is approximately what percent of sale of HTC in 2011?
   (a) 30%   (b) 35%
   (c) 42%   (d) 48%

88. What is the ratio of number of apple handsets sold in 2010 and 2011?
   (a) 10 : 3   (b) 5 : 6
   (c) 16 : 11   (d) 20 : 9

89. For how many companies the market share of handsets is decreased from 2010 to 2011?
   (a) 1   (b) 2
   (c) 3   (d) Cannot be determined

90. The together market share of L.G. and Lava handsets in 2011 as compared to 2010 is increased by how much percentage points?
   (a) 8 percentage points   (b) 10 percentage points
   (c) 12 percentage points   (d) None of these

KEYS

1. (c)	2. (d)	3. (a)	4. (d)	5. (b)	6. (c)	7. (c)	8. (b)
9. (d)	10. (a)	11. (b)	12. (c)	13. (a)	14. (a)	15. (d)	16. (a)
17. (a)	18. (d)	19. (b)	20. (c)	21. (c)	22. (a)	23. (c)	24. (d)
25. (d)	26. (c)	27. (c)	28. (b)	29. (a)	30. (b)	31. (b)	32. (c)
33. (d)	34. (c)	35. (b)	36. (a)	37. (b)	38. (c)	39. (b)	40. (b)
41. (a)	42. (d)	43. (c)	44. (c)	45. (c)	46. (b)	47. (b)	48. (c)
49. (b)	50. (d)	51. (c)	52. (b)	53. (a)	54. (b)	55. (c)	56. (c)
57. (d)	58. (b)	59. (a)	60. (c)	61. (c)	62. (c)	63. (d)	64. (d)
65. (d)	66. (a)	67. (d)	68. (a)	69. (c)	70. (d)	71. (b)	72. (c)
73. (a)	74. (a)	75. (d)	76. (c)	77. (c)	78. (a)	79. (b)	80. (b)
81. (b)	82. (c)	83. (a)	84. (c)	85. (b)	86. (c)	87. (c)	88. (d)
89. (c)	90. (a)						

SOLUTIONS

Solution 1

Total sale of Apple flavor = $(20 + 22 + 30 + 25 + 38 + 40) \times 1000 = 175000$ liters
Total sale of Orange flavor = $(30 + 34 + 36 + 40 + 45 + 55) \times 1000 = 240000$ liters
Total sale of Mango flavor = $(25 + 28 + 32 + 50 + 64 + 60) \times 1000 = 259000$ liters
Total sale of Cola flavor = $(15 + 18 + 22 + 35 + 43 + 57) \times 1000 = 190000$ liters

So, total sale is maximum for mango flavor.

Choice (c)

Solution 2

Required percentage = $\frac{25}{40} \times 100 = 62.5\%$.

Choice (d)

Solution 3

For the Apple flavor, there is not a continuous increase in sale as in the month of April, there is drop of sale compared to March.

Choice (a)

Solution 4

Required percentage = $\dfrac{60-25}{25} \times 100 = 140\%$.

Choice (d)

Solution 5

Difference = 43000 − 22000 = 21000 liters.

Choice (b)

Solution 6

Percentage decrease in price of J-1100 = $\dfrac{10000-5300}{10000} \times 100 = 47\%$

Percentage decrease in price of J-1300 = $\dfrac{15500-9300}{15500} \times 100 = 40\%$

Percentage decrease in price of J-1500 = $\dfrac{16400-7500}{16400} \times 100 = 54.27\%$

Percentage decrease in price of J-1700 = $\dfrac{18000-15400}{18000} \times 100 = 14.44\%$

Percentage decrease in price of J-1900 = $\dfrac{20000-13000}{20000} \times 100 = 35\%$

So, model no. J-1500 has maximum percentage decrease in price.

Choice (c)

Solution 7

Drop in price of J-1100 = 8400 − 7000 = ₹ 1400
Drop in price of J-1300 = 12200 − 11800 = ₹ 400
Drop in price of J-1500 = 11300 − 9400 = ₹ 1900
Drop in price of J-1700 = 16600 − 16200 = ₹ 400
Drop in price of J-1900 = 14500 − 13200 = ₹ 1300

So, model no. J-1500 has maximum drop in price between 2008 and 2009.

Choice (c)

Solution 8

Price drop between 2006–07 = 18000 − 17600 = ₹ 400
Price drop between 2007–08 = 17600 − 16600 = ₹ 1000
Price drop between 2008–09 = 16600 − 16200 = ₹ 400
Price drop between 2009–10 = 16200 − 15400 = ₹ 800

So, maximum reduction in price for model J-1700 was during 2007–08.

Choice (b)

Solution 9

Required percentage = $\dfrac{7500}{10000} \times 100 = 75\%$.

Choice (d)

Solution 10

Average price = $\dfrac{8400+12200+11300+16600+14500}{5}$ = ₹ 12600.

Choice (a)

Solution 11

Overall percentage of Eshant = $\dfrac{\text{Sum of score of all subjects}}{\text{Total marks}} \times 100$

$= \dfrac{240}{400} \times 100$

$= 60\%$.

Choice (b)

Solution 12

Average marks in maths = $\dfrac{88+92+46+63+75+86}{6} = 75$.

Choice (c)

Solution 13

Aggregate score of Bharat = 32 + 45 + 38 + 25 + 36 + 92 = 268

Aggregate score of Deepak = 30 + 64 + 46 + 28 + 37 + 63 = 268.

Choice (a)

Solution 14

Ajay scored less than 50% in English and History. So, he cannot be considered.

Bharat scored exact 50% in Chemistry, and less than 50% in History. So, he cannot be considered.

Chetan scored exact 50% in Chemistry and Biology, and less than 50% in Maths. So, he cannot be considered

Eshant scored less than 50% in History. So, he cannot be considered.

Farhan scored exact 50% in Physics. So, he cannot be considered.

Only Deepak scored more than 50% in all the subjects.

Choice (a)

Solution 15

Average score in English = $\dfrac{22+32+42+30+35+44}{6} = 34.17$

Average score in History (out of 50) = $\dfrac{1}{2} \times \left(\dfrac{46+45+84+64+44+59}{6} \right) = 28.5$

Average score in Physics = $\dfrac{28+38+44+46+18+25}{6} = 33.17$

Average score in Chemistry = $\dfrac{42+25+25+28+26+35}{6} = 30.17$

Average score in Biology = $\dfrac{34+36+25+37+42+41}{6} = 35.83$

Average score in Maths (out of 50) = $\dfrac{1}{2} \times \left(\dfrac{88+92+46+63+75+86}{6} \right) = 37.5$

So, best performance of students is seen in Maths.

Choice (d)

Solution 16

Percentage of qualified in 2007 = $\dfrac{136}{290} \times 100 = 46.9\%$

Percentage of qualified in 2008 = $\dfrac{195}{270} \times 100 = 72.2\%$

Percentage of qualified in 2009 = $\dfrac{170}{310} \times 100 = 54.8\%$

Percentage of qualified in 2010 = $\dfrac{195}{340} \times 100 = 57.4\%$

Percentage of qualified in 2011 = $\dfrac{210}{375} \times 100 = 56\%$.

Choice (a)

Solution 17

Percentage of qualified from Mechanical = $\frac{370}{500} \times 100 = 74\%$

Percentage of qualified from Electrical = $\frac{210}{375} \times 100 = 56\%$

Percentage of qualified from Computer = $\frac{210}{400} \times 100 = 52.5\%$

Percentage of qualified from Electronics = $\frac{325}{450} \times 100 = 72.2\%$.

Choice (a)

Solution 18

Required percentage = $\frac{120}{150} \times 100 = 80\%$.

Choice (d)

Solution 19

From the figures, it clearly seems that minimum number of candidates appear from Electrical branch.

Choice (b)

Solution 20

Required percentage = $\frac{275+195+175+215}{440+340+420+410} \times 100 = \frac{860}{1610} \times 100 = 53.4\%$.

Choice (c)

Solution 21

Travel time for Jet ⇒ Mumbai to Delhi = 2 hr 15 min
Delhi to Mumbai = 2 hrs 15 min

Travel time for Spice ⇒ Mumbai to Delhi = 1 hr 40 min
Delhi to Mumbai = 1 hrs 50 min

Travel time for Indigo ⇒ Mumbai to Delhi = 2 hr
Delhi to Mumbai = 2 hrs 15 min

Travel time for Deccan ⇒ Mumbai to Delhi = 2 hr 30 min
Delhi to Mumbai = 2 hrs 30 min

Travel time for Kingfisher ⇒ Mumbai to Delhi = 1 hr 45 min
Delhi to Mumbai = 2 hrs

So, the travel time for Delhi to Mumbai is more than Mumbai to Delhi for Spice, Indigo and Kingfisher.

Choice (c)

Solution 22

Spice airways can travel from Mumbai to Delhi in minimum time i.e. 1 hr 40 min.

Choice (a)

Solution 23

Deccan flight takes maximum time to travel from Delhi to Mumbai i.e. 2 hrs 30 min.

Choice (c)

Solution 24

Arrival time in Mumbai = 10:00

Latest flight to return back to Delhi is Kingfisher at 12:00

Choice (d)

Solution 25

Halting time at Delhi Airport = 7 hrs 15 min
Halting time at Mumbai Airport = 13 hrs
Difference of halting time = 5 hrs 45 min

Choice (d)

Solution 26

Average production of cloth = $\dfrac{20+25+35+15+50+65+80+60+45+50+40+55}{12} = 45$

So, from the graph it can be seen that for 6 months the production was above average.

Choice (c)

Solution 27

Required percentage = $\dfrac{80-50}{50} \times 100 = 60\%$.

Choice (c)

Solution 28

The bar graph clearly indicates that the percentage increase in production is maximum in the month of May as compared to April.

Choice (b)

Solution 29

The bar graph clearly indicates that the percentage drop in production is maximum in the month of April as compared to March.

Choice (a)

Solution 30

Average Production of March and April = $\dfrac{35+15}{2} = 25$

The production in the month of Feb was equal to average production of March and April.

Choice (b)

Solution 31

Average income in 6 years = $\dfrac{60+80+60+60+75+65}{6} = 66.67$ lakhs

The income is more than average for 2 years.

Choice (b)

Solution 32

Profit percent in 2006 = $\dfrac{80-60}{60} \times 100$
= 33.33%

Profit percent in 2008 = $\dfrac{60-45}{45} \times 100$
= 33.33%

Profit percent in 2009 = $\dfrac{75-50}{50} \times 100$
= 50%

Profit percent in 2010 = $\dfrac{65-55}{55} \times 100$
= 18.18%.

Choice (c)

Solution 33

Average expenditure in first 2 years = $\dfrac{50+60}{2}$

= 55 lakhs

Average expenditure in next 2 years = $\dfrac{45+65}{2}$

= 55 lakhs.

Choice (d)

Solution 34

In 2005 ⇒ Profit < 25% of expenditure
In 2006 ⇒ Profit > 25% of expenditure
In 2008 ⇒ Profit > 25% of expenditure
In 2009 ⇒ Profit > 25% of expenditure
In 2010 ⇒ Profit < 25% of expenditure.

Choice (c)

Solution 35

Total income of 2007 and 2008 = 60 + 60 = 120 lakhs

Total expenses of 2007 and 2008 = 65 + 45 = 110 lakhs

Ratio of income to expenses = 120 : 110 = 12 : 11.

Choice (b)

Solution 36

From the bar graph it clearly seems that the maximum rise in sale is in the year 2006, as compared to 2005.

Choice (a)

Solution 37

Total sale of CD = (40 + 45 + 50 + 40 + 30 + 30) × 1000 = 235000

Total sale of DVD = (30 + 40 + 45 + 50 + 55 + 60) × 1000 = 280000

Total sale of pen drives = (10 + 10 + 20 + 25 + 35 + 50) × 1000 = 150000.

As the total sale of DVD is more that the sale of CD or Pen drives, hence its average sale over a period of 6 years will be maximum.

Choice (b)

Solution 38

Pen drives sold = 20000 + 25000 = 45000

CDs sold = 50000 + 40000 = 90000

Required percentage = $\dfrac{45000}{90000} \times 100 = 50\%$.

Choice (c)

Solution 39

Required percentage = $\dfrac{50-30}{50} \times 100 = 40\%$.

Choice (b)

Solution 40

Average sale of pen drives = $\dfrac{10+10+20+25+35+50}{6} = 25$

For 2 years, the sale was more than average.

Choice (b)

Solution 41

From the graph it clearly seems that the maximum rise in production of CNG is in the month of Feb as compared to Jan.

Choice (a)

Solution 42

From the graph we can see that the average production of petrol and CNG is equal to production of diesel in the month of May.

Choice (d)

Solution 43

Percentage increase in production of petrol = $\dfrac{110-40}{40} \times 100 = 175\%$

Percentage increase in production of diesel = $\dfrac{120-70}{70} \times 100 = 71.4\%$

Percentage increase in production of CNG = $\dfrac{100-35}{35} \times 100 = 185.7\%$.

Choice (c)

Solution 44

Required percentage = $\dfrac{100}{40+60} \times 100 = 100\%$.

Choice (c)

Solution 45

Average production of diesel in 5 months = $\dfrac{70+100+120+130+120}{5}$ = 108 lakh liters

In 3 months the production of diesel is more than average.

Choice (c)

Solution 46

Average income through export = $\dfrac{20+10+35+15+30}{5}$ = 22 crores.

Choice (b)

Solution 47

From the graph it can be seen that in 2009 income through export is more than domestic income.

Choice (b)

Solution 48

If the percentage of profit is 25%, then

Income = $\dfrac{125}{100} \times$ Expenditure

$\Rightarrow 60 = \dfrac{125}{100} \times$ Expenditure

$\therefore$ Expenditure = 48 crores.

Choice (c)

Solution 49

Average domestic income in 2010 and 2011 = $\dfrac{25+45}{2}$
= 35 crores

Income through export is 35 crores in 2009.

Choice (b)

Solution 50

Total domestic income = 40 + 40 + 30 + 25 + 45 = 180 crores

Total income through export = 20 + 10 + 35 + 15 + 30 = 110 crores
Required ratio = 18 : 11.

Choice (d)

Solution 51

Sale of model 'E' Laptops = $\dfrac{30}{100} \times 12800 = 3840$ units.

Choice (c)

Solution 52

The ratio units sold by company in 2010 and 2011 is 2 : 3.
Assuming 200 units are sold in 2010 and 300 units are sold in 2011.
From the graph it seems that sale of model 'C' and model 'E' is decreased.
Checking for model 'C'

Units sold of model C in 2010 = $\dfrac{25}{100} \times 200 = 50$

Units sold of model C in 2011 = $\dfrac{15}{100} \times 300 = 45$

So, there is decrease in sale of model C.

Checking for model 'E'

Units sold of model E in 2010 = $\dfrac{30}{100} \times 200 = 60$

Units sold of model E in 2011 = $\dfrac{20}{100} \times 300 = 60$

So, there is no decrease in sale of model E.

Choice (b)

Solution 53

Share of model $C \Rightarrow 15\% \rightarrow 4500$

Share of model $A \Rightarrow 25\% \rightarrow x$

$\therefore x = \dfrac{25 \times 4500}{15} = 7500$.

Choice (a)

Solution 54

Revenue from sale of model 'A' = Revenue from sale of model 'C'

$\Rightarrow$ SP of A × sale of A = SP of C × sale of C
$\Rightarrow$ SP of A × 20 = SP of B × 25
$\Rightarrow \dfrac{SP \text{ of } A}{SP \text{ of } C} = \dfrac{5}{4}.$

Choice (b)

Solution 55

Required percentage $= \dfrac{30}{25+15} \times 100$
$= 75\%.$

Choice (c)

Solution 56

Required percentage $= \dfrac{60}{150} \times 100$
$= 40\%.$

Choice (c)

Solution 57

Average price $= \dfrac{60+50+75+80+115+140}{6}$
$= ₹\, 86.67.$

Choice (d)

Solution 58

Required percentage $= \dfrac{160-95}{160} \times 100 = 40.62\%.$

Choice (b)

Solution 59

From the graph it clearly seems that the rise from ₹ 50 to ₹ 75 in the month of June is the maximum percentage rise, as compared to rise in any other months.

Choice (a)

Solution 60

From the graph it can be seen that at 3 points there is a downfall in the price of share i.e. May, Oct, and Dec.

Choice (c)

Solution 61

As the percentage profit in the year 2000 was 20%, then

$$\frac{\text{Profit}}{\text{Expenses}} = \frac{20}{100}$$

$$\Rightarrow \frac{\text{Income} - \text{Expenses}}{\text{Expenses}} = \frac{1}{5}$$

$$\Rightarrow \frac{\text{Income}}{\text{Expenses}} = \frac{6}{5}$$

$$\Rightarrow \text{Expenses} = \frac{5}{6} \times \text{Income} = \frac{5}{6} \times 48 = 40 \text{ crores.}$$

Choice (c)

Solution 62

From the graph it seems that in the year 2004 the percentage profit earned was 40%, and it was 50% in its previous year.

So, this is the minimum ratio i.e. $\frac{40}{50} = 0.8$.

Choice (c)

Solution 63

As percentage profit in 2003 was 50%

$$\frac{\text{Income of 2003}}{\text{Expenses}} = \frac{150}{100} \Rightarrow \frac{\text{Income of 2003}}{\text{Expenses}} = \frac{3}{2} \qquad \ldots (1)$$

As percentage profit in 2004 was 40%

$$\frac{\text{Income of 2004}}{\text{Expenses}} = \frac{140}{100} \Rightarrow \frac{\text{Income of 2004}}{\text{Expenses}} = \frac{7}{5} \qquad \ldots (2)$$

Dividing equation (1) by (2)

$$\frac{\text{Income of 2003}}{\text{Income of 2004}} = \frac{15}{14}.$$

Choice (d)

Solution 64

As percentage profit in 2005 was 45%

$$\frac{\text{Income}}{\text{Expenses}} = \frac{145}{100}$$

$\Rightarrow$ Income $= \dfrac{145}{100} \times$ Expenses

$= \dfrac{145}{100} \times 60 = 87$ crores.

Choice (d)

Solution 65

As the income is not known in the given years, hence by knowing only the percentage profit the expenditure cannot be determined.

Choice (d)

Solution 66

Stock at the end of any day = Initial stock + Delivered stock − Dispatched stock

Stock at the end of Monday = 150 + 100 − 200 = 50 tons

Stock at the end of Tuesday = 50 + 200 − 50 = 200 tons.

Choice (a)

Solution 67

Stock at the end of Monday = 150 + 100 − 200 = 50 tons

Stock at the end of Tuesday = 50 + 200 − 50 = 200 tons

Stock at the end of Wednesday = 200 + 150 − 100 = 250 tons

Stock at the end of Thursday = 250 + 300 − 150 = 400 tons

Stock at the end of Friday = 400 + 250 − 300 = 350 tons

Stock at the end of Saturday = 350 + 350 − 200 = 500 tons

Stock at the end of Sunday = 500 + 400 − 300 = 600 tons.

Choice (d)

Solution 68

From the calculations in Solution 67, it can be seen that the stock was minimum on Monday.

Choice (a)

Solution 69

From the calculations in Solution 67, the quantity of iron at the end of Thursday was 400 tons.

Quantity of iron dispatched on Friday = 300 tons.

Required percentage = $\dfrac{300}{400} \times 100 = 75\%$.

Choice (c)

Solution 70

Total iron delivered in the week = 100 + 200 + 150 + 300 + 250 + 350 + 400 = 1750 tons

Total iron dispatched in the week = 200 + 50 + 100 + 150 + 300 + 200 + 300 = 1300 tons

Required ratio = 1750 : 1300 = 35 : 26.

Choice (d)

Solution 71

Average production of company B and C equals to production of company A in 2005 and in 2010.

Choice (b)

Solution 72

Average production in 2009 = $\dfrac{(40+60+80) \times 1000}{3}$ = 60,000 inverters

Average production in 2010 = $\dfrac{(55+70+85) \times 1000}{3}$ = 70,000 inverters

Difference = 10000 inverters.

Choice (c)

Solution 73

From the graph it clearly seems that the difference in production by company B and company C is minimum in the year 2007.

Choice (a)

Solution 74

Ratio of total cost of production by A and B = 2 × 30 : 3 × 10
= 60 : 30
= 2 : 1.

Choice (a)

Solution 75

Average production of company C from 2005 to 2011 = $\dfrac{50+60+60+75+80+85+90}{7}$ = 71.4

So, in four years i.e. from 2008, 2009, 2010 and 2011 the production of company C is more than average.

Choice (d)

Solution 76

Spending on education = $\dfrac{40}{360} \times 360000$ = ₹ 40000.

Choice (c)

Solution 77

Required percentage = $\dfrac{30+30}{90} \times 100$ = 66.67%.

Choice (c)

Solution 78

Required percentage = $\dfrac{60}{360} \times 100$ = 16.67%.

Choice (a)

Solution 79

Rent paid by Mr. Kumar in 2010 = $\dfrac{60}{360} \times 360000$ = ₹ 60000

Rent paid by Mr. Kumar in 2011 = 1.2 × 60000 = ₹ 72000

So, additional rent paid = ₹ 12000.

Choice (b)

Solution 80

Spending on food in 2010 = $\dfrac{90}{360} \times 360000$ = ₹ 90000.

Expenses on food in 2010 and 2011 = $3x : 4x$
∴ $3x = 90000$ ⇒ $x = 30000$

So, spending on food in 2011 = 4x = 4 × 30000 = ₹ 120000

Required percentage = $\frac{120000}{360000} \times 100 = 33.33\%$.

Choice (b)

Solution 81

Number of model C bikes = $\frac{60}{360} \times 64800 = 10800$.

Choice (b)

Solution 82

Required percentage = $\frac{90-60}{90} \times 100 = 33.33\%$.

Choice (c)

Solution 83

Revenue obtained by selling model A bikes = Units sold × SP of model A
= 120 × 1 = 120

Revenue obtained by selling model F bikes = Units sold × SP of model F
= 20 × 3 = 60

Required ratio = 120 : 60 = 2 : 1.

Choice (a)

Solution 84

Number of model D bikes manufactured = $\frac{40}{360} \times 64800 = 7200$

Number of bikes not sold = 40% of 7200 = $\frac{40}{100} \times 7200 = 2880$.

Choice (c)

Solution 85

Model A + Model E = 120° + 30° = 150°

This is same as:
    Model B + Model C = 90° + 60° = 150°.

Choice (b)

Solution 86

Percentage increase in market share = $\dfrac{20-15}{15} \times 100 = 33.33\%$.

Choice (c)

Solution 87

Number of Blackberry handsets sold in 2010 = $\dfrac{10}{100} \times 12500$

= 1250

Number of HTC handsets sold in 2011 = $\dfrac{20}{100} \times 15000$

= 3000

Required percentage = $\dfrac{1250}{3000} \times 100 = 41.67\%$.

Choice (c)

Solution 88

Number of apple handsets sold in 2010 = $\dfrac{8}{100} \times 12500$

= 1000

Number of apple handsets sold in 2011 = $\dfrac{3}{100} \times 15000$

= 450

Required ratio = 1000 : 450 = 20 : 9.

Choice (d)

Solution 89

From the pie chart it can be seen that the market share is reduced for Nokia, Samsung and Apple Company.

Choice (c)

Solution 90

Market share of L.G. and Lava in 2010 = 7% + 5% = 12%

Market share of L.G. and Lava in 2011 = 10% + 10% = 20%

∴ Increase in market share is by 8 percentage points.

Choice (a)

www.ingramcontent.com/pod-product-compliance
Lightning Source LLC
Chambersburg PA
CBHW080717300426
44114CB00019B/2409